Zolar's
Encyclopedia
and Dictionary
of Dreams

*Fully Revised and Updated
for the 21st Century*

Zolar

A FIRESIDE BOOK
Published by Simon & Schuster
New York   London   Toronto   Sydney

FIRESIDE
Rockefeller Center
1230 Avenue of the Americas
New York, NY 10020

This Fireside Edition 2004

For information about special discounts for bulk purchases,
please contact Simon & Schuster Special Sales at:
1-800-456-6798 or business@simonandschuster.com.

FIRESIDE and colophon are registered trademarks
of Simon & Schuster, Inc.

Designed by Christine Weathersbee

Manufactured in the United States of America
10 9 8 7 6 5 4 3 2 1

Library of Congress Cataloging-in-Publication Data
    Zolar.
    Zolar's encyclopedia and dictionary of dreams / Zolar.—Fully rev. and updated for
    the 21st century.
        p.   cm.
    "A Fireside book."
    1. Dreams—Encyclopedias. 2. Dreams—Dictionaries. I. Title: Encyclopedia and
    dictionary of dreams. II. Title.
    BF1091.Z65 2004
    135'.3'03—dc22

                                        2003070355

ISBN 978-0-7432-2263-1

This work is dedicated to Naisha Amon, and all
my Sisters and Brothers in Light in
The Hermetic Order Temple Heliopolis,
T.H.O.T.H.
www.zolar-thoth.org

Once upon a time, I, Chuang Tze, dreamt I was a butterfly, fluttering hither and thither, to all intents and purposes a butterfly. I was conscious only of following my fancies as a butterfly, and was unconscious of my individuality as a man. Suddenly I awoke, and there I lay, myself again. Now I do not know whether I was then a man, dreaming I was a butterfly, or whether I am now a butterfly, dreaming I am a man.

from *The Works of Chuang Tze*

Introduction

$\mathcal{D}$reams!

Is there anyone reading this who hasn't had them? Do you remember the very first dream you ever had? I don't! But I do remember dreaming as a very young child. Much like Chuang Tze, early on I became aware of the fact that there was a part of me that apparently lived not in one, but in two worlds. Still later on I came to understand that not only could I *move* between one and the other, but that I could actually *live between the two*, as well.

In time I came to realize that existing in such a state was not a blessing at all, but rather a kind of curse that accompanied special people, whom Colin Wilson would one day write about, calling them "outsiders."

And with this understanding also came the realization that if I had a religion at all, it was not the Methodism of my youth, but rather that I was a "mystic," the roots of which word originally meant "to be silent," no doubt referring to the inability of man to put into words his experience of the ineffable.

You see, it is not as the ancient Hebrews would have us believe, that it is a blasphemy to utter the name of Yahweh. But rather, that to do so is an impossibility . . . for the moment one speaks the name of God, he is no longer that which is being spoken of. Hence, the Taoists would write, "The Tao which can be spoken of is not the real Tao!" It is this very idea that led the mystic Joel S. Goldsmith to coin the phrase "The Infinite Invisible" to describe that deity which he perceived.

So you see, it is only in the dream state that we as mortals ever begin to come close to even the remotest comprehension of who and what our gods may very well be. This truth was well known in ancient times and led to the creation of "sleep temples," which allowed those judged ill to regain their health through divine intervention. It was taught that during sleep, the god comes to you, bringing his or her healing touch. Of all the gods and their temples thought of in this way, the sanctuary of Asklepios was held in the highest reverence, becoming the very apex of Greek healing practice.

But it was not until I met Erlo van Waveren, one of Carl G. Jung's direct disciples, that I truly came to understand how very important dreams were. As the analysand of van Waveren, I grew to appreciate and rely on the unfiltered wisdom that I could obtain from my dreams, if I could but perceive the meaning behind the various symbols, which would present themselves night after night. And it is here that the present work becomes important.

Over half a century ago, Bruce King, who founded Zolar Publishing, gathered together whatever ancient dream books could be found and created what would unknowingly become an indisputable classic in occult literature. Such quickly took its place by the bedsides of rich and poor worldwide.

And in fact, of all the Zolar books in print, it is the *Encyclopedia and Dictionary of Dreams* that is most often treasured and passed down from parents to children, much like a family heirloom.

In this present edition, I have, with the help of the skillful editing talents of Nadine Daily Papon, removed ambiguities and duplications found in the first edition and have alphabetized the meanings within dream descriptions to make them more quickly accessible. And to make them even more useful, we have added lucky numbers for each dream category.

And, of course, should any of these numbers prove "*prophetable,*" I will not be offended by the receipt of any cashier's checks that readers may wish to tender with their "thank you" notes!

Seriously . . . enjoy, cherish, and have as much fun with this book as I have had in presenting it to you. And for those of you who may wish to reach me personally, or who may be seeking instructions in metaphysics or the occult, my contact information follows below.

Finally, not to be forgotten, I offer a hats-off to Dominick Abel, my ever-tireless literary agent, and to Amanda Patten at Touchstone/Fireside, without whom this major undertaking would have not seen dawn's early light.

Zolar
Post Office Box 635
Ozona, Florida 34660
Zolar's Webpage: *www.zolar-thoth.org*
E-Mail Address: zolar.pub@verizon.net

A

A *A* *A* *A* *A*

A (the letter itself)
01-04-26-38-39-48
another person writing: indicates a first
  attempt at expression.
beginning of the alphabet: all things have to
  begin somewhere.
by itself: it is good business to be first in the
  phone book.
typing or writing the letter: an action
  that signals the beginning of communication.

ABANDONMENT
04-14-15-31-34-46
business: quarrels, if not squelched, will lead
  to distressing affairs.
children: any excuse will be deemed pathetic.
father: your foolish actions lead to difficulty
  in business.
friends: planning the future is impossible
  without the cast of characters.
home: open yourself up to new ways of relating.
husband: change of friends leads to
  freedom to be yourself.
influential people: a reconciliation cannot
  wait; each person must maintain his or
  her power.
loved one, a: you must work hard to recover
  lost emotions.
lover: separation anxiety is debilitating due to
  guilt about foolish actions.
mother: you are looking for freedom and
  return home to find it.
of: have liberty to explore having balanced
  emotions.
others: will have much affection for enemies
  when they fail.
position: when one door closes another
  opens.
relatives: establish a surrogate family of those
  who care about you.
religion: poverty results from your attacks on
  the wrong people.
ship: will have success if you reach the shore.
something dear: bad things do happen to
  good people.
  sinful: chance to make a move you have
    long planned comes along.

sweetheart: failure in one's affairs leads to
  great debts.
wife: the betrayal was your own, reconcile.
yourself: to receive love you must be capable
  of giving it.

ABDOMEN
06-18-32-33-48-54
big and not being pregnant: put all of your
  eggs in an infertile basket.
big, if dreamt by an unmarried woman: the
  centering of life: you will soon be married.
  emaciated: persecution results from your
    lack of defense.
growing, a: redouble vigor on labors
  instead of amusement.
large, having a very: the way to your heart is
  not through your stomach.
lover's: treachery from differing ambitions;
  balance them all.
married person dreaming of an: an unfaithful
  partner's other lover is gluttony.
moving in the, something: a long journey of
  hard labor ahead for you.
of an: great expectations that all of your
  talents will be utilized.
pains in the, having: will have business belly-
  aches, but good health.
rubbing a naked: money is recovered; a relief
  of tension will allow more to come.
shot in the, being: love hurts; take this lesson
  to be positive and move on.
small, a: the future cannot be absorbed before
  you digest the past.
swollen, a: serious contagious illness will be
  overcome.

ABDUCTION
02-13-19-33-40-41
being abducted: someone close to you is
  taking unfair advantage.
by force: unexpected demands, when met,
  yield fortune.
child of an: a mystery is solved changing your
  view of yourself.
woman, of a: any iota of affection can be
  misconstrued for your love.

ABORIGINAL
26-41-45-48-51-52
being an: use natural forces to cope with your
  difficulty.

1

cannibal, a: fear a forbidden activity will be found out.

    feasting off someone: are being devoured by lover; take yourself back.

fighting an: embrace your instinctual nature; dance to your own drum.

ABORTION
13-17-33-34-39-52

campaign against, mounting a: your courage will surmount all obstacles.

having an: are taking a fruitless path in life.

    others: loneliness and scandal will result from your rejection of others.

of an: love affair ends with difference of goals.

performing an: will suffer from inattention to your code of ethics.

successful: present project will result in disgrace

ABOVE
09-13-16-19-37-38

falling near you from, something: move money sideways to escape losses.

    others: beware, friends will turn into jealous adversaries.

hanging, something: you must rise to meet the challenges of the situation.

    hit by: implement that idea you thought was beyond your reach.

looking: have sense of inferiority toward those in charge.

    from: your conceptual mind can direct the accomplishment of details.

ABSCESS
17-19-22-25-37-51

having an: will recover from the absorption in poisonous thoughts.

    neck, on: opinions are being choked out of you.

    others: what they didn't tell you is worth a thousand words.

    tooth, at a: eating to repress anger only transfers the pain.

of an: your experience with bad friends has kept you from forming good ones.

operated on, being: an early painful experience must be reexperienced to be rebuilt.

ABSENT
19-25-33-34-36-40

father: reconciliation comes with an estranged loved one.

friend, death of an: an intimate friend is taking advantage of your emotions.

loved one: will be forced to bear the brunt of another's burdens.

mother: the unexpected will happen from a distance.

others: will have mastery over many matters.

relative, rejoicing over an: blood relations do not equate with trust.

    friend: a hasty action exposes a faithless friend.

ABSORBING
09-18-42-45-47-55

being absorbed into a group: merge all facets of your identity.

ideas: reinterpret them to make them your own.

information: all data must be coordinated into the whole picture.

something into yourself: are too focused on your actions to see the truth.

ABUNDANCE
12-14-20-43-45-46

having: will have an influential position among your contemporaries.

    money, an, of: will make money through bartering.

    others: success in love matters: conserve your capital.

    over: calm your bad temper over money lent.

    relatives: increase confidence in yourself to receive approaching money.

ABUSING
01-13-23-38-42-53

another: will lose money by acting according to another's will.

being abused: it is poor business to provoke someone.

    children, by your: your hostility is mirrored back to you.

    friends, by: refuse to obey one who believes he is your superior, and you don't.

    parents, by: false rumors may contain an element of truth.

    verbally: will be molested through lack of attention.

children, your: are wasting your energy forcing others to do your bidding.

verbally abusive, being: your inferiority complex compounds the issue.

ABYSS
03-10-16-18-52-55
escaping from an: your rigid system of beliefs has been dismantled.
falling into an: careful journey through treacherous transactions.
>   *but not hurt:* money lent will not be returned; confront your own emptiness.
>   *others:* be circumspect in all your dealings; face the fear you had abandoned.
in general: an indefinable relief that your potential can be realized.
saving others from an: a relationship with yourself required before taking risky action.
>   *oneself:* keep eyes wide open to face your shadow.

ACCIDENT
02-08-17-29-35-40
air, in: with sufficient oxygen your mind is vigorous.
automobile, in an: money will appear when you get over the shock.
>   *overturning in an, or truck:* health anxieties should be treated as fact until proven false.
being in an: your life is threatened by your preoccupation with the rat race.
>   *enemies:* your glee at other's misfortune will backfire.
>   *family:* will require welfare for not integrating all experience to a positive goal.
>   *friends:* will suffer humiliation, but must develop the aspect you've forgotten.
>   *injured:* there is joy and profit from insurance, but an ominous cloud is hovering.
>   *killed:* family unhappiness over your blowing unexamined fears out of proportion.
bicycle, on a: beware of team members' aggression.
in general: avoid a hasty decision to undertake unnecessary travel.
insurance: explain your failure to comply with another's request.

land, on: good ventures, if old ones are abandoned.
sea, at: disappointing affairs of the heart; a new life direction has been blocked.
walking across the street: do not fear taking on a new responsibility.

ACCLAIM
07-10-19-24-41-45
prominent person, a: another's success tears at your heartstrings.
receiving: have been deprived of original simplicity.
>   *others:* sorrowful consequences go along with the backlash from friend's double-cross.
showing: to gain acclaim you must spend the time needed on undeveloped characteristics.

ACCOMPANYING
08-12-16-27-43-51
being accompanied: in giving your self-power to another for a just cause, you still lose.
>   *by a friend:* your surroundings will change; love and support will accompany you.
musical soloist, a: taking responsibility for life's disasters brings a love affair with life.
stranger, a: enemies will expose themselves; must use your inner resources.

ACCOMPLICE
03-04-09-34-35-55
having an, with you: are guilty of spreading sad news before you have digested it.
>   *good, a:* being distinguished will cause you to embrace a higher goal.
>   *several:* a plan is as good as its weakest link; discard it and move on.
wrong things with an, doing the: you are suffering from your own foolishness by cutting off ideas.

ACCOUNTS
05-09-15-19-26-52
adding up: will lose money by extending credit.
accountant, being an: demand cool examination before you act.
bookkeeper, being a: will soon be free of added duties you have been forced to assume.
comparing: live within your means; balance the giving and receiving of your energy.

employer's, figuring: must justify the value of your work.

figuring another's: dignity is yours, but not the spotlight.

stubs of own checkbook: will have respect of others for a short time.

   adding figures in: will come to a realization of the truth.

   finding a mistake in: means death of a very dear friend.

     not: a rolling promotion in employment, if you make personal sacrifices.

working on: period of strenuous activity followed by financial stability.

ACCUSED

07-11-15-26-33-34

being: beware of scandal from false rumors.

   man, by a: find success through an unplanned argument.

     others: misfortune accrues to those who curry favors.

     secret service agent, a: be on guard and have firm allies.

     woman, a: it's probably true that disaster will ensue.

proving innocence when: even if you are exonerated, you still lose.

righteous accusation, feeling: only God can convince them.

   other's, against you: a breakup of a friendship occurs for justifiable reasons.

wrongdoing, accusing self of: live up to own morality despite justification not to.

ACID

08-09-13-14-17-43

being dissolved by: are contemptuous of your friends for corroding your trust.

   others: your friends distrust your ability to corrupt them.

being eaten away by: use a new appliance with caution.

cleaning with: a friend is eroding your confidence.

in general: own hostile acts bar your fulfilling your promises.

handled by others: the worst case scenario is true.

handling: danger ahead due to a promise.

of: a relationship threatens to encompass you.

popping: are destroyed by your own cynicism.

test, the: your true value cannot be destroyed.

thrown in your face, being: beware of the envious.

tongue, having an: attacking others corrodes your confidence.

using: a rescue from a present peril is at hand.

ACORNS

12-25-32-34-46-54

collecting: a legacy is received—the truth.

gathering: have pleasant gains after fatigue.

holding, in one's hands: nurture the seeds of your good fortune.

   ill person: an immediate recovery, when the real value of life is learned.

   lover: your relationship has great potential.

tree, being under an: an abundance of tiny ideas will prove fruitful.

   shaking, from a: will have rapid advancement to full creative power.

woman eating: will rise in life station through her children.

ACQUAINTANCE

07-8-9-22-43-49

new, making a: open yourself up to the possibilities.

of an: making a new friendship is a sign of good luck.

others being your: a vigorous mind does not get caught in an argument.

quarreling with an: there is a reason he is not your friend.

visiting an: a taste of goodwill turns you into a gourmet.

ACROBAT

15-21-25-31-33-50

accident, having an: will escape all dangers.

balance, losing sense of: someone is pushing you sideways.

being an: use your enemies' own tricks to overcome them.

   relative: will be deceived by a well-meaning relative.

performing acrobatics: claim independence from those who rob your peace.

watching an, perform: postpone your trip for nine days.

ACTIONS

09-19-24-31-34-35

bad: will be cheated by friends who think it is justified.

good: your assertions will bring financial gains.

immoral: rivals will take sweetheart's affection.

movie, producer of an: be wary of those too willing to help.

ACTOR/ACTRESS
05-07-18-22-39-43

becoming a famous: don't assume another's destiny; take charge of your own.

being an: loss of friends you cannot convince.

  actress: have much uneasiness about your inadequacies.

  comedic: self-gratification will come in present business.

  star: enjoy the limelight; the power will soon be off.

  tragic: unhappiness will be caused by envy—yours.

in a film: will be exposed as being hypocritical.

introduced to an actor, being: beware of gossip spread by you in envy.

  actress: humiliation will come through confrontation with actual self-image.

many, seeing: will work long and hard for little return.

marry an: own ambitions are suppressed to gain mate's fame.

others acting: expand circle of friends to those you honestly admire.

  fighting in a movie: are acting out what others expect of you.

    playing: listen for lies in casual conversation.

unable to perform: sign of a friend proving to be false.

  don't know words: apply for a job in a different area.

  lost emotion, having: don't put faith in promises, only actions.

    skill: return to school or the books.

    voice: cannot convince yourself that acting out your response is better than voicing it.

watching an actor: will forget your lines at a presentation.

  actress: will be unconvincing in your participation.

  children: need to mature your true self.

wearing the wrong costume, an: change your career to fit you.

  no: others see through your pretense.

ADAM
15-22-28-30-35-51

of: When one's father prospers, there's more work for the son.

speaking to: define your wishes, but be specific, they will come true exactly.

woman dreaming of: will give birth to a grandchild for her father.

  young girl: lack of self-consciousness can lead to downfall.

ADDICTION
05-22-23-29-43-45

to alcohol: depend on another's emotion to entertain you.

  illegal drugs: fear controls your will to live.

    over the counter: your overindulgence is frivolous.

    prescribed: another's will dominates your actions.

  food: your decisions are responsible and long overdue.

  sex: are co-dependent, to your detriment.

ADDRESS:
03-06-28-39-40-46

losing someone's: have ceased to respect their qualities.

writing an: be careful of risky speculations.

  another: indicates a friend's misfortune, call her.

  business, a: good luck and prosperity will come.

  love letter, on a: personal affairs will be misconstrued.

ADMINISTRATE
06-12-19-25-26-45

of an administrator: are a leader in affairs you may not believe in.

  summoned by: improvement in business relations is at hand.

others' affairs: will receive an honorable position.

own business: will receive an inheritance.

ADMIRAL
04-15-25-28-29-54

being an: danger in love matters through lack of respect.

commanding his fleet: will have a good future, if you relate to an authority figure.

company of an, being in the: can master abilities to command other's respect.

wife of an, being the: insurmountable obstacles accompany this honor.

ADMIRED

06-08-32-44-45-48

being: danger of degradation, keep success to yourself.

> *children, by:* your vanity blocks your making friends that respect you.

>> *someone you like:* friendship is genuinely in love with you.

others, admiring: will retain the love of a former associate.

someone: check their motivation before you commit to friends.

ADOLESCENT

08-27-29-34-37-47

accompanied by an: a mirror of yourself at that age.

being a teenager: discover who you are, your goals, direction, for the umpteenth time.

cherishing adolescence: are acting less than adult.

confusion of: physical adjustments take precedence over reason.

strong, angry, a: for most of adolescence nothing seems right.

ADOPTED

08-12-18-23-33-40

adopting, children: an auspicious time for speculation with a new aspect of self.

> *other children:* own children will dislike the adopted one.

> *someone:* relatives will ask for help; don't forget you have earned your independence.

being: emotional health of someone close to you improves.

child, being an: temper causes misunderstanding, lack of control, a complete break.

children, having: an old friend mistrusts you; a new friend becomes jealous.

ADORING

32-35-39-40-49-52

children, your: a symbol of who you would have wished to be.

> *husband:* your abilities need to be extended from yourself alone.

> *sweetheart:* the qualities she possesses, you lack.

> *wife:* wealth of beauty symbolizes your position.

God, and praying to: merging all aspects of self in a quality you can aspire to.

idol, worshiping an: affairs fail through lack of individual action.

ADULTERY

12-16-39-47-53-54

committing: your morals are excellent; your partner's are not.

> *husband:* an inheritance is received in the form of a little girl.

> *others:* loss of money through physical inability to merge with your mate.

> *wife:* quarrels with neighbors, who confront you with evidence.

contemplating: are following your pacifier polls instead of your sense of right.

morally outraged by an affair: desire to have the affair yourself.

of: end your ongoing affair or you will become ill.

ADVANTAGE

04-12-36-38-45-47

friends taking, of you: will lead a life of ease.

> *others:* small disputes over petty investments.

> *people, to get money:* family prosperity is in the future.

> *poor people:* give a percentage back.

taking: future improvement in affairs.

> *of others:* consolidation of business affairs soon.

ADVENTURE

06-07-08-34-40-54

being an adventurer: will be tormented if your life is not exciting.

exciting, having an: are easy prey for manipulation.

> *man, with a:* exercise caution toward new interests and surroundings.

woman: your reactions to a delicate situation are being observed.

risky, a: commit to long-range plans.

participating in an: are bothered by a woman screaming.

ADVERSARY
02-36-41-51-54-55

being persecuted by adversity: money is discovered.

fighting an: are doomed for designing villains.

having an: prosperity if you befriend your adversary.

of an: will win against rivals eventually.

ADVERTISEMENT
02-05-09-39-42-49

advertising a sale: items are lost, money is gained.

in the newspaper: your lack of inner growth will be made public.

looking at an: the merger offered is a trap; the message is no.

placing an: exposure of subconscious desires and drives.

>   *reading:* your plans are realized without your participation.

receiving a favorable: will have numerous social activities.

ADVICE
23-30-33-42-43-49

children, giving: it will take hard work to convince them.

>   *financial:* receive a large payment from a reconciliation.

>   *others:* friendship with many people, if you refrain from giving advice.

>   *professional:* make certain affairs are properly handled.

receiving: beware of friends, who will abandon you.

ADVOCATE
08-16-21-26-43-48

becoming an: an inferiority you feel does not belong on the stage.

child, being a: growth is a two-participant deal.

counselor, being a: others consider you wealthy.

hiring an, to defend you: will not have good results.

introduced to an, being: must justify your decision.

AFFECTION
02-8-21-29-41-45

exchanging: the affair will not last, enjoy it.

having: dignify your emotions by fulfilling yourself first.

>   *not:* a long life is ahead within the bounds of decency and restraint.

of: indulgence in indiscreet pleasures.

offended by: make situation into a comedy act.

receiving from children: will receive unexpected money.

AFFLICTED
04-18-23-39-41-48

being: a healthy success is certain.

>   *by others:* a change for the better is coming soon.

>   *husband or wife:* rapid success in business.

being in a state of affliction: happy destiny is in view.

>   *others:* money will be repaid at great personal expense to payer.

AFRICA
04-13-17-25-32-54

alone, taking a trip to: new friends will be made.

>   *others, with:* will act foolishly.

deported to: reinvent your skills in new environment.

of: financial losses result from being on jury duty.

returning from: large disappointment ahead.

seeing on a map: your fortune is advanced.

AGENT
07-08-23-46-47-52

being an: will influence people to do good acts.

having dealings with an: change of surroundings to come.

others who are: be circumspect in all your dealings.

soliciting an: good earnings on paper, little in your hand.

AGGRESSION
14-22-29-31-39-43

of: feel threatened, restricted, and confined.

>   *violent:* the vague apprehension deluding you may be justified.

of anger toward a people: are not considering your own individuality.

    a person: repression of an emotion can be damaging, acting it out will be worse.

of inherent: funnel energy toward constructive outlets.

of plans to kill: the battle is private, within yourself.

AGONY
03-04-09-34-40-42

agonizing over something: overcome your inertia by confronting your indecision.

    over someone: if you allow their offenses to haunt you, they win.

being in: torment over opinion, which you must change to succeed.

    children: your stubborn attitude creates its own blockades.

    husband and wife: weariness of pleasure that lacks substance.

    others: will recover from an illness, but not your friend.

    relatives: are in great pain holding in past emotional reactions.

personal: your apology will be accepted; your mission still to be determined.

AGREEMENT
21-34-45-53-54-55

canceling an: uncertain intentions bring uncertain profits.

making an, with the devil: big success for fishermen.

not going through with an: must build your credibility in a new area.

of an: reconcile your belief system with reality.

reading an, without signing it: don't sign unless mutually beneficial.

signing an: put yourself on the line and cross it.

AIR
02-06-32-35-37-44

atmosphere, of: prosperity in money matters.

    clear: happiness within the family.

    cloudy: are unable to discern faithful friends from deceivers.

    rainy: abundant means to nurture your creativity.

    very stormy: illness brings danger.

blue sky and clear: clarity will bring success.

brake hissing, an: a woeful miscarriage of justice.

calm: free your thoughts to accept another's viewpoint.

castles in the: actualize your dream one story at a time.

cold: unhappiness in family relations from business failures.

conditioner not working: important distant news has not reached you.

damp: misfortune ends optimistic hopes.

foggy: present plans should be reconsidered.

gasping for: are too involved in project and need fresh air.

hot: creating oppression causes strong reactions.

misty: are deceived and influenced against your will.

oxygen in the, in need of: are at a level of basic survival, begin anew.

polluted: release yourself from confinement.

    with detritus: beware of niggling problems.

soaring in the: beware of overinflating your ego.

take a deep breath of: connect with the Universal Spirit.

    releasing: individualize your being, then act on it.

AIR GUN
12-16-39-47-53-54

buying an: are being deceived easily for your lack of attention.

having an: postpone decisions until the complete idea pops into your head.

others using an: enemies are endeavoring to destroy you.

receiving an: will be double-crossed in love through idle gossip.

AIRPLANE
04-5-25-38-41-48

disaster but alive, being in an: fear of falling from favor, power or authority.

    killed: your vision makes a quiet retreat into yourself.

falling out of an: coming down to a more idealistic earth.

flies in wrong direction: freedom does not allow irresponsibility.

    in no fly zone: compete with those you have avoided.

and attacked by fighter jets: several months of hard labor until perception.

flying in a fighter jet: project must be fast-tracked.

hanger, being locked in an: rise in fortune.

    empty: confusion, dissolution and chagrin.

hydroplane: will float successfully through a perplexing situation.

landing an: beware of adversity from an unusual source.

    in distress: ambitious plans are beyond your power to accomplish.

makes effort to land but misses: supreme effort is needed to recoup.

    and just makes it: rearrange your itinerary with longer connection times.

    connection: take several deep breaths before each action.

    the return and are stranded: fear lover will leave before you return home.

searched, being: are denying ourselves needs for which we deeply crave.

SST, an: profitable speculation for fast return will also prove advantageous.

stewardess, divorcing a: will have large damages when a guarded secret is discovered.

    marrying a: people have nothing good to say about you.

sudden dip in an, experiencing a: reexamine yesterday's activities.

taking off in a small: loss through small investments, success in other enterprises.

    trip in an, taking a: many ups and downs will be experienced.

        family, with: will earn money from study of plans.

        friend, a: balance your priorities.

        lover: are guilty of foolish actions; spiritual awakening is the object.

wings of an: your glide through life may come to an abrupt halt.

AIRPORT

05-18-24-26-28-31

being delayed by ice: your one loyal friend will aid you.

    blocked at the departure gate, are: are avoiding going straight to the point.

caught at security check: if you don't feel secure, don't do the project.

choppy weather: trust your sense of direction.

crowded airspace: will trade favors with an influential associate.

disaster: are you speeding without hinking?

forgot passport: your transition cannot be rushed.

seeing the signal lights at the: need some form of release.

stopped at the arrival gate: major obstacles are being kept in the dark.

ticket, can't buy: business complications stem from your ill humor.

walking on the landing strip: plans made must be reexamined.

ALARM

02-8-18-26-38-51

giving an: hasten others to accomplish plans—their own, not yours.

going off: act swiftly on present project to prevent loss.

hearing an, while awake: are too late to repair the damage.

    asleep: time to replenish your energies, apologize.

setting an, yourself: your impatience is haunting you; use past insights instead.

    someone else's: the problem is not yours; keep your valuables close.

ALBATROSS

09-20-25-31-38-42

flying above: with freedom comes responsibility.

of an: a stranger brings weighted problems.

on top of the mast: your high and mighty attitude needs a rest.

several on the sea: are able to aid relatives seeking help.

shooting an: will not escape present peril.

ALCOHOLISM

01-04-07-21-22-33

excessive drinking, your: stimulation is in resolving your troubles.

    other's: the praise of your success is temporary.

hangover, having an: problems are not solved by hedonism.

of being an alcoholic: your habits fit your inner anxieties.

small amount of, drinking a: your heart needs to relax and allow your spirit to act.

in secret: express the courage of your convictions.

tipsy, being: your inhibitions are blocking your creativity.

ALIEN
03-05-28-34-47-48

being an: varying from the norm is your choice.

chased by: will be honored for innovative designs.

undesirable: difficulty in accepting shame and sorrow of past actions.

changing citizenship: your boundaries have been invaded.

foreigners, being in the company of: awareness of your own racial prejudice.

disliking a: undertakings will not succeed without facing the fear you have avoided.

falling in love with a: fear of what is foreign in yourself.

marrying a: will be fortunate in love affairs.

meeting: something that you do not wish to face, understand, or recognize.

introduced to an: a misunderstood part of your nature wants expression.

seeing little green: have out-of-character urges and desires.

ALIMONY
23-30-33-42-43-49

owing: no amount of money will pay spouse for your failed commitment.

paying: guilt at having visions of committing adultery.

receiving: the accountability lies close to home.

refusing to pay: have stolen your faithfulness to which mate had a right.

ALLERGY
35-38-40-45-47-50

being allergic: your body is persecuting you for what you put into it.

having an: a minor wrongdoing requires payment.

others: are anathema to one who is not your equal.

ALLEY
03-10-25-37-48-52

dark: neighbors gossip about your taking a devious route, to you it's unknown.

dead-end: fear of exposure has boxed you in a corner, the third side is still exposed.

of an: have no choice in way out of predicament but to totally redirect plans.

trees, lined with: transform the green reality with honor and dignity.

ALLIGATOR
05-21-26-36-46-48

being attacked by an: will be harassed and ridiculed by your enemies.

confronting an: your unconscious fears cause your irrational actions.

handbag, having: exercise caution with every step, care in each new speculation.

several: enemies surround you with their unconscious forces.

shoes, having: be fearless with each step.

wrestling with an: an argument with a close friend is a misuse of your verbal power.

ALMANAC
04-07-09-11-29-49

buying an: quarrels with lover over broken engagement.

consulting an: are sued for a debt, but will win the case.

of an: changes occur that affect your destiny.

owning an: your present actions will cause scandal.

ALPHABET
07-23-27-31-40-46

counting a foreign: a mystery is solved; write.

of the: an absent friend returns to share basic lessons of life.

printing the entire: worries are smoothed away.

writing: unexpected good news heretofore unexpressed.

ALTAR
06-08-18-21-27-43

boy, an: release from pressing worries to honor the source of love.

candelabra, at the, lit: your faith is the loftiest part of your inner resources.

being lighted: new plans for committing totally to yourself will be successful.

being snuffed out: humility is needed to solve problem.

confusion, in: need to let go of your defenses to negotiate with enemies.

constructed, being: awe at nature's ability to regenerate itself.

> *decorated:* a better understanding with those about you.
>> *with white flowers:* a wedding, joy, consolation and thanksgiving.
> *destroyed:* sacrificing all that was, to allow all that can be.

kneeling at an: secret unfulfilled desire sacrificed for universal good.

married and dreaming of an, to be: many small vexations at your choice.

of an: need to let go of something to be able to possess it.

outside the chapel, being: a large fortune if you cross the threshold.

AMBASSADOR
07-25-38-42-43-49

being an: present position will be lost though an official treachery.

conference with an, in a: keep faithful friends nearby and enemies even closer.

recalling an: social activities of a happy nature are exceedingly dull.

AMBULANCE
11-21-32-38-39-48

calling an, for a relative: financial troubles from large medical bills loom.

> *yourself, for:* help is available for impending emergency.

empty: a friend is lost through your careless words.

full: all desires are realized if you are discreet.

AMERICA
13-27-28-34-48-50

abroad from, going: ventures are far away, but close to your heart.

anthem of the USA, hearing the national: a temptation will come—follow it.

> *singing, at an official ceremony:* the bond of loyalty strengthens.

being an American: are grasping all material experience for survival.

being in: success in the world through own efforts.

deported from: are unable to feel gratitude.

returning to, from abroad: your prosperity must be appreciated and maintained.

deported: many people are envious of you.

> *seeing on a map:* all roads lead to where the money is.
taking a trip to, alone: leave the baggage of envy behind.
> *others, with:* unsettled future depends totally on your actions.

AMUSING
01-05-21-33-43-48

of a place of amusement: are going in circles; use time wisely to chart your direction.

> *park, an:* inhibitions thrown to the wind blow back in your face.

others, themselves: loosen up your seriousness to laugh in the light.

yourself: unhappiness unless you find new friends.

> *family, with:* arguments can be eased with a sense of humor.
> *friends, with:* if you can't laugh at yourself, others will.
> *sweetheart, with a:* will have very high hopes.

ANARCHIST
11-13-18-21-39-40

being an: giving way to your impulse will lose you freedom.

being killed: fully develop the new before destroying the old.

revolution, inciting a: your position will be restructured and you terminated.

several: use caution against those who want something for nothing.

ANCESTORS
04-05-12-13-36-52

genealogy, studying your: will marry beneath you and rue the day.

hearing the voice of an: whatever you were not going to do—do it now!

of: don't trust people who say they are in love without being empowered by it.

other's: cannot fake your heritage; carry on tradition, the root to your past.

remembrance of: your interests will suffer from many lifetimes of malicious gossips.

respect for: without their successful struggle for survival, you wouldn't be here.

reunited with one's: use of inherited talents, if you allow your wisdom to persist.

reverence toward: your movements are being observed by hostile critics.

ANCHOR
06-12-20-35-44-46

bow of a ship, on: your search for fortune needs a secure relationship.

   hanging on side: your prosperity is thwarted by your aimless drifting.

broken: being weighted down by circumstances brings a string of bad luck.

down in the water: those on whom you depend drag you down.

losing: momentum toward learning is mounted.

raising: follow direction decided upon to the letter.

throwing an: resolve to attain answers in the deepest part of yourself.

ANECDOTE
17-26-27-33-38-39

hearing an: will participate in a big social event.

   friend, from a: a puzzle must be solved before you can continue.

   someone on stage, from: are doomed for disappointment.

telling an: double entendres confuse your message.

ANESTHETIC
04-17-27-46-48-51

being chloroformed: a pleasant surprise when you realize what is going on.

   others: your control tower has been gassed.

giving chloroform: deadening your feelings does not overcome emotional sorrow.

going under an: are trying to escape a reality better forgotten.

ANGELS
06-31-42-44-46-52

cherubs, of: your guides through a propitious event.

   looking respectful: your actions leave a question as to your character.

   sorrowful: someone will inflict their anger upon you.

choir of, a: your strength of character will find the light of truth.

close to you, being: peace and well-being with your intuitive spiritual nature.

hair pasta, of: forgive the chef.

healthy person dreaming of an: a friend's health will improve.

   having wings: sick people on your watch will recover.

   ill person: the peacefulness of death.

      non-sinful: assure dead loved ones that they can go on.

      sinful: a demand for repentance; the message is for you alone.

several: you have inherited abnormal intelligence.

wings, an, with: your innocence makes you vulnerable.

   putting on: your actions now will not be considered interference.

ANGER
23-25-28-30-36-40

being angry: depicts genuine conflict with adversary, yourself.

   fighting, and: confront the issue or destroy the friendship.

   very: will be so upset you lose your breath; your life is at stake.

fighting with: no resolution without understanding of negative programming.

having a fit of: the antagonism is between factions of yourself.

   children: excessive love breeds violence, which results in physical disorders.

   enemies: will be annoyed by petty quarrels started by you and ended by another.

   husband or wife: a cover-up for inability to express love.

   others: illness is ahead, if you do not heed your conscience.

with a relative: will benefit from that person's refusal to fight with you; it isn't his fight.

ANIMALS
11-13-30-39-48-50

angry: your wrath is difficult to restrain.

another's: are a mirror of their emotions toward you.

baboons: a fleeting rise in status, try to maintain it.

beast, talking to a: hardship and misfortune come soon.

beating an: your sense of power is fragile at best.

  pigs: misinformation damages your own affairs.

  to death: get out of the business before you destroy it.

bleating: new concerns will be pleasant.

bones, gnawing on: will fall into complete ruin.

buffaloes: perseverance in the launching of your large enterprise.

buttocks of an: will soon have money.

buying an: are mimicking another, rather than sharing yourself.

carcass of an: long life and good perspectives.

caressing an: a big fortune is ahead.

chasing you: part of your personality is stubbornly demanding expression.

coyote: a trickster wants to pull you into loneliness.

dead: are ridding yourself of instincts no longer needed.

fangs of an, the: leave before you are kicked out.

fat: abundance during the winter.

feeding: someone is endeavoring to destroy you.

  on a carcass: gluttony of backbiting hardly fills the stomach.

furious: a friend is defending your name.

  in a cage, many: your offenses are gathering against you.

giraffe, a: keep your nose out of other's business.

gnu, a: take a walk in fresh air and natural surroundings.

gopher, a: family troubles are eating at your ability to perform in business.

gorilla, a: your actions are misinterpreted and unjustly criticized.

grunting: time to change your occupation.

head in hands, holding a dog, horse, or donkey: you will be enslaved.

hippopotamus, a: beneath your authority are unsteady legs.

  in a zoo: are bored with people from whom you cannot escape.

hoof of an: are in danger of being swindled by a lover.

hungry: greed interferes with your attaining allies.

hydrophobia, having: to play with sharks you must first learn to swim.

hyena, being chased by a laughing: others are useless, go it alone.

invading your car: others just want to get close to you.

  and attacking you: show them your license to proceed.

  and you drive off with them: bring your enemies into your fold.

large: your repressed cravings surface with hostility.

mountain, on a: loss of money in business.

octopus, of an: multiple deals that entangle you in an irreversible situation.

orangutan: a ruthless acquaintance will stop at nothing to make a fool out of you.

passionate: unfulfilled lust translates to rage.

paws of an: will be offended by a person's bad manners.

  domestic, a: friends far away are thinking of you.

  wild, a: joy of short duration.

poacher, being a: want to steal another's lifestyle.

polecat, being a: pick up the scent of deception and confront it.

pursued by wild, being: will be offended by a friend.

  and wounded: are opening yourself up to criticism.

pushing away an: will soon be divorced from your bitchy behavior.

resting in a stable: will be unfortunate in love, if you don't pay attention to it.

  field: financial gains, if you broaden your scope.

rodent, a: a pest that confounds the exterminator.

selling an: success postponed until more propitious times.

skinny: must endure starvation to get to the bottom of aggressive nature.

small: a younger sibling needs your attention.

standing in front of your car: other's concern is real and with positive intent.

stroking: fortune is ahead for you; don't grab.

talking: protect your flanks from vindictiveness.

   you, to an: will benefit by associating with people of society.

tame: keep your friends close; you are surrounded by enemies.

veterinarian, a: your basic instincts require remedial elevation.

walrus, a: your simple requirements for work still need refining.

wild, howling: enemies will get the best of your bigotry.

young: your parental love will bring about prosperity.

ANKLES
09-16-23-39-44-47

beautiful, having: will have excess money in old age.

   big: need basic support before beginning your plan.

   broken, bleeding: will die far from loved ones.

   large, extraordinary: happiness secured from people abroad.

   small, very: separation from mate in near future.

breaking an: death of someone in foreign land.

man dreaming of beautiful: what have you brought to the relationship?

own, of: a friend tries to help you secretly.

sprained, being: difficulty of movement followed by success of flexible movement.

   another's: mystery will be solved, when you discover the motive.

woman showing her: realization of her desires.

   dreaming of a man's: will lose husband and children.

ANNOUNCEMENT
06-13-19-34-35-41

edged in black, an: a social confrontation turns evil.

happy, making a: happiness is not always infectious.

   public: will need a shot of luck to prosper.

others making news, to you: a change in life will soon come.

wedding, a: take baby steps in announcing plan.

ANNOYED
07-11-14-17-26-45

being: all your plans will go through trials you can overcome.

   children: danger through holding on to a secret.

   others, annoying: invitation from a prominent person is received.

married person dreaming of annoying another: cannot save a marriage lacking love.

ANTELOPE
21-23-26-32-34-42

following a herd of: sudden improvement money-wise.

gazelle having lustrous eyes, a: will fall in love with love.

   young girl dreaming of a graceful: will have a rough suitor but true husband.

leather handbag, having a: money matters will prosper, but someone will persecute you.

of an: someone dear has placed confidence in you.

ANTIQUES
11-14-20-36-43-47

buying: wish to gain knowledge through other's life experiences.

losing: return to your heritage, the source of your happiness.

of: aspects of previous lives of yourself and others.

selling: time to share your hard-earned wisdom.

taking advantage of an antiquary in a deal: increased prosperity.

ANTS
17-23-25-28-48-49

anteater, of an: will go bankrupt to escape numerous petty irritations.

   eating, with wings: failure to perform your duties will cause a loss of real estate.

   worms: use radical measures to rid yourself of false friends.

antenna, an: your ability to transmit and receive energy needs fine tuning.

anthill, being in an: the workplace is too crowded with conformity.

bitten by, being: expect renewed energy at work.

body, on your: become more involved in business venture.

food, of an: heavy industry will ensure happiness.

house, in the: are examples of successful communal living.

   long line of, a: loss of individuality for a cause more important than you alone.

stepping on an anthill: your ambition has provoked animosity in coworkers.

tree, climbing a: vexations to come from new offer of employment.

   winged: carelessness at work.

work, at: trifling annoyances will detract from your progress.

ANXIETY

03-16-30-35-43-45

apprehension, having: do things your own way as in the past.

   children, over: will escape a present peril.

     finances: family quarrels.

     friends: expect too many favors for little effort.

being plagued with: don't let anger at past mistakes block your future.

chaotic life, about: be assertive in overcoming hurdles to your progress.

frantic, being: strenuous times followed by a peaceful holiday.

   others: advancement within company.

   relatives: will receive a small inheritance.

having: must recognize enemies before you confront them.

   painful, of the mind: what you desire is forbidden and wrong.

images of, about: expose your secret worries to your mate.

vibrating, some part of body: schedule a physical exam.

APARTMENT

06-24-28-37-43-51

another person, of: troubles ahead.

being in an, alone: be friends with yourself first.

   someone else, with: will find a friend you have been trying to locate.

owing the rent: will be persecuted to the extent of another's greed.

owning an: family quarrels over territorial imperative.

paying the rent for an: face eye-to-eye those who surround you.

   for relatives: return the favor of family ties.

   not: another will be persecuted in your stead.

penthouse, living in a: have overemphasized your importance.

   staying in an, with friends: are living beyond your abilities.

renting an: joy for the term of the lease.

APE

10-15-17-28-42-43

baby: have an instinctive purely physical love.

cage, in a: there is a mischievous opposition to your love.

chimpanzee, of a: your intelligence will play a trick on you.

   up a tree: will incur disease if you follow the wrong direction.

dancing: success in real estate will take some tricky steps.

imitating others: care to expose falseness in friends.

poor people dreaming of: buckle down and use intelligence to gain good earnings.

   rich people: guard against mischief maker in circle of friends.

APPLES

07-09-10-24-43-45

blossom, an: are a victim of deceitful charms.

eating a golden: wise gains in self-knowledge.

   red: go fearlessly ahead to new love affair.

   rotten: will have difficulty conceiving a child.

   sauce: change comes for the better.

   sour: the source of the contention is you.

   sweet: good means and a favorable end with your openness to new insight.

   with worms: frustration at lover's distraction.

giving an, to a woman: what negativity and decay has tempted you?

having an: time to realize big earnings with existing plans.

taking, from another's tree: the love you cherish does not belong to you.

tree in an orchard: are surrounded with friends.

bloom, in: opportunities in business abound.

harvest, at: long-term business plan coming to fruition.

ripe, high on a: your aim is higher than possible outcome.

APPOINTMENT
02-10-31-34-48-53

making an: business with untrustworthy person.

missing an: your insincerity will be exposed.
  others: be at an equal level of priority with your friends.

time of, changing: your enemies are within your home.

APRICOTS
22-27-35-37-51-53

brandy: will best your business enemies.

eating: calamity is nearly caused by a hypocritical person.
  canned or preserved: will be cheated by friends.
  dried: large annoyance to come.
  out of season: business prospers despite loss of hope.

picking: future prosperity in business and love.

spoiled in the hands, having: trouble and loss of a relative.

tree, growing on a: pleasure and contentment in the future

APRIL
04-06-33-37-38-53

1st, foreign nations' Labor Day: a trip abroad.

born in, having been: happy in love affairs.
  child, a: will have important position in life.

Fool's Day, fooling someone on: happiness in the family.

fool's joke played on you, having a: will have power over someone.

month of, during: success is postponed.

APRON
04-26-30-36-51-52

blue: will be annoyed by gossip of other women.
  losing an: stay out of the kitchen.
  lost an, having: will lose your sweetheart.

string, being tied to an: get to work on the family situation.

tying an: big honors are received.

untying an: a loved one is lost through censure from elders.

wearing an: happiness in covering something up.
  man: subject to wife's eccentric whims.

ARBITRATION
05-15-33-40-46-52

being an arbitrator: new responsibilities will be saddled on you.

losing an: will have future financial benefits.

of business: loss of money through injustice; and even more, trying to get it back.

winning: projects will not succeed.

ARBOR   04-25-32-43-45-46

being in an: personal secrets will be revealed.
  under an, alone: a marriage proposal will be received.
  with others: will be visited by a lover.

designing an: will win a lawsuit by straightforward presentation of the facts.

fire, being on: affliction in love affairs.

grapes from an, picking: will have a happy married life.

of an: will have secrets of many children.

walking in an: will receive good news for your artistic pursuits.

ARCHITECT
08-15-18-34-43-50

being an: surround yourself with visual pleasures and shelter.

of an: much pleasure in life will be yours.

talking with an, about construction: everyone is a frustrated architect.

with an, being: architects are just plain frustrated.
  with blueprints: will be cheated by land brokers.

ARGUING
04-08-11-21-34-45

friend, with a: your pride will be injured, but allow others' theirs.
  loved one: point out consequences of unwise action.
  others: you rationalize your own behavior by accusing others of it.

relatives: watch neighbors' behavior carefully but do not judge.

having an argument: will have a strenuous time opposing intimidation.

and being scolded: are too cocky about your ideas.

heated, a: will have difficulty in balancing the opposing facts.

others: one facet of your personality opposes the other.

ARK
01-07-15-22-32-43

having an: a safe haven from the passionate forces.

of an: beneficial and important events to come.

sacred place, in a: a long-comfortable, old-fashioned place with emotional balance.

Ten Commandments, of the: abundant means if you act according to rules.

ARMOR
05-12-24-28-34-38

armored car, in an: the only influence should be your own.

wearing: the frightened child needs to peek its head out of the shell.

others: shut out nasty people, expose your true spirit.

weighted down by: are stifled by negative comments from others.

in the mud: inappropriate rigidity will cause failure.

ARMS
09-13-15-17-34-47

accident with: ill health in family.

amputated, left, being: part of yourself needs reconstructive energy.

right: death of a male part of your personality; no longer an indiscriminate giver.

bearing: turning point at which you take control of your destiny.

small: will have plenty of money that you can't reach.

thin: soften your tactics to include tact.

breaking an: your loss of confidence causes your family big peril.

broken, both: loss of power to direct your life and extend your self.

broken, a man having: family quarrels.

woman: loss of her husband.

freckles on: displeasing incidents will be implied.

hairs, covered with: will be very rich.

having big: the power to construct or destroy is within you.

muscles: your accomplishments don't extend to your full potential.

skin disease on: will work hard without profit.

hugging you: a new friend will be a resource.

of own: victory over enemies.

one arm missing, having: your creativity is inhibited.

pain in your: unlucky in business.

Popeye's: have overstated your authority.

ARMY
03-04-23-35-44-46

colonel being stripped of his rank: intrigues will sabotage your plans.

country, of own: renewed hope after a painful but necessary decision.

drafted into the, being: mechanical employment, physical self-discipline.

fighting, an: treason and persecution within your family.

garrison of troops, a: express your emotions in a letter home.

caught off guard: the future starts now, prepare.

of an: caused by a mysterious occurrence.

officer: pay attention to your behavior that may upset others.

private in the, being a: an upsetting, dishonorable, but in the end amusing experience.

rations: your errors of judgment are minor but you exaggerate them.

several from different countries: fortune and joy.

ARRESTED
02-13-18-19-33-38

arresting others: you disapprove of their behavior, which prevents your motivation.

others, you: have endangered their moral principles.

being: misery from blocked actions followed by the joy of having a conscience.

others: be warned not to take chances until attitudes are in line.

 and released: unexpected and sudden success with new comprehension of the positive.

ARROWS
02-13-18-19-33-38

archer, being an: are unfitted to fill your position.

 hitting the target: unfaithfulness until you find the right spouse.

 married: danger is nearby, disgrace will soon follow.

 of an: your planned seduction will bring unhappiness in love.

 unmarried: engagement is near.

bow, a: to honor the God within.

 and: benefit from other's failure to complete tasks.

 stringing a: with steady effort you will accomplish.

breaking an: present failure in love is partially your fault.

broken, a: business failure.

bulls-eye with an, hitting: power to set your goals and the skill to carry them through.

Cupid's, being hit by: will be smitten with love.

hit by an, being: have the strength to redirect your performance back to its source.

hitting target with: a straight course with swift arrival at a clear accomplishment.

injury from an: your nerves are breaking down.

losing: difficulties because of carelessness.

many: messages, powerful and purposeful, are intended for you.

 having: friends are spectators to your money losses.

missing the target with: expect difficulties, misfortune because of an unsuspected person.

quiver full of, a: concentrate on your performance at work and a raise is in the offing.

shooting an, in self-defense: pending verification, you are the target.

splitting target in two: will alienate a friend.

throwing an: vengeance never clears up the injustice.

volley of: opposition from several sources.

ARSON
07-15-18-26-47-48

arsonist, seeing an: as the messenger you will lose your reputation.

clear flames in home, causing fire with: good employment.

 dark: financial ruin if you associate with women of loose morals.

 small: ignore men with no accessible past.

land, on: must have destruction to make room for the new.

others' homes, committed to: realization of an unworthy ambition.

sea, at: will have successful ventures while others flounder.

throwing a firebrand into a home: must make amends by saving a life.

ART
02-08-09-20-36-38

buying works of: will work hard but want another to give directions.

 selling: are ready to express your opinion.

dealer, being an: your diligence will be compensated.

of living: use creative expression from a masterpiece to an ashtray.

of works of: honor through use of refined taste in job.

ARTERIES
04-21-24-27-32-52

clogged, having: your fairness towards others is blocking your progress.

of a river: worries will flow to the next port.

own being cut: have many life-saving skills to gain.

strong, having: a message with good news.

 weak: slow recovery from an illness.

ARTIST
15-16-22-40-44-52

being an: your eccentricity will receive many honors.

easel, having an: a realization of self-expression in your hobbies.

 others: your potential needs development.

 working at an: your mind is concentrating on lofty meditation.

of an: fulfillment of irrational parts of self.

paint your portrait, having an: treachery if you allow others to express your creativity.

painting another's portrait: while attention is drawn away from you, act.

palette of all colors: will be invited to an underground party of people from all the arts.

student, having a private: will receive much consolation in love of your creation.

with frequent visitors: what appears to be true is not.

ASH
03-12-21-34-45-46

ashes: raw material of spiritual rebirth of the light of God.

sifting through: the purified remains of an imperfect life.

cleaning out, trap: your carelessness will cause financial woes.

coating of, having a: irritating, though temporal, reverses.

from which the Phoenix rises: receiving money from an unexpected source.

Phoenix rising from the ashes: move to a new height of understanding.

tray, emptying an: your concentrating on state of perfection misses the arrival process.

cleaning: your fear of error has blocked your utilizing your abilities.

metal: are traveling too fast and the repercussions are mounting up.

onyx: your life is based on solid accomplishments.

tree, of an: harvest the old, purify the ground and fertilize new growth.

Wednesday, observing: antecedent to a contented year.

ASHAMED
10-17-20-29-42-47

being: fortune in business.

actions, of: are stricken with a guilty conscience.

chastity, of: will meet a rich person.

children, of: listen to advice of friends.

mate being, of the other: separation will soon take place.

ASSASSINATION
13-17-24-27-28-51

being assassinated: proceed with utmost precaution.

committing an: luck in misfortune if you allow enemies to expose themselves.

of: are making a martyr out of a mediocre enemy.

bloody, a: all his negative energy will be transferred to you.

ASSAULTED
11-30-33-38-44-52

assaulting others: have deep-rooted anger at being rejected.

being: dreams won't stop until source of anger is discovered.

by many small figures: want to possess qualities from many people.

one gigantic: angry with outside overpowering authority.

children: feud is from your childhood and with yourself.

others: want to spread harmful information of another's character.

ASSISTANT
11-15-16-25-36-42

attendant, dismissing an: love affairs will be disturbed.

having an: advancement within present position.

others: will be cheated by friends.

being an: troubles ahead if you don't read minds.

needing assistance: success requires you to ask for aid.

ASTHMA
02-21-28-32-44-51

attack, having an: not facing your intuitive process is stifling progress.

contracting: fear has caused your lungs to paralyze themselves.

having: recovery from illness by changing one's state of residence.

others: your disillusion is fated by your careless treatment of your emotional overload.

of: schedule a deep, long breath between each action.

ASTROLOGY
02-03-10-16-17-21

consulting an astrologer: need reliable and useful assistance to determine your influence.

horoscope, following your: free will requires an understanding that timing is everything.

of: the patient search for the truth yields an orchestra of leitmotifs.

of an astrologer: the solution is in knowledge you previously rejected.

rich person studying: will sell goods below cost to enhance growth.

zodiac, of any sign of the: love and accept whom you are, first.

　your: your fortune is in attuning yourself to your harmonics.

ASTRONOMER
01-23-26-35-38-45

being an: projects will develop slowly and methodically.

　astronaut: are open to exploring the universe one planet at a time.

company of an, being in: enemies fail by limiting the scope of their research.

　others: good earnings.

of an: high ambitions are realized.

telescope, looking through a: will have your fortune told.

　handling a: difficulties will be lessened with care.

　　others: will be embarrassed by your exaggeration of trouble.

ASYLUM
03-08-10-19-28-45

being in an: serious troubles ahead will be resolved through careful analysis.

　placed, avoiding: must break with the past and take better care of your health.

lunatic in a, being a: will be guilty of foolish actions until you deal with your motivation.

of an: will live long, healthy life if you express your disagreement at work and at home.

requesting political: separation anxiety from those you left behind.

ATHLETE
16-23-27-28-38-42

becoming an: beware of overtaxing your strengths.

being an: financial problems until you are good enough to gain support.

　with: to compete, jump higher to develop balance, flexibility and stamina.

jumping higher: know your limits and reach for the next one.

training, an: consistency, commitment and awareness of your body.

winning the race: when the going gets tough, the tough get going.

ATOM
05-11-19-36-42-48

causing the end of the world: "and the next world is . . ."

bomb, the atomic: are searching for security, understanding and spiritual certainty.

　explode, watching an: your destruction is caused by yourself, as is your awareness.

of the: its enormous energy potential is the basis of harmony, or the split of a friendship.

splitting the: time for inner changes in response to the lowering of your income.

ATTACHMENT
04-12-23-32-41-42

bank accounts, of: change banks.

money due, having an, for: dissolution of hopes for future from fallacy of the past.

　unpaid taxes: financial embarrassments from faulty accounting.

putting an, upon others: ridiculous disputes over computer glitches.

ATTACKED
08-11-14-17-49-51

ambushed, being: problems are not solved in one dimension, but three.

attacking others: the integrity of your moral fiber is in question.

　women: need professional counseling and a new job.

being: danger is in who you are, not what you do.

　and calling for help: are being sabotaged by an associate.

　　being eaten by an attacker: are confined; leave the relationship.

　　escaping: save yourself, then fend for others.

　friend, by a: a legacy is received.

　　computer: you cannot reason with your own rigid mind.

　　machine: pull the plug on the funds for the project.

　　man: others scorn you for being enticing.

tiny but powerful figure: lack of attention to details does not hurt you.
    vague: profit leaks affect you
adversely.
    very tall: have overextended your-
self.
    unknown evil force: return to
the house of worship of your
choice.
    woman: female foes are not weak.
injured, and: will allow an insult.
counterattacking: mosquitoes should not be
killed with a machine gun!
running from being: the best defense is a
strong offense.
saving self from: have been outmaneuvered;
sue for peace.
    asking "who are you?": time to audit your
books and your life.
       "what do you want of me?": someone
you trust will betray you.
    befriend attacker, by: surround him with
white light and send him away in
peace.
victim of a, being a: your projects will
fail; taking charge will save your
plans.
wake up when dream of being: change your
locks and lock your windows.
woman dreaming of being: have indeterminate
fear of the male.

ATTIC
13-16-19-25-38-47
disorderly: family connections must
flourish to develop a higher level where all
relate.
    orderly: contented family gatherings.
married person dreaming of an: should avoid
flirtations, innocent or not.
    single person: have purely idealistic
approach to an engagement.
    woman: should avoid flirtations inter-
preted as social climbing.
of an: will escape present peril by sticking to
your loftier ideals.
others' homes, in: are confronted by a history
of insurmountable obstacles.
rummaging through an: a part of your history
is in each object.

AUCTION
05-10-26-46-49-50
antiques, of: your bid is too low to be competitive; you are resisting change.
art, of: are being falsely accused by an opponent bargaining to gain advantage.
being outbid in an: are denied quality
materials needed to finish task, then
degraded.
bidding in an: cannot accomplish project
without aid.
livestock, of: a raise in salary and stature due
to your intelligent plan.
no one is bidding on your treasure: others
do not value your ideas and
opinions.

AUGUST
11-14-17-19-28-34
born in, being: are self-confident and open
to new experiences; self-loving to
acceptance.
dreaming of, during the fall: are duly warned
of tests and challenges to come.
    month: fortune is received from parents;
desirability from yourself.
    spring, during the: a reformulation of
plans is required and a new adventure
begun.
    summer: an opportunity to express
yourself and be heard.
    winter: are harboring old ideas and
resentments.

AUNT
07-13-18-24-29-39
being an: the marriage, currently planned,
will be successful.
husband's: your good times are coming as
your idol arrives.
of an: will be accused of an action, not yours.
visiting with an: an unexpected legacy will be
received.
wife's: beware of individual who exemplifies
all you hate about yourself.

AUSTRALIA
12-13-15-27-31-40
being in: are a hardheaded practical oppor-
tunist.
deported from, being: affairs must be brought
into order.

to: exemplifies how easily or with what difficulty you are mixing up your life.

traveling to: social events will be turned upside down.

    abroad from: what cannot be explained is too easily doubted.

AUTHOR
03-12-14-44-46-52

being an: have the opportunity to express the diversity of yourself and be heard.

dealing with an: good times are coming.

of an: will have mental vigor and a prestigious social life.

promoter dreaming of, a: handle your business; let the writer write his life script.

AUTOMATIC
08-12-15-28-41-47

acting on: your weaknesses will be exposed but you will not see them.

    machines, handling: guard against commitments you can't produce.

power, having: guidelines have been set; limits given; move on.

AUTOMOBILE
02-05-18-34-47-52

accelerator, stepping on the: attempting to go faster than your capabilities.

accident, having an: prepare to meet powerful competition for approaching money.

    injured, and being: stretch your muscles and your world view.

    seeing an: unexpected hurdles interfere with your master plan.

antifreeze to an, adding: desire to prevent relationship from cooling down.

axle, breaking an: disaster from a source beyond your comprehension.

backseat driver in an: your mode of expression is to order others to do things for you.

bags in an, your: unexpected money arrives.

battery going dead in traffic: how to annoy the most people with one act.

body too awkward: feel inept and inadequate for job at hand.

    big: you can't handle life; simplify it.

    bulky: are carrying too much emotional and material baggage.

    designed with flash: a restless need to be noticed.

    old: body is deteriorating, get a medical checkup.

    rusted: indulge in armchair travel.

    small: feel cramped in hard labor for meager living.

brakes in an, using the: withdraw from business deal if your will is not in it.

    failing: false stops are draining your resources.

    installing new: put an immediate stop to a project you initiated.

breaking down on the road: journeying and changing will alternate in succession.

buying a beautiful: advancement at work will include stipulations.

crashing in an: have set yourself up for failure to avoid confrontation.

denting a fender of your: someone is endeavoring to destroy your pride.

    others, your: exercise restraint in criticizing others within the family.

departing, a: new burdens and responsibilities don't lessen dependence on others.

directions in an, being given wrong: don't move until you see way ahead clearly.

driver, with no: rethink the level of self-control of your activities.

    poor, a: slow down those around you from taking parts of your life.

driving an, alone: anticipate and take charge of your destiny.

    children, with: be concerned for other's first.

    friends: the degree of your self-control and self-responsibility.

    lover, your: passions must be controlled while driving.

    relatives: don't be manipulated into living the life they failed to do.

    sweetheart: your weaknesses will be known, your reputation scandalized.

    wife: cement your relationship before moving.

    fast, a: are making progress in trust and faithfulness but check the emotional weather.

    night, at: are keeping secrets from friends.

rain, in the: have been driven to new heights without preparation.

safely and skillfully: success through your own effort.

dying in an: become active in scene you avoided or it will haunt you.

by fire in the: regret a deed that foretold your disappointment.

an explosion: your enemies endeavor to thwart your affairs.

engine parts missing: do not have tools to finish the job.

responsive: are foiled in your attempt to forward your ambitions.

unresponsive: your inability to move your mind-set is blocking progress.

escape from path of an overturning: will succeed in harrowing schemes.

fender, standing on a: will soon travel to a foreign country.

find parked, can't: your business promotion will be foiled.

fuel gauge on empty: stop and rebuild your energy.

gear impossible to engage correctly: are struggling with an intractable problem.

headlights, seeing other's: can't see past a disagreeable solution.

many glaring: quick and decisive action can avert disaster.

own won't light: are forcing the issue.

hitchhiker in an, being a: will be criticized for being overly dependent upon others.

picking up: will have confrontations with creditors.

horn, hearing a loud: have taken an illegal turn.

idle, running in: create a constructive use for your energy.

ignition won't turn on: something fails to strike a vital spark.

impounded, being: your innocent action has been misread.

leasing an: will acquire an unfavorable reputation.

man, an, to a: sexual drive with power, mobility, dexterity and carelessness.

woman: ambition, assertion, desire to overtake the male, freedom.

night in an, spending the: helpful friends were overenthusiastic with their advice.

owning an: are stealing a reputation.

pedals, pressing the: your ambitions and decisive abilities will be acknowledged.

radiator in a, a: your hasty actions cause you to make the wrong decision.

rear view mirror, see danger in: go full speed ahead.

reverse, driving in: setbacks caused by people you have run over.

rolling in: your backsliding is self-induced.

riding in an, others: be on guard against false news.

woman, a: your name is scandalized; your weakness will be disclosed.

running over someone with your: are destroying a part of self with your blind ambition.

skidding: your judgment error endangers your family.

pulling out of a skid: your mentor will make a favorable turn.

speeding in an: pick up your opponent and include him in race.

and getting a ticket: displeasure with own sexual performance.

man: sexual euphoria, pause and appreciate yourself.

stalling on highway: unable to gain momentum, check the engine.

stealing your, others: traveling in uncharted business circles will prove costly.

steering wheel comes off in hands: the money you need is delayed being paid back.

stepping out of an: stagnation at the degree you are presently actualizing your potential.

tires flat: massage those thighs and walk every day!

blow out: check the air and rotate your tires, now!

van, getting out of a: plans for trip will not be realized; loss of employment.

others: do not act impulsively; good things come to one with patience.

vulnerable to damage, being: fear of inadequacy squelches your performance.

windshield, can't see through the: stop and look sideways.

winning a race in an: will make a swift disposal of the competition.

AUTUMN

16-21-22-24-45-50

in the: a harvesting of rewards from unexpected sources.

of: withdrawal from your surroundings.
>*in the spring:* unfriendly influences nearby.
>>*summer:* many ups and downs.
>>*winter:* love for a person is dying.

AVALANCHE

04-14-28-35-36-50

buried under an: your life is out of control, dig yourself out.
>*others:* change your surroundings for your health's sake.

mudslide, being under a: oppressive force threatens to overwhelm you.

running away from an: must avert impending danger before freeze sets in again.

rushing down mountain: the inertia of the rejected project must be blocked.

seeing an: insurmountable obstacles confront your rigid stance.

standing on unstable earth: break loose your frozen emotions and learn to fly.

AWAKE

07-22-25-30-42-48

being awakened: be aware of channels for your creativity.
>*an alarm clock:* are always half a step behind.
>*by someone:* staunch friends lead to good business affairs.
>*wide:* a problem must be recognized and solved.

dreaming while awake: are in the control seat; make your life.

having to wake up: are threatened by danger; be alert.

mind keeps you: admit your secret guilt and apologize.

others waking up: a trap is being laid for you.

AWNING

04-09-13-17-18-20

lowering an: improvement with change of occupation.

raising an: will receive many suitors and reject them all.

sitting under an: will escape an expected injury.

AXE

11-14-25-26-31-34

broken: loss of fortune through breakup with close friend.

lifting a sharp: someone who is threatened by you will strike back.
>*with blood on it:* will be blamed for other's mistakes.

man dreaming of an: separation of relationship through battle.
>*woman:* a wealthy lover will be eliminated.

owning an: danger is averted by own bravery.

rusty: your inconsiderate actions cause you to quarrel with people.

sharp, a: your influence is based on shaky credentials.

splitting wood: your emotions are divided.

swinging an: a business promotion through threatening your boss.

working with an: are not an innocent bystander anymore, but the perpetrator.
>*someone else is:* your actions have caused ill will.

BABY

05-13-39-47-51-52

another's: you have an infantile dependence on someone who does not know.

bald, a: you want to return to when bald was adorable.

beautiful, a: you need nurturing and encouragement.

buttocks of a: you are exhausted by constant failure to reunite your family.

carriage, being in a: your responsibilities will hamper your socializing.
>*with others:* jealous of a sibling; pay attention to your inner child.

crying, hearing a: disputes in the family will be remedied by an outsider.

diapers, changing: new growth opens to untapped potential.
>*refusing to change:* husband's job will take him from home for long periods.

drooling: party with your peers.

feeding a: you will eventually reap the rewards of your labor.

first steps, taking: your reluctance to act causes difficulties with associates.

foundling, finding a: take care of all children within your reach.

giving birth to a: start new, more productive direction now.

helpless, a: that of least account proves to be of great value.

many: your friend's refusal to grow up shouldn't stop you.

newborn, a: a union at the physical, mental and spiritual levels.

   in diapers: become open and not fearful of events.

nursery, being in a: things will not run quietly.
   bringing a baby home to a: disturbed love.

nursing, a: concern for your helplessness and wish to be loved.

rocking a cradle: forget selfishness to keep the peace.

sick, being a: your failure to overcome your basic instincts.

   and crying: feeling neglected but must take care of business problem.

sitter, a: be wary of your own security; you will be blamed for another's anger.

sleeping, a: your future looks bright if you accept your responsibilities.

smart, a very: struggle for the perfection of the higher self.

sucking milk from mother's breast, a: are too dependent on parental guidance.

   wet nurse's, a: are too reliant upon others who have no loyalty to you.

swaddling clothes, a, in: your ideas are squelched in early development.

toddling, a: sudden independence is intoxicating.

ugly, an: misfortune ahead from someone you trust.

your: a rebirth of self in a state of innocence.

BACHELOR
01-23-24-25-48-46

beating someone, dreaming of a: good fortune in love affairs.

being a: change in life, but on the safe side of the altar.

old, an: misfortune in an early affair has tainted your ability to love.

young, a: wish to return to person you were before marriage.

getting married: will find a rich woman to marry.

middle-aged, a: sudden change in circumstances; stay away from the ladies.

of a: beware of deceitful, desperate, designing women.

slapping someone on the face: an episode of reckless love.

BACK
10-11-22-33-36-48

backward, going: retrace your steps to find the flaw.

bare, a: vulnerability to illness, fraud and giving the wrong advice.

broken, being: you will have ulcers from being poisoned with jealousy.

looking at someone's: his true character is in what he cannot see or reveal.

of own: you will always be behind the part of yourself you have turned your back on.

someone turning his, on you: rekindle old friendship with present awareness.

sores, full of: hurts, repressed to your unconscious, fester.

spine, animals having trouble with: another has stood up for you and suffered for it.

   another: loss of wealth in an unsympathetic lawsuit blaming you for another's failures.

   children: standing up for yourself is an unpleasant task.

turning right side of the: your boss has a low opinion of you as spineless.

   left: a friend is acting superior to you; your strength of character is intimidating.

BACKGAMMON
02-17-21-29-32-44

game of, losing a: business loss expected through allying with wrong foe.

   playing: financial gains, but your affairs are still unsettled.

     others: unfortunate triumph over enemies leads to a strained friendship.

winning: expect an inheritance that will endure much contesting.

BACKPACK
02-03-22-24-47-49

carrying a: use contents wisely to further your position.

> *bending over from:* turn some responsibilities over to others.
> *soldiers:* difficulties ahead for a short time, but only in the company of friends.

of a: an enemy is seeking your ruin, but cannot disrupt your column of support.

old worn: each crease represents a distinct memory.

BACON
03-06-20-31-32-43

eating, alone: money comes easily throughout life.

> *rancid:* old trials become present worries.
> *with others:* wealth as long as your hands are clean.

frying: unexpected gift if you degrease your heart.

purchasing: improve conditions at home.

receiving as a gift: you will be highly compensated.

BADGE
04-09-10-12-15-47

enemies wearing: treason and unfaithfulness to you, honor to them.

of: you are being considered for a promotion; is that how you see yourself?

pinned on you, being: the possibilities to rise in status are endless.

> *others:* you will be warned of trouble ahead in crowds.

policeman, pinning a, on a: family reunion in the family profession.

BADGER
09-13-22-36-47-48

being chased by: starvation must be endured to get past fear.

feeding, a fat: abundance due to your business acumen.

field, resting in a: big work ahead in unfamiliar places.

killing a: luck after battles with hardship.

tooth of a: you will win at cards.

BAGGAGE
06-15-27-41-42-49

bags, paper: reluctance to face up to impending dangers.

> *tote:* have everything you want with you, except unexpected company.

car, in a: unexpected money.

carrying only one: many debts are incurred.

> *heavy:* your lifestyle is too excessive, your workload is heavy; keep your spirits light.
>> *lighter than expected:* you need to exert yourself; defining you is not easy.
> *others, your:* your dependence could prove positive.
> *several:* treachery from a friend, overwork from an enemy.

empty: valuables will be in an odd place, behind something.

find your, unable to: others provoke you and cause you to fail.

house, inside the: cancel your trip; change your locks.

leather: be wary of the envy of those you meet on unexpected trip.

losing your: you feel ill-equipped to face the situation.

other's: misfortune from unexpected company.

putting things in a: you are not contributing your fair share.

room, being inside a: a trip has been cancelled.

rummaging through: your character is sound beneath all the trivial clutter.

stealing: you are avaricious toward others' possessions.

street, on the: abundant burdens await you, as your belongings will be stolen.

throwing away: contents will return to haunt you.

wagon, on a: you are making something hard that is quite simple.

BAGPIPES
13-23-27-29-35-48

owning: lending support and leading the troops.

> *others:* perpetuation of matrimonial worries, if you do not get past sadness.

playing: you are greatly loved in distressing times.

others: a marriage proposal is received.

BAIL

03-05-07-08-25-35

bailiff, fighting with a: fury with own misdeeds, not the consequences of them.

forfeiting: striving for a higher place, you cannot miss any steps.

furnishing: trouble with an old friend and your money.

not granting: present condition in life will improve.

requesting: unforeseen accidents through unfortunate alliances.

BAKERY

03-13-18-30-39-48

baker, a: transmutes physical into wisdom you can digest.

at, a: someone will become rich at your expense.

at work in a: the unpredictable excites the mundane.

baking: your ideas have been transformed into palatable forms.

bread: be wary of losing ability to care for your family.

mince pies at Christmas: a potpourri of sweet thoughts are baked to perfection.

muffin: you will receive a small legacy and spend it on the home.

cake, missing a: a short-lived infatuation with sugar.

croissants: a delicate beginning in your uphill battle with home.

dough, kneading: you will be publicly humiliated until your creation is accomplished.

doughnuts, baking: build up your savings account for extensive worldwide travel.

eclair, eating an: you will meet old sweetheart and reminisce.

fudge, making: desire for revenge against those who thwart their ambitions.

gingerbread, baking: improvement in family's social standing through children.

of a: you will be rich with perseverance and avoidance of pitfalls.

of an oven: your finances will rise, if you use the right temperature.

owning a: outwit your foes by feeding their egos.

rolling pin, using a: the thinner the dough the lighter the mood.

throwing a: creative minds need to use their anger in their projects.

BALCONY

11-21-26-28-31-32

being on a: disagreeable news of the unsavory actions of absent friends.

person of opposite sex, with: the longer the separations, the greater the love.

crashing to the ground: heed the warning of a professional.

draped with a flag: mourning, leading to determination that you will succeed.

leaving a, with a loved one: big disappointments will be broadcast news.

lovers saying farewell on a: a long separation will follow.

recognizing another person on a: a happy reunion with a dear friend.

sitting on a: you will be unable to keep what you now have.

standing: present position will be lost, a preemptive strike is in order.

waving to someone from a: success through receptiveness to other's ideas.

on a: a new friend will have positive influence.

BALL

06-07-10-16-31-36

colorful, a: your affair is fleeting; love has roots.

different, a: friends are lacking in your competitive spirit.

globe, of a: it appears that fate plays games in the perfect sphere.

hand, playing: it takes physical courage to field whatever is thrown at you.

losing a: need a well-rounded approach to the whole.

playing, with partner: a new partnership will prove profitable.

many people: relate only to the universal forces of the world.

rolling downhill: you are your own contradiction.

BALL (Gala)

01-03-11-32-35-38

among the dancers at, being: good news is received.

belle of the, being the: many love affairs, but not without difficulty.

 dancing with: avoid rivals while enjoying the strains of entrancing music.

 neglecting: complicated social affairs.

dancing in a, room: your spirits will be lifted.

 man: obstacles are encountered.

 young girls: you will have plenty of money.

girls being at a: feel distressed at being left out.

married woman dancing with another man at a: gossip by friends, slander by enemies.

 unmarried, married: friends will cheat you.

 woman, her boyfriend at: you will encounter much opposition.

 husband: success is had.

masquerade, attending a: beware of a trap.

of a: plenty of money will be inherited.

 at which you are not present: you will soon be engaged.

professional dancer at a, a: you will meet a pleasant person.

room, a: renewing old friendship.

watching a, without dancing: a legacy will soon be received.

wedding, attending a: misfortune in one's affairs.

 well-dressed woman, with a: a betterment of your position.

widow dancing with a married man at: will soon divorce his wife.

BALLET

16-20-21-22-40-45

dancing: you are easily seduced into infidelity, failure and jealousy.

 daughter: you will marry a bandleader.

 many dancers: a childlike awareness of an uplifting fantasy.

 others: take directions, others and yours.

 young girls: health and prosperity are at the mercy of delicate movement.

doing a pirouette: much gratitude for dedicated hard work cannot match your joy.

dreaming of a, man: frivolous with your attentions.

woman: trouble from lighthearted affair with younger man.

young woman: your lover is unfaithful with an older woman.

on a professional stage: exercise more to forestall poor health.

watching a: being deluded by your partner will give momentary concern.

BALLOON

17-37-39-44-46-49

being in a: a release from captivity of your creative idea.

 ascending: a risk you take will compromise the venture.

 basket of hot air: slow but steady progress to unlimited heights.

 descending: unfavorable ventures unless you calm down and accept aid.

bursting: find the pieces and fit them together in a different way.

child's: you will quickly get over disappointment of losing job.

deflating: you have given reason for another to be angry.

floating: you need a stepladder to reach your goals.

of a: your inventive mind causes disappointment to others.

seeing a colorful: catch a discovery before it dissipates in thin air.

BANANAS

15-23-29-41-46-48

buying: none of your emotions can be denied, nor should your mate's.

decaying: distasteful affair will be undertaken.

eating: you will be imposed upon to fulfill some self-inflicted duty.

growing: a small business venture, if undertaken, will accumulate debts.

selling: unprofitable business is a disagreeable enterprise.

BANDAGE

05-06-16-27-40-45

gauze, of using: your mental torture and physical pain are relieved.

 throwing away: the residue of poisons leaking from within.

 other's: others are concealing their feelings for you.

having a Band-Aid: receive an unexpected visit.

> *binding a cut with:* you will improve your estate.

> *buying:* you expect too many favors from others.

> *handling:* expect congenial work and recovery from an illness.

putting on others: forgiveness of past emotional injury.

wearing a on your mouth: all past offenses must be forgiven and forgotten.

> *children:* expect news about an accident.

BANDIT
08-17-22-24-42-43

attacked by a, being: beware of accidents.

attacking a: rely upon own vigor and judgment.

of a: prosperity in one's affairs, but you will apologize for methods used.

robbing a bank: imminent danger from a visiting friend.

several: handling danger will advance you in business.

BANJO
08-13-25-28-47-48

owning, a: you must endure sorrow while enjoying this amusement.

playing, a: poverty, but a merry time of it.

> *others:* slight worries will soon fade in the distance.

stage, playing a, on a: a big consolation is in cosmic exchange.

BANK
05-07-11-21-28-34

being a banker: you wish to be respected for your financial advice.

being in a: false promises are received from your energy storeroom.

> *money changer's:* giving lavishly does not gain you friends.

borrowing money from a: financial losses ahead through your careless act.

dealing with a: sudden loss of confidence and emotional security.

hoarding money in a: fear you will lose virility if you share.

lien on your, account: disputes are not ridiculous when they can cross state lines.

operating an ATM: your emotions are secure.

> *and having it take your card:* confront one who risks your emotions.

owning a: friends make fun of your innate sense of responsibility.

receiving a loan from a: you feel insecure in balancing business and personal life.

sandbags reinforcing a: put pet project on ice and watch for time to reopen it.

BANKRUPT
01-08-11-17-22-30

being: extreme caution required for business to prosper.

> *others:* your business needs immediate attention of others.

going into bankruptcy: you will receive the esteem of friends and sneers of enemies.

> *declare, having to:* avoid speculation on what might have been.

BANNER
12-14-35-43-46-48

house, on a: failure of enemies to cause you to defect to their side.

raising your, in a battle: justify your action, which was ridiculed.

> *seizing:* painful dilemmas force you to take an alternate route.

> > *your enemies, their:* the challenge has been set.

receiving: your personal position is not good; promised gift will not be given.

red: help received from friends abroad.

ship, on a: you will take an ocean voyage.

BANQUET
14-19-21-29-37-46

attending a: pleasures will be costly, a depression victory.

> *political, a:* disappointment at not receiving an expected gift.

> *wedding, a:* good friends surround you, but do you admire them?

old person dreaming of a: a grave misunderstanding in what you value.

young person: you are enjoying comfort while others starve.

BAPTIZED
02-08-16-39-43-49

baptism of a baby: take responsibility for a new project.

another's: a friend's illness will awaken your secret strengths.

being at a: a new face creates a drastic change in your life.

   your: cleanse yourself of old negative emotions.

fire, by: intense purging will result in a refined character.

officiating at a: allow old insights to redirect your life.

wind, by: immersion in a desperate intellectual struggle.

having been: you are open to the possibilities of a prosperous life.

   own children: influx of your potential realized by your children.

   relatives: you will be disappointed by changes in your best friend.

BAR
12-14-40-41-42-43

being at a: you will cover up your loss of a loved one with deceptive plans.

drink at a, having a: anxiety caused by your sense of failure.

   alone: obstacles block your expression of illicit desires.

   company, with: control your passions without becoming rigid.

   others: more highly esteemed by friends than you realize.

   single women: have self-deprecating view of your sexual attractiveness.

going to a: you will be put in prison for actions of your acquaintances.

keeper, being a: provide others means to act out their conflicts, not yours.

miss transport home from a: time for another to lead your project.

of a: you will be guilty of foolish actions in a group.

people won't let you leave a: other's advice is not good for you.

stool, an empty: make room for new friends.

BARBARIANS
01-04-10-31-35-43

being with a: you will humiliate your inner self for social acceptance.

fighting: failure of enemies to practice temperance in advocating their opinions.

killed, being: desperate mental struggle to not defend mediocrity, even in friends.

man being barbaric: your strength will be transformed and resign itself to duty.

   woman: self-abnegation will create a lustful engagement.

BARBECUE
13-19-20-24-38-41

ablaze: heed sympathetic warnings and helpful suggestions.

charcoal unlit: body is unwilling to deal with barrage of fever.

glowing coals: your hospitality will be abused.

grille, cooking at a: an expansive social life is yours.

   brazier: warmth in auspicious affairs.

   poking food on a: intervene with the uninvited.

BARBER
09-10-20-24-27-46

being: you wish to reduce another's strength over you.

female, haircut and shave by: lack of confidence in relations with females.

going to a: arbitrate the hostility of the male and female sides of yourself.

hair cut by a: fear of being dominated by your temptations.

home, calling a, to the: wish to equal the odds in an argument.

shave at a, having a: feel strength to reveal yourself to society.

shop, being in a: difficulties in business with those who wish to control.

BAREFOOT
12-18-20-37-44-46

feet alone: expect trouble from polluted sources.

   and legs to knees are bare: social dishonor at your very basis.

     to hips: a small prison term will be served.

going, children: shame and sorrow of crushed expectations.

   man, a: success is postponed by meager increments.

   woman, a: evil influences surround your search for lasting love.

running, through wet grass: you are free to act on the possibilities.

walking: keep in touch with your roots.

   on clear water: your health will improve.

   over gravel: deal with each stone of conflict.

BARGAIN

19-21-25-30-31-45

being cheated out of a: your own home will be robbed.

having made a good: advancement within your position.

   others: you will have to get up a little earlier.

of a: trust only your own opinions.

splitting up the: you will be rid of an enemy, but not the petty annoyances of friends.

BARLEY

07-22-31-33-35-49

bread made of, eating: great satisfaction and good health.

buying: unhappiness that family cannot provide for itself.

eating: big satisfaction and rugged health.

growing, in the country: progress in city career.

handling, with the hands: joy and profit from quick and correct decisions.

lot of, having a: a mind organized with foresight succeeds.

malt from, making: a period of wealth.

selling: an enemy is very near, let him decay.

BARTENDER

07-08-11-14-26-45

being, a: you are the crutch supporting everyone else but yourself.

   married to a: partner is feeling used by you.

dating a: someone to satisfy your infantile oral needs.

having a need for a: you have a friend who is paid to be convivial and of service.

of a: childhood sensual comforts and exemption from responsibilities.

wishing to date a: attracted to fast life with irregular pleasure, not propriety.

BARN

06-17-21-22-26-49

animals invading a: prosperity is when everyone wants what you have.

being in a: you will win a lawsuit.

   with others: you will receive an inheritance.

constructing a: hard work will pay off in protection.

   others, for you: stop negating the value of neighbors.

empty, an: put your support in the other project.

   with doors open: misfortune leads a clear way in, nurturing without.

fire, catching: mislaid valuable papers should be stored in safe.

full, a: you will marry a wealthy person.

handling grain in a: use care in your diet.

hayrack, an empty: confront your career problem: you have an unnerving sense of rejection.

   full, a: a promise of a ripe and mature future.

Jesus in a crib in a: blessings will fall upon you.

BAROMETER

13-24-36-37-41-46

bad weather, registering: evaluate your emotions before you change them.

   fair: control your emotions, don't act on them.

   good: do not block this change in your emotional climate.

   rainy: put your trust in the other person.

   stormy: change in position will bring financial losses.

having a: air pressure is causing your headache.

rising rapidly: inner pressure of emotional conflict will come to a head.

BARRACKS

02-22-32-29-41-43

being lost from your: a restrictive relationship must change or it will end.

   blocked from: problems must be resolved before it is time to move on.

living in a: reexamine your motives for the differences you have with your boss.

   a soldier: difficulties will end with a change of venue, new ones will begin.

many: hard work under influence of authority.

BARREL

01-02-27-35-41-45

bottom missing: change jobs to get your promotion.

buying a: you feel sufficiently sated to share your wine.

empty: change your dissatisfactions.

large number of: abundance of money and merrymaking.

opening a: A new friend will be influential in expanding your horizons.

owning a: an unexpected gift.

rolling empty uphill: hard times to come.

> *several below the bar:* you are establishing a solid future.

upright and full: a lucky streak is about to begin.

BASEBALL
08-16-23-29-40-41

batting a home run: your business venture has turned to success.

pitching ball: your bad temper is the cause of your family troubles.

playing game of: future prosperity if you do not foul out.

> *good score, making a:* divorce is ahead if you don't squelch false rumors.

> *not scoring:* disappointments from false reports spread about you.

> *others:* cultivate domestic contentment by being a cheerful companion.

BASEMENT
08-14-21-30-32-39

entering a: you will benefit from several years of a frugal life

foundations crumbling: get new references to your degree of openness or suppression.

house collapsed into: too bad you bought the furniture first.

seeing a: poor circulation in your feet is a sign of gout.

trapped in a: your deepest feelings beg to be understood.

water seeping in: reestablish your credit base.

working in your: your patience will pay dividends.

BASKET
16-18-24-33-38-44

another's: your family will increase in number.

empty, having an: you will lose money through carelessness.

full: plenty in all its forms.

flower: another will have an accident.

full, of a: everlasting life through birth, death and resurrection.

giving away your: don't help that friend.

laundry: doubly confirm another's honesty before placing your trust.

BASTARD
03-05-11-41-40-47

being a: to overcome lack of love, you must give it.

> *ashamed of:* you will have trouble raising all of your children.

having a: dissatisfaction that another's way won't give you yours.

of a: other's discovery of your impurities obstructs your living up to your purities.

BATH
16-19-20-21-42-45

empty, an: don't proceed with your plan in anger.

lathering your body in a: good news is below the encrusted old.

preparing a: fight with the old to make way for the new.

> *children, for:* happiness is yours.

> > *mate:* high ambitions of self-indulgence will be realized.

robe, wearing a: need aid from relatives to cleanse family debts.

sun, taking a: lush green foliage and fresh country air.

> *being criticized for:* it is easy for others to condemn you for things they can't do.

> *with family:* unexpected advances.

> > *sweetheart:* warm affection previously unknown to you.

taking a, at bedtime: you will surrender to a lover.

> *cold water, in:* only direct involvement leads to success.

> *early in the morning:* old anxieties in your dreams will be washed away.

> *evening, in the:* strengthen outer self to allow cleansing of inner self.

> *ice water, in:* disgrace from prejudicial acts.

> *lukewarm water, in:* serious state of unwanted emotional dirt.

noon, at: the beginning of the healing process.

warm water, in: you will be separated from love through lack of interest.

BATHING

10-23-38-40-43-45

bathhouse, at a: clear up misunderstanding with friend.

canal, in a: satisfying logical research after intelligence.

cascade of water, in a: present projects will fail.

children at sea, with: happiness within the family.

clear water, in: danger in business situation is passing.

loved one, a: a miscarriage of fetus or of justice.

your mate: anxiety over adultery.

clothes on, with: you will have an argument with lover.

cold water, in: exercise your healthy body.

dirty: illness is creeping up on you.

hot: intrigues of salacious character will be offered to you.

with others: be careful in selection of your companions.

house, in a: avoid frivolous and immoral companions.

lake, in a: unhappiness will pass through no action of your own.

marsh, in a: forget lost loves, hurry on to earthly pursuits.

muddy water, in: a process of mental purification.

murky: get out of the negative environment, change friends.

nude, in the: an inheritance of spiritual dedication.

open sea, in: with endurance you will establish a large fortune.

others, with: go to the aid of your friends; defame your enemies.

river, in a: unusually good business ahead.

swimming pool, in a: much solicitude from one of the opposite sex.

waves, with: solve this problem and success is yours.

weeds, in water choked with: you fear loss

of good opinions through others' ill intent.

BATHROOM

19-23-29-31-38-45

basin, drinking from a: difficulties ahead in love affairs.

eating over a: you will not marry the person you love.

empty, an: you will incur many debts.

of a, full of water: joy within the family.

using a full, of water: you will have plenty of money.

woman: her graces will win her social elevation.

bathtub, being in a: moral cleansing of disappointments.

clothed, getting into a: purge yourself of moral impurities.

empty, an: business worries cannot be escaped.

of a: you will become very angry with your guilt.

one you love, being in a, with the: an inheritance is received.

undressing, but not getting into a: love troubles.

toilet: relieve yourself of another's emotional buttress.

BATS

05-06-08-20-21-38

black: quarrel and financial disaster awaits you when your conscience becomes aware.

gray: seek out less fickle friends.

hanging from the ceiling: proceed in the opposite direction.

many: if you follow your instincts blindly, evil abounds.

right side up: your debts will be paid; get a receipt.

sport's, a: defense against aggression should be a game, not real life.

white: a sick person does not recover.

BATTLE

05-06-12-26-28-35

alone, fighting a: things turn out right, if you are not the aggressor.

defeated in a: business dealings with others are unwise.

field: feel mental turmoil, with antagonistic impulses set to battle each other.

fists, with: double-crossed in love affairs.

guerrilla tactics, of: clandestine plans involving devious tactics.

invasion, being in an: interference, real or psychological.

land: identify your opposition, then decide.

naval: you will be triumphant in your maneuvers.

of a: you can only live up to your potential, not anyone else's.

regiment, being part of a: talk is safe in numbers, but one among you is a traitor.

watching a: you will be persecuted within yourself for not participating.

winning a: wish to forget real problems and destroy the enemy.

BAYONET

13-14-21-26-33-39

carrying in the hands: verify the correct enemy in your own enterprises.

having a: success is postponed until you see fit to seek it.

> *soldier:* mistakes need patching up to prevent separation of parties.

of a: quarrels with friends attack your heart.

others holding: you will be under the power of enemies unless you get the bayonet.

BEACH

15-17-33-38-44-53

bay, in a: the manifestation of mating.

finding garbage debris on the: take the opportunity others have rejected.

> *oil slicks:* have a healthy attitude toward sex.

naked on the, being: you have regrouped and are prepared for fresh adventure.

plodding through sand on the: you are walking the line between genius and insanity.

tanning on the: business will improve on hearing from a long-forgotten friend.

> *but not going in the water:* you are grounded, pulling away from all around you.

BEADS

13-28-31-32-46-48

buying: those in an elevated position will show you attention.

counting: immaculate joy and contentment.

finding: you will be molested on a short trip.

scattering: loss of reputation among acquaintances.

selling: the sum of money will astonish you.

stringing: favors from a wealthy person are received.

BEANS

05-11-29-31-36-38

buying: you will be criticized and slandered.

cooking: good business enterprises, but ill tidings from loved ones.

drying: disappointment in ability to acquire material possessions.

eating: a contagious disease is contracted.

growing: live modestly; worries and illness among children ahead.

having: a friend you trust is proving to be false.

lentil: assurance of a fulfilled home.

lima: disappointing reception of solid achievement.

picking: your selections are correct, keep contagion from spreading.

stalk, a: let your ambition reach for the sky.

BEAR

01-10-22-31-33-43

attacked by a: you will be persecuted by one who professes to love you.

being a: your vitality has returned to face major problems.

cage, in a: liberation from charges of complicity.

cub, of one: a friendly hint will be given; charming and cuddly are *in.*

> *many:* emotional sorrow from an overprotective situation.

> > *in a cage:* you are feeling possessed by your mother.

dancing: you will be tempted into speculations whose profit will be inconsistent.

> *with a:* your plan will endure with your strength.

dead: resolution of emotional ambiguities.

drinking, milk: others are envious of your power.

driving off an attacking: the darkness that occurs before spiritual rebirth.

eating, meat: a long illness will initiate you into next phase.

hibernating, a: a wish to retreat from reality.

killing a: defeat your adversaries with their own gossip.

man dreaming of a: create a distance from your mother.

of a: great competition in every pursuit.

polar, in a zoo: loss of heritage and solid foundations makes a path slippery.

   sunny habitat: must find your comfort zone between old and new.

several: people gossip about your raw primitive instinct.

standing: insecurities towards your mother.

transformed into a: you will be able to free yourself from your inhibitions.

woman dreaming of a: a rival will threaten your love.

working, a: the competition is overwhelming.

BEARD
22-25-28-34-35-42

black: success in business is promised.

brown: at the threshold of healing is sadness.

combing your: your vanity is detectable to former companions.

curly, having a: are you making the impression you desire?

cutting of someone you know: the real person is exposed.

full, man having a: you will gain unexpected courage.

goatee, a: a health scandal.

gray: loss of money, hard luck and quarrels.

   turning: you will suffer from gossip and slander.

hairs from, losing: loss of a female relative.

handsome, a: complete success in own enterprises.

having a: fierce struggle for mastery over financial distress.

   false: you are deceiving yourself about your health.

   long, very: prosperity will come and stay.

   not: large gain in business.

   shaggy: each split end is an abandoned dream.

man dreaming of a woman with a: your lover is hiding her innermost thoughts.

pulling off own: ruin and poverty; will have to pay creditors.

red: you are provoked and will lose money in combat.

shaving his, man: loss of virility.

short, a very: riches are short lived.

smaller, making a: in danger of losing wealth.

thin, a very: death of a family member.

trimming own: fear of castration and loss of male power.

washing own: anxiety over being obsolete.

white: great prosperity through conscientiousness.

   long: listen to the wisdom of the ages.

woman dreaming of having a small: an abortion will occur.

   a man with a beard: you will leave your husband.

      shaving his: looking for a gentle father figure.

BEAST
04-05-08-09-13-21

babbling noises, making: you will suffer grief.

beating a wild: damage in your own affairs.

   bones of: bad business transactions.

chased by a, being: vexation caused by enemies.

fight, a, starting a: you will be molested by friends.

fighting with another beast, a: you are likely to become ill.

running: only material pleasures will concern you.

scuffling with a: cruel suffering; if you attempt to rise above your station.

BEATEN
01-03-16-22-30-39

beating a child: you are taking unfair advantage.

   friend, a: contentment at a game well played.

being: home life does not support your inner nature.

   others: who is beating you at your own game?

married person dreaming of beating a spouse: both will be very happy.

   someone, you: an ambitious colleague must be matched.

35

others getting a beating: obstacles block your way.

giving a: despite adversities, your project will succeed.

BEAUTIFUL

07-09-21-22-40-42

being: illness from fear of losing desirability.
  with a, woman: will have agreeable past-times.

others who are: invalidism caused by jealous admirer.

BEAUTY SALON

05-06-10-20-31-42

being at a, to have hair done: beware of untrue friends and cherish the true ones.
  facial: embarrassed by the way you present yourself.
  friends: insurmountable obstacles confront you.
  waxing: you will complete your present plans successfully.

going to a: your partner's lack of attention is temporal.
  with a member of the family: watch your spending to live up to your self-esteem.

BEAVER

04-06-17-26-38-39

buying a, coat: you will be accused of improper conduct toward an innocent.
  selling: be cautious of overwork in business ventures.

friends having a, coat: a friend is industriously working against you.
  relatives: don't let spiteful gossip damage your emotions.

of the: be very diligent in planning meticulously.

owning a: a small inheritance through perseverance will not solve problems.

BED

07-18-19-23-36-46

arising from: sickness at loss of intimacy.

baby in, dreaming of a: someone with evil intentions is watching you.

burning, a: secrets are divulged that bring prosperity.
  own, but not being injured: tragedy will interfere with daily routine.

camping, a: you will go deep into the country to afford to buy real estate.

children going to: you wish to escape into a world of sleep.
  wetting the: anxiety from a domestic source.

disorder, in: secrets will be discovered by you, but not revealed.

empty, an: win over a person who in the past has been cool toward you.

four poster, a: private behavior needs to pause to look at itself.

hotel room, being in a: unexpected visits at inopportune moments.

made neatly. a: you will have a contented heart with new lover.

making a: change of residence caused by change in relationships.

old people going to: dead friends are near at hand.

pristine white, a: peace.

remaining in a, for a long time: you are unwilling to accept that the relationship is over.

resting comfortably in own: you will have security and love.

seeing yourself in a: you need solitude for your health.

sick in a, being: complications will develop from an illness.

sitting on own: beginning of a soul-to-soul contact of an early marriage.

sleep, being in a, but unable to: don't be too trusting of your rejection of dreams.

soiled, seeing a: negative people surround you.

strange, being in a: win over person who in the past has been unfriendly.

stranger in your: matrimonial unfaithfulness.

under the stars: future possibilities are infinite.

BEDBUGS

13-17-26-33-45-47

bedding, having in the: prosperity beyond fondest hopes.

bitten by, being: wealth and abundance of property.

crushing, and blood appears: serious illness deep within.
  water: you will have a nonfatal accident.

many: death of a relative provides the place for you to move.

   mattress, on a: you will be provoked by a friend.

of: you will be annoyed in a relationship.

BEDROOM
11-12-24-33-36-42

apartment, in an: family secrets are concealed.

bedclothes, buying new: big love and friendship.

   pulled from the bed: face the challenge.

being in a: feel relaxed and secure in health and income.

boudoir, of a beautiful lady, being in the: separation from your mate.

   making love in a: will soon be arrested.

   preparing a: good results in love affairs.

   ugly lady, of an: will have disputes.

friend's, sleeping in a: will become drunk.

hotel: stupid gossip about you is spread.

luxurious, someone's: delays in present affairs.

own, of: changes in one's affairs.

BEEF
06-11-16-39-40-49

boiled, eating: you will be in deep melancholy.

boiling water, dropping in: derive pleasure out of life.

bones, taken from: a loss of wealth is anticipated.

displaying at a show: actions will be rewarded.

eating, raw: your internal disorder spreads to family.

   roast: you will have a pleasant life.

   stew: you will be comfortably well-off; long-lasting happiness.

hamburger: be on guard as to bruises you can't remember getting.

meatloaf: evil, foreboding over a trifling matter.

more than can eat: may result in mysterious cuts and bruises.

purchasing to cook: winnings at gambling.

tartar, eating: bodily afflictions if you do not perform sensibly.

throwing away: imminent danger.

BEEHIVE
09-19-21-26-38-39

empty: your individuality excludes teamwork.

full of bees: flitting about from one thing to another.

   flying around their: productive business requires twenty-four-vigilance.

   work, at: you are in an industrious communal organization.

overturned, being: your stumbling is infuriating friends.

taking honey from a: an enemy will be successful in seeking your ruin.

without honey: dangerous undertakings will cause you extended worry.

BEER
28-32-38-39-41-45

bottles of: business loss, if you speculate with numbers.

brewing: you will be exonerated from unjust accusations.

drinking: lively interchange with friends will be decisive.

   ale: simple needs, hearty pleasures, thrifty grasp of power.

friends becoming drunk from: designing intrigues bring devastation.

full mug of: excitement is brewing, rise to the occasion.

   several: too complacent about your satisfying life.

making, people: master your business; for a life free of troubles will be yours.

malt, brewing with: fermenting good luck to one for whom you care.

others drinking, but not yourself: you will have a little money; great generosity of loves.

party, being at a: bet on your success, the odds from your loss.

picking hops for: an enticing love affair will cease as suddenly as it began.

spilling: someone will reveal your guilt in an intrigue.

BEES
05-12-22-28-31-47

being attacked by: you are too busy and over-committed to drudgery work.

bumblebees flying around: too distracted with unimportant matters.

flying in the evening: you will receive a well-publicized profit.

honey in your own tree or shed, making: enemies will be overcome with sweetness.

own property, on: enjoy the source of your success in business.

top of your house, on: you will be unlucky from a sticky situation.

house, coming into your: enemies will damage your reputation.

killing: you will be ruined for having destroyed the wrong perpetrator.

many: stay surrounded by your own kind.

honey, with: will accumulate money and those who want yours.

morning, in the: diligence, organization and being there first lead to success.

noon, at: good earnings attained through shocking news.

queen: enemies want to hurt you.

stung by: beware of letting minor stinging thoughts control you.

not being: a minor difference of opinion, a confusion of activity.

swarms, in: mass power with individual weakness lead to a profitable undertaking.

being stung by a, of: beware of your enemies interfering in your close affections.

wax: smoothing over the pain of some internal want.

BEETLES
07-12-31-35-44-48

catching a: quarrels with friends over small ills; the problem is solvable.

flying: exceedingly good fortune.

killing: admit your mistake and matters will be set right quickly.

of: money will come in spurts; monitor your spending.

scarab: symbol of resurrection; humility is in order, poverty is not.

watching scampering over you: financial shortfalls soon.

BEETS
14-18-20-21-30-33

buying: you will receive an expensive gift.

eating: love affairs will be stained with slander.

from dirty dishes: distressful middle of the night awakenings.

field, growing in a: your own affairs will prosper.

piled up, many: good dealings in big business.

BEGGAR
09-17-19-32-45-48

accosted in the street by a, being: you are hiding difficulties from yourself.

refused to give when: your actions are detrimental to your social standing.

aged, an: exercise economy or you will lose property.

assisting a: you will overcome uncomfortable situation.

begging, enemies: you will escape a present danger.

friends: dissatisfaction with present surroundings.

others, for you: you are not admitting your need.

people you know: will receive the help of a good friend.

street, in the: be where your enemies will fail to see you.

being a: need intellectual challenge to prevent being a selfish miser.

and begging: affairs are prospering; don't take undue risks.

crippled, a: feel inadequate in your disputes within family.

house, coming into the: trouble follows a surprise visitor.

many: your weaknesses need support, but management is poor.

money to a, giving: he expresses the thought you dare not.

of a: a period of sorrow from the revelation of your shame.

of one: unexpected help is received as scandals are proved wrong.

BEHEADED
05-11-31-32-40-48

beheading another: solve your own problems.

being: business deals are accomplished but alienate partners.

enemies: benefit from another's bad judgment.

murderers: you cannot force someone to take responsibility for his actions.

businessmen dreaming of being: making correct business decisions against your heart.

guillotine, by a: traumatic memories of misdeeds will endanger you to fatal illness.

losing your head: your rational thought succumbs to your intuition.

murderers, by: overwhelming defeat and loss of real estate.

BELFRY

08-34-40-42-46-49

bells ring from: be free from embarrassment; financial credit will be received.

cathedral, of a: you must accept your place in the bigger picture.

church, of a: unexpected disgrace will be announced to you.

demolished, partially: loss of employment through reaching beyond abilities.

fortress, of a: enemies' efforts can be resisted, if you are alert.

high, a very: a long life is promised; the bell has not yet rung.

BELL

02-12-13-26-38-39

announcing others with a: relate this dream to family member who appeared in it.

being announced by a: you wish your work would be noticed.

   others: another will get your dream house.

chimes: anxiety over distant friend is confirmed.

church without a: are impotent in advising others.

dissonant gongs from a: distressing news exposing your lack of understanding.

door: exciting sexual adventures will surprise you.

funeral knell, tolling a: a missed opportunity to better yourself.

hearing a church, ringing: be on guard against anxieties caused by hidden enemies.

   doorbell: warning of family quarrels.

   many: important friendships have been solidified and announced.

   one: the object of your seduction is listening.

Liberty Bell, The: the beginning of a favorable phase of your life.

looking at a silent: someone highly placed is manipulating your success.

man, being a: you will settle disputes amicably and reap fortune.

striking a: your presence will make someone happy.

BELLOWS

04-11-21-23-29-33

lending: good results in triumph over poverty.

many: a false report can be debunked by perseverance.

of one: absent friends are desirous of seeing you.

using on a fire: will be confronted with powerful occult knowledge.

   not: wasted energies under misguided impulses.

BELLY BUTTON

05-06-20-28-43-47

children playing with their: insane desires to return to the source of nourishment.

hurting, if: a reaction to the beginning of a project.

own, of: your creativity is begging to be expressed; the source is your childhood.

relatives, of: an influential person will assist you in an adventure.

study own: have respect of your colleagues.

BELT

04-11-13-18-33-36

black: damage to anyone who challenges you.

broken: damage received will require major surgery.

buckling a: your rudeness will put a brake on your rise to power.

   others: a stranger will create gossip around you.

finding a: you are gaining another's trust, honor it.

gold: big earnings.

leather, a: relaxation for a moment, then be on guard.

losing a: heartfelt misery.

new, a: you will meet a significant stranger.

old, an: hard work is for naught; bright ideas bring success.

sash, putting on a: present your best facade for important guests.

   children: charge them to retain the

affections of one they could inherit from.

taking off a: your comedy can be belligerent.

  children: desires will be met with affection previously concealed.

silver: you will go to court to protect your honor.

tying a: you are suppressing your erotic needs to allow a smooth operation.

  others: wish to influence another, but cannot hold three things together.

yellow: treason.

BENCH

13-25-27-38-43-47

of a: attend to work carefully or you may lose your job.

sitting on a: a chance to go on a trip you have postponed in the past.

  children, park: exposed to the game, but you are not allowed to play.

  others: distrust debtors and confidants who can't meet you in public.

  with sun shining: will meet new friends and soon disagree with them.

BENEFITS

22-29-30-40-46-49

conferring on others: fortunate investments.

family: angry that you have not been able to provide for them.

friends being beneficial: a mystery will be solved.

receiving: will have a trust estate.

  endowment, an: will be unable to live up to responsibilities.

BEREAVEMENT

08-14-19-26-36-47

loss of friends: extend your circle of friends by socializing.

  relatives: you have not received support from people important to you.

  work: make an effort to talk to fellow workers.

separating from children: breakdown of communication leads to failure.

suffering from death of loved one: disappointment in extensive plans.

  loved one, your: remove barrier from communication.

BERET

03-24-26-39-42-47

children's: are innocent of what you have been accused.

cotton, having a: friendship is being abused by a friend.

  silk: deeds are not practical, but for effect.

owning a: someone will attempt to pull a dirty deal, but you will break it.

BEVERAGES

01-02-13-27-29-33

foam on the top of a: pleasure with light-hearted companions.

jug, in a cracked: loss of virginity.

  liquid spilling from a: emotion wasted on the unworthy.

spilling over: emotions for an unrequited love overwhelms you.

BIBLE

01-02-11-33-40-49

believing in: enemies will be overcome by your perseverance.

buying a: stop trying to justify your actions; act genuinely.

letting fall on the floor: do not disregard well-meant sound advice to feel internal peace.

open, an: are tortured by lack of discretion of an elderly, well-loved relative.

reading the: seek the hidden meaning for all that happens in you life.

  children: joy without profit, or need for any.

  someone, to you: resist temptations to vilify your ethics.

taking to church: some innocent action will clear your conscience.

Testament, consulting the New: your mental outlook can change your environment.

BICYCLE

04-09-18-37-40-43

buying a: your solo activity will improve your physical condition.

  for children: advancement, if you make right decision.

falling from a: someone is causing you to lose your balance.

owning a: happiness with large investment of personal effort.

unicycle: going it alone will leave balanced issues unstable.

pedals of a: you are pragmatic and authentic with delusions of grandeur.

racer crossing the finish line with arms up: triumph of balanced energies.

repairing a: your nervy yet sensitive actions create a work of efficiency.

riding, a: hurrying your ambitions will cause failure, others cannot lead your way.

    downhill: misfortune looms over you.

    tandem, in: acceptance of parts of mate and self previously rejected.

    uphill: high energy is needed to take advantage of bright prospects.

selling, a: you are sensitive to other's needs.

sitting on a: expect others to lead the way.

wheels being punctured: you are letting down your body.

BIG

03-09-26-27-43-47

being a, person: your hanging on to your weight is not power.

    extra, and tall: you are emotionally invested in your view of yourself to the opposite sex.

    talker around women: your strong emotional words do not impact your inadequacies.

    visited by, people: your hospitality will not live up to their expectations.

BIGAMY

17-22-26-28-37-39

being a bigamist: the severity of the penalty reflects your feelings about your offense.

    not: are defensive about your own offenses against others.

    partner: fear you will be cheated out of fair share of devotion.

        not: wish partner would find another to free you of emotional responsibility.

committing: deceit is not guilt free.

    punished for: the offense was against yourself.

not believing in: eager for the comfort of absolution.

BILL

01-04-16-41-45-48

being handed a: your decision was wrong, reverse it.

bills, being solicited to pay: your boss dislikes you.

    overdue, having: others speak evil of you.

    paying: immediate financial gains through the karmic repayment plan.

        not: the consequence of earlier transgressions is now.

for past mistakes: make a serious effort to be fair.

paying a: don't take on any new responsibilities.

receiving a: promises must be kept, at all costs.

writing a: sign of insecurity that you will be paid.

BILLFOLD

14-33-32-38-40-41

finding a: luck and prosperity.

    and returning it: a showering of gifts upon you.

lady's, a: attainment of almost every desire.

losing a: quarrels with closest friends.

own: big joy tempered by emotional sorrow.

relative's: a discovery of a secret life.

BILLIARDS

09-13-20-25-32-48

of a: game has reestablished a friendship that needs to address its first demise.

playing: planned event will begin your dissipation of wealth.

    engaged people: will have opposition from in-laws.

    every day: are pocketing balls with usual skill.

    married: love of mate is sincere, yours for mate is not.

    single: deal with problems in a particular prescribed order.

    snooker: block the opposition's unfair advantage.

BINOCULARS

13-14-33-34-38-41

being watched through: think carefully and concentrate fully before acting.

broken: your financial future is unclear.

buying: a woman of poor morals is nearby.

enlarging: take things too seriously, when clarity will reveal all.

loved one through, viewing a: loss of a distant relative.

men looking through: fortune through another's scandal.

women: will be greatly compensated in life.

military personnel using: will be damaged in personal affairs.

owning: your vision of the future is correct.

seeing through: what you see of the future is minute.

BIRDS

11-21-28-29-40-42

aviary, at an: warning to stop leaving work for social events.

beak, seeing a: voice your solutions; you need some form of relief.

being bitten by a: keep your opinions to yourself.

bluebird, a: the spirit is in limbo, deciding which life to live next.

blue jay, catching a: immediate marriage.

buzzard flying above: an unusual scandal will make you vulnerable to loss.

away: decayed attitudes have been cleared; the solution is within your reach.

cackle at dawn, hearing: warning that care is needed.

evening, in the: big peril prowls around you.

noon, at: fights between relatives.

cage, putting in a: business will not live up to your lofty goals.

catching a: immediate marriage for the unmarried.

crane, a flying: a momentous occasion will alter the best-laid plans.

wading: bound to deal constructively, to crack open the energy within.

eaten, that can be: form a corporation.

emu in your back yard, an: will meet a fool with foolish proposals.

feet of: you have faithful friends who don't understand you.

fighting: you will change employment.

flamingo, pink: distant travel, exciting chance events.

flock of, a: will be part of those heard.

flying: your soul will be saved by a wave of prosperity.

away: freedom to aspire to greatness.

like a: any attempt at the impossible will meet with the probable.

greenfinch, killing a: you are confronted with insurmountable obstacles.

owning a Texas sparrow: stick to your work and undertakings.

head of a, the: change within own position.

herons, of: career will move faster with greater gains than losses.

hummingbird: rapid hovering over affair in multiple locales.

killing a, for sport: disaster.

ladybird, killing a: be cautious at a postponement in business ventures.

of a, others having a: postponement of happiness in love affairs.

macaw hopping around the cage, a: any excuse to avoid a long-winded conference.

many: big family reunion and gain of a suit.

migrating: visit your childhood home, pay homage, then be free of material ties.

mockingbird singing in the night: an extended period of calm contentment.

molting: inhuman treatment of those not up to your financial standard.

night, at: lasting joy of spiritual freedom.

oriole, being an: will move up in business in altitude and in stature.

pelican, a: thwart an enemy before he establishes a foothold.

catching a: you will be invited to a dinner by a fisherman with a full net.

penguin, strutting like a: are overdressed for an occasion.

phoenix rising above the ashes: spiritual rebirth.

flying: freedom from unpleasantness with a caretaker and nurturer.

on the branch of a tree: an overview to put others in their place.

plumage, with beautiful: a wealthy and loving partner.

poor people dreaming of: improve own circumstances with a caretaker and nurturer.

single girl, beautiful: are loved but do not control your fate.

unmarried woman: will be unable to escape marrying a wealthy man.

wealthy people: reverse of luck in business, with you dependent on another's money.

predatory: your enemies are perched for attack.

seabirds: freedom of intellect if you leave present situation.

seeing: are attempting to evade duties you find it impossible to perform.

during business negotiations: a foe will cheat you by demanding a judge rule in his favor.

singing, hearing: great joy is in store for you as you are pardoned for past offenses.

many: will be called upon to perform complex important tasks.

sleeping: important information has been overlooked.

tanager, a: a pleasant house party where you will meet many interesting people.

waddling, a: will conclude affairs satisfactorily.

injured, an: persecution by an enemy.

on land: uncertain affairs will turn out well.

wild: will be oppressed by people with obscure demands.

wings, of a: freedom may be your desire, but not of the one in control.

broken, a: you have lost your balance.

woman seeing, with brilliant plumage: see yourself or your husband being reborn.

wounded, a: deep grief caused by malfeasance of children.

wrens, watching: be certain your plans are well grounded.

hearing, singing: keep your happiness to yourself.

BIRD'S NEST
10-13-24-35-37-42

animal eating a: a change in surroundings soon.

bird's eggs in a: excellent engagement results in huge dowry.

broken, a: loss of balance.

chicks coming out of: good news will be received.

destroying a: a family member will commit an egregious act.

destroying birds in a: a youthful folly will continue to cause distress.

empty, an: termination of affairs.

finding several birds in a: a task near at hand requires caution.

one bird in a: a package with a gift will be received.

several: happiness within the family.

BIRTH
09-21-24-37-41-45

announcing, a: work out the future of your cherished possession.

assisting with a cesarean: your development will require assistance.

child's: joy and prosperity awaits your new self.

dead: present projects will fail when someone misunderstands your motives.

twins or triplets, of: anxiety over effect of child on relationship.

children, having: crave independent children who make their own important decisions.

control: have excessively high ambitions and will stop at nothing to gain them.

cutting the cord: your children are ready to leave the nest.

difficult, a: major issues will be resolved in your favor.

easy, an: a reprieve from long-held worry.

embryo, of an: a new idea is evolving in you.

endangering life of pregnant woman: settle in to your cool rational mind.

giving: promotion through job change will open up grand opportunities.

grotesque, baby being: fear monster or baby with defect.

father receiving news of a, while away: actual, infantile memories of birth.

labor, being in: your plans are incomplete; you are prone to be impatient.

man: will lose wife's affections from inability to perform.

unmarried: loss of reputation and abandonment by lover.

married woman dreaming of: no amount of accomplishments can equal childbirth.

miscarriage, having a: are justifiably frightened that your self includes your treason.

occurring: a painful process will result in prosperity and abundance.

of the embryo: regression to earlier levels of consciousness.

one baby being born, only: birth of one cannot help but be the death of another.

    twins: comfort when life seems overwhelming.

    your: have considerable resistance to pain and suffering.

premature, a: ambitions crowned with scholarly success.

relative's, close: separation anxiety from a loved one.

right, demanding your: innate abilities present at birth have been exploited.

stillborn, being: certain pursuits should be abandoned.

triplets, having: your judgment is solid, fair and wise; proceed with your plans.

    of different sex: dignity, happiness and pleasure will follow pain.

    same: enemies are conspiring against you with unjustifiable gossip.

watching animal give: begin a new phase with positive results.

womb, returning to the: growth is insufficiently developed, allow exposure.

BIRTHDAY

05-18-29-34-35-40

celebrating your: good health and tranquil existence.

    another's: that person brings job prospects.

children's: approaching money, if you are not too obstinate.

friend's: will benefit shortly from a surprise gift.

gifts: advancement through support of others, if you are sensitive to their needs.

husband's: an anticipated disappointment.

own: are feeling in control of your future.

presents, receiving: will earn many perks in life.

    giving: your presence will be welcome despite repayment of debts.

relative's: contacts must be remade after long absence.

sweetheart's: abundance of money coming soon.

wife's: good times are coming.

BISCUITS

06-08-34-36-44-47

baking: news regarding a wedding.

buying: your good appetite ruptured over trivial conflicts.

giving away: are prone to enjoy other's displeasures too much.

making: you will have a prosperous journey.

sea biscuits, eating: will receive a well-deserved distinction.

    giving, to sailors: a prosperous married life.

BISHOP

06-17-18-27-36-40

altar, at the: legal troubles are likely.

clergymen being with a: ill health to come from mental distress.

dressing a: a false friend will delve into your intimate worries.

procession, in a: are highly optimistic, continue.

receiving communion from a: wish calm serenity however fleeting.

BITING

02-07-15-40-43-49

being bitten by an animal: the truth is a frustrating solution to love.

    insect, by an: you feel attacked by anxious competition.

    man, a: beware of quarrels based on misinformation.

    several times: are being slandered by others from all sides.

    woman, a: a jealous person is threatening those near you.

of a bite: are about to sustain a loss through your lack of diplomacy.

someone else: will be embarrassed by your own lies.

tongue, your: have lost consideration from others and for them.

BITTER

09-15-17-30-40-41

children eating, things: their demands are difficult to swallow.

feeling: the taste in your mouth signifies success.

    others: cannot quell another's distaste for you.

medicine, taking: will quarrel with domestic help.

tasting something: will have a rash all over your body.

BLACK

07-15-19-23-46-49

animals: transformation of unconscious drives.

earth: inner ability you are unaware of is rich with possibilities.

seeing: obstructions through ignorance of that which you rejected through fear.

shadow, the: repressed facets of your personality screaming for attention.

wearing: an unfortunate depression over differences of opinion.

BLACKBERRIES

14-16-30-43-44-47

bushes, hanging on: many trials to endure before the plan will be ripe.

buying: will be wounded by overeagerness.

eating: will suffer great losses through discoloration of your character.

gathering: will be unlucky as thorns are intermittent with success.

married woman picking: will soon become pregnant.

BLACKBIRD

06-11-15-34-39-40

of a: death is needed for new growth to survive.

singing, a woman dreaming of a: will have two husbands.

man: will have two wives, his mother and the woman he married.

unmarried person: will soon be engaged with the shadow side of yourself.

BLACKBOARD

06-07-08-10-16-44

blank: ignore other's panic and start building your credit.

cleaning the: contest items on your credit rating.

wiping the: erase character traits that are not inborn.

writing on: hands will get dirty in the proposed deal.

BLACKMAILED

03-07-18-30-38-41

being: survival is enough money to get food on the table.

employer, your: a whistle-blower will have difficulty getting another job.

friend, a: a lack of self-confidence and wisdom.

blackmailing a dependent: vain overconfidence thwarts any hope of a relationship.

of: will be accused of a situation of which you are not guilty.

BLACKSMITH

05-07-16-18-38-46

anvil, hammering on a: an unexpected legacy from one you aided in need.

forging: serious quarrels over love affairs.

metal, a: strike while the fire is hot.

sculpting: develop new talents to your advantage.

being a: will soon lose self-confidence in the fires of life.

fire on a forge: will use your creativity as a weapon.

melting metal: unbend your rigid personality traits.

shaping iron: you will encounter a stubborn will.

red hot: frustration at another's immobility.

shoeing a horse: obstacles if problem is not approached correctly.

talking to a: people do not have faith in your ability to forge a true personality.

BLADDER

01-09-12-20-41-46

disease, having a: are unwilling to earn your worth.

having to pee in the middle of the night: finish your dream first.

in public: an embarrassment needs to be exposed and laughed about.

mate having, removed: will contract pneumonia.

of a: be careful how you exert your power.

operation, having a: disgrace causing failure of your expectations.

others: will have health setback if you overexert yourself.

BLAMING

05-07-10-15-25-47

being blamed for something: be humble toward superiors.

others, by: your peace of mind will be threatened with illness.

children for something: a gift from a foreign country.

  friends: you will be cruelly deceived into believing your guilt.

  others: observe and avoid the hypocrisy of friends.

husband or wife, each other: joy following an argument.

BLANKET
06-12-13-15-41-47

buying a new, middle-class person: change in conduct will improve conditions at home.

covering your head with: you are denying the truth with a cover-up.

looking for blankets: unexpected visitors are coming from afar.

old: an illness averted through the exercise of caution.

security, a: are nostalgic about the past.

wealthy person dreaming of buying a: expect a loss of money.

  poor people: take extra precautions with your ill health.

wrapping, around you: be careful to whom you open up.

BLESSING
08-11-14-27-44-47

giving a, to someone: are at peace with their transgressions against you.

receiving a: will be forced into a marriage you cannot condone.

  others: will be vexed by competing ambitions.

  priest, from a: your energies will erupt out from divine protection.

BLIND
06-11-30-35-45-49

baby being born: you did not want to be born in this body.

  someone: you don't want them to see traits you don't like about yourself.

becoming: what you refuse to see is limiting you.

  friends: trouble and desolation are around you.

man: be cautious that ambition does not replace intelligence in business ventures.

many people: be willing to understand enemies to triumph over them.

relatives: don't ignore family quarrels; what you don't see will hurt you.

woman: some worthy person will appeal to you for help.

beggar, giving money to a: play the lottery, the odds are better.

being: you will be double-crossed by someone close.

blinders on, having: failure to see the obvious leads you astray.

blindfolded, man being: wish to become a widower.

  others: a troubled conscience over a disturbing influence.

  people, among: sudden reversal of fortune.

  woman: disappoint others in your inability to face the issue.

eyes closed and running: danger at the race-track.

leading a, person: strange adventures, impossible to complete.

  dog, a: precautionary news.

losing own eyesight: time to have your eyes checked.

man's bluff: the blind are leading the blind in this enterprise.

young person going: are unable to agree with friends, who turn out to be false.

BLOOD
20-23-32-36-43-48

bad, between: animosity from a chemical imbalance.

bleeding: malicious reports will cause others to desert you.

clothing stained with: enemies are hampering your chance at success.

dried on cotton pads: choose friends sparingly and wisely at work.

drinking: use your enmity to create your own power.

flowing: symbol of rejuvenation after the fall.

  onto the floor: friends are sapping your motivation.

46

wound, from a: cleanse yourself of old diseased hatred.

girl dreaming of: the start of menstruation; your energy is being drained.

hands, having on: loss of strength through mental and physical overexertion.

    yourself: stay out of another's problems.

hemorrhaging: being drained of nourishment by loved one.

lack of: with loss of blood go burdens and active life.

    menopause: fear end of sexual life and the imbalance of emotions.

losing: frustrations reveal parts of your body prone to illness.

lost, having: the supreme sacrifice of moral strength; stick up for yourself.

menstruating, are: the fertile cycles of God's wisdom.

money, taking: will be betrayed as you have betrayed.

oath, a: pledge unbreakable loyalty, bond.

others, on: absorb the power of your enemies.

pulse, feel your own: your nervous system needs an overhaul.

seeing: symbol of life's vitality and ability to succeed.

    yourself bleeding: your emotional wounds have not healed.

        someone else: a close friend needs your support.

    spitting: have disregarded the manners you were raised with.

stained garments: strange friendships will destroy your opportunities.

tourniquet, applying a: luck will arise from a long-lost friend.

transfusion, of a: will expedite emotional support vital to your psyche.

    giving, for a: your vitality is weakening as a result of stress.

        animal, to an: must take some responsibility off shoulders to be able to function.

    receiving a, from a blood bank: are being bled financially.

        sick man: shame for your actions will turn others against you.

spilling, during a: disastrous foreign dealings.

BLOWS

24-31-33-42-44-45

receiving: reconciliation following a quarrel you provoked.

    enemies: change of surroundings will bring new respect.

giving, to others: good fortune coming from a friend's indulgences.

    children, to each other: advancement in own position.

BLUE

11-12-22-27-32-44

any shade of: a comfortable tranquil life full of generous acts of simple cares.

azure: calm, contemplative and peaceful relationship with your mother.

dark: your murky moodiness wallows in depression.

hit by a bolt from the, being: an exciting new friendship with truth.

mood: nostalgia brings on your depression of frozen emotions.

navy: will prosper through mysterious means.

sky: are embarking on an enlightening project.

BLUNDERING

19-22-23-25-30-32

about clumsily: dismal outlook for those in love.

    others: accord among friends.

    relatives: good times are coming.

of a blunder: will do unexpectedly well in new undertaking.

BLUSHING

04-06-25-28-29-39

children: will break up with a best friend over immature accusations.

pleasure, with: your awkward act will need a laxative.

shame, with: will have to offer explanations of false accusations.

sweethearts: will marry before the date that was set.

wrongdoing, when caught in: love from an older woman.

BOAR

04-08-14-18-25-45

chased by a: unsuccessful efforts to stay separation from lover.

in a meeting: another will undermine your project.

>*woods, the:* find the source of the hostility around you.

>*zoo, a:* a secret will soon be revealed, but contained.

killing a: advancement in one's position.

>*near the herd:* your trust in another is destroyed.

BOAT
07-15-19-30-35-40

aboard a large, being: will attain your aim in life, not another's for you.

adrift in a, being: difficulties ahead due to your lack of purpose, acquire one.

>*and overturning, and:* your tarnished ideals need an overhaul.

>>*reaching land safely:* happiness and riches despite all odds.

>*others:* changes in present environment.

anchored, an: are securing a stable relationship to accompany you on your mission.

arrives at wrong date: your timing needs to be reset; postpone your coming trip.

>*no one to meet you, and:* feel inadequate to steer your own course in life.

>*port:* life pulls you down for you to learn lessons at your own expense.

barge, an empty: troubles arise from prying into another's affairs.

fully loaded: will take a long journey.

barnacles on the bottom of a: meticulous labors will be compensated one at a time.

being at the helm: have strength to direct life and meet its challenges.

>*someone else:* another has mindset of control of your new experiences and lessons.

being in a: a happy marriage will take place despite disorganization.

>*in a storm, a:* an excessive degree of control is necessary.

>*on calm water:* prosperity in own enterprises.

buoy, securing your, to a: your emotions are moored securely, but they will die there.

capsizing, a: fear of being overthrown, but fortune will be regained.

clear stream, in a: things are destined to go well.

creeps along: slow down, nothing will ever be fast enough.

crew on shore, of a: your prospective events will come as a surprise.

>*on a vessel:* expect a trickster's work in your journey to a new phase of your life.

>>*in a storm:* life is full of unpredictable challenges.

crossing a river on a small: great difficulties tax your limited abilities.

>*with lover:* deal with emotional impasse to reach each other.

dinghy, on a: your advances are clumsy.

falling from a: dishonor at a misplaced attempt to regain a missed opportunity.

>*into rough water:* you can change negative emotional trip.

ferry, separating from dock: differences cannot be moderated; separate into a new realm.

>*leaves dock station without you:* are in deep trouble and are not ready to make a change.

>>*with your baggage:* independence includes loneliness from lack of identity.

halyard splitting while at full sail: will change plans radically.

hawser, towing a, with a: dire happenings will be inescapable.

houseboat, living on a: a disquieting event with unrestrained companions.

make effort but miss: need supreme effort to recoup from frustration at being left behind.

>*connection and are stranded, the:* fear that if you do not get home, lover will leave.

>*fall into the water, and:* take several deep breaths before each action.

>*just make it, and:* rearrange your itinerary with longer connection times.

motor, a: the isolation of leadership and freedom to act on your own.

stalls: will be a victim in a dispute with a disagreeable person.

moving slowly: patience in the voyage of life must be had.

muddy stream, in a: must journey through hell to get to the truth.

murky: a mishap on a trip from your rocking the boat.

paddle, a: choose your emotion's response and charge ahead to experience it.

passing through a strait: put worry behind you and concentrate on the essential plan.

piloting a: a well-driven boat is tantamount to a well-driven life.

propeller, having lost its: will fail to complete task at hand productively.

river, on a, in the: security if you travel the straight and narrow.

seeing a: a trip through your unconscious will change your life.

sinking: time for your children to leave the nest; your emotions will survive.

skiff, rowing in a: gain through simple acts and an unexpected aide.

and overturning: achievements must consider all aspects.

down a smooth river: will be helped by a prominent person.

spending the night on a: reflection of your need for solitude.

steamer, on a: have a solid emotional relation-ship.

Styx, rowing a, on the: a voyage into the after-life to gain rebirth.

taking a ride: are not pursuing your goals forcefully enough.

with lover: relationship has nowhere to go.

tugboat pulling a barge: dignity from doing work no one else wants to do.

ship: are escorting your venture for public reception.

in distress: will receive unexpected money as a reward for success.

yacht, sailing in a: have confidence your talents will gain you wealth.

BODY

01-07-11-42-47-49

amputation, seeing an: removal of old habit to allow talent to grow.

bleeding heavily from own: poisons are erupting in a bloody base, in unhealthy direction.

little, a: achievement of own desires.

bloated, being: secret bad news is exploding in you; will fall into a trap.

friends: dishonor is what they don't tell you.

bound with tape, part of a, being: must block premature exposure of your plan.

buttocks, own: self-disapproval.

colon, pain in: one's inner strength is being challenged.

dislocating a part of the: stall any venture requiring change of employment.

distorted, a: go for a massage.

injured, having been: too much negative energy, high strung, emotional outbursts.

navel, of your: your paralysis in the past is caused by bad management.

of own: happiness at your very existence.

children: will undertake a playful, intuitive journey.

deformed person: will have good fortune ahead.

man, a: good business ventures.

woman, a: people flirt with this woman.

painful or swollen: sadness due to parent's waste of an inheritance.

pimples on the, having: an indication of disgust in the truth will out.

seeing your own: the vision can be the reality.

as ill: deal with your emotional burdens before they do damage.

as too fat: reduce your food intake by 1/8 a week.

stiffness causing pain: will be molested.

trapped in your own, feel: treacherous territory, the ooze of the unconscious.

paralyzed and cannot move: particularly forceful and dramatic change is required.

BOILER

14-20-27-37-45-50

owning a: will make new acquaintance with the repairman.

boilermaker, being a: unhappiness under bad management.

operating a: don't listen to flattery; your hopes are useless without talent.

steam: business ventures may cause sickness.

BOMBARDMENT
01-10-11-31-39-47

aftermath of being in a: hard times are behind you.

 discover special power: ask someone you highly respect for advice.

being unable to disarm a bomb: your anger is out of control.

 disarming: your honesty will allow you to avoid danger.

being under: your anger may explode and do your marriage harm.

 others: deception in love matters.

bombshell, a: lawsuits extending over a multitude of victims.

dying in a: are deeply hurt.

 others: thanks to friends, you're rescued once again.

exploding bomb, an: a heated discussion with truce and settlement.

hand grenade, a: impending gift.

hurt, you are: are emotionally wounded.

 others: are not responsible for other's failure

immobilized in an, are: treat yourself for shock, then react.

of a: bad news that will cost you money.

seeing a bomb explode: turn your aggression into a positive force.

 people die: your problems are solvable.

smell gas in a: call gas company immediately.

throwing a bomb at another: returning hostility complicates the issue.

 another, you: an apology for your hostility is due.

town ruined in a, your: need to take charge of your life.

 all life gone: forward planning prevents financial loss.

  but you are unharmed: take charge of family problems and solve them.

trapped in a: both options are needed to solve the problem.

unharmed, are: you are the only witness to your life's indiscretions.

BONES
15-18-28-33-40-46

arthritis of the joints: your rigid attitudes and beliefs are met in their silence.

 flaring up: eliminate the nightshade vegetables from your diet.

bone marrow transplant: despite your help, another will feel only ingratitude.

breaking a: a legacy will be received, causing family discord.

chewing on a: your job is in jeopardy from your apathy.

dead person's: many troubles from absence of friends.

digging for: disarm your opponent by actively helping him.

funny: sudden humorous reversal of fortunes.

gnawing on a: anxiety is self-induced.

hiding: hold too tightly to old attitudes, which are not essential to your future.

joints, having pains in the: after an altercation will win affection of a loved one.

many, of: don't force matters; wait at least a week before completing them.

protruding from the flesh: do not believe those who sugarcoat the truth.

searching for: ask for support to solve problems with opposite sex.

throwing a, to a dog: overspending and frivolous actions will result in pain.

BOOKS
01-12-21-32-34-48

binding: something hidden away is found.

bookcase, buying, a: loss of employment to someone better educated.

 empty, an: will suffer from negligent and careless work.

 full, a: your life plan, your purpose, your knowledge accumulate.

 half-empty, a: your bad personality leaves you to converse only with books.

 selling a: financial troubles in business.

buying a: news will serve you well.

comic, reading a: a sense of humor to be taken with a grain of salt.

 collecting: see only the sunny side of life; forget calamities.

decrepit: anxious disquiet toward ideas presented.

encyclopedia, looking up a subject in an: wish to become a celebrated author.

forbidden knowledge, of: won't admit to secrets about yourself.

gathering many, around you: fear of intellectual failure.

papers: be careful of speculation.

home, at: wisdom creates happiness.

index of a, consulting the: are attempting to better understand the opposite sex.

lending a: too much giving with no return.

library, in a: an unexpected experience to solve intricate problems with a book.

lost, a: seek out hidden information.

mark, a: it's to your benefit to keep the appointment.

prayer: consolation through the mystical that needs cultivation.

carrying a, with you: attempting to keep evil from you.

press, own, going to: the market may only be you.

primer, of a school: good news, if you shun evil in any form.

carrying a, with you: harmony with youngsters.

publishing: unpleasant gossip of envious people.

review, a: it is difficult to acknowledge another's success.

reading: friends are lost, better ones are gained.

detective: a quiet life is led if you keep away from evil.

mystery: will receive consolation from friends.

religious: contentment at the paths not taken.

school: are creating your own prosperity.

science: he who views the wonders of the universe and has no joy is asleep.

seller, talking to a: will find comparable intellect.

store, visiting a: literary ambitions will hinder your career path.

writing a: your life needs to be rewritten.

BOOTS

19-23-24-30-36-38

bootlegger, being a: have no regard for laws you feel are unjust.

brown, having: good luck in new work.

galoshes, wearing: savings should reach a considerable sum.

leaking: will be called to defend missing work.

heavy: someone is treading on your reputation.

new: can rely upon employees' faithfulness.

another with: follow the practical and sensible action.

buying: business will be very good.

hurting the feet: loss of money due to carelessness.

old: disappointment in the trust you placed in a friend.

wearing: business will be good, but insignificant amount.

women buying: wish to make your definitive stance sexy.

your, on another: your lover has already left you.

BORDER

24-30-31-42-46-49

airplane flies over an international: approach the problem from your opponent's side.

being at the: are very good at adapting to various situations.

crossing the: require challenging intellectual stimulation.

boat crosses international: extend yourself, embrace others.

denied a visa, were: must make that public appearance.

forgot passport, and you: have not assimilated your purpose, thus have no direction.

officials allowing you to cross the: learn a new language.

not: your sentimental side is frustrating your advancement.

BOREDOM

09-10-14-26-34-42

having to talk with a tiresome person: beware, the sky is falling down.

present lifestyle of: lack the imagination to change.

BOSS

01-02-09-38-44-47

asking you to work late, the: added chores will be forced upon you.

being a friend: another's condescending attitude is degrading your ambition.

president, the: want your boss to lead from intelligence, not the popularity polls.

your parent: are manipulating your boss to act like your parent.

being the boss: independence is possible now, make it probable.

    and overworked: are the critic of your influences; your guidance is from within.

harboring animosity towards you: difficult period requires the calm of a storm's eye.

hovering over you: the prevailing major driving force is your ambition.

of your: feeling mentally insecure towards authority.

BOTTLE
05-08-25-37-41-45

breaking, a: not wise to ask for financial assistance at this time.

empty, an: misfortune from having drunk too much adversity.

floating ashore, a: God has given you the answer.

full, a: prosperity in business and conquest in love.

neck: are squeezing through a constricted scheme.

several: a party invitation will lead to prosperous engagements.

spilling the contents of: expect domestic worries.

BOUQUET
05-11-29-31-43-46

beautiful, a: your self-esteem needs micromanagement.

being handed a: from a stranger, your admirer will be revealed.

dried: a celebration of growth in perpetuity.

giving a: your lover is constant.

losing a: your love is unrequited.

preparing a: will be married soon.

receiving a: your friends will support you.

throwing away a: separation from a friend.

withered, a: illness and ensuing death.

BOWL
05-09-17-28-29-36

empty: the invitation is not coming; your ideas are unused and unneeded.

    half: replenish your inner resources; your self needs nurturing.

filled with food: be wary of giving advice to friends and getting blamed for the results.

hands surrounding a, your: an offer is coming.

many: beware of giving advice, it will be misinterpreted.

receiving a full: your family will flourish, others will demand their share.

    empty, an: must throw a dinner party.

small: live frugally now and it will be continually refilled.

    of cherries: symbol of eternity.

BOWLING
10-24-27-31-42-49

knocking down all the pins: high ambitions will be realized in final hours.

    most of: one factor will break up your relationship.

    not hitting any: defeat in business dealings.

lawn, playing: who are you obstructing?

of ninepins: a rival will take sweetheart's affection.

playing: your blind ambition should be wary of risks.

    and winning: will be robbed.

    with business partners: dissolve the partnership.

        sweetheart: will have disappointments in love.

playing skittles: affairs are unsettled.

    of this game of ninepins: a rival will take affection of sweetheart.

    others: will soon experience many ups and downs.

    sweetheart: will suffer disappointment in love.

BOX
02-19-21-24-25-41

admiring a: leave your youth to memories.

being given a, with an intricate design: this relationship is worth working for.

burying stolen property in a: will be blamed for circumstances you did not control.

cardboard, a: a limited protection against risk.

church charity: will have misery and disillusionment at work.

closed, a: another's secrets will harm you.

    with the key: are too eager to find other's secrets and less your own.

crate, a: your desire to fill it up with positive emotions drives you.

empty, an: have difficulty earning what you consider a decent living.

enclosed in a, being: don't select one action, do both.

full, a: a marriage proposal game has been established.

having a: business will fail without mature policies.

    empty, an: plans will be upset with crossed purposes.

open, an: someone wants to steal from you.

opening a: will take a long delightful journey.

Pandora's: evil will be unleashed upon the world.

strong, a: will be cheated by being denied the truth.

    robbing: will lose entire fortune by greed of wanting another's share, too.

tying a: putting your life in order.

BOXING MATCH
01-05-15-26-35-47

boxer in a, a: have difficulty choosing appropriate options.

boxing in a: shadow your opponent.

losing a bet on a: have one loyal friend.

pushed on the ropes, being: your illusions are suffering a reality check.

taking a part in a: loss of someone precious to you.

training for a: conflicts and friction in your own backyard.

watching, a: an astonishing announcement of wasted energies.

winning: exciting events bring accord among friends.

BOY
08-10-12-27-36-42

altar, an: are too impulsive and flighty.

boy scout, being a: are overprepared for your meetings.

    participating in a ceremony: something close to your heart will emerge victorious.

    seeing a: don't let others distract you from your goals.

crippled, a: troubles are ahead.

fighting, a: a good resolution cannot be made without understanding.

having a: a woman will soon become pregnant.

jumping, a: will collect money.

killed, a, being: parents cause misery.

rescuing a, from danger: will rise to eminence.

school for boys, a: exposure to a breadth of vision.

securing work in a store, a: unhappiness.

    working: good business will be enjoyed.

sick, a: obstacles are ahead.

young, a: will soon be married.

    dating, a: must keep house in better order.

BRA
10-16-22-36-47-49

another's: your strange ideas spark another's creativity.

buying a: your vigorous mind can make judicious decisions.

losing a: obstinacy causes you to hold on to useless opinions.

own, of: another person enjoys the fruits of your labor.

putting on a: your adaptability will serve you well.

small, a: are aggressively seeking a larger share of the pie.

sweetheart's: temptation will come with a person close to you.

wife's: avoid making false steps in front of rivals.

BRACELET
03-08-16-20-29-46

ankle, an: scandal will be exposed.

beautifully adorned, a: wealth is your silver lining.

being given a: new relationship with one of the opposite sex.

finding a: property acquired causes confusion of loser's intent.

losing a: relationship will end soon.

    young woman dreaming of: worry and vexation.

of a gold, wearing a: luck in unexpected financial affairs.

receiving as a gift from a friend: an early and happy marriage.

wearing a: be wary of jealousy.

beautiful: you spend more than you earn.

BRAGGING
03-07-16-28-30-52

you are: your impulsive act will cause duress to friends.

> *to your competitors:* are determined to win even by cheating.

BRAIN
04-08-09-14-19-33

animal's, an: extreme caution is needed with every mental step.

brains, eating: will profit unexpectedly from your ability.

> *elderly people:* return of selective memory.

of a: a disagreeable atmosphere irritates you into becoming disagreeable.

operation, having a: have a passionate rational mind.

> *enemies:* will enjoy good earnings.
> *friends:* will find a valuable hidden object.
> *performing a:* are expanding awareness of own power in its constructive use.

relatives having a poor: danger ahead.

sane, having a: good results in affairs due to great knowledge.

> *others:* balance your intellect with the logic of the heart.

sick, having a: meditation awakens the transfer from unconscious to conscious.

tumor, having a: your reputation has not transcended time and space.

BRAMBLES
21-27-32-45-46-48

cutting down: shame and sorrow through evil influences.

entangled in, being: malignant lawsuits that cannot be defended.

of: poverty and deprivation from unfavorable lawsuit.

pushing through without being scratched: interweaving of body, mind and spirit.

> *others:* will find your way through difficulties.

BRANCHES
12-16-25-41-44-45

broken, a tree with: misfortune from the absent.

burning: a new interest will arise once the old had been eliminated.

> *dry:* your negative character traits that you have worked through.
> *green:* your life experiences did not carry through.

cutting from trees: a small disagreement.

dead, a tree with: a friend secretly tries to help you.

> *dry:* have petrified a situation that can no longer exist.
> *fertile, many:* an unexpected legacy is received.
> *withered:* recovery from an illness.

gathering together: an operation.

> *dry:* your past still haunts you.
> *green:* will successfully complete your project.

green: your work has just begun.

hurt by, being: an accident.

laurel: will receive honors.

olive: make peace with your enemies.

BRANDY
09-13-19-20-42-49

buying a bottle of: unexpected good news is received.

> *owning:* possessions don't make you, you have to live up to them.

drinking: pleasant affluence with little regard for others.

drink to others, offering a: passions must be controlled or friends will avoid you.

BRASS
13-26-30-35-36-48

badge, a: your ambitious actions will be amply rewarded.

buying: advancement in one's position.

candlesticks: a native emotion burnished to show you the light.

instruments: blow your own horn, but privately anticipate failure.

made of, having something: a friend causes unhappiness.

of: rapid advance in your profession necessitates keeping a careful watch on associates.

selling: are being deceived and fear your downfall.

tarnished: will take polishing to utilize your
strong decisive personality.

worker, being a: will have much trouble.

BRAVERY

03-13-27-29-41-49

acting with: will have a nervous illness, until
you prove yourself.

being without: are apt to underestimate yourself.

showing courage and: a friend holds secret
enmity against you.

BREAD

21-31-32-38-42-52

baking: add the ingredients needed for
complete nourishment.

buying: others will share their success with
you.

carrying several loaves of: a recent request will
be granted.

corn, eating: a gamble pays off richly.

crumbs, of: this essential nourishment is a
clue to resolving a stale problem.

eating: will be helped by friends who visit
from afar.

black: business losses through hard reality.

dark: contentment in the support received
from acquaintances.

white: use your sensitivity and fragile
psychology for a large profit.

hard loaf of: physical well-being to all your
family but yourself.

hot, freshly baked: wealth and honor will
be yours if you maintain stable relations.

hardtack, chewing: be wary of allowing others
to push you to lose your temper.

men kneading: need the young woman on
your mind.

offering, to others: involvement with a larger
social context in near future.

pumpernickel, eating: all basic nutrients
one needs to survive in a harsh environment.

several loaves of: period of equanimity and
fearlessness is ending.

stale: domestic difficulty will be helped from
the granting of an old request.

watching others eat: your envy involved you in
bickering.

BREAKFAST

07-17-21-37-47-48

another's home, having, in: a trip is soon
taken, slow down and be aware.

coffee shop, having in a: will accomplish
hurried but propitious acts.

eating alone: a hasty folly will be committed.

with others: the trap is set for you to step
in, dispel the illusion.

preparing: misery and illness will result in
favorable changes.

BREASTS

04-08-12-21-41-53

baby on your, holding a: homesickness for
the nurturing love.

sucking a: are desperate for the security
of unconditional love.

beautiful and healthy, having a: big joy ahead.

cuddling in another's: seek to escape back to
the womb.

emaciated: rivals will assure your poverty and
misery.

enlarged, being: an illness is threatening you.

feeding: your creativity needs to be nurtured.

hair, covered with: success in love.

hair on her, woman having: her husband will
pass away.

inflamed, being: will have a tooth pulled.

painful: give to another only after you
have fed yourself.

large, having: your prosperity is rising.

man dreaming of a woman's: seeking nourishment.

man, of a: will soon be married.

mother holding her child against her: you
shield your child against the hardness of
this world.

operation: your eavesdropping will reveal your
shortcomings, you are being discussed.

resting on someone's: true and loyal friendship.

spot on, having a: presages an illness to come.

watching a baby nursing: strong need for
tenderness.

woman, of a: be wary of the ardent admirer.

swollen: desire to have children.

BREATH

05-15-17-35-44-48

bad, having: feel closed into a space you did
not choose.

children: will be abandoned in sickness.

others: a special friend wishes to see you.

fast, a: reorganized, revitalized, and conscious acceleration of power.

out of, being: catch it before it is taken from you.

slow, steady, a: relaxation of whole system for energy to renew itself.

    unable to breathe, being: remorse over past actions; balance speed with competence.

suffocated, being: accept the situation as is, but avoid claustrophobic conditions.

    others: feel smothered by a confinement not your own.

BRIBE
02-07-10-36-43-50

accepting a: upright and honorable conduct cannot stop rumors.

of: will be guilty of exploiting others for your selfish ends.

official person, of an: great sorrow from fake rumors.

refusing a: money will be repaid unexpectedly.

BRIDE
24-26-30-35-42-47

bridesmaid, being a: wish to leave home with the security of your family.

    girlfriends: are feeling smug with your relationship and their lack of one.

    not: feel that you are sexually unattractive.

    several: your contribution to the celebration is minor.

kissed by a, being: activates your inner intuitive sphere.

kissing a: wish to start afresh and do better this time.

man embracing a bride: renewal of love affair is foolish.

without bridegroom: chances are better without him.

young woman being a: a large legacy, long deserved, could come to fruition.

    bridal gown, displeased with her: marrying to get away from home is not an answer.

    pleased: are ready to create a new independent life.

BRIDEGROOM
13-24-34-35-42-47

being a: money from obscure source will aid you.

    nervous in ceremony: a momentous decision is in front of you.

can't find wedding ring: misconduct criticized by your manager.

having handsome, a: a higher awareness of masculine union of body, mind and spirit.

BRIDGE
04-21-36-38-45-47

broken down, a: project does not have the means to succeed.

built, a, being: complete your plans within a rigid framework.

burning, a: some friends are lost who had turned against you.

causeway, crossing over a: work will be of an artistic nature.

    not yet paved: will receive a letter with money.

covered, a: surprisingly pleasant, imminent emotional encounter.

crisscrossing highway, a: your fertile imagination makes life's journey complicated.

crossing a: move from one occupation to the next.

    man: change in one's residence from youth to adulthood.

    others: delays in one's business from state of conflict to solution.

    single person: move from one phase of life to the next.

    woman: social activities of a happy nature will be met on the other side.

curved, a: serious financial problems.

damaged, a: be careful with new plans, but make them now.

    under repair: mend the relationship and enter it anew.

driving over a: present plans should be abandoned.

falling from a: ambitions exceed abilities and possibilities.

falling while walking on a: the connection is lost, change plans.

foot, walking over a: have painted yourself into limited action.

many: choose your foundation of life and connect to it.

opens in the center, that: your creative intuition can't get your intellect's attention.

red, a: danger ahead.

standing at the center of a: are balancing emotions and actions.

suspension bridge, riding on a: rapid speed toward success.

   climbing the towers of: are at the height of your power, downhill from here.

   sliding down the cables: will be rewarded for daring efforts.

   while swaying: a preview of crossing from life to death.

unstable, an: a need for rethinking future plans becomes evident.

walking across an old: repair your relationship or it will break.

   very long, a: your future is one big adventure.

wooden, a: are lacking in will power.

BRIEFCASE
08-11-41-42-43-48

having a: will have the benefit of riches for a short time.

   full of papers: will neglect some of your own business.

      without any: good results in enterprises.

finding a: failure in all affairs.

   with money: will consider illegal actions.

losing a: will make good business.

opening a: someone trusts you with a secret.

BRIERS
02-14-27-38-42-43

being caught in the bush: enemies surround you to cause distress.

blood drawn by a prick: expect heavy losses.

passing through without harm: triumph over persecutors.

pricked by: will be injured by secret enemies.

   children being: will live a long life.

BRISTLES
02-09-19-28-29-37

being given a: your clearly analyzed planning needs input from the opposition.

handing out: a short-lived high followed by a small percentage of acceptance.

having: security in your own business.

others: insurmountable obstacles confront you.

picking off: are exposing yourself to new business proposals.

BROCHURE
01-03-14-23-24-43

political, a: your inner anger argues with the world.

reading a: a morbid curiosity of those you disagree with.

religions, a: are making hasty judgments without fair counsel and wise forethought.

BROKER
16-22-27-32-46-50

being a: earnings will remain constant for a short while.

dealing with, re: purchase: pleasure lies ahead.

   sale: loss of money.

   several: be cautious in affairs.

of a: will meet untruthful people in near future.

BRONCHITIS
01-20-24-29-31-33

having: an enemy seeks your ruin by causing illness.

   others: obstacles in business loom over your attempts to rectify them.

   relatives: the needed medical help will be given.

recovering from: great prosperity if you pursue your views only.

BROOK
01-12-13-14-30-49

bathing in a: are ready to accept resolve by your own effort.

calm, slow-moving: move on from your gentleness to emotional action.

changing to turbulent: your restlessness is causing your stress.

fishing in a clear: will have faithful friends who support your increased finances.

   dangling feet in a: analyze your direction thoroughly before proceeding.

muddy: loss of friends.

nearly dry: lost valuables are discovered.

near one's home: will receive an honorable appointment.

walking along a, with murky water: time is needed for your actions to settle.

winding through a pasture: deal with the distractions.

BROOM
07-09-19-36-41-43

hitting someone with a: a change for the better is coming, if you clean up your act.

new, having a: conviction is the first step to success.

   old: money wasted because of thoughtlessness on your part.

shaking out a: rid your soul of harmful spiritual dust bunnies.

stick, riding on a: job is in jeopardy by slanderous press.

sweeping with a: take care of every iota of responsibility for your success.

throwing away an old: disregard complications from unwanted people and things.

whisk, brushing with a: need extra effort to extract bad seeds that delay plans.

BROTH
02-20-29-32-35-37

boiling: marriage.

drinking: affairs will prosper through the support of friends.

giving to a sick person: abundance of money.

spilling on clothing: a high honor will be received.

BROTHER
09-25-27-38-43-52

brother-in-law, flirting with a: material indulgences put your reputation at stake.

   marrying a: are being taken advantage of by relatives.

   several, having: financial gains.

dying: one's enemies are destroyed.

getting married: family quarrels from your act of courage.

man dreaming of his: expect quarrels.

   woman, her: much domestic happiness.

quarreling with a: big fortune from black sheep of the family.

BRUISES
07-17-23-26-33-41

being bruised: will work hard for what you get, but be pleased with it.

others having, on their body: beware of enemies.

   face: a season of petty arrogances.

relatives having: troubles ahead.

BRUSH
03-04-17-21-38-49

brush maker, a: a mixed line of work will be assigned to you.

buying a new: will receive money from a debt long owed.

hair, a: sacrifices are needed for relationship to continue.

having an old: are too naively generous and open-hearted.

painting with a: your creativity is adventurous; your subject needs untangling.

   small: ignore stupid remarks, get your point across.

shop selling brushes: beginning of period of great creativity.

using a: are surrounded by simple people who don't brush real problems aside.

BUBBLES
01-17-20-47-50-51

bathtub, in a: your naiveté will find a protector.

boiling water, from: dignity and distinction.

bursting: your world may be transient but you are not.

creating: avoid wastefulness or you may lose a sweetheart.

emerging from a: unresolved anxieties about birth.

BUCKLE
08-11-18-20-32-36

broken, a: an enemy is seeking your destruction.

buying a: filling a desire for invitations.

fancy, having a: abundance of affairs in splendid chaos.

man unfastening a woman's: marriage will take place soon.

woman having an unfastened: troubles and difficulties ahead.

BUDDHA   02-20-27-28-39-43

praying to: lack the courage to express your heart.

sitting as a: spiritual guidance will emanate through you.

statue of: are unable to escape someone's influence.

talking to you: unexpected pure joy from blessings of wisdom.

BUFFET

25-26-28-37-42-52

all you can eat: guilt has to be digested.

can't decide what to pick: partnership is devouring you.

too much food at a: fed up with relationship with much action and little substance.

BUGS

03-15-18-27-30-37

being bitten by a: annoying people surround your energy field; swat them away.

house, having in the: success in business or worldly affairs.

killing: will have money from illegal sources.

others: will go to prison for abetting a relative's crime.

many: will have gold and silver given to you.

outside the house: do not place blame on friends.

seeing: your friends scurry around you.

BUILDING

03-16-21-24-33-40

aisle in a: will take a long trip.

alcove, entering an: someone is imitating you.

hiding in: secrets are sabotaging your relationship.

annex, an: are expanding to fit your enhanced ambition.

arch, of an: must bring diverse ways to meet at the keystone.

damaged, a: must mend ways of wasting effort.

passing under an: many will seek favors from you.

big, a: will have great opportunities to enhance your present life.

bricklayer, a: your professional career is stagnating; use your industrious imagination.

bricks, with: little deeds can slowly build a castle.

laying: a slow but steady increase in fortune.

burning: getting upper hand over situation with troublemaker.

collapsing, a: faith you placed in project is unjustified.

college: academic advancement will come to you.

demolished, being: will be accused of wrongdoings.

dome of a: will receive honors from high officials.

facade, of a: relate with outer influences hiding inner resources.

foundation being built: death of someone you know and a place among strangers.

other, of: will soon take a long trip.

haunted spot, finding a: emulate a quality in a dead relative.

Jacobean architectural work: will gain by experience.

level, at a specific: represents level of awareness.

lintel spanning an opening in a, a: will move to a larger building.

being under a: important changes.

lobby, meeting people in the: dishonor of treacherous friends who spy from afar.

mortar, mixing: an arduous task that will produce a bitter deal.

move a door opening in a: adapt easily to new surroundings.

new, walking into a: perfect each step you make in your new environment.

restoring a: your vivid imagination will realize your aspirations.

several: will become very annoyed.

small, a: present affairs will not prove successful.

steel beam: money is collected from across enemy lines.

riveting a: energy and support gained through defiance of evil foes.

trapped in a: new job may be difficult but new boss is worse.

rooms going nowhere: only open familiar doors, go back to your origins.

wall, in a: belief systems must be radically changed.

very tall: have tremendous potential and a superb destiny to accomplish.

wandering aimlessly in the hallways: have lost your time and thought process.

with faux materials: are unable to say "no!" to the wasting of your life force.

BULL

15-30-37-38-45-47

being chased by: your lover is overly optimistic about your sexual prowess.

fighter: will have an interesting friend from Latin America.

furious: your rashness is creating havoc in your love life.

goring you: bad luck will overtake you in your race to escape.

liver, finding a: will suffer a big business loss through hardheadedness.

many: will receive high honors with your brute force.

not running away from a: situation of envious competitors is harmless.

of a: will make good investments, but not in anger at the opposite sex.

BULLDOG

01-03-05-38-45-49

buying a: will be tempted to commit perjury to protect your desires.

owning a: a big protector will aid your advancement in own position.

selling the puppies of a: an enemy is seeking your ruin by adverse criticism.

street, attacking you in the: send the subversive intrusion back to your enemy.

BUNDLE

13-27-30-38-49-31

carrying a: unhappy days are ahead until an invitation is received.

   children: change for the better.

   others: you are being cheated by a friend.

   people: desires are achieved by diligence.

clothes, of: you will receive good news.

hay, of: you will have hardships if you give out confidences.

many people with: a gift from a friend.

sticks or twigs, many, of: you will receive false news.

BURDEN

04-13-20-17-29-39

carrying a burden: your strength will struggle to be independent of others.

   others: expect a large inheritance from a difficult job.

throwing off a: unjust favoritism toward enemies weighs on you.

BURGLAR

01-10-16-23-32-43

being in own house: beware of treachery to demand your virtue and character.

catching red-handed: are feeling guilty for a stolen love.

   handing over to police: want a reward for assailing another's good name.

coming into the house at night: are jealous that your father has your mother's love.

having stolen valuable things: take great care to gain high return on investments.

of a: want to steal something you can buy openly.

stealing money from a colleague: you envy his position and discount yours.

thief, you are a: exhibit extreme care dealing with strangers.

BURIED ALIVE

16-19-29-34-36-42

being: are about to give your opponents the edge by making a huge mistake.

   climbing out of: the crisis is over, renewal.

   enemies: you are burying a negative experience.

   others: if you deal with the world, you will have wealth and influence.

   traitor: dig everything up on your cheating friends.

   watching before: the fear and anxiety of mistrusting God.

burying yourself: are searching for your roots beneath the old emotions.

of someone who was: bidding farewell to terrible misfortune.

BURNED

04-05-15-20-27-41

alive, being: your ambitions will rise with your success.

because of others, being: approaching troubles.

burning, a house: relief from distressing problems.

   incense: sympathy from an unsuspecting source.

   oil: caution with volatile companions.

   up with fever: your sexual passion will be the source of your destruction.

   wood: inventiveness of mind.

cooking, being, while: will be jilted by a lover.

incinerated, being: in group projects you are
the one who will lose.
own body, having burns on: will have valuable
friendships during life.
others: prosperity in own affairs.
person burning himself: unhappiness and sickness for those around him.
scalded, being: high ambitions.
scalding own hand while cooking: misery or
sickness.
walking through hot coals, by: can overcome
any impossibility.

BURYING
15-28-34-39-45-47
money: dissolution of hopes.
of: invest your repressed feelings in real
estate holdings.
someone: your death wish for your relationship with that person.
yourself: overwhelmed with problems caused
by your misdeeds.

BUS
07-10-12-22-24-49
children missing school: time for children to
leave home.
connection, too late to make your: antics of
friends will cause estrangement.
driver can't find way: time to take over your
own creative development.
enemies taking a: an accident will occur.
going too fast: your determination will make
fantastic gains.
for curve: your finances are overextended.
jitney: will be required to entertain a visitor
with sightseeing.
many people riding the same: obstacles in your
path to fortune.
missing a: fear of oversleeping while hiding
from life.
of a: following a direction with company.
passenger bothering driver: for success in job
you must persevere.
riding in a: impersonal, relatively safe path
that is under collective control.
alone: you isolate yourself with your dated
points of view.
going in the wrong direction: you refuse
to agree with what others say.

with children: your ambition supports
your virtuous family.
with wife or relative: sickness in the family.
on the wrong route: collective action
according to polls.

BUSINESS
06-10-12-15-42-48
accosted by a, person, being: promise of profit
to another; pennies to yourself.
advancing to become own boss: success is
certain in furthering your own interest.
in present position: beware of jealous
friends, rival may do you an injustice.
adversarial partner, having an: will be unable
to meet obligations in a healthy manor.
adversity in: will realize ambitions, but not
escape adversarial gossip of your conduct.
approached by a, man: results in projects
through the intercession of an influential
man.
arranging: misfortune is not to be misunderstood but remolded to future.
arriving, people: will receive compliments
from a wily man; don't accept them.
assembly line, working on a: will succeed
and bring a partner with you.
attacked by a, person: will profit from
another's being cheated.
beginning a good: must fight for good results
at every threat that sorely affects you.
checking accounts: mental distress and illegal
actions by carelessness, not intent.
community, having a: will soon have a lawsuit
over an ugly love affair.
conference, participating in a: will be asked to
arbitrate a conflict.
director, being a: choose the correct leadership
quality to carry your business forward.
responding position as: hold your tongue
when you have been provoked.
dismissed, being: your illusions of your value
to the company were dispelled.
others: are doomed for disappointment
if you do not believe it could happen
to you.
doing: your total resources commandeered
to create something another needs.
executive ability, having: make well thought-
out decisions, then take the risks.

industrious person, being an: every effort put forth will bring additional responsibility.

industry, having an: will be very embarrassed by our period of rest and relaxation.

insolvent, being: your industry and enterprise will not allow you to fail.

inventory, taking: abundance will soon be yours.

losing money in: will lose your temper over untruthful gossip.

> *making:* will receive money from a friend without his knowledge.

lost own, having: will be humiliated in unhealthy and gloomy surroundings.

man, being: make plans for your own business; an important conference is imminent.

> *dating a:* your date will be honest and thrifty, but your transactions will bring discord.

> *dealing with a:* improve your intelligent support; their frankness may harm you.

partner, having a: are prone to arguing, but it clears the air of unwarranted suspicion.

person dreaming of retirement: your raise is a prelude to being knocked upstairs.

receiving compliments on: will enjoy good profits, but will overvalue your contribution.

> *bonus, a:* will narrowly escape public censure for an unsubstantiated injustice.

> *large:* your insecurities cause you to purport superiority.

BUSINESS DOCUMENTS
09-10-27-29-37-39

family, handling: will be a misuse of your intellectual forces to hunt for fraud.

> *partnership:* big profit will be accompanied by loss of esteem.

> *personal:* will receive a legacy, lose a lover, and incur distrust among close friends.

man handling: are willing to take responsibility for your own life.

> *notary:* be careful of financial speculations.

> *woman:* will reap what your male relatives have sown.

BUTCHER
03-25-36-38-41-53

arguing with a: pay attention to your own negative habits.

butchering: financial success comes with loss of reputation.

> *beef:* check your aggressive behavior at the freezer door.

> *lamb:* fear your own bloodletting with a blunt object.

> *pork:* perceived danger of contamination is real.

friendly with a, being: renewal of old acquaintance will prove valuable.

killing any animal: death of a close friend whom you fear.

of a: reveals pent-up hostility to carve up someone's life.

serving you with cut meat: have strength to do what it takes to survive.

watching a, work: disregard cold-hearted people.

BUTTER
01-06-13-20-36-40

churning: prosperity will attend you.

> *in own house:* surrounding yourself with tenderness.

churning, of: a difficult task of manual labor is ahead.

cooking with: will be fortunate in business.

> *frying:* will have a new admirer.

eating: good health from the purest nutrition.

fresh: everything is in balance, but instantaneously susceptible to slipping.

plenty of, having: good luck of some kind to come.

purchasing: will have a change for the better.

rancid: an intrigue is behind your being slandered.

selling: avoid financial speculations, gains will be small.

single man dreaming of churning: false flattery will not gain you a happy marriage.

> *young woman:* will have energetic, thrifty husband.

BUTTERFLY
18-29-36-38-43-48

beautifully colored, in the sunshine: happiness in love, but temporary.

becoming a: your metamorphosis will blossom into beauty.

catching, a: from the unpromising and ugly emerges beauty.

chasing, a: are surrounded by unfortunate influences.

cocoon, being in a: feel burdened with life and want to escape.

> *emerging from:* birth of new aspect of yourself to improve image.

flitting from flower to flower: flourishing prosperity through all of its journey.

> *around the light:* a short-lived victory from which awareness will emerge.

house, being in the: an inconsistency will cause a slight trouble.

killing a: your relationship is stifling your transformation.

on a lover: fickleness on both sides.

young woman dreaming of: transformative healing needs a safe environment.

BUTTERMILK
08-15-31-38-43-47

buying: will escape an imminent danger with a discreet maneuver.

children drinking: pleasant solution to salacious gossip.

> *married people:* will be called upon to enact offensive interlude.

> *single people:* disappointment in love if you continue this course.

making: big joy followed by soured experience.

spilling: will suffer because of own foolishness.

BUTTONS
03-06-26-27-29-44

buying: will have a vigorous mind; open it up to others.

loose, your: your social face is in meltdowns; button up and survey the damage.

losing: another's secret enmity could be detrimental to your health.

sewing a, back on: a futile pursuit of an unattainable ideal.

> *single man dreaming of:* delay in love affairs because you feel bound in.

> *woman:* be prepared for conflict with those close to you.

tearing off a button: obvious erotic significance to see how you will react.

tight, your: your tightly wrought social facade fears a crack.

CAB
07-12-13-17-18-38

alone in a, riding: are engaged in a suitable hobby.

> *woman:* will enjoy average success.

chased in a, being: disorder is running riot, apply the brakes.

chasing someone in a: a new romance.

driving a: an entry into society.

man riding with a woman in a: name will be connected with scandal.

riding at night in a: are keeping secrets from friends.

> *rain, in the:* correspondence with friends living abroad.

>> *friends:* discovery of a secret.

>> *relatives:* will encounter gossip in the future.

>> *wife:* will have a long life.

> *to meet sweetheart in a:* weaknesses will be known.

> *with children in a:* happiness within the family.

CABBAGE
31-34-36-42-48-49

boiling: your stagnation needs an emotional cleanser and healing agent.

buying: troubled marriage of unfaithfulness and want.

eating: certain health but uncertain livelihood.

> *sauerkraut:* a healthy meal and an evening of fine music.

growing: be cautious of extravagance in business affairs.

making a salad: abundant means by dealing with troubles in manageable form.

CABIN
05-08-20-29-41-49

entering a: seek protection from your harsh responsibilities.

family, being in a, with the: time to refurbish your home.

friends: danger in love matters.

lover: death of an enemy.

living in a log: will move to a larger home.

of a: too much time is being spent alone.

ship, being in a: viewing domestic troubles from a distorted perspective.

beach: premonition of petty behavior witnessed by an unstable person.

country: a slow recovery from an illness; your frugality will pay off.

CABINET

02-06-09-13-49-50

buying a: treachery from trusted people.

closing a: loss of a letter in the mail.

opening a: a long-awaited letter.

selling a: dissension within the family.

CACTUS

09-14-23-24-27-28

being punctured by a: your thoughtless actions cause harm.

others: your prickliness has isolated you.

buying a: beauty growing out of abundant negatives has poignant repercussions.

small, a: your stinginess causes injury to others.

watering a: your generosity is wasted on false friends.

CADETS

07-15-26-30-32-35

academy, at an: will be threatened by someone.

drilling: are in a line for a superb, high-paying position.

going home: must prepare yourself for opportunities in a foreign city.

graduating: will be cheated by a woman.

of a: hard work ahead.

relative being a: will receive news of the birth of a child.

CAFÉ

14-20-24-33-45-48

discussing philosophy in a: your philosophy of life is being challenged.

eating cake in a: can do whatever you wish.

ordering another espresso in a: null your addiction to coffee.

taking a coffee break in a: your search for knowledge needs a rest.

watching the sidewalk from a: have lost your direction.

CAFETERIA

7-16-19-32-45-51

adequate but uninspired food, with: your love life needs attention

college, a: eating enormous quantity without quality.

don't want to eat in a, you: sign of money difficulties.

nothing is appetizing: a career change is needed.

school, a: depersonalized emotional nourishment.

too much food: your health is in danger; you must lose weight.

want to throw it at someone: have faults that are blocking your success at work.

CAGE

12-16-18-21-24-47

being in a: social restraints question your morality.

animals: triumph over enemies is temporary, but only if they are restrained.

breaking out of a: the ethics of childhood support your escape from trauma.

empty: a member of the family will elope; take the easy way out of family feuds.

freeing someone from a: wish to help that person out of his predicament.

full of birds: are boxed in by your own inhibitions.

one bird in a: questionable situation will turn positive.

three birds in a: engagement will be broken by your antisocial behavior.

two birds in a: love affairs will bring wealth, but a confining marriage.

wild animals in a: danger of going to prison if your impulses are given full reign.

CAKE

07-13-18-21-44-49

baking a: your indulgence will turn your luck from luxurious to practical.

buying a: the affection of a friend will support your weakness.

eating a piece of: your self-aggrandizement will lose you your sweetheart.

frosting first: fear being trapped in yourself, set boundaries no matter how sweet.

pan: will gain a home in a legal settlement.

pound: a gentle pleasure upon which you can add any sauce.

sweet: promising future to those enterprising souls.

serving friends: are confronted with insurmountable obstacles.

walk, a: acquaintances are performing grotesque acts.

woman dreaming of eating her wedding: big peril of self-created prison.

CALCULATING
13-25-34-35-45-47

having calculated: the solution is in using your head.

> *expenditures:* expect bad news concerning business, others living at your expense.

> *other affairs:* new acquaintances will manipulate you.

> *wrongly:* damages in affairs add up to harsh judgment of yourself.

others, for you: asking for help will incur new enemies.

problem: frugal spending habits are needed to resolve your dilemma.

CALENDAR
03-11-25-26-31-32

buying a: make time for friends to visit.

of a: are prone to being too impatient and miss the present.

tearing off sheets from a: time is passing quicker than you think.

throwing out a: after a down period, your situation will improve.

worrying about a date: now is the right time to make hasty decisions.

CALF
01-07-12-16-18-32

belonging to others, a: worldly pleasure received from parents.

buying: will be madly in love.

feeding a: your generosity extends to the wrong people.

golden, dancing around a: leave friends behind in your search for luxuries.

head of a, the: big consolation of the gay, frivolous kind.

leg, the, of your: strength builds in your mission's flexibility.

married people dreaming of: youthful love and sensuality will last forever.

owning a: have massaged your physical ability to move up the ladder.

peacefully grazing, a: the early fortune of a loving mother.

playing, a: your attitude is superficial.

selling a: will soon be married.

several: are in a mischievous mood.

slaughtered, being: change to the opposite direction.

standing beside its mother: your leadership abilities have not been developed.

CALLING
08-16-25-28-30-44

familiar voice, you: a distant friend is in impending danger.

God's voice: will be asked to perform an important task.

someone: reverse your direction before acting.

> *your name:* await advice from your unconscious.

CALMING
02-04-13-14-24-29

calm after a storm: period of grace followed by an ambush.

friend, a: successful ending of a doubtful undertaking.

oneself in a stressful situation: must be unflappable to steady your nerves.

relative, a: have lost consideration of friends.

CAMEL
08-26-34-36-37-44

buying a: want to pay others to take your responsibilities.

caravan, on a: your trip through life will be a series of bumps.

carrying a load: your anger at your pitiful inheritance de-energizes you.

chewing: increasing your stamina takes patience and fortitude.

envisioning a: old problems caused by your blind obedience will return.

> *loaded with merchandise:* need to bear a heavy burden until each obstacle is overcome.

kneeling: in lightening your load you leave yourself no spiritual sustenance.

many: great financial gain, if you store up money for lean times.

oasis, a herd of, in an: will rebound in health contrary to all expectations.

of one: will have obstacles and unbearable anguish to overcome.

riding on a: will be wealthy through your forbearance.

seated on a: modesty and moderation rule your successful actions.

CAMEO
08-34-40-41-45-47

buying a: a sad occasion will dominate your interests.

having a: promotion in own affairs will become displeasing.

losing a: a death will claim your attention.

of a: will receive high consideration of others.

receiving as a gift: recovery from an illness.

CAMERA
14-19-21-24-28-31

being a, man: keep up with the motion; replay it for the lesson to be learned.

buying a: attempt to recapture fleeting moments to be repeatedly experienced.

looking into a: will be deceived by an old friendship in the immediate future.

owning a: will receive disagreeable news from the impressions recorded.

receiving a, as a gift: love troubles will subject you to an acute disappointment.

taking pictures with a: a displeasing occurrence not processed into awareness.

CAMP
07-11-19-39-41-48

being in a: transcendence in love affairs, but you can't name the wedding day.

friends: successful result of all ventures except marriage.

camouflage, in: are hiding within the elements and grounded by them.

going camping: time to move on from worries and accept a marriage proposal.

of a: uncertainty in domestic affairs as mate's name is vilified.

of camping: your resting from your long, wearisome journey will be temporary.

soldiers in a: the troops will increase their estates while yours dwindle.

surrounded by the enemy, a: line up your assets and stand firm.

CAN
15-17-22-23-28-31

drinking from a: laughter and music from a source not your own.

food, of canned: your laziness blocks your advancement, not your boss.

　eating: are satisfied with mediocre company, rusty beliefs and stale ideas.

　past the expiration date: true love will not be found hanging on to an old lover.

juice, buying several: avoid enemies.

many: will receive good news.

opening a: a rival will win the affection of your sweetheart.

shooting at a can: expect to take a long trip.

throwing away an empty: serious disaster ahead.

CANADA
02-06-08-12-36-47

being a citizen of: will make financial gains.

being deported from: will find a new lover.

　to: there will be much discussion about you.

going abroad from: worldly goods are assured.

　to, from abroad: have many loyal friends.

having business dealings with: will be implicated in a secret deal.

living in: opportunity for self-expression with little competition.

returning from a trip to: loss of business.

seeing on the map: will have a vigorous mind.

taking a trip to, alone: must endure a painful experience.

　with others: enjoy amusements too much.

CANAL
33-36-41-45-46-50

clean, clear water: fortune is easily accessible with little variance from the goal.

constructing a: transform your passions into intellectual goals.

covered with weeds: coming trouble you can't control.

full of water: security is forthcoming.

lock, traveling through a: eliminate the sour grapes among your friends.

muddy water: minimize quality of life now to save money for old age.

ships passing through a: new contacts will take you abroad.

walking along with a: your business affair has problematic illegalities.

mule, with a: transport your cravings into material goods.

water flowing in a small: your self-imposed emotional traumas need to flow.

CANARY
03-08-10-32-33-36

buying a: need to check for poison air before entering the mine.

dead, a: attaining your aspirations takes delicate careful steps.

having a, in the home: idle talk that is a hindrance to yourself.

owning a: play the music you want to sing and live the life you wish to live.

CANCER
03-05-22-28-35-42

body, having inside the: a disabling concern leaves your emotions in disharmony.

having: someone in your social circle seeks to destroy your success.

body, on the: are accommodating poisonous forces to match your self-hate.

face: are hiding your true character behind your anxieties.

neck, in the: a problem that is eroding your energy is lowering your resistance.

others: cells produce disease with each selfish desire.

relatives: others have been consuming your resources.

of: are short of money at present but will have plenty later.

CANDLES
02-07-17-18-21-33

being burned by a: the search for wisdom is not without nodes of distress.

blowing out: competition and rivalry at the end of a period of your life.

burning brightly: expect an invitation to a feast and accept it.

at both ends: your indulgences are depleting your physical resources.

quietly: your peace is within your innermost self.

businessperson dreaming of: attain prosperity with good business ethics.

sick: will recover, if you follow the good of the whole body.

unmarried: are craving for freedom from being married.

buying: are inclined to believe enemies.

candelabra, of a: your salvation is clearly guided through the unseen.

candlestick, of a: your spirit will be enlightened.

carrying lighted: a small effort produces remarkable results.

clear steady flame, with: will have a splendid marriage full of adventure.

colored, having: will become a widow or a widower prematurely.

corpse: let those who have died, go!

flickering: are being guided through the unknown of detrimental gossip.

going out: a measure of the time left in your life.

putting: your quarrel with a friend has passed, start anew.

lighting a: be more reflective and reverent with friends, start anew.

maiden, a: will have an affair against parent's wishes.

making: are seeking guidance in a time of spiritual darkness.

maiden, a: a marriage offer introduced by a distant relative.

of a small wax: wisdom comes in small doses.

carrying a lighted taper: good fortune will protect your course in life.

unlighted: it is the only burden you will ever carry.

having a small: indecisiveness with regard to proposal.

smoking: period of uncertainty, doubt and indecision.

CANDY
02-05-18-23-30-51

eating: loving pleasure in society without the balance of nutrition.

sour: long-held secrets will be exposed.

eating confections: will soon be in love.

others making: peace and happiness in another's home, not yours.

enjoying taste of: spoil yourself with indul-

gences, believing that security is forthcoming.

giving, as a gift: money long overdue will be
refunded.

receiving: will have much success with new
romance.

jar in your hand, having a: worry will be
smoothed away.

lollipops as pacifiers, using: will be elected to
prominence by your peers.

making: will reap profit in business.

dainty fancy desserts: will have pleasure
and profit.

nougats, eating: surrounded with exotic
flavors.

CANE
30-35-38-44-51-52

bamboo: will raise several children.

breaking a: dissension within the family.

carrying a, on your arm: good health.

cutting: absolute failure on all fronts.

hitting someone with a: will have domination
over enemies.

another, you: are being treated the way you
have treated others.

killing: will make good profits.

hit with a, being: forget revenge, learn your
lesson and go on.

leaning on a: a source of strength has pulled
out from under you.

owning a: you will be unhappy.

punish people with a, having to: financial troubles.

resting on a: illness in the near future.

small blowing, a: several dogs will be killed.

sugar, field of: advancement in business.

walking with a: your common sense needs a
steadying helpful influence.

wicker: are prone always to doubt others.

CANISTER
07-10-15-35-41-45

closing a: are concealing lessons you must
learn before venturing out into reality.

having: doomed to disappointment.

food in: will have a secret to keep.

opening: will discover a secret that will
easily nurture your emotions.

CANNIBALS
09-13-18-42-47-51

being a: are living off other's energies to avoid
evolving your creative energy.

animals: feel you are being eaten alive by
demanding overwork.

humans: insatiable lust to possess
another's life force.

cannibalizing yourself: deprive one part to
strengthen another, thus destroying
both.

of: devour abilities of enemies to acquire their
power.

recognizing a friend as a: throw the freeloader
out and produce for yourself.

CANNON
01-19-21-40-41-48

balls, of: aggressive destructive desires to
avoid situations you find uncomfortable.

being fired: quick reactions will avoid an accident.

hearing a: the deception of fleeting relationship will be exposed as meaningless.

man dreaming of hearing a, fired: overcome
risks before entering into a project.

woman: will marry a military man at great
expense to your emotions.

military man firing a: marriage to a beautiful
girl who will dump you emotionally.

of: will be called upon to defend your
country.

woman dreaming of a: are desperate to make
an impression on your partner.

CANOE
04-09-19-30-31-50

being in a: your leadership will solve business
turmoil.

calm water, in: focus your energy on one
path; no other is offered.

in rapidly running stream: stolen pleasures
of short duration.

loved one, with a: fragile home life, strike
out on your own.

overturning: have reneged on your emotional
balance.

owning a: lack of anything to share with
friends.

paddling in place: must define your goals
before you can move.

CAP
01-02-03-17-28-39

buying a: will receive an inheritance, capped
with a maximum withdrawal per year.
given to you: your marriage will be involved
in community affairs.
losing a: your courage will fail you in time of
danger.
miner's, a: fail-safe measures should be stud-
ied and memorized.
old and dirty: damages in business.
prisoner's, a: courage is failing you at a critical
point.
putting on a: have accomplished the mission.
selling a: are not operating your own business
well.
sweetheart wearing a: are timid and demure
in lover's presence.

CAPE
20-25-30-38-41-52
buying a: are wasting good time.
cloak, wearing a: need to protect what you
have covered up.
fixing a: will be exact in own affairs.
mantle on own shoulders, wearing a: dignity.
putting on a: will have new employment.
taking off a, from: will be disgraced.
new, putting on a: sorrow and grief will come
to an end.
old, of an: will receive good news from a friend.
tearing a: separation from all that is dear to you.

CAPTAIN
04-09-11-24-43-44
being a: advancement and prosperity, if you
can live up to the responsibility.
captain's servant: someone else is making
your decisions.
sweetheart: don't believe all that men,
any man, tell you.
wife: joy in the family, jealous rivalry
in the community.
marrying a: will be confronted with a big
scandal.
seeing a: the strength of your noble aspirations guides you through life.
frequently: take control of your destiny
and responsibility for your actions.

CAPTIVITY
01-10-11-12-17-24
animals in: your dignity and distinction are
destroyed by bondage.

being in: are a prisoner of your moral and
ethical belief system.
enemies: guilt about desires to trap others
into defeating themselves.
others: overstraining to subject others to
your opinions and emotions.
give yourself up to: misfortune if treachery
is not faced at the source.
taking one into: will fall in life's station
when you allow others to walk on you.
wife being in: husband will censure you for
your indiscretions.

CARDINAL
10-12-14-22-42-44
conclave of: progress in business affairs will be
stalled.
dying: misfortune in own affairs will cause
deportation.
many: sorrow caused by keeping a secret
while another is destroyed.
walking in a procession: important proposals will advance your career.
of a: advancement in profession will be
blocked by an evil adviser.
pope, being appointed: misfortune in
enterprises through conflict of
interest.
priest being made a: your downfall through
false promises.

CARDS
32-35-38-40-50-52
ace of: hopes that have kept you penniless will
be realized.
clubs: money will buy you a partner who
will question your absences.
diamonds: will attract a person who will
bring lucky changes.
hearts: holding onto clichés, your worldly
goods will be increased.
spades: "the devil made you do it" is an
unacceptable answer.
bridge, making tricks in: travel plans must
be reevaluated.
dealer, being a: you control the last card to
adjust matters to your advantage.
dealing: are investing too much emotion in
risky business with an unreliable person.
full house, a: fortune will follow you, until
she succeeds.

high-class lady dealing: have made mistakes in figures that will be noticed.

Jack of Clubs: a rival will create an obstacle to attainment of your goal.

Diamonds: some event will light your way out of darkness.

Hearts: a fair-complexioned person is tempting you.

Spades: will be in or witness an accident.

joker, being a: light company brings no good.

holding the: an energetic competition with double your effort.

playing the: indicates a suitable time to pursue courtship.

not: people will take advantage of you.

King of Clubs: much needed assistance comes from man in superior position.

Diamonds: the head of the family is in a forgiving mood.

Hearts: the grand passion of your life will be the danger of remaining king.

Spades: change of character and habits come through influence of a new person.

playing: are reckless with your all-consuming passion.

and losing: good business ventures fall away when competition supersedes growing.

and winning: troubles ahead from legal claims to your winnings.

Black Jack: experience of loss through robbery when focused on competing instead of creating.

others: will have quarrels over the quality of your intentions.

Queen of Clubs: aid comes from a woman in differences with others.

Diamonds: find continuous facets of minor deceit of one kind or another.

Hearts: innovation will restore your faith.

Spades: have arguments with a woman over her rise in power.

shuffling a deck of: will test the one you love for faithfulness and lose his faith.

solitaire, playing: rest one part of your brain while your creative juices flow.

CARNATIONS
2-15-21-26-29-30

as a boutonniere: settle for expedience; your vanity will not be satisfied.

striped, a: your attentions will be refused.

bluish red: gain prosperity through others.

man dreaming of: you desire to buy a woman.

picking, a: your thoughtless actions create a crisis.

pink: know glorious success.

red: start quarrels with friends.

white: succeed in undertakings.

wilted, a: close friend will desert you.

yellow: big friendship disdains you.

CARPENTER
06-09-13-22-23-45

auger, drilling with an: a tiresome companion will extend his stay.

bandsaw, using a: will win praise from your employer before long.

being at work: legitimate success in financial matters for shaping ideas.

chisel, using a: will mislay important papers that define your design.

buying a: will obtain desires through energetic work.

drawknife, shaving wood with a: heartening support will come from creditors.

drill, using a: are overcoming the shyness, which precluded your forming relationships.

fixing the house: forget frivolity, get straight to the source.

hiring: unexpected and pleasant occurrences arriving with a bang.

lathe, operating a: your fortune is in the ideas you favor.

lever, using a: your strength will be enhanced once the plane is level.

sandpaper, finishing with: your imagination covers too vast an area to be productive.

tack, pounding: care for your reputation; your quick, sharp wit may be infamous.

pulling out a: arguments with your employer.

vise, using a: a task being squeezed to a forced conclusion.

working busily: will use practical wisdom to unlock the intuitive unknown.

CARPET
04-13-28-40-45-50

carpeted room, being in a: expect good news from exposure of a cover-up.

cleaning a: an annoying visitor will step into your plans.

colorful, a: no time for boredom when you deal with complex situations.

burning: out of seeming chaos arises the superb design.

buying a: a mystery is being created by your cover-up.

exchanging for a new one: dissatisfaction in love is possible; watch your step.

intricately designed: a map of your life from the complicated to the serene.

laying a: big catastrophe ahead from your being walked on.

making a: a pleasant, profitable journey with grounding, insulation and protection.

Persian, a: sweep away your mediocre past to gain room for your ambitions.

several: danger for the one who owns the carpet.

worn out, a: will scrimp and eke out a living.

CARRIAGE

03-06-13-19-38-52

being a footman: a false friend is nearby.

　having a, at your service: unexpected troubles from your many visits.

　of a: feel disappointment at what you hoped to do.

broken, a: your aging body is no longer carrying you.

coachman, being the: will have and will be a faithful servant.

driving a: will reach goal despite sickness.

driving a coach alone: will have a power struggle with a person you least like.

　with others: beware past treachery does not thwart your advantageous position.

getting out of a: loss of an estate if you don't proceed with caution.

going somewhere in a: will have many pleasant memories.

long trip in, making a: will be slow to achieve fortune.

of a: beware wealth that will last for a short time only.

others driving a coach: disappointment.

overturned: misery for you, when you make a fool of someone.

postillion riding as a guard, a: will receive good news.

　being killed: expect domestic arguments, don't force conditions.

　falling from a horse: will receive annoying news.

　several as escorts: fortune.

riding in a: are subject to a short illness caused by lack of seriousness.

CARRIED

03-04-07-18-26-42

anyone, being, by: your personality that others rely on has an uncertain future.

　man, a: anxious days because of illness.

　poor person, a: burden you are carrying is someone else's.

　woman, a: new love affair after problem is solved.

child: will be charitable with your failure to complete the project.

load: will begin before sunrise and rest after sunset.

woman, carrying a: are overzealous in carrying the relationship.

CARROTS

04-06-14-25-29-36

cooking: abundance has to be experienced before it can be attained.

eating: good health for your eyes.

growing: don't be lured by friends into compromising circumstances.

having in the home: will ultimately be rewarded with healthy children.

of: profit through inheritance of worldly experience.

CART

17-19-21-24-49-53

being carried in own: will have might and authority.

covered, a: excess baggage will deter your completing a planned trip.

en charrette: your project will be overdue.

getting in a: loss of steady employment leads to constant search for work.

　out of: loss of dignity comes through machinations of rivals.

heavy, a: unload emotional baggage to attain success you merit.

loaded with hay, a: wishes will be accomplished.

stuck in the mud, a: reexamine your overloaded responsibilities.

to pull it, being tied to a: will be in pain and bondage.

CARVING

01-10-22-24-29-39

cooked meat: are in the grip of deceitful people, so carve a niche for yourself.

doing own: others will constantly hamper your prosperity.

for others: others will benefit by own actions; leave your mark on yourself alone.

fowl, a: your continued outbursts of temper will foil any plans.

others, for you: conceive new methods to improve state of affairs.

CASHIER

18-22-28-40-44-49

being a: friends view you as an unfeeling mercenary soldier.

box, full of cash: favorable expectations.
  empty: will receive meager reparations for past work.

of a: the deception of your effusive benevolence will be disclosed.

several, at a bank: are spending borrowed money from many sources.

stealing money from the: your deceit will gain material goods, but lose a friend.

till, empty, an: have disobedient help.
  filled: will have dealings with a wealthy businessman.
  man dreaming of taking money from a: will fall in love with a beautiful woman.
    woman: will marry a rich man.

watching a: freedom from want that an abundance of cash can bring.

CASTLE

15-32-36-42-45-47

ancient: long-term investments need to be reviewed.

being a guest in a: a distinguished person will influence you.

entering a: are madly in love with yourself; bring yourself into reality.

fortress of a: are walling yourself off from opportunity.

living in a: your overblown pride presages your fall.

looking at a: your expectations exceed your means.

of a: expect friends to visit your life of fewer restrictions and greater richness.

on fire: quarrels result from your bad temper; move to a better neighborhood.

residing in a: will receive recognition for your outstanding achievements.

small: your imagination needs some realism.

under siege: are defending your quest for creative freedom.

CASTRATED

03-13-16-28-37-42

being: triumph over enemies by undermining their vigor.
  animal: will be found guilty of causing a sexual trauma.
  lamb: give a large dinner party for repressed emotions, feelings and urges.
  mule: will be punished by a high official for inferiority.
  pig: unhappiness at growing old and at having to grow up.

man being: society will get along much better without your scheme.

woman dreaming of castrating a man: harsh desire to avenge his rejection of her.

CAT

01-17-23-39-44-53

angora, an: double-crossed by one who honestly envies you.
  black, a: illness from spitefulness is near.
  brown or gray: are being deceived by a trusted person.
  calico, a: see deceit where there is none.
  tomcat, a: artful deception upon your frequent trading of sexual partners.
  white, a: hide your great affection for someone; it will be a source of great sorrow.
  wild, a: will fight with neighbors over their pet; ward off complications.

attacked by a, being: driving enemies away makes them do desperate things.

beaten, a, being: treachery of one who accuses others of his own unpleasant thoughts.

being a: your desire for independence is wise.

birth of a: a sudden awareness of a part of the unconscious previously misunderstood.

claw of a, a: will be victimized beyond your conspicuous indiscretion.

defending yourself from a: will be robbed of your reputation.

eating rats, a: will receive payment of money loaned.

familiar, a: are in need of psychic self-defense.

fighting with a dog: quarrels with neighbors over who caused the fire.

food, eating her: a female friend slanders you, causing divorce and legal difficulties.

furious, a: arguments with lover will drive him away.

hitting a: will fall into bad company, who work harm on themselves.

kittens, delivering: divorce is near at hand whether married or not.

   being hurt: your evil thought manifests upon the innocent.

     not: will emerge from a present danger with your sensuality intact.

   newborn: can overcome great obstacles if you are not fooled by liars.

   with her: unhappiness in marriage through inattention to mate.

man dreaming of a cat: one misstep will end your affair.

manx, a tailless green-eyed: discord over your child's reaction to another's attack.

many cats and dogs: loss of profits in a business deal.

night, at: uncontrollable unpleasant thoughts.

playing, with a: will be visited at home by enemies.

pregnant, a: will be robbed by a sleek, slick burglar.

roof, on the: will need cleverness to succeed.

scratched by a, being: someone is seeking your downfall; cause them discomfort.

several: your lover is unfaithful to you with one of them.

Siamese, a: will obtain modest employment using half your effort.

a pair of: will never attain the prosperity of their secret.

sleeping, a: annoying gossip from artless friends.

CATALOG
21-30-38-39-41-51

clothes and shoes: friends will place blame upon you.

machinery: loss in personal affairs.

making a selection from: attempt to be diligent in future.

store merchandise: will enjoy large gambling winnings.

CATERPILLAR
9-22-24-42-44-48

catching a: talents you are saving should be revealed.

killing a: your distrust of hypocrisy is credible, in your worldly experience.

several: be careful of the spiritual blindness of those whose help you accept.

tractor, owning a: watch own actions, especially to whom you speak.

   of this piece of machinery: embarrassing situations will provide small gain.

   working with a: embarrassing situations with little chance of progress.

CATHEDRAL
12-16-26-36-39-41

apse in a, an: expect a miracle soon.

being in a: will receive honors.

gargoyle, on a: a prank will make you laugh and pray.

interior of a: take care of your own business.

niche, an empty: are hovering at the fringe of action, trust one close to you.

   Madonna in the: are too shy in expressing your feelings in a crowd.

   statue in a: will overcome your trepidations and act intelligently.

outside of a: good fortune.

CATTLE
13-18-28-29-30-31

black: troubles ahead in business.

drinking, one steer: object sought will be difficult to acquire.

driving: must work hard for future ahead of you.

fat, grazing: will have a fruitful year with a jolly companion.

fighting: happiness within the family.

fire, killed in a barn: infirmity and stalemate of affections.

followed by: correct your habits.

herd of, a: are entering into a contract that will gain you respect.

    gathering together: a fortune from sales of futures.

    many: will lose lover by not responding to his advances.

    milking: will earn money.

    skinny, having: will be very short of money from misspent youth.

lean: will be in want of provisions.

many: prosperity according to the number of cattle.

other colors, of: will be adored by a loyal society person.

running steer: must stampede to keep your career profitable.

CAULIFLOWER

05-09-10-28-34-45

buying: will have good health after recovering from illness.

eating: will marry for money to please parents and yourself.

growing: will be charged with dereliction of duty from a friend's treason.

of: a sign of second sight.

CAVALRY

06-07-24-29-38-43

belonging to a: will marry a beautiful woman.

married woman dreaming of a, man: will divorce her husband.

    single woman: will marry a rich banker.

of a: distinction in service and advancement in society.

CAVE

07-15-17-27-37-51

being in a: change and probable separation from loved ones.

    with others: abundant means if you seek refuge with friends.

being in a cavern: will remain poor and unknown in your expanding universe.

    of a: desire to relinquish responsibility

and to become totally dependent on another.

    very deep: death of a friend makes you contemplate the beginning of your life.

coming out of a, into the light: your depression is over; your self can emerge safely.

crawling into a: avoiding an overwhelming situation will not solve it.

digging a: feel the energy receding from you, leaving muscular aches from a wet chill.

escaping from: your deep stronger self is trying to locate you.

falling into a: returning to levels of consciousness where fear was founded.

grotto, having a big party in a: are happily absorbed in and engulfed by your lover.

    dining in a: your lover cannot replace your inability to deal with your world.

living in a: your insecurities are revealed in egotism.

taken by force into a, being: perilous journey ahead to the ancient level of being.

CEILING

08-17-19-25-26-29

colored, a: full of ideas that you project on it.

cracked, a: will have troubles caused by someone near to you.

exploding out of a: expansion is crucial to continued growth and well-being.

of own room being damaged: view of authority has been impaired.

ornate, an: shows fine artistic taste and the intellect to support it.

repairing a: protection against the elements.

white, a: the purity and romantic ardor of first love.

CELERY

09-11-15-29-31-47

buying: will escape from troubles and rise to your wildest dreams.

chewing on: will have a multitude of affairs.

    stuffed with cream cheese: a promise of luxury.

eating: will have domestic comfort, love and affection.

of: good digestive health and healthy finances.

CELLAR

01-14-32-36-37-48

cleaning out a: a healthy renewal of emotional strength.

cluttered, a: your retaining emotional garbage will become a physical ailment.

coal in: good news from far away will relieve your depression.

empty: being receptive to new ideas will gain you prosperity.

going into a: old storage is interfering with your progress.

many things stored in a: will lose property if you lose confidence in partner.

sleeping in a: significant messages from the deepest regions of your unconscious.

wine, a: are storing emotion to be enjoyed at a later date.

    woman dreaming of a: a gambler will propose marriage.

CELLPHONE
01-04-20-35-37-38

can't see numbers: research vital information.

connection difficulty: are not clear who is the object of your feelings.

    fuzzy: mate doesn't see that you want to leave.

disconnected, are: disregard what was said.

distraction: other people are interfering.

interference: relationship is between two people only.

redial doesn't work: face it, it's time.

trouble dialing, have: more effort is required for you to be successful.

won't work: try another direction.

CEMENT
12-17-31-32-44-49

buying bags of: are amassing wealth for an important event.

hardened concrete: reinforce substantial stability in business.

mixing: a nebulous acquaintance will solidify into an intense relationship.

wet: enduring solidity of love will conquer all things.

working with: will receive unexpected money from a new friend.

CEMETERY
02-06-10-30-38-45

accompanying a close friend to: will hear from friend you have mourned as dead.

unknown person, an: money is needed to resolve one's dead past.

being in a: attain your peace, prosperity will follow.

bride passing a, on way to wedding: will lose husband.

bringing flowers to a: release from anxiety over past problem.

cypress tree around border of a: protects the dead from evil.

flowers, children gathering in a: have sensitive, indecisive personality.

    elderly people putting: will have no grief if you resolve it.

lingering about a: hang onto unfulfilled dreams, there is still time.

of a: will regain lost property occupied by usurpers.

walking into a: uproot the anguish you have buried.

CEREMONY
02-13-33-34-35-49

government, a: have ability to react quickly to complex high-level situations.

military parade, a: feel pride for one's homeland.

participating in a: are a consummate professional.

religious, a: wish-fulfilling expression of inner values.

CERTIFICATE
06-28-30-40-42-44

birth, a: the powers of creation are just gearing up.

death, a: major upheaval in the family power structure.

giving a: people will recognize your innocence.

official: are in line for a promotion.

receiving a: do not see things from others' point of view.

    stock: financial losses.

CHAINS
02-11-25-29-30-35

bound in: your relief from burdens is imminent, but difficult.

cutting a: your opinions chain you to the wrong people.

    your: worries will dissipate, if you face the past.

enemies being bound in: are being restricted by deception.

    others: burdens are about to depart on the heels of your opponents.

    relatives: anchor your strength in several loyal friends.

flowers, a, of: stress will lighten up momentarily.

gold, around a woman's neck: the missing link to good fortune with lover.

iron: will escape from what bound you after extensive endeavor.

not being free of: the succession of torment is linked to a relative.

others in: will receive long-awaited news of the missing link.

person wearing, in jail: an anchoring of your basic needs allows victory over foes.

person with a: confront the person to finally break free.

pulling chain apart: your strength will free you from a confusing relationship.

reaction, a: line up the succession of events to the truth.

set free from, being: will escape in the eternal cycle of renewal.

shackles, bound in: your beliefs have burdened you with isolation.

sound of chains: will hear news that will limit your future freedom.

succeeding in breaking: will be free of social engagements.

wearing a: expect the limits of your ideas to hold you back in the near future.

CHAIR
12-14-15-19-40-44

arising from a: are entrusting your power to another.

beach, a: your fraud has been uncovered.

head of the table, at: your attitudes establish whether it is time for you to lead.

maker, being a: labor is comfortably nondemanding, your worries are.

man, being the: other's trust in your judgment will bring you distinction.

moved by others, being in a, and: will fail to meet an important obligation.

of an arm: will receive news of negotiations in your favor.

comfortable, a: need to overcome natural laziness.

empty: will receive news from an absent friend.

many: honor and dignity in your optimistic outlook.

sitting in an: will have high consideration by others.

    others: unwelcome guest will come to visit.

sleeping in a: have overstayed your welcome.

sitting down in a: relief from adversity by your own wise dealings.

stool, a: new friendship if you can expose your repressed anxieties.

tack for someone to sit on, placing a: a grave error in judgment will reverberate on you.

upholstered, an: improve your home with your raise.

worn-out: your immune system cannot fight emotional woes.

CHALICE
07-29-41-40-44-49

breaking a: disappointment in some cherished hope.

drinking from a: do not react, proceed with calm; there are serious flaws in your fun.

holding, with both hands: your soul has spoken, follow it.

CHALK
07-14-15-46-48-49

buying: will have a long life, if you can keep your hands clean.

handling: will soon be married above your station.

painting face with: are scheming for love, position and money.

writing on blackboard: ill luck at having been caught doing a childish prank.

CHALLENGING
01-04-17-32-52-53

being challenged: will reconcile with enemies after the duel.

boxing match, someone to a: will bring a public shame to community.

duel, someone to a: immediate death of a relative.

order to stop, defying: will bear defeat to spare others from dishonor.

others: in the future be prudent, apologize and keep the friendship.

CHAMELEON
23-26-29-34-40-47

changing color: your fickleness obstructs your progress.

> *skin:* changing values to fit situation leads to confusion.

hidden on a branch: your adaptability to give aid when and where needed.

scurrying off: return and face your indecision.

CHAMOMILE
13-23-27-43-44-50

applying a, poultice: deal with the depth of your wounds.

drinking: reduce your stress before you make a decision.

gathering: treat the sickness before it develops.

CHAMPAGNE
10-19-22-32-37-39

being at a, party: will be happy with lover.

breaking a bottle of: an imminent adventure.

buying: seek out only happy companionship.

drinking: charming people do not understand you.

> *by yourself:* will be unfortunate in love affairs.

glass of, a: short-lived good fortune.

tray of glasses of, a: rebellion against social norms brings loneliness.

CHAMPION
14-25-34-36-42-49

being a: financial gains are given to very few whose enthusiasm never wanes.

justice, of: need righteousness to be dealt in your favor.

of: pull yourself together and be more careful.

own team being: your commitment to excellence will bring lasting friendships.

women, of: your overconcern shows a guilt at feeling dishonor toward women.

CHANDELIER
06-12-35-36-48-51

candles, with: prosperity brings distressing responsibility for the not prosperous.

church: will go to prison for misuse of other's funds.

table with candles, over: your capriciousness destroys any stability in a relationship.

> *globes:* wealth into several generations reflected in your inner light.

CHANGE
04-05-07-13-29-41

changing one's mind about a friend: the misunderstanding has carried on too long.

> *conditions in life:* damages to present condition.

> *in crisis:* must take charge of what others are doing.

> *on impulse:* will be rewarded for displaying justice.

stalling: your failure has blocked your project's completion.

supplanted, being: are unfitted to fill your life position.

> *by force:* will be superseded and uprooted by a cheating friend.

CHAPEL
09-11-19-25-32-47

being outside of a: your multitude of friends block the serenity gained within.

kneeling inside of a: a moment of inner peace denotes business must change.

of a: reflect on only true friends, disentangle from false ones.

praying inside a: contemplate God's guidance.

CHARITY
03-05-09-18-22-44

bazaar, buying things at a: will realize high ambitions.

> *people selling:* will receive a proposal from an unexpected source.

being charitable: less fortune awaits you in business affairs.

clothing to, giving: people are laughing at your being a burden to them.

foodstuffs to, giving: work hard or you will be forced to beg.

giving to: long-awaited financial gains in near future.

> *freely:* your financial situation is deteriorating.

of alms: sorrow caused by affection for another.

receiving: feel you can't solve your domestic affliction on your own.

someone begging from you: misfortune if you refuse to give.

work without hesitation, doing: have a dangerous ally.

CHARMS
05-13-16-28-29-41

buying to ward off evil: are accepting easy answers without answering hard ones within.

receiving as a gift: will soon experience many ups and downs.

selling: beware of jealous friends bringing unhappiness.

wearing: will have an important decision to make soon.

CHASE
04-08-28-41-45-53

chased, being: running from a frightening situation.

> *by opposite sex:* are denying your own sexual drive.
>> *shadowy creature:* an early trauma is trying to be reheard and solved.

chasing: an elopement will cause much gossip; is that goal really yours?

CHEATING
06-18-31-38-50-53

being caught: wish your unfaithfulness were acknowledged, to end relationship.

cards, at a game of: risk losing the trust of your partner with lack of honesty.

contemplating: can't match up with the competition; try a different game.

feelings, of: worried about a project you do not have the heart to finish.

having been cheated: endeavor to trust friends; ferret out the false ones.

of: designing people wish to relieve you of your fortune.

CHECK
14-22-26-34-44-48

bad, giving a: what you are willing to resort to is what you will receive.

> *without funds to cover it:* an enemy is seeking your ruin.

checkbook, handling own: dignity and distinction.

> *losing a:* secret enmity of some person that you will escape easily.

writing checks from a: good times are coming.

> *others, in own:* business disappointments.

forgery, committing: friends are not revealing the whole truth.

> *signature on a, forging a:* are trying to be clear rather than right.

having a: a change in life will soon come.

losing a: a promise of financial gains will be reneged.

receiving a: a long-forgiven loan will be repaid.

returned without funds, a: are being deceived.

writing a: you will find it difficult to keep your promises.

> *knowing no money is in the account:* guilt.

CHEEKS
01-05-20-23-27-30

beautiful: joy and contentment.

man dreaming of his: narcissism is a lonely route.

> *woman, her:* will be loved very much for the wrong things.

painting the: deceit at the end of the day will be uncovered.

pale: will be in need of provisions.

rosy: are too shy to ogle the truth, preferring a colorful illusion.

CHEESE
08-25-35-38-45-51

buying: aspirations will come to fruition if you uncover those deceiving you.

eating: minor portions will bring health.

foreign: are prone to liking only the richest gourmet foods.

grated, having: opposition causes minor setbacks in love affairs.

homemade: good luck to one for whom you care.

limburger: your actions are foul-smelling and embarrassing to you.

made in own country: will refurnish your home.

of: worry caused through own hasty actions.

CHEF
08-10-15-20-36-46

being a: have transformed the toil of life into an enjoyable feast.

> *at a restaurant:* will be cheated by friends.
> *young girl:* will soon become engaged.

dismissing the: have been dishonest with yourself.

female: will break her engagement.

male: you expect too many favors of others.

CHEMIST
21-23-25-26-31-48

apothecary, being an: attend to your health and security.

  asking, to heal you: self-insight into wisdom heals all.

chemical reaction, causing a: your naiveté needs inner resources to adapt to convention.

combining solids: grounding in the material is required.

dissolving liquids: your spiritual life needs attention.

vaporizing: intense purification process.

watching chemistry experiments: a degree of self-responsibility in your transformation.

CHERRIES
04-18-28-47-49-51

bowl of, a: your life is your own destiny and no one else's.

cooking: are in possession of a delicious, much-desired object.

dark, having: will be sorry about present enterprises.

eating: will be agreeable in personality matters.

  in alcohol: will be cheated by best friends.

  sour: disappointments in love.

house, having, in the: your home is in excellent condition.

maraschino: a touch of class to land support in your favor.

picking: your desires will be fulfilled superficially.

  man dreaming of: will be deceived by women.

  out of season: annoyance from a former friend.

Queen Anne: you crave the succulence of elegance.

rotten: will be hurt by slander from a lover.

tree, climbing on a: a short-lived passionate affair.

  falling out of: affair ends in disappointment at your lover's lies.

hanging from: losses in business will come soon.

tree, in bloom: beautiful fortune ahead.

  without: your unselfishness will free your good health.

CHESS
03-35-36-43-46-48

king, the: highly developed critical faculties.

  knight: decisive astute personality.

  queen: are setting your sights too high in the game of life; you don't need that much.

  rook: think carefully, the way others see you.

losing a game of: dissect your opponent's thought patterns or squelch the deal.

  winning: use good sense to handle approaching money.

making a, move: increase your knowledge before you act.

  your opponent: notice how he thinks and act upon it.

playing: turn the difficulties ahead in your path to your favor.

  others: your fortune will depend upon results of the game.

CHESTNUTS
17-19-27-30-40-48

buying: will be disappointed by lover.

eating: turn advantages carefully to your favor.

having: domestic afflictions are caused by a supposed friend.

picking off the ground: use your ingenuity to solidify your love affair.

roasting in an open fire: life without your lover would be unthinkable.

sitting under a, tree: life has regained its possibilities.

CHEWING
05-20-22-23-27-39

children: break down issues to absorb all items.

gum: lesson must be pondered to be understood.

nails: are swallowing a problem that was never yours to deal with.

of: will have to overlook own faults to sample other's faults.

others: will have peace of mind if you realize the whole situation.

until your jaws ache: your sheer will persuades others to your interpretation of events.

CHICKENS

09-25-28-35-38-50

chasing a: stop those one-night stands and concentrate on one lover.

> *several:* are anxious at the extensive cost of your overdomestication.

cooking: will make considerable money from an opportunity you thought lost.

eating: your job efforts will find reward; your home efforts will fail.

hearing hens cackle at dawn: warning that care is needed to not be henpecked.

> *evening:* big peril if you do not exert henpecked power.

> *noon:* fights between relatives; don't let them take advantage of you.

henpecked, of being: be wary of being pushed to lose your temper.

killing a: your profit by taking advantage of another's cowardice will haunt you.

of a hen: overpossessiveness will yield financial gains.

> *cackling:* sudden suicide in neighborhood brought on by malicious fabricated gossip.

> *house:* many petty concerns ultimately twist to your benefit.

> *laying eggs:* unexpected money or child.
> > *sitting on her:* happiness at present comfort in life.

> *setting:* promises fulfillment of a long-cherished wish.

> *with her chicks:* your deed has caused another's displeasure.

of chicks: a family means you support each other.

> *eating a:* you see melancholia where fun exists.

> *feeding:* stop playing the martyr and keep your self-assurance to yourself.

> *killing a:* are blaming an innocent person.

of one fine: will be fortunate in the venture you are contemplating.

plucking a: seek higher compensation for your work.

several: good friends are around the corner.

> *chirping:* don't waste time on idle chatter

CHILDREN

14-15-30-39-51-52

alive, being: happy days ahead for your unrealized potential.

apology from, receiving: your relationship has a future.

apprehension over: present peril is escaped.

around with, going: seek to acquire much-needed skills.

arrival of: accept responsibility for that which is undeveloped.

bashful, having: your self-centeredness reacts immaturely to simple situations.

buying things for: buy that much-needed new outfit.

chagrined, being: experience awe, wonder and curiosity at not knowing something.

clumsy: the awkwardness of those who ask and seek to learn.

devotion for parents, having: are imitating them rather than creating your own life.

disgrace, being in: want another chance to attain your desires.

feeding small: have forgotten the child within your adult exterior.

> *others:* are being deceived.

having many of your own: the facets of your inner child are finally communicating.

killing a child: destruction of high ideals by own misdeeds.

moaning: be cautious in dealing with those caring for children.

neglecting your: have begun projects that need your attention.

of: a woman will become pregnant soon.

overturned while playing, being: an infantile rivalry reactivated in a new setting.

pretty: success if you express emotion and explore all possibilities.

prodigy, being a: are bored with present company.

several: will have abundance in life.

sick, being: emotional wounds need to be healed.

stain on clothes: melancholy over how one appears to others.

stiff, being: involve your children in their own raising.

strong, a: for most of adolescence nothing seems right.

talking to own: your trauma at that age needs expression

CHIMNEY

06-16-18-26-31-45

ascending a: will extract yourself from unpleasant scheme.

cracked: big catastrophe ahead bringing unexpected income.

falling down: joy that the fire was out before you jumped into the fray.

going down a: your untimely, indecent behavior will alienate your associates.

of own house: will receive short-term stability.

ship smokestack: new opportunity appears over the horizon.

smoke coming from: your affairs will turn to prosperity.

soot from a: cannot take credit for completing an unsavory task.

　covering you: a tabloid misinterpretation of the facts haunts you.

sweep, a: messenger of good luck in profession.

　clean your chimney, having: relief when family embarrassments are exposed.

　face all black, with: will do mediocre business.

　hearing calling for work: will make big profits with new idea.

　of a: will be bitterly disappointed at being falsely accused.

　work, at: positive change in your personal life.

tall: fortunate events from unexpected income.

CHIN

29-33-37-40-46-52

beautiful, having a: have been able to take life's blows gracefully.

　large: your sternness blocks the free flow of your intelligence.

double chin, others having a: will be complemented for doing good.

of own: your character just out for exposure.

others hurting their: obstinacy gets in the way of success.

tumor on the, a: illness to come.

CHINESE

05-18-29-33-49-53

company of, being in the: fear of being influenced by illogical foreign beliefs.

home, being in a: are looking for the mysticism inherent in wisdom.

people, several: fear the irrational; it is the unlimited universe that awes you.

Wall, the Great: the ultimate in protection and security.

CHOCOLATE

02-23-25-29-32-42

buying: a short period of major expenses followed by prosperity.

candy: use as a crutch to make you feel special.

drinking hot: will receive a marriage proposal that turns to disaster.

　sharing: you wish that person was more than a friend.

eating: a gift from a reliable friend who lacks restraint.

　covered desserts: embellish simple pleasures with overindulgence.

powder: will provide happiness and health for those looking for your support.

CHOKING

09-12-18-23-26-28

being choked: physical symptoms caused by your undesirable impulse.

children: recovery from conflicting decisions made growing up.

of: your guilt causes you to punish yourself by not speaking the truth.

others: extreme hostility causes an explosion that no one survives.

CHOOSING

08-10-16-18-28-48

employees: family disagreements have no place in the office.

of: will have a sickness that may result in an operation.

too fast: overexertion of yourself will cause burn-out and leave you further behind.

CHRIST

16-18-20-21-25-27

Antichrist, seeing the: an appreciation of what exists.

birth of: will have peace, joy, and contentment by surrendering your innermost self.

Christ consciousness: will have spiritual harmony.

crucified, being: your enemies will be defeated.

garden, being in the: will be highly esteemed and influential.

of: trust the higher power to reach wholeness.

resurrection of: are in harmony with yourself and your fate.

talking to: will receive a big consolation for bringing others uplifting experiences.

Temple, in the: unpopular but correct efforts will be rewarded.

CHRISTMAS
07-08-17-21-28-40

banquet, attending a: fulfilling relationship with those you love.

caroling, going: after your financial gains your situation becomes precarious.

church on, attending: will receive God's blessings and give love.

family reunion during: giving and receiving spiritual awareness.

of: will have happy family affairs and openings for new members.

party, being at a: are too cautious in your relations with new friends.

present, receiving; will have a pleasant reunion of friends.

    several: beware of person from whom you received them.

reindeer pulling a sled, a: prestige from the community.

    many: an investment you thought worthless will climb in value.

tree, a: after a long wait, the angel will light up your life.

    decorations dismantled, with: an emptiness followed by clarity of message.

CHRYSANTHEMUM
06-07-09-28-32-40

blue: clarity and purity.

light: slighted love through jealousy-motivated intrigue.

red: an expression of your love.

white: something must die for the truth to live.

yellow, deep: deep inside you is the solution to your slighted love.

CHURCH
15-17-22-27-41-49

aisle, in a: difficulties and misfortune will beset you.

altar: aspire to a spirituality fundamental to all life.

anthem in, hearing an: your prayers are being answered on your well-planned work.

blasphemy in a, committing: use violent protest rather than practical action.

building, a: are loved by God, love him back.

    several: happiness is buried too deep beneath your material ambition.

built, being: will surmount difficulties while remaining true to your innermost thoughts.

catechism, preaching from the: distinction of your future position.

    reading, a, manual: activities in a lucrative position.

    receiving oral instruction: you can accept strictures behind advancement.

caving in: have deep feeling of regret that you have lost faith in God.

choir, singing in the: a surprise visit of an old friend reveals lover's disloyalty.

    hearing a: a lack of tolerance for one another leads to gloom.

Christening, attending your child's: will achieve hopes and desires.

    friend's, a: contentment with new life.

    godparent, being a: be decisive in taking advantage of favorable opportunity.

communion, going to: will receive many blessings.

    children: guidance will be received through your third eye.

crucifix, praying to a: you will receive high honors.

    hanging a: will be involved in troubles you will blame on others.

deacon, a: your actions will be severely criticized.

decorated, fully: will receive an inheritance of spiritual nourishment if you atone.

during mass, in: your approach is tentative for fear of refusal.

entering a: your making amends will be received with kindness.

hearing a dispute in: conflict between daily life and spiritual values.

heresy, being accused of: will assert yourself and gain stature in community affairs.

Holy Communion: will make a friend who will stand by you for life.

Judgment Day, at: are resigned to pay for your sins and be credited for your conduct.

parish, of a: there are no clouds in your future.

praying in: will be kept from the wrong path if you cooperate with the family.

priest in, being with a: harbor guilt and shame for breaking important rules.

Sabbath, observing the: will participate in the ritual.

  reveling in the: will mock the very truth of your life.

sacrilege, committing a: will suffer much misery.

salvation, institution, joining a: a rude awakening for your family.

Savior, praying to the: desires will be granted in the future.

  granting wishes: spiritual healing has been earned, prayers are answered.

seated in: will change habits, with the strength of spiritual forces.

talking in: friends are envious of your relationship with the forces of life.

vicar of a, talking to the: people will cause anguish.

yard, being in: a sense of what is fundamental to all life and death.

  others in a: cycles of life and growth, reproduction and interdependence.

CIDER
01-06-07-09-20-32

buying: will gossip about your own private affairs.

having: your destructive habits are out of control.

making: be cautious with social contacts who are not worthy of your confidence.

people drinking: cheap pleasures are followed by rude awakenings.

selling: luring others into bingeing results in swift penalties.

CIGARETTE
06-26-28-32-35-42

enjoying a: no progress.

half-smoked, in hands, holding a: postponement of love.

lighting a: signifies negotiations for new projects.

loose cigarettes: disillusion and disappointment.

man and woman smoking together: conclusion of hopes.

rolling a: will never have to worry about squandering money.

smoking a: need to postpone appointment until you are better prepared.

  to the end: sense of prosperity is a ruse.

stubbing out a, with determination: good progress in trying to quit.

suddenly repulsive to you: quitting has to emerge from the inside out.

trying to give up: limitations don't reach goals, diversion does.

women dreaming of smoking a: troubles will soon vanish.

CIGARS
01-02-04-07-28-49

buying, in a, shop: your attempt to be economical is a ruse.

lit, having a: have hopes of prosperity, but should save money for a rainy day.

  cigarillo, a: your show has little substance, except for the value you give it.

  others: be discreet when you attend a big party.

  unlit, an: being dogmatic will bring misfortune.

CIRCLE
05-17-19-22-26-44

circling a: are stalled in a never-ending cycle.

crop: are under the influence of a power beyond your circle of friends.

drawing a: your thoughts are not goal oriented, but ritual.

mandala, a: a symbol of wholeness for protection from evil.

running around a: are solving problems you created, which create new ones to solve.

standing inside a: your higher state of consciousness comes at the price of loneliness.

universal man, with arms and legs outstretched: emotional symmetry.

CIRCUS
05-07-16-19-25-30

children to, taking: important and beneficial, but short-lived events.

in a: your frivolity is the sign to others of a potential victim.

juggler performing, a: deception of an imposter ready to take advantage.
   teaching you his tricks: an opportunity you should grasp with both hands.

of a: embarrassment will cause future unhappiness.

performing in a: have ignored the development of your other talents.

roller coaster, riding the: your erratic behavior, in search of excitement, is getting you lost.

watching a, performance: loss of money in an expensive enterprise.

CISTERN
02-05-18-21-39-47

brimful: financial matters are improving at the expense of friends.

drawing water from a: have an abundance while others are dehydrated.

half-full: unhappiness because of own careless improprieties.

nearly empty: unfortunate business return will bring sorrow.

CITIZEN
03-19-14-21-32-38

bad, being a: will pay a visit to a tomb.
   good: much ambition will bring excessive stress.

becoming a: will have hard work ahead.

fall into a: trouble from trespassing on other's rights and pleasures.

refused citizenship, being: will make money.

CITY
01-04-23-27-30-43

beautiful, a: slow recovery of business losses.

burning, a: poverty if you remain in present abode.

councilman, with a: insurmountable obstacles ahead if you speculate on real estate.
   dealing with a: will improve your estate.
   friends at a meeting of: new interests and surroundings.

others with: beware of friends whose allegiance can be bought.

ghetto, living in a: loss of home through mortgage foreclosure.

going through a strange: a friend will move in with you.

inhabited: with each soul comes the overcrowding of emotional baggage.

large, being in a: conclusion of hopes for diversion, not fruition.
   small: business ideals will be shortly realized for what, and all, they can be.

lost in the, being: feeling isolated by your outmoded social attitudes.
   an unfamiliar: the confusion will clear through cooperation with others.
   familiar, now strange, a: something that usually works no longer does.
   fog, in the: look even if you do not want to see.
   foreign, a: feeling out of place in society.
   in a dangerous area: proceed with caution in your risky ventures.

ruins, in: will have illness in the family.

seeing a, in the distance: a complex maze through which you must pass.
   small: your expectations are below your capabilities.
   with many towers: your life is too hectic to accomplish anything.

well situated, a: business plans will come to fruition.

CITY HALL
14-18-20-31-32-35

doing business at: your enterprise at work will allow freedom in life.

employed at, being: the challenging activity preoccupies you.

going to: victory over persecution by bowing to authority.

married at, being: unpleasantness results from doing things in a hurry.

mayor, becoming the: civic responsibility will be fulfilled with jury duty.

of: will attain desires slowly but surely in a highly vital atmosphere.

seeking aid from: forebodes legal entanglements with officials.

CIVIL SERVANT
34-42-38-45-44-48
being a: your right to some semblance of control.
dealing with a: worrisome problems ahead in a power battle.
fighting with a: legal issues won't be avoided by challenging them.
paying fees to a: will be taxed to the maximum.

CLAM
09-13-29-40-41-45
closing a: are vulnerable to exposure of your erotic desires.
digging for: are taking advantage of another's hard-earned affluence.
opening a: betrayal is a carefully guarded secret.
several in a pail: don't stop at your first attempt, verbalize again and again.
unable to open a: holding yourself together in the midst of chaos

CLAY
06-10-12-34-38-48
baking bricks of: your flexibility does not stop special interests from harming you.
   white: good business prospects if your ethics remain pure.
building a house of, bricks: your home is based on shaky foundations.
   putting a room atop: sheer will power is needed to overcome obstacles.
of: own ideas are too easily manipulated by others.
sculpting with: your ideas are precisely defined.
working with: are stuck with a pliable destiny shaped by events.

CLEANING
12-16-26-34-40-50
ammonia, with: a stinging resolution to adversity.
   buying: will be vexed through another's accident.
   using: quarrels with friends over your excessive drinking.
bathroom, a: your thoughts are crystal clear.
children: will achieve victory over enemies.
disinfectant, using a: cleansing fear and emotions of guilt.

drains: have clogged up, fragile spiritual connections.
mop, clean new: progress in new venture through fresh ideas.
   dirty: do not encourage evil rumors by repeating them.
of: embarrassment and quarrels from old dirt.
scrubbing: recollection of deep sin troubling you.
spot, a: are a good housewife and well fed, but your melancholia thwarts every move.
stain, a: a compelling instinct won't be erased.
toxic buildup: a memory you wish to exorcise.
vegetables: the healing power that arises from your depths.
washing machine, in a: your life is too repetitive.
with a dust rag: your inner vitality will stand you in good stead.
   broom: face emotions you have hidden and make a fresh, clean start.
   sweeper: are blowing your problems out of proportion.
   wet: remove stains on your character.
yourself: are constipated, with unhealthy attitudes.

CLERGYMAN
01-09-26-28-30-38
company of, being in the: an honorable position will cause you mental distress.
confiding in a: a confusion of ethical playgrounds.
curates, many: will receive a disappointing letter from abroad.
delivering the sermon: will be lead out of your predicament.
many: will receive a letter from abroad; burn it.
of a: disappointment in love affairs caused by earnest endeavors with evil motives.

CLIFF
06-08-12-13-25-32
at the very edge of a: any business risks will cause a radical change.
climbing up a: will venture into unexplored territory for the conclusion of your affairs.
   down a: hidden dangers will cause defeat at the slightest misstep.

descending from a: fall from powerful achievement to a vacuum of activity.

jumping from a: problems are surmountable,
the difficulty is within you.

others, being on a, with: fear of falling in
another's esteem; getting back into
control.

pushing someone from a: unconscious sense of
difficulty causes your indecision.

standing on top of a: face your fear of not
being able to achieve.

CLIMBING
26-30-41-42-45-46

Alp, an: your social stature is rising, bring
up the rest of your growth.

difficult: solve one problem, out of many,
at a time.

effortlessly: your project is reaching its conclusion; watch the last rung in the ladder.

ladder, a: each rung must be stabilized before
stepping on the next one.

to upstairs window: will take unfair advantage of the secrets of friends.

mountain, a: conclude obligations to reach
the top distinction.

steep: new viewpoints are lateral, spiritual
renewal is straight up.

of: will overcome the obstacles to your prosperity in business.

unable to climb, being: have set unrealistically
high expectations.

CLOCK
03-04-08-13-35-48

alarm ringing in a: need more balance and
discipline to your spurts of willpower.

broken, a: trouble from a backbiter.

church or city: are part of an ever-changing
present, bolstered by past deeds.

grandfather: time has gone by and you are
still not finished.

large hand moving swiftly: your impatience
causes your dissatisfaction with life.

loss of a: feel time is running out on you.

minutes, counting the: can no longer delay an
important decision.

stopped: a situation has reached its end and
will finally bear fruit.

before noon: will be spared from illness if
you face your decision.

stopping a: are trying to stall the process
towards death.

strike the hours: your life-changing decision is
marriage.

wall, buying a: plan a business enterprise with
small steady successes.

having a: plenty of time to solve a problem.

winding a: are finding difficulty in catching
up with the self you feel you are.

CLOISTER
01-09-37-42-44-46

being in a: crying out for peace of mind does
not gain it.

reading in a: seek no counsel about your
confusion but your own.

sitting within a: emotional distress requires
solitude before reacting.

walking around a: silence will renew your
spiritual strength.

can't find way out of: you feel trapped in
a situation that has gotten out of
control.

CLOSET
06-10-23-25-36-48

casually dressed: listen to strangers, but confirm
their allegations from a trusted source.

casual for formal occasions, wearing: your lack
of inhibition damages your reputation.

formal for casual: you act too stiffly,
with ideas above your station.

changing: will receive a large damage
assessment.

closed, a: only you can order your personal
life.

clothes hanging in a: they don't help you
there; get out and wear them.

cypress, buying a dress made of: advancement
in financial position.

dressed in white: loss of friendship.

forget to put on: feel ill-equipped to cope.

giving, to charity: people are laughing at you.

halter, of a: a former playmate will become
your marriage partner.

halter straps worn by women: will overcome
obstacles.

taking away your, someone: an admirer
will haggle with you.

hamper, an empty: will have a jealous quarrel
with sweetheart.

hang up own: must control your project, every step of the way.

children's: avoid rivals.

visitors': change in your own environment.

hem, taking up a: will attain respect for completion of a credible job.

impeccably clothed: sense of inferiority blinds you.

linens in a: share the happiness in your home.

money in a, having: have squandered your talent by keeping it for your own pleasure.

open, an: your life is too exposed to envy.

scarlet-colored: will have sorrow.

    evening gown: dignity and distinction.

    silver-colored: happiness is assured.

    white: happiness in love.

    yellow: warning of troubles.

    black: unhappy events in near future.

skeletons, in the: are scaring people by unveiling previously hidden aspects of self.

CLOTHING
04-15-25-28-34-51

arranging: you receive an unexpected visitor.

alterations being made: adjust your outward appearance to match inner changes.

    children's clothes, to: happiness in the family.

    others making, for you: the acquisition of an immortal body.

    various, on: a prompt engagement.

badly dressed, being: are dissatisfied with your attractiveness to others.

buying: the persona or face you are willing to reveal.

    blue: will have a vigorous mind.

    brown: joy without profit.

    crimson, dresses of: dignity and distinction.

    gray: important and very beneficial event to come.

    green: financial gains.

    many: a conquering of the material.

    mauve: being sexually inviolate.

    pink: recovery of lost money.

    red: will receive a sad letter.

new, of: domestic troubles that concerned you are at an end.

nightcap, wearing a: abundance in business.

no, wearing: will receive plenty of money.

others: gossip spread by you is just as wrong.

overalls, having dirty: watch your diet for a fancy dress occasion.

    woman dreaming of a man in: doesn't know her loved one's character.

    working in: will be repaid for your kindness with admiration.

overdressed: self-protectiveness.

partly dressed, being: are behaving in an irrational, irritating manner.

plenty of, having: are seriously intent on your ambitions.

putting on: the virtue of each piece of clothing must be discerned.

selling: losses cannot be recouped by selling your possessions.

show window, wearing, from a: unexpected death of a relative close to your heart.

soiled: have raw creative power; use it.

spot on, having a: what you desire has one major flaw; get to work and repair it.

tattered, wearing: you emphasize work at your expense.

    collecting: appreciate every single thing you have.

    ragged: a conspiracy is under way to harm you.

    selling: your deception is obvious to others.

teenagers: immature attempts at self-importance.

    throwing away: your enemies triumph when you reject a friend's assistance.

tight: your attitudes restrict your emotions.

unable to get clothes off: lacking ability to conform to social norms.

unwilling to take, off: refusal to reveal real character.

    other's: want to adopt aspects of their life.

wearing wrong, for occasion: what you want versus what others want of you.

    above waist only: a warning against snobbery.

        below: are uncertain of your social identity.

    accessories, odd: you do not have to attend the occasion.

baby clothes: feel childish in adult occasion.

camouflage: are hiding something.

kimono, wearing a: will attend a fete where you meet your destiny.

    soiled: a love affair of haunting consequences.

no blouse: feel you have inadequate breasts.

no pants: rebellion against authority.

no shirt: have trouble fitting in.

no skirt: a new lover awaits you.

not your own: show admiration for that person.

overalls: are undertaking a dirty task.

plaid: a hearty fortune from activities outdoors.

too big for you: role is overwhelming you.

too much clothing: feel exposed and vulnerable.

too small: role is too limited for you.

weird outfit: are an outsider because you wish to be.

without any, being: pure you; make your appearances what you will.

    missing specific: exposed body part is vulnerable.

CLOUDS
01-03-09-10-12-14

beautiful white: will be problem free when sky is clear.

clearing away: your disagreeable attitude keeps the problems, problems.

downpour of rain from: illness will cause hard days ahead.

dull: feel overshadowed by someone.

lightning bursting from: an unexpected disappointment will raise your anger.

lowering: an emotional downpour due to bad management.

passing away: clearing up obscure issues.

stars, lit by the: your realizing the sparkle will be short-lived.

stormy and dark: your becoming a miser will bring sorrow.

sun covered by: your strong sense of duty is practical.

    moon: patience and perseverance will help you overtake present problems.

up in the, being: break through your illusions.

very black: the sense that someone is disappointing you is long overdue.

CLOVER
02-29-38-39-43-48

being in a field of: love which develops in a well-rounded way.

field of, a: an event will change you and your enemies' lives.

in blossom: misfortune from too much of a good thing.

of: industrious undertaking will create a magical future.

CLOWN
11-18-20-23-33-48

being with a: troubles from ridicule unless you learn to laugh at yourself.

    dressed as a: try too hard to make others like you.

hurt, being: fear of ridicule from vexed associates.

making love to a woman: have many hypocritical friends.

meeting a: your astuteness and shrewdness are misdirected.

performing: are seeing things superficially and therefore they are seen as wicked.

CLUB
03-20-28-37-49-52

being hit with a: would like an invitation to hit back.

being in a: will meet acquaintances of long ago.

belonging to a: wish deeper friendships with fewer people.

hitting with a: are creating your own potholes of adversity.

meeting friends in a: listen to your own counsel, not another's.

party in a, being at a: financial losses with other than your group.

refused admittance to a: take good care of the business you have.

CLUMSY
06-14-18-23-46-50

being: will overcome troubles in business.

    employees: don't confide in relatives so much.

    others: good results in love affairs.

COAL

02-17-22-28-35-36

burning brightly: are underestimating virtues of people you work with.
  fireplace, in a: will be tenderly loved and enjoy pleasures.
  slowly: minor irritations caused by employer.
  stove, in a: beware of untrue friends, compromise with true ones.
buying: will be justly rewarded for being industrious and conscientious.
children, playing with: reflect carefully before making decisions.
completely dead: troubles ahead as shame is exposed.
extinguished: are losing a job because of unfounded jealousy.
fiery: reputation is in doubt, change it.
handling: grief will occupy the void left by your heartless recklessness.
pit, being in: use your insight to avoid grave danger.
receiving, in Christmas stocking: another's opinion of you is greatly amiss.
selling: will have enough money to live comfortably all your life.
sitting in a bin: waiting for a lover who has abandoned you to return.
swallowing in medicines: secret affection.
wet, non-burning: are concerned about a project that is stalled.

COAL MINE

10-17-28-31-45-47

being in a: will not be fully satisfied in own affairs until you dig deeper.
blackness of a: contentment will be disrupted.
digging coal from a: abundant means through energy stocks.
working in a: accident will bring out unknown talents.

COAT

01-14-23-35-38-41

buttoning up your: careful restraint is required in speculations.
  high against the wind: adversity causes upset in business.
children's: substantial means.

buying a: will be a person of honor in family arguments.
  outworn: are disillusioned by insincere romantic gesture.
dirty, getting your: will lose a good friend due to your hypocrisy.
fleece, lined with: will be depressed without the sun.
losing a: speculation will cause your financial ruin.
mackinaw, bright plaid: outdoor activities.
  worn out: accidents come when defenses are weakened.
of a new: your innermost feelings, if exposed, will receive honors.
old, an: prosperity comes with the truth; your help will be sought.
overcoat: how you wish the world would see you.
poncho, a: aid is on its way.
purple, and hat: others regard you with respect.
rain, buying a mackintosh: great strength of character blocks any tendency to steal.
wearing a new: take a fresh view of business troubles for unforeseen gain.
  another person's: will be forced to seek a friend's help.
  old: a turn for the worse due to others' dishonesty.
  rain: attain an attitude to protect yourself.
  torn, a: others will siphon off your profits; they will fall into disgrace.

COAT OF ARMS

10-11-12-13-29-41

having a: will be highly honored by women.
magnificent, a: seek out those whose ambition matches yours.
of a: the keepsake in the attic will lower your opinion of your ancestors.
own, on door of home: a business failure from inflating your importance.
stained: are ashamed at having sullied the family name.

COAXING

01-11-28-30-36-45

being coaxed: immediate marriage to your chagrin.

89

of: a dangerous request will be made of you.

others: will have emotional sorrow.

COBWEB
02-25-17-38-34-35

destroying a: misfortune is near.

seeing and brushing away a: are discarding valuable ideas for lack of impetus.

spider, with a: are being used by a cynic.

   without: your abilities are under wraps, waiting to be distributed.

spinning a: people dislike, criticize and slander you.

COCK
01-09-14-21-39-49

dead: your aggressive pursuit of power will no longer get its wake-up call.

fighting: will have quarrels that lead to separation.

hearing a, crow: your great prosperity will be due to your machismo confidence.

   while you are asleep: are overachieving on thankless tasks.

in the house: will get married and that's a warning.

laying eggs: luck in the lottery, all else is impossible.

COCKATOO
04-06-13-30-32-34

buying a: will have arguments with friends.

hearing a, talking: a false friend is nearby.

keeping a, in a cage: will realize your own indiscretion.

of a: discovery of a secret.

COCOA
03-12-15-24-28-40

buying: happiness in the family is disrupted by ardent intentions of friends.

drinking: stand up for your right to a very good future.

making: abundant means, but below expectations.

of: cover up distasteful friends for your own profit.

COCONUT
04-10-20-29-41-50

buying, a: will have a love affair.

eating, a: will receive a large sum of money.

large tree full of, a: women are gossiping.

tree, a: will receive a fortune from parents.

CODE
11-22-27-35-43-49

business: you know more than you reveal.

consulting a law: your communication is too roundabout.

deciphering a: are manipulating news of improvement in business to impress others.

Morse, in: ask dream for a decipherable signal.

tax: advantageous events in business.

COFFEE
12-20-28-32-35-42

being in a, shop with good people: highly considered by friends.

   with strangers: other's plot to gain your possessions.

boiling: emotional sorrows from searching for things past the limit.

burning: family trouble can be avoided with proper call.

buying: will have the best reputation in business.

drinking, alone: friends are gossiping about you.

espresso, drinking strong: need an additional thrust of energy to complete project.

grinder, a: avoid gossip by changing your behavior.

grinding: will overcome obstacles by being discreet.

grounds: happiness interrupted by illness.

growing: financial gains through substantial credit.

maker, new: will change your residence.

   old: will refurbish your present home.

making: getting what you want, not what you need.

mill: be alert to any misstep that could give your enemies an edge.

of a, shop: will be deceived by the social ritual.

   being a waiter/waitress at a: are serving savory food to unsavory people.

      customer, a: your friend is trying too hard.

   eating in a: have an ache from evil pitted in your stomach.

pouring: security is forthcoming.

roasting: are preparing to give affection to a visitor.

selling: expect financial losses.

serving in a: your independence is at stake.

sweet: your empathic, cooperative nature yearns for affection.

COFFIN
07-16-26-35-38-45

being in a: a deadened dull state lacking spirit.

    friend: serious illness of a dear friend that will end an era for you.

    lowered in a grave: restriction of expressing one's self physically.

dead person in a: financial drain from a decaying situation.

elaborate, an: death of one partner, birth of another.

empty: will live to a ripe old age.

head of the family, of the: must contend with squabbles over the will.

lowered, being: changes you are powerless to avoid, are almost upon you.

lying in a: breaking a bond will bring a triumphant end to hopes.

    friend: advancement in own position through mistakes of another.

    relatives: a legacy is received through another's sorrow.

many: will incur large debts to failed lovers you have failed.

of a: will soon marry and own your own house with water in the basement.

own: someone is attempting to cheat you.

someone else's: inheritance may be unavoidably lost.

stealing a: are ashamed of receiving a fortune.

COINS
07-18-20-31-34-39

assembling all kinds of: unexpected news.

    seeing: promotion in own affairs.

collecting: an unusual event pursues you.

copper: sickness from the layers of corrosion on your conscience.

counting: will make a considerable profit.

finding: good fortune in domestic affairs.

foreign: a stranger will play a vital role.

giving, to others: others will take your money.

gold in the hands, having: may see Seven Wonders of the World.

nickel: good work will be your fortune.

of: great financial gains.

running through your fingers: are perfecting a useless, frivolous skill.

silver: strife and contention in the family.

    girl dreaming of: will be jilted by her lover.

spending: will risk failure in your own plans.

stealing: deeds well done.

COLD
02-19-29-31-32-39

bad, having a: are depressed and anxious, but security is forthcoming.

    children: all the deprivations of your childhood are reenacted.

    mate: disloyalty causes emotional estrangement.

cold climate, in a: others withhold their emotions and things don't go your way.

feeling cold: kick off the blankets and secure your finances.

huddling in the: have an obligation to carry out.

COLLAR
18-19-28-34-35-39

dirty, having a: shows fickleness on the part of the loved one.

fur collar, woman's: have control of a man's affections, use it well.

high, a: embarrassment from honors you did not deserve or earn.

man's: gains in speculations that have just been completed.

putting on a new: showing restraint means you have control of your destiny.

tight, a: restrictions on feelings put constraints on a relationship.

white, on her dress, woman having a: prosperity in a confining relationship.

COLLEAGUES
02-03-14-15-18-44

dealing with: will be treated with disdain by big business gossip.

death of a: unhappiness.

having: will have litigations.

hitting a, in anger: birth of the first son in the family.

COLLECTION

11-17-19-34-36-41

agency, a: have failed to return an affection.

contributing to a: owe someone something.

making a, for poor people: trying to obtain affection before they leave.

others contributing to own: have gained respect from a devious action.

COLLEGE

10-19-27-33-48-53

child going to: will receive well-deserved eminence.

dormitory: through mental application goals are reachable.

dreaming of being at: the position you deserve.

man dreaming of being inside a: something you missed will be learned.

   woman: will have a chance to expose your talents.

COLLISION

15-24-28-32-50-51

dying in a: are unable to decide which life to choose.

hurt in a, being: disappointments in business become physical.

   unhurt: will make a love conquest, several.

of a: will have a serious accident.

COLONEL

09-16-24-30-35-43

being a: will be surrounded by evil that you are expected to destroy.

   Southern: business trip will follow to a solution of financial woes.

in uniform, a: dissatisfaction that love is not prominent in your social clique.

unmarried woman dreaming of a: will marry a banker to best your friends.

woman dreaming of being married to a: save money for old age.

COLONIES

07-16-22-42-43-44

being in the: don't take offense at fancied slights.

deported from the, being: danger is ahead.

   to the: will hold a religious mission.

going to the: good financial affairs.

of the: will receive an unexpected visit.

returning from the: will have an important result.

COLOR

21-31-37-39-43-50

amber: will receive a letter that will transform you.

bright: emotions are churning to the vibrations of light.

brown: are concealing a romantic emotion.

discolored, any part of body being: your pretense will cause a social setback.

gold: Christ consciousness.

gray: a colorless existence full of invalid thoughts.

indigo: wisdom, listen to it as you cruise in southern waters.

mauve: warning against pride in cheating others out of their possessions.

pink: glorious resurrections of love from the material body.

several colors mixed together: you have false friends.

silver: divine protection.

turquoise: healing spirituality.

violet: spiritual purification and illumination.

yellow hair: be wary of the envious as you pursue your objections.

   painting a room: important but bad changes will occur.

COLUMBUS

07-08-13-15-20-32

celebrating, Day: will be going fishing.

discovering America: good business transactions.

fleet of ships of: rapid success of hopes and desires.

statue of: postponement of success.

COLUMN

04-20-39-41-46-50

broken, a: hopes are shattered by best friend.

erecting a: abundance of money through your efforts alone.

falling, a: your rigidity has caused your stability to topple.

leaning on a: others depend upon you, as you on them.

of any kind of a supporting: are holding up under the burden of supporting others.

standing next to a: support is there if you are desperate.

   on top of: a stab at romance has deluded you.

steel, a: your increased value to the community will earn your stripes.

COMB

08-17-23-29-42-46

being combed by a beautician: self-preservation.

   others: loss through someone trusted.

   rich woman's hair, a: big fortune ahead.

borrowing another's: loss of money unless serious affairs are resolved.

broken, a: serious rift in the family.

buying a: not taking care of own affairs leads to unexpected change of address.

combing a boy's hair: friendships are solid and secure.

   curly: are emotional and impressionable and want it your way.

   long: your new friendship will last, which is what you want.

   others, their hair: have a generous, reflective nature.

   own hair: your vanity is counterproductive, tidy it up.

   young girl's hair: good relationship with someone you love.

losing a: your love for someone is not as strong as it once was.

own, being borrowed by others: difficulties through a strained friendship.

teeth missing, with: some points need clearing up.

using a: affairs are in confusion, tidy them up.

COMBAT

08-24-47-48-50-53

engaging in: are enterprising and enjoy taking risks.

   and being successful: stealing love is not gaining love.

   unsuccessful: pay attention to presence of enemies in lovers.

helping others in: reconciliation with enemies, if you stand your ground.

watching a: are risking your good name by being indifferent to current events.

COMEDIAN

09-22-24-38-49-52

being a: you harbor bad desires in your mind.

   harlequin: your passion will allow you to be ensnared in a contention of sins.

jester: it's a wise adviser who doesn't take himself too seriously.

mime: words not spoken reveal new friend is unworthy of your trust.

   gesturing: major problems daunt partner who needs your support.

poor, being a: loss of money and disgrace.

   female: results in affairs are a mockery.

   male: will handle heavy criticism of business automatically.

COMEDY

03-13-14-40-43-48

acting in a: be prepared for repercussions from your frivolity.

   friend: beware of friends who take themselves too seriously.

of a: will rise above mediocre with a long-awaited letter.

reading a: security is forthcoming; laughter heals.

watching a: you waste time indulging in temporary pleasures.

writing: a visit from an unwelcome guest with cruel intentions.

COMET

02-14-27-28-35-40

falling: influences from within ground you for uncertain times ahead.

   several: change of personality will overcome poverty.

of a: unusual distinction will come when you unleash your tremendous creative potential.

streaking across the sky: upsets causing external changes reveal your new personality.

   several: approaching sorrow if inner changes are not made.

COMMAND

15-26-35-39-48-53

being commanded by others: your anger at authority is noticed.

commanding others: unexpected reward conferred on you.

   children: fear is not a constructive learning process.

receiving a government: your glee at the death of an enemy will backfire on you.

COMMANDER

07-12-18-21-22-26

being a: will be ordered around by those who have earned the right.

of a: will receive words to the wise; follow them.

promoted to a, being: you triumph over mistakes in your own affairs by abstinence.

vessel, being of a: a love conquest obtained through an error in judgment.

COMMERCE

13-21-27-47-49-51

being an important Chamber of Commerce official: will be robbed.

having dealings in fabric: afflictions are overcome by wise use of profit and pleasure.

of: death of people doing distasteful labor.

own, having: will receive a favor at a crucial point in the near future.

small trade, doing a: treason and persecution from those who want your business.

steel trade, being in the: loss of friends who can't live up to your rigid ethics.

COMPANION

02-03-06-08-15-43

being with a pleasant: their presence blocks you from performing your obligations.

unpleasant, an: another's anxieties cause a temporary reprieve from work.

conversing with several: heavy rain places you in peril.

driving, to airport: illness will separate you from your anxiety.

joins you on a walk: a new friend to enjoy your sordid pasttimes.

who does not recognize you: have matured past the friendship.

COMPASS

01-08-17-20-29-36

checking your bearings on a: follow the direction of your true self-expression.

arrow points to you: no one can help you but yourself.

point of a, walking to each: have ability to persist in face of opposing external events.

East: long-standing projects will be recognized.

North: major longterm success in direction you are not taking.

South: avoid getting unnecessarily jealous of your partner.

West: new interests and initiatives are being taken.

holding a: this problem's solution is a life changer.

losing a: your life's direction has disappeared.

COMPETITION

02-03-08-09-16-32

others competing with you: inordinate amount of energy for little return.

taking part in a: tact and diplomacy succeed better than defeat.

children: big joys if you don't try to play their game for them.

tournament, being in a: delinquency will be recompensed.

losing: will take a trek of renewal before beginning a new season of practice.

winning: will lead a mysterious life until your fiancé exposes you.

COMPLAINING

09-11-30-37-39-46

making a legal complaint: important event, very beneficial.

of: you become angry over unimportant things too easily.

to others: your hopes have no foundation.

receiving complaints: your grasping for favorable opportunities shows your desperation.

COMPOSING

06-10-12-14-28-44

being a musical composer: believe you can create and direct your life.

literature: vainglory reflecting jealousy and discord.

musical composition, a: an inspired song should be written down.

music yourself: solving difficulties will take your supreme effort.

printing a composition: extravagant in spending money.

COMPUTER

08-12-15-21-26-39

comes apart and breaks down: a state of depression with little outlet.

condenses two or more programs: someone plots against you.

crashing: your action has not been properly planned.

distorts: take time to do it right.

doesn't respond to command: goals you have set are unrealistic.

explodes: slow down; you are overextended.

goes out of control: time to take back your power.

internet: have unlimited knowledge at your fingertips.

keyboard: a misunderstanding with a loved one.

malfunction: don't be put off with minor failure at work.

melts: a secret enemy plots against you.

monitor: your plans need to be reexamined.

mouse: create and manipulate your reality.

mutates: be careful that you are not cheated by business partner.

not enough memory: demoting someone brings a period of emotional difficulty.

odd shape or appearance: make sure you back up your hard drive.

operator can't see screen: the skills of associates are underestimated.

parts are missing: your accountant is failing you.

software: decide what you want and you can have it.

  is not compatible: expect difficulties in your relationship or marriage.

something loose inside: choosing a job below your capabilities thwarts your career.

speakers order you around: are not calling your own shots.

won't boot up: nothing will happen unless you make it so.

won't shut down: are so insecure about your job you won't leave work.

won't work properly: give credit to others where it is due.

  fingers don't work: a vacation is long overdue.

  lacks vital operating information: computers are not a substitute for wisdom.

CONCERT:
09-13-37-38-43-47

being at a, as a participant: your entrepreneurial personality is stubborn.

singing: your presence in the public eye will be short-lived.

invited to a, being: others hold you in high regard.

listening to a: a new atmosphere will enrich your independence.

others at a: an inheritance will support your entrepreneurial ventures.

sick person dreaming of a: will soon recover through your obstinate inaction.

CONDUCTING
09-10-11-30-36-47

affairs correctly: inheritance is the positive effect of self-directed energy.

  wrongly: will have many changes.

being a conductor of a train or bus: you will receive an inheritance.

business: happiness.

conduct, having bad: loss of a friend.

military troops: good changes ahead.

orchestra, an: teeter between accepting weighty responsibility and exhibitionism.

  fanfare: plan and direct your level of awareness to new heights.

CONFESSING
01-09-16-38-42-44

cheating on a mate, to: forgive yourself first or mate never will.

children to their parents: recognize behavior that is deleterious to your health.

friends, to you: will take part in the creative adventure of sharing faults.

going to confession: will soon be told a secret, causing your deprivation.

  receiving, from others: others will reveal their secrets to you.

sins to a priest: ethical business will be put in order after you lose your lofty ideas.

someone else: correct your behavior towards that person.

CONFETTI
11-17-21-36-42-52

purchasing: social disappointment.

throwing: will receive a letter with good news.

  others, at you: love and happiness.

  people, into a crowd: big business profit.

CONFIDING
11-16-17-22-33-53

in others: settle pace of your life to a canter.

children: important and beneficial event
to come.

your mate: rely upon own vigor and relax
your dependence on mate.

news in a friend: misfortune in love affairs.

others, in you: holding their secret puts you at
considerable risk.

CONFISCATION

01-15-27-36-40-42

being released from: will make an unexpected
gain. ·

confiscating another's things: own affairs are in
confusion.

having own things confiscated: dangerous
enterprises ahead.

property, of: premonitions will be realized.

CONFLICT

06-14-27-28-30-48

having a: will participate in dangerous affairs.

legal: will soon be tricked.

losing a: will make unexpected earnings.

winning a: will make a profit through
speculations.

with a friend: your emotions are torn.

CONFUSION

11-18-26-28-32-40

being confused: will make an unexpected, big
profit.

of: will be defrauded of money.

others being in a state of: will be deceived.

relatives: family arguments.

CONGRESS

04-05-30-46-48-52

attending a congressional session: will soon
be cheated out of your possessions.

being a congressman: loss of hope in business;
switch to the business of governing.

being in: family will be ignored and misused.

legislation, enacting: make strange alliances
for a fair balance of power.

preparing law for: consolidating a multitude
of needs into practical use.

CONSCIENCE

02-09-16-20-22-27

another's: they have to live with it, let God
take the toll.

clear, having a: aid from the goodwill of others.

worried: your temptations should put you
on guard.

CONSPIRING

02-09-14-22-45-47

being a conspirator: will be badly burned in a
fire you created.

of a conspiracy: are compromised to the point
where your plan is unfeasible.

being the object of: your directions are
questionable, be the first to question
them.

others, against you: you labor under an illusion that all is well.

with others: bring on troubles with your
misapprehension of events.

CONSTIPATION

03-15-26-30-35-40

being constipated: life's poison is clinging to
you.

of: are squirreling away the nuts of your ideas
and experiences for your use only.

paralyzed with: withholding self-expression
limits your self-esteem.

taking a laxative for you: a formerly stingy
person will treat you generously.

CONSTRUCTING

12-14-17-37-38-47

bulldozer, driving a: destruction of that
limiting your reconstruction.

crane, operating a: take responsibility for the
advice you drop.

lifting weights with a: will lose personal
property in unusual ways.

derrick, using a: have the power to build or
demolish your future.

docks: will have many things on your mind.

girder swinging into place, a: scrimmage and
blockages on way to constructive union.

home for others: annoyance.

other things: big profit ahead.

own home: are rebuilding who and what you
are.

roads: confusion in business affairs; yours.

tombs: sickness.

CONTAMINATED

12-22-28-34-36-40

foodstuff being: loss in business through your
misrepresentation of yourself.

other's things: will have hard times if you
take on more burdens than your own.

things: future disgrace.

having, things: danger from a life-threatening illness.

CONTRABAND
04-06-16-28-34-51
being apprehended while smuggling: doomed to disappointment.
having partners dealing in: worry will be smoothed away.
of making: danger through a secret.
selling the smuggled: a serious disaster is ahead.

CONTRACT
10-12-18-26-32-48
canceling a: uncertain profits.
drawing up a: ill health.
making a purchase: will have good health right up to death.
not performing a: hard work awaits.
of a: dignity and distinction.
others making a: will pass away very soon.
reading a, without signing: friends will cheat you.
signing a: success of your plans.
  of sale: will be informed of an accident.

CONTRADICTED
22-25-26-34-37-52
being, by mate: will collect articles of little value that later are worth a great deal.
  friend: jealous people are nearby.
contradicting others: business will be satisfactory.

CONVENT
04-08-14-17-24-40
becoming a nun in a: happiness, though not a wealthy marriage.
being an abbess: have high ambitions with an interesting future.
  meeting an, after an illness: are reactivating, integrating your spiritual growth.
  of a bad monastery: your friendliness should bypass conflict.
being in a: fear your ethics and chastity will be questioned.
  church: a happy engagement with openness and generosity.
  others: coming ill health from guilt over confining others.
of a superior nun: peace, contentment and awe.

CONVERT
07-31-36-42-43-50
foreign money: will fall into disgrace.
of a: must endure tribulation.
others to own ideas: very beneficial and important event to come.
religion to another, from one: will have a quiet, happy life.

CONVICTS
09-13-25-33-39-46
being a: be wary that your behavior does not slip into illegality.
  others: feel trapped and wish to find another to take your place.
being convicted in court: your antisocial desires have been fulfilled.
  not: fear recrimination for unsavory thoughts.
  others: clear up your mistakes before they are blown out of proportion.
escaping from prison: wish you could entrap your trapper.
of a: feel thwarted in struggle to attain your objectives.
who are in prison: have strong antimoral impulse that needs to be checked.

COOKIES
01-12-24-34-38-44
buying: must rely on own good judgment.
giving as a gift: should mend your ways in life.
  receiving: will have a prosperous married life.
making: will receive good news.
  others: you enjoy sports.

COOKING
06-17-26-43-45-50
appetizers, making: are easing your entry into a social circle.
basting meats: will undermine your expectations with misplaced trust.
cauldron, in a: transforming inedible ambitions into palatable possibilities.
  boiling on the fire: a lucrative business deal will amount to nothing.
  of water: your worries are transitory.
  overturning a: plans slated as profitable amount to nothing.
  witches brewing in a: are disturbing the

ingredients of a healthy family relationship.

cook at heart, being a: successful future as a caterer.

eating: will receive a large amount of money from reunion of friends.

enamelware, with: friendship turns into a constant thorn in your side.

fritters, making: new work without additional compensation.

gourmet meal, a: are attempting to make your life experience palatable.

grease, with: a stupid move could splatter fire.

  stain, having a: a distraction will keep you from making a mistake.

    several on the cook's clothes: don't accept offers from older men.

hash, eating: petty vexations and pressure from rivals.

  making: unexplained visits by several family friends.

hearth, on the fire of a: acquaintances who had little regard for you will visit.

lard, in: a rise in prosperity does not equal arise in social stature.

man: will be invited to a party; take your positive attitude.

of: anxieties over family's nurturing may cause you to burn yourself.

others: no use creating love, if you don't serve it.

pots and pans: will rush to the aid of a dangerous felon.

recipe in a contest, entering a: your decision will prove correct.

  using a: past financial setbacks will be reconciled in your favor.

  writing a: have misjudged one who highly respects you.

seasoning: a means to adjust your family to your capriciousness.

several people at the same time: grasping for love, any love.

stew, a: beware of receiving violence from someone.

stove: irritability of hungry people will be quelled with your presence.

  cleaning a: too quick to accept any friendship; you lost important one.

woman: beware of treachery, caused by your temper.

COP
12-17-19-22-29-34

being a: troubles caused from prying into others' affairs.

being with a policeman: ambitions of using your original ideas will be realized.

  policewoman: an object of criticism and gossip in your relations with your partner.

others with a: good news is on the way if you return to earth and common sense.

wrestling a jaywalker: will have a serious altercation over a slight infraction of the law.

COPPER
01-09-20-31-30-47

buying: refined appearances must be well-grounded in fact.

coin, being given a: another will aid you in finishing your project.

handling: unexpected visit of important person brings period of discomfort.

of: ungrounded fears make present desires impossible to realize.

selling: have been deceived into believing minor crisis was major.

wire, installing a: a curious oppression will finally be lifted.

COPYING
01-12-28-39-43-47

being in the, business: a plan thought favorable will become unfavorable.

legal papers: are in struggle with stronger opponent.

letter: anxiety over contents needs to be put in perspective.

others: emotional sorrow when you see your extravagance exposed.

picture, a: would prefer a clone would take the flack for you.

signature, another's: copying another's behavior leads to ridicule, your own.

text, a: solve your problems before they get out of hand.

CORAL
08-18-21-24-26-37

buying: a letter with money attained by your perseverance.

black: invisible illness from the depths of your emotions.

pink: inspiration to create new experiences.

red: love yourself first.

white: use your intuition for guidance.

reef, a: danger for love boats.

selling: an old friend will return, weak and distraught.

wearing: the inspiration for a beautiful inner experience.

CORD
08-15-28-47-49-51

among your tools: project will not be completed.

around your neck: servitude to the malicious interests of the devil.

breaking a: become independent of the authority you resent.

holding a: a friend will come to your rescue.

knotting a: friendships will be strengthened.

unraveling a: an engagement will be broken due to dissipating interest.

> *many knots in a:* weaving together dissimilar strengths to one purpose.

CORN
04-08-11-18-33-43

eating: sustenance and strength in times of trial.

feet, on the: enemies endeavoring to undermine you.

> *getting rid of:* a legacy from an unknown source.

field with large ears of: will rejoice in prosperity of a friend.

> *small yield of:* expect trouble in your love affairs.

> *without ears still on the stalks:* a plethora of worldly experience available for harvest.

grinding: are in this life for the duration.

growing: your gentle elegance can sway with the winds of action.

harvesting: your investments are sound, but must be cultivated.

hominy, eating: dull days of boredom that need spicing up.

husking: level of success will vary, your pleasure in it should be constant.

meal, eating: throw up obstructions to make the boring, easy tasks into a challenge.

planting: future success is secure, if others bid high.

tassels: advancement within your own position.

CORNER
03-07-21-33-38-46

being in a: doomed for disappointment unless you change your attitudes.

> *children:* are not sincere in your approach; change it.

> *others:* trouble smolders in loneliness.

grasping the, of a blanket: free yourself from the limits of your insecurity.

huddling in the: are hurt by assertiveness of the person you love.

pushed into a: revise your own actions by changing your direction.

putting articles in a: a mystery will be solved; the traitor is your lies.

CORONATION
03-15-19-41-42-51

beauty contest queen, of a: are deceived by people in authority.

daughter being crowned queen: neighbors can be relied upon.

king or queen, of a: will receive an unexpected fortune.

CORPORATION
03-04-21-24-36-48

armed people, of: will have good enterprises.

businessmen's, having a: don't be swayed by present events.

having a: you enjoy amusements too much.

strong: will have dominion over people.

CORPSE
06-12-27-30-36-41

animal, of an: need to face up to the fact that the current project is a dead end.

clothes on, with: old problems can be solved despite a disappointing friend.

cutting open a cadaver: leave old conventions buried.

dragging a suitcase with a: your conscience is getting heavier.

lowered into a grave, being: realization of mortality and lessening of bodily functions.

morgue, at a: death of a marriage that you do not want.

others, of: wish to rid that person and his bitterness from your life.

relative, of a: fear you are losing control of your love affair.

rigor mortis, in: fear has armored you against your own feelings.

rotting, a: others are disgusted with your disregard for your health.

seeing yourself as a: an apology from one who has deeply wronged you in the past.

several: feel peril of death from those you have harmed.

walking around: will be required to perform a disagreeable duty and die prematurely.

water, in the: wish death to escape from an intolerable mental outlook.

CORSET
05-24-39-41-46-50

buying a: your vigorous mind frightens others who wish to rein it in.

losing a: will find a new person for whom you care.

others, of: will be jilted by lover for the slightest provocation.

own, of: another person is enjoying what you desired.

sweetheart's, of: financial matters may cause a delay in plans.

unlacing your: freedom from a troublesome relationship.

having difficulty: quarrel with a friend over the slightest cause.

wife's, of: your efforts are for naught, the quarrel will ensue.

COSTUME
06-26-34-38-41-47

man in a riding: a great effort will be required of you.

woman: pleasant play.

masquerade, having a: are discontented with your image and fear repercussions.

officers in uniforms: need discipline and a code of justice to realize high ambitions.

others in different: escape an unhappy position before they do, and blame you.

priest, of a: avoid rivals who claim innocence.

several different, having: have an identity problem.

COTTON
02-15-17-36-39-51

bale of: advancement toward good fortune.

buying: will overcome enemies with a superior product.

selling: approaching money for all concerned.

field: abundance for the economy.

polishing with: it's dangerous to let the genie out of the lamp.

using, pads: bloodstains can be wiped clean.

wadding, employees: business will prosper.

large quantities of: troubles will cause you to lose weight.

COUCH
02-03-07-30-49-52

arising from a: an unexpected letter will improve your social standing.

lounging on a: have a false impression of the circumstances behind an event.

watching TV: be alert to altering surroundings.

of an empty: trust, relaxation and openness if you are willing to accept it.

sitting on a, alone: disappointment and loneliness.

children, with: the prospect of your great willpower needs to be nurtured.

dog, with a: have faithful friends.

friend, with a: hard work awaits.

husband, with: change the slipcover.

loved one, with a: a sudden trip will secure your future.

with a loose spring, a: perhaps now is the time to reconsider your diet.

COUGHING
05-18-22-30-32-33

children: good earnings; buy a humidifier.

hiccupping, having a siege of: a warning against consuming too much alcohol.

of: indiscreet people are nearby, observe their habits.

others: are intertwined in a delicate situation, rise above it.

serious fit of: something you had to digest at work is regurgitating on you.

that you are: good health, it you pay heed to first signs of illness.

COUNT

02-05-09-14-30-34

being a: people are testing your character, test theirs.

    friendly with: your soul will go to prison for your morbid wishes.

    in the company of: do not speculate thinking you have his support.

dealing with a: opposition in love affairs.

of a countess: humiliation at forced idleness.

COUNTERFEIT MONEY

10-16-26-28-41-47

handling: will be asked to help a recalcitrant teenager.

making: will receive a promotion, be careful of who didn't get it.

receiving: the mystery is solved; everyone wants more money.

COUNTING

05-14-18-26-28-39

different items: propitious losses must be stopped before all is lost.

finding items missing: results in business are unsure.

men: jealousy will bring you back to reality.

money: take a more composed attitude toward paying your debts.

objects: are perfectly able to meet obligations.

of: ambitions will be satisfied with a calmer attitude.

others: discard your usual emotional response.

people: will receive orders from a superior who wants to discipline you.

sums, making mistakes: are much too stingy with your relationships.

    correcting: will experience ups and downs in a dangerous friendship.

women: will be tormented by a lack of understanding.

COUNTRY

02-17-27-31-34-52

being in, with the family: profit provides freedom from financial anxiety.

    bright sunny day, on a: illness of the mind.

business in another, having: conceptual awareness of life beyond your present milieu.

company visiting you in the: good health.

family giving you a fine piece of, property: will have a beautiful wife.

going to the: danger of losing an estate.

    big city, from a: a letter with sad news.

    small town, from a: will take a long trip.

large piece of property in the, having a: riches in proportion to size of property.

living in the: persecution by those trying to take an estate.

lost in the countryside, being: make your own path.

night, at: melancholy and weakness.

picnic in the, going on a: a pending decision could cost money you do not have.

property being very fertile: satisfaction and comfort of having a good and honest mate.

    barren: period of desolation.

    well-situated: happiness.

vegetable garden in the, a: unhappiness.

COURT

02-08-22-28-29-36

acquitted by a, being: failure of enemies to condemn you.

    guilty people: slander causes your ups and downs.

    not: come clean with your responsibility.

    others: make up your mind of their guilt.

        not: need to defend yourself from injustice.

    punished by: accusing others of prejudice implies your prejudice.

bailiff, being a: are prosecuting and judging yourself.

    custody of a, in: advancement within position.

    talking with: unexpected money will come soon.

    trouble with, having: memories of mistakes have surfaced.

being in: your conscience is communicating events to come.

    contempt of: your indiscretions will be challenged; your exile is imminent.

    unable to defend yourself: an inner rottenness needs to be extricated and dissected.

convicted, being: wasting time waiting for gratitude for your actions.

documents, seeing: authorities will challenge you in court.

having been in: past mistake will cause loss of prestige.

jester, being a: will ignore responsibilities while exploring silly reunion with friends.

judging another: feel injured, but not ready to confront the culprit.

martial, a: extenuating circumstances will not be considered.

ordered to appear as a witness, being: friend desperately needs your aid.

requested to go to, being: high consideration of others will result in their belief in you.
  going to: are struggling with guilt and loss issues.

spectator in a, being a: face the unconscious memories haunting you.

standing in front of a judge: measuring your recent actions against universal morality.

subpoena, being served with a: are reaping what you have sown.

witness, being a: must overcome an unrecognizable obstacle.

yard, a: a shelter from past dangers not subject to the winds of change.

COURTED
02-30-32-41-44-52

being: your romantic illusions are doomed for disappointment.
  married person, by a: the abundance of marriage cannot be shared.

courting someone else: love affairs are not good when lovers are incompatible.

COUSINS
13-21-42-44-48-49

being in the company of a: distress over inability to enjoy your communication.
  of all: unexpected danger in love you thought was shared.

of a: relatives will ask you for help, tell them to help themselves.

several: misfortune in love affairs with close relations.

COW
03-12-21-24-41-49

barn: a haven from illness.

being a: your sexual urges are patient and calm.

being chased by a: a friend's sheer stupidity puts you in danger.
  but escaping: watch your own affairs carefully.

Guernsey, a: feel like a small loan bank.

herd of, a: pay little heed to other's opinions.
  grazing in the field: stop and chew your cud, then make your decision.

milking a: your attitude towards motherhood will bear fruit.
  watching someone else: someone is taking advantage of your maternal instinct.

several: great prosperity in all ventures from well-nourished investments.

tripe at dinner, serving: an asociate will undermine you to get your position.
  malnourished: pain at losing your maternal instinct.

worshiping a: are malnourished of mother love.

CRAB APPLE
19-24-41-43-48-53

buying. a: profit in small amounts.

eating, a: will be wounded and have unhappiness.

having a: will be happy in love affairs, if you let expectations be what they may.

tree, a: splaying your pain around only hurts you more.

CRABS
02-18-36-37-43-47

crawling: are compelled to solve more complex mysteries.

dead: your guilt at sensual pleasures destroys love.
  boiled: will lose all you have hoarded.

eating: tensions in your abdomen are caused by your cynicism.
  others: time for evasive action, rivals are sure to cause you pain.

live: a new lover will save your sanity from your possessiveness.

many: distractions keep you from finishing a project.
  in a fish market: many people claw at your energy.

shell, creating a new: resurrection from a tenacious clinging partner.

soft-shell: clinging to old resentments does not justify angry actions.

CRADLE
04-06-29-31-35-39

baby in the: delicately dissuade someone from talking.

being taken from the: consider yourself a cradle robber.

doll's, a: unrealizable goals.

empty: misfortune due to health problems.

rocking a: have power to control others or nurture them.

   baby in a: don't divert your focus from real matters at hand.

   own: don't suspend your healthy suspicion of illness in the family.

young woman dreaming of a: present conduct will bring 20 years of responsibility.

CRAMPS
01-06-20-24-37-50

having: a painful short-lived affliction will cause you to have a fit of temper.

   children: riches.

   others: worry.

   relatives: family quarrels.

   stomach, your: anything can be eaten in moderation.

CRAWLING
10-13-16-38-44-45

of: love affair will not prosper with your humiliation of your lover.

others: doomed for a big disappointment at censure of friends.

rough places, over: good opportunities have been neglected.

CRAZY
05-10-21-29-41-48

acting: refuse to participate in the strictures of living with others in community.

being: will be the object of much flattery.

   others: others will solve a pressing problem for you.

situation, in a: are acting on a whim and wasting a bit of talent.

CREAM
01-06-14-20-30-39

buying: will have a bright wholesome future.

eating: your allusion to riches will be resented.

   sour: must absorb the acrid with the luscious passions.

of: are hated by others for your association with riches.

using a soothing: true friendship will realize financial gains.

   others: will experience irrational ill humor over the wrong purchase.

CREDIT
03-09-10-22-23-43

being a creditor: money worries are close at hand.

   pursuing your debtors: money owed to you, at the end of the day is still not yours.

being harassed for payment: capture and humiliate the man dunning you.

   many people, by: big misery and harassment bring nightmares.

   partner, by a: misery for a short time, good expectations in business.

   relatives: serious troubles you cannot rectify, nor ease.

discharged interest, being: will have reason to be jealous.

harassing a partner: beware of damages if you have overspent.

pursued by creditors for payment: they smell your approaching prosperity.

receiving payment of money owed by others: security in business.

CREMATION
01-02-15-17-36-47

ashes being put in an urn: lost opportunity of approaching money.

   of a relative: will live a long life.

being cremated: will have business failure if advice of others is followed.

   mate: will possess abounding health.

   member of the family: will receive a legacy.

collecting, ashes: inheritance is imminent.

   disbursing: final request of a loved one.

requesting at death: abundant means.

CREPE
01-03-05-24-33-45

black, hanging from the door: bad omens.

handling: lovers' quarrels and separation may follow.

person dressed in: must endure deep sorrows.

widow: will have a happy life.

CRIME

14-16-19-28-39-48

committing a: an appalling secret needs to be rectified.

   accused by others of: doubts will beset you about a debt you may have incurred.

   being caught while: will be sorely tempted to lose your temper.

   confessing to: beware of your unconscious brutality.

   for honor: major misunderstanding of the law.

   others: danger through a secret, changing things for the worse.

   political, a: your hatred for the other party stems from your inabilities and anger.

of a, being committed: another person is enjoying what you desired.

CRIMINAL

02-24-38-40-43-50

abetting a: are cheating yourself of your potential.

being a: feel guilt at breaking your own moral code.

being arrested: annoyed by friends who use your influence for their personal gain.

   executed: triumph over enemies who have committed wrongs against you.

being chased by a: may come into areas that will jeopardize your freedom.

   with chains rattling: make the information public and let credit lie where it may.

harboring a: an unscrupulous gang will treat you as their partner.

of a: cunning friend wants to use your influence.

   murderer: unexpected help from an ally you deemed mediocre.

CRIPPLED

08-20-27-39-46-49

being: your psychological depression is from disregard for your moral health.

   children: you depend heavily on your family.

disabled: presenting a frightening view of yourself to others.

friends: will become a beggar, if you don't recognize kindness.

members of family: expect too many favors from others.

others: would like to distort another's life in revenge.

relatives: someday you will be rewarded for your kindness.

yourself: a part of your nature has been blocked from growing naturally.

   badly: annoyances over a prolonged lawsuit.

children: are caught in a dispute between elders.

deformed, being: are without a viable remedy for emotional injury.

disabled, being: presenting a frightening view of yourself to others.

man in prison: someone seriously brought your business to a standstill.

   woman: will be duly punished for wrong-doings.

of a, person: will be asked to give help from an unexpected source.

   limping: are talking falsely against someone close to you.

several, people: triumph over enemies by building your self-esteem.

taking care of a, person: a remorseful person disturbs you.

wearing a brace, and: beware of false appearances.

CROCODILE

03-04-27-31-41-44

bitten by a, being: a dangerous situation is stifling you.

   others: evil-minded people are around you.

having a: avoid gluttonous rivals and cease your own gluttony.

killing a: defeat your most powerful enemy: your own negative feelings.

many: big catastrophe ahead driven by your loathsome impulses.

of a: are in the grip of hypocrites.

stalked by a, being: your own greed will swallow you up.

CROSS

04-07-22-28-34-45

Christ on the: your fortune will be shared in comfort and security.

having a, on the feet: prepare for emotional sorrow.

in the church: great joy.

of a: trouble in integrating extreme behaviors.

on a grave: request help to moderate your emotions.

praying on a: are trying to forestall a hopeless situation.

side of the road, at the: rely on your own strength to get through hard times.

wearing a: reconciliation with friends.

> *others:* will have the protection of foundation and stability.

> *gold:* keep favorable energies surrounding you.

CROSSROAD

09-26-28-36-43-44

floundering at a: fear of taking the wrong path obstructs your decision.

friends being at a: secret enmity of someone has to be uncovered and resolved.

> *relatives:* will recover from illness if you change doctors.

married person dreaming of a: convergence of different desires causes loss of mate.

> *unmarried people:* fear engagement will be to wrong person.

standing at a: a postponed decision must be made to forestall more troubles.

CROSSWORD PUZZLE

10-11-17-20-27-28

completing: speculations are realized.

> *not:* your argument is missing one word.

> *others:* a lover will jilt you.

puzzling over a: unnecessary fears plague your indecision.

verse, if in: don't make hasty decisions.

CROWD

15-25-26-34-41-42

attacked by a, being: view public opinion as threatening.

being in a: distinguish yourself to advance your position.

> *enemies:* nervous about being trampled by jealous people.

friends: have to shout to be heard in present social circle.

lonely in a: you isolate yourself by preferring to make decisions yourself.

chased by an unruly mob, being: someone known to you creates the tension.

hiding in a: wish to camouflage your actions from public opinion.

of a: many people are swallowing up your time and energy.

CROWN

02-37-40-46-48-49

being crowned: initiation into a league of important people through your achievements.

Christ's, of thorns: another's glorification is significant to you.

cross on it, with a: benefits through another's death.

damaged: your need to be admired is falling on blind eyes.

flowers, of: a creative venture will be a huge success.

head, on the: will benefit through distant relatives.

> *gold:* great protection of high officials.

iron, of: beware of business transactions that appear to be righteous.

placing on another's head: are worthy of social advancement.

royal: expect a great task from which trust will be gauged.

> *king's, a:* need too much reassurance from loved ones.

> *queen's:* feeling neglected and wish to escape.

thorns, of: are at the threshold of initiation into martyrdom.

tiara, wearing a: social activities of a happy nature.

> *girl, a:* her ambition is beyond her reach.

tin, of: your hopes for success are dashed.

CROWS

12-22-31-43-44-49

catching a: your future fraught with conflict.

cawing: impending ruin through loss of mortgage.

flying: others may persuade you to join their venture against your better judgment.

overhead: under influence of a scheming liar.

hearing their squawk: conflict over who caused children illness.

large flock of: plan a family reunion before time is lost.

man dreaming of: poor harvest.

    woman: early death of her husband.

    young girl: will rush to become engaged ahead of love.

of a: a herald of disappointment.

CRUMBS

01-25-34-35-37-43

birds eating: will receive valuable gifts, if you take on added responsibility.

cleaning, from the table: big joy when you receive an unexpected offer to travel.

cooking with bread: must rely on own good judgment.

feeding to birds: temptation will come.

CRUTCHES

23-29-32-35-41-44

being able to walk without: will receive plenty of money from charity.

seeing: be wary of others causing you to be incapacitated.

throwing, away: will be self-supporting in a difficult situation.

using: are too dependent and morally lame.

    others: will achieve all you hoped from your labors, yours alone.

walking on: only self-reliance will spur you ahead.

CRYING

01-29-33-43-48-49

baby, hearing a: disputes in the family.

crocodile tears: your time for sorrow is now.

of: a happy, domestic life will subside into gloomy trials.

    others: will have to render aid to others in deep distress.

members of the family: great empathy for another's loss.

tears of sorrow: there is a clown in your future.

CRYSTAL

11-31-38-45-46-48

ball: others are deluding you.

being given: giver proves true friendship.

breaking: your carelessness will lose you friends.

buying: will receive a gift of delicate and fragile wisdom.

having: the correct course of your life has been determined.

    dirty: others will misinterpret your actions.

jewelry: see the inner clarity of present situation.

rock, wearing a: are supported and guided in your goals.

CUCKOO

02-05-15-17-31-40

catching a: others' gossip is cruel, but you know the truth is worse.

killing a: will interfere in another's business and with another's emotional life.

many: sexual promiscuity leads to eggs in the wrong baskets.

of a: a selfish person will insinuate himself into your family.

    singing: your lover is a fickle freeloader.

shouting: do not accept another's responsibilities as your own.

CUCUMBERS

05-08-14-19-21-47

buying: recovery from an illness to excellent health due to your iron constitution.

eating: a friendship will be betrayed in a violent love.

growing: good health if you surround yourself with prosperous, happy people.

using to make a salad: avoid spending money for foolish things.

CUP

04-15-16-28-31-40

breaking a: death of an enemy.

broken, a: your opponent would rather die than you have power over him.

chalice, drinking from a: you require others to suffer for you to gain pleasure.

china, a: expected appointment will be delayed.

drinking from a: good times are coming.

    gold: advancement in own affairs.

    many drinking from a: your health depends upon its contents.

dropping to the floor: your newfound vitality will be short-lived.

having an empty: spiritual consciousness will fill it up.

elegant: fortune in love affairs.

overflowing, an: favorable, cheerful rule of the heart.

receiving a, as a gift: one you regard highly will improve your life.

seeing a: a friendly visitor.

CUPID

14-18-31-39-45-48

of: will receive sad news.

several: will find a hidden treasure.

shooting an arrow: stay out of others' affairs.

at you: a flirtatious short-lived romance.

Venus giving birth to: infirmity or death.

CURBSTONE

10-15-20-38-39-43

bank of a lake, on the: will have fun with friends.

house, of a: someone is attempting to bring harm.

riverbank, on a: an outsider is interfering in affairs.

street, of a: must complete the present job in a hurry.

CURLS

07-21-23-42-44-48

curling daughter's hair: will have great motherly love.

cutting off another's: someone wants you to get lost.

others, their: a trusting friend confesses a secret love affair.

dark: will be relieved of some blame by antagonistic confessor.

having: complete change in your own affairs.

others: will have emotional sorrow.

man dreaming of someone curling hair: his wife is unfaithful.

many: love life is confusing.

others putting up your: suitable time to push your suit.

putting up own: new environment and better times in view.

rolling up: loss of a friend.

woman dreaming of curling her hair: overly dependent upon her partner.

CURSE

22-27-40-41-46-51

being cursed: ambitions of your inner fears will be realized.

cursing: are denying your anger, others will act out theirs.

friends, you: if you change your approach, your enemies will fail.

hearing a: difficulties have been surmounted with great embarrassment.

hearing others, you: troubled love affairs lie ahead.

name of God to, using the: will have fortune tainted with evil.

others taking the name of God in vain: difficulties are surmounted.

CURTAINS

02-08-16-23-24-35

closed: trying to hide something from others.

of many: own curiosity will bring damages.

pulling aside: a revealed secret will warn you in time.

others: warning of trouble, if you extend your performance.

putting up new: will entertain a prominent guest.

colored: a modest life of calm serenity.

white: overwhelming responsibility.

tassels on: will be required to do a difficult job for no remuneration.

CUSHIONS

01-10-17-18-26-39

belonging to others: discord among friends.

having a few: will make a substantial, not wealthy marriage.

plenty of: difficulties and business worries will be relieved through your cunning.

lying on several: change to protect yourself from being a perpetual freeloader.

ruffles on: attitude toward friends is narrow, biased and contemptible.

CUT

15-16-21-26-35-49

being: evil deeds of supposed friends will hurt you.

children: approaching money.

yourself: will be rushed into a bad decision on an imminent problem.

gash, a deep: are harboring grudges over hurt feelings, yours, not theirs.

healing, a: will have good earnings from career advancement.

not: will be paid for your services.

treating a: sever a relationship that brings continual grief.

CUTTING

07-17-18-21-37-52

being a cutter: infidelity will sever a relationship.

grass and shrubs: wish to cut off another's fortune in business for yours.

off the head of a bird: wish to silence one who is chirping about happiness.

   animals: must detach yourself from the situation.

   another person: revenge will be sought for the destruction of long-cherished ideals.

stones: to continue your latest project is self-destructive.

with a saw or file: unpleasant events are ahead.

CYCLES

03-09-10-24-33-35

interplaying: the interdimensional communicant who contains all.

life, of: the kinetic picture of the changing seasons.

time, of: the roundabout route; the process that is your life.

CYCLONE

18-27-30-31-36-38

being in the area of a: warning of troubles.

of a: intense sorrow will come to you.

property being damaged by a: social activities of a happy nature.

   ships at sea: death of an enemy.

typhoon, being caught in a: disturbed wild thoughts.

DAGGER

07-11-12-28-45-46

aiming at someone: your aggression covers up your weakness.

attacking someone with a: own plans will be threatened; more so if you attack first.

being wounded by a: another person is enjoying what you hoped for.

blood, covered with: you now have the strength to conquer your rivals.

carrying a: will be a victim of your own hostility.

defending yourself with a: your courage will face a difficult matter.

hilt sticking out of a body: impending danger; your actions must be above reproach.

many: beware of treachery, leading to an unfortunate affair.

of a: hostility from an absent person may soon apply to you.

stabbed, being: a heated argument brings repercussions.

   in the back: your treachery leaves you vulnerable; evil thoughts attract another's evil.

stabbing: your immature, quick resolution creates more conflict.

DAIRY

19-28-31-41-44-47

allergic to: a startling affront to your safety from temptations offered in marriage.

buying produce from a: will never reach the height of your ambition.

cottage cheese, eating: an aggravating matter can be turned to your advantage.

cream, eating: don't be selfish with your advantages, or public with your indiscretions.

of a: a nauseatingly pleasant life full of emotional advantages.

working at a: will be courted by dissolute wanderers who want what you have.

DAISIES

02-24-27-38-40-41

black eyed-Susan: a rival will wrench your lover's heart.

in a garden: success is participating with those who share your sentiments.

   field: a gift of something you never expected to have.

   vase in the home: salvation from the loss of innocence.

picking apart: great happiness in love whichever way it turns out.

DAM

08-12-13-31-42-46

bursting, a: can't hold back the fury; release the stored-up wrath.

standing at the top of a: feel like crying but are holding back tears.

water flowing over a: impulsive actions bring drastic results.

    calm with sun shining: bliss cannot be reached by repressing feelings.

    turbulent: losses due to community action without due consideration.

DAMASK
07-16-17-28-43-45

buying woven silk: a wedding will bring a faithful lover.

flowered pattern, with a: within the weaving will be a wealth of your intrigues.

    deep pink roses, of: as affairs boom, memories of destroyed hopes will loom.

soiled: will never live up to your in-law's expectations.

tablecloth: a dignified prosperous and worthy life; dispense your beneficence gracefully.

DANCING
01-02-11-14-42-44

alone: sadness at not attracting a particular person's attention.

being a dancer: will endure long periods of work for intense moments of pure passion.

    led by a: accept the situation; the problem doesn't desist when you dance around it.

children, little: a spontaneous outburst from a contented home.

fancy dances: big prosperity if you keep your balance.

great grace, with: need to connect with a carefree, uninhibited spirit to solve dilemmas.

hulahula, the: a string of tantalizing love adventures.

jazz, to: will borrow carfare home for safety.

jig, man dancing a, with a woman: he is in love with her, her purpose is more basic.

    married woman: are light-hearted and gay and love your work.

    others: must control your passion for being too easily benevolent.

    woman, with a man: a life of simple pleasures will come soon.

    young girl: will win favor from elder for inheritance.

of: freedom of movement from earthly limits.

others: performing steps you should do for success in business.

polka, the: a good, heart-felt, kind, instinctual exercise.

quadrille, the: off with the old love and in with the new.

    with sweetheart: gracefulness in creative expression.

    with your wife: unity is the only solution to boredom.

rings around your partner: are pushing too hard to have your way.

school, attending a: entanglement into an already complex love affair.

sick people, before: need to keep emotional distance.

steel rope, on a: seek conditions that prevent unity while saying you want it.

tango, a: will be too occupied with nightclubs and places of amusement.

    dancing a: intense passion dissipates into intense regret.

teacher, woman dreaming of a: rivals will step up at every lull in the music.

    man: have difficulty choosing between love offered.

watching friends: joy of transiting from one phase of life to another.

    others: reflects your emotions toward them.

whirling in ecstasy: contact with the divine harmonic.

DANGER
03-08-11-17-27-28

avoiding: moderation in the midst of primordial chaos.

being in: destroy the old to build new aspects of yourself.

facing: expect success, one small danger at a time.

immobilized by: a high wage may not justify working in a job you hate.

impending: look before you leap and leap anyway.

jeopardy, being in: will meet an emergency no one could have predicted.

lover in: taking undue chances with life will prove hazardous.

married person in: heartaches from jealousy will break an engagement.

others rescue you from: psychic reordering in the absence of monsters.

rescue another from, you: emergence of self from spiritual rebirth.

try to save yourself from: with your prudence you will make major gains.

   fail: your dark night of the soul; exercise caution.

   succeed: a part of yourself is glowing under the light of spiritual illumination.

DARK
03-04-12-16-20-23

being in the: insecurities about the difficulties ahead, leave present problems unsolved.

   children: suffer from an obscure illness from fear of the unknown.

   others: an emotionally dangerous situation must be resolved.

cave: use your fear to determine how to outflank your attacker.

closet: use your anxiety of another's hidden intentions to block their carrying them out.

falling and hurting yourself in the: unresolved fears from a depletion of energy.

find light and follow it: lucidity becomes more difficult to grasp.

groping way out to the light: the passing through intellectual darkness to clarity.

night: afraid of living to your fullest, when parts of self are dark.

passage, being in a: your options to shed light on situation are limited.

room, photography: a mystery, long troubling you, will unravel.

small light: help for your distress is approaching; turn on your inner light.

suddenly growing: listen to message and carefully watch your surroundings.

very dim lighting, lost in: go only on your own power to explore the darkness.

walking in the: lack of comprehension of intuitive function.

DATES
16-18-19-38-41-49

buying: will be admired by a member of the opposite sex.

eating: will experience want of several lovers when you meet an old flame.

giving a gift of: will have to take a disagreeable journey.

   receiving: troubles on a long journey caused by false companions.

growing on a palm tree: fertility, prosperity and a significant marriage.

making a: feel unattractive and unwanted to the point of distress.

unable to make a: lover will forsake you for another.

DAUGHTER
05-09-13-14-15-22

adopted: serious disaster ahead if you do not limit your generosity.

disobedient, a: uncertainty over the security of her future.

mother dreaming of her only: pregnancy will bring unexpected beneficence.

own playing: worries that she will imitate your faults, are only beginning.

parent, a: will wear pleasure and harmony in the home with dignity.

several, gathered together: the lover you desire will scorn your attentions and intentions.

talking to a: will suffer increased sorrow over transferring your sorrow to your child.

DAY
05-18-27-30-34-45

dawn, cloudy at: your distress will be progressively relieved by good work.

   rainy: will lose large contract you need to stay afloat.

   very clear: splendid spiritual life to increase consciousness.

dusk, being in the: struggle against the adverse and early decline of unrequited hopes.

election: do not despair, troubles will soon be over.

holiday during the week: fortune, with a new understanding and value of it.

   on Sunday: will receive money from a new start and, after a prolonged effort, profit.

own name: beginning of understanding, if you choose to look.

pay: will receive an injustice from which you will emerge absolved.

your birthday: be warned: your life may be short.

DEAD
05-06-09-19-32-47

being: shed tears of profound sympathy over death of one whom you asked for aid.

alive at the expense of others: will be short of money to ensure project's success.

enemy, an: a grieving process for a battle well fought.

person, in the company of a: are harboring a death wish to join your friends.

bodies: a wedding will take place; a divorce process will begin.

feel anger toward a, person: rid yourself of their quality.

death, a: regain the part of you that you gave up at their death.

friend's, a: you shun friends in your nervous and agitated state.

delight: are able to say good-bye again.

fear: report of a friend's death is highly overrated.

grief: apologize for your pessimistic behavior; say your peace and forgive.

regret: are in possession of the powerful will of one dead, that you would prefer he had.

fighting with the: are battling a contract, rightly so, because it is flawed in your disfavor.

fish being afloat: your life will devitalize to a lifeless routine of business with strangers.

friend, a: replacement of an existing relationship with one worse for its idiosyncrasies.

gift to the, giving a: your fear of exploring darkness is gone; are restored to youth and vigor.

receiving, from the: slow recovery from the destruction of a prior stage of your life.

helping to put the, in a grave: your prosperity will be ruthlessly yanked from you.

kissing the: a spontaneous expression of a happy home.

letter, a: a chance has been lost by your carelessness.

person, seeing a: the spiritually alive message will guide you.

afloat in sea or river, being: the transformation to gain your destiny is complete.

dying after already thought to be: slow down your ambitions or your health will suffer.

husband: a widow's grief process is complete; an opportunity for a new life.

lying in an open coffin: indigestion and a chill will possibly cause permanent damage.

near a beach: your inattention to your affairs will depreciate their value.

receive comfort from a: offer a neighbor compassion when called for aid.

that is really alive: loss of legal matters, if they are not sorted out immediately.

and does not talk: are threatened by one who previously supported your actions.

touching a: are weighted in helplessness and misery at the ill luck of those close to you.

unknown, an: a loss of kindred spirits to help explore beyond your destiny.

who is always loved: feel watched over, but that security if challenged will prove false.

appears as an angel: have resolved the grief and accepted their death.

criticizes you: a loss of one you can live without in your future.

curses: ask pardon and accept forgiveness and be done with him.

entices, toward dying: can cope with their loss, but not yours.

holds: a deathlike illness from which your slow recovery will bring vigor.

is reborn: a peaceful resolution of grief with tidings of good health.

orders, to avenge his death: be wary of the influence of the accused, evil or good.

praises: reinvest emotionally in your life and your absent friends.

threatens: encourage him into the light and bid him farewell.

urges, to go on with your life: eventually you will unite.

warns: take heed of the message; disastrous consequences could be averted.

wife, of a: simple, calm plenty makes showy poverty insufferable.

pet, a: volunteer at the ASPCA or buy a pet at the pound.

relative, a: mend family fences, however haggard and unkempt.

   defy demands to protect yourself from a: do not turn aside ambitious struggle, ever.

   speaking to: news from a living relative preparing for transition.

stranger, a: have dealt successfully with a difficult separation.

talking with the: are asking for the best recommended accommodation.

thinking of an elderly person now: prospect of death more appealing than disquieting.

   famous: what is no longer obtainable must be re-created.

   healthy: are learning things you wish would remain unknown to everyone.

   sickly: a desperate illness, untreatable as yet, will cause a drain on your finances.

DEAF
13-20-28-34-35-46

being: are closing yourself off from reality and its truth.

going, very suddenly: advancement in own position by avoiding a scandal.

others who are: your opinion of others defines you, not them.

trying to talk with a, mute: disillusionment that others are closed to your ideas.

turning a, ear: accept another's comments or advice and not your own.

DEATH
01-07-35-40-43-46

accidental: a vital element breaks away to synthesize with sperm of the new.

adult, of an intimate: reactivate missing qualities in yourself you admire.

   not: weed out last remnants of quality in yourself you dislike.

announcing a: existing experience regroups, realizing new possibilities.

criminal before execution, being with a: innate qualities move into expression.

decapitation, by: mind feels body has betrayed it by feeling.

decay after: blackening phase destroys before wholeness can be created.

Doomsday: another will stop at nothing to gain your material and emotional possessions.

dying relative, being with a: wish to mourn the loss of one you secretly hope dies.

going to your: this phase of your life is over; an inheritance will transform your life.

grim reaper: great burden is lifted from your shoulders.

hearing a, march played: good luck for one for whom you care.

   playing the: are spreading equally your vengeful stress and upheaval.

      military people: mortal wounds transformed into renewal.

keeping a, watch: the eleventh hour will arrive before you are ready.

pregnant woman, of a: will be released from unpleasant, manipulated bonds.

several people, of: social breakdown leading to social development.

someone coming to life after: death of old form leads to production of new ones.

wanting: will have good health unless you wish another's accidental death.

warrant, a: the need to reactivate the cycle of change and explore difficult passages.

young girl or boy, of a: don't get lost in despair; rewrite your project and resubmit it.

DEBATING
16-24-30-31-36-49

as opposed to discussing: your informality has a chance at agreement.

con: must be more flexible in your thinking.

judging a: superiors are evaluating your behavior.

man dreaming of a woman: forceful persuasion is temporarily effective.

   a man: a promotion will be gained through thorough attention to details.

pro: caution is advised in expressing your opinions.

woman, a man: must exert yourself twice as hard to make a point.

DEBTS

04-07-13-27-37-49

being in debt: pay yourself more consideration; reap from your own crop.

having no intention of: catastrophe
ahead from not living up to your mark.

others repaying, owed you: feel you owe
them.

owing, to others: are not living up to your
expectations.

paying: are not returning favors and good
works in kind.

DECEMBER

07-14-19-20-24-45

being born in: will live a long life with continuous gain and loss of friendship.

children: their affection for you will be transferred to an alien.

of the month of, during that month: rapid
success in life.

of, during other months: good financial
revenues.

on the 25th: will have blessings from God.

DECORATED

02-14-23-32-40-45

being: difficulties and troubles ahead.

others: death of a relative.

decorating your home: changes in circumstances to gay and festive times.

children's room, your: copious productive
study and uninterrupted social invitations.

with wallpaper: improved social status,
but not from use of your talents.

DEED

22-23-27-31-42-44

good, perform a: will receive an unexpected
personal kindness.

having already signed a: loss of money
through unfavorable legal action.

receiving payment of a: will have good health
until death.

signing a: the attorney you selected makes
you appear to be a loser.

others, to you: loss of affection.

DEER

06-26-28-31-34-46

antlers: your presence causes vexation in
others.

several: a painful, unrequited love who
refused to be your trophy.

buck, a: be wary of making a stupid appearance in unwanted territory.

doe, a: an encounter in peaceful surroundings
detracts from needed actions.

killing a, while hunting: are accusing the
wrong person; engagement is broken.

driving: are acting one-dimensionally.

many: are offending the hospitality of
your friends.

tame: don't be afraid to show your vulnerability.

ears of a: are often hurt by other's criticism.

head: triumph over a gentle, harmless self
is no victory.

eating the meat of a hart: partner is betraying
you.

venison: complete victory for your
enemies in their particular objections.

fawn, a: a severe danger to your relationships,
if you allow your quality of life to suffer.

herd of: great friendship with messengers
from the unconscious.

running away: grace and gentleness and
fertility.

horns of, having the: will be bound and gored
by backbiters.

skin: will receive inheritance from an
elderly person pre-death.

jumping: diversionary tactics will gain you
the contract.

killing a: will be called to court by best friend.

hart: will receive an inheritance after
battling for your rights.

male: an invitation to the ultimate stag
party.

others: postponement of the event aids
your opponent.

rabbit and, on the run: run with the opportunity in front of you.

running at your headlights: are headed into
conflict with another by your own acts.

several: want freedom to roam with the
messengers of your unconscious.

shouting because of missing a shot at a: will go
into bankruptcy with an unfaithful partner.

stag high on a forest hill, a: pride rules your
actions.

venison, eating: an invitation from a distinguished person.

DELAYED

01-19-31-35-36-41

appointment, being, for an: your considerable
skills are being tested.

being: decisions cannot be put off any longer.

by others: your support is unprepared; change
it and begin again.

check, a: it is worthless with no money to
back it.

others: will not enjoy peace of mind until you
confront your pain.

DEMOCRACY

28-35-37-41-45-47

belonging to a: false friends are undermining
you by antagonistic criticism.

  democratic party: all for one, but not one
for all.

fighting for: the rational negations will fail at
the edge of deceit.

forming a: to defend against a threat to values
we cherish.

living in a: will battle amongst yourselves, but
defend it to the death against outside
attack.

DENTIST

07-18-39-42-44-49

being a, and enjoying it: are fearsome, hurtful
and to some degree, destructive.

chair, being in a: will have cause to question a
friend's sincerity.

  children: feeling helpless next to authority
figures.

  friends: fear of losing a vital part of yourself.

  others: are mismanaging business partners
with opinions better left unsaid.

hitting a tooth nerve: contentment and good
fortune.

making a, appointment: face the consequences
bravely.

DEPARTING

08-17-18-27-32-43

date of, deciding on a: ambitions are lofty, get
to work.

loved ones: problems are remedied gradually
and permanently.

of: will barely avoid an unhappy event to gain
legitimate aspirations.

others, unwillingly: surprise visits from old
acquaintances.

others, with: an interesting suggestion will
resolve your financial difficulties.

place of pleasure, for a: danger of losing
property.

DEPRESSED

25-26-28-31-39-44

being miserable: set yourself up to regain a
cheerful state of mind, as well as a dour
one.

feeling: restrained by fear of punishment for
your inability to feel respect.

going to the depths of: deepest layers must be
healed to begin anew.

others being: profound reflections of the past
will be smoothed away.

DESCENDANT

02-04-10-13-21-43

first in line of, being the: belittle the deepest
intuitive continuity in your life.

of a: your undeveloped talents, misfired
ambitions and misdirected hopes are
in them.

others, of: decline of energy or status, as it is
split among your children.

talking to a: fear of falling from favor if you
discontinue the journey of self-discovery.

worrying about your future: what you have to
add to your heritage may not be monetary.

your: will be forced to yield your progenitor
rights to your progeny.

DESERT

03-04-16-19-35-45

bad weather, crossing a, in: intuition, feelings,
logic and reason must work together.

  sandstorm: impotence to activate your
cherished plan.

being thirsty in the: a drink of energy will
push you to productivity.

island: romantic isolation in barren cheerless
place.

lost in a: bring your own protection from the
empty isolation.

others crossing a: friends are depriving you of
companionship.

stranded in the: are being baked in horrifying
seclusion.

traveling across a: with slow, painstaking effort you will succeed.

walking in the: withdrawing from people enhances loneliness.

with others, crossing a: accord among friends, if you are resourceful.

DESERTION
02-09-33-34-35-42

army, from the: feel isolated in a crowd; involve yourself in the argument.

defecting from a foreign country: don't sacrifice your convictions for approval.

wife: will discover the truth of a secret.

your business: a temporary respite from problems, large losses will recur.

> *children:* must fight to combat adversity from an absent friend.

> *home:* a mirage of happy distraction is what you need to keep your life.

DESK
02-17-18-26-29-47

accountant's, an: overwork on scientific matters.

an open desk: keep mouth firmly closed for the duration.

at home: avoid fruitless discussions and hurried decisions.

closed: will have emotional sorrow.

lawyer's, a: advancement in own position.

others, several: friends will solve a mystery for you.

working at a: unanticipated extrication from irksome family affairs.

DESSERT
08-09-17-33-38-45

alone, having: will be able to enjoy luxuries you have denied yourself.

> *with others:* accord among friends after accomplishment.

not enjoying a: no celebration until the project is completed.

others eating, without you: leave the overindulgence to others.

sherbet, eating: restrain yourself from falling for someone in a romantic daze.

spilling on your dress clothes: a respected friend will look upon you with suspicion.

DESTROYED
08-16-25-27-31-46

army: small fights in the future.

of demolishing: people are talking against you.

of destroying something: big catastrophe ahead if you let it happen.

> *others:* negative influences block your building.

of destruction: process neither continuous nor smooth requires an urban renewal project.

> *causing, to many things:* will have fights with friends.

others: have foolish desires.

someone having, your things: are threatened with a rare strain of a common disease.

something, having: warning of troubles from being too quick to take offense.

DETECTIVE
11-14-15-16-24-34

being a: irritating troubles can be overcome in your search for insight and answers.

being blamed by a: feel you deserve punishment for misdeed.

> *interrogated:* the wrong people are inquiring into your credit.

> *questioned by a:* wish to unburden your guilt, but not for the crime in question.

inquisitive about your affairs, being: cannot know the future but plan for it anyway.

interrogating a suspect: relationships are stunted by your invasive questioning.

others being with a: will lose reputation and friends will turn against you.

> *taken away by a:* your friend is not guilty, do not abandon.

DEVIL
02-05-20-35-40-48

agreement with, signing an: beware of the shadow side of your illusion of reality.

being among demons: emotions will break through your denial.

big horn and long tail, with a: your weaknesses, vices and sins are your torment.

chased by the, being: temptations have serious consequences.

> *and running away:* will be punished for legal attachments.

conversation with the, having a: will be cheated by friends, seduced by enemies.

elderly sick person dreaming of the: expect melancholia; find the source.

poor person: big catastrophe ahead, if you fall for temptation.

young girl: guilty feelings about sex are obscured by possessions.

fighting with the: can overpower the diabolical influence that threatens your security.

hitting and vanquishing the: major temptations are avoided to triumph over enemies.

of the: develop spiritual power by wrestling with consequences of desires.

seeing the, while praying: will resist temptation to sin and hate, but must admit past sin.

sick person dreaming of the: are led to do things you, deep down, do not wish to do.

spear, with: an uphill battle to regain composure against the ignorant part of yourself.

taken away by the, being: the promptings of your deepest nature.

talking to the: will never be short of money or evil thoughts of the enemies.

wounded by the, being: your negative thoughts are festering in you.

wounding the: promptings of own deepest nature to battle for own life.

DIAMONDS
03-06-10-24-31-32

buying: look at various facets of your emotional experience; polish each one.

carbon changing into: experiences transmute to wisdom, if you open up to the concept.

fake: bragging is overcompensation for inferiority.

finding: hypocritical behavior by a distinctive and wealthy man.

having: fortunate dealings in business and speculations.

losing: separation from loved one brings poverty and ill health.

of: drive for power extends to spiritual perception.

others wearing: make a big profit from false friends once they are exposed.

owning many: success and honor will be conferred upon you.

receiving, as a gift: your social status will have a short-lived improvement.

selling: exercise great care in selecting a mate.

stealing: will have big losses if you marry a social butterfly.

wearing a: your overly developed ego hides your insecurity.

DICE
08-20-26-40-44-49

playing with: your carelessness will cost you family happiness.

losing while: losses through speculation on unlucky numbers.

others winning: recovery of money from blind chance, not your own will.

cheating: your trust in people is a naïve illusion.

winning: rid yourself of lover who is guilty of dishonorable actions.

DICTIONARY
06-09-10-24-27-31

buying a: an intellectual inquiry that lacks emotions and empathy.

children studying with a: your thirst for knowledge will impress your superiors.

consulting a: a wordy argument with an opinionated pedant.

others: intuitive direction can only be realized in the self.

DIETING
21-26-27-32-33-34

anorexia, having: deprive your body of nourishment and it will deprive you of meaning.

being weak from: are measuring out affection.

broke diet with disastrous circumstances: are allowing your emotions to control you.

friends: feel resigned to pointless anxieties over self-punishment.

of: dissolution of hopes if feelings are not expressed.

others who are: are restricting the extent you allow your emotions to show.

too much: danger of sickness from holding back feelings.

DIFFICULTY
11-24-36-42-46-47

being in great, of any kind: your reflective frame of mind loses in the execution.

business, having: temporary embarrassment.

   financial: are subconsciously aware of hostility towards you at work.

   others: are overinvolved in someone else's dispute; it's time you dealt with your own.

   personal: need to explore different avenues before you return to the present one.

   relatives: in spite of strenuous efforts you will not reach agreement.

   sweetheart: repressing a problem to be kind and agreeable does not solve it.

dangerous, in own life: quarrel with long-standing friend who became untrustworthy.

DIGGING
05-30-31-33-38-44

dead person's body, up a: your dishonorable deeds have resurfaced.

graves: dredge up little-known facts before proceeding.

holes for trees: go to root cause of your integrity to solve the problem.

of: level of success varies with level of difficulty.

others: advancement in own position if you apply yourself diligently.

professional digger, of a: your inquiring mind needs discipline.

soil, in: with hard work your task will turn a profit.

   good: reactivate character traits you've forgotten.

   loose: your plans will ease your unconscious.

DILIGENT
02-10-32-34-44-49

being: present sacrifices made will lead to an important relationship.

   with personal affairs: long-awaited solution to a personal problem.

children being, at school: will be offended by others.

   employees, at work: your suggestion will receive enthusiasm.

DINNER
04-10-14-24-30-48

having: warning of trouble through a quarrel with friends.

friends for: triumph over enemies through teamwork.

over the sink: others are planning to steal from you despite how little you have.

relatives for: must control your nerves and accept hospitality, as it is well intended.

with a large group: the decision should be joint, or pleasant courtesies turn sour.

Last Supper, The: love will support you through sorrow and worry.

others giving a, party: one loyal friend does not replace mother love.

restaurant, at a: settle down and let another serve you, for once.

tête-à-tête with a high-class person, having: advancement or promotion at work.

DINOSAUR
10-16-21-29-41-43

being chased by a: are driven by a compulsion to accomplish something.

   several: collectively imposed discipline on an ancient part of yourself.

   who catches you: are limitations to your acceptance of society's rules.

    wounds: punishment for a destruction not accomplished.

DIPLOMA
06-07-15-38-42-43

being handed a: own talents are being neglected; use tact to allow their exposure.

having a: your pride presages your bitter downfall.

   children: a delicate situation has come to fruition.

   others: temptation will come to you, act with distinction.

DIRT
07-14-28-33-37-43

being dirty: illness allowed to fester through hereditary lack of immunity.

   clothes: will escape some contagious disease.

   others who are: will suffer abuse for illness in the family.

being thrown at you: early warning of a diseased state of mind.

church, in a: expect punishment for your recent actions.

created by humans: discovery of lost valuables among the undergrowth.

falling into the: your affairs lack the requisite growth to prosper.

stepping into: will be leaving your abode for a larger home.

throwing, at others: cleanliness is not gained by transferring guilt to another.

DISAPPEARING
02-11-22-26-31-47

act: magicians do it for applause, you to escape facing reality.

friends: sickness in the family; which they do not wish to spread to yours.

mate: would prefer mate vanished rather than face divorce.

money or jewelry: all gems hold their history close; they are wrong for you now.

of: realizing things are: are bewildered at being robbed; face the robber.

DISAPPOINTED
02-07-35-41-47-48

being: success in all hopes dreamed about.
   lovers: danger through a secret.
   others, in you: are in the grip of deceitful people.

others, disappointing: misfortune in love affairs.

DISAPPROVING
08-17-26-35-40-48

of: disagreements in the family will cause unhappiness.
   of others' opinions: honor and consideration.
   others: will be involved in a car accident.

receiving disapproval of family: will enjoy good results in business.

DISASTER
19-22-30-38-39-43

are rescued from: ask for help even if you think you don't need it.

being in a: loss of sweetheart by accident you controlled.

lucidity after, complete: a sudden change will quickly reorder your life.

man dreaming of a: profound anxiety over ability to cope.
   woman: suitable time to pursue endeavors toward wedding bells.

rescuing others: look at your relationship from another perspective.

try to save self from: inner turmoil over life's passages.
   fail: save yourself before helping others; otherwise you both go down.

wedding ceremony: take a greater part in the planning.

DISCIPLINE
02-07-10-13-28-29

being disciplined: by bending the rules your deal will become fortunate.
   others, by: will be frightened by coming events.

disciplining children: must be more cautious with your investments.
   others: are imposing guilt for your own failure on another.
   prisoners: could benefit from being a disciple of one in confined pain.

of: will be reprimanded by an authority figure.

people ignoring: an enemy desires to become a friend again.

DISCOVERING
07-14-16-27-29-44

money: far-reaching changes in recovery from a major upheaval.

something: be careful what you rely on; evidence may be uncovered to the contrary.

valuables: your search is theoretical, not empirical; the new is unearthed with dirty hands.

yourself: have fully adjusted to your new identity, whose evolution is unstoppable.

DISEASE
06-07-10-27-36-42

causing pestilence: will undertake a very tiring business.
   friends: will squander fortune.
   others: must rely on own good judgment.

colon: life for you is too much to digest.

convulsions: your predicament can be alleviated with a strong will.
   others: are indirectly connected.

convulsions: one has neglected his/her spiritual life.

diabetes: the love you are seeking must first be found within.

118

epidemic, of an: transform your mental obsession with materialism into spiritualism.

euthanasia, considering: are pleading with yourself to make a change.

having a: warning of treachery, not yet apparent.

    appendicitis: financial success if you keep your own counsel.

    arthritis: put on an extra blanket.

    brain: will be fortunate and honored.

    cancer: your creativity and sexuality are blocked.

heart: are not being honest with your feelings.

liver: must live your own treaty, not someone else's!

lovers dreaming of a: good times are coming.

measles, having: fretting and worry will interfere with your solving tribulations.

    others: will be asked to organize a charity ball and hone down the guest list.

    relatives: approach them for amends, not with anxious care.

of pestilence: beware of revealing personal affairs.

others: will be exposed to a contagious disease; confine yourself.

Parkinson's, shaking from: control must be surrendered.

psoriasis: enemy is attempting to defame you to a friend.

    scarlet fever: have faith in your determination to live.

        children: things will turn out for the best.

    stomach, in the: waste of money through overmedication.

    terminal, a: there is no death, only transition.

    unknown, an: heralds symptoms of future disease.

DISFIGURED
01-20-21-28-32-36

being: unexpected happiness from your own self-criticism.

    relatives: luck and prosperity.

disfiguring a lover: have one loyal friend.

others who are: see a repugnant part of their personality in yourself.

DISGRACE
03-10-17-25-34-39

children being in: every negative memory long forgotten will surge in your heart.

    others: are surrounded by enemies; a challenge to your integrity will spark you.

    relatives: hard work awaits you.

having been in: accord among friends; difficulties with lovers over morality.

others disgracing you: are prosecuted for not living up to a reputation you did not foster.

DISGUISED
03-04-13-20-30-43

disguising yourself: will have troubles that are not yours.

    fancy costumes, with: underhanded dealings with rivals.

having, yourself: will take a long trip and change residence.

others being: be perfectly open and aboveboard.

    relatives: important and very beneficial events to come.

DISGUSTED
09-15-18-31-33-49

being: people you respect will aid you in accomplishing your goal.

    with the attitude of others: infidelity.

        others, toward you: will have misery from friends in foreign countries.

        other's succeeding: will lose a loyal and influential colleague.

    relatives: will not accomplish plans.

DISHCLOTH
09-11-16-23-28-37

ordinary, an: will have a small, unimportant argument.

rough material, made of: unknown person will give you good advice.

throwing away a: be careful of heart condition.

washing a: desire to clear wounds from business ventures.

washing with a: will receive important and good news.

DISHES

04-06-16-20-24-28

breaking: outsiders are causing your domestic troubles.

    others: must control the passions you incite in others.

    porcelain: replacing the old with new, with generosity and enthusiasm.

bull in a china shop: family problems are caused by you.

buying china: expansion of the tranquil peaceful love of family.

    single people seen together: their marriage is imminent.

chipping a baked enamel: emotional agitation will bring plenty of money.

dirty: insecurity with members of family due to unexpected moves.

dropping a plate on a scale: are denying the need to proportion your nurturance.

of an empty plate: your delegation skills leaves your desk empty.

    full to the brim: the world is your succulent oyster.

    half empty: are being unreasonable in demanding it's half full.

of own china: financial gains from a faraway place.

    fine: emotional aspirations are overly ambitious; social ones are not.

DISOBEDIENT

13-17-20-30-33-36

children being: prompt engagement in an interminable battle.

    husband or wife: loneliness and trouble ahead unless you can prove order was unjust.

    others: will be accused and have a big quarrel.

    relatives: long sea voyage among vacationers is prescribed.

having been: a difficult choice is before you to change occupation.

DISPUTE

01-17-19-40-41-43

having a: good times are coming from the discovery of lost valuables.

    business: disastrous investments in a depressed industry.

others: will be snubbed by a woman of prominence.

relatives, with: obstacles will be avoided by calming nerves before you act.

over trifling matters: are creating the issues for the credit you gain in solving them.

DISTANCE

12-19-23-27-34-35

being at a, from family: a big catastrophe ahead won't be resolved quickly or by you.

    husband: strangers will be instrumental in the outcome.

    wife: another person is enjoying what you desired but left unattended.

friends being at a: will be disappointed if you expect your friendship not to wane.

others being in distant places: travel on a journey far more momentous than planned.

DISTRESS

11-20-27-40-44-46

being in: your immoderate behavior and lack of responsibility are at a high cost.

    children: are not aware of a child's agitated state.

    others: your combative frame of mine takes things out on another.

    wife or husband: will have emotional sorrow from upcoming argument.

cries of: being vigilant with the validity of early warnings.

    children's: no questions, just act.

helping others in: will have success where you had feared failure.

    putting: warning of trouble.

indifferent to, are: misfortune at not noticing first signs of illness.

DISTRICT ATTORNEY

35-40-42-43-46-49

accused by a, being: will be amorous, have happiness and delight.

of a: unexpected worries.

policeman, being brought before a, by a: satisfaction and moral content.

presence of a, being in the: will have self-respect.

DITCH

03-07-10-28-34-37

attempting to jump over: step back before you purchase anything.

being in a: rapid recovery of good health.

digging a: discovery of a secret will overcome troubles and allow prosperity.

hoping someone will fall in: your revenge will be exposed, causing degradation and loss.

jumping over: cease to speculate with such diversions present.

others in a: will have financial difficulties, not your own.

pushed into a, being: beware of unexpected difficulties.

standing at the edge of a: think hard before you proceed.

very deep: are prone to exaggerate adversity to inflate your ego.

walking through a: your behavior ruts and outmoded habits prevent your progress.

DIVING
05-09-18-34-36-48

bell: sharp dive of stocks, which will rise again slowly.

children: a favorable ending to the ordeal could be reversed.

into a calm lake: the auspicious search requires humility; find it at the bottom.

members of family: business undertaking will be risky, love affairs illicit.

of: loss of reputation unless you change your ways.

others: warning of troubles if you do not throw yourself into work.

sky: current business conditions require that you take risks.

snorkeling: are exploring deeper layers of your soul.

underwater: consider the other person's objectives before dredging them through the mud.

DIVORCE
16-19-27-34-45-47

being divorced: acknowledge partner's faults and forgive.

children: imitation is the sincerest form of flattery.

enemies: restate your vows against the jealousy and unfaithfulness of others.

friends: listen only to your own counsel when selecting long-term companions.

obtaining a: confess your actions to your spouse before they are irreparable.

and receiving alimony: prosperity in present marriage.

relatives: bad gossip causes discontent with in-laws.

wanting a: a love affair will put your domestic happiness at risk.

DIZZY
05-06-11-14-34-48

being: hard work with no results until you take a plane trip.

children: hard work will bring a change for the better.

feeling ill or: get back into the control seat of your conscious acts.

from effect of alcohol: fear of falling out of love with yourself.

members of family being: sense of strain from lack of order.

others: responsibilities overwhelm one on the edge of love.

of being: check out possibility of hereditary illness.

giddy: this momentous decision will alter your future.

DOCK
04-17-24-41-43-44

being on a, alone: must endure grief before a pleasant surprise.

with a sailor: a secret enmity will cause an unpropitious journey.

with workmen or stevedores: good business prospects, if you stay in full disclosure.

longshoreman, of: will be doing things for others.

yard, being in a: a safe zone for reevaluating your past and steering your future course.

sailors on a: a fight with your best friend will begin in earnest and dribble to laughter.

workmen on a: watch your footing, your flanks, and listen to the messages from above.

DOCTOR
06-09-22-32-35-40

becoming a: relief from a pain that is unconsciously experienced.

being a: depend on your higher self to heal you.

calling a, for children: every healing force of your being is mobilized.

  friends: seeing others in need brings out your caring nature.

  relatives: rapid recovery from fear of illness or death.

  yourself: open your total awareness of your body's function.

going to a: wish to find a powerful person to love.

need of a, being in: unwise ventures will have a distressing ending.

others calling a: troubles ahead when you don't trust your own opinion.

seeing a, socially: better business prospects, but medical bills will be erratic.

visiting patients, a: suffer from over-benevolence; need a gentle, inner healing authority.

DOCTRINE

11-12-13-15-43-44

enforcing government: a corporation will be dissolved; suitable time to pursue endeavors.

learning the principles of: an arrogant idea of self becomes offensive to friends.

teacher of, being a: will have opposition, hard times and poverty.

teaching testament: an honorable position in a far-off land and a new, kind friend.

DOG

04-21-26-31-34-45

attacked by a, being: feel threatened, your own animal urges will overpower you.

  chased by a: are being distracted by those you feel are your inferior.

barking, a: beware of quarrels, make friends of your enemies.

  at you in a tree: a person who shouts, threatens you with rage.

  friends, at: expect agreeable happenings from friend's action.

  hearing: instinctive advice of friends should be taken.

  several: risks of going with the pack must be essential to the outcome.

  your: think hard and long before you act on your angry aggression.

bastard, a: faithfulness between lovers; doggedness in a relationship.

beaten, a, being: fidelity surrounds you; concentrate your energies and be true to them.

belonging to others, a: warning of trouble from those who bare their teeth.

  big: an inopportune time to do business with wise and humane partners.

birddog: an old lover still stalks you with exposure of your illicit connections.

biting others, a: are at the end of your resources; take your dog for obedience training.

bitten by a, being: will be double-crossed by someone you trust, injuring your reputation.

  poodle: look past another's appearance before you act.

black: beware of friends who cannot necessarily be trusted.

brown: are mistrusted by someone.

bulldog: will express hostility with girlfriends; it's better left unsaid.

buttocks of a: will soon be visited by thieves, part of a desperate effort to overthrow you.

castrating a: your obstinate nature is making your life difficult.

cat, playing with a: sickness spread among children causes big love disputes.

  fighting with a: expect to quarrel with a neighbor.

causing destruction, a: your arduous efforts will force strained alliances.

courageous, a: a guide to your unconscious, personal and collective.

ears of a: honesty between husband and wife or a deplorable tragedy will occur.

English: will receive an invitation to a party of those possessing solid wealth.

German: will be deeply in love.

fighting, a: beware of thieves having a sudden burst of temper.

foam coming out of a dog's mouth: are not fitted to fill your position.

French poodle, a: are overdressed and overly-made-up for the occasion.

friendly, a: all will be well if you take care of basic needs.

frightened by a savage, being: will have an affair with someone with a ferocious mind.

frothing, a: prosperity to the limit of your endurance; fortune and various favors.

gray: a faithful friend is constantly nearby.

greyhound: will be seduced.

growling at you, a: encounter with one you dislike for reasons unknown.

guard: a disconcerting situation will turn to your advantage.

guarding a wounded person, a: affairs will be useless if you are totally exhausted.

happy, a: are at the mercy of designing foes; take your dog to the vet.

harness for a, a: an introduction will lead to friendship, profitable dealings and pleasure.

head of a, the: a falsehood unmasked will ruin your contented future.

howling: will receive a message of another's misery and pain.

hunting: a stranger will tempt you with what could cause your downfall.

hydrophobia, having: guard your treasures; your friends stop short of full protection.

kennel, a full: do not go it alone to avoid quarrels; go where you are invited.

leash breaks: unpredictable events in your love life; unusual briskness in business.

litter of: many talents are yours, but you must choose one and run with it.

   runt of the: must work harder than others to prove yourself.

lost, a: loyalty must be earned; if not, it will be tempted away.

mad, being bitten by a: destroy your enemies' threat before it can be activated.

   killing a: are on the verge of insanity and don't wish it pointed out to you.

male, playing with a female: appetites are sated with unrestrained, exaggerated pleasure.

   loving a: realization of all desires; lovers are cheating on each other.

mange, having: environmental issues foil physical ones.

mountain: will have trustworthy friends.

muzzle on a, putting a: a safety precaution to save him from basic survival instincts.

police: aggression redirected to positive actions.

pretty little: will be visited by an unwelcome guest carrying illicit goods.

owning: an unfair accusation will be used to implicate you in a scandal.

Pekingese, a: your neighbors complain of your constant chatter.

petting a: are repressing sexual urges, transferring them to an unconditional lover.

   small: your sweetheart is unworthy of the love you give.

playing together: are reverting to childhood, with staunch friends and adventures.

pug, a plump asthmatic: will be accepted by an angry medical miracle of unknown age.

rabies, with: will succeed in overcoming evil tendencies.

   attacking you: an unexpected foe is redressing you behind your back.

racing: loss of a lawsuit when you manage too many branches of business at once.

sad: fear of persecution and abuse.

seeing-eye: sudden loss of freedom is in the offing in a long separation from friends.

several: are going along with the pack despite your misgivings.

shaggy: a meager inheritance and a drudging life.

sheep: will encounter deceitfulness leading to your uncovering fraud.

single person dreaming of a: will be seduced and become selfish and narrow-minded.

sleeping with a: need have no fears; he will awaken at the first scent of attack.

small: are high-strung and frivolous with your constant need to be pleased.

spaniel getting his ears in his food, a: a liaison at work is ill-advised.

spoken of in Dante's book, the: will experience a journey and rise above mediocrity.

talking to a: are sniffling out your quarry with sociable means.

tearing clothes: gossip among your own family will ensure unalterable misfortune.

unfriendly, an: will receive help from a good friend over a quarrelsome companion.

untying a: a marriage will take place.

watch: innocent lambs will suffer from others insinuating themselves into their life.

white: your fortune is soon to be realized.

yelping: imminent danger, as someone is subduing him to gain access to you.

DOLLS
14-21-28-30-32-37

belonging to others: fashion, beauty, manipulation and revenge.

buying a: avoid being involved in disagreements with a new acquaintance.

girls playing with: manipulation of your childhood memories to be your ideal person.

having: are prone to flirt with aspects of your personality.

of: belittlement of the flaws in your domestic happiness.

DONKEY
10-12-19-24-36-45

bray, hearing a: disgrace and loss of friend caused by a lewd unscrupulous foe.

castrating a: a big affliction is to come from a dispute with one's best friend.

chasing a jackass: scandal is being spread about you.

children sitting on a: flattery will gain you healthy obedient children.

dead, seeing a: will be haunted by fear of a stubborn betrayal.

ears of a: a great scandal confronts your stubbornness.

feeding a: people are laughing at your stupidity in helping them.

hitting a: unpleasant news is received by a kick in the buttocks.

kicked by a, being: misfortune as clandestine affair is disclosed.

killing a: your fortune is gained, if you stop your stupidity.

leading a: your good nature is being exploited by evil women.

loaded: have a foolish attitude toward hard work.

loading a: determination does not equate to money.

many: save your effort for several friends, not the universe.

many: your meekness will not prevent a lover from jilting you.

moving very slowly: much security is forthcoming before bad news is received.

others, belonging to: your whimsy will be gratified at the expense of another's duties.

owning a: your lack of humility is no benefit within quarrels.

pulled by a, being: are being used for other's goals, not yours.

purchasing a: are slow moving through unexpected difficulties.

riding on a: though sturdy, you will fall into disgrace.

selling a: buyer will be humble, but you will sustain a major business loss.

shoes on a, putting: future hard work will not be futile, but you will be dishonored by it.

stable, in a: your intemperance and greedy disregard for others will ruin your business.

thrown from a, being: quarrel with sweetheart over your hiding a personal matter.

wild: are not operating your business rationally.

DOOR
05-13-17-33-44-49

back, friends entering by the: caution must be used to avoid imaginative gossip.

letting lover out: a repression of expression; the opportunity is no longer available.

relations: your vain attempt to avoid family arguments over backbiting.

robbers breaking down the: foes slander you with unpardonable offenses, not your own.

using the: life changes from unsuccessful attempts to be profitable.

banging, a: imminent unpleasant events cannot be avoided.

blocked from entering a, being: speak up about the treatment of a friend.

bolts, attempting to open: a new start will be made elsewhere.

closed, being broken: are prone to greed and selfishness.

fastening: will be offended by the actions of others.

locked by others, being: knowing their secrets is a burden to you.

locking a, with: your gullibility has caused your frustration.

breaking down a: regular methods will lead to opportunity.

broken, a: will receive news of a job from a person far away.

bumping into a: will be cognizant of a friend's horror but be frigid with fear of helping him.

burning, a: a cancerous injury threatened your friend due to your ill-fated advice.

carried across the threshold, being: someone is expecting great things of you.

city, to a: populace shows their disapproval of your ideas by refusing to open the door.

closed, a: make an effort with your neighbors.

closing, a: are shutting someone out of your life.

doorman, being a: will be obedient and passionate in protecting your family.

giving orders to a: will be persecuted for what you failed to see on watch.

doorway: the juncture to your fortune is near at hand.

entering own house: friends will cheat you out of your harmony with a partner.

hinge, a rusty: difficult personal social affairs.

squeaky, a: physical and mental cruelty will be perpetrated upon you.

house with many: will lose your money through slanderous gossip.

knob, a: a new business will climb steadily to success.

locked: replace your poor conduct with positive actions.

open and entering, being: long, emotional and satisfying relationship.

opening, a: a warning to shut up with a new acquaintance at work.

another's: new opportunities for a departure from the mundane.

by force: be careful of your violent tendencies while preventing the perpetrator's escape.

own: another chance will be given to you to make good.

portal, a glowing: your transformation has succeeded.

revolving, being stuck in a: three others are blocking your ability to use your resources.

ringing a, bell: have clear vision of the development of your future.

slipping through a: it takes two willing lovers to have an affair.

stepping through a: the matter resolves itself despite interference.

threshold, crossing the: the difficult part is over; now get to work.

unable to escape from a, being: major change of course before it's too late.

unlocking a: how secure is your future?

DOUBLE
06-07-20-21-26-45

bicycle, two children riding a: will have honest, reliable friends.

going somewhere on the: will enjoy good food.

of anything that is: don't place too many hopes in the future.

marriage of family members: are unfitted to fill your position.

yoked egg: a member of the family will have an accident.

DOVES
11-12-15-22-35-38

cooing, hearing: make peace with someone who is dying.

delivery of a letter, a: a misunderstanding will be healed.

dovecote, in a: long line of visitors to your contented home.

feeding: follow the advice given; lovers will reconcile.

flying: new contacts are important to attain your potential.

Holy Spirit, as the representation of the: peace and love.

on a roof: be satisfied with the partner you have, despite the note of sadness.

white: bountiful crops and the reconciliation of faithful friends.

pair of: peace, innocence and spiritual salvation.

woman dreaming of: fortunate affairs at home.

DOWRY

01-03-04-08-21-28

daughters, giving a, to: will earn more money.

filing to give a: impoverishment in the cold, cruel world.

man giving property to his bride: expect much uneasiness.

widow's: will make a good change in your life.

woman giving a, to her husband: a man of ample means will take good care of you.

DRAGON

03-22-23-26-31-40

being chased by a: materialism surrounds itself with covetousness.

fighting with a: have a negative relationship with your mother.

and winning: are mastering the powers of your unconscious.

being injured: a powerful enemy will attempt to hurt you.

man: fear of being devoured by a woman.

flying in the garden, a: a voyage to tropical islands to be governed by your passions.

killing a: rid yourself of your heartless, disdainful attitudes or be avenged for them.

many: big disappointments when you try to dominate in love.

military man dreaming of a: will be visited by a harbinger of spiritual awakening.

rescuing a maiden from a: are preserving virtue from the forces of evil.

slaying a: conquer your inner darkness and master yourself.

DRAPERIES

08-13-27-30-38-44

draper, of a: must control your passion.

being in the company of a: prompt engagement.

being a, and dealing in cloth: a change in life will come soon.

faded: the transience of prosperity.

flowered print, with a: a dinner invitation from prominent people.

fringe, with: will have an ill-defined future.

married women dreaming of: will give birth to many children.

of one color: are hiding from problems.

silk: are covering up your feelings behind a life of luxury.

DRAWBRIDGE

01-06-11-16-19-32

closed: will realize high ambitions and a wide separation from friends.

drawn up, being: projects will peter out in midstream.

lowered, being: far more favorable projects are on the way.

open: will pardon enemies, but they will not pardon you.

DRAWERS

20-25-30-33-35-41

man dreaming of his drawers: want to forget shame and sorrow, which are still close.

woman, her: will be unfaithful to the man who loves her.

open, of an: suitable time to pursue ordering your internal chaos.

opening a: money you lent is about to be repaid.

locked: dangers lurk around the corner, but you can't confront them.

unable to open a closed: have a complicated, introverted personality.

DRAWING

09-18-21-26-40-41

finished, a: others are controlling you.

in pencil: tentatively apologize for weaknesses.

charcoal: express your strengths on paper.

sepia: unusual efforts are rewarded, if you expose them.

perspective, a: cope with all dimensions simultaneously.

room, formal: aspirations will be exposed before they can be realized.

DREAMING

09-20-25-27-28-33

city, of a: a real-life problem if dream becomes a tolerable fantasy.

consulting someone about your dreams: expect news from far away.

family of children, of a: difficulty with authority.

legs won't run, that your: the present situation will develop into a fruitful one.

magical place, of a: are refreshed; allow your soul to be.

neighborhood, of a: lack of attention to everyday affairs.

nice things, of: have impossible desires.

nightmares, experiencing numerous: time to relinquish one's lifestyle, it's excessive.

   having a: treachery from one you trust.

      including others: will be confronted with abundant worries.

         children: your disappointment would dispute hallowed ground.

others, of: will have emotional sorrow.

poor, of being: change in your position.

recurring dream, a: reveals the innermost contents of your being.

rich, of being: will be disillusioned.

series, in a: there is a thread connecting all parts; find it!

DRENCHED
03-05-23-26-28-41

being: danger of fever for you or someone nearby.

   others: expect too many favors of others.

causing someone to drink: a false friend is nearby.

drenching by force: it is safe to rely on a good friend.

DRESS
10-23-29-37-40-43

beautiful, a: will become socially prominent.

   receiving a: will be helped by an unknown man.

changing a: will suffer because of your own foolishness.

cleaners, taking a, to the: are spending time with those who will ultimately harm you.

closet full of dresses, a: constant love of social pleasures.

   without: will have difficulty picking appropriate attire.

cross-dressing, a man: are jealous of mate's success.

   woman: have a selfish, presumptive personality.

dark, a: financial gains if you make the correct impression.

designing a: will receive a proposition and turn it down.

dirty, a: will be blamed for business woes.

disorder in your: someone is taking unfair advantage of you.

elderly people, of: will attend a baptism.

jet sewn on a: a luxury connected to a love affair with a person of wealth.

lining out of a, taking the: beware of rivals.

losing a: expect too many favors from others.

loose, a: will be cheated by friends.

new, buying a: health and happiness.

nun's, a: will receive great honors.

out of style, a, that is: the hostile situation is self-inflicted.

owning a: an unpleasant moment must be delicately handled, to keep it from being exasperating.

   black: sadness and grief.

   blue, light: promotion in own employment.

   brown, a: will have a high social position.

   embroidered: will receive favors from an unknown person.

   fancy, a: presumptuously arriving where you do not belong.

   gold, a: will not shy away from burdens placed on you.

   gray, a: will receive a letter with good news.

   green, a: expect the fortune you wish for.

   house, a: are very neglectful.

   mauve: expect unhappiness.

   mourning: death of a relative.

   navy blue: misfortune will be avoided.

   nice dresses: efforts will succeed.

   pink: a glorious success.

   purple: happy marriage and death of a friend.

   red: will be respected by others.

   short: will do anything to attract attention.

   simple: will have success in love.

   tight: are being unrelenting in your control of others.

   various colors: will meet a nice person.

   white, a: people appreciate that your intentions are pure.

partially sewn, a: will be disregarded by friends.

pregnant woman wearing her, loose: are being unthinking in your relationships.

127

shop window, in a: your ambition is inspired, follow it.

staining a: people are talking against you.

stealing a: want respect you feel you can't earn on your own.

taking off a: forget frivolity, trust only your own counsel.

   black: your state of depression cannot be shaken off easily.

   blue: unreasonable contempt for danger.

   red: will lose your temper.

   tan, a: financial gains.

   yellow: become jealousy.

tearing a: your fortune is in danger from your overreaction.

   others, your: will receive the help of a friend.

tear up a, desiring to: success in love affairs.

torn, sewing up a: are neglecting your own children.

train of your dress, having a long: unhappiness.

   someone stepping on the: will have a new love affair.

washing a: be more financially frugal.

wearing an azure blue: a change for the better.

   black, a: a marriage will take place soon.

      at a funeral: inheritance.

   black silk, a: will receive what you desire.

   cheap, a: friends will turn their backs when you are in need.

   daring evening dress, a: sickness.

   daring evening gown: your selfish, presumptive personality shines.

      others: will be shamed for hiding your feelings from those around you.

   gold-trimmed, a: want a higher social standing.

      with furs: abundance of money.

   red: your arrogance will come back to haunt you.

   too large, a, that is: will have good employment.

   torn, a: are unaware of good fortune.

   white, a: big fortune.

   yellow, a: your honor will be deceived.

DRINKING
03-04-11-16-24-35

blood: quenching your spiritual thirst.

breaking a glass, and: will suffer a broken leg.

company of friends, in: beware, your flirting is sending the wrong message.

excess in: drinking partners will take advantage of your indolence.

getting drunk from, sweet things: longing for a wealth that cannot gain you love.

liquor: beware of an accident caused by your desire for oblivion.

milk: abundant means and thoughtful occupations ahead.

moderation, in: are engaging in practices that will discredit you and enjoying them.

nectar: will accumulate honor and wealth, possibly through marriage.

others: want to be relieved of the responsibilities of adulthood.

out of a clean cup: immediate employment.

relatives: prompt engagement to old-time acquaintance.

soda fountain, at a: will be asked by a neighbor to join a lodge.

someone: will add degrees to your name, but still feel helplessly dependent.

something sweet: will be violently loved and engage in pleasures insinuatingly offered.

until satisfied: will be required to go with a relative to a boring, tiresome party.

water from the side of the boat: someone wants to pour salt in your wounds.

   clear spring: will be very richly nourished in the future, health and happiness.

   muddy, dirty: are overinvolved in your matters.

   pitcher, from a: will have pleasant companions.

   pure, from a glass: a thirst for spiritual experience.

   spring, from a: complete recovery from an illness.

   very cold: triumph over enemies.

   wanting a drink and cannot find water: misfortune.

   warm: you have loyal friends.

wine, red: escape and nourishment.

   glass half full of, from a: your self-esteem is lowering.

   white: happiness.

DRIVING
02-08-13-23-26-35

along an open road: a passionate weekend awaits.

busy street, a: family responsibility is weighing you down.

backward: are overwhelmed by impulses toward decadence.

changing course while: will be exhausted in difficult activities that appear undignified.

dead end, into a: poverty and unfortunate circumstances until you turn around.

downhill: press more lightly on the pedal, if at all.

drunken driving: ecstatic and frenzied release of repression.

loved one: hopeful implications if you avoid rivals.

not being able to stop: avert disaster by quick reactions and skill.

of: discovery of a major solution, which was troubling you.

others: expect monetary losses, if another chooses the purchase.

recklessly: are losing control of basic cravings; attracting unjust criticism.

relatives: listen to the suggestions and profit from superior knowledge.

running out of fuel: will spend a large amount of money unnecessarily.

sports car, in a: belief in own mastery of your independence.

SUV, in a: will realize your moderate ambitions to become a prominent citizen.

with no map: feel you have little control over own destiny.

without a license: look at yourself as a grown-up, and drive your wishes with maturity.

wrong direction on purpose, the: difference of opinion with loved ones is your choice.

speed: must avoid impulse to have a hasty, thus unfortunate, marriage.

DROUGHT
10-23-28-34-38-44

dry, parched fields: another person is enjoying what you hoped to win.

lengthy dry spell: will soon experience ups and a lengthy damaging down.

of a: beware of business losses; menial labor with no viable opportunity to advance.

rain falling after a long: supplies will be brought in, disaster relief will reunite families.

DROWNING
11-14-18-23-29-30

able to breath underwater: current events weigh you down; shocking how able you are.

afraid of: misfortune in love is around the corner.

awakened upon impact of cold water: are unable to function without a jolt.

before: are afraid of losing your identity.

being drowned alive in water by others: be aware of clues to your enemy's identity.

murky: hard to see what to do, but you know what you want to forget.

businessman, a: are forced to face issues of bankruptcy.

can't breathe: situation seems life-threatening; are grossly overextended.

capsized boat, in a: are helpless in changing your life's direction; ask for aid.

children being rescued from: will have prosperity and appropriate high position.

falling into the water, by: immersion in the unconscious to bereave a loss.

car plunging, in a: are overwhelmed with unconscious, repressed issues.

jumping: are forced to face issues previously left untended.

husband or wife: serious disaster is ahead; loss of stability and balance.

others: joy and triumph is yours.

own children: anxiety of childbirth—your own.

people clutching at you: save yourself first; then return for the others.

reaction to near drowning: terror at your own ineptitude in coping with your emotions.

are saved: friends will help you get through problems in one piece.

die: bitterness is debilitating your will to live.

feel calm: overwhelming situation will become manageable.

give up: will lose all that you have, to make room for bereavement and despair.

lucidity: with your ill-thoughts submerged, hope can emerge from the deluge.

save self: will go the distance; keep your eye on your sweetheart.

terror: prospects and ease after seemingly hopeless struggles with fortune.

try to swim: take lifeguard lessons now and save yourself!

  yell: no one can rescue you from your current situation except you.

relatives: big ruin ahead through this dreadful calamity.

rescued from: expect help from a friend.

rescuing others from: a friend will reach a high position.

trapped underwater: are overwhelmed by impending doom.

DRUGS
03-05-15-32-36-43

cocaine, taking: self-afflicted damage to your brain.

doctor, being given, by a: will have the protection of friends.

drugged, being: enemy is watching his chance to harm you.

giving, to children: successful speculation.

  relatives: are surrounded by much gossip.

having: infirmity in your illusions; come down to earth.

  medicine chest full of: good business but no profit.

making: loss of money.

ordered to take, being: morale will be raised.

refusing to take: affairs will be in confusion.

selling: a dishonest man is nearby making money off of you.

store, a: will begin a new business.

taking: affliction of a potentially dangerous situation.

  others: are putting money in something giving you a poor return.

DRUMS
05-15-23-29-42-43

bass, beating on a: will achieve favorite ambition at your own rhythm.

buying a set of: are at a loss trying to keep people in step; send out an SOS.

hearing: unrest before you arise to your aspirations.

playing a: march to your individual beat.

  children: calamities await them who wish to unify youth.

  marching in a parade and: luck and prosperity and overindulgence.

  others: bring another around to your point of view.

sticks: boastful statements lose credibility when they are not fulfilled.

tom-toms, playing the: a disagreeable experience that is hard to defend to your peers.

DRUNK
10-26-30-32-37-42

being: your indiscretions and lawless behavior will drag you to ruin.

  children: wish to return to your youth of no responsibility or self-control.

  enemies: will be slandered and disgraced through another's forgery and theft.

  feeling sad, and: treachery by relatives.

  heart pains, and having: infidelity of a lover; a suitable time for flirtation.

  husband, constantly: shift responsibility from your overdependence on mate.

  others: will lose money through another person.

  person, without liquor, a: are unable to extricate yourself from a predicament.

  relatives: riches and improved health will be yours.

  several people: will be guilty of overindulgence.

  water, from: will become rich through literary pursuits.

  woman, a: will commit some immoral, shameless, dissolute action.

cheap wine, becoming, with: your fleeting pleasures leave you in poor physical condition.

  fine wine: will make acquaintance of a high person, fortunate in trade.

hangover, and having a: any false moves are asking for trouble.

music, getting, on: have considerable

degree of sensitivity; use it in aesthetic experiences.

seeing a: your job is on shaky ground from your cultivation of illicit immoral pleasures.

    yourself: sober up for arbitration; shift your energies into more healthful conduits.

sick from drunkenness, being: are squandering household money gambling.

    others: have little self-confidence in your skills and abilities.

DRYING
02-18-23-30-31-42

children: riches and profit.

clothes: will be visited by an unwelcome person.

dishes: hard work will bring good returns in money.

others: prosperity.

pots and pans: will receive news from far away.

yourself: joy.

DUCKS
01-17-29-31-34-38

attacked by wild, being: employer will have trouble in business affairs.

catching a: are scurrying when one direct step would work.

    many: malicious gossip by friends will not deter your dinner date.

drake waddling, a: festivities are about to begin for a fine harvesting of your talents.

eating a: have a great deal of honor and fortune to be thankful for; be thrifty with it.

flying: in your wisdom you will cause the failure of enemies.

hunting: have the intelligence to reflect upon whatever is below the water level.

killing a: will have a disaster in traveling across the sea; fortune in short journeys.

roast, a: the fat has left your wallet; foes have meddled in your affairs.

    eating: your family should let go of the unnecessary.

swimming: unfavorable danger to your own business will be displaced.

wild, dead: don't forget who your friends, and enemies, are.

DUEL
01-17-29-31-34-38

challenged to a: step back and regroup in battle.

having a, to save your honor: beware of your rival.

    friend, with a: keep your tongue in check and reconcile.

    others, their: stay out of others' squabbles.

    swordsman, with a: a romantic adventure will embarrass the family.

    walking stick, with a: will dominate friends.

watching, from a distance: resent not being the center of the action.

winning a: trials and tribulations must be resolved first.

wounded in a duel, being: damage to your standing with others.

    killed: warning of trouble.

DUET
11-13-15-32-38-44

playing a: a mild rivalry of sorts creates a harmonic interplay.

singing in a: good fortune in love, a peaceful existence in marriage.

    hearing children: a mystery will be solved; a new pleasure will replace the old.

        friends: temptation will come to you to compete and wrangle with authority.

        others: domestic happiness is disrupted by unpleasant news from the absent.

    quartet: your harmony and congenial company make life come alive.

DUKE
13-18-22-40-41-43

being a: failure of plans due to your inability to make sound judgments.

dating a: new love affairs are in sight if you stop flirting.

Duchess: will attend a gala with distinguished guests.

meeting a: will be guilty of improper actions requiring correction of your erring ways.

DUMB

15-19-23-25-28-29

ass of yourself, making an: your circumstances will improve with speech lessons.

being: expect to have a family quarrel.

  members of family: a child unable to express feelings will be born.

  others: do not discuss your business plans with your usual glib tongue.

unable to speak, being: will meet new like-minded friends; avoid speculation with them.

DUMPLINGS

20-21-30-39-40-43

eating: aspirations will be realized from seemingly innocent, innocuous sources.

  others: success in all affairs.

making: fortune will change with five seasons of abundance.

  from potatoes: pleasant surprise awaits.

DUNGEON

04-10-19-21-30-38

being in a: visit from wealthy relatives who pass judgment on your circumstances.

  others: have many enemies who wish you to lose your acceptance by honorable people.

escaping from a: have loyal friends who with willful indiscretion will set you free.

unable to escape from a, being: entanglements cause losses due to your misjudgment.

DUSTING

04-08-09-10-21-37

bin, a: feel that your moral rightness was valueless.

blowing dust: good news is received from your inner nature.

books and ornaments: happy days ahead, if you simplify your life.

covering your dust: will be tainted by proximity to another's ill dealing.

feather duster, using a: are attempting to hide wrongdoing; use judicious means.

furniture in the house: ideas without feeling, dried up; set sights on a newer flame.

off clothes: good business ventures, if you deal with discomfort.

DWARF

11-12-28-30-41-44

being a: are being outclassed and over-powered in another's pursuits; try your own.

  friend: wish to cut your inadequacies down to size.

gnomes: face the music now or you will have the tune forever on your mind.

of a male: will have a vigorous mind and stunted emotions.

ugly, an: the future is menaced by one with ominous wishes.

unknown, an: fear the part of your self yet undeveloped.

well-formed female, a: the elements are there, but lack substance.

DYEING

04-05-08-21-28-44

clothes: business is very confused.

  making a mess while: expect a very expensive present.

dyer, a: must endure a long infirmity.

indigo, others, things with: immediate success; prosperity will be long-standing.

  in water, putting: will take a journey over water or seas.

light colors, with: sickness is forthcoming.

  yellow or dark: family member will have a high fever.

materials: misery.

others, their hair: will suffer through your own foolishness.

own hair: warning of trouble.

  another's: joy without profit.

DYING

07-09-11-22-24-32

children: dreamer wishes to die in child's place.

friends: you will triumph over enemies.

kissing a, person: are so disgusted you feel you should die.

of: an early death makes a martyr; a late death, all your sins will die before you.

  being abandoned by someone: lessening the intensity of the sorrow when awake.

parent: wish to have all of your other parent's affections for yourself.

relatives: emotional value of separation anxiety is devalued.

you are: your spiritual rebirth will not manifest without your close attention.

> *others:* recent plans are doomed to disappointment.

DYNAMITE
01-20-32-34-38-43

being blown up by: your material force is opposed by vicious enemies.

hurling sticks of: expressing anger as directed by your mental outlook.

sitting on a box of: precaution, in an explosive situation, is the best medicine.

sticks everywhere: wipe out the old, but be stingy with what new you let in.

watching, fuse being set: can renege on this deal before it gets out of control.

DYSENTERY
05-12-16-22-27-30

having: will receive a very costly gift; the purging of your outdated affairs.

> *children:* will attend a banquet that will encompass a new realm of opportunity.

> *entire family:* a secret enemy will disclose himself at his most helpless moment.

recovering from: will receive news of a marriage.

taking medicine for: enemies, after helping you, will extract payment again and again.

EAGLE
19-21-28-37-39-43

attacked by an: your partner sees your contribution as interference.

bald: after great difficulty, will have a more prominent political position than you do now.

cage, in a: your friends restrict your vision; impending death of one of them.

carrying you, an: shame and sorrow through serious accident you caused.

catching prey: a stronger person makes you feel physically inferior.

dead: decline of your physical strength amidst victory.

eaglets, birth of: will have a very prosperous future in a foreign country.

> *in a nest:* great responsibility will be entrusted to you with wise counsel.

falling on you: the threat is in your inability to relate to yourself.

finding your hiding place: will be exposed by fierce competitors.

flying: yearn for freedom that others have taken.

high up on a statue: your farsightedness will realize high ambitions.

killing an: nothing will prevent you from achieving your goal.

landing: the spirit of the mind has descended to supervise mundane needs.

> *on your head:* the power of inner life to carry us away.

owning an: honors and business profits will be quickly squandered.

perched on a mountaintop: victory of the loftiest elements of power.

> *on top of your head:* present your problem for group solution, so that you control.

standing up: many soldiers will die in triumph of spirit over matter.

woman dreaming of several: will have famous sons of liberty.

wounded, a: have lost your ability to perceive that you cause the loss of love.

EARRINGS
03-08-20-21-30-42

another's, of: unpleasant judgments are made about you by detractors.

giving own, to someone: finally getting the message after a big quarrel.

losing own: a period of sorrow caused by your laziness.

of own: congenial work that requires greater effort than you are giving it.

receiving, as a gift: someone's affection will bring rivals of a low order.

wearing: will be cheated by friends, but will win the lottery.

> *attractive woman, an:* will have an affair with an adventuress.

EARS
01-08-14-16-28-42

being pulled: listen to criticism and advice, and pause.

boxed: are fighting with the wrong team; your conversations are not your own.

boxing someone's: express your anger constructively.

broken eardrum, a: defend yourself with fists, peace is attained with words.

cleaning own: your mistrust was justified, your friend has let you down.

clogged: breakup with a friend who abused your trust.

cupping your, to listen: your actions should be directed by common sense.

cut in an, a: disappointment through a friend who let you down badly.

cutting your, off: a fit of creative expression with no outlet.

feeling own: startling news by mail that will turn profitable.

having big: your intelligence is overtaking your practical wisdom.

long: public shame and sorrow.

small: friendship with a wealthy person.

stopped up: are unwilling to listen to domestic troubles.

trouble with own: new project from an unexpected source you have discounted.

many: gossip is about you; don't listen.

one, being stopped up: troubles are from partner's acting unpleasantly toward you.

pulling another's ear: their blunder is the cause of your woes.

pierced, having your: have been inattentive to the whispers of your conscience.

something heavy hanging on the: your inner self has to struggle in life.

EARTH

06-15-16-24-29-34

black: your inertia in solving problems brings sorrow.

burrowing in: your anxieties have no constructive outlet.

digging in the: someone is burying you in work.

eating the: long sickness over emotional matters.

escaping an eruption of the: are grounded in a good work ethic.

farmer working the: big profits coming from continuous effort.

footprint in the: complicated life fraught with burdens.

full of corn, wheat, rye or grain: are receptive, nurturing and maternal.

of vegetables: are in the grip of deceitful, materialistic friends.

kissing the: will be humiliated for not honoring Mother Earth.

lying on the: a solid foundation from which you build.

Moorlands, walking on the: an unknown enemy is plotting against you.

observing through a telescope: a legacy will be held up in probate.

of the: the source of your physical strength.

owning good, or land: insufficient concern for your roots.

pleasant pastures, with: will have children grounded in natural instincts.

pulled down to, being: no matter your spirituality, keep your feet grounded.

put under the, being: your history is layered in your consciousness.

sitting on cold: don't let your shyness keep you from paying attention to your health.

tilling the: a steady income from hard work.

EARTHQUAKE

01-11-16-29-30-31

area of an, being in the: insecurity at the loss of a close friend.

building during an, being in a: will withstand shakeup and financial upheaval at your job.

city destroyed by an: a sudden change with prolonged ramifications.

earth trembling from an: work to gain solid feet on the business ground.

feeling an: will be badly shaken by intense turmoil that needs expression.

ground moving under you during an: resist your insecurity toward action.

injured in an, being: upheavals in your social structure can be life threatening.

occurring in the East: old difficulties must be left for others to overcome.

North: will rip the foundation of your life apart.

South: will have emotional cleansing of original horror.

West: warning of troubles, changes will occur in your absence, let off steam now.

watching an, on film: turmoil between multiple actions brings the entire world to risk.

EARTHWORMS
01-16-22-23-24-41

area full of: will have a contagious illness.

bait, using, as: have unscrupulously followed your ambition.

body, having, on the: don't disregard the contribution of others to your riches.

coming out after a rain: humiliation caused by friends.

of: secret enemies are endeavoring to cause ruin.

EAST
01-14-30-37-43-44

being in the: a rebirth of your mystical side.

> *others:* irrational actions can bring important results.

of the: are about to be sent on a long journey to your immortal self.

returning from the: you will gain financially.

EASTER
08-14-17-25-26-42

eggs, eating: your unchecked passions could lead to pregnancy.

> *giving:* will surrender to a respectful love.

> *hiding:* your honesty is in question.

> *receiving:* a person loves you, but you can't return it.

> *searching for:* love in all the wrong places.

Good Friday: your patience and care will be rewarded.

having a happy: pleasant social gatherings.

Lent, giving up something for: will easily overcome insurmountable obstacles.

Mardi Gras, celebrating: a document declaring your independence will be tossed to you.

others celebrating without you: good times are coming.

parade, being in an: temptation will come.

> *others:* danger through a secret.

spending, with others: bad days are ahead.

EATING
06-17-21-29-32-44

alone: unfortunate woes can be handled by you alone.

being eaten by a lion: a prominent person will take credit for your actions.

> *shark:* are devoured by your inner anxieties.

belching after: thank the hostess before you display a lack of manners.

diet, on a: pare away your anxieties one at a time.

dreaming of, while fasting: your emotions need to be nurtured with other than food.

empty table, at an: find the source of your energy depletion.

> *large, a:* are saddened at your love life and need to socialize.

family, with the: happy environment and profitable undertakings.

> *relatives:* nostalgia for past relationship before vexations from your dependents.

fat things: warning of an illness from absorbing others' pain as yours.

floor, on the: someone has taken something from you; the loss makes you melancholy.

fruits: food is being withheld from you, which you justly deserve.

full, until you are: losses and depressed spirits won't be alleviated by overeating.

hands, with your: a would-be lover is proving elusive.

human flesh: are shunned by society and rightly so.

meal, a big: are unable to share the discovery of valuables.

> *gourmet, alone:* your lack of empathy has lost you friends.

nibbling, of: be careful what you write and sign.

> *in public:* be careful in whom you confide.

others: are angry and disillusioned with your partner.

> *in company of:* will soon receive what you desired at the expense of what you had.

overeating: are being devoured by another's voracious love; are emotionally starved.

salads: healthy overindulgence is still overindulgence.

salted things: personal prosperity retained against threats posed by grasping friends.

secret, in: deep-seated desires and longings are not being fulfilled.

sharing good: have enough to feel comfortable giving to others.

small portion of food: apologize or you will be shut out of a friendship.

standing up: are doing things too hurriedly without thought.

suffocating while: take a deep breath before and in the middle of each bite.

unable to find food to eat: make a radical change in your diet and your companions.

EAVESDROPPING
07-17-18-19-27-31

friends, on own: approaching money.

of: dilemma of a distressing dispute from which you cannot find your way out.

others, on a secret: money is coming to you.

secretly, on a conversation: should be tarred and feathered and run out of town.

EBONY
02-13-17-19-25-43

being given things made with: will have good earnings.

buying: your intensity will bring success in business.

having: will meet someone from abroad.

of wood or tree: will write a letter that will cause you no end of notoriety.

ECHO
08-13-19-21-26-29

hearing an, in a cavern: an inner response to your outer action; magnified for clarity.

   close by: hate breeds hostility, acceptance influences power.

   faraway: listen carefully to what you are saying.

   in the woods: being alone but not lonely; losing your job but not your talent.

   of your words: your gossip will boomerang back to you.

ECLIPSE
15-30-33-35-37-41

end of an: the threat is gone; begin anew.

moon, of the: state of being completely in accord with what the universe offers you.

   watching the, with the family: stillness with no conflicts within; without is reverence.

    loved one, a: are experiencing only one sphere of emotions.

sun, of the: will incur losses furthered by your own forebodings.

EDUCATION
02-13-15-16-27-33

children having an: three make an education: the teacher, the child and the parent.

not having an: will suffer through unwillingness to accept that another could teach you.

restricted, having a: the greatest cruelty is to limit what one can learn.

seeking an: fortune will smile on your efforts, but not increase your culture.

EELS
16-23-26-30-35-37

catching a dead: warning of another suffering envy; maintain your grip on him.

   live: new business proceeding positively over slippery slopes.

dead: expose another's inveigling to vindicate himself.

holding an: hold on to what you are afraid of until the fear goes away.

many dead: beware of the real threat when you get out of prison.

many in the water: are overworking the wrong people, but lauding the correct ones.

   live: desire to participate in an orgy of pleasures that gradually dissipate.

of one: slippery unseen dangers lurk, awaiting one error.

squirming: an envious smooth operator who will add hazard to your courtship.

   out of your hands: hold tight to your wallet in the wake of maliciousness.

EGGS
01-06-25-34-38-41

beating: a speculation will attract a business proposal.

broken shells: your basic core has been cracked.

brown: will be threatened by someone.

buying: infidelity by a loved one.

chickens laying: properly enriched, your creative juices are ceaseless.

colors, of different: don't put all your eggs in one basket.

cooking: will receive some advantageous news.

decorated: a creative response to being confined by weather.

eating: foretells a permanent relationship stigmatized by profligacy.

> *hard-boiled:* have a high regard for the staunchness of justice to allow love in the world.

empty shells of: financial ambition is aiming too high.

fish: are spending time with those appearing to be more influential than they really are.

fresh in a nest: profit from a new venture, going to the source.

making a mess with: showing disfavor for other's vices and actions.

many broken: latent tendencies to multiple love affairs break through your fear of love.

nest of, a: unexpected money; make good use of it.

nog, drinking: the settling of peace of your lofty spirit within your home.

omelet, breaking, for an: a sacrifice to break through to the truth.

> *flat, heavy, a:* will be manipulated into kissing someone; stop it there.

> *light fluffy, a:* sudden elopement to bliss.

pastries with, making: all undertakings will be accomplished; all speculations, profitable.

poached, eating: will display wealth of questionable origin.

poaching: guard your speech.

raw: will attain a substantial amount of money.

rotten: begin your inner process of resurrection from degradation.

> *thrown at you, having:* will be attacked from your side.

yolk, with a double: discovery of lost valuables and legacy from distant relations.

ELASTIC

17-24-31-40-42-44

corset, having an: the ability to adapt to worldly experience is constrained.

of: will stretch the rules to aid a friend.

putting, bands on bundles of things: beware of jealous friends.

snapping: your courage will be challenged, whetting your appetite for more.

something made of, having: good times are coming.

ELBOW

02-13-20-30-36-37

breaking an: are nimble and adaptable to the extreme in a loveless marriage.

dirty, having a: are pushing beyond your capabilities for insignificant gains.

> *nice:* your nimbleness allows you to advance; your toil will be transferred to another.

elbowing through a crowd: are willing to withstand an invasion of your privacy.

> *another, his:* your temper will cause you a lawsuit.

pain in the, having a: difficulties from another pushing you into an unwanted marriage.

> *children:* use caution with younger colleagues to prevent a lawsuit.

ELDERBERRIES

10-15-22-28-40-44

buying jam: will make a friend of an old vigorous mind.

eating: abundant means.

picking: social activities and domestic bliss of an agreeable pleasant country home.

wine: will clean up litter from the wedding of an unrequited love.

ELDERLY

04-11-23-32-36-37

man, being an: will be challenged to prove your competency, honor and distinction.

> *dreaming of courting an old woman:* good business enterprises.

woman, being an: freedom from troubles.

> *belonging to an, club:* jealousy of friends.

> *dreaming of being courted by old man:* her love is faithful.

> *at a party:* good family reputation.

ELECTION

04-07-12-19-23-36

assisting with an: rapid success of your hopes of appointment to office.

filling an office after an: change the environment to suit your purposes.

others at an: important and very beneficial events to come.

winning the: a false friend will cause your business failure.

ELECTRICITY

13-26-38-39-40-43

appliances won't run on: check your wiring; your inner spirit needs power.

fuse, blowing a: your energy is not fully utilized on a worthless project.

handling electrical devices: your energy is not fully contained.

   others: listen to another's sudden intellectual power.

shocked by, being: are close to losing your patience with cheating friends.

sparks: your adventure will rapidly end on the heels of shocking news.

using: will be greatly surprised by an electrical storm.

ELEPHANT

02-05-09-26-38-39

being free, an: will enjoy much independence and influential connections.

circus, at a: danger of a relative's death through foolishness.

   escaping from an: be steadfast and patient amidst family quarrels.

feeding an: a person of solid character will befriend you.

giving water to an: will be of service to an influential person.

mammoth, of an Indian: obstacles confront you; sit high and watch the conflict.

   cage, being in a: the power of spirit manifesting.

   trained, being: your unconscious needs conscious direction.

many: your remarkable memory will lead your prosperity.

others with: fear and danger for those who would not allow positive thinking.

poor person dreaming of an: with cooperation you can achieve tremendous prosperity.

riding an: your reckless brute force can cause damage.

ELEVATOR

18-21-27-34-41-44

ascending in an: increase in wealth and advancement in position.

   descending: overwhelming misfortune through unsettling investment climate.

being out of order: warning of troubles in the face of fortune.

changing shafts: alternate energy or status.

dropping to the ground floor: are losing altitude in a rising career.

   which is full of water: submerging into the depths of the subconscious.

family, being in an, with the: need their support to proceed with life.

   others, with: defy your rivals and appear where you were purposely uninvited.

   clinging to you: are being engorged by parasitic weaklings.

in your house: wish for too much, too quickly with little effort.

moving sideways: are indecisive as to which goals to pursue.

riding in an: feel secure in accessing various levels of your psyche.

stuck between floors in an elevator, being: will have emotional sorrow.

ELM

11-19-20-28-31-36

being under an, tree: use cold caution in social activities.

   others: doomed for disappointment.

   relatives: responsibility requires endurance.

diseased, an: continual petty annoyances.

of an, tree: rapid success of your own hopes.

ELOPING

03-06-16-24-26-29

children: a head in the clouds does not see reality.

friends: a sentimental journey is best left to the head.

married person: are unfitted to fill your position with your disorderly affairs.

   mate: your marriage has lost its commitment to honor and obey.

single person: your lover holds a place in your heart he is not willing to fill.

young girl: are acting as someone you are not; loss of reputation will follow.

EMBALMED

02-06-13-22-35-42

animal or bird, an: expect too many favors from others, who will cease to give them.

body, an: desire for immortality despite present life.

dignitary: are doing work with diligence and courage.

relative's body being: must rely on own good judgment to remain in the status quo.

EMBARRASSED

05-14-18-26-27-37

being: the more embarrassed you are, the greater your success.

children: are acting too old-fashioned.

friends: rely on own good judgment and practical mind.

members of family: disputes with mother-in-law will be advantageously concluded.

others: proposals must be set in concrete before presenting them.

EMBRACING

04-08-15-19-23-39

being embraced by others: another wants to possess your lover.

unknown person, an: is a suitable time to pursue flirtations.

children: will be given a secret which if exposed would destroy your family.

friend, a: treason from previously honest and challenging friendship.

mate, others: will have a fruitful emotional life.

relatives: will be accused of indiscretion upon no evidence.

someone else, your mate: loneliness and trouble.

stranger, a: an unwelcome guest will criticize you to balance the praise.

EMBROIDERING

09-14-17-23-33-41

dress, on a child's: the embellishment of details enriches a young life.

linens, on: a true marriage requires simple truths and wise economical actions.

loved one, for: will be accepted in society for your talent for embellishing all you touch.

napkins: a marriage will take place soon.

of: your innocent peccadilloes will cause others to plot against you.

EMERALD

10-11-14-15-26-36

buying an: emotional imbalance from a person far away.

having an: your power of consciousness brings great fortune.

lover already: your love will be displaced by a wealthier suitor.

of an: will experience difficulty over an inheritance.

selling own: separation from a loved one who didn't live up to your expectations.

EMIGRATING

02-06-09-21-42-43

of: will receive a letter from a friend in a foreign country.

others who are: watch out for treachery that will put you in need.

trouble with immigration authorities, having: big joy is ahead.

refused admittance by, being: danger through a secret.

EMPEROR

01-15-17-19-20-44

being an: your ambitions are unrealistic; your search for power is not.

empress: loss of your lover to gain an empire and much pride and prejudice.

married to: happiness is assured even with the disparity of wealth.

married to an, being: your reputation will be lost.

mistress in the court of an: a person of authority supports you; his minions do not.

presented before an, being: will take a long journey in the loss of dignity.

EMPLOYER

01-10-17-27-31-41

argument with your, having an: present a viable alternate route to a solution or shut up.

employees being idle: request assistance for those who are in poverty.

insolent: must answer for a misdemeanor to your boss.

employing others: their interests clash with

yours; their offensiveness disagrees with you.

employment office seeking a job, being at: use close contacts to create a bonanza.

   being unable to find: go after the job you want, not the one you know you can get.

   finding, for others: your project will create many jobs; most importantly, yours.

   having good: laid off in a slack period; your conscientiousness will cause your rehiring.

fired by an, being: a mystery will be solved with the egg on your face.

going out of business, own: have a vigorous mind, but misplaced confidence.

hired by an, being: must mend your ways; are too impressionable.

of own: will have a unpleasant change in your position, if you don't fulfill contracts.

receiving a gift from an: will lose your job, if you question his motives.

shaking hands with your: don't burn your bridges when you leave.

speaking to own: will be advanced shortly through excellent prospective project.

unemployed, being: your failure to work to your capabilities will abort your mission.

   while others are scurrying to work: will attract only disdain from others.

EMPTY
01-02-19-29-32-44

barrel, having an: big poverty; work on the little things first, then expand.

emptiness: seeing no results for extensive effort; a glass half-empty.

home being: big catastrophe is ahead, with nothing left to sell.

jar, pouring from an: unexpected gains are a futile hope.

ENCHANTED
03-05-14-16-25-26

being: evil influences that don't relate to self.

   others: are emulating one who enchants you, but are failing to enchant yourself.

   relatives: loss in business matters can be

regained with your willingness to share freely.

enchanting others: will realize high ambitions by your own broadmindedness.

resisting an enchantment: your advice will be sought by many, except yourself.

sorceress, by a: your sloth will attract unsavory people with corrupt intent.

ENCOURAGING
02-14-24-35-37-39

being: will be offended by the discovery your intentions were selfish.

children: will have arguments with mate over child's temptations.

friends: will have sorrow because of your own actions.

needing encouragement: are being unjust because of jealousy.

relatives: are losing someone you are particularly attached to.

sick person, a: will receive monetary assistance, which will entrap you.

END
04-08-09-10-18-29

hearing the, of something: are highly motivated to take on a new project.

others, of: recovery from the defeat of outmoded attitudes.

watching the, of a play: a difficult predicament needs resolution.

world, of the: extreme emotional conflict.

ENEMA
02-06-17-20-21-23

being given an: unhappiness at enforced childhood trauma.

giving an: your love affairs will make you sick.

   of the syringe used in: confusion in business.

taking an, yourself: will be short of money.

ENEMY
01-12-21-24-37-41

being in the company of someone disliked: mistakes through ill-conceived actions.

being taken away by an: will be embarrassed by an inimical force.

conquering an: business success can be surmounted using utmost caution.

fighting with an: enemy reveals fears of you in decisive encounter.

hating an: protect your fortune from another's malice.

killing an: your intentions are in question; your process is adverse.

meeting an: avoid deceit by thinking only good fortune.

overthrowing an: physical complications are too involved to be overcome.

speaking with an: be cautious in dealings until you understand your motive.

winning out over an: lawsuit will create unfortunate experiences.

ENGAGEMENT
02-21-32-33-36-41

becoming engaged: expect troubles within the family.
   friends: will realize high ambitions.
   relatives: family arguments.

betrothed but not engaged, being: will have troubles with lover.

broken, a: may have to endure disappointments.
   of others having, an: make a commitment before it's too late.

celebrating an: couples everywhere are making you lonelier.

returning an, ring: a change in life will take years to come.
   wearing an: big joy.
      others: will be a nuisance to your friends.
      relatives: their happiness is assured in the dullness that is their life.

social high-class: your parameters for a relationship block your having one.

strong, beautiful engaged person: dishonesty.
   quiet or simple: future will be good.

ENGINE
07-12-15-23-24-32

difficulty starting, having: build up your motivation and your team.

driving an: own ambition must be skillfully controlled.

engineer, being a: unpleasant trip that is destined for success.

gas, a: important and very beneficial event to come.

in motion: expect difficulties in the near future.

of an: must endure trials in pursuit of your goal.

out of order, being: watch out for treachery.

steam, a: money will come easily during your entire life.
   releasing: exercise before you confront the problem.
   under: you overemphasize the wrong thing.

top speed, at: your project is full steam ahead to the finish line.

ENGLISH
02-21-23-26-28-32

going to England: creditors will press for payment.
   living in: desires will not be realized unless you look at it from all sides.

love affair with an, person, having: will have an unknown sickness.

many, people: false friends are nearby; diplomacy and tact will resolve it.

of an, person: a good friend has ulterior motives in his mind.

ENGRAVE
05-08-24-26-28-31

being an engraver: cannot finish job with your lack of ability.
   seals, of: misfortune in love affairs; concentrate on your career.

hard wood, on: are eagerly awaiting social activities with a blind date.

metal, on: change of work.

ENLISTING
02-06-10-15-28-44

children: family quarrels from curtailment of income.

man dreaming of: postponement of success.
   woman: will take many years to find a fine husband.

others: advancement within position.

relatives: a false friend is nearby.

ENTERPRISE
01-08-19-38-39-41

beginning a new: be prudent in order to avoid ruin.

forced into a bad, being: will make a great deal of money.

others being in good: big changes awaiting.

undertaking a good: sad news awaits.

ENTERTAINMENT
13-15-16-18-25-42

enjoying good: warning against imitation of star's extravagance.

  others, themselves: reckless living and loose morals cast great shadows on a reputation.

  yourself: nothing more offensive than another's joy when you are done for.

entertaining a relative: change in a complicated situation in another's favor.

feeling uncomfortable at an: big joy and money ahead.

leaving before, is over: will miss a good opportunity.

liking the: sorrow caused by your own carelessness.

nightclub, being in a: decadence is free for years; the balloon payment is deadly.

others at an, being with: will soon have money.

  relatives at an: joy without profit.

ENTRANCE
02-15-21-23-24-33

making a grand, in society: at hearing of a death, seek birth of higher knowledge.

  solemn: the weight of the world must be spread around.

private place, going through an, of a: will have a glorious future with yourself.

  public, ornate: desires of higher learning will be realized to your great profit.

refused entry: someone wishes to keep you at a distance.

  for lack of funds: deep-rooted inhibitions are obstructing your advancement.

ENVELOPE
03-11-26-27-32-34

buying an: anticipation of lonely outcome after an opportunity is missed.

closed, a: difficulties are ahead that preoccupy your tenacity.

mailing an: will receive sad news, but depression will fade soon.

opening an, and removing the contents: are concerned that secret will be revealed.

putting a letter in an: discovery of lost opportunity and allowing another to find it.

receiving an, with many letters: disappointment in love letters, love returned.

sealing an: will meet addressee in an obscure place.

tearing it open: tell the person your ominous news before it becomes public.

ENVIED
15-18-23-28-29-34

enemies, by: are being watched by one with evil intentions.

envying others: ill temper sees friends as enemies and enemies as fodder for ambition.

friends, by: your vigorous mind is respected for its liberal deference to others.

others, by: have a hard time resisting the efforts of others to cater to your wishes.

relatives, by: strength of character will reduce tensions of those competing for your favor.

EPILEPSY
08-10-12-30-35-43

being an epileptic: will have sudden large gains after years of laying fallow.

having a, fit: the forceful breakthrough of unconscious material.

  children: will be frightened that the solution is not yours to be had.

  others: an homage by your mental faculties to the body's unsavory tasks.

  relative: the corruption of your worries and cares; to be taken care of by others.

EQUATOR
03-12-21-23-32-36

of the: will have new happiness in life.

others passing the: your indecision on which course to pursue gives enemies an edge.

passing the, on a ship: will be baptized again on the ship.

  not, on purpose: a fine opportunity has floated out of reach.

EQUIPMENT
04-07-11-18-27-32

buying any kind of: will receive unexpected money.

getting, for the house: are jealous of neighbor's good fortune.

  for a store: good business is ahead.

of any kind of: poverty.
selling business: will receive a valuable gift.

ERMINE
07-19-20-25-30-39
fur coat, buying an: save money by allowing
others to pay for your presence.
   owning an: will invest in real estate and
     live in a wealthy barrier to your misery.
   selling an: will be cheated as the buyer,
     if expecting your honor in the bargain.
   wearing an: a false friend is nearby, as is
     one of purity and faithfulness; choose.
of: big wealth and riches, if you don't give
them away.

ERRAND
04-11-18-20-34-37
going on an: harmony in the home; congeniality and communality of purpose
without.
incomplete, an: happy adjustment of difficulties with silly busybodies.
sent on an, being: your selfishness will alienate
your lover.
successfully completing an: expect business
troubles, move to politics.
   unsuccessfully: important and very benefi-
     cial event to come.

ESCALATOR
10-12-13-15-36-43
riding an: want the prize without participating in the game.
   down: must climb backwards to rearrange
     priorities.
stepping up an: support from others will
speed up reaching your goals.

ESCAPING
05-11-14-22-24-30
accident or injury, from: a seemingly unfortunate decision will prove correct.
confinement, from: a rapid rise in the
commercial world.
difficulties, from: climb out of the chasm, no
one needs to face that issue.
drowning, from: success must travel through
a series of anxious moments.
fire, from: your explosive spewing of
repressions creates more enemies.
furious animal, from a: your lack of scruples
will lose you money.

others, from danger: making progress with
deep-rooted psychological problems.
   relatives: financial gains will prove short-
     term with the upheaval you have
     evaded.
unable to escape, being: the illness is upon
you; recover quickly and run.

ESTATE
11-14-25-40-43-44
another person's: your disappointing inheritance will be a devoted marriage partner.
having an: must face reality and enjoy yours.
manor house, entertained at the: will receive
favors from distant relatives.
owning an: your preoccupation with yourself
is self-destructive.
selling an: your net will be a poor provider
and a dozen emotionally deprived children.

ETIQUETTE
18-20-31-34-35-40
observing rules of: public snubbing of you by
one you wanted to impress.
   not, with strangers: your inferiority
     complex aggravates your chances.

EUROPE
10-20-24-25-26-34
European country, being a citizen of a:
unpleasant notoriety to befall you.
   deported from: a change in social
     surroundings.
   to: danger through a secret.
   returning from: quarrels over your inabil-
     ity to see qualities beyond your own.
   seeing, on a map: advancement through
     your ability to see beyond your job.
   taking a trip to: will meet important
     acquaintances and acquire their
     mannerisms.
     with others: a rival will take your
       sweetheart.
   visiting several: a rise in financial affairs
     through multiple contacts.
     having business with: failure of enemies.

EVACUATING
05-10-14-27-38-40
house, a: will receive bad news.
household items from rooms: will have
unhappiness.

others, your furniture in payment of debts: death of distant relative.

others, your property: will lose money by gambling.

place of business: will make money in the future.

EVAPORATING

21-22-26-39-42-43

ether or alcohol: will live a long life.

of things: will fall into poverty.

perfume: liking someone you're meeting and receiving a kiss.

steam: must rely on your own good judgment.

unpleasant odors: disappointment in love.

EVE

05-09-14-20-30-43

being: a new beginning in paradise, in which you wish to remain.

being, and being naked: desire to outsmart your friends by authenticating your doubts.

man dreaming of: give a big family dinner; keep the opulence close at hand.

speaking to: are spiritually conscious but self-conscious.

   young man: find new employment where you know whose money started it.

young girl dreaming of being: purity and simplicity is ripe fodder for temptation.

EVENING

03-18-21-26-41-44

being tired from an exciting: your energies are depleted when they should be heightened.

having a wonderful: shame from loss of love, a brighter future is still awake.

   of celebration: danger through a secret complicated with love.

prosperous, spent with others: worries will end, if you change your childish behavior.

star, an: will perpetuate your belief in love at first sight.

twilight, at: rest on your accomplishments and rejuvenate yourself tomorrow.

EVIL

04-10-17-22-23-44

person, being taken away by an: serious disaster is ahead.

spirits, causing sorrow: will be cheated out of your ambitions; try a new career.

driving, away: will be mystified by unaccountable horror.

impairing happiness: will have mastery over many matters.

EXAMINATION

01-06-07-08-40-49

answering all questions correctly on an: need self-assurance to resolve job confusion.

   not: your boss needs to know your version of the truth.

can't finish the: are self-controlled and over-disciplined, which leaves no room to learn.

entrance of the: face the difficulty you have getting started at the onset.

failing an: overconfidence causes failure; you will pass.

fear of failing: in turmoil over having wasted time when you could have prepared for life.

forgot had class: an unexpected challenge presents itself.

late to take an, too: go back and study to prepare for project.

location of the, can't find: feel pressure about a performance.

missed the: puzzled over how to handle challenge, study.

missing pen or equipment for an: are facing a situation for which you are unprepared.

nervous in, are: are a well-balanced, conscientious person.

never read books for the: are puzzled over how to handle a challenge.

not recognizing material: regret for not having finished your education.

oral, taking an: an associate's invasive behavior must be dispelled quietly.

   loss of voice in: are too proud of your ambitions and lack accomplishments.

passing an: move on to new projects with renewed self-confidence.

   children: have difficulty keeping house in order while realizing high ambitions.

   others: if you can pass the test, you are not doomed for disappointment.

proctor won't let you start the: are ill-equipped for your chosen field.

read the wrong books for the: fear you will appear stupid, as in grade school.

taking an: fear you are unfitted to fill your position.

too hard, is: need to think more seriously before acting.

EXAMPLE

05-16-22-35-36-37

children, being an, to: will obtain a high position.

of: will be a model in your life.

people being good: will make a success of business.

bad: will write a death sentence.

EXCHANGING

05-10-11-12-25-36

articles in a store: discovery of lost valuables will rearrange your plans.

with another person: expect business losses.

with family members: a pleasant surprise to mutual benefit.

blonde for a brunette: will marry again with the same circumstances repeated.

wives between relatives: rapid success of hopes that your happiness is with another.

EXCITED

04-19-25-30-43-48

happily, being: postponement of success.

others, being, by: poverty.

others exciting you to anger: will suffer starvation.

unpleasantly, being: successful completion of plans.

EXCUSES

20-30-40-42-44-49

making, children: your firm decisiveness needs a dose of flexibility.

friends: avoiding enemies does not mean being antisocial with friends.

others, to you: will live a long life.

partner: are obstinate and tenacious.

making an: will suffer loss through your own foolishness.

EXECUTION

07-15-24-30-31-49

attending an: will best your adversary.

being executed: others debase you, change that element in your life.

executioner, being an: death of a small child in the family.

failing in his duties: wish to rid yourself of destructive impulses.

of an: catastrophe and ruin to the enemy within.

preparing to kill someone, an: desire to eliminate someone from your life.

guilty person, of a: triumph over enemies in unusual places.

friend: doubtful success of undertakings; that friend is lost to you.

innocent: will be jilted by a lover, because of your poor health.

lethal injection, by: investigate all routes of responsibility before investing.

lover, of a: will suffer through own foolishness causing misfortune to others.

own: must control passions or will suffer a prolonged illness.

stay of, a: miraculous timing of new evidence, which will connect your foes to the crime.

sweetheart, of a: your loyalty and faithfulness will be repaid.

EXERCISING

12-17-30-43-44-46

aerobic: there is something in raising your heart rate, exercise.

enjoying vigorous: will eventually rise to the occasion.

feeling tired from: beware of monetary losses.

lifting weights easily: are bravely confronting the task.

with difficulty: weight of labor is Herculean.

members of the family, with: fortune and joy.

of: are on the fast track; get out of your intellect for a moment, and take a recess and play.

others: sum up your condition and balance your personality.

powder keg, exploding a: a disconcerting radical change leaves you perplexed.

treadmill, running on the: are circling; not spiraling in growth but in tedium.

wife and husband: persecution and treachery.

EXHIBITION

06-20-26-29-42-45

of an: well-deserved commendation for your achievements.

visiting an: increase your powers of concentration on financial losses.

   with family: warning of troubles.

   with others: unexpected good fortune awaits.

EXILE

12-15-17-18-31-42

being exiled: serious losses from being misunderstood.

   guilt, because of: will have a skin disease for years.

   home, from your: bad financial conditions.

   others: must sacrifice pleasure to take a trip where you will receive plenty of money.

being in: discontent over business politics brings much hostile antagonism.

   forced to accept: the accusations will be unjust, but your actions will be indefensible.

returning from: unworthy friends abuse your confidence and have their rights infringed.

EXPERT

01-02-03-13-28-48

being an: will have a good harvest.

   witness: digging out the rotten part to leave the truth.

of an: the intellect within which answers all.

taking advice from an: will be humiliated.

talking with an: stupid gossip is being spread about you.

EXPLORER

13-17-27-40-42-47

being an: will soon have many new, trustworthy acquaintances.

discussing a discovery with an: strange merchandise will turn a hefty profit.

going exploring: success in uncharted waters, fear in the future.

of an: friends do not comprehend your sense of adventure.

on an expedition: adventure in the unfamiliar; marriage.

EXPLOSION

13-15-17-20-44-48

dead after an: will escape from danger unscathed and free of barriers.

detonating the fuse: will trigger a long-standing depression.

enveloped in flames after an, being: friends trespass on your rights.

face being scarred by an: will be unjustly accused for a short duration.

guilty of causing an, being: friends lose confidence in your explosive temperament.

imploding an old building: don't end your life; restructure your finances.

injured in an, being: an endured vexation has gone out of control.

of an: friends disapprove of your restless actions.

others being in an: express yourself in no uncertain terms.

sitting bolt upright after a dream: your nerve endings are ragged; release emotion daily.

suffocating after overexertion: switch to yoga.

witnessing an: an alarming, unexpected event threatens you.

EXPRESS

08-15-22-25-40-47

bus, traveling on an: an enemy is seeking your ruin.

letter, mailing an: danger through a secret.

   receiving: will be cheated by friends.

train, traveling on an: be careful not to offend superiors.

EXQUISITE

03-05-07-13-19-20

lady of, beauty: will incur many debts.

man, meeting an: joy without profit.

taste, having: will be sorry for present actions.

woman, flirting with an: will have a sad future.

EXTINGUISHING

02-06-11-14-31-34

fire, a: end the affair before it devours you.

   in your home: will prevail over difficulties.

flame, a: will not have sufficient money.

lawsuit, a: will be persecuted by a woman.

light, a: serious quarrels over love.

EXTRAVAGANT

10-23-26-36-37-42

being: shame and sorrow from scandal of which you are its center.

   husband: use caution in business ventures.

others: financial gains.

wife: will realize high ambitions.

EYEGLASSES
03-05-19-20-27-35

breaking your: unexpected fortune and the end of a love affair.

buying: your refusal to see the truth will cause your failure.

children: clear up other's distorted view of the situation.

enemies: obstacles block your progress, but you will come out well from present peril.

goggles, wearing airplane: your boldness gets in the way of your refusing bad advice.

looking through rose-colored: reality includes everything.

losing your: intrigues and lies surround you; beware of passions leading you astray.

monocle: own faults will determine your future; you need a new prescription.

   others: must rely on your own good judgment to not miss out on a favorable opportunity.

   sunglasses: be wary of hidden motives when you are optimistically self-confident.

repairing: an unexpected agreement in a long-standing dispute will bring a payment.

sunglasses: are afraid to expose your intentions with friends you no longer care for.

wearing: will reach agreement and have an honorable, moderate position.

   another's: are being intimidated into hiding your inner vision.

EYES, EYE
07-14-15-22-37-38

beautiful: beware of passions leading you astray.

big: have a breadth of vision, explore it.

black: need an eye test.

blinking: diplomacy and tact are greatly needed to carry out any intention.

blue: your envy drives you from distraction into depression.

brown: a romance disappoints you with deceit and a deliberate breaking of faith.

brows, bushy: financial gains using sinister methods.

falling out: will try to no avail to separate yourself from an irascible sycophant.

narrow and colorless: envious altercations at the instigation of the blonde-haters.

children's: financial gains.

closed: are avoiding intimacy with a serious family situation.

crossed: your view of reality is distorted to balance your knowledge.

doctor, an: a change of point of view could change your occupation.

eyesight, having good: have clarity of spiritual understanding.

   losing your: refusal to accept reality of your guilt.

farsighted, seeing: the answer is right in front of your wisdom.

glass eye, a: have lost your ability to see clearly though you can see everything.

gray: your weakness is predisposed to attract flattery.

green: unexpected big wealth of another through your perceptiveness.

grim: are groping in the darkness of blind ignorance.

hazel: must envelop all sides in your argument to gain true enlightenment.

laughing: an uproariously amusing scene for which you will have to atone.

lids, lashes on: a secret revealed will be to your disadvantage.

   small: even with your considerable fortune; you are naïve and childish.

   unusually expressive: repetitive, pointless argument will destroy confidence.

looking at you, an: a secret admirer—God.

loss of sight in left: are unaware of how you appear to others.

   right: refusing to accept the reality about yourself.

nearsighted, of being: are being watched by one with evil intent.

   children: the problem cannot be solved without the big picture.

   getting glasses to cure myopia: take a closer look at things.

   others: change your focus to a neglected situation.

of many: are preoccupied with having others notice you.

one-eyed man, the: have great insight; use it.

patch, an: look for a more challenging position, like exotic swashbuckling adventurer.

red: illness from overstraining to reach an acceptable level of accomplishment.

small: unconscious fear that you will lose your sexual power.

third eye: are seeking transcendent wisdom, but will be unable to focus on a ruse.

wide-open: intellectual insight will change your direction.

worried about your, being: the trepidations of consciousness expanding.

> *children's:* someone is working secretly against you.

your wife, admiring the, of: are unfaithful to your wife while a rival has eyes only for her.

> *husband:* may expect a baby.

FABLE
15-27-30-33-34-38

hearing others tell a: time to mend your ways and change your behavior.

reading a: a sharp lecture enumerating your faults.

telling a: a romantic homage with a literary bent.

> *children, to:* big joy.

FABRIC
17-19-23-31-33-49

azure blue, of: happiness.

brown, of: will be double-crossed by employees.

calico, buying: unhappy events within twelve months.

canvas: an unexpected all-expenses-paid shopping spree.

chiffon: frivolous.

crimson, of: good times are coming.

cutting on the bias: a friend in distress.

cypress, having: delay in the conclusion of your business.

> *of this heavy rich satin:* troubles caused by prying into others' affairs.

dyeing colors: put too much trust in the wrong new acquaintance.

frame for making: efforts are being wasted.

fringe, adding: have knotted up the beauty of your sex.

gingham, bright colored: must choose love of your life now.

gray, of any: wealth.

> *green:* abundant means.

having lightweight: will be molested.

Indianhead: wrongdoings will be recognized.

indigo, dyeing, with: will have a long stay away from home.

khaki uniforms, of cloth for: are surrounded by anxieties.

lavender, silk: are blessed by the church.

> *any other:* success in own affairs.

linen: will make certain and secure profit from sustained health.

> *white, buying:* money will come easily during life.

lining, of, used for: vanity; an imperfection within yourself that needs mending.

> *buying:* will receive an unexpected visitor.

loom, making yarns into, on a: a promising career in the arts.

> *of a:* recovery from an illness.

mauve: warning of troubles.

of: the wearing of the pattern of your life experiences.

pinking, of: will receive consideration from others.

pink of any kind: will have a happy family life.

> *others':* certain and secure profit from sustained health.

> *that has been pinked:* joyous times and new clothes.

plaid: kind companions who will stand by you to the death.

purple: loss of friends.

red, of any: misfortune.

satin: don't be deceived by flattery; bring the project to your conclusion.

> *wearing:* all misinterpretations are deflected off of you by your confidence.

scarlet-colored, of any kind: danger in love matters.

silk: creating beauty out of chaos.

silver-colored, various: will have many friends.

striped: face up to deep-seated problem before it resurfaces.

taffeta, blue: will resume being damaged goods.

velvet: will have an amorous conversation.

white-colored, various: have unjustified negative thoughts.

woolen: will make profits from your own products.

yellow, of any kind: will have sorrow.

zephyr, buying: will have a serious accident.

FACE

02-03-27-34-40-47

acne on your: exposure of inner turmoil; breaking out of constraints to agitate enemies.

> *picking:* illness will not go away easily.
> *pimples on the, having:* will have good earnings in real estate.
> *squeezing your:* will have a large amount of silver.

bearded, having a: a traveler will return.

> *beautiful:* quarrels that resolve in love.
> *blemished:* a character defect has become obvious to others.
> *bright happy:* don't take yourself too seriously.
> *clean-shaven:* will be too ashamed and not stay long in one area.
> *complexion, a beautiful:* how you appear to others.
> *dimples:* several affairs will deplete passion to simple flirtation.
> *features, smiling:* only a sincere wish will be granted.
> *jowls, heavy:* will meet with threats and narrowly escape.
> *mustache:* will have disagreements and disputes with employer over proper conduct.
> > *woman admiring a:* guard her virtue or you will be publicly disgraced and lose her friendship.
> *pale:* life's energy has been drained.
> *spot on the, having a:* someone desires to make love to you.
> *swollen:* your idea of own importance is highly inflated.

ugly, an: conflicts in love affairs; your repentance for sins will be considered insincere.

blowing in someone's: a woman is deceiving you.

brow, furrowing your: your true nature is exposed.

child's, a: postponement of success.

coloring your: your lies about your heritage will catch up with you.

> *creaming:* your desire to appear well-groomed.

facade, hiding behind a: your social self hides a quite different personality.

facelift, having a: appearances fade after the first meeting; character sustains the second.

> *facial:* cover up your indiscretion before it is exposed, or better yet, expose it yourself.

forehead, smoothing a wrinkled: your influence at work will be significant.

grimacing your: face up to the situation; don't hide your fear.

makeup, with too much: friends are lying to you.

mirror, seeing own, in a: pay attention to physical symptoms.

painting the: image of how you would like to be seen.

> *with pitch black:* your selection of friends leads to imminent scandal.

stranger, of a: that face will encounter you.

> *absolute:* secret project is about to be presented to you.
> *not remembering a:* important introduction to a teacher or a mentor.
> *repulsive, a:* a failure of enemies.

washing own: unaccustomed pleasures through refreshingly new friends of wise counsel.

FACTORY

02-06-14-22-25-40

being in a: a life lacking in individuality.

belonging to others: are not using your opportunities to your productive advantage.

building, a: respect from the community for financial gains rendered.

> *closed and deserted, suddenly:* that phase of your life is empty; move on.

clothing, a: congenial work and good
activity in making money.

dish, a: will live a long life.

glass: sights must be lowered with regard
to risky project.

linen, a: use caution in business ventures.

paper, a: affairs will prosper.

pottery, a: will be visited by a good friend.

silk, a: affairs will go from bad to worse.

velvet, a: will entertain an unwelcome
guest.

workers entering a: beneficial activities of
industriousness and productivity.

buying a: will be blessed.

chimney smoking, a: new plans will disrupt
your peace.

owning a: your investments yield little profit
without your mastery and energy.

selling a: loss due to inattentive and narrow-
minded management.

working in a: the hectic tense situation is part
of a good job; to correct it is your job.

FAILURE
09-19-31-32-38-41

being a: will realize high ambitions with
common sense, not over-perfectionism.

enemies: will be stricken with muscular
affliction.

husband: your lack of good judgment
makes you unfitted to fill your position.

others: postponement of success through
present discouraging news.

relatives: reverses with speedy recovery
and lessons to be learned.

FAINTING
19-23-26-34-48-49

children: a sign of the onset of illness; preven-
tive measures are in order.

having fainted: a dizzying and disastrous love
affair designed by you.

member of the family: distressing news from
the absent, caused by careless ways.

of: foretells possible poor blood circulation.

others: postponement of success until you rid
yourself of frivolous ways.

suffering injury from: are temporarily freed
from responsibility.

another: money will be requested of you
to care for a profligate other.

FAIR
03-04-10-23-38-42

being at a: social activities will provide opportunities of advancement for you.

others: a profitable business venture of
short intense duration.

going to a: avoid unnecessary expenditures
that charge double their worth.

with the family: postponement of success
until tomorrow; today is for congeniality.

friends: will have emotional sorrow
from a usually jovial, even-
tempered friend.

FAIRY
12-13-19-20-36-48

goblin, a: your affair is in danger of being
discovered.

land: sustain your artistic talent to profit.

listening to a: guidance is available if you
listen, but you will have to fix the problem.

of a: long-cherished wishes come true, if you
don't include rivals as your support.

children dreaming: return to your natural
spirit and nature forces.

elf: suffer from an inferiority complex.

FAITHFUL
11-15-18-19-22-23

being: only faith in yourself will lead to the
success of your plans.

faithless: at each opportunity a friend will
prove undependable and dishonor-
able.

children, having: rivals hold their children in
high esteem and yours in lower.

friends: do not demand from others their
faith in you, to their detriment.

mate, a: happiness between children and
parents.

relatives: happiness is assured.

FALCON
02-03-19-24-34-49

flying, a: ascension through all levels of
consciousness.

holding a, on your wrist: thieves will dishonor
you; remain firm.

others, their: are surrounded by enemies
who are envious and malicious in their
intent.

of a: own fortune will increase, but rivals will be plentiful, as will their false rumors.

FALLING
03-04-13-28-35-46

amusement park ride, from an: let yourself enjoy the struggle as you do the solution.

bridge, a: will sink as low as your highs were high.

high place, a: feeling emotionally out of control, now that warranted fright is absent.

medium height: lack of support will cause you to activate your true strength.

arising again, and: keep re-experiencing unfinished deed until you accomplish it.

dying: ask friend to subsidize your project; but not to fail in your place.

awaking with a start, in the ocean and then: loss of faith in yourself.

children: anticipate the breathing process stopping until assured that the child is well.

ditch, into a: salvage your reputation from your low opinion of yourself.

enemies: do not confide your secret fear of not being in control.

floor, to the: are menaced by the danger of total isolation.

friends: fear of being deceived will make you so.

frightened, and being: will experience an obscure guilt for a moral lapse.

from the edge of a cliff: the status you have reached needs basic human contact.

black hole, into a: are highly sensitive to your environment.

into the rocks: some obstacle is hindering your presentation.

water: seek spiritual insights now.

ladder, a: one rung does not a failure make; step up and try again.

roof, a: your mental equilibrium is going, going, gone!

space, outer: unfulfilled desire for support and affection.

grave hole, in a: have lost your sense of self-worth and mental equilibrium.

hurt, and being: financial losses are imminent if you repeat past mistakes.

children: will make the wrong move; put off your decision.

injured, being: will endure hardship from having lost the esteem of friends.

without: will be victorious in your struggles and hardship will turn to care.

ocean, in the: will be ill until you immerse yourself in healing your mind.

others: a timely unmasking of your enemies as you sustain a fall at their expense.

over something: let go of that object or situation you have lost control of.

physical act of: sense of coming back into reality after a dream trip.

relatives: loss of esteem among those you love and respect.

stumbling, and: have put distorted value on a chance of trouble.

without: can salvage a tricky situation, by returning more gently each night.

thrown in the ocean by enemies, being: will be persecuted for loss of self-control.

water, in the: risk the fulfillment of a death wish for your enemy.

FAME
12-18-20-32-38-42

being famous: losses through following a mistaken ambition.

children achieving: rise from obscurity to highest aspirations.

husband: he is in love with another woman, in himself.

others: others use your abilities to gain their fame.

someone else: will rise from obscurity through your own work.

having: will have dealings with authorities for robbing another's tree.

FAMILY
16-20-27-31-40-41

announcing, affairs: probable divorce or a bidding of farewell.

arranging: major sacrifices will fill each soul with caring encouragement.

arguing with: your tactful diplomacy will lead to a constructive plan.

awakening from sleep: prying into affairs of others causes trouble.

being happy: wish fulfillment for an unplanned, undesired change in your environment.

chagrined, members of, being: disputes with mother-in-law over raising of children.

convulsions, members having: disheartening failure in otherwise good financial matters.

destitute, a: upheaval in national interests causes your business to not be remunerative.

   feeding a: are sufficiently self-confident to extend your civic responsibility.

large, having a: prosperous times are in store.

   no, or relatives: are being deceived by members of the opposite sex.

   rich: your excessive vanity, gloating on success encourages a scourge on your family.

   small: a friend is trying to help.

of own: be cautious, not unhappy and pessimistic in your ventures.

old member of: approaching money from those you have been faithful to.

others, of: your failure to acknowledge others makes them argumentative.

refuses to accept: financial woes make responsibilities overwhelming.

FAMINE

02-10-27-31-33-45

continued: reduce food intake by half, then half again.

enduring a: triumph over enemies by teaching them to be your friends.

having plenty following a: are searching for a natural leader.

   others: revival of an old friendship that may end very profitably.

FAN

06-24-28-40-47-48

dancing: jealousy leads to unwarranted ridicule.

having a: news of a pleasant nature will come soon.

mail, receiving: your lover is fading from your life.

others with a: are warding off evil forces fanning your flame.

   rival: competition is imbued with the life force; healthy rivalry takes work.

single lady fanning herself: will soon form profitable acquaintances.

woman losing her: a close friend will drift away into lack of self-confidence.

   buying a: sudden insertion of energy into your interest in another man.

young woman dreaming of being fanned: old-fashioned variety of daydreaming.

FANTASY

09-22-23-29-31-44

beautiful woman in a: will soon love someone else.

handsome man in a: loss of money.

of: will enjoy a fortunate business venture.

seeing things in: will be very disillusioned.

FARM

03-11-14-15-27-40

being a farmer: are well-grounded and in tune with life's rhythms.

belonging to others: congenial work, profitable production and neighborly support.

burning, a: repression of your natural inner-conditioned growth.

buying a: a well-tended farm brings a big harvest for the farmer.

empty field: others have harvested your crop.

farmer dreaming of the Greek god Bacchus: nurturing growth and natural pleasures.

farming, of: simple joys, salt of the earth and robust health.

   difficulties with: arguments due to vanity forestalling the development of your potential.

   money in, making: success through cooperation with Mother Nature.

      through, losing: fateful event will thwart highly anticipated gains.

   new in the, business: have an advantage others don't have, a fresh viewpoint.

fertile meadow, walking a: symbolizes the characteristics of learning and unfolding.

fertilizing a field: unpleasantness forces you to attain growth; insight is not that easy.

field yet to be harvested, a: hard work equals abundant harvest.

gleaner, being a: are completing the process of transition and establishing your rights.

   gathering grain after a reaper: are completing the process of transition.

harrow, drawing a: cultivation of the personality.

hiring people to work on a: will be helped by people with more expertise.

hoe, cultivating with a: will be competent in the sale of farm and dairy products.

hothouse, of a: are nervous and irritable in an overheated argumentative atmosphere.

making paths on a: reaping benefits of hard work ahead.

measuring farmland: diligently represent your sensual, aggressive or animalistic urges.

others visiting your: rapid sowing and reaping of mutual affairs.

owning a large: the cultivation of your goals are on solid ground and rising.

   small: will realize high ambitions.

pitchfork, a: a lengthy burdensome task will increase prosperity by a small amount.

   being chased with a: creditors!

prosperous, a: advantages in business, matrimony and inheritance.

relatives working on a: will take a safe journey.

scarecrow, seeing a person as a: he has no good character traits.

selling a: profit from astute business dealings.

   animals for slaughter: don't underestimate the value of your talents.

sickle, cutting grain with a: brandish insults without caring who you hurt.

silo, feeding animals from a: belly up to the bar doesn't mean you drink everything on it.

   on fire: are hedging your due dates to your detriment.

tractor, driving a: will accomplish exactly what you have sown, no more.

vacant, a: a run on the bank and loss of money.

visiting a: unpleasant arguments with narrow-minded people.

withered crops, with: homeland needs planting of the seeds of insight.

working a, all alone: material success for your simple needs.

young, working: a burdensome life for a peaceful old age.

FASHION

12-13-21-37-38-49

haut couture, being dressed in: will be prominent in social activities.

models in a store window: family quarrels.

out of fashion, being: take an interest in your own life so others will.

show, others being in a: watch out for treachery.

   taking family to a: postponement of success.

studying a, magazine: danger through a secret.

watching a, show: will have a long life.

FASTING

01-06-28-29-38-47

according to own religion: your happiness is assured.

dreaming of eating while: your emotions need to be nurtured.

fast, a forced: self-denial and lack of self-love destroy physical energy.

members of family, with you: hereditary instincts bring big wealth.

of: cleansing of character from greed and unrealistic impulses.

reading cookbooks while: your decisive personality has a vivid imagination.

FAT

04-14-17-18-42-43

children getting: the results of your forgotten actions are visited upon your children.

cooking with: tendency to overspend in business ventures.

   lard: are in the company of doubtful morals and questionable ethics.

eating fatty foods: redirect your hunger to cleanse yourself of error and sickness.

greasy stains on clothes: allowing your greed to taint your opinions.

land, living off the, of the: have made a fortunate move to prosperity.

man dreaming of growing: too much emphasis on material values.

   married woman: impending loss of freedom.

   woman: will be abandoned by your lover.

     really: inability to harmonize your sensual desires with your ambitions.

young girl: will be married with opulence.

other women being: dishonest and dangerous activities are hidden in sloth.

others who are: postponement of your success while they enjoy theirs.

relatives: fear people see you as disgusting, as you see them.

FATE

08-17-25-49-50-53

against your desires, is: brush out the cabinets and take advantage of the day.

played into your hands: an opportunity arises to create the life you want.

FATHER

05-28-35-46-48-49

being a: a responsible and respected position to create and sustain life.

dead, being: a conscience catastrophe over the qualities of protection you must now have.

  poor: fear that you have brought shame to the family.

father-in-law being alive: live up to the responsible father you wished you had.

  dead: are subject to enthusiasm soon passed.

  of own: take the commonsense advice with a grain of salt.

    another's: it will be difficult to escape approaching troubles.

homage to you, paying: will not be accepted without unsolicited advice.

of own: there is safety and security in the advice of elders.

others: will benefit from group support and mentors capable of wise counsel.

own, passing away: faith in yourself is waning; you need it to succeed.

talking with your: need for forgiveness and guidance on both sides.

FAVOR

08-12-28-30-35-47

asking for a: loss of social stature and trust, which you sorely need to push on.

for others, doing a: a loss of friendship, if you expect to be paid in return.

friend, from a: have straightforward, thinking friends who do what has to be done.

  mate: an enemy's influence on your domestic bliss proves self-servingly insidious.

  relatives: warning of arguments, which will taint future cooperation.

others doing you a: will receive a compliment from someone you respect.

FEAR

11-14-16-33-34-38

great, having: are a person of extraordinary courage; make the decision.

  not knowing reason for: one you now trust is untrustworthy.

of something, having: someone will take care of you when plans come to naught.

  persisting, a: have not developed ability to cope with the cause.

overcoming own: bring fears into the open and deal with them.

  others: past must be clarified and rectified for peace of mind.

retribution, of: a form of self-punishment before the real punishment is meted out.

FEAST

03-19-22-26-28-31

having a: expect difficulties in the near future, and plenty thereafter.

  children: happiness, you have done something very basic, very well.

  enemies: misery is being painstakingly prepared in your honor.

  others: joy and contentment.

  relatives: will receive happy news.

preparing a: another person is enjoying what you desired and worked so hard to earn.

FEATHERS

05-13-21-33-35-45

being covered with feather plumes: egocentric satisfaction of rising to power.

black plume: burdens and postponement of profits will be borne with aplomb.

breath of God, on the: the uplifting thoughts to holiness.

brown: your fortunes have been clipped by petty annoyances and unrequited loves.

collecting flying: your vain money hopes are futile.

eagle: access to the heavens for the realization of your ambitions.

gray: false pride will limit your journey through life to you alone.

light blue: realization of own ambitions to become socially popular.

molting: don't act if you doubt; a new opportunity is offered in the morning.

ostrich: fortunate business transactions, if you keep your head high.

pillow of down: fortunate affairs of pride and purse.

pen, a: an apology, due to you, brings an upturn in financial matters.

people wearing, in hats: rapid success of own hopes for a job well done.

   tuft of, a: great honors will crown you.

red: irritating friction from coworkers.

wearing a plume in own hat: will gain favor, but your methods will be contemptible.

   daughters: public honor for a talent well developed, especially if white feather.

   friends: will be tortured with inability to gain honorable long-lasting friendships.

   others: vanity brings unhappiness yet your aspirations are attainable.

   relatives: unexpected gains.

white: the accusation will be proven false.

FEBRUARY
02-07-08-10-31-45

being born in: the price of maturity is greater responsibility.

   children: will succeed in political life.

month, of, during this: good month for business.

President's Day: take what you want in life and pay for it in cash.

FECES
08-14-22-23-32-43

animals, of: will make a big profit with your new project by using the work of the old.

any other kind of: a gift you are waiting to receive is highly valued.

babies' diapers, in: your basic self-expression flows unrefined.

defecation: production from the bowels of one's being.

diarrhea, having: an ungovernable flushing of nefarious thoughts at the wrong time.

feeling dirtied by: a long-repressed shame needs airing.

handling your own: have driven into an emotional ballast.

of: purge yourself of sexual repression; clean it up before you discard it.

passing stool: relief is gained by sitting still.

playing with: an infantile pleasure search drives your materialism.

stepping in: matters left behind cannot be resolved in your favor.

   others: cause trouble unintentionally, by not dealing with it.

FEEBLE
08-11-26-29-37-47

being: will be approached continuously for aid when you have all you need.

   always: must gasp for air to breathe in your toxic occupation.

   children: a disappointment that will inconvenience you very much.

   others: use cautious expressions or may fail to influence the person concerned.

FEET
01-22-24-27-32-36

amputated, being: no one wins with brutality.

arthritic: are relishing pleasures that make your age beyond your years.

bare, your: lighten up, look up and laugh; you are grounded.

   many: competition makes your present position insecure; keep in touch with the earth.

bathing in a basin: your greed increases your anxiety and needs healing.

   ocean, the: shame and sorrow bring much vexation.

   river: basic feelings upon which your love rests will be molested.

blister on a: you lack the self-confidence to find the source of your irritation.

   popping a: the problem at work is not physical.

bunion, suffering from a: humiliation will stem from family quarrels over control.

   friends: are confronted with insurmountable obstacles.

   inflammation leaving, the: with return of the foot traveler; you will have a new admirer.

burning own: you walked too close to an emotional fire.

children's: you never wanted dependency, but found yourself needing it.

cloven, a: investigate strangers and observe friends for ill will toward you.

corns on the, cutting: struggle to remain stable in the common walkway of life.
> *others:* you have a loyal friend.

cutting the: you are troubling about trifles while lust for life passes you by.

deformed: disturbing gossip distorts the truth of a hereditary illness within the family.

dirty: your conscience is begging you to come clean.

footbath, a hot: pull yourself up to undertake a new project with enthusiasm.
> *cold:* are not ready to proceed as troubles creep into family.

having a big: the lowliness, the earthiness, from which your life is built, comes out.
> *broken, a:* are relinquishing too much energy without replenishing it.
> *fractured:* obstacles will come from unexpected foes.
> *lame:* you are unable to proceed to the first step and allow others to receive.
> *small:* worry will be smoothed away, one small step at a time.

heel, having a wounded: what you leave out of a proposal is as important as that left in.
> *being down at the:* a long-established friend needs attention.
> *pain in the:* are being oppressed by a contemptible, despicable person.

hurting your: humiliating troubles are likely over an unexpected challenge to your values.

itching: make the move; you know the direction.

kissing the, of another person: are a smooth talker around ladies; change your conduct.

measuring distances in: expect happiness and good humor.

moving: are trying to escape your responsibilities; find out what they really are first.

narrow: can never stray from your path.

pedicure, having a: the foundation of your principles and jealousies will be challenged.

scratched by others, being: do not pay attention to enemies.

see, can't: are unable to see the end of the path.

toes: a tiny adjustment will balance your center.
> *twitching:* are traveling astrally in your sleep.

washing your: a therapeutic detour will clear up a bad conscience.
> *another's:* being repentant for past misdeeds does not allow others an advantage.
> *in the sea:* others are mystified by your actions.

FENCE
01-06-22-23-34-47

blocking you: reexamine the inhibitions blocking your self-expression.

boundary: are avoiding making a decision to act upon.

climbing a: your courage will challenge your restrictions.
> *getting hurt:* will attain your goal but be disappointed in the methods you used.
> *others:* an enemy is imposing limits on your work.
> *through a:* will obtain money in questionable manner.
> *warily:* an enemy is trying to entrap you.

falling from a: are attempting more than you can complete.

looking at a: solve a side issue first, then aim for the height of your ambitions.

open, an: feel you should be restrained from your exotic desires.

picket, being caught in a: a minor error places you in jeopardy for major misdeed.

reaching the border: others are defining your boundaries for you.

selling jewelry through a: are protecting yourself from being exposed for your mistakes.

stile, falling from a: will be in mourning over the death of a relative.
> *stepping over a:* your way out involves climbing.

FERRET
05-15-16-26-37-41

hunting rabbits, a: search out denied emotions from your unconscious.

rats: will have emotional sorrow.

of this small animal: watch for an inquisitiveness that can injure another's feelings.

using a, to hunt: will have a vigorous mind.

FERRYBOAT

17-19-21-30-31-47

alone, being on a: will be baffled by the
breadth and depth of danger.

   family, with: your rewards will be
commensurate with your effort.

   others, with: erase your past emotional
reactions; listen to your heart for new
ones.

at dock: your inertia blocks your momentum
toward success.

enemies being at a: are being watched by one
with evil intent.

   friends: well-meaning friends block your
maturity.

others on a: triumph over fun-loving diversions from your goal.

FESTIVAL

15-19-30-31-34-49

children, being at a, with: enjoy happiness
until you must face life's cold realities.

   enemies: will survive a stage of dissatisfaction and impatience.

   others at a: are unable to express the joy
and contentment of your spiritual side.

   relatives: will receive happy news.

preparing a: another person is enjoying what
you desired.

FEVER

15-20-23-29-40-47

having a: unconscious is fighting repressed
fears that affair will go awry.

   children: have mistreated someone, causing temporary fever to a dependent
upon you.

   friends: will be cheated by friends; go back
for the win.

   relatives: friends will tell you lies about
their financial gains.

   very high: crisis point leading to renewed
energy and vitality.

suffering from a: are wearing down your
nerves by letting petty worries bother you.

   enemies: your fiery mental attitude causes
an array of disharmonies.

FIANCÉ

04-17-19-20-24-44

another person's: will have a vigorous mind.

daughter's: an argument will soon be overcome.

of own: will have sad experiences if you stay
in this relationship.

son's fiancée: a disagreement will not be
settled until the future.

FIASCO

05-06-21-34-35-45

making a ridiculous failure: will realize high
ambitions by first getting out of debt.

   children: bad business ventures.

   husband: are unfitted to fill your position.

   others: postponement of success.

FIELD

06-10-17-18-19-42

being in a: find the activities of which you are
most capable.

buying a: will have much hospitality.

crop circles, with: a message from a higher
power.

devastated by hail: nature destroys in order
to rebuild.

fertilizing a: a vigorous venture back to the
womb.

going around the fields: grounded in natural
elements.

lain fallow, a: have allowed an opportunity
to be missed.

neglected, a: what you have repressed is draining your inner resources.

of a: a good marriage requires your conscious
interaction.

   of corn: good earnings.

      grain: pleasant friends and great abun-
dance.

      oats: prosperity.

      wheat: prosperous trade if you are
cautious about traders.

sowing a: your strength is emotionally rooted.

working in a: hard work is ahead; your
endeavor will benefit many.

FIGHT

07-10-11-17-34-40

being beaten in a: are powerless to the opposition of your love affair.

fighting with a wild animal: feel conflict with
an irascible savage part of yourself.

of being in a: your battle with yourself will bring on an unfavorable peace.

   others: have plenty of scope to improve your projects.

participating in a: will gain honorable wealth despite lawsuits threatening you.

   on a battlefield: hate and envy make life difficult when they fight within themselves.

struggling to save yourself: will suffer abuse you have forced upon another.

watching a: don't involve yourself in another's ugliness.

winning a: conciliation with yourself will overcome your sense of your unworthiness.

witnessing a: your smugness will regurgitate on you.

FIGS

26-28-32-38-39-49

eating: are squandering the wealth of your intuitive faculties.

having dry: time for the second advent of your health and wealth of being.

of, during their season: the seed of birth and the lusciousness of life.

   when out of: idleness allows the barrenness of unrequited love.

of a tree: will take a trip after an argument and it will end the relationship.

receiving, as a gift: a friend wants to intensify the relationship.

FILE

01-20-24-25-37-45

filing cabinet, a: discovery of lost valuables misfiled; unpaid bills long overdue.

   putting papers in a: are confronted with disquieting organizational obstacles.

   several: will realize high ambitions by lowering your moral standards.

   taking, out of: will misplace important documents, causing debate over your intentions.

filing metal: success through hard work and imagination.

   piece of wood, a: root a tenuous situation in logic.

   your nails: boredom is a product of your mind.

using a: reconciliation with the energies.

   machinist's, a: unpleasant news will arrive soon.

   nail, a: a mystery will be solved.

FILLING

12-17-19-25-29-45

bottles: happiness for the woman of the house.

gas station, at a: increase of income for little price.

handbag, a: will receive a gift of jewelry.

hole, a: enjoy amusements too much of the time.

of: will be involved in a secret transaction.

pockets: honor.

up: satisfaction breeds laziness.

FILM

18-22-29-41-42-49

buying: go back in time to foretell a journey abroad in the near future.

having: new projects are of utmost importance to your cause.

spliced, a: have secure, unassailable prospects.

using: guard against malicious remarks to those who respect you.

   others: much discussion concerning you and your interpretation of life.

FINDING

07-14-15-28-39-47

child, a: will have a very complicated lawsuit.

gold and silver: will have many worries from hidden secrets.

someone naked: will find new employment for old talents.

   lost in a forest: will have an unsettled future.

tree, a: dissolution of that which you care about most.

valuable article, a: big misfortune in business.

   things, others: shame and sorrow.

various other things: are decisive and confident in your infidelity.

FINGERS

03-07-18-19-27-39

bleeding: will lose money at the rate of flow.

bowl, a: money from a surprising source; will gain notoriety for your benevolence.

breaking the: your intent for a good marriage has been ruptured.

burning the: are envied by many people who scorn you.

cutting the: caught between gossip and the truth; point your own direction.

dirty, a: patience and understanding in non-winnable quarrels.

gold rings, being covered with: will be married soon.

having, cut off: have failed to grasp the enormity of the situation.

less than five: joy and love are not options until you cultivate them.

long: marriage will not last long with your accusatory nature.

more than five: the regenerative, healing power of touch.

nails cut: dishonor in unpleasant wrangles with lover.

pains in the: accusations against your supposed misdeeds.

short: inheritance has been decreased; new goals must be set.

index finger: only methodical patience, without relying on another's favors, will succeed.

little: a period of stagnation; must rely on own vigor to emerge from it.

middle: be cautious how you expend your work ethic.

ring: will receive support from artistic community.

mouth, over your: the truth is best kept to yourself.

nails back, bending your: period of agitation caused by fault-finding relatives.

breaking off: a certain matter should not succeed, no matter how much you desire it.

cutting your: unveil the motives of an arrogant person; accept your own.

others: will be neglected by those you considered friends.

extremely long: dishonor in family reveals another's bite into your legacy.

painting, with red polish: conduit is lowering moral standards.

scratching you: someone is out to seriously hurt you.

you scratching another with: deal with intellect sharply and literary works thriftily.

nice: are overly timid and indecisive in your charitable work.

pale: your love will not be reciprocated.

point a, at another: the guilt is yours for not pinpointing the problem when you saw it.

pointing at you, others: will have to learn how to make deals more lucrative.

prints: peace, when you accept others' individuality as you accept your own.

thumb: stubborn fighting spirit against the evil eye needs to change paths.

FIRE

05-15-16-28-43-48

afraid of: commitment is a dirty word for your intense psychological ordeal.

artificial, an: dries up water; excesses of your unconscious.

ashes: last chance for resolution of a relationship.

being fired: your inattention will lose your job.

firing another: need person more than you admit or realize.

being in a: your plans will mature to triumph, if the impetus is continually stoked.

burned: business damaged, but unforeseen fortune will bear you up.

killed: confront anger with compassion.

relatives: will soon have a high fever caused by various passions.

blazing, a: nostalgic regret for past mistakes and present state of affairs.

boat spraying water on a: nervous disorders need natural remedies.

bonfire, a: have regard for those blocking exposure of the truth.

standing in front of a, brightly burning: victory in bringing invulnerability to any situation.

throwing books in a: rebellion against teaching principles.

brush, an uncontrolled: the destruction a released spirit creates on its barriers.

under control, being brought: sins have been purified in harmony with your innate nature.

burning inside you: your obsession must become reality to burn itself out.

burning without smoke: need help to put out your emotional blaze.

caused by an electric spark: beware of secret enemies.

dancing around a: your passions are unburdened from the past.

dead, a: after a rest your neighbors will help you rebuild.

extinguishing a, completely: disapproval of another's point of view.

  by throwing water on: scrap the old and build the new.

    urinating: a rejection of the message; deceptive practices will lose a lawsuit.

falling from the sky: desolation of overambitious ideas; rebirth and renewal.

falling into a, someone: transmuting influence of your internal energy or spirit.

false alarm, a: anxiety over an unnatural rage.

fireman, a: an exclusive stag party of those capable of dealing with burning desires.

  saving a woman: a very peculiar situation for love to blossom.

flames, bright: extinguish the maliciousness before it gains headway.

large: a selfish expression of the life-giving energies.

  smoking heavily: your ego is clouding your vision.

  without smoke: keep your passions under wraps.

lighting a: a spark from across the room will ignite into an affair.

lives lost, no: confusion at work will be sorted out without your involvement.

lots of smoke: people around you are covering up their motives.

  but no flames: will be disappointed in their intentions.

ordeal by: test of instinctive and mental energy to gain spiritual purity and initiation.

setting something ablaze: will allow yourself to be seduced in a futile fight against fate.

stove, on a: someone is pregnant.

  putting out a: a slow-growing illness will be revealed.

taking something from a, with hand: your vulnerability cannot surmount obstacles.

throwing logs on a: your effort far exceeds your profit.

unaware of a, being: do not overestimate your importance.

FIREARMS
04-15-21-27-30-38

ammunition shells: a painful encounter with a dentist.

armed people: will be visited by army officers.

armed with, being: a good opportunity to gather positive resources.

  others: worry will not be smoothed away easily; complications expand the issues.

armory, in the: others are menaced by your self-protectiveness.

artillery shooting: must choose a single career.

bullets coming toward you: warning of immediate verbal violence.

carrying: will have a lawsuit if you attack another.

cartridge, an empty: you foolishly vary your alliances; they have united against you.

grenade, a: check your angry, violent, explosive emotions at your own door.

half-cocked: be wary of being incited to lose your temper.

  firing: are bound to reject impulsive act.

machine gun, firing a: your enemies' reliance on uninhibited aggression bears down on you.

  hearing a: injured by injudicious actions of friends; watch for who exudes guilt.

owning: financial gains through a miraculous turning of affairs.

revolver, shooting a: lost valuables are discovered.

  rifle: another person steals your winnings.

  shotgun: two lovers are one too many; decide whom you want!

selling: are in the company of ruffians.

FIRE ENGINE
08-20-21-40-44-46

chief, being the: riches and fortune.

fireman on a, being a: will realize high ambitions.

going to a fire: will have peace.

  returning from: will receive a big disappointment.

hydrant, connected to a: good luck to those who are in danger.

    bursting: a disquieting experience will prove oppressive.

FIREPLACE
01-07-08-16-20-47

andirons, a pair of: a high promotion much to your chagrin.

ashes, of: loss through carelessness.

    in own: loss of money.

cinders, of: expect a big disappointment if you get burned.

    blowing out a: gossip about you is being spread.

    throwing away: success in business of a mediocre level.

        others: are wasting time with irrelevancies.

empty, an: something will be lost.

fire burning in a: intimate family gathering.

fireside, sitting alone beside a: will be happy in love.

    with others: are being deceived by friends.

        family: will live a long life.

        fiancé: will soon get married.

hearth, in the: control the inflammatory remarks if you wish to advance in own affairs.

mantel, of a beautiful: beware of treachery.

    clock sitting on a: beware in whom you place your trust.

poker, chasing a robber with a: an ill-tempered action will need much justification.

poking up a fire in a: have no control of your temper.

smoke coming from a: your family problems will be exposed.

FIREWORKS
09-27-28-34-36-43

display, watching a: will suffer through being the center of attention.

    children, with: your energy is scattered among your progeny.

    relatives: family celebration for a job well done.

firecracker, a: an irritation, interesting but deadly, of a purpose misdirected.

of: a rude awakening that your partners are con artists.

FISH
18-21-30-39-45-48

anchovies: suffering through memories of first lover.

aquarium, being in an: are constricted by your inability to express emotions.

    darting back and forth: time for you to leave present position.

bait: a lure is no substitute for solid facts.

barracuda, being attacked by a: must change environment to succeed.

birth of a: the treasures or sustenance of your inner, unconscious life.

boiled, eating: spiritual surrender to God's will.

bones of a: survive the emotional state and rationalize it continuously.

carp, several: your chance to win a contest.

cod, a: will have an unexpected visitor.

cooking: freedom from detestable work to quest your own enterprising talents.

cuttlefish, buying: an important decision must be made in a hurry.

dead, in a store: the nourishing influence needs your vitality to actuate.

    stream: a distant dire calamity has echoed into your water.

flying, a: travel to odd places with even odder experiences.

    several: will enjoy pleasures that will cost money.

fried, eating: will find a lost trinket among the bones.

hatching: will have difficulties in bearing a child.

jellyfish, having: support you expect, will dissipate along with the indecisive people.

kingfisher, flying across the water: recovery of lost money through conscientious effort.

mackerel, of a: expensive pleasures cause quarrels and suffering.

many colors, of: expect to quarrel with your partner.

market, a: will obtain a highly honorable position among the wealthy and powerful.

mermaid, of a: are deceived by a lover under false pretensions.

pickerel, a: trouble with a lover you should never have trusted.

red-colored: are fishing for compliments.

salmon: lighten up and your deep emotional conflict can be solved.

salted: will have to fight to avoid misery.

several: your presence of mind to play the lottery will tide you over the rough times.

shallow water, in: warm reputation and lasting friendships will taint you.

story, the, that got away: extracting yourself from an enmeshed love triangle is futile.

sushi, eating: will require uncooked, spiritual food.

swallowed by a, being: period of terrific and terrifying introversion into madness.

swimming freely about: seek and bring to light your inner spiritual realization.

swordfish, angling a: a battle of elegance; the nobility of capture.

  eating: will gain riches by changing sources.

  offered: will be complimented by sincere friends.

tuna, eating: your lively independent mind needs to mediate out the fishy order.

  tinned: extreme shyness intermittent with bursts of outrage.

FISHING

09-12-29-35-39-47

angling: your ingenuity is needed to attain your ambition.

bait: are manipulating another to initiate the plan you want.

  fishhook, putting on a: will love those involved in a family dispute, to your opportunity.

  others putting out: disappointment with the advice you have given.

canal, in a: will realize high ambitions.

  pond: must rely on own good judgment.

  river: downstream, ideas can now be put into action.

  sea, the: be on the lookout over new horizons for treachery.

catching a fish: success for something recently begun.

  and it getting away: expect to find something you mislaid.

  but not: enemies cause risk to your health.

flounder, a: your project will flip-flop.

in your hands: are wasting your talents.

  small: ruin in proportion to size of fish.

  throwing it back: money will come to you another way.

deep-sea: will be alone and annoyed with interesting news.

enemies: your efforts to gain wealth will be stifled at every turn.

fisherman, of a: needs enlightenment for your properly employed emotions.

  being a: emotions are not being properly employed.

  in the company of a: unexpected fortune will take years to absorb.

  many: a large measure of prosperity awaits.

fishmonger, being a: can count on everyone's trust and support for new venture.

  scale, weighing in a: are short on initiative and bore those at work.

  unloading: mistake cannot be put right without major sacrifices.

harpooning: increased earning capacity enlarges home.

nets, with: will do business with a smart woman.

pearls: are in over your head with details.

rock from a, extracting a: will do anything for a compliment.

rod, a: your solution follows a circuitous route; keep fishing.

  casting a: someone is attracted to you from afar.

  throwing a: a close person is deceiving you; search for your own deceit within.

tackle: will discover lost valuables on your hook.

telling others of going: they will gossip about you.

trident, spearing a fish with a: will be sincerely loved in body, mind and spirit.

FISTS

14-30-31-38-41-45

children hitting with their: the selfish arrogance of insecurity.

clenched in front of your face: an ambush from one you thought was a friend.

against someone else: you hog the limelight, grasping for a sense of yourself.
double up a: aggressive tension can be
released in small degrees.
hitting someone with your: will enjoy a very
long friendship.
opening another's tight: your strength will
remove obstacles.
others fighting with: will have a delay in business.
using your: aggression, anger better left unexpressed.

FLAG
04-09-15-24-31-43
American, waving an: will perform a difficult
task with honor and dignity.
hoisting: may fight amongst yourselves,
but close ranks against any outside
attack.
black, a: your hostility will rupture confidence among friends.
brown: big friendship.
gold: will do business with people far
away.
green: good fortune in love affairs.
light blue: promotion within employment.
navy blue: will have prosperity through
others.
red: warning of quarrels with friends.
white: success in own undertakings.
yellow: important changes in your affairs.
carrying a: respect will come to you.
floating in the breeze: will escape from threatened misfortune.
half-mast, at: a calamity beyond normal
sympathy.
lowering a: regret your actions.
pole, a big: admiration for a victorious
soldier.
breaking a: hard work.
signaled with, being: failure to observe the
terms and conditions of your good name.
viewing a display of: triumph of your territorial imperative over enemies.

FLANNEL
04-10-24-27-35-42
of: hopes are temporarily being dashed.
suit, a: will have unpleasant events ahead.
wearing, underwear: sickness.

wrapping something in: are guilty of wrongdoing.

FLASH
14-17-27-36-39-46
buying a flashlight: are being watched by one
with evil intent; your light is within.
using: a secret will be solved; look
closely.
of light of a: cash in on your creativity; the
light will awaken it.
torch or searchlight, from a: news from
unknown part of yourself causes success.

FLASK
10-16-27-36-44-45
breaking a: losses.
drinking wine from a: troubles caused by
drinking too much.
others: be on guard against gossip.
empty, an: disappointment in love for your
petty-mindedness.
full of water: will be rich.
of a: will ignore your friends.
owning a: enjoyment.

FLATTERING
08-17-27-35-38-41
being flattered by others: their attention is false
and insincere.
fiancé: boasting about your wealth attracts
ill will.
friends: will experience many ups and downs
from boasting about your friendship.
others: will be defrauded by their ostentatious
behavior.
your mate: flaunting your talents is useless
without action.

FLEA MARKET
13-20-30-39-40-46
being at a: happiness in love.
buying things at a charity: high ambitions will
be realized.
selling, people: a proposal is received.
of a: will waste your luck and prosperity
on petty ventures.

FLEAS
03-14-18-20-25-43
bitten by a, being: bothersome, negative
people harass you over petty things.
catching a: one worry is over; more petty
annoyances to come.

children, being on: will entertain an unwelcome guest.

jumping: think before you leap into the deal.

killing a: will encounter obstacles for energies desiring revenge.

many: mind jumps too rapidly to accomplish your goal.

woman dreaming of: unhappiness if you enact your revenge on an inconsistent lover.

FLEEING
05-20-25-34-42-45

enemies, from: danger will be smoothed away in time.

friends: expect too many favors from others.

someone: irritation from close associates may cause you to exhibit your temper.

helping friends flee: your Good Samaritan act will be turned against you.

others: will be cheated by friends.

FLEET
10-12-18-27-37-42

anchored, an: contentment today, worries for another day.

merchant marine: brisk activity of commercial import.

naval, of a: will receive a letter from a loved one confirming rumors of foreign wars.

foreign: will entertain an unwelcome guest.

on maneuvers: will be victorious in any battle for contention.

in a parade: are being deceived.

FLIES
01-17-29-36-37-39

around food, being: a major worry at postponement of success.

bitten by a horsefly, being: disgrace and unpleasant sorrow is about to come.

wasp: will be persecuted by the envious, whom you have just terrorized.

catching: stop the gossip before it stresses you.

dog or cat, on a: goes with the territory.

firefly in the dark: will be repaid later.

killing: unable to avoid distasteful situations.

lover, on: will insinuate yourself ingeniously into lover's life.

many pesky: aggravating gossip from irritating close associates.

mouth, in the: unavoidable problems with impertinence.

of: will be annoyed by friends who can't keep their illness to themselves.

trap, a: facing quibbling predicaments will ward off larger issues.

FLIRTING
03-05-13-19-30-34

divorced person, with a: will realize own ambitions, short-term.

married woman: beware of treachery.

man: suitable time to pursue a courtship.

unmarried girl: will be pursued by the wrong man.

man: will be deceived; she has no money.

widow: financial gains.

widower: will be guilty of foolish actions.

others, with you: flaunting yourself brings ill-will.

FLOOD
04-07-11-26-39-44

being engulfed by rising water: overwhelmed by out-of-control, intense sorrow.

causing devastation: head out of bitterness to higher spiritual ground.

deluge, crops being lost in a: have the ability to stay on top of your sensitivities; use it.

of rain: an overwhelming release of emotions.

others being in: love affairs at this time are unfortunate.

flooded, being: will quietly retreat within yourself.

own home: a friend is trying to help you secretly.

land: worry will be smoothed away, if you stop the drain on your finances.

flooding house and ruining furniture: temporary illness to be replaced with love.

you out of own house: have not been able to express your emotions.

heavy rainstorm causing a: an overwhelming release of emotion.

of a big: will be jilted by lover when you have major financial worries.

others being in a: bothersome pleas and petitions.

relatives: their nature has gone on a
rampage.
outrun a, trying to: your anxieties must be
faced.
ruin caused by: are moved by passing feelings
instead of by inner purpose.
saving yourself from a: your one loyal friend is
hopeful and buoys you up.
tidal waves inundating town: in danger of
losing your head over a designing lover.
viewing much flooding: to be engulfed by
others' uncontrolled emotions.

FLOOR
29-31-33-35-38-47
arising from: affliction from being overpow-
ered by the gravity of material life.
dirty: feel morally degraded.
first: leave out foods from your diet that you
crave.
ground: take a walk in the morning before
work.
laying a tile: alliance that will bring an active
profit.
middle: check out that rasping in your
chest.
repaired, having the: have a delicate constitution from being trod upon.
sitting on the: are anxiously awaiting arrival of
an old acquaintance.
sleeping on the: will take journey you have
always wanted to take.
sweeping your: be cautious that the foundations laid are clear in your ventures.
upper: your third eye is not easily influenced.
washing the: have an untroubled frame of
mind.
wooden: sympathy is being reciprocated.

FLOUR
02-05-10-25-42-43
buying: will be making money.
clothes, on your: another's deception will
cause your mate to question your honor.
cooking with: a contented home, abundant
with comfort.
dealing in the, market: will make risky
speculations in your usual frugal life.
grinding: will share your wealth.
making pastries with: a happy life is ahead.

FLOWERS
10-16-19-40-41-43
acacia, smelling an: must control your
passions with chaste love.
allergy to flowers, child having: will be afflicted
with skin rashes.
pollen in the air: your dreams need to be
fertilized to be realized.
amaryllis: pride, a love affair that will transform you inside out.
artificial: are astonished at the exorbitant
price for services rendered.
aster, picking an: a long-awaited letter is
received; be true to the end.
azalea, receiving a bouquet of: your plan will
flourish, if you use temperance.
buying and planting: expect communication from long-lost friend.
beds: allow a cautious exposure of your
talents; success soon comes.
begonia, a: will receive criticism for your
ostentation, not your dark thoughts.
blooming: a new relationship with what is
latent within.
bluebells, a bouquet of: many are envious of
your constancy in love.
bud, a: a love relationship is germinating; be
patient.
holding in your hands: your love affair will
turn sinister.
bulb, a: the unfolding of the layers of toil, as
the flower is more able to fend for itself.
buttercup: precious childhood memories of
gaiety.
camellia, a: delicacy is reassuring; unpretend-
ing excellence is intense but short-lived
joy.
clematis: your mental beauty is suggesting
poverty before you reach prestige, lofty
goals.
cloudy sky, under a: hard work with little
reward; sorrow falls like a blanket.
columbine, having a: your youthful folly
obstructs your advancement.
cowslip, picking: a pensive winning grace
before the battle is on.
crocus, giving a bouquet of: do not abuse the
fresh naïvéte; mirth is not youthful glad-
ness.

cut: artificial emotions do not make an impression, nor do they last.

daffodils, growing in the garden: your chivalry will be held in high regard.

dahlias, in a vase: instability in financial affairs will settle down.

dandelions fluff blowing in the wind: time to fertilize and weed the lawn; heed its oracle.

dead: regret for unfulfilled ambition.

decorating yourself with: your relationship is deepening.

delivering: someone needs clarification of your intentions.

destruction of: expect respect for being in the wrong position at the right time.

florist's yard full of: seek out an oracle for guidance in love affairs.

forsythia on the lawn, yellow: joy will visit luxurious surroundings.

foxgloves, receiving a gift of: your insincerity makes you unfitted to fill your position.

fragrance, a pleasant: your lover will be impressed with your good taste.

   offensive, an: your recognition will be formalized in the face of slander.

fragrant: festivities of the young; enticing advice best left unheeded.

fuchsia, a: need a new teacher; have learned all you can from the last one.

gardenia, a: passionate embrace of intoxicating aromas.

garland, having a: hurdles can be jumped with flying colors.

gathering: good relations with future in-laws.

gentian, a: pleasures of life are in touch with the natural; yours are unjust.

geraniums: will be visited by a beloved person on a long stay.

giving a gift of: your passions must be controlled.

gladiolas: another's firing will give you added responsibility and compensation.

goldenrod, a: use precaution in meddling in other's concerns; encouragement only.

gorse, yellow: luck and prosperity.

hawthorn, smelling fragrant: with quick-sightedness you bring accord among friends.

heather, lying in a field of: simple pleasures in succession, lasting a lifetime.

heliotope, a: quiet devotion of a sensible love is secure in the future.

hollyhock, a: happiness is fertilized even in your present state of poverty.

honeysuckles being in flower: will move to a contented home and life with new neighbors.

hothouse, in a: an advantageous deal dependent on outside forces.

if in season: great disappointments ahead.

in the house: your sweet disposition will make the most out of every opportunity.

iris, a: peace and plenty with a faithful mate.

jonquil, yellow: will receive a passionate love letter.

juniper, eating blue berries of a: be cautious in all your dealings.

laburnum, of a: your forsaken demeanor has a bright yellow glow of pensive beauty.

lavender dried, amid the linen: exciting adventures surrounded with pleasure.

lotus blossoms: will be fortunate in gambling with an ecstatic romance.

magnolia, wearing a: will lose your heart to a Southerner.

marigolds to others, giving: grief cannot block your giving from your frugal side.

   receiving a bouquet of: will incur debts when you overspend unexpected money.

morning glory, a: an elegant, carefree, full energy climb to heaven.

neighbor's flowers in blossom: vulgar minds wish to influence your failure.

nosegay, being given a: debts will be incurred.

of: hopes will be short-lived blossoms; take this as a suitable time to pursue courtship.

oleander, fragrance of white: a blissful marriage.

out of season: your wishes are realized.

own, in blossom: danger because of a secret.

passion, smelling a: must control your sacrifice and sorrow to inherit wealth.

peonies: an annoying suitor; anxiety from a secret admirer.

petunia as a boutonniere: a drooping emotional life.

picking: big benefit from a steady friendship.

pink: lots of party favors and good eats.

primroses, picking: a small indication of inconstancy in your flourishing love affair.

purple, having: loss of own estate.

receiving a gift of: have a loyal admirer in love with you.

    from far away: will be an heir to a fortune.

    young woman dreaming of: will have many suitors.

red: dissolution of the family.

ripping up, plants: are the source of your own destruction.

roses: joy from an exquisite pleasure that's not fleeting.

smelling perfume of: enticing advice best left unheeded.

    scent of, coming from the yard, the: loss of friends.

throwing away: will suffer violent quarrels from own carelessness.

    trees in blossom, all sorts of: much recreation is enjoyed.

tiger lilies, a bouquet of: will be invited to a round of stupid boring parties.

tulips, gathering: will have a proposal of marriage.

    receiving: a recurring friendship that begins where it left off, no matter how long ago.

watering: care for your beauty.

water lilies, picking: an acquaintance will cause your desires to be out of reach.

    putting in a vase: your purity of heart will gain the confidence of others.

white: small difficulties.

wild: an adventure with the relaxed beauty of nature.

wilted, a: break off a dead-end relationship.

withered: many suitors, all after the wrong thing.

yard full of: will have weakness in your body.

yellow: big difficulties.

FLUSHING

04-05-11-18-39-48

boiler, a: fortune will arrive a little late.

of, the toilet: be on guard against spiteful gossip.

pipes: will fall into poverty and misery.

water from a sink: family unhappiness.

FLUTE

03-05-09-10-27-31

fife, having a: will be called to honorable duty in advancement within your position.

    others: others will attack your character; your staunch honor will remain intact.

of a: money will come easily through embarrassing situations.

played, hearing a: will take a trip to see a relative in the army.

playing the: harmony of the soul with your feelings.

    children: the expression of the spirit upon all of your faculties.

    others: difficulties from child in the offing.

FLYING

06-14-16-20-35-38

clouds, in the: overcompensation for lack of sexual experience.

free: an incentive to put others in your place.

high altitude, at a: are too conceited to dominate others and too confident to realize it.

    low: ruin is caused by your playing it too safe.

of: congenial work and last-minute action will bring acclaim.

off the handle: rage is good as long as you act it out alone and silently.

others: problems are dealt with, look out for hovering treachery.

out of control: low self-esteem, as you do not see ambitions realized.

over an abyss: a disembodied spirit looking over a detached body.

    in: equilibrium between your conscious and unconscious, on which you base your life.

skydiving: gain control; direct movement in time and space.

soaring: burdensome restrictions have lost their learning curve.

space, in: your behavior is insufferable and annoying; your foundations will crumble.

FOG

03-09-22-28-30-34

clearing away: your intuition clouds your judgment.

to sunshine: your introverted, mysterious personality needs airing.

dense: nebulous indicators of the direction to be pursued stall your business.

emerging from a: can no longer hide your intentions.

ground, moving into the sky: family concern will take patience and tact to overcome.

horn blasting, a: one direction giving speedy relief, another lacking clarity.

lost in a fog: don't ignore the rewarding empathy offered.

surrounded by pea soup: postpone decisions without sufficient data.

traveling through a: confounding suspicions lead you astray.

> *thick:* be over-careful not to allow your confusion to obscure your purpose.

FOLDING
01-06-18-36-45-46

clothes: will realize high ambitions.

household linen: your lack of commitment alienates love.

others, things: will succeed in your business.

something: a period where everything seems to go wrong.

FOLIAGE
02-03-04-11-12-47

brown: quarrels and broken engagements.

crown of, having a: big honors.

dead: undertakings will not succeed.

dry: sickness.

eating boiled: dissension within the family.

fallen, of: dangerous illness.

figs, of: people are envious of you.

grape: will lose your temper.

green: pleasures are in store for you.

FONT
03-33-34-40-43-47

filled with water in a garden: a change in life will soon come.

inside a sacred building: will be abandoned by lover.

of a spring: important and very beneficial events to come.

public park, in a: have one loyal friend.

FOOD
02-03-16-19-33-39

appetite, having a big: loss of relatives.

> *big feast, for a:* loss of money.
> *losing one's:* the need for satisfaction in some sphere sickens you.
> *small:* ill health ahead.

being supplied to you: their intentions are ambiguous.

boiling: much happiness will be yours.

buying: will have an average success.

casserole: use your pool of ideas.

cutting up: a successful completion of your project.

> *yourself:* affair will fail as you predicted.

eating: to absorb, understand and incorporate into your way of life.

> *cereal:* the beginning.
> *custard:* making a new and rather valuable friendship.
> *like a glutton:* hunger for affection, self-confidence and recognition.
> *many victuals:* one man's food is another's poison.
> *not being satisfied, and:* feeling of loneliness and emptiness.
> *others:* rapid success of own hopes.
> *that has gone bad:* loss of money that will be hard to bear.

foam created from cooking: will be surrounded with cheerful friends.

giving to charity: will have hard work ahead.

leftover: are accepting less than you deserve.

not having enough: painful arguments with partner.

nutrition plan for children: dignity and ambition.

of: happiness is nearby.

people selling: will receive some money.

porridge, eating: do not maintain friendships with those addicted to liquors.

rancid, animals eating: will endure persecution, but not slander.

> *buying, unknowingly:* an unknown enemy will cause much damage.
> *eating:* will have good health.
> *of:* will disregard a proposal of love.
> *throwing away:* will have misfortune for a short time.

serving, to others: social pleasure.

stew, a: life is quietly cooking.

supplying food to hotels and restaurants: riches.

tamales, eating: will be asked to go on a hunting or fishing trip.

tasting the flavor of: petty annoyances of situations that are never finished.

FOOLISH
15-18-27-29-37-46

actions, having committed: don't take yourself so seriously.

   others committing: joy without profit.

     children: will receive money soon.

folly, fool's: experience you do not understand, but enough to make use of.

lover being: mend your ways, laugh at yourself.

playing the: kicking yourself for mistakes doesn't solve the negatives.

two engaged people: both will suffer from their foolishness.

youthful: knowledge you have not yet applied.

   mate: the use of mate's ideas will bring financial gains.

FOOTBALL
08-23-24-32-46-48

fullback, being a: be on guard against unscrupulous men.

game, winning a: future is secured.

   not scoring in: someone did not pass you the ball.

   others scoring in: a friend will refuse to be part of the team.

gridiron, a: success requires calling the right plays.

playing: good business ventures.

   children: a friend is trying to help.

   husband: triumph over enemies.

watching a, game: may expect worries from quickly found friends.

FOOTPRINTS
06-09-19-22-28-41

animals, of: unfulfilled ambition, rightly so.

   children: will surmount difficulties.

   man, a: use caution with your stern, unbending personality.

   others: a friend is secretly trying to help you.

   woman, a: rapid success in a difficult but important victory.

in front of you: follow the pathway presented to you.

own: appreciate the positive process and what you have gained.

FOOTSTEPS
13-27-33-36-42-43

following another's: have limited your ambition to a half-life.

neighbor's home, of a: a foundation for communication.

own house, of: your mental sense blocks your sense of balance.

stepping up on a: have committed yourself to great success; live up to it.

   down from a: will hear good news.

FOOTSTOOL
09-25-27-28-39-44

hassock, of stuffing a: are ceding your strength and will to another.

   feet on a, having: a gathering of young people from many origins.

   praying: beware of rivals.

of an empty ottoman: warning of troubles; if you foster your strong-willed independence.

sitting on an ottoman alone: an enemy is seeking your ruin.

   children: peace after a period of distress.

   friend, a: hard work awaits you.

   husband: have a great deal of willpower to triumph over enemies.

   loved one, a: danger in love matters.

   with a dog: have faithful friends.

FORCE
14-21-25-35-42-45

against a prisoner, using: despair.

   others: your hopes will be realized.

forcing others to do your will: allow others to dominate you.

   safe, open a: will buy an old-fashioned safe.

police: your accountant must be supervised.

using great strength to, something: strictures to which your nature cannot comply.

FOREHEAD
04-06-23-26-29-33

fine, having a: will attain power through your wise judgment and integrity.

   large: will enjoy high spirits and intelligence; use them to the advantage of all.

ugly: vexation as your detachment does not lead to truth.

wounded: will discover an unknown treasure from a venture indiscreetly conducted.

of others: will receive sincere admiration for the quality of your friendship.

FOREIGN COUNTRY
04-26-29-31-34-46

alone, being in: searching for a part of your heritage to change your life.

lady, with a: will be guilty of foolish actions.

loved one: luck and prosperity.

man: must control passions.

others: will have new business ventures.

going to a: déjà vu; a return momentarily to a life past, lived into the present.

FOREST
09-10-26-27-39-40

alone, being in a: social activities are no substitute for a relationship.

others, with: will be cheated by friends, breaking a solemn promise.

relatives: be attentive to physical symptoms that are hereditary.

edge of the forest, the: a risky love affair is over; a comfortable refuge found.

fire: expect savage behavior from otherwise civilized people.

going around the: avoiding your shadow still brings sad news.

lost in the, getting: project succeeds by working your way out of the dark.

of a dense: your unshakable faith will attract supportive people.

ranger: homesickness in the throws of Mother Nature.

strolling through a: puzzling and disturbing message dredges up a past wrong.

unusually high trees, with: unresolved emotions need to be aired.

wandering around in a: so many experiences, so little time.

FORGET-ME-NOTS
28-29-34-37-42-44

giving, as a remembrance: important and beneficial event coming.

having: someone's past neglect is still with you.

of: are beloved and remembered by many.

receiving a bouquet of: a faithful friend loves you despite your neglect.

as a gift: big gain in love if you forgive.

FORGETTING
24-32-37-40-41-49

date, a: are causing another a disappointment in love.

elders, your: the source of your feeling abandoned is your rejection of your roots.

forgotten, being: sense a well-hidden resentment toward you.

loved one, a: your feelings of neglect are from your childhood.

mail a letter, to: are afraid that you will receive news that you have been forgotten.

of: business will not improve by obliterating the opposition.

pay a bill, to: refuse to pay back for a happy childhood you didn't have.

FORKS
01-15-22-23-38-47

cooking with: probe the root of the parasites causing big family quarrels.

dropping your: resolve the conflict that distracts you from your goal.

eating with a: happiness is assured after the battle.

guests: reconciliation with an enemy is impossible.

of: probe the root of big family quarrels.

receiving a gift of: doomed for disappointment.

road, in the: take the road that you and you alone decide should be traveled by you.

stabbing yourself with a: be wary of someone's desire to deceive you.

someone else: another is shamelessly exploiting you; leave your position.

FORT
11-18-22-26-42-45

being in a: avoid the hostility of rivals, but not the demands of life.

with others: will forgive someone in disgrace, as you have forgiven yourself.

blockade, a: hunger within boundaries if you erect barriers against life.

command of a, being in: increasing responsibility, with the salary to match.

destroyed, a: a past memory is the source of your lack of self-worth.

fortress, living in a: are protected as long as you stay home; is that all you want?

    looking from a: venturing out from overprotection to heal constructively.

    unable to open the lock of a: are deliberately erecting barriers against life.

    under siege: high morale and optimism that the cavalry will come.

honored when entering a, being: your selfabsorption blocks out relationships.

mines, surrounded with: a prickly fear of danger behind the facade.

of a: protect yourself from the troubles and losses in store for you.

under construction: time is of the essence to quell the state of fatigue.

FORTUNE
05-07-24-33-34-35

being fortunate in business: gay occasion to come.

fortune-teller, being a: trust in your first impression.

from relatives, receiving a: success in everything.

    love: will lose plenty of money through gambling.

    politics: will have a steady position.

reading a, on a spinning wheel: beware of danger.

receiving a: trouble and losses.

telling another's: special activities of a happy nature.

told, having own: great struggle in real life.

told to others, hearing a: have a loyal friend.

FOSSILS
15-25-28-29-32-42

called a, being: perk up, your laziness might cost you your job.

digging, from the earth: will hear of the illness of someone.

many qualities of: a mystery will be solved.

possessing: will meet an old friend.

FOUNTAIN
16-20-34-41-47-49

clear water, being at a, of: rejuvenate your talents; make them sparkle and shine.

high sprays, with: an unusually uplifting event will happen soon.

littered: an intellectualized examination of self misses the point.

muddy: good luck to come later.

sweetheart, with a: great happiness in love and success in marriage.

dry: period of frustration, desolation and cessation of joy.

full: self-expression is the key to happiness and long life.

large: sexual emotion overflowing in an illadvised assignation.

life, of: the fertile powers of rebirth, eternal life.

pen, a: have literary aspirations of an intellectualized examination of life.

sacred, of a: devotion will bring success.

sunlight, a, playing in the: pleasantries from a multitude of sources.

washing yourself at a: your joy and love will be reciprocated.

    drying: poverty or death.

youth, of: pamper yourself to renew your love.

FOWL
01-15-20-31-35-44

beautiful bird: will stand erect with head high in any group.

of domestic: will enjoy eventful life without ups and downs.

giblets, cooking: listen to sound advice based upon common sense.

many: considerable earnings will assuage your anxiety temporarily.

owning a: will receive a favor from an unknown person.

FOX
05-07-30-38-40-43

beautiful coat, with a: beware of the deceit of seductive charms.

buying a: be on close lookout for other's potentially dangerous activities.

catching a, in a trap: will uncover a clandestine relationship.

children playing with a baby: people are abusing your kindness.

hunt, participating in a: are being outmaneuvered; step back and redirect.

killed, a, being: will overcome the threat of a clever foe.

killing a: success in undermining a quick-witted opponent.

many: enemies are inventive in their sneakiness.

of a: an enemy's rival is among your acquaintances.

sly, a: a crafty enemy will subtly amaze you.

surprising a: beware of baseness and trickery on the part of thieves.

tame: your love will not be misplaced and betrayed.

terrier, a: put your hyperactive nervousness to work in the stock market.

FRAGILE
01-05-15-16-29-39

breaking something: hopes will not be realized. *mailing:* happiness.

receiving a, gift: will make resolutions to form your beauty into consciousness.
  that is broken: your vulnerability has been breached by a caring friend.

FRAUD
07-12-15-16-26-40

being defrauded: big treachery will expose your foes and gain you honors.
  others, by: enemies try in vain to cause loss of your reputation; will lose it yourself.
  relatives, by: deception in love; will not lose your ability to give and feel love.

committing: your lies will be uncovered; your indulgence in pleasures will degrade you.

defrauding others: lose a too-trusting friend for a bit of money and a lot of vengeance.
  catching someone in the act of: gossip about you has become nasty.

FRECKLES
23-28-29-35-37-40

all over the body, having: your vices will be uncovered before you can cover them up.

children having: discovery of an enemy who has insinuated himself into your life.

face being covered with: unpleasant discovery about a friend becoming a rival for lover.

looking at own in a mirror: loss of a lover whom you had only in your heart.

FREEZING
10-14-21-31-39-47

being cold: will be compensated for having a kind heart.

coat on, without a: must attempt to regain stolen things.

feet: are slipping out of control.

hands: acquisition of doubtful benefit.

others: are painfully unfeeling to others.

things, in a refrigerator: will receive false information through lack of communication.

FRENCH
07-09-13-18-28-45

being a, man: are undecided in business matters.

divorcing a, woman or man: will go to prison.

going to France: own future is uncertain.
  sightseeing in: your resolutions are wise; be determined about them.

Jacobin society member, of a: an abundance of love.

marrying a man: must control passions to enjoy exuberance.
  woman: will have plenty of clothes and linens.

nationality, being of: danger through a secret.

speaking: success in love affairs.

FRIDAY
10-15-19-26-29-36

Good: will have prosperity in the family.
  attending church on: must bring domestic affairs into order.

of: dignity and honor.

things to happen on following: will be falsely accused.

FRIENDS
13-19-31-32-34-41

accosted by: expect to receive a legacy soon.

apologizing to: a former friend returns with all of the relatives.

apology from a, receiving an: a change of companionship without changing the friend.

apprehension over: too many favors are expected; too little returned that you need.

approached by, being: a legacy of the dishonor perpetuated in edgy affairs.

arrival of a: an ebullient act in flaming colors making a statement you don't wish to hear.

bashful, having: listen to the one who does not form his opinions on a whim.

compatible relationship with a: emotions balanced with an even-tempered, staunch friend.

  chagrined: rely on own judgment about involving yourself in their questionable activities.

  troubled: sickness is near at hand over the alienation of a long-time associate.

laughing with: will dissolve your partnership with others but retain this friend.

lost the friendship of, having: painful experiences will cause you to move.

making new: a projected quality you did not realize you possessed.

meeting a: think before you take action against an affront; is the argument with it?

  at an alehouse: interests beyond present pursuits and surroundings of more distinction.

parting from a: will have a life of vexation as annoyance at petty acts controls you.

spending the night with: are not as abandoned as you think.

taking advantage of you: will seek changes in the relationship, or not at all.

trouble, in: will receive unexpected good news.

FRIGHTENED

04-09-17-18-22-23

being: an announcement will please you.

  badly: great success if you take a vacation first.

  children, by: will prosper with perseverance; your fears are temporary.

  your sleep, in: will discover a secret.

frightening others: a change in life from suffering serious reverses.

FROGS

03-07-21-28-37-40

being given: will receive an unexpected strange inner power.

buying, in a store: will meet people who admire your cold-bloodedness.

catching: a self-inflicted injury when leaping from pillar to post.

dissecting a: get to the crux of the problem with learning and resolution.

eating: don't create an excuse for others to gossip.

hearing, croaking: pleasure awaits if you ask for it; be specific who shares it.

killing: many sincere friends are concerned about you.

tadpole, of a: your transformation has begun; fate is smiling on you.

watching: looking to escape a situation, but it keeps escaping you.

water, in: your reputation blends in with the crowd.

woman seeing a bullfrog: marriage with wealthy widower with children.

FROST

12-20-22-23-24-28

covered landscape: stop mourning the unworkable; the pleasures were masochistic.

damaging your plants: have closed doors to your emotions.

frostbite, having: a misunderstanding will exile you where you can be at peace.

  of: your desires endanger your health and put any possibility of love in jeopardy.

melting under the sun: your behavior may fool friends; past indiscretions do not.

of a: your energies are too immobilized to travel abroad.

thick: stay within own position, as you are restricted from any other.

windowpanes, on: an ennobling experience of emotional dependency.

FROWNING

04-19-23-31-42-43

children: advancement within own position.

friends: misfortune in own affairs.

of: confrontation with an officer of the law.

others: confidence will break down if pressure is brought to bear.

FRUIT

16-19-21-32-43-45

avocado, eating an: will be loved by many but love only one.

basket, offering a: fear your lover's rejection; will be reaping what you have sown.

berries, of: social activities of a happy nature are enjoyed.

buying: misfortune in love affairs.

> *currants, buying dry:* a surprising proposal for your future career.

cantaloupe, eating: warning to watch your diet or you will have stomach disorders.

damson plum, eating a: troubles caused by false companions.

display at market: transactions will attract your business.

eating: a luscious love, a prosperous present and uncertain future.

> *dried:* missed your chance.
>
> *mixed:* an argument will be resolved to your satisfaction.
>
> *rotten:* your lover leaves you fulfilled.
>
> *sour:* stimulate from within to solve what overhasty actions have blocked without.
>
> *sweet:* powerful creative period.
>
> *unripe:* plans are premature; your health will suffer.
>
> *wild:* unfortunate speculation upsets the cart, allowing smaller sources to be able to buy.

grapefruit: being drawn in too many directions to ensure your ability to succeed in any.

huckleberries, eating: a slight illness from unsanitary handling of your food.

jelly, making: accept the invitation to the neighborhood party.

mango, eating a: delays and annoying obstacles impede your project.

marmalade, making: even the sourest experiences can come out sweet.

> *eating alone:* preserve the labor of love amidst untrue friends.

mulberries: a bitter disappointment; will comfort others and not be given comfort.

out of season: struggles and unpleasant things to contend with.

peeling: must extricate yourself from a difficult situation.

picking: experience gained will support positive changes to the relationship.

> *off the ground:* adverse efforts turn to fruition.

wild: rapid success, even quicker loss, and desperate attempts to regain plan.

pineapple, slicing: will receive a social invitation of dubious value.

> *eating:* an overdose of nutrition you can live longer with.

preserves, making: recent practical successes denote many sales with little profit.

prunes: obstacles and trials that will clear in a short time.

> *eating:* creative blockage undone.

selling: are trying too hard to win favor, to sell at the right stage of ripeness.

FRYING
03-21-26-27-31-47

chicken: will live a long life.

eggs: forget your reservations; take a vacation from your lover.

fish: are gambling with the future.

food for a party: your enthusiasm turns into an unfortunate quarrel.

of: will be taken care of during old age.

potatoes: forget the malicious gossip, will be loved dearly by someone new.

FUN
18-28-30-33-41-47

expense of others, at the: losses.

friends: change for the better.

having lots of: rapid success of own hopes.

important people: honor and happiness.

others having: money will come easily during life.

relatives: happiness in various matters.

with children, having: doomed for disappointment.

FUNERAL
06-08-34-44-47-48

attending a best friend's: support but do not ignite the situation.

> *brother or sister's:* prosperous days ahead.
>
> *clothed in black:* are assuming too great a burden of responsibility.
>
> *enemy's, an:* scandal and underhanded practices.
>
> *friend's:* embarrassment in affairs.
>
> *mate's:* profound shift in emotional stability.
>
> *mother or father's:* are expecting an inheritance.

relative's: death of a friend.

yours: letting go of past and accepting what it taught you.

bier, lying in a: sad rites performed in dismal surroundings.

friend: advancement in own position.

relative: will receive a legacy.

black colors at a: ominous and unpleasant news will arrive soon.

casket, ordering own: will be married soon.

close friend to a cemetery, accompanying a: riches and fortune cannot replace lost love.

coffin and its litter, of a: will adorn the casket of a friend.

condolences, expressing: sickness.

receiving: death through fortune.

eulogizing at a: your hypocrisy will defeat you ultimately.

family to a, going with: congenial family turns sour over loss of a friend.

loved one, a: are envied by enemies.

hearse conveying the dead: worries smoothed away when bitter enemy is overcome.

at the church: prepare, old habits die hard.

driving a: increased responsibilities lead to a sudden trip.

laughing at a: your past has caught up with you.

someone: others are too involved in your life.

your: are unwilling to be released from the past.

mortuary, being in a: difficult period from which you will emerge triumphant.

mourning, attending a woman in: unhappy married life.

others to a, going with: good health.

own, attending: riches, happiness, legacies and a brilliant marriage.

pallbearer at a, being a: will do something foolish.

procession, accompanying a: involved in approaching change.

unknown person to a cemetery: your mother controls your life.

pyre, building your own: have breached your ethics.

rainy during a: those absent will have an adverse fate.

shroud covering the body: lack of perseverance and cohesive thought toward others.

sunny during a: the sunny relations will be in good stead financially.

FUR

04-15-16-23-24-32

covered with, being: being reclusive will ensure your health.

owning a, coat: protection from the cold winds of want.

fox: treachery by friends who are envious of your success.

mink: people are being false to you; you are being evil toward them.

sable: your ethics are not properly appreciated.

skunk: some man will fall in love with you.

worn, a: singled out for honors from well-thought-out ideas.

possessing: are wasting time on risky adventures.

rabbit: multiple children will give you credit.

raccoon: will go back for a higher degree.

receiving a, coat as a gift: make yourself approachable for a marriage of sorts.

stole, of a priest: will be frightened by a ghost and have remorse of conscience.

selling a: someone is attempting to cause damages to you.

wearing a: are attempting to hide wrongdoings.

FURIOUS

09-11-31-35-39-47

person, being a: will be compatible.

an exceptionally: people are gossiping against you.

woman being: jealousy over your lover.

children: are disliked by your neighbors.

man: unhappiness in love affairs.

others: are hated by people.

two beloved people: joy and long happiness.

FURNACE

26-27-29-31-36-44

blast, a roaring: rapid advancement is intricately sloped, worthy only of sideways moves.

dead fire, with a: your physical potency is cooled; help, even hired, will be lost.

burning: present your new idea, but keep control of its patent.

lighting a: troubles caused by own children, who wish to overpower you.

> *someone else:* your servants are not faithful; you picked ones incapable of it.

putting out a: your emotional energy is restrained by your logic.

FURNITURE

07-16-17-23-27-30

armchair: whoever uses it most frequently exercises his slanderous tongue.

beautiful: productive work on solid objects brings innocent well-being.

breaking: quarrels within the home.

bulky, business girl dreaming of having: will earn own living.

chest, having a big: will overextend your credit for treasures unearned.

> *empty, an:* are too overwhelmed with hiding ideas to nurture them in peace.

> *full:* the possibilities are endless; pick one at a time.

> *small:* you want little in life and will get it.

common: will be a person of the working class.

common person dreaming of nice: the method you have picked to define yourself.

ebony: will accomplish intuition through diligent work.

favorite piece of your: encouraging news regarding feasibility of plan.

Jacobean furnishings, of: will enjoy a quiet life.

mahogany: will inherit the estate of a distant relative.

maple: pleasant extended family connections and reunions.

table, break a marble: changing your mind on a tricky question will bring good luck.

wealthy woman having nice: will do something foolish.

FUTURE

03-05-20-23-26-40

of own: patch up old quarrels, relive losses and build on that clarity.

own, not being good: an assessment of damage from injurious toxic prodigality.

own children's: in defense against your subdued adolescent behavior as an adult.

G   G   G   G   G

GABLE

01-14-24-34-44-46

many, house of: each gable tells an adventure story.

of a: good advice will be given to you.

of others' homes: warning of trouble.

window, being at the: will lead to good fortune.

window of own home, the: discovery of lost valuables.

GAIETY

04-12-20-37-46-48

being in a place of: advancement within own position.

enjoying, with your mate: good times are coming.

> *lover:* danger in love matters.

of having: big catastrophe is ahead.

GAIN

11-18-19-28-30-46

being a dandy: your lack of concern for your appearance left you in an inferior position.

making a big, a: misfortune in love affairs.

> *by cheating:* shame and sorrow.

> *through gambling:* will have good friendship.

> *using unfair advantages:* recovery from an illness.

real-estate, making a: will be fed well during life.

successful business: a big catastrophe is ahead.

GALLANT

02-07-24-31-32-38

being, to a lady: satisfaction and good health.

dandy, being a: your lack of concern for your appearance creates your inferior position.

man being, to a young unmarried lady: inconsistency in love.

> *widow, to a:* good results in business affairs.

married woman being, to a man: good fortune in business.

GALLERY

10-15-20-24-28-44

being in a: a merry chase will lead you to a crescendo of financial gains.

commercial: fortune in business affairs.

falling from a: family quarrels.

of a: a false friend is attempting to bring harm to you.

paintings, of: an old and desirable acquaintance will be renewed.

GALLOWS
01-09-15-20-33-49

building: unexpected constructive changes stay the execution of emergency decisions.

die on the, having to: much suffering until you obtain an honorable position.

hanging on the: lynching by a man your actions made angry.

  another: your adversary will soon say "uncle"; victory in all spheres.

  relative: will be persecuted if your petty crime is uncovered.

  someone you know: dispense with some bad habit before it is found out.

of a: major adjustments on your part are needed for you to acquire happiness.

public: ultimate condemnation of your action or thought.

GAMBLING
06-08-25-26-27-47

baccarat: a succession of tormented situations, some serious.

blackjack, playing: be wary of being tempted into losing your temper.

bookmaker: careful of a rapacious friend whose advice is selfish.

cards, with: are taking unwarranted chances with loss of prestige.

  checkers: feel you cannot make your own choices unless they are limited.

  chess: are wasting your time; life itself is the most challenging game.

  dice: guidance, not the roll of the dice, is your aim.

casino, in a: the people involved aren't any clearer than you are.

cheated in a game: are confronted with insurmountable obstacles.

checking numbers: your appetites will create enemies.

children playing childish, games: fortune in own affairs, but selfishness to others.

craps: will use immoral means to obtain money.

friend and winning, with a: loss of a beloved one to his obsessions.

  losing: other tries to wring money out of you with a cunning deal.

gambler, a: affairs will divert your attention in an illegitimate direction.

handling chips: will collect money soon; be prepared for its power.

  playing with: will win a wager, but business success will be postponed.

    making a bet: do not allow others' opinions to influence you.

    others cheating in: are taking unwarranted chances with your life.

having been cheated in: use caution in engaging in new business affairs.

losing a bet: your acting on your imagined weakness makes you weak.

losing at: will be relieved of the pains of living beyond your means.

lost, having: enemies are trying to divert your attention from their misdeeds.

lottery, winning the: enemies are distracting you with false hopes.

making a bet: do not trust your own opinion against the pros.

of: immoral devices will be used to wrestle money out of you.

pinball machine, at a: are tempted to fight with the enemy.

roulette, at: your careless lifestyle results in vain hopes.

  losing at a: will receive money from an elderly person.

  people gambling at a: are tempted to fight with an enemy.

  table, of a: will have arguments with a friend.

  winning at a: will prove your innocence to others.

selling: are deluding yourself that someone loves you.

slot machine, at a: doomed for disappointment.

spinning wheel, at a: are waging against calculated yet overwhelming odds.

wager, accepting a: are very confused in your thinking.

　losing a: will acquire wealth dishonorably.

　making a: are uncertain of what you are doing.

　winning a: act cautiously and fortune will smile upon you.

GAMES
02-10-12-30-37-44

acrostic composition in verse: don't make hasty decisions.

　completing an: realization of speculations.

　　betting on outcome of a: are involved in a risky, uncertain matter.

　　bingo, playing: don't gamble a huge amount on your dream being accurate.

　　bull's-eye, hitting a: attunement of actions to your ideals.

　missing a: will have rivals in love affairs.

　　not: will be jilted by a lover.

　others: be careful to whom you give your confidence.

checkers, playing: serious disagreements with strangers.

　winning at: will accomplish a superb plan whose basis will become questionable.

children playing: your delusions will make you very unhappy.

　blindfolded: are being deceived.

　hopscotch: simple pleasures provide hours of entertainment.

cribbage, losing: important decisions need to be made to avoid troubles.

　watching a: your advice will be sought.

　winning: will escape present danger.

dominoes, playing: will have a small triumph in a large-scale competition.

　losing while: will be offered a useless article that you refuse to buy.

　winning: happiness is assured.

　loved one, with a: unhappiness in love.

jigsaw puzzle: a broken engagement that can eventually be mended.

keeper, a: will lead a pleasant, well-mannered existence, spiritually and financially.

　billiard balls, with: unstable relations with the opposite sex.

darts: have great ambition to score a hurtful thought.

　falling short of a bull's-eye: undreamed-of success followed by failure.

losing: are gaining the upper hand over enemies.

　others: worry will be smoothed away.

　　winning while: misfortune in business; hopes are not being realized.

　by a wide margin: differences with your elders.

playing, in general: heated arguments with those close you.

raffle, buying a ticket for a: cannot always predict results of your actions.

shuffleboard, playing: financial improvements.

whist, losing a game of: will have arguments with friends.

　winning: will receive a better position.

　　watching others: change in environment.

GANG
10-12-14-18-19-52

being in a: lack of initiation caused by submission to a stronger rule.

　head of a: income based on ability to intimidate others.

　threatened by a: unrest and calamitous period ahead, if you accept intimidation.

gangster: easy money, even easier death.

　captured by a: torture is mental; distress can be turned to positive action.

wanting out of a: great will erases despondency and rebuilds your ambitions.

GANGRENE
03-11-13-30-43-46

having: are being confronted with clawing dependents draining you.

　others in family: you choice to retrieve and to return a favor of love.

own leg being cut off because of: your handicap forces you to push above previous limits.

　another's: disloyal friends malign you to others, yet in need you will support them.

GANGWAY
04-21-25-28-30-35

coming down the: social disgrace and disadvantageous industry in every realm.

others: loss of friends' confidence.

crossing a: will receive hostility from a rival.

going up the, of a ship: a transition out of a difficult past into an adventure.

    others crowding to be: turn back, don't change; make the best of the status quo.

    sailors or officers being on a: being restrained by your environment.

GARAGE
22-30-31-37-40-48

burning, a: congenial work and good news.

empty, an: either husband or wife is cheating on the other.

full of cars: an older person will surmount difficulties for you.

    old, in disrepair: will gain only by cooperating with another.

of a: affairs will take a turn for the better in near future.

putting a car in the: money will come easily during life, if you go in search of it.

GARBAGE
01-27-34-42-47-48

being dumped on you: another who is cheap and trashy causes your burden.

can, picking up a: are being aided in your disposal of excess.

falling into: reassess your assumptions, fertilizer is decayed garbage.

    over: honor your painful past emotions; each is a seed to a bright future.

surrounded by, being: rid yourself of deep-seated irritation, your own sordidness.

trash: separate out what is emotional garbage and what is recyclable.

truck: past actions are foisted back on you, to dispose of yourself.

GARDEN
03-14-29-31-33-37

barren, a: have serious intentions for your project to succeed.

beautiful, a: the growth of perennial ideas and habitual emotions.

beautiful flowers, with: imminent matrimony; it takes time to grow a life.

composting vegetables: your energies can be remolded, regurgitated and reused.

digging up a: will uncover unwanted materials; discard those you cannot reverse.

disorderly and dirty: will go into bankruptcy: your soul's.

Eden, of the, of: a suitable time to pursue an affair; an inauspicious time to consummate it.

fenced in: are in denial because you cannot accept the vulnerability of your true feelings.

friend's: your social life is too organized, leaving no time for openness.

neglected: spiritual matters need to be fertilized; nothing grows without love.

neighbor's: will have prosperity and expansion of the family.

overgrown: will weed remorse for what you failed to do.

planting seeds: ideas nurtured with a well-planned controlled attitude will grow.

relative's: success in spite of present difficulties; in a crunch, blood is your only support.

ruined by weather: period of confusion with no time for idle pleasure.

    insects: are behaving in an irrational and irritable way; redirect your energy.

taking care of a: increasing security through a positive constructive life.

trees, full of: your support and help are needed by an old acquaintance.

walking in a: your work is your wish fulfillment for pure decorousness and contented mien.

watering flowers in a: expect too many favors from others.

well-kept: well-handled advantageous deals are productive.

working in the: a good harvest of congenial activities and the fruits of your labors.

    with a pickax: have not begun to dig deep enough.

GARDENER
20-35-37-41-45-48

another person's: are communicating on a deep level with a friend in trouble.

being a: are having problems with someone you love.

not taking care of a garden: remove decay and debris to facilitate growth.

of a: present activities will soon make you rich.

of own garden, being the: how you cultivate or neglect the possibilities in your life.

pruning trees: remove the unwanted growth to allow what you want, to be.

GARLIC
06-09-12-15-29-48

buying: against what irritation do you need protection?

cooking with: are disliked by those working under you.

eating: recovery of your health, which you thought you had lost.

giving children, to eat: will realize high position through repelling deleterious forces.

growing in a garden: people detest you; those with evil intent, even more.

hanging: protection from those who wish you ill.

of: discovery of the secret to robust health.

people who don't like: are unfitted to fill your position.

seasoning with: your system will repeatedly say thank you.

GARRET
02-29-30-38-42-44

being in a public: advancement in position will come soon.

living in a: your intellect is pristine but incomplete without emotion.

of own house, being in the: happiness was assured in past easier circumstances.

of this watchtower: gains through pure intent and unselfish commitment to true knowledge.

writing in a: are living totally in your head, for which you will gain truth.

GARTERS
07-08-25-30-39-49

bride, pulling a, off your: can no longer take foolish chances.

falling down: are on thin ice, which threatens to break.

loosening: loose morals must meet with your disproval.

lost, being returned: your future will hang in the polls of public opinion.

losing: will have a jealous lover who finds suspicious data everywhere.

not: will realize high ambitions toward a lover and low expectations in love.

someone picking up your: will have a loyal friend in the betrayal of multitudes.

woman giving her, to a man: a token of eternal faithfulness through all adversity.

GAS
14-17-21-24-26-29

asphyxiated by: guard against double cross of your own intentions.

benzene, the smell of: stay cool and don't light any fires until you find the toxic source.

buying: need a vacation from your disadvantageous opinions of others.

log, a: a convivial gathering of artificial hopes.

mask, a: creditors will find you behind your disguise.

meter, a: disentangle yourself from receipt of another's bill.

of: harmful thoughts insinuate evil masquerading as spirituality.

of petroleum: danger of family trouble and source of energy.

others buying: expression of emotions under pressure.

running out of: low sexual energy and a struggling competency.

selling: rapid success in business bringing dispute with business associates.

smelling: keep to your own business and call the gas company.

station: recharge your batteries, refuel and fill up your tires.

stove, lighting a: slow, steady commitment to progress.

GAS LAMP
16-19-40-42-43-45

already lit: passion and loss of hope in love.

decorative: people are telling you lies about the source of their subsidy.

of others: good love affairs and domestic happiness.

flame, blowing out a: are being destroyed by your own negative thoughts.

   being low: your interests will suffer from oppressive ill luck.

   lighting a: threats avoided by surreptitiously allowing enemies to foil themselves.

going out suddenly: business will come to a standstill; expect a catastrophe.

soot from a: a forced error could lord over it truth.

GATE
04-05-07-16-19-40

broken: your favorite engrossing endeavors will fail to pay for themselves.

closed: are oppressed with difficulties that only climbing the fence will alleviate.

locking a: various business affairs can no longer be ignored.

of a: are very much in love and wish to contain it.

of others, the: opportunities to participate in other's projects.

open: others welcome your visit and offer opportunities.

opening of a: time to move forward.

others being at your: untrue friends lead a sparkling social life; don't join them.

passing through a: will be shocked with receipt of bad news.

GATHERING
02-13-22-24-38-46

former classmates, of: slow and difficult ascent to popularity.

love letters: a secret opinion weighs heavily on your conscience.

others' things: postponement of success until trials are overcome.

various things, of: will be used, then abandoned by your love.

GAUNTLET
13-14-16-26-29-35

flinging down the: arguments fail; arbitration leads to a future.

running the: must accept criticism and responsibility for each wrong.

take up the: will accept challenge to defend ally.

throw down the: your protection in battle.

GEESE
14-23-30-35-41-46

eating a stuffed goose: good fortune with golden eggs.

   others: great joy is yours.

flying: will take an extensive journey with friends; a pleasant but unprofitable pursuit.

plucking: your friends forget you in your unworthiness; will return with your inheritance.

quacking: a death within the family circle will improve your present circumstances.

swimming: fortune will decrease through foolishness and increase with sensible actions.

wild: misfortune at sea if not watchful; possessions left at home will be sold at auction.

GEMSTONES
01-05-17-29-35-38

amethyst, buying: will be jilted after lover conceives of contentment in intellectual fancy.

   aquamarine: having the affection of a youthful friend.

   bloodstone: will love one friend and gain a better one.

   lapis lazuli: sensibility, physical vitality.

buying: the untouchable center of your soul has been reached by another.

fake, of a: malicious gossip is circulating about you.

losing: unexpected good fortune.

opal: purification through survival of peril.

putting, around the neck: an unexplainable happening will delight you.

receiving a gift of a: danger through a secret causing your depression.

relatives having: sickness within the family.

selling a: disappointment in love leads to disposal of all gifts; misfortune in all affairs.

wearing a: are comfortable with your importance to the giver.

   blue: an unexpected, hopeful message.

   others: discovery of lost valuables within the reaping of the harvest.

   red: a romance as you see it.

violet: are filled with peace.

yellow: avail yourself of a multi-
   dimensional opportunity.

zircon, selling a: your friendship is badly
   placed; they will be ungrateful.

GENERAL

01-08-22-24-39-40

army, being an: demand obedience of yourself; mobilize your will.

artillery, being an: your arrogance has become
   dangerous.

being a: honors for performing a clandestine
   task.

friend being promoted to: sponsorship from a
   high official indicates your energy level.

marching in a parade: use caution in your
   ventures, an incentive to grow.

GENTRY

11-13-20-33-36-47

being with the: a change in life will soon
   come.

country girl dreaming of the: will work in a
   large city soon.

lady: will marry a nobleman from abroad.

courted by women of high class, being: misery
   and wrongdoings.

GEOGRAPHY

24-27-30-42-45-46

book, of a: your love will be refused by someone.

buying a, book: present worries are needless;
   foreign travel is imminent.

studying: be very cautious in everyday
   affairs, that you don't enact your mind's
   explorations.

   children: will be afflicted with minor pains
      from time warp and jet lag.

teacher, being a: will find your commanding
   presence in other territories.

GHOST

03-15-17-33-37-39

apparition, of an: recriminations against your
   lover's unpredictable behavior.

   dead relative, of a: temptation of the allur-
      ing sides of evil doers.

   robber, of a: will be decoyed into the hands
      of evildoers.

being frightened by a: expect troubles ahead in
   your exceedingly happy marriage.

disappearing: look behind reality to your
   shadow qualities.

dressed in black: great sorrow is ahead for you,
   unless the past is dealt with.

   white: big consolation for your dangerous
      illusions.

frightening a: that something is no longer
   attainable; keep affairs closely supervised.

ghouls robbing graves: hopes are stolen from
   you; take them back.

having no fear of: will pull through difficulties
   that others will not notice.

hobgoblin: an overindulgence in overrich
   spicy foods.

of a: immediate mobilization against ill will
   of those who plot against you.

speaking to you: a dead relative returns to
   advise you that you are in danger of malice.

GIANT

05-08-09-25-30-31

being a: one insignificant affair becomes a
   gigantic obstacle.

killing a: have come to terms with your inferiority complex.

meeting a: your fear that has become too big
   for you to handle.

monstrous: kill the beast for unexpected
   personal success.

with a, being: be careful whom you trust in
   making mountains out of molehills.

GIFT

12-20-23-27-42-46

Christmas, receiving a: take as great a pleasure
   in giving as you do in receiving.

   relatives: take a long hard look at your
      many admirers.

giving: are an idealist with many delusions;
   are prone to hasty actions that backfire.

   relatives, to: one you disliked will prove to
      be a loyal friend.

receiving a: in your involvement in work you
   have neglected yourself.

   confections, of: take your friend to dinner.

   from a daughter: will receive a marriage
      proposal you are overjoyed to accept.

      important person, an: need recognition
         and praise.

      loved one: be generous with affection

and aware of the ingratitude of
others.

relatives: will soon find a favorable
position within the family fold.

son: tribulations through his opposition to the low amount.

woman: depression and emotional
upheaval will not be assuaged.

several: beware of person from whom you
receive them.

GIN

01-02-09-14-45-47

breaking a bottle of: will be visited by a friend.

buying: will have many changes in life.

drinking: will have a short life.

friends, with: have deceitful friends.

loved one, with a: fleeting pleasures.

giving a gift of: false favors.

receiving as a gift: family quarrels.

serving: you have false friends.

GIRL

05-07-08-27-34-49

amorous young, being an: will marry the
wrong person.

beautiful, exceptionally, an: increase in
romantic fulfillment.

crying, a: will be embarrassed by a major
financial problem; relax and play a little.

in a window: big disputes over unexpected
expense.

single man: new conquests on the romantic front.

intelligent: big fortune and bright future
prospects.

kind: immature but maturing female sexuality.

kissing several: encouraging prospects and
many joys.

man dreaming of being a: will play a female
part on stage.

married person dreaming of kissing a: domestic troubles.

saving a, from danger: latent possibilities in
your own nature will be extremely loved.

surprising news from a, receiving: a long-
delayed reply will arrive.

talking to a: keep a tight rein on your actions.

ugly, an: your love attentions will be refused.

unmarried, dreaming of beating a man:
success in love.

young, dreaming of being in an asylum: will
meet an unanticipated obstacle.

of having a small beard: matrimony
nearby in an uncongenial union.

of a man with a beard: will marry the one
you love by standing firm against all
suitors.

receiving attentions from a man: is exposing his feelings about her with clear
intent.

GLACIER

18-19-27-38-40-49

moving: your frigidity is cracking; warm up
to the possibilities.

standing on top of a, alone: adversaries are
gone, deal with your own adversity.

at foot of a: your repressed emotions need
to be vented.

with lover: impending separation, take a
trip to the North.

GLADIATOR

01-11-14-16-17-40

being killed: unhappiness.

festival, being at a: something will happen to
cause sorrow.

in combat: will have plenty of money.

several: change in environment.

GLASS

02-19-20-34-48-49

bar, at a: a vindictive argument with one
equally inclined.

being offered a, of water: birth of a child.

blower, a: a promotion through merit foretells injury from accepting flattery.

breaking a: your actions will cause the
breakup of your affair to your distinct
advantage.

and spilling water: children will be healthy
but business results prove unfavorable.

on clothes: favors from a stranger in
exchange for arranging their illicit
pleasures.

full of water: death of a mother and ill
health for children.

businessman dreaming of breaking a:
unfavorable termination of fruitless
speculation.

chewing: are so angry the verbalization is
garbled; spewing out cutting remarks.

cutting: forthcoming break leads to a postponement of a wedding.

dirty: congenial work in a subordinate position requires no real effort.

drinking a, of fresh water: have a clear
conscience as to the dangers of prompt
matrimony.

empty, an: adjust your lifestyle to hard times;
your marriage will be sorely tested.

full, a: time to do some speculating with your
vivid imagination.

goblet, breaking a: your very existence picks a
quarrel among those despondent.

    drinking out of a: sit with your back to
the wall and let the enemy drink the
first sip.

        beer: are welcome anywhere and
humiliated anytime.

house: your frankness with what should be
hidden will cloud your fondest hopes.

plate, seeing your reflection in a: the image you
think you project.

    breaking a: will save another from the
distress you caused.

GLOBE
09-14-19-23-24-41

falling to ground: your lucrative projects are
turning sour.

globe-trotter, of a: be aware of the unpredictability of Lady Luck.

holding a, in your hands: your complete
nature, symmetry and proportion.

    one hand: are taking the risk needed to
rule your work.

made of glass: your ambivalence will create a
crisis; make a decision.

    iron: with courage you will face every
challenge.

map: divisions denoting the aspects of nature.

of a: wide travel and adventure in an ideal
universe.

taking a trip around the: stationary success is
still stationary.

    others: your friends are spinning out of
control.

GLOOM
01-18-21-22-26-37

being in very dark: don't hesitate to grasp an
opportunity.

feeling gloomy: will soon hear discouraging
news.

    others: much unhappiness from severe
headaches.

of the: the something eating you is the source
of your woes.

GLOVES
04-25-29-32-47-48

buying: you don't make friends by hiding
yourself behind caution.

carrying, in the hands: honor, pleasure and
prosperity; economical but not mercenary.

dirty, getting: are protecting yourself from
shady business.

dropping a: a potential love affair should be
handled with the utmost diplomacy.

finding a pair of: don't dare get your hands
dirty on that project.

losing own: frustrations will throw you onto
your own resources.

maker, being a: your lack of contact does not
fit one of high position.

putting on: insularity against the world;
avoiding intimate contact.

    mittens: at times aggression is needed; add
a bit of playfulness to simmer it down.

receiving a gift of: politeness will get you
everywhere; openness, overexposure.

throwing a, at someone: a velvet touch solves
the issue until the smoothness wears off.

too big: have taken on more than you can
handle successfully.

    small: your dissatisfaction is confining you
to a downward spiral.

wearing: are hiding your iron fist.

    kid: need to handle the situation of your
shame with particular care.

    new: promotion and social prominence.

    old: will be betrayed and suffer a loss.

    others: matters are being brought to
conclusion, not yours.

    torn: melancholy and dissatisfaction.

GLOW
02-13-15-17-34-42

expression, having a glowing: a change in life
will come soon.

feeling a very hot: the actual form symbolizing
your soul quality.

of passion, feeling the: a part of you is relaying direct spiritual guidance.

scene, of a brilliant: improvement in fortune from the expression of your inner light.

sensation after exercise, feeling a glowing: triumph over enemies.

GLUE
06-14-22-23-28-34

becoming unglued: wish to scatter your energies but see something painful in it.

buying: program yourself to make positive connections to keep this job permanently.

glued to television, being: refusal of emotional environment, beyond what you will risk.

sniffing: cannot escape from your challenges.

spilling: that which is broken cannot be fixed.

stuck on your hands: the consequences never leave the act, nor do your motives.

using: have a faithful friend that you can trust.

   others: are deceived by best friends in unwise investments.

GLUTTONY
11-15-19-22-25-41

being a glutton: feel you are in danger of poverty, if you do not consume all in sight.

   children: will lose all of your estate unless your cultivate yourself to fit your task.

   others: success does not bring sincere friends of unselfish principles.

   relatives: do not expect any money from a person of wealth.

of: are expending unwarranted emotion on distinguished presence who batters you.

GOATS
07-24-35-38-44-46

baby: resistance to a God that has to be sacrificed to.

being a: realization of a dream of rampant sexuality.

being butted by a: can be persuaded of anything with no indigestion.

billy, a: be alert and listen attentively to the herd.

black, a: unreliable friends portend your failure.

black and white spotted, a: use caution in own affairs of lust.

drinking, milk: will marry for money and attain full health.

female, a: will overcome enemies with care and prudence.

fighting: your stubbornness is making another miserable.

herding: will climb difficult terrain.

horns of a: poverty through money lost in gambling.

keeping, in a pen: cannot contain the ecstasy of nature without repercussions.

killing a: stop resisting progress; make your choice.

listening to: others' needless complaints surround you.

many: hardy ability to accept almost anything.

milked, being: modesty becomes you; humility is far-fetched.

of a: adversity being overcome through powers of patience.

owning many: abundance and riches from sturdy investments.

play, at: your boisterousness decreases your credibility.

scapegoat, being a: are looking for someone to accept your burdens.

white, a: luck at meeting important people will be very erratic.

GOD
08-11-13-17-40-47

face to face, seeing: question how you can be of use to the world.

Goddesses: power to manifest spirituality.

godparent, being a: recognition of past kind deeds.

   another: take advantage of this good period.

   to a relative: be astute and decisive with the opportunity offered.

granting you what was desired: will realize ambitions of being better, holy and sinless.

name of, others taking the: drop personal desires to acquire God.

parent, a: all support and advice to be found within God.

praying to: you grow stronger with your moral responsibility.

putting his arms around you: will receive that prayed for in discrete form.

speak to you, hearing: intense sense of well-being and vigilant energy.

talking to: act on the advice from above that is within you.

worshiping: desire to act with wisdom that touches the center of your being.

GOLD
12-15-18-39-45-49

brick, buying a: hiding a secret for fear of exposing the shame.

burying a pot of: will avenge yourself for some petty deed.

business venture, handling, in a: have no luck in games.

buying clothes of, color: wish to expose your intellectual gifts.

gilt articles: a deep and durable love, a flattering future.

color of: will do business with people far away.

counting: are attempting to deceive friends.

dancing around the golden calf: your superficiality denies your inner qualities.

digging for: unexpected fortune will come through own efforts.

exchanging: be discreet with the information you offer.

finding: your superior skill gives you an advantage in the game of acquiring wealth.

golden fleece: divine protection.

imitation: will be plenty rich for appearances only and lose the chance for real honors.

losing: financial distress will reveal a deep and durable love.

materials of any kind in, color: expect abundant means.

melting: someone is doing you wrong.

mine, discovering a: a big fortune is ahead.

belonging to others: are being cheated by friends

mining: are avaricious and mercenary.

mixture of, and silver: will take a large loss.

plating: will receive high honors; every enterprise will bring success.

resembles, having something that: your castles are built on shaky foundations.

rings from, making: love divinely bestowed on you.

stealing: are trying to get ahead by sheer force.

throwing away: friends will convince you to lend them money.

wearing clothes embroidered with: are highly thought of by others.

lace, covered with: great honor.

working as a gilder: an uneasy horror will be thrust upon your privacy.

others gilding: friends have ulterior motives in keeping opportunity from you.

working with: truth to the mind does not allow usurping the rights of others.

GOLDFISH
13-18-20-27-33-43

buying: matrimony within the family.

children playing with: much contentment.

dead: disappointments to come.

having, in a bowl in own house: financial gains.

married woman dreaming of: close the shades from Peeping Toms.

young woman: will marry into wealth and a pleasing man.

GOLF
05-09-11-25-26-44

better scores than you, others making: will be humiliated by an aggressive look.

bogey, making a: chance of miscalculation does not need to be broadcasted.

bad score: humiliation at being the object of scorn.

caddy, using a: spiritual passage to the game's heart for the pain of nonparticipation.

playing: skill takes a careful study of form.

spending much time: transient wins take needed attention away from business affairs.

with friends: much joy.

playing on a, course: want to be identified with a wealth you cannot attain.

enemies: warning of a mistake opening your actions up to sensationalism.

with others: are unfitted to fill your position, which will dash hopes for advancement.

winning a, tournament: important and very beneficial event to come.

GONDOLA
03-09-11-16-21-44

being in a, with your mate: good days are
ahead.
   with a lover: love will not last very long.
of a: happy but unromantic life.
others being in a: will honeymoon in Europe.

GONG
02-03-08-22-27-34

hearing a: an exciting event will happen in the
family.
in own house, having a: pleasant work and good
news, which makes loss even more vexing.
of a ship, the: avoid trifling with problems in
present job; return to old one.

GOOD
21-36-38-41-46-48

children doing, things: a baby will be born late
in life.
others doing, to you: profit and gains.
saying, things about others: will be embarrassed.
   people, you: will be deceived by friends.
things, of: misfortune in love.
to others, doing: joy and pleasure.

GOOD-BYE
12-21-27-41-44-45

bidding your children: worry will be
smoothed away.
   mate: good times are coming.
   relatives: will receive painful news.
   someone else: be cautious in business
ventures.
mate saying, to you: a false friend is nearby.
   others: a long and tedious journey.
   parents: their worry is a product of
loneliness.
   stranger: examine how well you know
your friends.

GOOSE
02-06-23-33-40-48

big fat, a: opulently fertile proposals yield
high profit.
buying a: are being taken for a fool.
eating: be alert to your diet.
   others: joy.
fattening a: all your work will result in profit.
flesh, having: your secrets are making you
sick.

flying, a: take an extensive journey.
gabbling: listen carefully to the gossip about
you, but don't respond.
gander, a: your weight should be proportionate to your height.
killing a: increase in money.
   the golden: your ethics have been
corrupted.
of a: opulent fertility.
plucking a: inheritance.
quacking: avoid the company of one-
dimensional people.
swimming: fortune is increasing.
tending a flock of geese: a friend you have
cared for will desert you.
wild, a: your friends have forgotten you.

GOOSEBERRIES
03-04-14-27-33-46

buying: patience will help you avoid your
loneliness and trouble.
eating: are doomed to have a combative mate.
gathering: brighter business prospects.
having: will receive an unexpected invitation.
jam of, making: avoid rivals.
   pie: will be jilted by your lover.
picking: will be publicly ridiculed for deed not
yours.

GOSSIPING
05-11-41-42-45-47

about others: are undergoing an annoying
anxiety.
being the object of gossip: pleasant surprises
are in store.
   telling others: will be making an important
change shortly.
enemies, about you: will suffer through own
foolishness.
   friends: your confidence is being deceived.
   relatives: family arguments.
friends, from: beware of deceit, and trust
few people.
of hearsay: unhappiness in the home.
others, from: unhappiness in your business.

GOURMET
05-07-12-28-35-47

aspic, eating foods in: an invitation to an old-
fashioned dinner party.
being a connoisseur or fine gourmet: will be
jilted by lover.

enjoying fine food yourself: must control passions.

epicure, being an: practice restraint in your diet and safe sex.

fine: have one loyal friend.

others being a, of fine foods: good times are coming.

GOUT

15-21-25-29-31-42

having, in a joint: vexation at financial losses caused by a relative.

    for a long time: must avoid overstrain because of weakness.

    old person: will have misfortune in business.

    young person: are in danger of expending your health prematurely.

on the hands, having: will soon have an illness from toxic gossip you are spreading.

    feet: walking away from your problems only brings them along.

GOVERNMENT

11-16-18-42-46-48

authorities, being called before: will tell you something you already know.

    others: danger through a secret.

    persecuted by: advancement in your career but not this position.

    seeking help from: will receive insults and incur debts.

being offered a, position: good times are coming.

embassy, entering an: responsibility to represent yourself respectably.

emissary, being an: catastrophe of worldwide influence is imminent.

governor, meeting with the: will soon buy a new automobile.

having a, position: the inner forces that govern your health.

    others: troubles are ahead.

influential male in, an: will be persecuted.

losing a, position: will soon experience many ups and downs.

people in high office: honor and dignity.

persecuted by, authorities: advancement with your position.

sanctioned, being: infidelity.

enemy: their public disgrace, your joy and prosperity.

seeking help from, authorities: debts are incurred.

GOWN

02-13-20-33-41-42

being pulled away and left naked: will be superseded in the arms of your lover.

own shabby: are provoked to exasperation over the inabilities of those identified by you.

    torn: secret will be exposed, limiting your advancement.

wearing a beautiful: your need to be the center of attraction limits your love affairs.

GRACE

10-13-15-25-35-49

asking, for a prisoner: abundant means.

asking God for: will have important changes in life.

receiving: will make good earnings.

saying, on food: will be returned to perfect health.

GRAIN

17-29-30-32-42-45

buying: problematic process to emotional profit.

    carrying bags of, to the barn: relative's visit will be a shifting unstable situation.

catching fire: serious disaster ahead as plans will not succeed, but important things will.

chaff of, storing the: will have a vigorous mind full of useless information.

ears of corn, wheat, rye or other: will have abundant means.

feeding, to animals: prosperity from an opulent harvest.

granary, a full: forthcoming abundance.

    empty: are insecure about a problem that will prove temporary.

harvesting: expect robust health for some time to come.

    millet: expect great gains in your work.

selling large amount of: financial gains will continue.

    small: troubles are ahead.

separating chaff from the seed: only do important things.

sowing, in a field: good marriage and good business.

standing: will receive plenty of money.

GRANDPARENT
03-04-22-45-47-48

being a: will inherit wisdom of their past without regressing to childhood.

grandchildren being with a: advancement in health condition; a plethora of experience.

great-grandparents: non-life-threatening illness to come; heed their advice to prevent it.

speaking to a: have made a wise decision; follow through with it.

talking in the dream to: expect help in living a more prudent life.

GRAPES
12-13-17-28-42-46

black: be cautious in your business affairs, do not allow your creativity to harden.

buying: physical life without the influence of spirit has a short shelf life.

destroying: should mend your ways in life.

dry, having: sacrifice the poisonous for the voluptuousness of full bloom.

   large: considerable fortune; set aside half for emergencies.

   raisins made from: a stranger will have a profound affect on you.

eating: reaping the intoxicating fruits of your labors.

   children: will have a wide influence and bright promise.

   sour: a bitter argument over your bitterness.

harvesting ripe: a big fortune is ahead from unexpected meeting.

making wine out of: abundant means through your strong business acumen.

of a field full of: the spiritual strength to live a long life.

on the vines, handling: preeminence in the bounties of love will be yours.

red: the outlook worsens from a small contradiction.

selling: business affairs, but not your health, are at risk.

white: victory over enemies through your sacrifices.

GRASS
08-11-26-36-45-49

artistic person dreaming of: reduce materials to manageable proportions.

cutting the: rake up the cuttings for the only profit you will get.

dead: rely on tried and true methods and work exceedingly hard.

dew on the, at dawn, seeing: the innumerable thoughts that can spring to life.

   falling refreshing: abundance through marriage to person of means.

dogs or animals eating: overgrown egotism that needs cutting.

dried up: health of loved one has taken a turn for the worse.

eating: are starving financially.

green, flourishing: make money in unison with making love.

literary person dreaming of: simplify your material life for intellectual strength.

lying in the: your peace is momentary; others will walk all over you.

of: wealth to those in business.

very long: will be taken for granted in uncharted territory.

GRASSHOPPER
08-13-19-34-36-37

in own yard: bad omen for sick people; adjust with caution to turn your fear around.

killing: arrival of one whose indiscretion will amaze and embarrass you.

   others: expect the arrival of a thief dressed impeccably.

of: will enjoy a short period of fancied success, then perplexing complexities.

GRATE
03-15-19-28-45-47

barbecue: will have the love of a rich person.

breaking a: worries ahead.

   cooking fish on the stove: sickness followed by death.

      meat: will enjoy liberty again.

of a: unhappiness at many jolly acquaintances and no good friends.

GRATITUDE
06-10-21-26-41-43

being grateful to someone: surprising events will happen.

189

others expressing, to you: events will happen to a loved one.

receiving, from children: will live a long life.

GRAVE

09-14-23-42-44-48

decorating a: will have very little joy from another's broken vow.

destroying a: a wedding will take place soon, leading to an unfortunate marriage.

digging a: big obstacles you create to cause others harm will destroy you.

newly prepared: will suffer through the sins of others and succeed using their success.

of own: enemies are trying to bring disaster to you; shoulder it and toss the dregs back.

of your father: unpleasant tidings about your inheritance; the oppression has lifted.

space being open: will receive news of hopeless despair from afar.

   enemies': are submerging you in distress with no hope of extrication.

   standing before an: confess your complicity before you are accused.

   visiting relatives': sorrow from promises not kept at a big matrimonial dinner.

walking on a: are weighted with the debt of worldly experience.

   another person, your: death or an unfortunate marriage is very near at hand.

GREECE

04-06-18-24-28-32

being a Greek: intellect under the influence of emotion.

going to: your proposal will be criticized technically, discussed practically and used.

Greek marrying a foreigner: gossip by the women makes communication impossible.

   other nationalities marrying a: humiliation for not living up to ancient expectations.

traveling in: meet disagreeably rude and pompously polished natives.

GREEN

2-8-23-24-36-50

landscape of: are in tune with the development of your environment.

painting a room: receptiveness to intellectual inspiration.

wearing: reconsider your potential growth only in projects you are enthusiastic about.

with envy: reassess your opinions and achievements.

wood, burning: your extravagance is allowing your imagination to run rampant.

GREETINGS

10-24-32-37-45-47

receiving, from friends: have gained well-deserved recognition.

   people abroad: loss of present position.

sending, to friends: will be involved in long-complicated discussions of your motives.

   businessmen: will come out well from present peril.

GREYHOUND

03-07-16-21-45-47

belonging to others: will win at a lottery.

of a: will overcome enemies and transform them into friends.

owning a: walking a slender fence with the threat of a sudden collapse of fortune.

racing: will win at the races; a legacy from unknown bettors.

GRIEF

02-15-26-27-42-43

bereaved, being: marriage of one you wished to marry will soon take place.

of moaning: guilty for behavior toward the dead.

suffering: someone else will benefit by your actions.

   children: joy and merry times ahead.

   enemies: foe's accusations are not easily digested.

   relatives: something good will happen to a loved one.

   others: a loyal friend is nearby.

GRINDING

09-12-14-37-38-45

coffee: troubles at home.

colored stones: derive great pleasure from simple things.

corn: good fortune.

grain: rectify your habits or irritated people will reject you.

190

machine, of a: will speculate wildly and lose your estate.

materials for dyeing: discord within the family.

pepper: a worrying piece of news of sickness and sorrow.

GRINDSTONE

09-14-22-23-46-48

of a: battle until even the tiniest problem is solved.

    machine: find the core of the problem, contain the energy and build on it.

using a: good fortune will attend your efforts, insignificant but honest profit.

    children: life of great activity with financial success.

    others: loss of the friendship of several friends and the gain of a worthy mate.

GROANING

03-06-10-11-34-47

hearing children: will live a long life with pleasant and frequent return of children.

    enemies: have one loyal friend who cannot stop the scourge of enemies.

of, in a dream: someone will investigate your work, nit-picking their way to a flaw.

relatives: an unfulfilled wish will become unwanted and a new wish fulfilled.

GROCERIES

02-12-17-21-36-46

buying: your calm state of mind will lead to a life of ease.

    others: expect a project you are involved with to come out well eventually.

eating the: need love and must pay to get it.

relatives: annoyance and disagreements within the family.

well-stocked shelves: your initiatives have a good chance of success.

GROOM

17-18-25-27-30-46

being a: legal affairs will be made known to you.

bridle of a: incomplete and inconstant drains of emotion in service of others.

currying a horse: will take an overland trip and many strokes before project is completed.

of a stable: are in favor with fortune.

others working as a: change of surroundings.

several: will have to contend with ruffians.

taking care of your horses: abundant means.

GROUND

09-18-28-40-44-46

digging in own yard: must rely on own vigor to increase your fortune.

hog: will fall in love with a loner genius.

kissing the, of own property: happiness within the immediate family.

stretched out on the, being: degraded and humble status for some time to come.

GROWING

03-14-20-24-30-31

being grown up: will shortly be disillusioned about something.

children: pleasant family news arriving very shortly.

good stuffs: riches.

of: will become an important person.

taller quickly: your self-confidence and self-respect have not caught up with your height.

GUARD

04-09-12-15-29-47

against danger, being on: avoid uncouth speech in confronting dealings.

being taken away by a: will have a secure fortune.

    night, being a: a big sorrow is ahead.

guardian, a: criticism from all sides is less than constructive.

    of a young person: must protect minor from the possibility of theft of resources

hitting a: are being illogical in your behavior.

killing a: social pressures are too much for your embryonic spirit.

night watchman, being a: fear for your property is thrust into his every move.

    feeling you need a: someone is preventing you from carrying out certain tasks.

park, of a: have a good heart, but cannot wait for useless help.

presidential: fortify your honor against serious flattery and poignant persuasion.

security, being a: fear of losing respect or social standing.

taking away a prisoner: will be insulted by
friends.

GUESSING

10-17-23-34-40-48

about peoples' personal affairs: are the deceitful friend.

about you, others: will be cheated through
misunderstanding.

ages of people, the: come back to earth after a
period of illusion.

correctly: will have a good adventure.

of: are desirous of knowing future but unable
to do so.

GUESTS

01-09-14-43-45-47

being a guest: adventure at new location and
foreign soil.

call on you, having a: important and very
beneficial event to come.

crossing your doorstep: accept this unwanted
responsibility to make affairs harmonious.

many: you will lose your judgment under the
wiles of a seductive woman.

others having: part of self brought out for
special requests.

unwelcome: unhappiness in love affairs that
you don't wish to face.

welcome: at the beginning of an important,
fascinating project; will be courted by foes.

GUIDE

08-14-16-32-36-49

being a: depend on the principles that guide
you.

book: the principles that give you social structure.

by others, being guided: pay attention to
suggestions of a friend.

guiding people around: go for the thing only
you can do and patent it.

GUILTY

01-04-17-30-34-44

being: must endure tribulation for some
misdeed.

   enemies: are unusually oversensitive and
intolerant.

   mate or lover: will receive inheritance
from an old lady.

   others: are in an unaccustomed situation.

GUITAR

18-28-30-31-44-46

hearing a, played: a vigorous life until death:
harmony or disharmony—your choice.

music, being pleased by: are in process of overcoming difficulties successfully.

music being interrupted: friends will interfere
in your closest affections.

playing a: unreliable whimsical behavior that
needs sharp tuning.

   Spanish: go your own way with determination.

soft strains of a: fortify yourself against clever
wiles of a seducer.

young woman dreaming of hearing a: temptation through flattery.

GULF

05-06-12-17-18-24

being in a: only time well spent with lover will
prevent her departure.

boat in a, being in a: will overcome troubles
by giving others care and attention.

of a: separateness, separation from the life
you are living.

others being in a: sad parting from someone
you love.

port, landing at a: joy without profit.

GUM

03-06-11-12-32-49

chewing: someone will stick by you, but not
your best girl.

   others: may have cause to regret actions.

drops: return of childhood friend.

having: financial delays are indicated; watch
or you will get stuck.

GUMS

03-21-28-40-42-45

children's, being sore: will receive an unexpected guest.

inflamed, being: unfavorable results in affairs.

of own: discord among the family.

treated by a dentist, being: death of a friend.

GUN

20-26-33-35-43-46

buying a: be wary of whose face you see
during target practice.

double-barreled: worries and conflicts to
come through bad management decisions.

fired, hearing a: financial problems need to be sorted out before they snowball.

firing a: your physical fitness and mental energy make it an auspicious time to start a project.

handling gunpowder: your adventure is inherently explosive.

    having: should mend your ways before they explode on you.

having a: signifies your present problems incessantly on the verge of dishonor.

hunting with a: are putting off profound decisions in favor of life or death.

loaded, a: unfortunate feeling that violence is your only defense.

machine, a: feel weak and drained of strength.

man dreaming of gunpowder: your recent cantankerous behavior.

    woman: are nervous and restless and will divorce your husband.

    young girl: fear of sexual activity if she marries a soldier.

merchant, a: will dissolve a corporation.

others firing a: will feel invalided for some time.

receiving a, as a gift: keep your impulses under control.

revolver, firing a: full of brilliant ideas.

rifle with a bayonet: mistakes need patching up to prevent separation of partners.

shooting a person with a: can put that unpleasant episode behind you for good.

    an enemy with a: a lawsuit will end a harmful relationship.

    yourself: can stand alone against any attacks.

shot by a, being: a serious illness of the heart threatens.

traveling with a: fear of violence.

trigger against the enemy, pulling: will be greatly criticized.

    married woman: dishonor in love affairs.

    teenagers: are pushing your actions beyond your ability to be responsive.

GURU
07-12-14-18-27-47

attending an ashram: are viewing your life from a higher plane.

being a: power to direct all facets of self to reach your destiny.

connecting with a: change goals through forgiving yourself.

consulting a: peaceful dealings with mentors ungenerous with their advice.

meeting a: trust the guidance offered by a wise soul.

GUTTER
01-06-18-28-34-40

being in a: hard times to come from low self-esteem; degradation takes your participation.

    enemies: take a trip to triumph over contemptible enemies.

    friends: will cause others' lives to roil in turmoil and laugh.

cleaning out the: will climb up on solid foundations, but your rights will be questioned.

finding something valuable in a: will receive a financial reward

GYMNASTICS
10-14-16-26-29-35

doing, in a gym: lasting and faithful relationship with partner.

    children: will gain a respected position in society.

    handspring, a girl: are wary of behavior in front of men.

        a boy: keep your mind on task at hand.

    horizontal bars: your courage will be challenged in the face of danger.

    open air: unexpected trip will broaden your horizons.

    relatives: holistic experience of body and emotion.

    trapeze, swinging on a: cover all the ground intelligently, incisively before deciding.

owning a gym for: attending to business will gain you a respected position in society.

GYPSY
39-42-44-45-48-40

hearing, music: free your slate for a romantic adventure.

married woman, telling a fortune to a: an early and unwise marriage.

    man: will be jealous of wife without cause.

    woman: affairs will intensify, then dissipate.

of a: are prone to change your mind very often irresponsibly.

paying a, for a reading: your naïveté has made a fool of you.

speaking to a: your assessment and plan of action are correct.

ᚻ   ᚻ   ᚻ   ᚻ   ᚻ

HABITS
02-16-22-32-41-51

bad, having: some venture you are involved in is coming to an end.

  good: slow and unrelenting career progress.

  others: will have social troubles, if your habits don't return to normal.

  relatives: will be humiliated by an uncomfortable situation.

  special, a: will be welcomed, wherever you go.

nun's, a: who you are speaks through all the layers, and what you are stands firm.

HADDOCK
13-20-24-28-41-48

buying: will have mastery over many matters.

cooking: have more friends than you thought.

eating: accord among friends; disruption within marriage.

fishing for: own stupidity will cause you danger.

HAILSTORM
02-07-12-41-42-54

being caught in a: a dispute with someone out for emotional revenge.

  in a car during a: your affair will be exposed loud and clear.

  others: offer a friend shelter from the cold.

crop being ruined by a: sow seeds in another venture; this one won't succeed.

of falling hail: a barrage of highly strung, restless attacks upon you.

  in a distance: future separation from source of financial support.

HAIR
06-18-22-31-45-54

allowing, to be cut up to your ears: unhappiness.

another's: own affairs will need careful attention.

beautiful long, having: want a sexually vibrant lover.

  black: in a car accident an old acquaintance will be renewed.

  blonde: get on with the onerous task of proving you are not dumb.

  brown: will be a voluptuous person; whatever it takes.

crew cut style, a: your liberality with your money, once exploited, leads to frugality.

handful of, a: will become poor by being overgenerous to annoying friends.

long: will receive something important.

  as her body, as: are being deceived by mate's cowardice and effeminacy.

  conductor's, a: will be cheated by those with a lot of hair.

red: are telling an untruth for the right to act according to your own morality or immorality.

white: dignity as your physique weakens.

  very long: high hopes, but your lover is married.

woman dreaming of: an inappropriate overevaluation of your personality.

bleaching your: despite the hype to the contrary, gentlemen still prefer blondes.

blonde women, men dreaming of: reversals of inattention to the whole person.

braiding your: have overromanticized your affair.

  unbraiding your: begin your new adventure into womanhood.

brushing your: are recharging your energy and centering your growth.

bun, wearing in a tight: restrained from inter-relationships.

burning: death of someone you know will cast a pall over your aspirations.

caressing: will earn love and trust of mate despite yourself.

combing lover's hair: any sex problems will be solved.

  another's: warning to those who would be unfriendly to that person.

curly, of: will be antagonistic and surly until you are with the right mate.

    black: will deceive with your charm to gain trust; then will betray it.

cutting: fear losing your spotless reputation.

    off your braids: reevaluate your habits; expect an explanation.

dandruff, having: wipe out past offenses before approaching another.

falling out: loss of friendship will solve some annoying problems.

golden, woman with: an audacious predator in the chase; a true woman's woman.

gray, turning: must endure difficulty in choosing a partner.

    being in the company of a person with: love after many rebuffs.

    comparing dark to: to keep youth you must choose a path; one will age you faster.

groomed, carefully: fear sex as contaminating.

growing from the edge of the mouth: accept advice in the spirit given.

    on the back of the hands: will offend discriminating society with your indiscretion.

    on the face of a woman: danger of losing fortune; will have to support yourself.

man having lost all of his: fear your impotence will be bared to the public.

    forcibly shaven: will lose your love from a sudden change to a pledge of celibacy.

    long: false dignity leads to weakness of character.

    short white: the wisdom that comes only with age.

    very little: want independence from moral taboos.

    woman, her: are mentally and physically overextended.

of own: continued prosperity in a new sphere of life.

    cutting, with scissors: will be called upon to help someone.

    getting thin or falling out: tend to split hairs; your disdain will lose a worthy lover.

    mussing up: family quarrels will be minor squabbles on close inspection.

putting up: invigorate your soul with patience; engender your trials with fortitude.

satisfied with the way, looks, being: will be pleasant in your life journey; thus fortunate.

washing: sorrow in dire happenings.

worrying because, is turning gray: separation from family; displacement of lover.

ponytail, in a: your vain desires are tempered with liveliness and enthusiasm.

prisoners, of: will be victorious over enemy's shame, but indiscrete in yours.

putting a net over own: will have a terrible headache, which will signify an unworthy ally.

short, very: your emotions are too controlled; it will not lessen the depth of your grief.

snarled: a long legal action will be the end to bad business and a burdensome marriage.

someone pulling your: enemies are trying to harm you.

tidying, at neck: get rid of characteristics that can't handle the danger.

trouble taking your, down, having: you emphasize your intellect to hide your emotions.

unkempt: are practicing unsafe sex; have lost or will lose control of your future.

washing your: deliverance from overwhelming misfortune.

well-combed: your advancement will be neglected through your loss of mental fortitude.

wild, of an assailant: disdain for society's reaction to your image embroils you in issues.

HAIRDRESSER

01-10-22-29-40-44

being a: prepare for and be ready to face attending a large ball.

conversing with a: careful whom you allow to influence you.

dyed auburn, having hair: will be renounced by lover for unfaithfulness.

    black: give a mystery party for others.

    blonde: the only dumb blondes are bottle blondes; wouldn't you rather be a brunette?

gray, to cover: wish to be more sexually attractive.

henna, with: confronted with society's scorn and enemy's destructive reputation.

red: exciting, but you will run the risk of losing a friend.

white: dampen your enthusiasm for an unrequited love.

enemies being at a: your image is doomed for disappointment.

hair done at a, having: postponement of success until work is done.

friend, with a: have power to change friend's image.

man getting a short haircut at a: are afraid of subjugation.

permanent, a: there are repercussions in repeating scandalous gossip.

red-haired woman, a beautiful: unexpected impassioned news reads as simple grief.

dying her, blond: will manipulate new men to her wishes.

style, changing your: the external expression of inner change.

taking daughter to a: don't allow anyone to meddle in others' squabbles.

wig made by a, having a: your false attitudes put you in imminent danger.

woman at a: a symbol of the level of her attractiveness to men.

HAIRPINS
21-25-30-34-45-52

buying: calm and fruitful married life.

man watching a woman handling: will visit a novel place of amusement.

rival woman, finding, of a: will be guilty of foolish actions.

using to unlock door: a friend is watching you.

HALIBUT
01-22-38-43-52-56

buying, in a fish store: will be generous to friends, but mate will be shiftless.

catching: will damage someone by exposing a confidence.

cooking: expect pregnancy in the near future, or a weakness all your own.

eating: good luck to one whom you have overconfidence in.

receiving, from others: will realize high ambitions and darker reputation by misspeaking.

HALL
04-09-13-23-38-51

being in a: a two-faced companion will injure your reputation.

alone: be prepared for extended period of illusive anxiety until you reach insight.

with others: transition from one group of friends to another.

having a meeting in a, with friends: conversion is made complex by conflicting ideas.

enemies: advancement within own position leads to pessimism about the future.

HALLMARK
05-09-13-17-24-42

missing on your gold articles, being: will fail to accomplish your designs.

of a: reputation will be injured by a two-faced friend.

stamped on gold and silver, being: loss through negligence of underlings.

possessions: will be forced to grant privileges to unworthy characters.

HALLOWEEN
18-21-23-25-43-53

costumes, on wearing: your inner fears and desires are not recognized by you.

high jinks in: increased influence in social circles.

mischief on, creating: will intrigue against innocent people and be caught.

without a costume, being: pretend to be and act the role of who you desire to be.

HALO
5-12-19-32-43-46

of a: present troubles stem from your "holier than thou" attitude.

seeing a lunar: bring foreign influence into your home environment.

solar: rapid advancement of own hopes in business.

surrounding something: emotional sorrow at death among your circle.

your head: your intermittent search for perfection brings emotional sorrow.

HAM

02-21-37-40-52-54

baking a: a difficult situation that will ultimately prove positive.

boiling a: small profit, but sweet, from the enterprise and perseverance of others.

buying a: incurring debts does not build wealth.

eating a: sensual gluttony and a business gamble won.

serving, to others: family quarrels will be eased by sharing your hospitality.

slicing a: all opposition treacherously used against you will be met.

smoking a: plenty to be shared from year to year.

HAMLET

09-17-27-37-42-48

of a small village: defeat to long-standing sensitive project.

Pied Piper playing in a: will be disappointed in the character of the actual deceiver.

reading Shakespeare's: will have comfort in conversation with the author.

seeing the play at a theater: a rival will steal your sweetheart.

HAMMER

15-16-19-31-35-51

hammering, furiously: curb your anger before you act.

  hearing many people: just because the idea has been spoken, doesn't make it true or yours.

  on wood: your irritability works to your rival's advantage.

  others: financial condition will be better in the future.

in own hands, having a: power to forge dreams into innovation.

others holding a: others will try to influence you by force.

sound of a, being used to the: failure to agree causes numerous stoppages and reverses.

HAMMOCK

06-08-31-37-40-48

being in a: happiness with lover is assured in wholesome recreation.

  children: succession of irritations from your selfish attitude.

others: bad management will disturb an otherwise placid existence.

relatives: will have emotional sorrow from misfortune in love affairs.

sleeping, in a: are floating, wrapped securely, while in the throes of your life.

HANDBAG

2-10-16-21-42-49

buying a: are confronted with an unsolvable problem.

finding a: bankruptcy, but a great love life.

  coin purse in it, with a: good results in business to forestall your burden.

  empty: good results in enterprises to forestall your boredom.

  full: all your sympathies, though neglected, will be played out.

giving a, as a gift: will encounter opposition to your success in undertakings.

  receiving: irritation and loss of temper with unworthy servants.

losing a: someone is trying to take your lover.

of a: passing riches as affairs go well.

stolen, being: others are taking advantage of your indecisiveness.

HANDCUFFED

21-24-35-37-40-51

being: ruing your past mistake will not return a lover; only limit self-expression.

  dangerous prisoner: will receive a letter with money, but no release to move ahead.

  enemies: others will be greatly vexed by your own good prospects.

  lover: an elusory love has captivated your heart.

  others: will conquer all obstacles, including in-law complications.

  relatives: will be criticized for fumble by boss, then promoted.

handcuffing others: forced love will return to break your heart.

releasing yourself from: outfox your enemies by turning their plan on them.

HANDKERCHIEF

06-15-22-27-28-53

buying a: be careful of new flirtations and that ensuing affairs don't taint your old ones.

embroidered: are prone to conceit with little competition otherwise.

giving a, as a gift: will cry for a long time over your corruption by seductive forces.

   receiving: will allow other's degrading remarks to force you to participate in deviant behavior.

linen: will have an interesting, though not passionate, affair.

losing a: broken engagement through the machinations of a jealous admirer.

putting a, around the neck: will be loved by people who will increase your income.

silk: are egotistical in your belief that your magnetic personality can spread cheer.

torn: serious troubles between lovers; a counselor should be called in to arbitrate.

using a, to blow your nose: will be defiled by your inability to state your correct case.

wiping sweat away with a: troubles are ahead which are solvable.

HANDS

05-8-9-13-17-38

amputated, being: death of an enemy; loss of an expressive part of self.

arthritic: relief from financial worries; affairs will have no hindrances.

big, having: your heavy-handed manner pushes others into deceit.

   blister on a, a: your actions are blocked by your indecision.

   blood on your hands: contention in family over deeds ill done.

   bloody: are guilty of what you have done and what you are thinking of doing.

   cold: will fail to communicate the wealth of your true intentions.

   full: others overload you with their chores to escape blame for being unable to do them.

   small: others will succeed at what you have been unable to attempt.

   swollen: others' envy is forcing you to defend a correct decision.

   tied: a relative is in difficulty; you cannot save him.

blowing on, to warm: a brief depression clouds your alertness at work.

burned your, having: a business associate seeks to limit you.

child's being cut off: the child will elope and you will celebrate with festivities.

   man's: have overreached in your push for a score and will be penalized.

   woman's: will be covetous of another's husband, thus pushing yours to run away.

clasping hands: unity and completeness of purpose; the natural leader will lead.

in front of your eyes, your: tolerate another's mistake as you would your own.

kissing a: an elegant way of expressing an eloquence words cannot.

   being kissed: will be seduced into actions that are fodder for the gossip mongers.

knocking with knuckles: your affections are not required.

   wearing brass: take control of those wishing to handle your life.

left, working with the: contrariness leading to an artistic creation.

   right: are expending energy without allowing replenishment.

losing a right: disturbing news from father brings difficulty in sharing with others.

   left: mother's illness prevents your receipt of a benefit.

own, of: perfect accord between husband and wife.

   being cut: will incur debts out of your control; stop the flow.

   burning: are unable to perform task, which would prove disgraceful and unprofitable.

   clean: will overcome troubles with the resolution of honest friends.

   dirty: the sentence for dishonest affairs is hard labor.

   palms: the pattern of your life is exposed; have only to seek it inside.

   strong, your: favorable outcome if you finalize the deal now.

   tied, are: any chance of creative expression has been denied.

   washing: are limiting growth by discarding aspects of self before examining them.

shake, a: begin new project and another, at the point you fully trust your partner.

> *firm and friendly:* your balanced attitude will force others to desist in their arguments.

> *pressure so hard you feel the pain:* are under pressure to accept the wrong thing.

> *weak and clammy:* lack enthusiasm and are received in a half-hearted way.

shaking: outrageous demands cause your suffering.

thumb, cutting your: prevent your business from overspending.

ugly and malformed: feel constrained from acting in your own interest.

unmarried people dreaming of their: will love and be loved with sincere regard.

watch or clock, of a: rapid progression of your affairs; are you ready?

wringing: worrisome issue needs to be worked through.

HANDWRITING
02-06-12-13-18-24

letter, a: take action at once on seeing older relatives.

others, of: will need aid in deciphering legal documents.

seeing, on paper: will make excuses to people, but not for them.

speech, a: your opponent will exaggerate your words to advance in the polls.

wall, on a: will find out the truth and rise in rank and position.

HANGING
11-30-34-41-51-55

criminal, a: will make money in a shameful manner.

effigy, in: disclosure of dishonesty from one you trusted.

freed just before, being: will realize own ambitions with a long-term lack of money.

friend, a: will subdue those persecuting others to gain in stature above them.

hangman, being a: be wary of being overcritical of anyone.

laundry on the line, the: are ready to reveal your sensitivities.

man, a: have passed a level of consciousness and a step on the social ladder.

relative, a: good luck to the person in the dream; exceptional honors will be yours.

sentenced to, being: forerunner to a succession of grievous offenses against you.

> *someone who is going to be:* will enjoy excellent meat at meals, your last.

stranger, a: hasty actions bring dire results; false friends solidify your alibi.

> *without cause:* are prone to be stingy with fortunate matrimonial alliance.

HAPPY
03-16-28-33-34-54

being: approaching money, better times to follow.

> *children:* rapid success of own hopes; cannot be overscrupulous in their morals.

> *employees:* pleasant social activities and congenial companions.

> *friends:* a false friend is nearby giving grief to a loving heart.

> *husband and wife:* joy and success; affairs have no hindrances.

> *others:* pleasant associations with strangers who become fast friends.

> *relatives:* worry will be smoothed away along with your selfish, unbecoming conduct.

delighted, being: people are endeavoring to destroy you for enjoying too many favors.

deliriously, being: use caution in speculation as you are tempted to go with your passion.

Hallelujah, saying: a successful culmination of a fervent love affair.

increased happiness: bad business ventures according to the degree of happiness.

jolly, being: many friends cherish your respect, spirit and leadership.

of being: wish-fulfillment does not replace realization of your ambitions.

HARBOR
06-13-23-29-35-46

aboard a ship, being alone in a: financial opportunities will allow a trip abroad.

> *with loved one:* falsehoods to be exposed; safety in that emotional storm.

far away: a sanctuary in a never-ending journey.

jetty extending into a, being on a: a longed-for trip will finally take place.

    falling from a: time to examine your accountant's efforts on your behalf.

lake, being in a, of a: will take a trip to the wrong location and rise above it to distinction.

    ocean: a place of security in which to reconnoiter and reorganize.

    sea: will discover a secret and successfully meet your obligation.

with ships: your venture is on solid foundations; sail to continue your growth.

    without: misery: no rest for the weary, no place for the restoration of energy.

HAREM
11-17-21-40-41-53

being in a: upsets in love life lead to inconsistent love.

    eunuch, a: are holding back your emotions to separate you from love.

    foreigners, a: accuse others of what you are desirous of doing.

    other women: your base pleasures are the consuming subject of gossip.

keeper of a, being the: are squandering your talents on vulgar pleasures.

living in a: overindulgence in pleasures that may terminate disastrously.

of a: are prone to luxurious living at the expense of another's marriage.

HARES
08-10-21-27-41-53

backyard, having, in the: a big relationship with a prolific artless plain-spoken friend.

chasing: are ready for adventure; protect your valuables.

cooking a: pleasant surroundings at the dinner table; concern yourself with relations.

running: don't spread rumors; their harm increases with each telling.

several on the run: very good business ventures through mysterious means.

shooting: a friend is leaving you; violent measures to waylay the departure are needed.

HARMONICA
02-10-27-33-45-55

buying a: a vivacious lift to your economic livelihood.

hearing a, played: a big fight is ahead over your beloved.

playing a: will receive unexpected good company.

    others: arguments within the family over illness of the father.

HARMONY
02-16-40-46-49-53

being in: joy and contentment.

    others: a friend is helping you secretly.

musical, hearing: happiness, pleasant hours.

within the family, having: change in environment.

HARP
07-16-23-24-32-49

broken, being: disassociation from a lover.

    played at a concert: reawakening of spiritual life of one loyal friend.

harpsichord, playing a: the tingling chords of love.

    jazz on a: a puzzling interplay of discordance.

playing a: do not overtax your nerves with faithless friends.

    daughter: she will not have a happy marriage, through misplaced trust.

    enemies: expensive pleasures from a favor of considerable importance.

    others: will view a normal affair as ethereal.

HARVEST
11-17-24-43-45-48

abundant, having an: nature favors your laborious but profitable task.

disrupted by bad weather: brothers battling brothers bring business difficulties.

moon: friends will regret their former extravagances and keep their eyes on one another.

    mist on the: quarrels should not be pushed to seriousness.

poor: are allergic to the diet you are now eating.

workers harvesting: are reaping the culmination of labor done by yourself long ago.

resting from: have traveled an extended, eventful journey to this point.

HARVEST FLIES
02-20-22-34-43-47

catching a: will suffer hunger from nauseous lack of appetite.

   not: your own laziness is keeping you from healing.

jumping: are surrounded by boisterous people.

killing: will receive news of another's operation.

singing, hearing many: arrival of an unwelcome guest.

   at noon: arrival of musicians prone to laziness.

HAT
   08-20-24-32-51-54

black: false friends of the opposite sex.

bonnet, wearing a: much slander from envious friends.

floating on water, your: be wary of the philosophy behind a friend's mental health.

hatbox, closing a: will be called on your indiscretions.

   empty: worry will be smoothed away with reasoning and logic.

   full: disappointment concerning a party.

   opening a: a gay occasion to come where your presence will be marveled at.

hood, hiding under a: secrecy and concealment behind cover of perfection.

losing a new: freedom from old-fashioned authority.

   your: have lost your position of power at work.

making a: your thoughts on a creative job will be requested.

man's: useless work will lead to emotional sorrow.

milliner, of a: your vanity brings easy money.

   buying a, from a: will encounter debts, despite business being to your great advantage.

   selling a, to: will have money coming in the near future.

off to someone, taking your: humility towards a success is not humiliation.

taking off a: a conscious show of respect resulting in advancement.

wearing a big: are trying to conceal your lack of self-confidence under extravagance.

   new: wish attention were centered on you, and it will be.

   not, when appropriate: your thoughts are uncontrollable in the winds of truth.

   old torn, an: physical damage and dishonor to your soul.

   Panama, a: will crash parties you could not afford to give.

   pith helmet: will visit a tropical country.

   someone else: cowering from a situation.

   straw: are prone to a conceit that irritates your associates.

   top: expect to hobnob with the magic of royalty.

   turban: a long-awaited arrival bringing most wanted supplies.

   woman, an unusual: big admiration for finally exposing your true self.

wind blowing your, off: perplexing puzzle will require skillful handling.

   young woman: prone to flirting and will be called to account for it.

woman's: sign of status and pride.

HATCHET
06-13-32-41-44-46

enemies with a: make amends with a more vulnerable enemy, making him an ally.

   friend: will be in danger from a mysterious source.

   others: warning that your life is at risk; anxiety and trouble with machinery.

owning a: it is not impossible to reconcile with enemies.

rusty, a: disobedient people undermine your ability to work.

HATE
16-29-30-42-45-50

being hated by others: the source of the hatred is within you.

detesting a particular person: good luck to the one for whom you care.

getting rid of: enemies will malign you, but it is they who are maligned.

hating others: be careful not to do them wrong unconsciously.

enemies: will win a lawsuit once you recognize their deception.

some of own relatives: others' sadness can be barred from your domestic affairs.

malice without reason: difficulty could be avoided with forethought and care.

by friends: working in a slapdash manner produces sloppy results.

HAWK
02-04-08-11-16-53

chasing a small animal: fight with those of your own intelligence.

dead, a: will contest your enemies and subdue their objection to your actions.

flying: losses caused through intrigue can be retrieved by diligent attention.

over you: stop hovering intently; perceive and process the situation from a great height.

of a: your fortune will increase through your ability to see the whole picture.

over her roost: allow freedom, but watch from afar.

several together: will be shot in the foot by your protégé.

shooting a: no obstacles will be insurmountable if you waylay suspicion.

sparrow, killing a: warning of a period of depression; don't succumb to it.

several: enemies are conspiring against you, soar higher.

HAY
03-12-19-22-27-35

cart, coming down off a: unhappy termination to affection.

full, being: will produce great dividends from your initiative.

loading hay on a: working too hard for too little money.

cutting: seize the moment to your advantage.

fever, suffering from: to keep your health you must guard it.

field of, a: exceptional prosperity as crop yield is copious.

harvesting: a relationship will deepen with an influential stranger.

haystack, finding something in a: are laying the foundation for a prosperous future.

losing: are being deceived when you offer aid to one you assume is in need.

lying on a: simple tastes equal simple cares.

with sweetheart: must rely on own vigor to withstand the enthrall of an evil woman.

loft, playing in the: ease and freedom, young love does not replace recognition or profit.

smell of: good health will lessen the effects of a small accident.

rotten: will receive money from unexpected source.

stack of: will render your services to a person of consequence.

HAZARD
01-09-25-31-45-55

building being a safety: will go into bankruptcy, if you do not reexamine your precepts.

escaping from a: will be involved in car accident, but not hurt.

hurt by a, being: desperate measures are extorting your possessions and finances.

of a: slight ailments will afflict a loved one; look for the source out of the box.

HAZELNUTS
01-22-26-31-32-41

buying: productive arguments and discussions over business ventures.

cracking: stop the dissension before it has time to fester.

eating: joyous occasions with ebullient sterling friends.

picking: father or mother is in danger of death.

tree before picking: difficult problems turn into assets.

HEAD
04-05-34-37-40-55

ache: keep your business plans to yourself or they will cause violent fever.

migraine, having a: your pet project will succeed, if you keep your own counsel.

bald, being: have disregarded virtuous teaching and are envious of another's hair.

back of the, on the: your ideas are barred to the public.

going: society's esteem increases for an

attraction emanating from an internal source.

left side of the, on the: death of a relative who squandered his life on illicit pleasures.

> *right side:* death of a friend who committed indiscretions and did not return to favor.

woman going: after 50, who you are cannot be hidden from your face.

cut off, having your: trust your intuition or you will create new enemies.

> *another's:* will surpass your friends in success.

> *chicken with its:* others will decide what to do next.

> *in half, a:* will win legal conflict with powerful people of vast influence.

> *stranger's, a:* will defeat an unknown adversary.

dead person's, a: will discover the secret of servitude, pain and misery.

facing your back, your: your thoughtless stunts create long-term pain.

foreigner, of a: will take a long journey and be unduly influenced by others.

holding own, in hands: will have a brain disease and subsequent nervous disorder.

hunter, being captured by a: be wary of associating with wild unruly savages.

large rounded: dignity and esteem from good business transactions.

many: must meet dishonor in love with fortitude and good sense.

of own: will receive something good unexpectedly.

> *being turned sideways, a one-eyed Jack:* are too preoccupied with seduction.

round, having a: extract yourself from your involvement before it defeats your heart.

savage, of a: your base desires will keep you hovering at the bottom.

severed, a: fresh bitterness over dashed hopes.

sick person dreaming of a large: will get well soon if you are not obsessed with worry.

small: beware of those whose pleasure is undermined with ulterior motives.

smashing your: resolve conflicts one step at a time.

three-headed person, of a: honor and money immediately upon changing your occupation.

torso without: your rapid rise is based on unstable probabilities.

without a body: a mildly amusingly experience will prove your future.

HEALTH

10-15-17-18-19-50

advocating a healthy life: be wary, you are eating too much.

children being in good: keep things right and care for new ones well.

> *family:* will attain fame stepping up over a friend's injury.

food store, being in a: exercising your right to question the source of all you eat.

healing another: need the emotional support yourself.

of promoting good, by exercise: will have a good position in life.

poor, being in: will be saved from a big peril by increased vigor in business.

> *children:* fortune in their undertakings, lack of harmony in their home.

> *friends:* death of a friend whose wake brings joy to bright companions.

> *husband or wife:* feel bitter resentment for previous iniquity.

> *relatives:* warning of troubles from persecution.

recovering after an illness: must rely upon business intelligence.

selecting vitamins: vitality needs boosting because of overindulgent life.

spa, being in a hot springs: career will have its ups and downs.

> *lolling in waters of a:* your partner's trust is at risk; find ways to reassure mate.

taking exercises for: are too active in affairs to spend time with yourself.

taking the dip in the: will journey to a new home across the sea.

teaching children to live a healthy life: their happiness is your obligation.

HEART

08-38-39-45-48-51

being out of breath with, trouble: will surpass friends if you stop empathizing with them.

big, having a: sickness within the very life force that centers your energy.

    disease: are being disarmed emotionally by others' high drama trips.

    happy: good business, happy and productive living, positive lessons of growth.

    wounded: better times through release from unnecessary annoyances.

bleeding, a: your sacrifice was rebuffed, rightly so, as an insult to another's abilities.

blood passing to, slowly: have failed to compliment your best friend.

burn, an attack of: return to the blander simplicities of a contented life.

eating: happy love affairs as you meet a new, eligible lover.

heartless, being: triumph in business cannot be attained without truth and love.

losing your: the death of your courage is near; suffocate your pain.

man, of a: will love another woman, which will lose you your true love if not quelled.

    woman: will leave your husband if you allow your energy to be drained by another.

    unmarried person: elopement and a particularly insensitive marriage.

pains in your, having: long sickness from the breakage of romantic bonds.

palpitating, feeling your: fear losing your temper when reprimanded by boss.

pulse, checking your: push yourself to your limit, no further.

suffering from, palpitations: are likely to outlive your children.

HEAT
18-24-26-35-45-55

being very hot: your body is reacting to distressing physical symptoms.

heater, buying a new: are prone to frivolity towards your physiology.

    lighting a: looming tensions are temporary; advancement within own position.

    putting out a: apologize to another for ill-considered comments.

in your face, having: friends are letting their negative imagination run riot.

suffering from a, stroke: have no willingness to worry about another's travails.

very heated place, being in a: a profound imagination with transient emotions.

HEATHENS
06-16-20-24-27-30

being among: a return to home values and nurturing feelings.

priest going among: dignity and distinction at the center of sacred beginnings.

referring to one of another faith as a: that you be so judged.

savage country among, going to a: will enjoy contented home life.

HEAVENS
02-13-27-30-32-41

ascending to the: success too late in life to allow a full family.

being clear: escapist wish fulfillment of grandeur and glory.

    dark: a new and more complicated, but better project.

being in: are going helter-skelter; settle into an immediate marriage.

climbing a ladder to the: your accomplishments are at that rung in the ladder.

    unable to: will meet with losses, passionate, heated arguments.

of the moonlit: financial gain, understanding and love, as you rise in stature, is exposed.

surrounding the earth, of the: your reunion will reveal losses; reconcile and continue.

viewing the, with a loved one: prosperity, bliss and contentment.

    free of clouds: enlightenment will bring comfort and love to you; hold it.

    obscured by clouds: fail to benefit fully from your toil; the carrot of joy is ever ahead.

without the sun: recovery from an illness; have turned off that emotional faucet.

    stars: will receive bad news; need regrouping of your loving support.

HEAVY
13-14-19-21-35-43

being crushed under a, load: do allow yourself to be dominated by friends.

carrying something: children will be born into the family; your burden is to raise them.

children carrying, bundles of books: big honors and stooped shoulders.

friends carrying, things: a poor showing in business affairs, even with the use of caution.

    laborers: remove the weights and allow yourself to be courted.

    others: will receive unexpected money; delegate that responsibility.

of, heavy articles: wealth will assume a gloomy cast.

HEIGHT
01-44-47-48-49-50

fear of: will fall from feeling above it all, to participation in new challenges.

reaching the, of your career: are striving for ambitions beyond your capabilities.

    depth: should strive harder to comprehend motives of those you dislike.

HEIRLOOM
04-10-25-31-46-53

having a personal: establish dignity within your social association.

putting an, away: will be humiliated by another's social error.

receiving property as an inheritance: will lose present affluence and gain responsibility.

HELICOPTER
18-22-29-33-42-46

landing in a: are a special person with unique talents; use them.

pilot of a, being the: are in control of your life, like never before.

ride in a, taking a: have become frivolous in your spending; stop it at once.

someone else flying a: competitors are causing you to lose business.

HELL
17-20-22-39-41-44

being in: the pain will continue until you choose the right path.

cavorting with Hades in: worst kind of suffering and torment in the future.

    dealing: once emotional power is relinquished there is no escape.

enjoying weird pleasures in: sins against the Universal Will must be redeemed.

hearing the people in, groaning: your purification process has begun.

of: succumbing to temptation has brought you a complete description of life.

returning from: hate decayed your hope and created your own hell.

running away from: denied pain spreads like gangrene.

HELP
03-16-34-40-45-49

asking for financial: are in position of gratitude from influential people.

firing: you expect too many favors of others; will be constantly changing jobs.

hiring: your hard work will earn respect of associates.

receiving, from a dog: will be double-crossed by a woman in ill temper.

    friend, a: your SOS in the near future will be answered.

reliable, having: must account to your employer for unseemly actions.

requiring: attempt to understand the hearts of your acquaintances.

HERBS
01-03-13-41-52-53

balm made from: your extended family expands.

basil: sweetness, kindness and deep affection.

collecting: heal yourself naturally; nourish your rest.

cutting: will have a long life of pleasing adventures.

eating fresh: use a natural solution; be wary, every leaf has a differing medicinal value.

ginger, tasting: your passion is misplaced.

growing vigorously: will be contented in everyday life with abundant means.

potion, an herbal: your resoluteness will gain a decisive victory.

    bitter: your presence is felt, the caustic one.

    sweet: sacrifices and condescension will win your partner back.

with their flowers: abundant means of therapeutic care.

HERMAPHRODITE
04-7-15-16-32-41

being a: must behave more judiciously in company of opposite sex.

both male and female reproductive organs,
having: will have many disgusting
emotions.

others being: will be guilty of foolish actions,
causing distress.

sailing vessel with two masts: will take long
journey with all parts of yourself.

son of Hermes and Aphrodite joined in one
body, the: companions will be provocative.

HERMIT
07-16-18-36-43-49

becoming a: your lack of faith has caused
you to withdraw.

being a: much misery caused by unfaithful
friends; pursue your own research, alone.

in tattered clothes, a: your reserved and self-
centered efforts will bear no gains.

of a: if you had been more daring, you would
have gained more.

HERO
04-07-12-40-50-53

being a: are more successful than you realize.
heroine: emulate the characteristics you
admire.

with others hissing you: will be disappointed with a new ally.

hissing a: are not being truthful about your
envy.

leaping, a: look first, confidence heeds
warnings.

of a: one who is treating you coolly will have a
change of heart.

that you admire: listen to advice as
presented; act on advice from your
heart.

relative being a: be aware of the overall
danger.

HERRING
04-07-09-18-25-32

buying: will be generous to friends who will
be suspicious of your actions.

catching: desires will be satisfied after a slight
predicament.

cooking: expect pregnancy in the near future.

eating: good luck to one for whom you care.

given, by others, being: will realize high ambitions and monetary pinches.

smoked: conquer overindulgence in cheap
wines and liquor.

HIDING
02-17-22-39-42-45

from attacker: will have explanations to give
for your eccentric doings.

small ominous figures: fear of dealing
with little problems makes big ones
impossible.

going around: persecution of your thoughts
and ideas.

money: apprehension, to the deleterious
effects of others' influence.

others: tend to disallow development within a
relationship.

place, being found in your: your secrets are not
securely protected.

and killed: are accusing others of your
own prejudices.

relatives: are being deceived by those prejudiced against you.

HIGH SCHOOL
01-18-25-35-55-56

being in: quarrels will end with people of
inferior intelligence.

children going to: will get no satisfaction from
modesty.

graduating from: will distinguish yourself
by an intellectual achievement.

highbrow clique, being in a: will be shamed
by one for whom you have little
regard.

teaching: will be happy at your innocence of
the real world.

HILL
06-24-31-48-51-55

climbing up a: will gain confidence
when your future good fortune is
surmountable.

having difficulties: must overcome
being weakened by fallout, inner
and outer.

others: the path to the unattainable
begins with one loyal friend.

with relatives: financial gains with
established income and contentment.

hiker, meeting a: change course to the
one providing physical and mental rejuvenation.

on a path: be patient, slow determined
progress recharges you with each step.

reaching the crest of a: will have to fight against envy, other battles are easy.

several: will have easy earnings and an opportunity to climb to new adventures.

HIPS
01-23-29-31-42-52

admiring your husband's: he is cheating on you; handle situation with care and calm.

　wife: will have love affair in a foreign land, to her great disappointment.

breaking own: sickness and loss of children cannot be replaced; hips can.

injured and bleeding, being: mate will cause family embarrassment and large losses.

of own: slow but sure progress in a succession of seemingly unrelated problems.

　enemies: triumph over enemies in their loss of reputation.

　fat: animalistic pleasures.

operation on, having an: misplaced surety, that mate is leaving you for physical reasons.

HISTORY
01-09-12-20-23-36

consulting a book on ancient: your fortune is at expense of others.

of past: big honors if you learn judgment from studying the past.

reading a, book: be ready to go into the bankruptcy of not knowing before you can learn.

　modern, books: don't believe lies being told by another.

teacher, being a: intensive research leads to a comprehensive analysis of disorder.

HIT
04-06-15-24-51-53

bandit, being, by a: changes in personal relations from an imagined wrong.

　enemies: your surroundings are changed, which will bring improvement of personal situation.

　friend: reconciliation after a quarrel over your supersensitivity.

　others: good fortune comes from a friend.

　wild person: will gain the love of one you desire.

hitting someone: present situation will get worse unless you rise above it.

each other, people: shame will fall upon your worthless accounts.

　children: will advance in their own position, not an extension of yours.

HOGS
01-05-08-22-26-36

bristles: brisk and violent dangers of prickly import.

buying: are conceited, selfish and unreasonably rude.

many: will receive money after the death of a relative.

others who have: will be introduced to a new factory business.

selling: will be hated by friends for a successful sale.

squealing: irritating revelation of muddied facts.

thin, being: children will cause petty vexations.

　well fed: prosperity from your poor showing after an altercation with a woman.

wild, a: a friend will try to cause harm to your ability to organize.

HOLE
04-14-19-26-33-45

clothes, in your: your debts must be paid.

creeping into a: will come in contact with undesirable people.

darning a: an old disagreement must be settled.

falling into a: your harming another will cause you to recoil.

making a: be wary of the authenticity of a stranger's opinion.

　others: good times will come in the future.

peering into a: a previously unknown part of yourself.

　out of a: the trap has been set for a situation you cannot easily climb out of.

shoes, in your: your troubles will not walk away.

HOLY GRAIL
06-15-24-27-32-42

of the: your estate will touch everyone involved.

quest for the: your mission is the only thing that matters.

searching for the: your efforts will procure great rewards.

seeking holiness: peace and accord with your family and friends.

HOME

03-06-37-47-50-54

angel coming in your: are relinquishing your strong-willed opinions for superficial gains.

another's: will have a lawsuit over property disputes coming up.

arranging things in a: desires will not be realized; time will fill up the emptiness.

attic of another's: indefinable obstacles will confront your spiritual awareness.

bedroom, missing a: wish sex with your partner would cease and he would find another.

> *bathroom:* cleansing is futile in a tainted atmosphere.

big fire burning a: friends are being disagreeable; replace them with congenial strangers.

> *with dark smoke:* a mystery is ahead, if you follow your head, not your heart.

breaking any household object: home life frustrated with difficulties from outside party.

bric-a-brac in a: good fortune if you break the set.

building a: honor without joy in an unwarranted legacy.

collapsing ceiling, your: support is lacking; have lost your spiritual connection, meditate.

deluge, own, lost in a: slow down and take time to smell the roses.

dilapidated old: lies are being told about your family; a relative will die.

entering your dream, on a sunny day: happiness is nearby; buy real estate.

fire in your: follow your head and not your heart.

> *another's:* a friend needs your advice.

fitting into a small: prosperity, especially for lovers, if you solve one problem at a time.

floor, missing a: your solid foundation had been reduced.

rots: take more time for yourself.

friends visiting your: sorrow.

going in own, having a: pleasant work and good news make loss even more vexing.

going upstairs in a: dependence and independence alike found here.

ground floor of own: your daily inner strength and grounding for communal living.

homesick, being: your past as seen through rose-colored glasses will ruin your future.

> *leaving home:* your regret for what you left behind can be used to your advantage.

>> *for good:* are at the threshold of a fervent and fanatical passion.

>> *returning:* your refusal to extend travel will turn to regret of lost opportunity.

housewife with, in disorder: a former suitor will try to lure you away.

hut, living in a: it isn't much, but it's yours.

kitchen, missing a: are cooking up a cabal of plots and spicing them.

living room, missing a: emotional contact in the hearth of happiness.

locked out of own: avoid needless risk-taking; you are ready to move on.

lost own, having: be more careful of financial matters.

mosaic, laying a: profit is insufficient compensation; are overcomplicating a simple task.

others coming to your: will have much consolation if you search for your soul mate.

> *uninvited:* sorrow and tears as your personal space is being taken over.

receiving a, as a gift: return to childhood desires that need to be expressed.

refused admission to your, being: be cautious with plans and their planners.

shelter, being thrown out of a homeless: your courage is all you have left.

someone trying to break into your: others jealous of your success seek to destroy you.

> *rattling your windows:* your path to success is being blocked.

>> *battering down the door:* have enemies; be on guard.

stoop, sitting on the: your life is out of control; rein it in.

seeing others: friends come forward to assist you.

strange, entering a: new undertakings in disordered affairs.

termites in a: are physically exhausted and far too scattered in your personal life.

trembling: small loss of money; large loss of comfort.

visiting an old: will have cause to rejoice with a visit from friends at sea.

wallpaper, hanging: you are seeking to hide recent indiscretions.

walls collapsing in a: are physically exhausted and must rest.

war zone, own, being in a: violent invasion of private space.

HONEY
09-23-28-31-40-42

being given: your fitness allows you more independence and health.

eating: lack of self-knowledge will deny you the sweet smell of success.

fingers sticky with: some of your group are so slow and deliberate they are embarrassing.

honeycombs: your vulnerability threatens your honesty in community affairs.

making, in the yard: your mate is kind, affectionate and attentive; honor that.

HONEYMOON
02-09-14-23-25-43

being on own: an undertone of the illegal is the means of your abundant material gain.

children going on their: joy without profit; prompt flow of marital bliss.

    friends: disappointment in the financial stability of mate.

    relatives: will take a small trip to a remote place to settle accounts with God.

going on a: will be prosperous in your work and contented in your marriage.

HONOR
01-09-10-26-35-41

being honored: beware of false promises; celebrate the true ones.

defending your: violent emotions in support of your right to a life.

famous person: a slight acquaintance esteems you higher than you think.

giving your word of: be cautious in legal matters.

losing your: your confused depression should be professionally analyzed.

    others, to: sad consequences to follow bad management of your ethical affairs.

others showing you: their insincerity magnifies slight disputes into adversities.

receiving an: the original simplicity is deprived of a respect for honorable actions.

    others: will lose money invested in their worthless accounts.

HOODLUMS
10-13-24-26-32-43

being a: infidelity from those whom you have trusted.

blackmailing you: will be shamed and held up for public scorn.

having dealings with: one you thought was dishonest is honest and loyal.

of: someone will steal from you by luring you from virtue to obligation.

HOOK
06-16-19-29-34-38

being hooked: your bad decisions are better than others making them for you.

catching things with a: will squirm until you master many things.

fish, a: a secret passion swells in you for a long-time acquaintance.

having a: the source of a generous gesture will surprise you.

using a: are obstinate about unworthy projects.

    rock climbing: someone close to you is worried about your cavalier behavior.

wriggling free from a: success will bear the expense of your grief.

HOPE
17-18-32-41-44-45

having: have strong resources of character to support your actions.

    good, for family: your nervousness will cause you to fail to act.

    relative: are easily led, without a distinctive personality to monitor you.

losing: will defend your interests at all costs.

success of children, for: arguments with rela-

tives over new horizons opening up for
you.

HORNS

07-11-23-24-26-37

animals with: the dilemma is a wake-up call
for you to listen to your inner voices.

blowing a: extended social activities of a
happy nature; hasty news of a sinful
nature.

> *while hunting:* useless chatter will distract
> participants from the matter at hand.

bull or cow, of a: have an unusual degree of
stolid organizational ability.

buying: good business transactions through
your strong willpower.

hearing the sound of a: the cavalry is coming
to your well-deserved aid.

man, having, on his forehead, a: danger of a
disease that brings death.

> *others:* clashes and conflicts over an-
> other's problems.

receiving, as a gift: feel cheated at every
turn; are more anxious for marriage
than love.

HORSE RACES

02-11-24-29-35-40

derby horse win, having your: you have many
enemies.

> *lose:* a keen regret for an unworthy action.

galloping, a jockey: great profit in a perilous
adventure.

> *trotting, a:* increase your pace if you
> expect to complete your work before
> sunset.

loved one, attending a derby with a: who you
are seen with defines you to strangers.

> *others:* failure of enemies in every direc-
> tion in a compromising situation.

watching a derby: a luxury you cannot afford
to bet on.

> *others:* choose one of your enemies to aid
> in your triumph over the other.

HORSES

04-07-10-26-30-42

being a: have not realized your physical energies.

black, a: your mourning and grief for being
molested will separate you from others.

> *dark, a:* a season of discontent, hard train-

ing and spirited counsel; a victory so
sweet.

> *other colors, of:* good business is on the
> way to you.

> *tan, a:* will realize own ambitions; be care-
> ful handling ideas.

> *white, a:* joy, but not at other's expense;
> commingling of congenial friends.

breaking a wild: another is resisting your
attempts to be a friend.

bridled, a: animal side of nature needs to be
reined in.

bridling a: your success will be tainted by
having to pay off your enemies.

buying a: will profit from a property sale and
be lost in an emotional vacuum.

castrated, a: will lose a valuable but after
much anxiety will find it.

coach, pulling a: will meet a distant relative
who will insinuate himself into your life.

dead, a: forfeiture of a pleasant marriage and
fortunate enterprises through intemperance.

driving a team of: success for plans of good
harvest and domestic happiness.

falling off of a: jump out of the project before
it crashes.

foal, a: postponement of success with advantageous news.

> *running after his mother:* striking new
> beginnings improving your home
> life.

> > *sucking milk from:* triumph over
> > enemies, if you meet only honor-
> > able obligations.

friends riding a: a friend will make love to
your mate.

gray, a: money will come easily during life.

halter on a, putting a: will control destiny in
time, despite those working against you.

> *leading a, by the:* evaluate decisions care-
> fully before deliberate actions.

harness, a: advancement of a minor nature in
own love affairs.

> *buying a:* will be tempted by a new love.

hitting a, to make him obey: will injure your
friends with selfish acts of arrogance.

horseshoe, finding a: good luck to one for
whom you care.

losing: others will advance with the profit from your enterprise.

kicked by a, being: faulty overconfidence with strangers.

limping, a: will encounter opposition; start your own project.

livery servant, having a: triumph in life with faithful assistance of friends.

losing a: others will advance with the profit from your enterprise.

mane: a struggle to raise yourself with an invitation into society.

mare, a: will be married to a beautiful lady in near future.

mounted on a, being: wealthy marriage; sexual energy is well-supported.

mouth, foam of a: have loyal friends who have a difficult time keeping to the truth.

neighing, a: an unwelcome guest will be entertained and intimidated into leaving.

several at once: a predator is approaching your stable.

Pegasus: your imagination is fertilized by your instincts.

pulling a wagon: free yourself of the constraint of others.

reins, putting on: needless worry about another's health you can't change.

holding tightly on the: your intellect should temper your emotional urges.

ridden by a man, being: another has control of his life and yours.

woman: will be reconciled with friends after yielding to importune advances.

riding a: steady reins and firm heart will raise you a step further in life.

apprehension about: take action to improve this sphere of your life.

bareback: independence and codependence can coexist.

dangerous: your worrying, lack of confidence and confusion leave you open to harm.

equestrian, the hounds, an: unexpected dividend from a worthless stock.

fearlessly enjoying yourself: a rewarding relationship with your community.

not belonging to you: are unable to commit yourself to a partner.

overturned, a, a woman being: marriage will not last long.

racing: quarrels with friends over control of your vitality.

rocking, a: your indecision is costing you.

stallion, a: your social climbing will not bring you peace.

thrown from a, and being: use caution against scandal and disgrace.

runaway, hiding a: are challenging tradition without support of your superiors.

selling a: your generosity and unselfishness towards mate are appreciated.

shod, being: interests will advance beyond wildest expectations.

showing, at a fair: will handle affairs through turbulence to prosperity.

spurs, having: should accept other's attempts to bolster your confidence and composure.

fastening the: anxiety over results in business dealings.

raking a horse with: are nagged by one who does not have to do the work.

stirrups, fastening: will be forced to travel to regain fortune; the trip will be delayed.

having difficulty: profiting from other's ill fortune causes violent quarrels with a friend.

unfastening: a series of unlucky incidents add up to success.

tail, with a long: friends will help select your wife.

short: friends will desert you when you are in misery.

trading: are setting yourself wide open for deception in tricky business deal.

visit on horseback, someone coming to: expect a courting of your favor.

whipping a: your fury and disapproval are with yourself.

wild, restless bucking a: your overcoming great difficulties will be rewarded.

wounded, a: desires will be difficult to consummate in the enterprises of friends.

HOSPITAL

03-15-24-26-38-41

being in a: solution will be found to a long-standing problem.

another's: misfortune to the entire community.

children's: starvation of love in one's future must be fed.

enemies': misery without the push to the competitive edge.

mental: conflict between intuition and actions must be mended.

oxygen tent, in an: are being nurtured by those standing by.

relatives': someone will be highly considerate of you.

religious: your imperfections need attentive prayer.

to visit a friend: must explain misdeed to one outside the family.

very ill: news will be difficult to bear; project as now planned will fail.

cafeteria, eating in a: it isn't the food but the atmosphere that causes indigestion.

confined in an MRI: are being exceptionally decisive with your improving health.

an iron lung: are stricken with worries only gargantuan efforts can solve.

lead object on your chest in the: situation weighs you down, confining your rejuvenation.

leaving a, completely recovered: a good friend is relieving you of a difficult task.

nursing someone in a: are expressing an imprisoned part of yourself to another.

back to health: and succeeding.

of a: misery is yours right now.

patient in a, being a: the obstacles are too high to hurdle alone.

strapped to a, bed: strong family relationships, but they are not listening to you.

stretcher, being carried on a: argument over important matters in own ambition.

carrying a: your need their talent and they need your management skills.

surgeon operating: a profession is always messy; a work of art takes time.

using a lance: friends avoid you for unexplained reasons.

surgery being performed: your misdeeds are known to everyone, though not spoken.

on another: loss of a friend through tragedy.

trapped in a: get a second opinion and you will be better off.

treated by religious person at a: will be helped by God.

wandering in circles in a: are missing someone lost to depressed melancholia.

HOTEL

09-21-22-28-29-32

living in a: your life of ease will be more expensive than you thought.

making your home in a: delightful experiences with new friends.

of a: escape your present situation by rising above it.

owning a: success brought about by massive personal effort.

spending the night in a: overspending your income.

suite, being alone in a: family disagreements will be hampered by old-fashioned ideas.

going to a party in a: will be highly considered by others.

very fine: will take a long journey not available to everyone.

working in a: will find a more lucrative position and better chance elsewhere.

your sweetheart, being in a, with: your affair should remain secret.

HOUNDS

01-09-28-30-32-45

at work: will have luck and prosperity with no emotional involvement.

blood, a: a faithful friend will search for your venture and prosperity, but there is a limit.

following the: others are doing the same research; try another path.

owning a: success will come after much struggling.

riding to: make good use of your leisure time.

pursued by, being: if you slack your pace, you will suffer a breakdown.

HOUR

02-10-12-21-29-42

clock chiming the: wait until the last chime to make major decisions.

cuckoo giving the: unexpected wealth through your forwardness.

eleventh, the: anxiety before a deadline.

hourglass, of an: are running out of time to save your relationship.

> *with all the sand at the bottom:* concentrate on what you have achieved.

seeing the, on a clock in the street: for the stability of your life, donate to charity.

> *wristwatch:* will lose a friend with your inability to arrive on time.

HOUSE
05-08-10-18-28-37

arranging things in a: desires will not be realized.

back door of a, using the: wish to return to childhood candidness.

baggage inside a: a trip is canceled.

beam, rotten old: resolve the core problem before proceeding.

being torn down: short, mad love affair will ruin your marriage.

belonging to others: have let an enemy see your privacy and will be harmed by it.

bricks, setting: build on your intellectual talents.

> *owning:* your finances are secure enough to start your remodeling job.

building a new: honor without joy through a wise change.

> *addition, an:* begin a new exercise regime.

>> *to a unstable house:* reverse your recent decisions.

> *with others:* will have a big consolation; value your present support group.

burning, a: are blaming the wrong person.

> *own:* wild parties damage your soul.

car crashes into a: plans for the future will be changed at your impetus.

changing houses: apply for your mortgage, then find the right house.

cleaning: will receive news from an absent person.

commercial buildings around: important decision will change your emotional situation.

cottage, living in a: life lived on one level practically and emotionally; tranquility.

> *empty, an:* low income brings loneliness and trouble.

crowded out of your, being: relief will allow ventures to prosper.

damaged by animal invasion: abandon old habits that failed you.

> *earthquake:* lack basic support structure to present your venture.

> *insects:* are allowing petty annoyances to destroy your peace.

> *wind:* your sanity at risk from wild thoughts.

decorating a: have confidence in your own abilities; use them.

empty, an: you rue missed opportunities as you view the walls of your soul.

fine, a: have proper regard for yourself.

foundation of own, is sinking: basis of your faculties needs constructive support.

full of people, a: good relationship with family and friends.

gazebo, during a rainstorm, in a: others can read love in your silence.

lintel, being under a door: will move to a larger home for greater protection.

lost through bankruptcy: will have arguments about money and material objects.

> *foreclosure:* your demands on your energy exceed your supply.

missing a part of your: have unfinished business with a parent.

odd, an: be the black sheep no more; problems must be sorted out.

old, an: considering the alternative, aging is OK.

razing a: your strength has exploded from within.

roof shingles, leaking: a crack in your security, leaving your domestic bliss incomplete.

> *looking at:* physical security is at a premium.

shanty, a: live simply and sufficiently but do not disregard your health.

sold out from under you: return to your house of worship.

trapped in the: need to seek some counseling.

> *closet:* family secrets need to be revealed.

> *in an opening:* this is the time to examine all you are doing.

> *under an object:* your plans exceed your resources.

tree falling on a: have health check-up by your physician of choice.

under attack: your mind is being threatened by those who want what you have.

wallpapering a room: design the whole space first, all walls.

   many: changing your image must come from within.

walls give way: have taken on too many responsibilities.

water flooding: feel overwhelmed with tears for a sadness from long ago.

wrong with the, something: take back control of your life.

HUMOR
14-15-17-24-29-46

bad, being in a: false friends are nearby awaiting your taking yourself too seriously.

   boss: will receive an invitation to dinner and an agreeable proposal.

   husband or wife: foolish gossip is being incited by your attacks on mate.

   sweethearts: will encounter someone you love even in the worst of worlds.

good, being in a: disagreements and unhappiness if you cannot laugh at your own acts.

   sweethearts: will make a long trip on a slow boat.

HUNCHBACK
01-07-08-09-14-18

being a: will be humiliated by inabilities caused by poor health.

female a: many trials with strange but likable people.

male a: changes to come, bringing financial fortune.

talking to a: pleasant news of personal success.

HUNGRY
01-22-25-31-40-42

being: malicious gossip obstructs your being accepted.

   children: are starving for recognition of your spiritual substance.

   enemies: their battle with you has just begun.

   others: a cry for acceptance for your achievements and to gain new ones.

feeling hunger pangs: the lack of affection makes you feel hungry.

HUNTING
08-11-14-18-28-48

actually: are struggling for a majesty you cannot gain.

being on a, party: intrigues involving one who does not acknowledge your love.

big game: are manufacturing prosperity out of the residue of destroyed animal urges.

changing your place of: success in manufacturing when you change location.

decoy: deceit of someone for whom you have affection.

elk: will have an awestruck influence over women, leading to intrigues.

fox, a: will conquer difficulties of lack of trust in close associate.

going: will be accused by friends of unbecoming behavior.

many people: your endeavors are too weak to conquer obstacles; will be scandalized.

missing an animal while: failure of own desires to find the truth.

small animals: jealousy, resentment and petty intrigues.

trip, returning from a: are worried about responsibilities left behind.

women: see women as prey, not companions.

HURDLES
11-21-26-31-32-41

fixing: must clear yourself of false suspicions.

jumping: chance of advancement where a risk taker is valued.

of: will be unjustly accused of not taking the straight and narrow.

others arranging: will hear from an old acquaintance.

HURRICANE
05-07-08-25-34-40

being in a: nothing will avoid this complete disruption.

   the eye of a: impending crisis of belief system solved with the advice of friends.

devastation from a: one wrong step will be calamitous; a mystery has yet to be solved.

losing property in a: will avert business trouble by sheer luck.

roar and wind of a, the frightful: will suffer tortuous thoughts to avoid failure.

HURRY

05-07-08-12-22-47

being in a: danger of an accident you can avoid with quick action.

    children: important and very beneficial event to come.

    enemies: are doomed for disappointment with your selfishness.

    friends: will live a long life if you aid your grateful friends.

going somewhere in a big: you are a very happy-go-lucky person.

HUSBAND

12-13-19-21-22-38

beating his wife: are laying yourself open for criticism with your behavior.

    caressing: will be advantageously married within a year.

    divorcing: if you can relieve the bitterness, a reconciliation is possible.

calming one's: will have a violent family quarrel.

checking on: unfitted for position of loyal married person.

good, having a: a meaningful relationship will develop and last.

losing a, by death: important and very beneficial events to come.

love with another, is in: be prepared for the worst by taking care of your needs.

marrying a second: mistreatment; the foibles of first marriage tarnish the second.

nagging his wife: events occur over which you have no control; allow her that.

neglecting your: you are not being supported by your husband.

of a, when unmarried: are not ready to commit to marriage; or no one will commit to you?

others flirting with your: will live together all your life, yet he seeks pleasure elsewhere.

someone else's, liking: immediate congeniality impossible with emotional baggage.

wanting to divorce your: must control your passions until harmony is reinstated.

wife nagging her: circumstances will improve after a visit with the doctor.

HYACINTH

07-13-34-39-42-49

enemies wearing a: misfortune of those who are endeavoring to destroy you.

given to you, having a: unexpected guests become unwanted very quickly.

of: your faithful husband will improve your finances.

on your clothes: will have an everlasting marriage.

smelling a: a heartrending separation will prove positive, eventually.

wilted: your high expectations from a friend will be dashed.

HYMNS

10-11-12-16-31-37

hearing others singing: a constructive occupation within the community.

    foreigners: contentment at recovery from an illness.

singing: plans will require your courage and bravery.

    in church: own affairs will develop into a journey.

sung by friends, being: fair business prospects through mutual cooperation.

HYPNOTISM

07-13-14-20-35-37

being under another's influence: face disaster with the determination to survive.

mesmerizing others: your subtle influence will triumph over enemies.

of being hypnotized: confidence will be betrayed; sin can no longer be hidden.

others who are mesmerized: your confusion will clear; continue paying your debts.

HYPOCRITICAL

08-10-16-20-21-23

being: a false friend is cheating you by jumping to a quick conclusion.

    in love: your reputation destroyed, your chances at love are diminished greatly.

person, having dealings with a: will be undermined and exposed bare to your enemies.

realizing that you are: will lose your security in business through your own deception.

HYSTERICS

07-17-18-34-40-45

children: do not allow yourself to be dominated by one closest to you.

having: block being forced into anything, but listen to advice.

mob hysterics: national calamities are fed by the bitterness of a few failures in their lives.

relatives: be firm in order to achieve success.

ICE
08-14-24-25-43-48

breaking through the: an association based on a common ground.

businessman dreaming of: inability to break through obstacles in affairs.

> *farmer:* good harvesting is your job; the weather is God's.

> *ladies:* cannot cope adequately with own cooling emotions.

> *merchants:* are taking a risk for improvement in business.

> *military men:* promotion within their ranks or death on the front lines.

> *working people:* feels bound to follow leaders who cannot aid him.

> *young people:* threatening danger if unacceptable impulses are not controlled.

crystals on the window: your beautiful emotions are unrequited.

falling on the: a slight bump in your progress is a dealbreaker.

> *in the:* a secret adversary undermines your efforts.

floating in clear water: your happiness is surrounded by jaundiced eyes.

iceberg, of an: don't be frightened; it is all a part of your unconscious.

icicles, hanging from the eaves: distress will soon melt, leaving new sensations.

> *melting and dropping water:* your life is out of your control and into Mother Nature's.

melting: frozen emotions previously restrained take form.

of many: big business prosperity freezes over, no movement up or down allowed.

refrigerator, in own: discomfort during warm weather.

running on the: restlessness, waiting for deception in love.

sliding on the: a new, exciting, fast-tracked disaster threatens.

storm: those in distress will attempt to injure your creative effort.

vessel used to break up: make big efforts and you will triumph.

walking with others on the: waste time and money on temporary daring.

ICE CREAM
02-24-26-33-40-49

buying: danger through an overindulgence in your secure relationship.

eating: a love affair satisfies your cravings, not your emotions.

> *children:* childhood should be left for the young.

> *enemies:* they must endure starvation, according to your cold expression.

licking an, cone: greed and lust are complexes to be overcome.

> *others:* a naïve acquaintance idolizes your guidance.

making: restrain yourself from proposed action.

ICE SKATING
02-06-19-25-31-49

being injured while: your aloofness harms all those around you.

braking through the ice while: not following bad advice will bring you to your mark.

figure: an artistic relationship with skill demands unique discipline.

in competition: a bold confrontation shows your mettle.

rink, in a: risky business requires skilled support.

watching others: combine technical skill with artistry.

wobbly on skates: jumping without the expertise leads to disaster.

IDIOT
02-09-11-16-17-46

being an: are on the way to receive a cabinet post.

> *child:* will have a prominent place in life with their particular intelligence.

many: are exaggerating issues beyond their worth.

of an: unexpected fortune waits for you to deal with affliction.

IDOL

02-07-28-29-39-41

being idolized by others: are apprehensive over difference with a business associate.

idolizing a saint: are due for an increase in wages for your mastery over self.

an image: serious mental distortions lead to ill luck.

your children: must conceal your expectations; they will weight them down.

imitating an: your mysterious personality is jealous and unlucky.

movie star: are about to meet with major disapproval and discontent.

of an: intentions are to commit an injustice against another.

sacred cow, a: jealousy will arise between you and warm friends.

Superman: moodiness at being unable to reveal yourself.

IGNORANT

01-12-33-37-41-47

being: success will crown your efforts if you acknowledge your ignorance.

children: exposure of secret you would prefer hidden.

dealing with, people: will have to prove your identity in court.

unable to read or write, someone: will take an added responsibility at job.

ILL-BRED

02-25-31-33-46-47

friends who are: control your temper with those who harass you beyond endurance.

people: be threatened with embarrassment of an accident caused by others.

people, being among: success in your affairs will foster those who prefer your downfall.

person, being an: don't let others assail your conduct and reputation.

ILLNESS

01-07-15-24-25-49

brain, having a: self-punishment for guilt over hostile resentment.

chilblains, having: your anxiety pushes you into deceptive dealings, which leads to illness.

constipation, suffering from: memories must be re-experienced before they can be let go.

convulsions, having: your predicament can be alleviated by strong will.

others: much underhandedness among your fellow workers.

cyst, growing a: a morbid collection of energies unable to harmonize.

delirium, having: danger through a secret not kept.

children: enhanced prospects for the future.

others: a new colleague will betray you once your guard is down.

edema, suffering from: all your nutritional indiscretions will turn on you.

fits, having: are unable to attend to your duties because of illness.

flu, suffering from the: take a long rest after you are well.

frailty, of: feel you can't match another's expectations.

gallstones, having: a bright future after obstacles are passed.

germ, of a: the inner manifestation of a good or bad growth direction or idea.

having an: move out of the restrictive atmosphere.

children: my consolation is that you are the one who is distressed.

disability: apply for a complex job that you haven't done before, though you want the challenge.

enemies: great temptation will not be favorable for you.

indigestion: your pessimistic thoughts make life difficult to swallow.

nonfatal: take a multivitamin complex.

others: someone you know will go to prison.

relatives: arguments with loved ones will worry you.

sweetheart: must forego some anticipated pleasure to gain future ones.

unknown: diagnosis is positive for new love.

woman dreaming of: despair at inability to improve another's welfare.

head cold: are germinating an excuse to not do an arduous task.

hemorrhoids, having: have foolishly exposed yourself to parasites.

hoarse because of a cold, being: being disillusioned by the words of others.

　others: put additional energy and nourishment into love matters.

　speaking with a, sound: will lose an opportunity from inability to express your views.

infirm, being: mischief makers can plot against your affectations, not your actions.

influenza, dying from: faithful friends will show compassion toward you.

jaundice, having: a warning to check out your yellowness with a doctor.

　mate: quarrels with sweetheart over unfaithful heart.

lockjaw, having: will marry a nagging partner and grind your teeth, not state your case.

　dying from: inability to speak your mind will destroy your life.

many people in a hospital with: an epidemic of petty proportions affecting a multitude.

mentally ill person, a: thrive among the chaos or harm will come to you.

　seeing yourself as a: overly imaginative people build sham castles.

nervous condition, having a serious: will discover a treasure among frayed minds.

pneumonia, of: will have a lengthy illness as long as you do not follow your better judgment.

　dying from: will suffer big losses; dissolution of own hopes.

prickly heat, having: a confluence of toxins are attacking your nervous system.

spleen, having an enlarged: malice, spite, illtemper, melancholy and ennui.

stomach, having a: are weak-willed and easily persuaded to stray.

swollen glands: a clue to a significant illness, which needs to be eliminated.

visiting people with an: will find a way to attain your own goal.

IMAGE
08-20-32-39-43-45

dead person, of a: expect the death of a relative, physically and emotionally.

　relatives, of: postpone important decisions on unsettled business, official and personal.

of an: guard against judging others, even if your actions are above reproach.

own children, of: many attempts to make them in your image will come to naught.

saint, of a: an irrevocable impropriety done in haste will cause years of repentance.

several beautiful: friendship slides away with disillusionment and failures on every score.

IMPALED
07-08-15-18-38-46

being tortured or punished: errors will cause pain and heartaches.

escaping from an, condition: feel you should be punished for an act you have not yet done.

upon railings, being: will be threatened by enemies and suffer for their faults.

　others: your repressed anger has reached certifiable proportions; seek help.

IMPATIENT
06-19-20-21-37-45

being: will reach own goals slowly but surely, but never quick enough for you.

　business people, with: feel restrained from indulging in creative schemes.

　children: a letter containing money from a source you expected to be paying.

　friends: feel another deserves to be restrained.

others: will get away with an act but will receive punishment from God.

IMPORTERS
15-25-31-35-40-43

being an: be diligent in your own work to secure your enterprises.

different animals, being, of: will enjoy much wealth; others will dispute your attainments.

　general merchandise: will be ashamed of actions; outwit your enemies to rectify them.

others being: will come into possession of valuables of questionable ownership.

IMPUDENT

13-17-21-31-35-45

being: be prepared to resist strong temptations put in your path.

    another, one, to: are in line for social advancement if you get past the folly of vice.

    others: will be cheated by friends over your lack of modesty.

        to you: are making excuses for being remiss in business transactions.

insolent to you, being: new position improves your finances, responsibility and respect.

    children: will have a vigorous mind if you keep your temper at bay.

INACTIVE

01-25-30-38-41-45

being, and unable to move: impediments are self-created.

    man: expect unhappiness in love.

    others: will lead a worried life if you allow everyone's troubles to be yours.

    woman: will not have a boyfriend or husband who can hold down a job.

properties, having: will fail to accomplish your designs.

INCENSE

04-05-06-30-41-42

before the arrival of a loved one, burning: pleasing adventures with lover.

church, burning in: lowering your standards does not bring success any earlier.

    own home: must explain something that will embarrass you.

myrrh: exceptional experiences from contact with a new social circle.

of: your hopes can be put into practice.

others burning: you will receive pleasing intentions.

unburnable: are surrounded by false praise and untrustworthiness.

INCOME

20-26-29-34-43-45

comfortable, having a: should mend your ways in life until you receive what is due.

insufficient: additional troubles with relatives over uncollected funds.

friends with a big: loss of temper merely reveals your envy.

own, getting very low: are up for a raise, but expect more than you will receive.

receiving a refund on: success in own enterprises.

relatives with a big: use caution in ventures; your deception will reflect on relatives.

INCREASING

06-08-19-32-36-45

bank account: the vanity of many is expedient; if one falls, the other may rise.

family, the: overexert yourself to become more agreeable in an amenable situation.

financial standing: be careful of expenses and present financial pinch will be loosened.

own business: warning against getting cocky over next deal.

INDECENT

17-25-29-31-32-35

being: will be put in your place when trying to lay an indemnity on another.

    friends: will incur debts from moneylenders.

    put in jail for: live strictly for success of business.

    woman: will be double-crossed by several sweethearts.

INDIA

02-07-08-11-32-38

being an Indian: mystical ideas do not provide financial gains.

being in: a big catastrophe if you don't keep both feet in reality.

going to: will have emotional sorrow; upon returning, happiness is assured.

native of: will have a mystical journey of spiritual union.

relatives being in: will receive message from unfriendly woman.

rubber, stretching: will expand affairs beyond that which you can do well.

traveling to, with sweetheart: are in the grip of deceitful people.

INFLATION

26-29-30-34-37-49

economy in period of: invest your money wisely or lose it.

imminent: your ethics need a revolution, as do your morals.

situation, of a: will be blamed for actions you have not done.

unable to buy food during: profound crisis of ennui; you know you have earned enough.

INFLUENTIAL

07-20-24-26-31-33

being: will be offended by an inferior person on an impressive occasion.

people, other: expect solicitousness towards you by dignitary.

dealing with: will be told of termination of your job.

position, acquiring an: will marry a beautiful rich woman.

INHERITANCE

07-16-17-29-30-38

cut off from an, being: will fall into misery, which will show you what you are made of.

receiving an: death in the family will cause conflicts.

not: will lose a sizable amount by your high-strung actions.

small, a: affliction, until you accept it as seed money for your own enterprise.

squandering an: are apprehensive about your ability to handle money.

INITIATION

03-40-46-48-49-50

going through an: evolving to a new spiritual level with aid from adepts.

leading an: sound friendship based on loyalty and honor.

participating in a: a new career is opening up for you.

INJURY

05-20-36-40-41-45

children having an: friends will look upon you with favor.

enemies: feel inadequately prepared for advancement within own position.

relatives: freedom from troubling pricks to your reputation.

hurt, being: will be plenty rich, if you learn how to cross the street.

injured by someone else, being: don't let a sour apple defeat your trust in love.

injuring someone else: danger is ahead if your unfairness is not rectified.

yourself: are hurt by circumstances that you could have controlled.

INK

05-09-12-30-40-49

blot, an: clear your bad conscience over being the cause of another's loss.

blotting, on an important document: your irritable behavior is hiding an adversity.

writing, a check: you resent having to pay the bill.

buying: be sparse with your confidences, all of them.

changing colors of: your indecisiveness fuels family quarrels.

children writing with: have one faithful friend within petty spiteful meanness of others.

drinking: will seek to stain another's reputation with your spite.

indelible, erasing: will battle with landlord over increase in rent.

inkblot on colored paper, making an: an extended trip distorts power in the near future.

clean white: fulfillment of fondest hopes; will sleep in a strange bed of your choice.

of a bottle of: make peace no matter what the cost.

spilling: prolong vexing, spiteful actions by the covetous.

stain: illness possibilities increase the longer it is left untended.

writing love letters with a pen and: your love is not reciprocated.

business letters with black: it is premature to sign agreements.

red: your discreditable associates will debase your affairs.

young woman dreaming of: will be slandered by a contender for lover's affections.

INMATE
15-22-39-40-43-47

being killed in prison: sins must be so offensive even inmates condemn you.
　long-time of a, a: are ill-disposed toward friendships that support you.
escaping from prison: plentiful means will bring appeals from the poverty-stricken.
executed, being: beware of illness depleting your ability to earn a living.
　released: the small fortune to be earned must be split among your creditors.
killing himself in prison: only everlasting friendship possible for you is with God.
　another: big arguments will cause an endless round of fruitless battles to be heard.
of a prison: accord among friends will turn disagreeable and destructive.

INN
18-19-21-26-41-47

beautiful a: will be tormented with overwork to keep your life commodious and well dressed.
being at an: will have emotional sorrow through those who are turned away at the door.
　celebration held, a: will have misery through major business failure you caused.
　regular customer: your partner will go off with another.
dilapidated seedy, a: are struggling for an impossible success.
friend at an, finding a: contentment with advancement within own position.
resting at an: you possess great courage; take care where you use it.

INNKEEPER
04-20-22-23-37-42

being an: will undertake affairs that will fail to profit.
female, acting immorally: will be unable to defend yourself from maliciousness.
having a fight with an: fruitless arguments over petty misunderstandings.
not paying the: a rival will take affection of sweetheart; gossip will injure prestige.

INSANE
04-17-28-41-42-47

committing something: big quarrels in virtually every aspect of your life.
divorced woman being: will give birth to a child whose suffering will cause you guilt.
　man: will divorce his wife, who will be left in great jeopardy.
　woman: will be a widow and receive your husband's promotion.
　young girl: an untenable conference with hostile relatives.
　young single woman: her child will be prominent and reject your motherhood.
of being: a sad ending to your newly imagined concept.
　cured of being: drastic improvements to your healthy outlook.
　friends: a long-enduring relationship will be impaired.
　relatives: will have to contend with an extended illness over a long life.
others who are: your perfectly simple plans will prove impossible to finish.

INSECTS
01-07-18-22-30-35

being bitten by a large: the insignificant becomes significant.
cockroaches, of: your work is contaminated with your undesirable motives.
　killing: survival is temporal, if you repress your shadow.
cricket, rubbing its forewings: unpleasant foreboding develops into melancholia.
　in the house: good luck, if you do not catch it.
dragonfly: your casualness is easily drawn away from dealing with real problems.
firefly, a: your conduct will be severely criticized.
fly, a: are losing your temper over petty annoyances.
　killing a, with a, swatter: annoyances through minor afflictions and skin irritations.
　　flypaper, on: will have to defend yourself in court for repeating gossip.

gnats, of: thoroughly investigate project before you invest.

being on others: pangs of conscience are showcased in others' looks.

killing with poison: a friend is trying to help you secretly.

swarming around you: dissension with an irritating neighbor.

having, in own house: be considerate of family.

katydids, hearing: a quarrelsome and unusual dependence upon others.

killing, inside own home: are plagued with guilty thoughts.

outside: financial gains.

with poison: a mystery will be solved.

ladybug, of a: luck with your family.

dirty: gold and silver in abundance.

spiders: annoying empty gossip.

tick, a: the tiniest of issues unsolved becomes an infected bite.

INSTRUMENTS

12-21-22-29-39-42

of: will make an advantageous marriage.

medical: warning of dangerous situation created by own family.

nautical: request aid in resolving the effects of your mistakes.

surgical: will endure pain securing aid when you need it most.

using: must expect dissension within the family.

various other kinds of: big reunion of the family.

INSULTED

19-25-30-35-37-44

being, by enemies: a grave situation is surrounding you; change your occupation.

friends: troubles are ahead as friends refuse to back up your character.

others: a season of sorrow is coming as you cultivate and defend your illicit pleasures.

relatives: passionate outbursts will estrange you from family.

but not resenting it, being: beware of partner's betrayal; love is not enough.

insulting enemies: will incur a grave calamity that will lose you a friend.

friends: will suffer foolishness, an illness which threatens your further communications.

others: lack the courage to set him straight.

you: your shaky self-worth needs bolstering; clear up the matter of deceitful friends.

receiving an insult: major upheaval will change your total environment.

friends, from: will be censured by those you care most about.

relatives, from: are including you in their own wrongs and deceit.

INSURANCE

11-13-15-21-23-39

approached by an, salesman: will be offered a new position through a friend's sympathy.

turned down for: ill health taken care of, outlasts good health abused.

buying a policy: the possibilities are endless if you are open to them.

auto: a rival will take what you desire while you are waiting for a quote.

disability: a difficult time financially for the family.

fire: new opportunities to make money, arson not being one of them.

health: preventative measures and diligent watch toward self-sufficiency.

INTERNET

03-08-22-23-35-40

disconnect: make effort to communicate with your boss.

e-mail, receiving: a new sexual liaison awaits you.

virus attacks: have overextended yourself to the wrong people.

weird action: check distortion in your thinking.

appearance: need to slow down and prioritize your thinking.

INTERVIEW

03-17-33-47-53-54

being interviewed: warning of outcome of being judged by others.

giving an: are questioning your motives and actions.

interviewing an entertainer: have difficulty seeing people as they really are.

politician: be prepared for a debate on your rebelliousness.

stammering during an: are hesitant about making decisions.

INTESTINES
08-11-21-24-31-37

diarrhea in public, having: your depression needs reformulating to cleanse your image.

eating the, of animals: conquer your archenemy by spreading cancer within his ranks.

of your: wretchedness, wallowing in despair, unwillingness to finish the job.

pains in own, having: are trying to digest your misfortune in love by overexertion.

   child, a: the dissolution of your complete dependence on a parent.

   enemies: unfavorable affairs unless you act with compassion and contrition.

   sweetheart: must forego pleasure to allow a slight hope of fulfillment.

removed, having part of own: illness will persist until you see a doctor.

   another's: sadistic torment to further your gaining complete control.

   children: are doomed for disappointment in the growth of your child.

tapeworm, having a: a small inheritance hangs on the wrong situation.

INTRIGUED
02-06-19-22-33-37

being, with gambling: a lethal addiction vies against an even more lethal foe.

   conceited person, a: ridiculous arrogance of destructive and dangerous thoughts.

   lottery, the: treason, a disassociation with reality, pleasant but gone in an instant.

   science: will have hard times proving your theories are worthy of testing.

instigating a cabal: your suspicions are completely unfounded.

married man being, with a woman: short-lived relationship creates ramifications.

   women, a man: much gossip about your affairs, to your detriment.

others being: cause affliction and misery by your pointless gossip.

unmarried people being, with opposite sex: despair.

INVALID
01-02-04-10-11-14

being an: partner is not strong enough and bars your intellectual freedom.

   children being: slow down for expected difficulties with enforcing your expectations.

   enemies: ignore the displeasure of those interfering with your interest.

   for the rest of your life: will soon receive money.

life of an: feeling your hopelessness has crippled your performance.

recovering from an, state: postponement of success until all your own affairs go well.

taking care of an: will receive financial support from an anonymous source.

INVENTOR
15-17-18-20-23-29

being an: high honors in whatever unique work you are engaged.

children becoming: will receive what you most desire.

other: will be well compensated through their designs.

INVITATION
16-20-33-36-38-42

accepting an: expect an inheritance; an additional expense will be incurred to retain it.

businesspeople, sending an, to: will be entangled in intricate and perplexing conditions.

   friends: expect delight from actions previously bringing despair.

   prominent personality, a: a mystery will be solved through a long and tedious journey.

   relatives: quarrels within the family over guest list.

receiving a business: disillusionment when great energies are invested in barren projects.

   loved one, from a: interesting acquaintances but no financial gains.

   printed, a: shame and sorrow with failure

to reach the summit of your
ambition.

relative, from a: be wary of why they are
inviting you.

written, a: expansion of area of influence
to include a more practical bent.

IRON
01-05-07-10-18-26

angle bars made from: accord among friends,
distress among enemies.

bars: discovery of lost abilities in new projects.

black: your great physical strength is misused.

buying: a slow steady progress to prosperity.

*collar for execution by strangulation, having on
an:* a strong will won't help you now.

criminal, a: a violent opposition to your
opinions will affect your fortune.

others with an: be firm in convictions; you
are right.

cutting: spiteful remarks will cause more
suspicion.

gray: must control your irritable gruffness;
work is your sustenance, as is pleasure.

hammering: your mental perplexities and
material losses must be sustained until
solution.

melted: an important agreement will be
reached, a ray of hopefulness in a dim
outlook.

plates, of: will need strength and willpower
for difficulties are ahead.

red-hot, touching a: incessant lack of pleas-
antry from even the smallest event.

selling: money will come easily; your friends
will be of notorious repute.

stealing: will not be able to avoid an onerous
responsibility or unpleasant duty.

IRONING
09-11-14-21-28-41

clothes: will experience trouble because of a
rival.

dresses: will be relieved of quarrelsome long-
suffering burdens.

iron mold, of an: dissolution in love as temptation will come to you.

stamping linen with an: serious illness due
to misapplied preventative measures.

linen: keep yourself free of any ties, if you
wish to change for the better.

man's clothes: comfortable home and increasing love and salary.

silk materials: delicately explore the effects of
your moves before proceeding.

starched clothes: minor problems untended
become permanent wrinkles.

ISLAND
03-06-10-12-15-32

abandoned, an: need a break from the stress
of your hectic life.

being alone on an: your pioneer fortitude is
stifled by overwhelming loneliness.

family, with: wish to concentrate on the
supportive whole.

others: rapid recovery from an illness.

relatives: your conscience is not clear
on your exciting and dangerous
adventure.

covered with green vegetation: pleasant travel,
profitable ventures and honor.

escaping to an: need the peace of solitude to
sort things out.

heavily populated, a: must struggle alone for
prominence in life.

leaving an: wish to come out of isolation and
deal with real-life situation.

relatives on an: must struggle to rid yourself
of unpleasant hangers-on.

ITCH
02-04-14-17-19-29

children scratching an: unhappy departure of
a friend; your fears are groundless.

having an: will be misused harshly and
incriminate others in your defense.

friends: will be happy with condition
until you fall in with dissolute
companions.

irritating rash: unexpected arrival of
friends who influence you in the
wrong direction.

sore caused from itching: unimportant but
irritating troubles from several
women.

itchy feet: wanderlust to escape contact with
distressing endeavors.

hands: money to raise yourself in higher
social circles.

nose: will enter into a fight, which will be a
great mistake.

IVORY

12-15-17-33-36-41

buying: have one true friend who trusts your honesty and ability.

giving as a present: accept offer from wealthy relative and the friendship it entails.

possessing: your literary talent will give you more pleasure than possessions.

selling: money will come easily during life; use it with compassion.

IVY

01-16-20-23-39-42

growing: beware of a broken engagement souring your marriage.

　trees, on: clinging friends give you grief; loves, scandal.

house, on a: are looking for a constantly faithful lover but being inconstant yourself.

　friend's: will enjoy rugged health and prized distinction among those you trust.

pot in the house, having in a: happiness is ensured with your continued growth.

spreading: in fear you latch on to the first person available.

J　J　J　J　J

JACKAL

10-12-13-24-31-36

attacking you: an opponent is stalking you, awaiting your weak moment.

children being with a: a loyal friend with good intentions watches you.

owning a: your tenaciousness feeds off others.

　others: your cowardice will postpone your success.

　with a yellow color: will be made to look foolish by one whose esteem you desire.

scavenging dead bodies: the transformation into your worst nightmare; seek help!

JACKET

15-19-20-30-32-36

dark-colored, wearing a: infirmity if you do not keep danger at bay.

　evening: will be invited to an elegant party with expensive favors.

house: infidelity in a happy home with dissident friends.

sport: financial gain through the congeniality of fellow athletes.

waiter's: a serious suggestion is being made; accept it.

tailcoat, wearing a: need to upgrade your image with a touch of class.

taking off a: are exposing yourself to darted eyes.

worn out: are too emotionally spent for the next party.

wrong sleeve, arm in: the information baffles you because it is incorrect.

JADE

02-05-17-25-27-41

buying: financial gain through intellectual success.

ears, having, ornaments on your: will receive unexpected news from foreign visitors.

necklace: marriage will last forever, from lifetime to lifetime.

selling: will contribute gains to a UN relief fund.

wearing: prosperity to all who come within view of your jade.

　green: arduous undertaking requiring intense analysis.

　others, ornaments: will gain only by tapping into another's dream.

JAIL

01-02-04-21-25-38

being a jailer: keep an immoral or improper impulse in check.

being in: resent being guarded from your criminal impulses by others.

　dark, a: look well into matters before you leap and are called to account for them.

　enemies: a short-lived fortune from your reluctantly granted favor.

　for a long time: feel trapped in a jail-like relationship.

　　life: will answer to your employer's criticism for going on a jag.

　friends: wish you were in charge of a particular person's actions.

　　wrongdoing, because of: will be caught in a white lie, which becomes a big lie.

sweetheart, your: will be gravely embarrassed and disappointed in lover's character.

woman dreaming of: must endure much suffering from an unknown source.

released from, being promptly: are in danger of contracting an infectious disease.

JANUARY
08-16-17-21-31-32

being born in the month of: the cold reality will be faced with stern survival instincts.

children: they will like sports, be rude to company and encouraging to prospects.

of, during the month of: financial gains amid temporary endeavors.

of, during other months: others will not comprehend your insistence on success.

JASMINE
03-11-14-21-34-42

blossom, in: will realize high ambitions and win your heart's desire.

bouquet of, having a: health, wealth and peace of mind.

eating out of the: incessant pangs of loneliness make you argue with yourself.

widow dreaming of: will be married within the year.

young girl: will soon receive proposal of marriage.

JAW   01-15-26-32-38-44

beast, being in the, of a large: perplexities caused by ill will between partners.

beautiful, and lips: changes for the better in own affairs.

deformed, a: use caution, as someone has whispered a grave lie about you.

flabby, a: spiritual indigestion from bad advice.

injuring the: disagreements with lover prove humiliating.

recovering from: have conquered initial difficulties; deal with ill-feeling of friends.

relative, of a: expect financial gains.

solid, a: will carry through vexations and perplexities with determination.

JEALOUS
03-05-14-21-28-41

being, of children: unpleasant family quarrels caused by your burst of despondency.

husband: home actions are fodder for ill-timed jests in company.

sweetheart: enemies are interfering to cause your good intentions to go wrong.

wife: pleasant social activities cannot repress malodorous emotion.

your religion: hope in God, that you snap our of your fit of the blues.

JELLY
04-08-14-20-30-35

eating: long-term trusting relationship in family life.

having: sure sign of long life past the present unhappiness in the family.

making: many charming friends will introduce you to your future mate.

receiving: accept the invitation to a neighborhood party.

JERUSALEM
08-19-21-26-29-31

being in: dignity and command within the center of your universe.

going to: will take a long journey to stay with a relative.

many people worshiping in: children will have abundant means.

of: will have bitter experiences suffering an injustice and the misery of loneliness.

praying in: will be respected in society and hated by your family.

JESUS CHRIST
06-17-27-29-32-35

of: peace of mind and contentment.

offering prayers to: will become a celebrity and a guiding light.

thanks to: will give charity to needy people.

talking to: will be consoled with full hope for the future.

JEWELRY
11-14-15-17-26-39

admiring jewels: will experience extravagance tempered by your rational mind.

agate, wearing: be careful when called upon to arbitrate quarrels.

amber, giving a gift of: obstacles between you and loved ones.

226

amulet for protection from evil, buying an: uncover the obstructer and confront him.

   receiving an: a price will be paid eventually through the high office of a friend.

   selling, to another: relieve yourself of the conflict of interest.

   wearing: eventually your vulnerability will be uncovered.

buying: are decorating yourself to gain attention.

cuff links: a formal matter of courtesy to respect your higher position.

garnet: the fertility of substantial labors for little return.

giving a gift of: indication you have precious feelings for recipient.

   receiving: admirer feels more than you do; their estate will threaten you.

gold ring: earnings will be just but lack in satisfaction.

having: an abundance brings continuous threat of their theft.

honest, an: date needs to be set to aim for finishing your plans.

   dishonest, an: will receive an expedient offer to add prestige to your work.

inherited: pay attention to your soul, with your risk of rank and satisfied ambitions.

iron ring, buying: will not receive the value of your worth.

jeweler, being a: will cheat friends and speculate with enemies.

   dishonest, an: will receive an expedient offer to add prestige to your work.

   honest, an: date needs to be set to aim for finishing your plan.

locket, breaking a: your partner will turn fickle, irresolute, bringing instability home.

   losing a: much travail will daunt your path as you fall in love with a stranger.

   receiving a family: early union with soulmate and numerous offspring.

loss of: your ability to operate is curtailed by those who flatter and deceive you.

   a gift: relationship with giver is over, to your great detriment.

platinum: your tension has tainted your efforts.

ring, losing a: will apologize to love of your dreams for not being perfect.

   receiving: keen disappointment in the actual value of money.

rhinestone: don't ask for a reference unless you are sure it will be a good one.

selling: will answer for peccadilloes you have kept hidden.

stealing: are in danger of committing some disgraceful act.

trinkets, buying: don't wear your heart upon your sleeve.

   receiving: your loved one is vain and fickle.

turquoise, of: natural healing.

wearing: will suffer because of envy and your foolish actions.

   other's: taken in by appearances and cheated by friends.

wristwatch: social activity among community-minded persons.

JILTED
12-19-24-26-36-40

man, a woman, a: are faltering in intentions to keep a judicious arrangement.

married man being: will have happiness in his married life.

   unmarried man: will have good luck with many women.

   widower, by a single woman: high finance would be the price of the relationship.

married woman jilting a secret lover: inability to connect feelings with actions.

   unmarried woman, a lover: timing and connection of the emotional dots are essential.

   woman, a man: frivolity in investments still yields a high return.

JINGLE
11-13-17-21-32-43

hearing the, of a dog's bell: imminent engagement in innocent flirtation.

   cattle: pastoral amusements with a person of the opposite sex.

   silly, a: will receive a wedding announcement from long-forgotten confidant.

   sleigh: will realize high ambitions of a semi-business nature.

JOB
11-23-28-39-44-53

challenge, as a: a stepping-stone in the larger attitude of life.

drudgery, as: your perception rules your success or failure.

gaining a job after months of trying: will find personal valuables of wealthy owner.

losing: prevent losing your temper with those you think responsible.

JOCKEY
03-06-15-23-25-38

being a: adjust every sliver of movement to obtain your desires.

losing a race, a: fall off the bandwagon and start your own project.

winning: a civil service exam will be passed with high marks.

underwear: translate instincts and vitality directly into victory.

tagless: will be called upon to aid a stranger; do it.

woman dreaming of a, at full speed: unexpected proposal from a less-expected source.

young girl fascinated with a: proposal of marriage from above; status.

JOKES
06-15-19-20-23-29

at the expense of others: there is no humor in this.

hearing and laughing: will be forced to receive an unwelcome visitor.

children telling: need to return to where you were not the joke.

listening to a good: extreme misery over disappointment of a trusted colleague.

telling a: need relief from overindulgence in one's work.

dirty: wrong will commingle with merriment.

very funny, a: will endure affliction for the ability to bring laughter to the weary.

JOURNEY
26-30-33-37-38-41

enemies: failure of enemies; bury them before they threaten you again.

failing to reach goal on a: change what you have the power to and move on.

others: business worries will take long plodding to straighten out.

going on a: will carry out your purposes and gain profits as journey is unpleasant.

armed with a sword at your side: will soon get married.

disagreeable: growth or disregard, depending upon your perception.

walking all the way: hard work is ahead; pleasant profits gained from the journey.

long, a: a nervous disorder requiring medical consultation.

on a rough road: everything will turn out well, speedier than required.

horseback, on: will surmount your disagreeable obstacles with your active power.

planning a, but not going: focus energies on one thing you do well and proceed.

relatives: will go into debt for frivolous, useless trivia.

steamer, taking a, by: companions are more congenial than ever before.

plane: family quarrels.

stormy weather on a, having: malcontented and thwarted hopes sabotage your wholeness.

JOYOUS
08-11-13-31-34-43

being very: good health and a Midas touch.

children: home circle needs expansion to make room for the joy.

joyride, taking a: will abandon your discretions to emotions.

when despondency is more appropriate, being: your indiscretions are best uncovered.

JUBILEE
04-08-12-21-39-40

being at a: a fortune will be left to you by a rich relative.

married people going to a: your hopes of an all-expense paid vacation will be realized.

of a: celebration of long and faithful service and devotion.

young woman dreaming of a: will become engaged in a close comfortable environment.

JUDGE
01-08-10-14-19-27

acquitted by a, being: are seeking sound judgment in justification for guilty actions.

found guilty: your high social standing seeks punishment for petty misdeeds.

punished: condemned for the spontaneity another can't allow himself.

summoned: criticized for being unruly and frivolous by one who is not.

being a: do not trust without evidence to back it up.

arbitration, in an: do not unquestionably accept your own judgment.

making decisions, and: are reminded of responsibility to society.

gavel, a judge's: wrong will be righted if you stand firm to your own course.

inquest, conducting an: your love life changes for the better.

being ruled in your favor: prosperity as you assume new responsibility.

not: a business associate betrays you.

in your favor, a: need to have your senses convened by an esteemed source.

justice of the peace: hard times for the jilting lover, not you.

juvenile correction, sentences you to: don't succumb to obstacles around every corner.

magistrate, of a: wish progress in own affairs were not condoned.

being before a: the problem, as now decided, needs reevaluation.

JUG
01-14-19-30-31-41

already broken: an angry exchange whether fortune is good or bad.

breaking a: will be assigned a thankless task that entails extensive work.

drinking out of a: much health and strength to get you through next phase.

water: a mystery will reveal optimism and fresh challenging ventures.

distasteful: find pleasure in all circles, along with disgust in some.

having a: loss of money because of another's sickness and failure.

JULY
01-09-12-18-23-43

being born in: will rebound from gloom with a rapid success of own hopes.

children: will have good earnings through need to complete your home.

during other months: use caution in your affairs as others cannot feel as you do.

of the month of, during: will meet your destiny at the postal service.

JUMP
05-06-15-25-29-30

failing to make the: life will be almost intolerable with disagreeable affairs.

jumping in the air: loss of present position to gain another, better one.

jack: reassess yourself through honest eyes and regain your friends.

kangaroo: pleasant social activities through your achievements.

others: will overcome enemies with perseverance.

precipice, into a: bad speculation, grave disappointment.

presence of others, in the: will lose a lawsuit due to your idleness and trivial pursuits.

water, in the: will be persecuted for trying to improve status.

making a: are very inconsistent in love affairs; for them to be serious, you have to be.

high: will meet your challenges and outwit them.

over a ditch: an enemy is seeking your ruin by challenging your reckless ventures.

hurdle: a steady unambitious progress will not gain you love.

JUNE
04-10-14-18-40-43

being born in: must rely on your own good judgment to make any gain at all.

children: will realize high ambitions in all enterprises.

during other months: sorrow and loss through drought and deluge.

of the month of, during: will have good earnings with advancement in job.

JUNGLE
06-11-14-25-34-40

being in a: economize while there is still time; leave your inhibitions at home.
> *others:* major obstacles block your way to discovering lost valuables.

killing a wild animal in a: social conditioning would never allow expression of this.

machete hacking way through, using a: close relations will regurgitate animosity.

of a: chaos in financial affairs will cause anxiety.

JURY
01-19-29-31-34-39

acquitted by an, being: be calm, over-excitement will backfire.

appointed to a, being: are highly esteemed by your employees.

formed, being: will overcome difficulties to be taken on as a partner.

pronouncing their verdict: fear of relying on courts to make the right decision.

seated in the court: weigh the evidence, persuade with tact and reach your verdict.

К К К К К

KALEIDOSCOPE
01-17-23-33-37-42

handling a: integrate your inner and outer self with a new wardrobe.
> *others:* colors chosen reflect each part of your personality.

losing colored glass fragments from a: parts of the puzzle of your whole life.

of a: great fortune will be yours.

KANGAROO
04-18-21-38-40-42

attacked by a, being: exercise great care of reputation, while being upwardly mobile.

cage, being in a: another's hostility that you may have contained will cause great anxiety.

dead: a big catastrophe of enormous power is ahead; conserve your strength.

parking in the pouch of a: leave others' secrets to them; succeed in spite of them.

KEG
05-11-15-26-32-38

empty: don't spoil today by yesterday's transgressions.

fish, being filled with: present difficulties are imaginary.

liquid, filled with: will attend a party with free-flowing drinks.

of a: will masquerade as sober in your drunkenness.

KETTLE
01-07-13-31-33-42

boiling water, of: there's difficult work ahead to widen your social horizons.

bright, that is very clean: big losses in business, but material and spiritual riches.

empty: a change awaits from boiling woes.

of a: hard work awaits.

KETTLEDRUM
02-05-27-32-36-42

buying a: change of surroundings from overindulgence in food and liquor.

having a: your ambition hides behind your enthusiasm.

playing a: your arrogance brings notoriety.
> *others:* don't fight, arbitrate an amiable compromise.
> *roll:* announcing a hanging or a crowning.

KEYS
12-16-29-34-39-41

finding several: have the power to unlock the peace in your home.

giving, to someone: in your carelessness you missed your turn.

having a: the solution to the puzzle is in your hands.
> *broken, a:* uncover the secret that will squelch their deal.
> *lover's, a:* will come out well from a present danger.

hole, peeping through a: things undreamed of will impair your route through shame.
> *enemies:* desire to lock opponent and all he stands for into a steel safe.
> *others:* profitable dealings of the heart.
> *relatives:* will be rebuked by one you admire for ignoring the truth.

losing own: your feelings can no longer be kept under lock and key.

KICKING

10-15-18-20-34-36

animal, an: organize every iota of evidence before proceeding.

being kicked: will have many powerful adversaries.

enemies: conflicts within you need to be resolved first.

friends: a friend is trying to help you follow office discipline.

someone else: will be reprimanded by superiors.

KIDNAPPED

02-03-10-28-42-43

being: change in your environment, buying outward wealth and inward misery.

  boy: your spirit, agility and quest for life have been disregarded.

  girl: your lovability and ability to love have been beaten.

kidnappers being arrested: your most treasured possession lies buried in an unmarked grave.

ransom, for: one who has owed you for a long time wants to make compensation.

KIDNEY

10-11-17-22-31-39

buying: unhappiness; physical deterioration of glandular function.

eating: will be visited by an uninvited person who will stay too long.

of: will be in mourning over involvement in an indecent, racy intrigue.

operation, having a: will invest in a useless stock of a toxic substance.

others refusing to eat: a sensational denial will prove to your detriment.

pains in the, having: you trust yourself too much, to the disgust of an officious person.

KIDS

07-16-27-34-39-44

another's: do not accept in others what you do not accept in yourself.

goat, baby: will meet a sage of great wisdom and knowledge.

of a: will be childishly careless in your moral pursuit.

own: will break their hearts with your immoral behavior.

relatives': joy without profit; your home is their home.

KILLING

08-10-19-26-28-39

animal, and then eating an: big profit from gaining their life force.

beast, a: in self-defense, victory and high position.

being killed: are naïve, impressionable and irresponsible.

  children: are relinquishing your childish behavior.

birds or bees: will be terrified witness to big damage in business.

businessman, a: are harboring unjustified suspicions and jealousy.

defenseless person, a: dead cells die to allow growth of new ones.

enemy, an: warning of trouble, if you move from your home.

father or mother, your: your unpleasant remarks will ruin your relationship for good.

friend, a: are destroying your ability to relate.

others, each other: will be criticized for malicious manners.

serpent, a: separation from the incentive and enthusiasm for life.

someone, of: your death for the dreamer, through your own anger.

someone wanting to kill you: they want your life but are unwilling to earn it themselves.

KILT

11-23-30-33-38-42

highlander in a: at news from abroad you will buy luggage for a trip.

wearing a: a whirlwind love affair.

  man: are dealing with someone who wears his character on his sleeve.

  woman: an old and trusted friend will return to fill your life with happiness.

KING

11-21-22-25-30-44

being a: how you use your power, wisely or foolishly, is your decision alone.

going to see a: a speedy solution will reap high rewards.

interview with a, having an: your overblown ego does not hide your inferiority.

of a: will encounter deceit in love matters as you are struggling in the wrong direction.

of the church, the: will be pardoned for your sins, but leave a revolution at your death.

sending a letter to a: careful what you wish for, because there is danger in what you get.

surrounded by his court: conspiracy undermines you, conceived of by a trusted friend.

KISSING
13-15-24-31-36-41

backside of a person, the: are deceived by your base passions and perverted integrity.

brother or a sister, a: sincerity and genuineness and your unyielding support.

dead person, a: emergence of a new love affair from those relatives left alive.

earth, the: humility for the vastness of glory and respect for its custody of your person.

father, your: an illness in the family will preclude his aiding your affairs.

friend, a: failure in your affairs through spiteful envy of false friends.

hand, on the: desire another's fortune but will attain the unhappiness of an unrequited love.

husband or wife, a: marital happiness and contentment will be your prize every day.

mother, your: are longing for tenderness that now only your friends can provide.

of a kiss: much affliction if you give vent to your sexual appetites.

   you don't want: minor illness full of emotional highs and lows.

single woman, a: are honored and beloved by your friends and deceived by your lover.

stranger, a: a brief acquaintance leads to loose morals and a deceptive honesty.

sweetheart in the day, your: honorable intentions, sincere love and responsible support.

   at night: danger from engaging improper energy; betrayal exposed after a deep sleep.

KITCHEN
04-18-26-34-36-43

bare: your conduct will estrange you with minor problems of a temporary nature.

being in your: nurture yourself first, then others.

coal stove in the: pamper your loved one; friends will unite to back you up.

Cuisinart, using the: wish to dissect feelings and rearrange them in a new recipe

   blender: family needs require greater diplomacy.

   grille: time to take charge of your affairs.

cupboard, an empty: business cannot prosper without investment.

   full: are emotionally starved but can't eat enough to be sated.

fire lighted in the: will have changes in your help to enjoy robust health.

   breaks out in the: check small appliances in the only place you have peace.

funnel, pouring liquid through a: gossip by friends is difficult to prove or justify.

   other: are incorrigible in working toward your goal.

gas range being in the: a gourmet meal is an option.

get out of the: stop interfering in others' concerns.

jars in the, a row of: will find a pleasure in catering your friends' social activities.

   empty: precarious success may lead to impoverishment.

ladle, using a: danger through a secret revealed in news from an absent friend.

   others: unhappiness through a secret exposed.

male chef preparing meals: will receive an invitation to a dinner of congenial guests.

of a: will be subject to unkind gossip from your own kin.

preparing a meal in the: mold your affairs into a palatable meal.

   menu: confused about multiple choices and fail to meet ensuing emergencies.

   others: notify others of your life before the gossip destroys it.

recipe, being given a: a successful future leaves out no ingredients.

refrigerator full of food: are being too stuck up with your neighbors.

spatula, of a wooden: will profit through

hard work; will survive if you avoid
neighbors.

untidy, dirty, an: will receive threats from the
health department.

very neat: arrival of a friend who will appreciate your spirit of accomplishment.

KITE
09-12-20-21-28-32

flying easily in the breeze: expect success, but
work beyond your capabilities.

> *low:* use poor judgment in disposal of
> limited funds.

> *very high:* big joy and extravagance; free-
> dom to soar to new heights.

making a: will risk all through speculation
and, as luck will have it, will fail.

> *for your lover:* are set for disappointment
> if you expect love for this.

KNAVE
05-10-17-22-34-38

employing a: your gift of gab will get you into
trouble.

male servant: dignity and distinction can only
be gained willingly.

of the, on cards: extract yourself from the
most complicated situation.

several: disputes with friends over doing
something against your better judgment.

KNEELING
03-10-20-25-33-34

church or tabernacle, in a: it is to receive the
message of the mission given.

enemies: they have their own mystery to be
solved; allow them thus.

friends: will be cheated by the friend you have
harmed.

in inappropriate setting: are breaking your
vows of honor.

relatives: humility solves more than
confrontation.

to pick up something: take advantage of the
tiniest opportunity.

to pray: happiness and honors come after
your confessional.

> *another:* ask another forgiveness for
> wronging him.

> *children:* stop a moment and tithe the
> spirit.

KNEES
02-17-26-40-42-44

animals, of: hard work awaits.

bandaged, a: take things easy on a long
journey.

bent: long illness has made stiff pain and
fearful calamity.

dimpled: liaison with a foreigner will not woo
you to marriage.

dislocated, having a: things will take a turn for
the worse before they get better.

falling on the: the last resort against your
rapid dissolution of fortune.

knock-kneed, being: are made a scapegoat for
another's ill luck.

> *another:* criticism of another is aimed at
> you but misses.

own, being badly injured: will suffer humiliation of your ardent hopes.

> *slightly:* affairs will turn out all right even-
> tually.

quaking: recovery from sins takes kneeling
before God.

recovering from a cut: fortune and joy.

swollen, a: are surrounded by unhelpful advice.

KNIFE
04-09-24-28-39-41

being stabbed with a: caution would be the
expedient route.

broken: your fear needs to be pruned to its
source.

butcher's, a: positive aggression is the basis
of primitive survival.

cutting yourself with a: wish your deepest
fears would bleed away.

dull: will be strained to make enough to put
food on the table.

finding a: failure in business from the selling
of your soul.

jack: your preemptive strike will be accused
of being two-faced.

kitchen: quarrels with friends about disobedient children.

large, searching for a: sever your participation
from the calamity.

many, having: quarrels with those slashing
you with words.

missing its mark: deviously performing a
straightforward task.

of a: will be invited to a big dinner where someone will try to swindle you.

pocket, having a: strife leads to a separation of lovers.

rusty: discontent and vexations at home from a stab in the back.

sharp: separation anxiety tears at your heart and an unhappy union.

stabbed in the back, being: are a victim of verbal violence.

stabbing another, your: have a poor sense of right and wrong.

table: a cordial invitation, well meant and offered.

two knives in the position of a cross: someone will be killed through your base acts.

wounded with a, in the neck, being: will be insulted by friends.

KNITTING
10-15-22-29-35-42

children: prosperity in the home, with delightful pleasures.

dropping a stitch while: you were tactless; don't scatter yourself; begin again.

enemies: undertakings will be crowned with success.

fancy, doing: making something simple, complicated.

mother: will have obedient bright children, thrifty with solid use of prospects.

muffler for her lover, woman, a: will lose his commitment to relationship.

of: peace in the home comes with attention to details.

others: are being deceived by friends.

scarf for a boyfriend, a: will alter his feelings to the negative.

worsted yarn, with: will inherit more than you earn; invest it well.

young woman: will make a hasty marriage that will reverse your ill-fortune in love.

KNOCKING
07-10-15-17-25-44

down a person with your car: your chronic fatigue is no excuse for violence.

enemies: dispute over something you once had and need aid to reclaim.

of: guard your tongue for all fortune to shine on you; spread only grave tidings.

others: feel nostalgic in re-creating the past, and fear for the future.

relatives: are enterprising in including your family in your approaching money.

repeatedly: a mysterious stranger will remain mysterious.

KNOTS
08-13-26-35-45-51

made by others: their history is revealed in the knots they pick.

making: a rhythm and a flow, a twist and a turn and a wrap around your madness.

> *enemies:* will have reason for anxiety, but not for trifling affairs.

> *relatives:* constraints of one's traditional values in the face of modernity.

> *sailors, in ropes on a ship:* feel control over your thoughts and actions.

string with many: have woven a tangled web of infidelity; refuse to be nagged into it.

> *loose:* have ignored valued relationships for the sake of independence.

> *undoing a:* leave no past issue unraveled, nor any present flirtation not reprimanded.

tying: will soon meet one who will be a true friend.

untying: will escape some danger if you refuse to go horseback riding.

LABORATORY
21-25-39-50-54-59

being in a: empirical data must support your actions.

beyond reasonable time: will unravel a long-standing mystery long after anyone cares.

experimenting in a: your intense exertion is wasted on fruitless ventures.

of a science: big peril with liquids in combination and emotions in disharmony.

working in a: have outmaneuvered your inner feelings, beliefs and fears.

LABOR DAY
15-19-32-38-47-50

laborers fighting on: will eat more than usual in the future.

of: your exhaustion from overwork has

pushed you into depression.

parade, being in a: staidness and conformity are practical necessities.

working on: will receive a good deal of money.

LABORER
01-25-27-39-44-56

angry at having to be a: the deterioration of your mental facilities and will.

fighting: infamy and disrepute due to laziness and inaction.

firing, a: will undergo a public crisis, allowing someone else to judge your value.

hiring: profit signifies profitable toil and the robust health of those doing it.

paying: without mutual respect for a hard day's labor, no money is enough.

punishing: beware of persecuting neighbors in backlash against an irrational attack.

resting, a: lack of willpower and enthusiasm leaves you in stagnation.

tilling the ground, a: solid blending of heavy burdens and well-done accomplishments.

working, a: prosperity in own business through your own enterprise.

left hand only, with: will have momentary troubles adjusting to unjust labors.

right: can organize the world but not create a new one.

LABYRINTH
08-14-19-35-42-50

becoming confused in a: are trapped in a lateral play; go back.

being in a: step back until you see in perspective.

battling wild beasts: enemies feed your angry foes with rancid words.

finding the way out: your perplexities will be happily solved.

not being able to: beware of domination by untrue friends.

maze: endless hide and seek on simple issues faced indirectly.

of such a place: follow the progress of chaos into consciousness.

surrounded by a: the solution is where you would never expect it.

LACE
01-02-32-33-36-39

buying: danger through a secret; your lure is not with the gown.

dress: your vigorous mind will realize your most ambitious goals.

stole: frivolity, but no question of your right to give orders.

giving a gift of: misfortune in love affairs, but prosperity will be your best friend.

making: lovers will prostrate themselves in awe of your imperious charms.

young girl dreaming of: will have handsome, devoted, caring and wealthy husband.

receiving, from sweetheart: lovers and every desire will be realized in a sincere love.

LADDER
01-17-25-27-28-50

breaking while climbing: backtrack and change course.

carrying a, with you: will rescue some fear within you that haunts you.

climbing a: your humility will bring unusual happiness and prosperity.

circular: your one-dimensional goal is causing you to miss opportunities.

house, a: take the nearest opportunity to rise from humble beginnings.

others: wish to achieve an authoritative position over faithful friends.

rope, a: profits interwoven with so many conditions that the bottom line is zero.

stepladder: your unexpected good fortune is good for six steps.

descending a: are going the wrong way in dealing with disappointments in business.

circular: worry will be smoothed away, but honors will not bring serenity.

dizzy when on a, being: an important and beneficial event will soon come.

falling from a: your arrogance will cause your failure.

another: your most stable friend will fail you.

fortress, of a: an advantageous lawsuit will guard your perilous path against strong foes.

jumping from a: will obtain a good position and be jilted by your sweetheart.

raising a, up to a window: will encounter a tender person on your climb to prosperity.

tall, a: your preposterousness will raise you to prominence by a narrow margin.

LAKE
05-17-30-35-41-49

clear, a: your emotional resources will attend every venture to success.

fishing in a: advancement within own position and in other's estimation.

lagoon, a: apprehension and discomfiture through misdirected intelligence.

large, a: a difficult period of your life is just ahead; get centered and plod through.

muddy, a: trials in business that become worse the more you stir them up.

rain falling on a: will overcome worries with patience, eventually.

rough water, with: are faced with scooping out others' problems from your boat.

smooth: will be jilted by your lover, which will allow you to meet your real love.

sailing on a: expect conflicts within the home, congenial friends without.

rowing: success in business if you don't catch a crab.

stormy, a: the source of your woes lies within, the monster deeper within.

LAMBS
01-06-23-30-40-51

bleating: your generosity will be pleasant and turn your simplest needs into profit.

buying: no small devotion will be denied these objects of your affection.

carrying a: prosperity, good future and devotion to chaste friendships.

eating a, on Easter: lasting friendship and contentment may be sacrificed for prosperity.

field, in a: much tranquility, comfort and pleasure appropriated by others.

finding a lost: good nature will not win your lawsuit; care for your conduct.

giving a, as a gift: others will increase your possessions.

herd of, grazing in a field: will be frightened by too much merriness.

killing: innocent ones will be tormented through wrongdoings of others.

owning: profit and consolation over the welfare of children.

selling: must sacrifice amusements and infatuations to reach your goal.

shearing: are taking advantage of wayward people under your care.

slaughtered, being: contrary to others' belief, you do have compassion.

LAMP
10-25-35-45-48-49

breaking a: your indifference will cause harm to your hopes.

bright: happy revelations of paths to success in a small venture.

homes of others, in the: warning of spiritual knowledge needed to solve their woes.

lamplight going out: wish you had seen the light of coolness in love.

very dim: will work hard and face difficulties carrying out your own ideas.

lighted: passion will turn to frigidity with one quick flick.

lighting a: will have to offer explanations for your independence at all costs.

many: your path in life will be highlighted by bright mentors.

plain unlit: business will come to a standstill, if you continue to fail to take advice.

post, leaning against the: are inebriated from trying to expand family circle.

broken, a: serious quarrel with neighbor over your independent connections.

turning on a: a casual friendship is intensifying.

LAND
05-22-35-47-52-58

barren: a stranger will become your staunchest ally at your most despondent time.

landscape, fine open: dignity, distinction and tranquility in love.

obscured by hills: will spend numerous hours second-guessing troubles and obstacles.

ugly: will suffer bitter aftertaste of dashed hopes.

with a clump of trees: will act promptly on your well-considered decisions.

landslide, of a: are overloaded, emotionally overwrought and carry the trust of others.

   causing a: triumph over enemies by being sensible and intelligent.

   repairing a: discovery of lost valuables in the rubble.

looming above the surface of the: money will come easily during life; watch over it.

moving away from a: expect changes in occupation.

ordered off of, by owner, being: expect bitter disappointment with a desired friendship.

possessing: loneliness and trouble through a cheating incident conceived of by you.

reaching, from water: your projects have found sufficient foundation.

LANDING
05-07-13-38-44-48

fall from bed: things are not what they appear to be.

hit bottom injured: future plans lack depth and understanding.

   die: a new opportunity will soon arrive.

   survive: caution is not advised in business expansion.

   wake on impact: a long vacation is called for.

     before: a change of career is around the corner.

important personality, an: successful completion of your work towards higher ambitions.

plane, from a: out-of-control issues still up in the air are progressively being grounded.

softly with a parachute: great happiness lies ahead.

try to grasp for support: self-reliance is called for now.

LANDLORD
06-08-11-17-22-41

being a: have loyal friends who know people who know people.

handyman to make repairs, paying: difficulties with tenants are from own miserliness.

landlady, being bawled out by a: rapid success of your own hopes for the right home.

   discussing business with a: will gain down payment for your home.

rent, collecting: good earnings and profit are gone before they can be invested.

   freezing the: at the point at which you lose money, leave.

LANGUAGE
07-12-20-34-51-52

foreign, learning a: get assistance, rather than aggravation, from your dreams.

   children: should practice modesty with your investments.

interpreter, being an: are not putting across ideas coherently.

needing an interpreter and one appears: was message understandable?

speaking in a foreign: are too muddled and confused to be understood.

   hearing others: an unfavorable turn will make you a victim of circumstances.

   in own: break through your inhibitions to state your view.

LANTERN
02-14-15-21-48-51

beautiful flame inside a: with insight you will reveal yourself.

blown out, being: will have trouble with the law and fail to gain prominence.

dim, a: domestic disquiet over aiding someone who will cause your family harm.

extinguishing, a: be careful of deceit through taking an unfavorable turn.

going out by itself: your understanding of another's situation is distorted at best.

magic, a: will suffer dissolution and reappearance in a new life.

putting out a: hopeful intentions will take an unfavorable turn.

signal, a: will have important and responsible position.

swinging a: are in grave danger from scheming, cunning women.

LAP
02-09-18-26-36-57

dog in your, a: whom you protect will in turn be your protector.

   cat: will be humiliated at the hands of a seductive enemy.

   dead: loss of whoever held your leash allows prosperity.

serpent, a: tempting prospects will distract you from your essentials.

married man holding a woman on his: humiliation and criticism from a jealous woman.

mother holding children on her: a pleasant security.

sitting in the, of opposite sex: a great need for compassion from the opposite sex.

stenographer sitting on the, of boss: an enemy is seeking the loss of a good position.

LARK
07-43-46-49-52-57

cage, in a: failure of own plans through the selfishness of control.

dead, being: someone is endeavoring to agonize over your experience; don't let them.

high in the sky: a positive outlook toward attainment with grace.

of a: will be bathed in the light of fortune and earn the right to honor.

singing happily: joyous, innocent experiences in the creation of new ventures.

LATE
06-15-26-30-55-56

being: your opinions will be sought; time to be a good scout and be prepared.

employees: undisciplined and irresponsible behavior.

friends: are deceived into caring for public welfare of ones who can help themselves.

meeting, to a: are confronted with obstacles caused by missed opportunities.

others: your loss of money will be condemned by enemies far above its worth.

LATIN
02-18-21-38-39-44

learning: expect to find new, profitable employment.

children: will have a strong character able to sustain your opinions.

reading: triumph over subjects of grave interest, which are usually avoided.

speaking: beware of having a failure to communicate thoughts worthy of distinction.

LAUGHING
09-16-21-28-30-48

children: approaching news of fundamental differences between you and offspring.

enemies: a rival is undermining your work and calling your accusations ridiculous.

former friend: old passions reverberate long after the affair is over.

giggling at a solemn occasion: your debts must be paid before your honor can be saved.

schoolgirls: invitations will have many motives; don't take them so seriously.

hearing: feel you are being mocked into a speedy rupture of amicability.

laughed at by a woman, being: she has deceived you and gloats over it.

several people: take precautions against gossipers with introversion and unsociability.

someone: only idiots laugh all of the time; make yours healing, uplifting energy.

with others: profitable investments in the work of others.

your: are hiding your burden from others with frivolity.

LAUNDRY
01-09-32-36-56-57

by hand: will be unusually happy in the company of people.

dirty: relationship is in doubt, with problems undermining you.

doing own: someone will render service to your physical health.

hanging, out to dry: exposed problems have no power.

laundromat, doing, in a: clean up your superiority act and stuffy attitude.

of a: of a public: will see an unknown dead person whose stain rests on you.

on the line: time to expose your psychological strengths and fix the error.

reconnecting, by: an old friend is gained through exercising your health.

washing under a fountain: sharp warning against local, festering gossip.

sweetheart, of: will cancel marriage when you meet a traveler with common interests.

LAURELS
11-16-20-22-30-37

branch as sign of peace, holding a: advancement from own position to superior rank.

given, being: will receive money from relatives and an unexpected gift from a friend.

leaves: joy from being honored for the final victory in winning your fortune.

plant, of the: everlasting pleasure, success and fame built on integrity.

picking: fools pick it to laud themselves; faithful men receive it from a lover.

smelling perfume of a: are in danger of losing something valuable in a fleeting moment.

tree, of a: will fall to temptation of fortune in enterprises where there is none.

wearing a laurel wreath: your craving attention fuels your ambition.

LAW ENFORCEMENT
05-16-21-30-38-49

aiding and abetting a fugitive: the cops are not after you; set out on your own adventure.

being a, officer: will have obstacles to overcome, not that you have a goal.

bailiff: clean up unfinished business, the poison of public opinion.

bondsman, a: will soon be free of duties you have been forced to assume.

fugitive from justice, being a: violent confrontation with family forum.

innocent, being: are a passionate person whose opinions get distorted in others' minds.

knowing you're not: will be exposed at a crucial point in an important position.

lynching, taking part in a: death to freedom; what you have done will be done to you.

observing a: disgrace among your peers, that you made no step to bar.

something is impounded: will seek to expropriate another's possessions for yourself.

LAWN
01-10-17-20-23-34

children playing on a: will receive an unwelcome guest; get them a puppy.

cutting own: will receive an unexpected visitor.

others, their: a false friend is nearby.

dog sleeping on a: approaching money from a latent source.

green, a: in an unexpected encounter you will win back lost love.

man mowing his: successful domestic life and amusing social engagements.

woman, her: the man rules the house until long-term prospects come to fruition.

needing to be cut: there will be cutbacks at work.

others, of: postponement of success.

sprinkling own: on own good judgment as to the limit of your investment in an idea.

walking on a: your anxiety with relatives will be relieved.

LAWSUIT
01-17-32-42-43-54

advancing in a: will lose the case unless facts are discovered.

against you to get money owed: you spend money too freely in careless acts.

appealing a: will be cheated by friends through unpleasant notoriety.

beginning a: use caution against unfavorable happenings in business ventures.

business transactions, starting a, for: will suffer losses from legal entanglements.

others: involves money losses from enemies influencing others against you.

losing a: will have a passing temptation to lend a friend money; don't.

man starting a divorce: people will think little of your harassment.

woman: is standing up for principles long since lost, as will lover.

recover money owed to you, to: success in business; is the battle worth the fight?

winning a: avoid speculation, money will be lost; concentrate on what you can earn.

LAWYER
01-10-20-23-29-31

adversarial, having an: your guilt is overwhelming you; you need your own lawyer.

advice from a, receiving: will be humiliated by your loose morals.

arguing with a: bureaucrats will cause an unexpected melancholy.

being a: will realize high ambitions if you can interpret both human and Universal law.

child becoming a: your highly developed sense of observation is hereditary.

consulting with a: your worries on a legal matter must be confronted.

court with a, being in: avoid stock speculation; the jury is unpredictable.

dealing with an opposing: disadvantage of deviating from conventional and correct behavior.

dismissing a: are too ambitious and impractical to expect to reconcile with an enemy.

evidence, giving, in court against a criminal: your reputation will be saved by a friend.

others giving, against you: watch out for treachery.

grand jury, being in front of the: your chance of winning malpractice suit is slim.

hiring a: acquaintances will take advantage of you; will not have good results.

introduced to a, being: subdue characteristics and actions that will cause criticism.

in a black robe: will receive the justice you seek.

litigation, beginning a: your own strength and energy will benefit your case.

marrying a: will be caught in an embarrassing predicament.

meeting with a, having a: your strong willpower will cause friction with your consultant.

of a: your prejudices against the law will become very weary.

opposing, dealing with a: have lost trust and respect of others.

others starting action against you: consider plans well before acting.

paying a: a lawsuit will fail if you do not gain support of a woman.

receiving a legal document from a: bad news turns into disaster.

sitting on a: a conflict of interest will lead to double-dealing.

writing a letter to an attorney: know exactly what you want before starting; be specific.

LAZY
17-26-35-47-55-57
being: trouble for those near you if you don't allow them to help you.

children: will marry wealthy people who will take you to task for your idleness.

employees: business will suffer through lack of attention to details.

husband: an unknown person is working against you by not working.

others: are being overly competitive on minor matters.

wife: dignity and distinction will not deter your family difficulties.

couple, a: a matter of your unwitting indiscretions will end in marriage of opponents.

LEAD
08-19-22-31-44-53
bars of: have grievous weights on your shoulders.

boxes out of, making: accord among friends will turn to suspicion of what you are hiding.

buying: will receive news from abroad of unnecessary burdens.

hammering: business upsets, yours or others.

melted: are weighted down by issues beyond your control.

pressing: the threat of serious accident oppresses your every move.

selling: money will come easily, as will accusations of foul play.

sheets of: are shielding your problems from the forces that can solve them.

LEAK
04-24-30-37-40-45
gas, a: your impatience will bring about more failure than patience.

leaking, bathtub: take stock of the situation and repair it.

boat: in an accident the owner of the boat who rescues you owns your boat.

car: have a faithful wife and are loved by those around you.

faucet: are accountable for your every word.

overshoes: much energy is being sapped out of you in emotional worry.

pipe: should find a wider scope for your activities.

radiator: will meet an important personality; the birth of a child is near.

roof: are wasting your time in love; concentrate on the material plane.

LEANING

04-05-10-46-50-56

another person, against: will receive substantial assistance.

　wall: help those near you who are in need of money.

children, against you: happiness.

people, against each other: will receive a letter from abroad.

LEAP

14-17-23-25-39-45

failing back from a: life will be almost intolerable without social prestige.

high, making a: will come out of present danger with a promotion.

of leaping: are very inconsistent in your love affairs.

　into water: will be persecuted and lose your present position.

　others: will overcome enemies with perseverance.

　over a ditch: an enemy is seeking your loss in a lawsuit.

LEAP YEAR

14-30-33-45-52-59

being born in: will live a long life.

children getting engaged in: will never marry this person.

getting married during: marriage will not last long.

relative dying during: will inherit money from a relative.

your being single, being, and: marriage within the year.

LEARNING

16-25-28-29-46-48

children, their lessons: will have few difficulties in life where you can't meet the challenge.

experience, of, something by: good luck to one for whom you care.

foreign language, a: will not be a love affair, but a new trusted friend.

life, a lesson in: are undertaking more than can be completed in your grade.

mentally, something: a healthy self-criticism so long as it is easily learned.

new trade, a: superficial attachment to established knowledge.

quicker than your peers, of: don't stuff what you know down their throats.

relatives, of the arrival of: unexpected sadness with your elders.

write, to: the secret of knowledge will be revealed to you.

LEASE

02-03-30-43-55-59

asking someone to sign a: going to prison.

canceling a: uncertain future, but will increase your income.

house, taking a, on a: avoid rival's persecution by legal means.

　land: will be fortunate in love affairs.

　shop: business is secure.

suing someone for a: reconciliation with an enemy.

LEATHER

18-34-37-38-42-55

buying: your family is firmly grounded in reality.

giving a gift made of: family quarrels over overdue bills will not corrupt their gratitude.

harness, handbag or belt of, having a: financial gains in speculations.

of a, shop: failure of enemies through your steady climb to prosperity.

selling, products: faithful love.

working with: advancement through unremitting, long hours of toil.

LEAVES

08-09-10-22-31-49

blossoms among: two people are very happy together.

collecting: money approaching from a wonderful accumulation of business.

covering the earth: illness, warning of future health liabilities.

dry: people are malicious toward your harmonious family relations.

falling autumn: will have a dangerous sickness; healing comes from an uplifting spirit.

grape: are prone to losing your temper over small delicacies.

seasoning, using, for: you like to eat too much; it is no substitute for love.

stem with fruit, on a: emotional and intellectual growth in a happy marriage.

tree in full leaf: important and very beneficial event to come.

wilted: you decide on old data, your emotion an old love.

wind blowing: God is directing your life.

LECTURE
07-26-39-41-50-56

delivering a harangue: will earn a civil service job.

giving a: will be disappointed if you do not control your tongue.

> *long, in public:* will become tangled in litigation.

> *political lecture:* your vanity creates rivals.

lecturing to children: your actions will prove unwise as criticism implodes.

misreading your notes during a: speak thoroughly or not at all.

public square, hearing a, in a: are disappointed that thought isn't given to the speech.

receiving a, from a superior: the novelty of learning something with substance.

LEDGER
02-08-17-23-27-55

balancing a: discovery of own errors, listed and categorized, made in life.

cash book: have a perplexing puzzler and a continuously moving target to contend with.

figures on it, with: discovery of lost money through a devious pattern of miscalculation.

finding mistakes on a: finances will suffer from careless neglect.

writing on a: will collect money by combining business with pleasure.

LEECH
02-11-15-19-23-56

killing a: strive against enemies meddling in your concerns.

many, being around: loss of money through parasitic relationships.

of this bloodsucking worm: doomed for misdiagnosed health problems.

> *applied to your body:* are causing immense distress to friends.

LEFT-HANDED
15-31-33-37-49-55

being: the rational, intellectual approach softened by the intuitive and creative.

boxing: take the off chance that surprise from another quarter could dip the bell.

driving a, car: the future is clear for you; find where yours is.

eating: control your manners and sit on the left.

fencing: will call upon strenuous, exacting artistry to react with precision and grace.

side of street, walking on the: face your day head on, nights with the headlights on.

traits, developing: develop your artistic, mechanical, three-dimensional, kinetic design.

working: combine right- and left-brain activities in a profitable venture.

writing: will catch others unaware of your attention or intentions.

LEGS
02-19-26-33-50-58

amputated, being: face responsibility squarely, despite not accomplishing your ambition.

beautiful, man dreaming of: nonsensical acts over the object of your fantasy.

bow, man with: reexamine your current behavior and its effects.

breaking a: will be reprimanded and discontented for a deed poorly done.

bruising own: self-punishment for financial difficulties.

injured, an: have lost your dignity due to financial difficulties.

limping: are going in circles feeling like an emotional cripple.

losing a: change directions, back to solving your issues.

married woman dreaming of having beautiful: will take a long trip of social enterprises.

running on healthy: don't run from what you want, walk to it.

swollen: loss of money.

thin: will be ridiculed for the poverty of your soul.

unable to run: an inner inflexibility towards solving outer problems.

well-formed, of: will win some contest and regain control.

women marching with pretty: have too many irons in too many relationships.

wooden, a: will lower yourself in the sight of friends.

LEMONS
03-16-27-33-51-58

blossom, a: will take a trip abroad to find fidelity in love.

drinking juice of: good health, cleansing, healing, clear throat and an avid mind.

eating: disparities in official papers will cause trouble.

 sweet: are not looking after your health.

lemonade, drinking a: shallow frivolity leads to temporary emotional health problems.

 hot: improvement in health and respect among friends.

 making: replace unsupportive friends with those who know the meaning of SOS.

making medicine from sweet: are forced to tolerate a bitter experience.

of a tree: are reprimanding another for an unproven charge.

ripe: will fall in love and become unpopular with your professional peers.

squeezing: get rid of those who take advantage of you.

sucking on a: your altercations with your partner persist.

unripened, an: frivolity before earning the joy of accomplishment.

LENDING
07-19-44-47-48-54

articles: friends seek your ruin by playing on your generosity.

being a usurer: business will cause much worry, as those you persecuted return the favor.

 going to a, to borrow money: are ashamed that with your profits you still need cash.

 having a, for a partner: are disliked in the community, but loved by partner's family.

clothes: trouble is ahead, the borrower wants your life.

machinery: make it mutual or you will never get over it.

money: will want money yourself before long for private debts.

others, you money: true friends won't want it back; false ones will be lost to you.

refusing to lend: will amass much wealth and few friends.

your car: insist it is returned with a full tank of gas.

LEOPARD
08-20-22-24-33-41

afraid of a, being: will be persecuted by enemies.

 attacked by: success through a series of trying experiences.

 triumphant over: avoid the routes of rivals, routes to achieve your ends.

cage, being in a: enemies seek to cause injury but will fail.

 tied with chains: a surprise is received from an enemy.

cub, a: joy and happiness.

dying: death of a prominent person.

killing a: will have many changes but finally victory, for which you will be embarrassed.

of a: victory over enemies will result in going abroad on business.

roar, hearing a: will suffer grief, verbal abuse and slander, but live on.

running: a promising venture with an exciting colleague wins your respect.

scuffling: a playful interchange, an enthusiastic debate, turns violent with the wrong move.

skeleton of a: will be bared down to your minimum before you can start route to success.

surprising a: your cocksureness is misleading in that it does not include all of the threats.

LEPROSY
07-17-29-47-57-59

becoming a leper: your true self is hidden behind your mistakes.

 seeing a: your emotional garbage separates you from those around you.

 yourself as a: those around you do not accept you.

children having: will have no end of guilt and remorse for child's pain.

enemies: misfortune in own home affairs cannot compare to the despondency of others.

man dreaming of having: are wasting your talents and abilities by denigrating them.

   woman: will be helped by a wealthy man, ruing the indifference of the one you love.

others: it is within own power to overcome worries.

relatives: will have good earnings sent after bad to care for another's agony.

LETTER

05-14-23-25-33-48

delivered by hand, your: your troubled conscience should redeem itself.

destroying a, of business: insurmountable obstacles confront you for lack of loyalty.

exchange, having a, of: unexpected profit from a number of exciting opportunities.

hiding another's: beware of a fair-haired rival; a stack of overdue letters will arrive.

love letters: frankness is an admirable quality when expended with passion.

mailing a: will receive interesting news with little trauma.

reading a chain: unpleasant accusations from one you know is in the offing.

   interesting, an: will battle for your reputation against potential evil.

   others, your: take precautions against being deceived by using simple routine information.

   political: will be assisted by a conceited, malicious person.

   refuse to read a: shame, loss of social business standing.

   romantic: will forget your troubled conscience and gain your fondest desire.

receiving a: great wealth awaits you emotionally, if you allow relief to be rendered.

   anonymous, an: disagreeable, imaginative injury creates tensions in every move.

   children: are embarking on a risky deal that is certain to fail.

      friend: a visitor brings hopeless mistakes; identity issues harm your reputation.

relatives: will come out well from a present peril with sensational charges rendered.

   suitor: prompt engagement, but fiancé will lure other offers.

business: don't rise to riot swiftly; the nasty situation will turn in your favor.

money, with: are in the center of a heated difference of opinion.

open it with eagerness, and: a message you communicated.

   put it aside: don't want to hear the truth rewarded with jealousy.

registered, a: a breach of durable confidence through unstable finances.

   receiving: the deal offered empowers your confidence in your competence.

return receipt, with a: will not stand up to legal or ethical standards; dishonor comes.

wife or husband, from a: separation with accusations flying and reproofs stampeding.

   lover: will be slighted out of an advantageous marriage, with accusations flying.

sealing a: will be successful in all your affairs until its contents are revealed.

sending a: be careful not to betray your secrets, yet be forthright in your offer of hospice.

   business: be careful that in your warning of troubles, envy cannot be detected.

   children, to: pay attention to finer details to raise the child.

   fax: some element of your life demands immediate attention.

   friend, to a: will take an extensive voyage after an attempted suicide.

   husband or wife, to a: regret for worry done long ago has had time to heal.

   lover, to a: the air around a recent heated but friendly discussion needs to be cleared.

   relatives, to: quarrels over being harassed by creditors for your debts.

shuffling out of another's sight: where there is money, there is treachery.

suitor, to a: your intuition overcomes your enemies; don't condemn without evidence.

tearing a: a rival will take the affection of your sweetheart.

writing a: overinvolvement in your own point of view.

anonymous, an: cannot accept the receiver's preeminence; destroying it won't help.

LIBELED
09-12-13-14-23-53

being: be careful that any remark may implicate you further in scandalous recriminations.

others, by you: humiliation through cunning fraudulence.

having others: a tenuous victory full of arrows about to boomerang.

wife or husband libeling each other: own responsibility or accusations lead to divorce.

accusing another of, your: will reject previously unknown actions and forgive.

LIBRARY
16-24-32-34-39-54

borrowing a book from a: make sure the opinions you express are yours.

consulting books at a: contact your innate cleverness through the collective unconscious.

of a: will make rapid progress in your hunger for ideas.

owning a: will need to consult a judge to seek out new meanings in life.

returning a book to the: are astute and not fearful in your coming problems.

LICE
05-07-21-27-29-50

hair, finding, in the: dishonor within the ranks; the source is unaware of his complicity.

killing body: will be surrounded by sycophants, each tested as to value and discarded.

many: emotional unrest through deep-seated insecurities.

own clothes, finding, on: pleasant news brings money and ensuing responsibility.

body: an unscrupulous individual will tempt you with a dishonest alliance.

others: eliminate the keen disappointment caused by freeloaders.

LICENSE
06-10-17-31-35-51

applying for a: new opportunities to make money in a questionable venture.

granted to you, being: a contract is a license to sue.

obtaining a: will have to defend your character from a vicious attack.

others receiving a: give yourself permission to leave the incessant quarrels to others.

being refused a: choose from options that are safely within your capabilities.

LIES
02-15-20-24-48-53

children telling parents: will suffer accidental injury from guilt.

husband or wife, each other: will suffer from own folly at great expense.

of telling a: will live a long life with a weight on your shoulders.

in court: will have trouble caused by own misconduct.

others, to: will make enemies in your failure at an important enterprise.

to you: will raise funds for the personal enjoyment of others at your expense.

to protect friend: will save friends shame and embarrassment and gain their loyalty.

told a, by others, being: absurd jealousies confronted and explained are never pacified.

LIFEBOAT
06-10-13-27-29-43

aboard a ship: will have opposition in all your affairs, but demand sufficient fail-safes.

buoy, at a: another will cause you great inconvenience by remaining at a distance.

built, being: own affairs advance by your building cautious foundations and well-funded ventures.

smashed: offers that appear distorted and unnatural probably are.

floating at sea: safety in emotional turmoil.

many: a mass of ill luck of which you are a small part.

launching a: will embark on new venture freed of the weight of the old.

saving lives of people, a: save yourself first, then others who contributed to your success.

sinking, a: at the first sign of failure others will beat you from their boat.

LIGHT
03-14-22-45-50-56

bright: a too-obvious issue will shed light on the situation.

dim: will have sickness that will handicap your abilities to move forward.

distance, in the: a safe return from extensive travel where dispersed funds seed the future.

going out: danger in love affairs when meeting with jealous exes.

illuminated house, being: will discard misery and affliction, which should be devalued.

  enemy's: be on the lookout for treacherous activities in the shadows.

  halls: will be requited when perplexing problem is solved.

lighting a lamp: bringing order to chaos is your spiritual journey.

  putting out: bad news is received from a friend faraway.

obscured: what is not seen cannot be understood.

on: the correct path will be revealed to you.

prison, through a: transmit your energy, each chakra at its own time.

ray of: your self-confidence is bolstered by mentor at work.

  broken up into a spectrum: have opened up to colors, their availability and meaning.

  ship in the distance, on a: wait for arrival of an important person soon.

turning on: success in business through a plethora of new ideas.

turning out a: warning of a small operation proving your lover has cheated.

warm incandescent: understanding and wisdom in the comfort of the soul.

LIGHTHOUSE
07-16-30-40-51-56

being in a: clarity in this warning against distress.

flashing: advice of friend will save you embarrassment.

going to a: an urgent message that favor has been reversed.

of a beacon: intermittent accord among friends publicly declares your vexations.

  watching a: attempt reconciliation of tumultuous quarrels by offering safe harbor.

returning from a: will receive guidance through dark rocky water from a relative.

seeing a, in a calm sea: insecurity over a seemingly benign person.

  its bright light: seek spiritual guidance for a prosperous voyage.

  through a storm: disappointing communications will gain new impetus on solid ground.

LIGHTNING
14-20-21-47-51-54

bolt of, followed by thunder: your bolt from the blue of spiritual insight is now.

of: a chance to solve unpleasant problem leads to high honors.

rod on roof: obstruction from an obscure, mysterious source.

storm, a: the mystery will be solved by your purification and purging.

striking a house: impending illness if not checked in this early stage.

  at night: quarrelsome revenge of a stranger.

  killing animals in a field: idea flashes will change structure of plan.

  trees: sudden revelation of the source of discord between partners.

struck by, being: a vivid warning of an approaching ambush.

  others: will meet a lustful woman for only a short duration.

  pain from: unexpected severe weather will cause hardships.

  water: success is certain, after sudden awareness dissolves tension.

LILACS

06-26-35-39-50-52

of: your conceited need for affection bars any sincere attempt to love you.

perfume, having: will receive a gift from a friend.

picking: the fragrance of budding love; the humility of inexperience.

receiving a gift of: you do not care about appearances, but should.

wilted: your ecstatic passion will fade in but a glint of your eye.

LILIES

12-15-31-40-47-59

buying: your remoteness discourages help from others.

growing: an early marriage will take place and continue in good health.

receiving a bouquet of, as a gift: elegant frivolity amidst fragile constitutions.

season, of, in: purity and modesty will enhance your mental attitude toward source.

    out of: misuse of power through vain aspirations.

selling: must depend on your own efforts to transform peace to bliss.

throwing away: thoughtless actions will cause your downfall.

valley, of the: the scent of hope should last as long.

withering: are guilty of foolish grandeur and will be punished with sadness coupled with joy.

LIME

04-44-46-49-54-59

buying: advancement within own position will limit you to that position.

drinking, juice: approaching money will revive your plans.

large heap of: small property soon to be left to you that holds no immediate value.

powder, handling: people will put your feelings to the test, situation will prostrate you.

squeezing a: a peculiar oddity will cross your path, relieve the scurry.

using, in work: be on guard against those who will not benefit from you.

LIMOUSINE

09-16-20-32-34-41

being a chauffeur: driving through power struggles and territorial imperatives.

partying in a: control is in the hands of whoever is paying the tab.

riding in a: are being driven with extreme skill; how you paid for it will return on you.

LIMP

07-11-21-42-45-52

of limping: your misuse of funds will dishonor you, detracting from your honors.

    enemies: be cautious in all your dealings, so as not to cause offense when not intended.

    relatives: restrain yourself from speculations until they actually confront you.

rest because of a, having to: hard work awaits; small failures interrupt progress.

unable to travel because of a, being: favorable business ventures are handled remotely.

LINEN

27-36-37-51-58-59

changing clothes: expect to overcome worse difficulties with domestic industry.

children: in their innocence they will feel your kindness.

dressed in clean, being: much joy is ahead for you; just be.

    others: will inherit money tinged with sorrow and guilt.

flax, of: will make much success out of little resources in all you undertake.

    spinning: will have a long life of industry and thrifty ventures.

hamper, having an empty: will have jealous quarrel with sweetheart.

    being full of: shame and sorrow at the sowing of joy and gain.

    taking, from a, to wash: cherished work will confront you; its finishing will touch you.

hanging up to dry: end of your troubles as you hand power over to the sun and the wind.

napkins, of: will be visited by a socially prominent person.

receiving as a gift: will receive a long-desired invitation.

rinsing washed: change of venue in new attire brings fresh insight.

stained, being: misfortune in love affairs whose delicate beginnings can stand no taint.

LINGERIE
03-04-09-38-42-43

taking off: dissolution of love in the throes of passion.

washing: social advancement and a large trousseau.

wearing a: share your sexual needs with your lover.

    bra: are warned against loose talk in intimate situations.

    chemise: will hear gossip concerning yourself or those Peeping Toms.

    enemies: will strive for money rather than honor.

    girdle: a period of sexual restraint.

    item that shows, an: adventurous companions in your nightlife.

    panties: a new lover sparks your interest.

    young woman: vanity as outer facade does not bring about inner changes.

LION
03-10-24-29-44-52

angry, an: daring strength and ferocity cannot quell jealousy.

being afraid of a: your persecution by enemies will be blocked by strong leadership.

    attached to: will baffle your enemies' decoding of your plans.

    chased by: an impending attack, exercise caution and protect your flanks.

    triumphant over: your opponent will not know what hit him.

cage, in a: enemies will fail to injure you when facing your massive cognitive powers.

cub, of a: will have a valuable friendship that needs your leadership.

cutting his mane: your success depends on your ability to undermine your opposition.

dying, a: death of a prominent person known for aggressive anger.

head of a: your bravery will make you an important person; intellect will solidify it.

hearing a, roar: will suffer grief from your own evil instincts.

killing a: many changes will finally achieve victory through your personal magnetism.

lioness, attacked by a, being: only her young are worth that dangerous affront.

    dying when in cub birth: your upwardly mobile path threatens your ability to reproduce.

    playing with a lion: glorified physical contact, courage and persistence.

    her cubs: cannot allow a minute of detraction from your obligation.

of a: future dignity with present strength of character and great determination.

playing with a lioness: powerful physical contact confronts success and will win.

skeleton, of a: will soon have money, which had previously been inaccessible.

surprising a: be on the lookout for deceitful friends in your drive to power.

tied with a chain: a powerful enemy, temptation, has been subdued.

LIPS
07-28-37-45-48-52

beautiful: will have mastery over the harmony of plenty.

children's: postponement of success through a long growth of harmony and affluence.

man kissing a woman's: sensuousness locked in familiar expression.

    woman, man's: defeat in a struggle to otherwise gain his attention.

of own: your basest and most lusty thoughts are showcased.

pale: denial of yourself does not lead to love.

pressed tightly together: are allowing another's hate to hurt you.

repulsive: failure of enemies through their own envy.

sore: poverty unless your read another's lips.

stranger's: will have to solve a connection disruption.

thick: unhappy marriage through unfeeling actions of love.

thin: vexation at being prissy, perfect and impossible to be with.

LIQUOR

04-10-28-35-38-55

abstaining from: your overindulgence is blocking you from important events.

  friends: beware of jealous friends in the fast lane.

  relatives: are ignoring principles that have guided the family.

applejack, drinking: humiliation through ill-considered remarks.

barrel of, having a full: will keep home congenial and comforting at all costs.

champagne, getting drunk on: the euphoric is momentary.

  others: feeling bitter and disappointed that you were left out.

cocktails, having: you make friends jealous of each other by not treating them all alike.

distillery, a: a change to a more profitable business to support your bohemian lifestyle.

drinking: loyal friends will not let you drive; false friends will drive you themselves.

  female friend, with a: women of questionable character will manipulate your thoughts.

    male: need to present your ideas without allowing intimidation.

  large glass, in a: suffer self-delusion that hangers-on are friends.

  small glass, in a: are hiding from reality in a shallow-minded good nature.

  with ice: must endure painful comments to avoid reacting to rivals.

drunk on, being: unhappiness does not end with joy, but a dull numbness.

empty bottle of: your courage is depleted, seek it elsewhere.

  full: marry a mate of wealth and the intelligence not to drink.

gin, drinking: surprises in a disturbing situation toughen form.

intoxicated by looking at, becoming: are concealing your plans by deceptive actions.

mixing drinks: are flooding your mind with visionary ideas and missing the real ones.

moonshine, making your own: beware of accusations of illegal activities.

refusing a drink: your image as a serious student is not believed.

rum, offering: will make friends, which you change frequently.

several highballs: an argument with an associate.

thirsty for, being: misfortune at ignoring your upbringing.

LISTENING

05-13-23-33-45-57

advice of others, to the: are not hearing the poverty of their plea.

  important people: take heed to advice given; deny your unhealthy urges.

behind closed door: prying in others' affairs brings blame to you.

children: are making excessive demands on your time and emotions.

mate: are confronted with problems different from emotional ones.

others, to: are heading for deception in the image of love.

someone, to you: don't let people get the best of your mastery of intricate subjects.

LIVER

04-06-07-20-44-57

animals without horns, having, of: inheritance to come after long period of discontent.

  with: have absorbed the poisons of others.

buying: improvement in health through positive reinforcement.

eating goose: pay attention and you will have good health.

  calves, with onions: are being taunted maliciously by querulous busybodies.

  enemies: to win a lawsuit does not halt your opponent's discontented disapproval.

giving children, to eat: denotes your naïve impressionability that health is easily attained.

plenty of, having: illness through misuse of drugs.

  spoiled: misery is not quelled by alcohol.

LIZARD

13-15-19-32-34-48

bag made of, having a: will have money from an unimportant misdemeanor.

belt: marriage will last until death or the annoyance is dead.

shoes: will be very healthy, but watch your step.

friends having articles made of: treachery through those in whom you trusted.

in a cage: secret hostilities cause you to explore injury.

killing a: will regain lost fortune and a reputation through unpleasant encounters.

LOBSTER
09-12-18-33-36-50

eating: your love affairs will be destroyed by your over-familiarity in public places.

   children: richness in the family; great favors from influential friends.

   enemies: opponents are endeavoring to ruin you with underhanded insults.

   friends: have only one loyal friend, the rest associate too freely with sensual pleasures.

   relatives: others take the prominent position; you will command your subordinates.

of a: domestic happiness through payment of long-overdue debt.

LOCK
03-23-29-38-45-58

finding the key for a: your negative attitudes offend others, leaving you alone with them.

   unable to find: inability to obtain your wishes; heaven's doors have no locks.

having keys for a: avoid speculations until you unlock your abilities.

latch, a: will respond to another's SOS with refusal to be duped.

   broken, a: a disruption of your comfort zone.

locked out, being: fear of losing your position in life.

of opening a: the expression of your talents is your only security.

   man: are flirting with several women and suspicious of mate.

   woman: will be unfaithful to the man who loves her.

opened, an: a suitable time to pursue your courtship.

possessing many: your very stingy relatives need to be confronted and dealt with.

to open a: beware of trouble opening inhibitions.

pick a, to: will be reviled and scorned in the love arena and run afoul of the law.

LOCUST
06-21-25-29-36-42

honey, having: the nectar of the devastator can still feed the gods.

of the plant: happiness will be short-lived, depending upon the year in the cycle.

picking, flowers: ambitions will be thwarted by the elegance of another.

swarm of locusts: your entire harvest will be devoured.

LONELY
08-09-13-23-27-33

being: isolation will lead to misfortune; attend your community church.

   and not seeking company of others: approaching money will bring out old friends.

   others: someone holds a secret enmity for you sharing only with his silence.

of loneliness: improvement in affairs relies on your facing public exposure.

LOOKING
06-07-13-15-17-41

down from a hill: your ambitions interfere with and depose your restless desire for love.

   window, a: do not go too far in your schemes, or act, if you can't enter by the front door.

forward to something: your hopes, hinged on one act alone, sway in wrong direction.

glass, a: more than you would have thought you could or wanted to see.

person with a side glance, at a: thoughts and lies are reflected in your eyes.

staring into space: your inner compass is reorienting you.

straight in the eyes of a man: true success assumes an improvement to all classes.

   woman: if she doesn't blink, it is a suitable time to pursue courtship.

up at a home: good luck is coming to you.

monument: what trials had to be mounted to attain the worthiness of this stone.

mountain: hard work awaits, as do the snow-capped heights.

sky, the: proceed with plans with all confidence that your guidance is divine.

window: must control your passions and leave the results to be reciprocated.

LORD
01-09-32-36-38-44

reciting the Lord's Prayer: concentrate on practical expression of your thoughts.

listening to: need an alliance; pick your allies carefully.

speaking to a: acceptance of self-worth will lead to social success.

others: a high authority acknowledges your true inner value.

woman: the support and sustenance of a guiding light.

young girl: personal matters are dwarfed by the counsel you are about to receive.

LOSING
05-19-20-39-40-48

argument, an: a business trip where you must defend your opinion.

being lost: can't escape fate; you must make that presentation.

don't know way: will attract attention when you are forced to ask directions.

in dark conditions: go with the prevailing winds; use your other senses.

no one willing to help: find your loved one and apologize.

unable to run: time to take responsibility for your life.

bet, a: your arrogance and presumptiveness are blindingly offensive.

boyfriend, a: what in yourself did you love that his presence elicited?

child, a: no greater terror exists than the loss of your creation.

clothing: be willing to give the shirt off your back, but grasp it if another turns to take it.

game, a: are encouraging bad habits by allowing yourself to be a victim of schemes.

girlfriend, a: will suffer because of own foolishness.

home, a: stop, go within and find your self.

husband, a: temptation will come to you to leave him first.

own car: your mobility has been stunted but not crippled.

dog: the unquestioning love of adoration.

shoes: time to walk in another's footsteps.

reputation, your: have nowhere else to run; rest awhile, take deep note and begin anew.

voice, your: are losing yourself in malicious gossip.

wife, a: beneficial changes are in the offing if you allow her to go.

woman, her wedding ring: will intensify your marriage through the expression of sorrow.

LOTTERY
14-23-28-36-41-43

drawing, a: the odds of being happy and settled are not in your favor.

interested in a, being: unknown obstacles block your romance.

lotto, playing: will be in disagreeable company.

winning at: are just beginning a black period that will be short-lived.

lovers holding a ticket: an unhappy association is out of control.

numbers being upside down: engagement to a worthless person.

of a: will be held up to ridicule by traitorous friend.

picking numbers for a: overblown hopes that your partner will win.

playing a: small risks from your own delusions multiply in time.

tickets, holding: your optimism will not bring good luck.

LOVE
12-14-17-32-33-37

advancing in a, affair: act on your third rational sober thought.

adversity in: be on guard for spiteful gossip bringing conflict into your relationship.

being in: friends are jealous of your concentration on your new love.

yourself, with: vanity, faith and confidence will be abused.

company of a lover, the: freedom from anxious cares.

being loved: satisfaction with your contentment in present home life.

  children, by: quarrels over which child is loved most.

lover, accepted, being: affairs do not prosper because you scorn them.

  afflicted, being: if you can't help publicly, leave to make room for someone who can.

  angry with: the nagging question is where this will lead; if nowhere, give it up.

  arrival of a: a special gift to your inner self is of little value when vengeance is paid.

  back door, letting go out the: seek an idealized, unrealistic love.

  bath for a, preparing a: will have a life of luxury.

  beating his mistress: this affair in its secrecy allows no rational advice from an outsider.

  giving a promise to a: suitable time to pursue courtship of everything surrounding you.

lover's quarrel, a: harmony in the relationship must go through discordant tones.

loving your children: it is impossible for them to do anything to sever that bond.

  partner: will succeed in present project through true grit.

    not: disappointing search for contentment lacking at home.

    others: will live happily together all your life.

  relatives: a secret love will be revealed.

  work: prosperity is ahead if you trust in your fortune.

not succeeding in: be happy with what you possess; not dissatisfied with what you don't.

trying to make, to someone: partner will succumb to romantic interlude with another.

unwanted, being: heart trouble will be shortly resolved.

LUGGAGE
11-18-21-33-44-48

easy to handle: everyday difficulties are easy; long-standing problems take awhile.

finding own: difficulties in your path are weighted by the heaviness of your luggage.

  losing: family quarrels over an unexpected expense.

leaving your, behind: are overly possessive and want to own everything everywhere you go.

light, having: will receive money to pay off your debt.

  very heavy: emotional baggage is bogging you down.

lovers losing their: broken engagement means time to move on.

  relatives: beware of business speculation when conscience is weighted down.

porters unloading your: are shoving responsibilities on others while you enjoy pleasure.

LUMBER
07-09-19-21-26-34

beam: of a heavy: will have burden to bear.

  light: a well-merited award is received.

buying: will be in need of money for your disruptive home affairs.

cedar: incorruptible strength.

gathering: good friendship and increasing business prospects.

owning a, yard: do not allow others to lead you; make your own inevitable errors.

  planing boards: a stubborn person must be put in their place.

  sawing: a death in the family causes squabbling among the survivors.

poles, breaking: an unwise stunt has made you climb too high for your slenderness ratio.

sandalwood: don't hesitate to take in the aroma and feel the smoothness.

LUNGS
14-17-25-34-36-40

black, having miner's: your employment will be terminated.

  congested: your conduct severely affects your health.

smoker's: consult with the physician of
your choice.

strong healthy: will be called upon to
perform a strenuous task.

can't breathe: have lost your connection with
the God in your heart.

removed, having a: disappointment in desires,
with loss of health and property.

spitting mucus from the: will suffer big losses
to clear the way for fresh air.

wounded in the, being: domestic loss.

LUXURY
08-10-28-38-39-42

being in: misfortune in wallowing indolence.

in love: in your temporary weakness a rival
will take sweetheart's affections.

life of, losing your: loss of money through bad
debts for things you bought on credit.

luxurious surrounding, having: will be humiliated by financial losses.

family life: domestic quarrels over jealousy
are based on your lack of love for
yourself.

receiving a: let no family quarrel interfere
with your advancement.

things, showing off: your ego will make
many enemies.

LYING
05-22-25-34-41-45

children, to parents: the friendship in question
will harm both.

dishonest, being: a pertinent document
proves your unusual acts were of great
benefit.

family: misfortune in love affairs due to
your lies.

others: are in the grip of deceitful people;
snap out of it.

down: at your most vulnerable your integrity
is being investigated.

friend, to a: your concealed hatred for one
who has not been given a word.

husband or wife, to each other: will suffer from
the confusion of keeping your lies
straight.

others, to you: will be cheated by friends if
you don't resolve a difference of
opinion.

M M M M M

MACARONI
06-11-15-16-26-37

buying: will be invited to a rousing musical
dance show.

cooking: persevering at work may not bring
joy, but will keep food on the table.

eating: will never be hungry or rich; small
losses will be exchanged for small gains.

making: will fall in love with a stranger as
young as yourself.

of: are prone to being an inquisitive parasite.

MACHINERY
04-05-15-26-34-41

afraid of, being: new ventures but continue
to live the routine of a proper life.

automatic: attention must be paid to details,
for a change for the better.

breaks down: your sabotage of your employee
will cause a disastrous collision.

bulldozer, driving a: all your problems swept
up before you.

buying: an investment that will be paid over
time.

demolishing, people: your bulldozer self-image
is in need of repair.

handling: receive recompense for solving
complicated issues.

inadequate for the job: a rock is undermining you; take your thought process
back.

others: your inability to finish things yourself will ruin friendship.

idle machine, on an: either step on the brakes
or rev your motor.

injured by, being: failure in own purpose, but
good profits by supporting your
employer.

leasing any kind of: be practical and cost effective with your resources.

mechanic running: vain struggle to maintain
love will be worth it in the end.

operator can't operate: have physical difficulty
that cannot be relieved practically.

repairing a piece of: dignity and distinction
will come from caring for all around you.

running: the continuous hum of an active,
smooth life.

steam, by: richness and happiness come from clean efficient fuel.

runs wild: time to slow down and examine your life.

selling: prosperity; expect change in your future plans.

stops: a new career opportunity soon appears.

won't work properly: difficult emotional communication resumes; you are stalled.

wrongly used: inappropriate solutions create new problems.

MAD
01-09-11-13-31-37

becoming: will have intelligence, a secure business and your health.

being insane: will overcome adversity, through life changes, to the present happiness.

dog, killing a: past misdeed will haunt; enemies scurry to attack that one flaw.

man dreaming of being: your deep-driven love is ruining your reputation.

woman: will have a son who becomes famous through extravagant actions.

young girl: will marry soon if you avoid careless fickle friends.

person being, in the street: others give hostile gossip to people you do not know.

raving, person: your actions have caused another unjustified humiliation.

straitjacket, in a: your nerves are in shreds, your mind in pieces.

MADONNA
05-14-21-25-32-41

of a: abundant energy from the goddess principle of the mystical Mother.

picture missing, entering a church and finding: shield yourself from dishonor with love.

picture of a: no more tears; blessings, light and beauty.

statue of a: will win love of a gifted endearing offspring.

talking with a: do not let your conceit be your undoing.

MAGGOTS
05-06-32-35-38-44

killing: harboring a grudge won't gain you justification.

many: your mental condition is disturbing at best.

meat crawling with: others exercise shameless exploitation of you.

of a: change your behavior before you become what you hate in your enemy.

MAGIC
01-07-11-14-32-43

being an alchemist: transform human attitudes to spirit.

casting a spell: be careful trusting one who influences you.

conjuring up: negotiation relies on skill, not solid facts.

discussing: loss of a friend who adamantly refuses to enlighten their thought.

events, being involved with unpredicted: progress in enterprises will become evident.

of: a change will come in your affairs when you act on your interest in the supernatural.

performing: your base qualities can become golden ones.

potion, making a: the deception of non-reality.

drinking a: will gain fortitude and support from your destiny.

making another drink: your error in judgment cannot be relieved by others.

reading about: you keenly see an unexpected source of unfavorable news.

sorcerer, being a: are taking advantage of others, because of disillusionment.

using: careful with what you do not understand.

wizard, being a: family prosperity through your intervention.

MAGICIAN
05-14-23-38-40-44

being a: you overestimate your social standing; magic is a higher form of nature, not you.

and performing tricks: a mystery will be solved with the wrong evidence.

others: your advancement in position will not be helped by believing others.

performing tricks: an unexpected event is not all it was touted to be.

MAGNET

01-21-26-39-47-49

attracting objects to you with a: your greed is alienating others.

being attracted by a: your heart is doing cartwheels over another.

man dreaming of using a: loss of honorable life through a woman.

　woman: wealth will be hers through power games, which must continue to be won.

of a: security in business if you are not reckless with important connections.

using a: an elevated trend in your affairs to come.

　professional people, for work: exert control; persuade one to bow to your will.

MAGNIFYING GLASS

03-33-34-38-43-46

buying a: discovery of lost items that are not as valuable as you claimed.

of a: careful not of enlarge your business past its market.

reading with a: may read between the lines, but they are still your words.

using a: a small incident will have a massive significance.

MAGPIE

13-14-29-39-42-43

cage, being in a: cannot give anything up after it has lost its usefulness.

cawing: quarrels leaving unpleasant shivers of disdain.

evening, in the: will be badly cheated by vicious chatter.

　morning: problems are brewing; guard your envy in thought and deed within your family.

of a: someone is trying to steal something from you.

MAID

16-17-25-29-34-46

being a: if you resent being a servant, you cannot respect who you really are.

chamber: be polite, then scheme behind your employer's back.

elderly woman dreaming of being a: increasing income but criticism from family.

　girl: are being harassed by those who want your money.

married woman: at a school reunion you are still lowly regarded for your ill temper.

honor, being a, of: will be disappointed in love.

marrying a: your employer will fall in love with you.

several, having: the issue you are dealing with is trickier in quantity.

MAILING

02-22-31-38-40-46

documents: will overpay for unwanted merchandise.

items of value: will spend extravagantly on useless things.

letter with a check, a: an irritating obligation must be met.

mailbox which won't accept: the answer is already "NO!"

package, a: false hopes guide your actions; self knowledge brings hope.

postcard, a: the simplest token renews an important relationship with the mailman.

MAKEUP

06-11-23-29-34-37

arrogant, conceited woman applying: danger of burning a hole in your clothes.

artist applying your: trying to convince audience you are not yourself.

　mascara: are avoiding facing the facts.

beautiful woman using: something hidden will reveal your guilt.

　plain: after fifty, even plastic surgery cannot hide the truth told in your face.

being made up: trying to convince audience you are not yourself.

buying: a change in your appearance will benefit you.

face powder, buying: will be extravagant in spending money.

　lipstick: frivolous, vain desire to attract attention.

　rouge: will give children a higher education.

overly painted lady, an: are putting on your best face, which isn't true enough.

putting rouge on cheeks: are covering up a health issue.

wearing lipstick: treason and friendship based on false values.

woman dreaming of using: discomfort at revealing herself to the world.

   man, a woman: loss of authority in the community.

     who steals another's: you envy her beauty, not her inner worth.

MAN
04-05-07-17-47-49

accosted by a, being: will be scorned by others for too much mental work.

amorous, being an: be careful of relationships with others; stay platonic.

Cain, dreaming of: retrace footsteps, then tread a different path.

carried by a, being: will have anxious days because of illness and dependence.

child, with his: your riches from within can't help but be imitated.

conquest of a wealthy: avoid rivals and play the real game.

fat, a: bad ventures in worshipping the wrong idol.

gentleman, an invitation from a: his courtly manners may rub off on you.

   meeting a: forget inferiority and jealousy; confront your admiration.

Greek god Bacchus, dreaming of: are worshipping the wrong talents in yourself.

handsome, a: big satisfaction and joy through rich possessions and richness given.

haughty proud, a: one who loves you secretly will not succumb to your mistreatment.

horrible-looking, a: cannot be a friend to yourself.

man dreaming of an unknown man: improvement in own business, glory and honor.

prominent, talking with a: an abundance of possibilities to explore.

   speech by a, hearing a: dishonor in speech because the audience can't hear it rationally.

short, a: have an adaptable commonsense nature.

strong, a: beware of cheating on the part of your mate.

   kicking sand in your eyes: aims have been dashed by the competition.

tall, a: boundless wealth; are setting your sights too high.

young, a: the contrast of ages causes discomfort to others, not you.

   being complimented by a girl: your prosperity should not take advantage of a peer's feelings.

MANDALA
01-03-10-11-13-38

cathedral rose window, of a: follow the journey of your psyche.

creating a multicolored: self-realization can restore healing, harmony and order.

focusing your mind on a: reflection of positive changes to be experienced.

MANICURE
13-26-30-31-33-36

having a: will have to reduce your expenses.

   hands beautifully manicured: will rapidly reach distinction in your calling.

   woman: will marry a man much older than herself.

manicurist, being a: will be required to meet overriding expenses.

of a: will have to act to reduce your expenses.

MANSION
06-08-11-14-16-36

being in a: someone will fall in love with the true you.

   others: are surrounded by jealous people.

burning, a: foolish to assume a status not earned.

demolishing a: someone will take something from you by force.

in a city, having a: will spend much money.

living in a: sorrow that own home is not imposing.

owning a: pleasure of short duration as people will be ungrateful to you.

   regal, having a: will be molested by those jealous of your travel.

seeing a distant: advancement when you reach its doors.

MANURE
04-05-22-26-33-44

buying: a particular notion needs fertilizing.

handling: a solution only through a difficult route; proceed.

of fertilizing soil with: germ of an idea will grow in importance.

selling: distance yourself from bad company.

shoveling, on a dunghill: malicious gossip and slanderous accusations.

stepping in a pile of: your odor will repel unwanted people.

MAP
03-07-10-11-27-39

atlas, buying an: are being shown the long trip abroad in your head.

  consulting an: will have plenty of money for the adventure planned.

  of an: social activities leads to a change of residence, which better fits your needs.

buying a: are being shown the long trip ahead.

colored, a: marriage across ethnic and racial bounds.

consulting a: are looking for changes in new employment, experiences and horizons.

  unable to locate place: are willing to abandon the present to rise to better surroundings.

studying a: your past and future life's journey will provide growth experiences.

MARBLE
01-18-19-25-37-49

buying: will attend the funeral of a cold person.

column: your substantial success is jeopardized by your inflexibility.

playing marbles: your behavior is immature and in defiance of all social codes.

polishing: are investing in receiving an inheritance.

quarry: your fantasies will come out solid; past love was never lost.

scratched, being: affection for childhood memories will brighten your life.

sculpture: friendships are not cast but finely chiseled.

things in own house, having: are taking risks that will pay off.

MARCH
04-15-22-25-29-44

being born in: at each ending there will be a beginning.

of the month of, during this month: expectations are raised, then dashed, to raise yours.

  during other months: will compete for favors from a newcomer you introduced.

children: should consider all aspirations before deciding on the height.

MARCHING
06-16-18-45-46-47

alone: pick your beat and work with it; your honesty must be above suspicion.

fast pace, at a: an unexpected windfall will lead to an advancement in business.

flags, with: define an ancient tradition.

soldiers, with: your ambition for participation on a team can be in many venues.

women, in the company of: should study all the options, in good time, before deciding.

MARIJUANA
03-11-12-31-37-44

being addicted to: postponement of everything as life passes you by.

buying: serious illness undetected will cause grievous, graceless acts.

smelling: will have much protection.

smoking, alone: will envision unattainable things and missions not attempted.

  opposite sex, with one of: security in love lasts as long as the euphoria, no longer.

  arrested for, being: your love of amusements will harass you more than anyone can.

  cigarette of hemp or: prompt engagement.

MARKET
05-08-17-22-41-47

being in a: your worth is who you are, not what you own.

  small: short-lived infirmity from imminent betrayal.

going to a fish: have a high degree of flexibility that will lead to a prominent position.

gourmet: your delicate tastes are being overloaded.

meat: will receive honors for keeping a fresh imagination.

idly looking through a: your open-mindedness allows forming long-lasting friendships.

of an empty: feel emotionally inept—but will soon fall in love.

purchases at a, making: nurture your recent acquaintance with an invitation to lunch.

selling something at a: the balance of trade is wobbly now, at best.

MARRIAGE
04-10-11-15-21-25

announcing one's own: friction from resentment of enemies will last over time.

annulled, becoming a bachelor after an: have a strong, outstanding personality.

assisting at a: will have pleasing news of little importance.

bridesmaid at a, ceremony, being a: will marry soon if sincerely happy for the bride.

    bride or groom: major financial loss affecting living standards and health.

    children: have a naïve enthusiasm toward a new project.

    daughter away in, giving a: good times are ahead; freedom from responsibility.

    sister: unexpected big peril of serious incestuous entanglements.

    flower girl: will have a happy future from the care and consideration of family.

    maid of honor: will accept nothing less than the truth.

getting married: melancholy for the guests with unrequited loves.

honeymoon, a: looking forward to future activities.

infidelity: accusing yourself of being unfaithful to an idea.

money, for: your nervousness and irritability are not ways to avert your financial loss.

others announcing their: disagreeable news from those absent.

partner being suddenly grotesque: question if this is the right choice for you.

priest in a, of the: sit back; you're into obsessing over other's lives rather than living own.

relatives, announcing to: immediate recovery from being overly committed.

second, a: inner marriage of formerly disjointed aspects of one's self.

    to a younger man: facing a delicate mental outlook that needs restructuring.

secret, a: a disappointing love affair leaves you uncertain and confused.

virgin, to a: frigidness and lack of sympathy from mate.

widower dreaming of: some things cannot be replaced.

wife and husband restating their vows: happiness is ensured until death.

will, against your: a lively and eventful period of excessive responsibilities.

woman dreaming of, to an old man: are tired, sick and stressed from trouble ahead.

    young, being an unhappy bride at a: enemies seek her downfall, adding burdens.

MARSH
02-18-31-36-40-45

getting out of a: situation is hopeless if you allow your mental outlook to deem it so.

    to firm ground: being fraught with emotional woes leaves you stronger.

having a tract of, land: temptations in love will be abundant but few long-lasting.

of a: will ruin a constant friendship through long illness.

others sinking in the: promises must have substance to be believed.

stuck in a, being: your positive attitude will attract animosity; meet obligations anyway.

walking across a: difficult problem must be tackled, not bemoaned.

MARTIAL ARTS
02-18-26-34-47-48

karate: every move had intellectual implications.

judo: simple moves with strength outwit opponents.

MARTYR
17-22-24-29-35-48

being a: your generous, honest sacrifice will not be appreciated; neither will anorexia.

    eagerly: your decisive altruism will be rewarded with public probation.

making a, of someone: their backlash will attempt to oppress you.

    children: stinginess will exaggerate damages well out of proportion.

    innocent people: will make great sacrifices for noble causes.

others, of you: your decisiveness will save you from failure of your projects.

MARY

05-10-16-35-42-44

daughter named, having a: must rely upon own vigor to protect her from the cold.

   loved one: will receive a large favor from someone for which no return is requested.

   mother: much happiness within the family.

of the mother of Jesus: will have fortune in business with your own guiding light.

   wife: honor without profit; blessings every day.

women named: a big fortune is ahead for you.

MASCOT

03-07-12-30-33-45

having a: will come out well from a present danger.

   in own car: serious argument with the driver over being under the wrong banner.

of a: unexpected news will change your future prospects.

   ship: important and very beneficial events to come.

MASK

03-06-11-37-39-45

face is a rigid, your: false persona to protect yourself from ridicule and scorn.

of a: analyze your friends' motives to uncover your own.

wearing a: hide faults and defects behind your cynicism.

   enemies: play treacherously upon the superficial attractiveness of others.

   others: will be injured through feigned sincerity and envy.

   someone: beware of duplicitous and secretly jealous neighbors.

MASON

03-06-07-17-19-39

being a: warning of troubles caused by your impatience.

employing several: losses due to illness of those depending on you.

freemason, being a: will be misunderstood; profit from ensuing estrangement.

becoming a: will have new, loyal-to-the-death friends.

other fraternal members: will be surrounded with protection from life's evils.

of a: distinction in work will result in increased quality with less man-hours.

several, building a house: will rise in dignity within the family.

work, at: will be guilty of foolish actions in other places, not with bricks and mortar.

working as a: build your life to your specifications alone.

MASQUERADE

12-14-21-25-32-47

being at a, party alone: you will have sprightly music and amusing companions.

   group, a: your conduct will be misinterpreted and maligned.

   loved one, with: a successful life ahead with no other options.

party, at a: someone will trick you by pretending to be something he is not.

queen of a, being: enemies seek your downfall, but your problem was self created.

MASS

06-07-09-13-17-25

attending: good sign for future well-being of your family.

   alone: your conscience is not clean and you will attempt to blame another.

   every week: will receive what you desire, for your actions are guided by spirit.

of a, of things: a close friend who has been unfaithful will return in good faith.

others being at: will combat falsehood and bring dignity and distinction to your life.

priest telling, a: will be freed from work to attend those in temporary trouble.

MASSACRE

20-22-27-38-39-40

hearing of a: spend money at the dentist to keep from grinding your teeth.

many being killed in a: contend with competition on the playing field, not the battlefield.

massacred, being: damages in own affairs from those you have ill-considered.

massacring others: extreme anger over others feelings entitled to what you don't have.

MASSAGE

01-04-06-08-46-47

giving a: the situation needs to be manipulated, by someone with the right expression.

   sick person, a: unattended symptoms will lead to health problems.

of a: leave your emotional tension on the table, you will be trained to handle it.

public place, having a, in a: your public image needs to be freed from taint.

MASTS

07-12-13-21-22-30

climbing a: your mastery is an enormous accomplishment.

   sailors: will live to a ripe old age in happiness.

of the, of a ship: will take an important journey giving pleasure for a greater goal.

   without sails: your ventures are at a standstill due to lack of proper equipment.

very high: your pride won't bend for anyone; live up to it.

MASTIFF

01-21-32-45-46-49

being bitten by a: a most trusted friend betrayed you in love affairs.

of this smooth-coated dog: beware of false suspicions, but keep your guard on watch.

two fighting: one you thought of as an enemy harbors strong feelings of love for you.

   playing: have armored yourself with defenses so that you can't see potential friends.

MAT

21-34-35-36-40-47

braided, a: your careful planning will bring prosperity.

door, being at the: indicates trouble from unwanted visitors.

exercise: increasing responsibility over which you have no control.

green, a: a growth of circumstances conspiring to do you harm.

straw, a: warning of poverty if you continue spending.

wrestling: are overconfident in your abilities.

yoga: to stretch further in ventures, keep to actions that are supported by previous ones.

MATCHES

04-07-15-33-45-46

box of, in pocket, having a: financial gains are at hand, grasp the opportunity.

buying: your love will create a happy home life for you.

home, having, at: misfortune in love affairs will cause you to make a painful sacrifice.

of: own efforts will bring riches, if you are able to keep plans secret.

playing with: toying with the passions of others will backfire.

MATHEMATICS

01-05-17-24-32-43

abacus, using an: financial success is in the painstaking details.

adding figures: personal difficulties need to be mastered.

arithmetic: problems may be difficult but are solvable.

formula, a: a convoluted lesson must be learned.

multiplying: an acquaintance is spreading harm to your reputation.

solving an equation: are overlooking a simple error that devalues your whole attitude.

   not: have little hope of fulfilling your plans; revisit their worth to you.

working in decimals: a message you discounted is happily received.

zero hour, it being the: will have success in all ventures in eternity.

zero of a: will have a small unhappiness, if you pass this test.

   double: will be double-crossed by a friend.

   three: will have great wealth.

MATTRESS

13-16-19-23-24-25

buying a: an easy life does not come from lack of initiative.

having a: worries caused by your firm indecision.

of a: perform heavier responsibilities and duties that cannot be avoided.

repairing own: desires will be accomplished, if you accept advice.

MAUSOLEUM

02-03-07-16-30-42

being entombed in a: relax and stop fretting over egotistical actions.

   others: death of one they emulated; trouble of a prominent friend.

of a: unhealthy, insincere attentions to rich relations for an inheritance.

visiting a: long sickness of the heart from memory of the dead.

MAY

06-16-24-32-33-35

being born in: undertakings will be successful through your stubbornness.

   children: will live a long life of pleasure you obstinately support.

1st being International Labor Day: will work hard in life and be blessed by it.

flowers blossoming in: disappointment is wisked away with the flick of a cloud.

of the month of, during this month: do not be discouraged; every blossom will open.

of, during other months: financial losses from an inability to start things happening.

MAYPOLE

02-06-25-30-47-49

dancing around the: the coming-out party of the common girl.

many, in an open area: will have a quarrelsome, sullen lover when harmony is expected.

tall, a: arrange your entanglements to be patterned with a definite purpose.

wreathed in flowers: joy without profit; beauty is in every eye, waiting to be expressed.

MEADOW

04-22-27-30-33-48

being in a: happiness and trust of partner are reciprocated.

buying a: will give much hospitality and accumulate much valuable property.

grass growing in a: illusions and vain hopes block your altering a good marriage.

   dried up to hay: leave old ideas as fodder to others.

of a: undertakings will bring reunions of bright promise.

sleeping in an open: your space is restricting your being able to experience happiness.

walking through a: your staid and conventional rigidity.

MEASURING

02-11-24-32-34-48

anything: lack of attention is detrimental to your own affairs.

clothing, own: only you can support the being that is you, to full fruition.

fabric: your pretentiousness covers your insensitivity to yourself.

Golden, the: become like a God who "numbers" the universe.

house, own: you may lose more than you save.

ingredients for cooking: be delicate in your balancing of the elements of life.

size of own body: tend to superficiality when your defenses expose your fragileness.

temperature, the: are oversensitive to your milieu and selfish in keeping it to yourself.

MEAT

17-21-24-26-36-48

bones taken from: will be busy with projects for a long time; give what's left to others.

breaking bones of: will have all kinds of losses beyond what you have to lose.

butchering raw: a friend would like to become a lover.

buying: will gain money in gambling on a wise stock.

carving cooked: must join forces with a rival on your ambitious quest and share success.

cooking, for yourself: minor difference of opinion over unrequited love.

   but not being allowed to eat: your "daily bread" is always provided.

   others: a bold and hearty grasp of your needs in love affairs.

eating beef: will have an easy life like the carnivorous mammal you are.

   boiled: melancholy from disagreements leads you to overanalyze your problems.

broiled: are getting to the heart of the matter, one side at a time.

fried: will be paid well to kill someone's spirit; others will be the spoils.

raw: will receive discouraging news of the death of a friend.

roasted: will receive God's blessings and affection from a friend.

rotten: your luck has turned on you and left you at risk.

sausage: are in a combative mood toward your career.

veal: will cheat someone, when they unexpectedly change plans on you.

frozen: falsehood and deception frozen out of your consciousness.

throwing, to a dog: danger is very close to you; who has it in for you?

MEDALS
07-17-21-23-25-44

earning a: you will be honored for the application of your talents.

Malta Cross, civilian being decorated with the: luck and prosperity.

being presented with the: will have good fortune by merit made bitter by loyal friends.

of a: will arise from a present peril with distinction for what you have accomplished.

Victoria Cross, receiving the: will win your advancement through your own merit.

wearing: have confidence in your potential that detractors can't quell.

army and navy personnel: preserve your energy and intelligence for the real battle.

someone else: danger of revealing unwarranted jealousy.

MEDICINE
21-30-33-36-48-49

antiseptic, applying: your negative intentions need a new scab.

bitter: success does not come out of misjudging those who would hinder you.

chest: troubles are not serious, but will strengthen your relationship.

disease: someone exerting power over you is causing you discomfort.

drops, nurse measuring: will soon have a small sum of money left to you.

others: don't keep track of small monetary values without registering the effects.

giving medicine to children: if they like the taste, illness will subside.

friends: your advice will bring accord among friends.

relatives: be cautious in all your dealings, to not cause disappointment.

hospital: signals the onset of a physical complaint.

injection: take precaution with what you ingest.

inoculation: cleaning the slate for new buds to bloom.

morphine, taking: face disagreeable duty and tackle it with initiative.

putting medicine, in water: advancement within position.

tablet, taking a: avoidance never solves or rids you of the issue.

bottle of: the bitter taste in your mouth should lead to optimism.

cold: have lost your lover through your vagueness and indecisiveness.

overdosing on: your self-indulgence is self-destructive.

sleeping: dreams are the window to the soul, don't close it.

take, refusing to: ill humor and irritability mean your body is rejecting the medicine.

taking: your body's healing mechanism has been activated.

bitter: will attempt to injure one who trusts you.

pleasant: healing guide will end troubles for ultimate good.

tasteful: the check will not be in the mail; you look ridiculous expecting it.

vaccination, getting a: take precaution with your health.

MEDITATION
10-18-19-21-37-46

of a: purification and cleansing of all belief systems to open you to higher knowledge.

trance, in a: have not grounded your insight with empirical knowledge.

tune in an: will receive wisdom from
expanded states of consciousness.

  out: are always at some level of attunement; each level needs its turn.

MEETING
04-06-07-14-43-44

being in a: neglect has tearful consequences
because of lost opportunity

friend, an old: news from distant past changes
your direction.

holding a: you wish to control an explosive
situation

of a, place: others are envious of your faithful
friends and sense of responsibility.

sudden unexpected, a: accidents are opportunities in disguise.

MELANCHOLY
09-12-14-21-29-44

being sad yourself: a lasting reflection of a
national tragedy.

state, being in a: will realize high ambitions
and calm happiness.

  married people: pleasant home life with
troubling business.

  others: separation of lovers dwindles your
income.

  young girl: disappointment from an
engagement thought to be made in
heaven.

MELODY
6-22-27-30-31-37

hearing a pleasant: influential, agreeable new
friends will attend you.

playing a: affairs will prosper with beloved
enduring friendship.

singing a: refreshing incidents of romantic
vision.

  hearing others: certain and happy marriage
for them, which you can aim for.

MELONS
07-12-16-23-27-44

buying a: are ready, finally, to commit to a
love affair.

eating: hopes for consistency in love are in
vain.

growing: your quick judgment bars intelligent
analysis.

having a: a long-standing dispute can now
be solved.

of: don't belittle true friendship or you will
lose it.

sick person dreaming of eating: with proper
treatment you will emerge healthier.

watermelon, giving: will receive a gift from an
unknown person.

MELTING POT
01-09-18-21-30-35

brewing a: a successful recipe uses intuitive,
rational and emotional thinking.

  at a hectic pace: your childhood was
wrought with explosive situations.

  steady: moderation is the key to peace,
acceptance to prosperity.

ethnic mix: don't take chances in a crowded
thoroughfare.

witches brew, a: resolve contradictions within;
a top deal with financial woes, without.

MEMORIAL DAY
03-06-12-14-36-48

attending church on: a chance to answer
persistent appeals for aid among the
survivors.

decorating graves on: will enjoy security for
a long time from their actions.

of: will have good health and blessings, but
cannot live up to greatness.

visiting a relative's grave on: face future deceit
by acquaintance with kindness.

MENDING
09-15-23-35-45-49

children's clothes: have a strong sense of
responsible common sense.

fences: trust cannot be abused and remain
true.

of: will have an inferior and miserable position before your well-deserved promotion.

others: be cautious in love adventures to
attain person you have desired for so
long.

others, your clothes: family quarrels will end
in a period of everything going your way.

young woman, clothes: will be of great assistance to her husband.

MERCURY
04-07-12-20-28-33

being: are a self-centered trickster who
controls others' actions with devious
devices.

controlled by your impulses: the truth communicates better when faced from the soul.

dominated by his appetites: listen well to what is offered, then kill the messenger.

buying: a negotiation will divert you from your real mission.

handling: loss of friends through false reports, but gain others.

others: gossip is being spread about your careless behavior with the opposite sex.

of: will be invited to a big festivity, but will not have money to attend.

God, the: don't shoot the messenger who brings reason to you.

taking in medicine: will become disgusted with the poison spoken by friends.

walking on: your life is in considerable flux.

MERIT

05-16-20-28-35-37

accomplishments, being given, for: hard work with a reasonable income.

receiving: will have to answer publicly for misdeed.

children: are at their mercy; give them what they need.

someone, without deserving it: will suffer a keen displeasure; leave it to be rectified.

MERRIMENT

02-18-23-30-33-34

having much: will suffer because of own foolishness, but enjoy it for a time first.

others: a distinguished outsider will court you.

merry-go-round: are going around in circles but making no progress in life.

of: expect difficulties in life if you don't share your accomplishments at home.

participating in: good married life full of arguments and good times.

watching: misfortune, as a refusal to take reality seriously overcomes your reason.

MESS

05-18-25-28-46-47

making a, of things: will be made love to by unexpected person.

children: will receive a legacy that cannot relieve the sense of abandonment.

sailors', hall: will be very fortunate in business transactions.

things being in a: idolize money, ignoring the organization's purpose to support its continuance.

MESSAGE

02-04-05-11-46-47

of a: conveying a truth so we can understand it.

receiving a: secure the problem in your thoughts before you reply.

relatives, from: an important and very beneficial event accompanies the small ones.

sweetheart, a: a big catastrophe ahead can be averted by challenging the source.

sending a: take notice of unpleasant circumstances in life.

taking a, to Garcia: must prove you can do mission before you are assigned it.

METALS

05-08-22-23-39-41

anvil, hammering metals on: will lose money gambling; invest in own chances.

molding: gains through patient work; proceed one step at a time.

working on an object on: will not succeed by forcing the issue.

another: good times ahead with partners.

bells, making large: do not be concerned with idle talk of others who can't act.

burrs on, irritated by rough: avoid those who take advantage of you.

seeing: avoid being too close to false friends.

buying: put your effort on the personal sensitivity of your humanity.

foundry, of a: will receive compensation for economizing on expenses.

molten: a major transformation is taking place; be part of it.

nugget of precious metals, of a: amazing the wealth within others, as within yourself.

several, of different metals: hard but malleable strength of character.

radium, handling: money will burn a hole in your palm.

selling: are confronted with insurmountable obstacles.

uranium: the ideas you are considering are explosive.

using base metals: seek function rather than form.

    aluminum: one should not use willow when oak is called for.

    bronze: your warlike passions are ready to plunder.

    platinum: out of gloom comes a chance to demonstrate your work and worth.

    statue: aim for the ideal rather than the reality.

welder, being a: be cautious of the oppression of your superiors in your business affairs.

METAMORPHOSIS
05-11-21-28-37-43

animals changing to humans: to earn a place in society, modify defensive instincts.

humans changing to animals: will improve present position by rectifying old offenses.

insects experiencing, a: the natural progression of a universal order.

plants going through: oh to be a bee; so much pollen to gather.

METEOR
05-12-31-33-34-38

landing in your backyard: a gift has been bestowed upon you.

streaking across the sky: wishful thinking solidified for a short duration.

METER
02-07-09-10-14-32

reading a: allow your emotions to flow too freely.

    not: advice should at least be listened to.

running, a: you talk too much without thinking.

MICE
16-29-38-39-44-49

cat killing: victory over insecure friends.

caught in a trap: will be slandered unless you foil your enemies.

dog catching: will be put to shame by being thought to be lesser.

fear of: your energy is being siphoned off.

mousetrap, of a: your inability to hurt another is not universal.

of: troubles through a business associate can be challenged with notarized letter.

only one: your scurrying, flitting and running about to avoid troubles is futile.

playing: your timidity will bring dishonor.

squeaking: an avoidable danger can be faced with a new outfit.

MICROSCOPE
17-20-25-26-35-41

of a: good intentions must be acted upon in full agreement with subject.

using a: a mystery is not there to be solved, but to show life in perspective.

    chemist: dignity will be gained through relinquishing your skepticism.

    doctor: recovery from an illness despite your distrust of his methods.

    jeweler: abundant means if you are able to discern what things are really worth.

MIDWIFE
14-17-27-28-33-46

being a: a narrow escape from an untimely incident is your gain.

doctor using a: will suffer for your expensive habits.

helping a: will quarrel with your husband about money.

of a: discovery of a secret illness that could have brought you to death's door.

seeing a: seek relief from your conscience and distress perpetrated by others.

MILDEW
06-10-20-23-45-46

developing: will be introduced to an attractive stranger; don't trust him.

removing, from vegetables: rapid recovery after drinking clear, clean water.

something going: disintegration of private papers and a friendship.

MILESTONE
07-13-28-37-38-41

of a: secret enemy will follow you on a cross-country trip.

placing a: can overcome obstacles by the courage of your convictions.

    several: will break with past limitations to achieve your new you.

MILITARY
01-05-13-14-21-25

being in company of an army adjutant: will be respected by neighborhood.

high-ranking adjutant, a: friends will be advantageous but not remunerative.

cavalry, of a: unreturned affection will be your fate.

disarmed, being: dignity in the midst of disaster and shame.

enemies: will have money difficulties for a long time.

thieves: the rate of recidivism proves they will soon be robbing again.

duty, being bound by: compulsive control issues you wish to live up to.

leave, being on: relief from pressing obligations.

major, meeting a: will be invited to a civic duty.

mess hall: preparation for a special event does not include a menu.

parade, viewing a: be prepared for danger in the immediate future.

veteran, a: lasting friendships transcend any period of discontent.

wounded, a: must succeed in jumping a few hurdles before life can return to normal.

volunteer in the, being: will lose your life in a battle of differences.

of a: will soon be in the armed forces; adjust your reaction to them.

woman dreaming of an officer: romance outweighs practical fortune.

MILITARY ACADEMY
14-15-18-20-39-48

cadet at a: humiliation must be endured to gain the strength of integrity.

married at a: enemies are overcome by perseverance.

officer at a: discouragement in your affairs.

professor at a: rigid authoritarianism is a matter of life or death.

unmarried at a: upcoming marriage filled with adversity and emotional repression.

MILK
05-25-32-37-38-46

cow, milking a: peace and plenty and pleasant journeys are coming.

getting lots of, from: enjoy the simplicities of life; prosperity in love affairs.

donkey, of a: deep inner nourishment has been reserved for your use only.

drinking: nurture the flowering of your personality.

empty udder, an: your energy is insufficient for successful completion of the project.

goat's: your naïve immaturity leads to childish behavior, embarrassing but fun.

large container full of: unexpected fortune from a dear friend.

large quantities of, having: possessions and loving support will be withheld from you.

malted, making a: your success is assured.

married woman having plenty of: will be pregnant again.

old woman having: big wealth will provide a safe journey for the traveler.

others, giving, to: will lead a charitable life in a caretaking profession.

pail, carrying full: good news concerning a birth.

empty: will be tormented with trivial inequities, forgetting the whole picture.

selling: will win by remaining independent of others' persuasion.

large amounts of: abundant harvest and prosperity for the farmer.

souring: have left your vigorous mind to wallow in minor disputes.

spilling: a slight tiff at home over your continual faultfinding.

woman selling: large profits for highly esteemed businesspeople.

young girl milking a cow: possessions are being withheld by greedy, jealous brother.

MILL
08-09-16-18-24-40

cloth: production of comfort through thrift and creative enterprise.

grinding grain: shame and sorrow of ego's false beliefs in self.

miller, being a: hard work awaits you.

woman dreaming of a: will marry a man poorer than she thought.

using a: take better care of your dealings.

new: dividends from investments long forgotten.

old: will overcome enemies with perseverance.

saw: take precautions against commitments you can't fulfill.

stone, around your neck: old convictions are strangling you; take care with present deals.

timber: disintegration of the nitty-gritty to build the new.

waterwheel, a: will unexpectedly receive money due to you.

   broken, being: old flaws in your friendship resurface.

   turning: your greater industry leads to higher wages.

      not: project has hit a roadblock; your love matters are in stagnation.

wind: will be badly deceived; project will bring you respect and promotion.

MILLIONAIRE
02-14-16-18-22-44

of a: do not act on other's advice without a second or third opinion.

receiving money from a: you will be exhausted from hard work.

   favor, a: a happiness short-lived because of deceit.

returning money to a: don't let people cheat you or let yourself cheat others.

MINE
03-04-11-25-39-47

big coal, having a: a rational plan for risky work includes the worst case scenario.

   gold: use your analytical skills to avoid future mistakes.

   iron: dwelling in uncertainties is particularly harmful.

closing a: a catastrophic end to love and the ability to sustain it in the future.

coming up out of a: your spirituality has matured sufficiently to be exposed.

deep shaft, in a: are desperate to make more money; there are more secure ways.

digging for a: your plate is overloaded; learn to say no.

entering a: the truth is deep inside you; enter with caution.

excavating a: resolve deep-rooted problems for unpromising expectations to turn bright.

field: potential dangers with each step.

going down into a: trust only proven friends; hidden dangers lie in wait for you.

miner, being a: danger in others meddling with your opportunities.

of a: mine the valuables from the inner terrain of your subconscious.

owning a: promise of future work will be dashed by unanticipated trouble.

trapped in a: be on constant guard in dealing with strangers.

   with ceiling collapsing: are overextended everywhere in your life.

   with no air: have lost your spiritual connection; pray.

   with no heat: examine your diet; make positive changes.

   with water rising: worry from indiscreet thoughts and warring actions.

MINISTER
09-11-15-24-28-31

black clothing of a: danger of dealing with the depths without wise counsel.

company of a woman, in the: financial frivolity on her part, social concern on his.

giving advice: true friends hold your advice in high esteem.

judge, being with a: expect serious disappointment; sins must be atoned for.

outside a church: clear up outstanding debts to society before entertaining an entry.

preaching: your promotion will be envied and criticized as usurping another's rights.

MINK
06-25-28-31-33-46

coat, buying a: be warned your husband is deceiving you with unscrupulous behavior.

   receiving, as a gift: increasing popularity among those you associate with.

   selling: will have a new husband who will treat you better.

   wearing: are ready to take on all dissenters.

      hat: a rival will take the affections of your sweetheart.

others: are in the grip of deceitful
people; refuse to do their bidding.
relatives: abundant means from working overtime, and overwrought.

MINT
11-13-20-28-31-36

Building, The: troubles caused by prying into
affairs of others.
working at: others will be serviced and
touched daily by your efforts.
julep, drinking a: initiation into the world
from another viewpoint.
minting coins: your fingers have immense
power with an intricate movement.

MINUET
01-24-35-41-49

dancing a, with your wife: domestic happiness
with a lilt of folly contains a pattern.
friend, a: congenial and sincere actions
from companions.
handsome man, a: approaching invitations
multiply with each event.
sweetheart: danger in love matters that
you do not commit too soon.
of a: social prospects increase with each
step.

MIRACLES
10-16-20-22-36-49

believing in: when there is nothing left to
cause recovery from an illness.
of a: unexpected events will astonish you for a
while, then believe.
others telling of being present at a: face insurmountable obstacles with confidence.
witnessing a: allow divine intervention into
your consciousness.

MIRAGE
06-12-21-22-40-45

business executive dreaming of a mirage: your
staff is not honestly confronting tasks.
lover: your sweetheart is not faithful;
face it and move on.
man: be wise in business ventures; bad
fortune is too easily obtained.
woman: friends are cheating you;
don't let that stop you from succeeding.
young girl: it is advisable to change
boyfriends.

MIRROR
11-20-25-32-46-47

broken: unexpected death of a relative brings
friction in the family circle.
clear, a: reflects one's inner depths uncovered
to their free expression.
cloudy, a: the distortions you project onto the
world are there to be viewed by you.
cracked, a: try to see yourself as others see
you, flaws and all.
looking at oneself in a mirror: what appears to
be reality is not the truth.
business executive: disloyal staff members
worm their way into your confidence.
husband, your: will be unfairly treated for
undesirable news relating to his
actions.
loved one, a: self-deception with your
flighty character.
lover: sweetheart is not really faithful;
neither is your eccentric behavior.
man: take stock of yourself to notice a
mistake before it happens.
married woman: are unfaithful to your
husband, or will be soon.
others: someone is making you aware of
your unhappy marriage.
widow: find out your ulterior motives
to match your selfish ones.
woman: are admired by men you don't
even know.
young girl: are shy about changing
boyfriends.
of a: are frightened that your self-knowledge
includes your own treason.

MISCHIEF
02-09-20-24-25-39

being an imp: serious changes and grave
disappointments.
dishonored, being: great scandal, sorrow and
unlucky events in near future.
getting into: will do wrong to others who
are menaced by danger you perpetrated.
children: arrival of a friend will turn out
very well.
husband: will abuse the confidence of
others in your postponement of a trip.
others: your misery and annoyance from
infidelity in their family affairs.

MISER

01-06-30-39-47-48

being a: have highly inflated your importance and are unfitted to fill your position.

    with children: will make martyrs of people.

    woman: taking from men and not giving in return is not tactful conduct.

counting money near his safe: inheritance will not come to you at the last codicil.

gloating over his money: manner in which money is obtained speaks volumes.

hoarding more money: variety of problems will be solved without partner's knowledge.

MISFORTUNE

01-05-12-23-34-45

having, yourself: your standard of punishment meets your standard of ethics.

    enemies: are being accused by your enemies of actions your enemy would do.

    lovers: afraid of being punished for another's guilty action.

    others: danger if you don't keep your misdeeds under control.

    relatives: self-punishment for what your family has done.

MISSIONARY

20-24-33-34-37-40

being a: overly zealous at trying to influence others.

converted to being a: give ten percent back in gratitude for what you received.

going far away with a: will fail in local enterprise.

of a: change to more interesting work for little or no pay.

working with a: unhappiness because of desertion of business principles from work.

MIST

16-22-25-27-31-36

clearing away: troubles will be passing ones; outcome will be favorable.

enveloped in a, being: unhappiness in the home caused by your dilemma.

loved one, being in the, with a: one of you is not telling the whole truth.

of: approaching money will require the utmost patience and skill to obtain.

MISTAKE

05-11-18-25-32-36

accounts, making a, in: what you desired will not be realized.

committing a: happy adjustment of difficulties with silly busybodies.

having made a: avoid conceit that you couldn't possibly have erred and admit it.

others making a: be sure of your information before acting, and pay for it up front.

    wife and husband: take a deep breath and an ounce of forgiveness before taking action.

speaking out, by: an ill-advised affirmation of an unrecognized mistake.

MISTLETOE

01-15-17-31-33-43

giving, to others: good luck and prosperity to those who receive your gifts.

hanging: will win a zealous and bewitching lover.

kissing under the: an emotional whirlwind has begun.

picking: will yield to wills of scheming lovers.

receiving, from someone: happiness must come from within yourself.

MISTRESS

04-12-23-26-45-49

concubinage, being member of a: have little self-respect nor care for public opinion.

having a: great danger and dual life will bring public disgrace.

household recognizing a: old enemies will be faced by entire family.

of a: security needed to keep true motives hidden.

MOCKED

09-14-15-17-35-40

being: take care not to be swindled out of your honest modesty.

    by friends: are in the grip of deceit; do not be overly suspicious, just careful.

    children: do not neglect your own affairs for those of your offspring.

    others: will be asked to assist others, but distrusted by those you know best.

MOLD

01-07-21-23-24-28

cooking, a: do not speculate in your affairs with lack of enthusiasm.

fungus on food: insidious illness underlies your health.

    cheese: time of stagnation has ended; take action.

molding bread: inheritance coming to you from a friend.

    food: save your money; with your careless habits, you will not keep it long.

shape of a: financial gains are coming your way.

used for casting metals: want to hide your emotional problems behind an iron mask.

MOLE

06-10-12-24-26-37

body having moles: the unknown is interfering with your reaching your desired esteem.

catching a: will not rise to prominence by working underground.

digging: a colleague will outdo you for a job.

internal spies: what appears to be a failure will ultimately succeed.

killing a: cannot see another's error for your own guilt.

of a: your burrowing for other's hidden agendas will not be acknowledged.

MONASTERY

10-12-22-36-43-45

being an abbot: passions should be calmed for quiet strength with meaning.

    bad behavior, with: friends pity your self-hatred, poor self-image and denial.

    desire to be an: loss of friend's trust by renouncing the world.

    meeting an: recovery from illness having endured pain and suffering.

being in a: protect yourself from outside troubles for the inner qualms to evolve.

building a: will endure many afflictions and angry deviousness to follow your vision.

conversing in a: after a vow of silence will soon commit another sin.

decorated fully: will be forced to go to trial over your inheritance.

entering a: release all pent-up emotions to attain inner quiet.

graves in a: the entire substance of your life must be worthy of such hallowed ground.

occupying a: freedom from anxiety, smooth sailing in business.

seated in, being: change in affairs after being accused of deception by your superiors.

talking with others in a: a major error in judgment; the only conversant should be God.

worshiping in: plentiful peace in a silence beyond despair.

MONEY

12-19-20-21-24-27

apprehension over: family quarrels only exacerbate the situation, blocking a solution.

assembling: will have ample money for your needs.

borrowing: one's inner resources have been depleted.

burying: dissolution of hopes and emotional barrenness.

changer, of a: difficulties are your own fault, as reverses made you avaricious.

collecting for charity: are full of pettiness in a desperate bid for affection and control.

counting: wish to raise your station in life; period of financial stability.

    miscounting: urge to increase all revenues is unfounded.

deducting amounts illegally: time-consuming manipulation to return books to correct.

    from bills owed: will soon have a family argument.

        others, you: assist one who needs money.

desiring: have a lavish feast at a gourmet restaurant.

finding: danger and business loss if you do not return money to rightful owner.

gathering: your patience and honesty will hurdle difficult tasks.

handling foreign: an interesting job with a small income.

    checks: will be unable to meet monthly debt payments.

    stocks: risk of failure, shame and blame and an unexpected gift by airmail.

losing: time for lean cuisine.

missing: illegally obtained cash in your hands is still illegal.

paying: your debts bother your conscience; pay them regularly.

    back borrowed money: your finances sail smooth waters.

receiving: impending changes in level of your expectations are disappointing.

shiny new: will be criticized for being a mercenary.

silver dollar: luck throughout unfortunate circumstances.

spending: will risk failure of plans for comfort.

stealing: long sickness from unguarded actions.

strewn across the street: a well-entrenched, civilized situation will be upset.

MONK
03-07-08-24-31-37

being a: will suffer through spiritual disciplines and asceticism to discover inner wisdom.

celibacy, practicing: integrate your energies before attempting to share them.

conversing with a: are seeking spiritual guidance.

meeting several: will have easier pain and a lessening of grief.

of a: using your sexual energy to expand your intelligence.

several: travel that will prove unpleasant.

wanting to become a: must control your passions and turn them to a greater use.

MONKEYS
01-13-23-26-41-43

cage, being in a: an encounter will embarrass you; suspected deviousness is real.

chattering: will be flattered by sycophants to advance their interests.

    children dreaming of: enjoy your animalistic tendencies while you still can.

climbing: hostile competitors are wise enough not only to win, but to seek your ruin.

dancing: are surrounded by instinctual lies and deceit.

face of: be wary of superficial, deceitful friends who flatter you to further their own interests.

feeding a: betrayal by a trusted friend through slanderous gossip.

of a: social activities emphasizing your bad habits meet with treacherous opponents.

MONSTER
03-12-18-30-34-44

facing a: are being confronted with some ugly and scary aspects of yourself.

of a: success is yours, if you redirect your hatred to constructive goals.

    in the sea: expect emotional misfortune for subduing parts of your nature.

    on dry land: reduce fear to acceptable proportions by writing a description of it.

    being killed: turn and face your enemy.

pursued by a, being: your sorrow and pessimism overwhelm those you meet.

    attacked: are depressed at inability to complete the project you initiated.

MONUMENT
08-10-15-28-29-34

cemetery, of a prominent person in a: discovery of lost valuables, honor and great fame.

    epitaph on a statue, an: for dignity and distinction you bask in another's shadow.

    soldiers' graves, on: are not willing to do the work to support your lifestyle.

made for you, being: your arrogance will be ridiculed.

stone tablet, a: your inflexibility and refusal to adapt are etched in stone.

tombstone of someone you know, visiting a: eradicate your attitude toward that person.

    with loved one: kill those qualities in yourself and attain ones from past relations.

    with others: reconsider your attitude toward charity.

MOON
01-20-26-36-37-43

blood-red, a: indicates strife, a battle engaging everyone.

clouded over, being: interruption in comforts of life with a gloomy weight on you.

eclipse of the, an: expect reverses in affairs and an opportunity to create a better venture.

dark actions: a contagion will ravage your society; illness of the brain or eyes.

free of clouds, being: no discouragement by others can stop you now.

full, a: intense enjoyment by fulfilling a worthwhile destiny.

going to the: your desires seem impossible, but are far from improbable.

half moon, a: foreign travel if you refrain from complaining to your boss.

   obscured by clouds: dissatisfaction with position is unwarranted.

illuminated by the, being: will receive big favors from a woman.

moving toward the sun: sudden rise in money matters from mysterious sources.

new, a: situation is propitious for you to conceptualize your plan and begin.

rays: are too easily manipulated and led into emotional trouble.

reflection of the, in water: will fall in love with feminine energy.

shining brightly: your desire for emotional contact will develop into a relationship.

sunset, at: death of a prominent person who is ready to meet his maker.

waning: any projects begun will meet hazardous circumstances.

waxing: clarify mental confusion and finish existing projects.

MORALS
7-12-21-31-37-47

going around with people of loose: advancement brings many opportunities; choose well.

questioning, of friends: pick your friends and see them as mirrors of yourself.

   your own: keep to your high standards through thick and thin, sickness and health.

MORNING
03-12-16-21-27-44

arising early in: new beginnings will make plenty of money.

beautiful, of a: your fate is protected by the gods.

cloudy, a: big profit from your youthful energy.

foggy, a: be confident in your creativity and vitality.

rainy, a: will have many advantages in life.

MORTGAGE
11-15-16-33-44-49

giving a: financial crisis in your affairs causes many sleepless nights.

holding a: will have plenty of money to pay all debts.

   others: misfortune in your business has been covered, even more embarrassing.

others paying you a: have sufficient funds to cover debts.

paying a: a heavy burden is troubling you; your faithfulness will be rewarded.

MOSQUE
03-12-17-29-44-48

hidden, a: beware of ignorant people, even more so of those who hide behind ignorance.

of a: ignorance keeps you from being a firm believer of your faith.

Omar at Jerusalem, of: will come out well from present danger.

worshiping in a: many faithful friends will bring renewed interest in your own religion.

MOSQUITOES
05-16-31-33-35-46

being bitten by a: restrict inviting those with enmity into your home.

bite, of a: irritation may spread disease if scratched.

flittering around your head: your generosity is being exploited.

killing: will undermine opponent's venture, as he has undermined yours.

MOSS
11-13-14-31-36-49

having: your lack of purpose hides your fear of failure.

of a, plant: someone is attracted to you and won't let go of you.

receiving, flowers: write guardedly; seal and post your love letter carefully.

   seeing: take care of your correspondence and return all borrowed things.

MOTHER
02-11-15-18-28-32

altercation with: will take patience and an apology to quell animosity.

anxiously watching her child: are over-
involved in another's misfortune.

being dead: danger to property and you,
personally.

　and speaking with her: are following the
　　wrong path and need to correct direc-
　　tion.

　crazy: your business holdings are in
　　danger; seek aid only from the family.

　healthy: a family gathering gives you guid-
　　ance; care will take place.

　in danger: your careless words are
　　regretful; do better with your actions.

caressing her children: need comfort and
protection from anxious days of illness.

crying, your: must not let problems last past
your childhood.

embracing own: expect good fortune and
support from home.

hitting own: a catastrophe is ahead; must turn
back to heritage for emotional security.

holding you in her bosom: sexually insecure
men can relate more easily.

homage to your, paying: peace and tranquility
with pleasant memories.

in-law: an argumentative environment
precipitated by you.

killing your: an inevitable death in the family,
keep your anxieties quiet until then.

lap, sitting on: are hiding from the responsibility of ending an estrangement with
her.

living with own: a security full of compromises and limited functions.

of own: need someone to tell you it will be
all right.

seeing own, while far away: will return to
shelter, love and nurture your children.

step: the flexibility and adaptability of
situational comedy.

MOTHS
09-10-14-16-38-44

destroying things: have tried to stop the exposure of condition, but ultimately will fail.

eating clothes: someone nearby is causing
your family harm.

fluttering around a light: minor conquests in
lace are short-lived.

home, being in the: rivals will attempt to
visibly harm you; be careful with your
speech.

house, having, in the: your actions are
insufficient to deal with problems.

killing: expect quarrels with your sweetheart.

throwing away, -eaten clothes: your help is not
faithful; your enemies don't give up.

　wearing: your finances are unreliable; your
　　sadness will not go away.

MOTORCYCLE
03-15-19-23-41-44

accident, being in a: major obstacles to your
stable financial situation.

buying a: notoriety is yours, well-deserved.

driving a: feel in control of your life and in
touch with the universe.

race, in a: will be extricated from predicament with help from unusual quarters.

selling a: all investments will climb again to
recoup your losses.

speeding in a: have doubts of a new acquaintance with no justification.

watching a speeding: will succeed where
others have feared to tread.

woman riding a: appearances expand a minor
confrontation to serious consequences.

MOUNTAIN
02-10-22-24-31-33

climbing a: difficulty is no obstacle;
hindrances won't stand in your way.

　Mt. Everest: there is nothing you can't do,
　　including erasing your melancholia.

coming down the: will reap the benefits of
timidity and caution.

covered with snow, being: don't commit to
a job you are not sure you can accomplish.

falling down a: ruin of a prominent person
with fallout on your reputation.

fire on top of a, seeing a: a big catastrophe only
makes the challenge more interesting.

high, a: will struggle in your affairs to reevaluate a major decision.

pass, climbing through a: is the grass really
greener on the other side?

seeing from a distance: have a long way and
many reverses to go.

small: will undertake a short trip while letting
go of insurmountable issues.

snow-capped, a: have seen the future now; live up to it.

trapped on the mountain, being: stop to take a breath before you climb.

very high: will ascend to top of your career.

MOUNTAIN CLIMBER

03-28-34-39-44-46

ascending: delivery of a baby will be very painful.

climbing and reaching the summit: will receive a visit from an unwelcome person.

but failing to reach the: cherished plans have to overcome your weaknesses.

descending: success of small importance in one's affairs.

lost in the mist, being: the ground you stand on is always holy ground.

of a: be on guard for spiteful gossip.

MOURNING

14-20-31-38-40-44

being in, over parents: an early wedding of which you are the planner.

relatives: invitation to a dance that will produce congenial company.

wife or husband, each other: emotional sorrow revisited frees a way for better times.

wearing black, clothes: foreshadows the emergence of a creative force—you.

MOUTH

04-28-30-31-42-48

big, a: loyalty to a friend is worth more than popularity.

closed, a: unjustified, untenable fears.

tightly: unconsciously ashamed of your part in a sticky situation.

dirty, a: desperation for nourishment.

food, full of: your current actions are sated with ridicule.

wine: big pleasures to come and happiness for lovers.

gag, having a: will soon be kissed by one who takes your fancy.

unable to free yourself from a: expect serious trouble with your self-presentation.

grimacing, a: lack of flexibility to allow others their mistakes.

halitosis, having: a social obstacle needs to be overcome.

being rejected for: your self-assertiveness offends those you don't wish to alienate.

infected, an: public shame when you talk out of context.

of a: will become drunk with covert meaning.

animals: starvation of malicious gossip from your mouth.

children: person you relied on least will be firm, dependable ally.

enemies: quickness to criticize brings speedy regret.

friends: misfortune will follow your dissatisfaction with your lot.

others: are hurt by insinuations from those you rely upon.

open, an: generosity and misplaced destructive chatter.

own: guard your tongue and your giggle.

pulling objects out of your: the source of the venomous words of your outburst is you.

toothless: will outlive your teeth.

unable to open the mouth: peril unless you spit out the truth.

very large, a: an abundance of talk does not make a friendship.

small, a: in stillness your innate abilities reveal themselves.

MOVIE

03-04-22-25-36-42

beautiful, a: others want to lead you, obstacles should be yours alone.

being chased by a, monster: give Bambi a hug.

going to a, alone: are being kept in the dark about the slander.

friends, with: don't trust appearances; an enemy is seeking your ruin.

sweetheart, with: beauty is in the eye of the beholder and the soul of the beloved.

of: frivolous invitations from oversolicitous, beautiful people.

performing in a: need to make a stronger impact.

someone you know: present work will not be permanent.

slow motion, in: your anxiety is not for what is happening, but what is not.

standing in front of a, theater: confront those who keep secrets from you.

taking a video: need to capture a particular scene.

    fuzzy: deal will fail to materialize satisfactorily.

unpleasant, an: will be guilty of foolish light-hearted actions.

writing a scenario: should change your career to creative writing.

MOVING

10-18-21-24-30-46

being prevented from: inhibition prevents need to move on.

from one house to another: anxious nerves displaced by contented health.

    apartment: are leaving loneliness for trouble.

    city: an attitude change will ensure your happiness.

    furniture: social activities of a happy nature; a full change for the better.

    store: business obstacles are rising in complexity with the rise of your position.

others: are being deceived by best friends.

MUD

12-14-17-33-34-38

bath, taking a: wallow in your dirty secrets and cleanse them.

being in the street: advancement within own position, adjustment to new circumstances.

having, on own clothes: your reputation is being attacked, shaking up your health.

    others: surrounded by those of questionable morals.

playing in the: break down your negatives into simple, solvable units.

    stuck: be still, make your plan, and struggle to activate it.

    walking: a painfully slow resolution of family disturbances.

    working: turn your labor into a silk purse of opportunities.

scraping, off own clothes: will escape from the slanderous intrigue and plotting of enemies.

MUDDLE

02-07-15-21-46-49

making a, of things: pleasure from a re-established friendship.

of things being in a: take no risks at all in business until clarity begins.

    business: business will take a turn for the worse.

    others: your debtors will influence your supporters against you.

    own affairs: watch your footing, especially in high places.

    own mind: dire circumstances if you fall down on your quest.

MUFF

02-08-23-41-47-48

buying a: unfaithfulness on the part of someone trusted.

owning a beautiful: will have no relationship beyond this.

wearing a: promises a life free from continual changes.

    others: be on guard against spiteful gossip.

MULE

10-18-31-34-35-41

female, a: business will increase after ridding yourself of wasted efforts.

kicked by a, being: your foolish maliciousness will be kicked down professionally.

of a: beware of sickness through your stubbornness.

owning a: disappointment in an insecure marriage.

riding a: will be confused, then annoyed, by others' mental stupidity.

using a, to pull a cart: profits will arrive after argument with friends.

MUMMIES

05-11-13-15-25-47

embalming: danger if love is not allowed to move.

of a: a change in life from gossip questioning your uncovered past.

seeing, in company of your sweetheart: wish to preserve lover in that exact minute.

well-preserved: be confident in your ability to grow.

MURDER

04-05-06-11-30-48

being murdered: an enemy is attempting to injure you through your friends.

    others: triumph over enemies is a pipe dream, because it raises the ante.

committing a: acting on your anger openly backfires.

helping someone commit a: disgrace through another's dishonorable act.

manslaughter, being found guilty of: under whatever influence, death is still death.

    innocent: beware of all within your 360-degree view.

of a murderer: repressed guilt causes multiple explosions.

    being arrested: an enemy will pay for his crimes against you.

planning to commit a: harsh reality won't ease emotional turmoil.

    friends: must avoid a danger that will ruin your reputation.

    others: getting rid of the competition won't get you promoted.

seeing a, committed: sorrow because of the actions of others undermining you.

MUSCLE
01-18-21-26-27-42

being unable to move an arm: are too scrunched.

    leg: will suffer because of own foolishness; the pain repeats long after the act.

children having sore: excitement of challenge has to be tempered with steady progress.

having a pain in the neck: your dishonorable deed is stuck with this throbbing remembrance.

own hurting: your evil adventures leave a stigma that will continue to be felt.

spraining a: will be recruited to run for political office.

MUSEUM
03-06-12-13-29-41

being lost in a: your mental storehouse of past happenings is in disorder.

of a: discovery of lost valuables that will prove important to future career.

visiting a, alone: your boredom is self-induced and self-resolved.

    family, with: are striving too hard to build a team out of the wrong athletes.

    loved one, with a: your love is not matched equally by lover.

MUSH
04-07-16-17-24-28

cooking: varying fortune, depending upon added ingredients.

eating: will enjoy your money, not your visit to the dentist.

giving to children to eat: will be invited to chaperone a school trip.

of this cooked cereal: the warmth to enjoy good times is ahead.

MUSHROOMS
01-06-21-26-35-40

collecting: take your profits from intelligent chances, a little at a time.

digging many from the earth: your potentially dangerous ventures will be fortunate.

    only one: a corporation will be dissolved in humiliation and disgrace.

eating: big distinction with social life will aid your finances.

    business partners: be cautious in dealings with them, some are poisonous.

poisonous: large-scale money transactions draw out the worst.

sprouting: big advancement for healthy desires and natural haste in all your affairs.

MUSIC
17-22-28-29-41-49

accompanied by: a mysterious music is food for your soul.

ballad, composing a: relaxation level allows acceptance of pure pleasure.

    hearing: are playing your emotions off of another's.

    singing: your sociability and outgoing behavior has opened up your horizons.

barrel organ, hearing a: take control of the project in unfamiliar surroundings.

baton, brandishing a: a loved one thinks unkindly of your anticipated pleasures.

being in the band: different facets of self, playing in harmony.

box, playing with a loved one, hearing a: frivolity.

    favorite song, your: change of surroundings.

buying: will be very uncomfortable when forced to face your reality.

encore, demanding an: will recap benefits of hard work over and over again.

enjoying good, at a theater: consolation of misfortune.

hall, attending a, alone: a cunning and underhanded renewal of an old adversary.

hearing harsh and unpleasant music: tension among friends, friction in the family.

  jarring: let others display their anger, but don't react to it.

  jazz: gaiety will cost you more than you can afford.

  melodious, at a concert: expect great pleasures in life.

  opera, and singing: a relationship that will fortify your life.

loss of instrument: a lessening of control where you once held influence.

  voice: will become very uncomfortable when forced to face the reality of your life.

musician, being a professional: a move to another district; a showdown with your lover.

playing an accordion: sadness amidst the gaiety; stillness amidst the dancing.

  barrel organ, a: a rollicking festival.

  bassoon, a: are wasting energy on remote causes.

  bass viol, a: will get to the heart of the matter straightaway.

  cornet, a: discovery of lost valuables through the kindness of strangers.

  double bass, a: your deep-grounded personality is calm and composed.

  dulcimer: highest wishes are exalted over petty jealousies.

  fiddle: attempting to cheat only makes rivals more competitive.

  lute, a: auspicious surroundings attract undivided attention and undying love.

  lyre, a: hypnotic bliss of pastoral, romantic encounter.

    breaking a string while: your evil intents cannot be furthered.

    out of tune, being: a discordant menace to your emotional life.

  mandolin, strumming a: a short whirlwind romance unfolds into a blissful marriage.

  piccolo, a: a close friend should follow your advice.

  saxophone: will be blatantly taking over another's territory and laugh.

  wrong instrument, the: must follow the beat of your own drummer.

singing without remembering the words: only Superman moves at the speed of light.

  or music to be performed: be cause—not effect!

  poor voice, with a: the impossible is possible with training.

    alto: are always in the right place; know and accept this.

    bass: an inconsistency in business brought on by deceit.

    soprano: only through practice does one reach the high note.

    tenor: being rare is not necessarily the road to happiness.

  recital, at a: rely on a few supportive people only.

stereo, playing records on a: are in a one-sided, obsessive love affair.

  others: a discovery received from afar.

trombone, sliding the tube of a: control the gossip about you; reach to be heard.

  several playing at once: everyone wants your attention—remain firm!

writing music: your secrets will be revealed in each leitmotif.

xylophone: rivals are playing a different tune and succeeding.

MUSSELS
04-11-18-28-31-36

buying, in cans: will change to a better position.

  fish market, at a: someone will make a proposal to you.

cooking: failure of enemies.

eating: popularity and stature within your social circle.

gathering: lead a carefree life of sufficient abundance.

giving, to others: will come out well from a present peril.

MUSTARD
07-10-11-20-41-49

buying: beware of friends making hasty decisions causing you to suffer.

cooking with, in powder form: warning of bad luck.

eating: will deeply repent repeating confidences to new love interest.

table, being on the: will have arguments and disputes to spice up the conversation.

MUTINY
03-10-15-22-33-39

of a: beware of untrue friends accusing you of double-dealing.

overcoming a: advancement within own position.

taking part in a: will be harassed for your convictions and convicted for your harassment.

others: friends will cease to annoy you.

watching a: be cautious with business matters.

wounded in a, being: find the source of infidelity and those who would do you harm.

MYRTLE
09-17-24-31-32-39

blossoms: will have pleasures that you desired.

crepe: patience first; profit second!

picking branches of: gratification of desires, luck and prosperity.

withered: your misconduct will prevent further fortune.

MYSTERY
02-18-22-26-28-41

explained, being: excessive worrying over important matter out of your control.

hearing of a: your loyal friends will straighten out your dilemma.

mysterious friends, having: will suffer because of own foolishness.

affair, being inveigled in a: will be hounded and goaded by strangers.

of a: something will happen that will puzzle you.

MYTHOLOGY
05-10-23-34-39-40

being a character in: will be fortunate to love one who expands your horizons.

centaur: are an exhibitionist who integrated physical and spiritual energy.

followed by a: aim is brutish, sexual frenzy.

minotaur: a dangerous instinct hides deep in your being.

unicorn: gently woo by placing head in lap.

being chased by a mythical creature: discourages your present attitude toward life.

being immortal: happiness in the family.

eternity, living into: validates your belief in timelessness.

Ν   Ν   Ν   Ν   Ν

NAILS
12-17-24-27-29-41

biting down to the quick: are brought to the limit by disparaging remarks about you.

breaking own: misery and affliction, briefly; things will go back to normal.

buying: your reputation for being high-strung and irritable is not in dispute.

carpenter: have laborious duties to continue; don't make it harder than it is.

copper: sorrow with your preoccupations; step out of them for a while.

horseshoe: will be worried by bad news, which you will turn around.

iron: solution will be found by solid, heavy-duty research.

steel: the solution will be uncovered in a pinhole and solved with a rivet.

children's, growing: you, or someone dear to you, will have an accident.

cutting own: an accident for a man; a quarrel for a woman.

others: dishonor in the family; unusual associations prove disastrous.

extra long, woman's: big profits do not come from small minds.

false fingernails, using: your mistakes increasingly occur due to lack of concentration.

hammering, in wall: the truth will out; tell it first.

hangnail, having a: prompt attention must be paid to the tiniest detail.

of own finger: to continue your abundance, stay frugal.

others': a high achievement for a woman to protect the tender parts of herself.

people chewing: will be shunned by the higher class for perceiving yourself as lower class.

pulling, out: your extreme sensibility makes your actions careful.

selling: your concise analysis will tie loose ends to a solution you can share.

tearing off another's: a sadistic approach exposes a domestic bliss.

toenails, biting your: are about to be exposed for abetting a crime.

very short, having: have not established your own opinions or point of view.

NAKED

06-09-11-21-26-34

beautiful, woman, a: people have a higher opinion of you than of themselves.

plain: high ambitions are causing you to be overstressed at their being unreachable.

ugly: will be humiliated for your indulgence in illicit desires.

being, at school: your talents will be revealed; concentrate on your skills in using them.

at home in the tub, but seen: a woman faces her presence in you, as you do in her.

at work: your inadequacies have been exposed; trade on your adequacies.

at the airport: check your suitcase; carry little else on; you are sufficient in yourself.

in public: have been found out for what you are; live well with that.

swimming pool: desire to expose yourself, but are still hiding in your unconscious.

in the street: have doubts of your sexual capability; are grasping at less-noble instincts.

on a beach: will be cheated by a lover who treats you as one of many conquests.

concealing nothing: be equally forthright, awake and wise in your actions.

counting, people: beware of whom you meet by chance; illicit pleasures are expensive.

man dreaming of being: designing person is attempting to cause you public disgrace.

woman: are vulnerable to how others see you, when they never ask.

married people being: plenty of wealth and inferiority complexes, mutually discounted.

men and women, together: are exposing themselves to well-deserved criticism.

relative: will have a quarrel over your scheme being better than his.

wife: relatives are talking about your not being up to their standards.

public reaction to your being: are anxious of another when your own welfare is at stake.

horrified: are searching for death as a place to hide, but it is evading you.

ignore you: are nervous about communicating with people who offer clothes, shelter.

laughing at you: feel ashamed at being found out; find out first.

running: a return to childhood; lack of ambition and inhibitions.

sleeping with a, person: big commotion and setbacks in the relationship.

woman away from home: someone is doing you wrong by sullying your reputation.

streaking across the stage, and: your lack of freedom is pushing you to great lengths.

stripping: personal freedom is to live without moral restrictions.

unrequited lover: your stated feelings have changed.

walking around the streets: what made you lose your edge and fail?

your reaction to public: horror at being exposed at the most primal level.

feel proud: impossible to return to childhood innocence; soul discretion is advised.

hide: are stripped of all your pretensions; charm can be honest.

search for clothes: cannot live without encumbrances and inhibitions.

young beautiful girl: it's arrogance that your mere presence is capable of such control.

NAME

10-23-26-28-38-40

being written, own: with recognition comes responsibility.

calling sweetheart's: will be visited by one who cares for you.

　children's: they will become prominent people.

　someone by: look for important news to release you of burdens.

hearing own, called: your high-strung irritability leads your difficulties with success.

others calling your full: will receive a visitor with whom you have lost contact.

married person dreaming of hearing, called: will soon divorce.

　single person: will have to explain questionable conduct to family.

using another: fear exposure of an aspect of your past that could be misinterpreted.

　others: concentrate on commission in front of you.

wrong, being called by: are unable to identify with your true self.

　several people: will be insulted by your inability to recognize others.

NARCISSUS

05-07-30-39-41-42

admiring yourself in a mirror: are likely to be restless and anxiety-driven for a long time.

giving, to others: beware of overconfidence in your self-esteem.

keeping, indoors: happiness is not certain, nor can it be contained in a pot.

picking: will be fortunate, if the flower is not kept at home.

receiving a bouquet of: will fall for a wealthy man and win a fortune by your charm.

NARCOTICS

03-22-29-35-36-42

being an addict: a warning—anything can be and become a drug.

　others who are: reduces the amount of help you can get from the dream.

experimenting with heroin: will be despised by another whose high opinion you need.

of: keep your ability to follow through on your promises.

taking dope: a moral weakening in face of everyday challenges.

　an overdose: are working too hard at possessing someone.

NATURE

11-17-30-31-32-40

being bad-natured: your disruption, anxiety, complexity and war are waged on others.

　mate being: people nearby are trying to destroy happiness.

　relatives who are: in the lion's den tearing apart another's life; laughing at another's pain.

being good-natured: relieving others' pain will give you calmness, simplicity and peace.

　mate being: be able to experience a long life, leaving the pain in your wake.

　others who are: important events will soon transpire because you want them.

of: a coming expression of basic instincts—freedom and restoration.

NAVY

07-09-25-29-33-39

being in the: will suffer from seasickness, but opposite sex loves you on land.

　boys: travel to far-off land with a new and kind friend.

enlisted, personnel, of: a victorious undertaking leads to business ruin.

high-ranking, officers: troubles in love from long journeys.

husband dreaming of being in the: need self-discipline; your wife is cheating on you.

　wife, husband: victorious tussles with offensive thoughts that you'll commit adultery.

naval battle, winning a: do not take the world's burdens on your shoulders, not all of them.

　falling in the water during a: a long life, with fortunes improving at each turn.

　losing a: a great service will be rendered by a relative.

navigating a small vessel: will spend long hours and extended travel to study navigation.

large, a: your changeable humor will be shunned by women.

navigator, being a: abundant problems causing constant vigilance to solve.

noncommissioned, personnel: obscure defenses must be faced to obtain your goal.

released from the: many struggles and untruthful friends.

NECK
10-11-17-20-22-37

aching: fear of getting caught in a secret mission you can't control.

bandaged, being: covering up to keep your actions from being condemned.

   strangled: you are a yes person; take the risk to say what you think.

   tied up by the: will be the slave to your inability to see your freedom.

children, of: will be proud of their intelligence and leery of their use of it.

infected, an: will receive news of the death of an idea you fostered, then left to others.

necking with emotions: a steady married life is based on the willingness to share.

   after covering, with scarves: are hiding the impressions of a romantic interlude.

of others: are too deeply in love to see who you are in love with.

of own: false friends surround you; will you be able to let the true ones in?

   injuring: your worldliness has opened your home to query.

small, a: will meet with opposition and lose money in the process.

stiff, having a: your rigidity will complicate your business ventures.

swollen, a: someone is trying to strangle your career with toxic talk.

tall, a thin: don't stick your neck out for the possibility of admonishment.

three heads on one, seeing: to see, hear and speak evil keeps evil with you always.

unusually large, an: honors will make you largely uncomfortable.

   long, an: social advancement if you can keep your head above the clouds.

very flabby, a: due to your lackadaisical attitude your affairs are delayed.

NECKLACE
05-07-14-19-36-37

beautiful, of a: realization of desired love of a distinguished gentleman.

children, for: you are a virtuous person; let them imitate that.

giving a, to your sweetheart: wish to make a slave of the object of your love and own it.

husband giving a, to his wife: a luxurious home life with total commitment established.

losing a: will receive a visitor who will bring bereavement.

receiving a gift of a: will possess your lover, after you question the motive for the gift.

wearing a: are stating your claims to your identity and enhancing it.

   another's: jealousy and resentment, and fear you may have to pay to replace it.

   pearl: gloom and despondency, after which comes pure wisdom.

NECKTIE
08-13-26-36-38-41

cutting your: are losing your virility to a decadent lifestyle.

difficulty putting it on a: a relationship that should be broken off.

having a: will have a sore throat until you loosen it up.

loose, a: have done your internship and are now in control.

numerous: some freedom will soon be lost, in that only one can be chosen.

selling a: someone will have to take care of your business.

stain on a: be sure to accept coming promotion.

taking off a: loss of employment; are too tightly knotted to perform your job.

tight, a: feel trapped into making an inoffensive appearance.

tying a: will recover from rheumatism, if you step back your aggressiveness.

wearing a: luxury, grandeur and unexpected fortune will come to you.

NEEDLES
03-06-13-28-33-35

darning: will be introduced to a new way to give service.

finding a: have appreciative friends; don't test them with your temper.

having: intrigue in a season of distress leads to revealing applications.

knitting: your egotism will return to pinch you.

losing a: indications of bickering prove disappointment in love.

made of steel: are suffering keenly from others' lack of sympathy.

of: are greatly annoyed by the trials and persecution of love.

pricking yourself with a: your affection hides your hostility toward a relative.

searching for a: you worry without cause and search without having lost anything.

sewing: you give too completely and tell it as you see it.

threading a: family burdens will require patience to repair unfinished business.

trying to thread a: problem is intractable; leave it alone.

NEEDLEWORK
04-10-17-25-30-37

crocheting, breaking the chain while: will be troubled for prying into another's affair.

  others: quarrel will require a change in environment for one of you.

  sweetheart: your overconfidence blinds you to potential problems best solved now.

darning: a careful, saving attitude before recycling.

doing: should distrust one that you now trust; carefully reveal who.

  others, for you: fix your own problems that have come unraveled.

  young girls: are attempting to hold onto the gentleness of your handiwork.

giving a gift of: have high hopes of renewal of an old romance.

hoop, handling a: assurance that your present job is secure.

NEGATIVES
01-14-26-29-32-33

burning: too much drinking to avoid seeing the negative, thus missing the positive.

buying: pay attention to subtleties of the contract and take them all.

developing: your disappointment in married life will be revealed in your close-up shots.

of something: big dissolution as your negation disproves any position.

photographic: have the ability to see and avert danger; don't hesitate.

printing from a: are surrounded by people who adore you; keep reminding yourself.

NEIGHBORS
08-17-18-20-35-36

helping, in distress: for aid at a propitious time you will receive a legacy.

meeting a: are confronted with unwelcome guests full of bitterness.

own: are a total nuisance, wasting your time in idle gossip.

very friendly with neighbors, being: loss of humility that would allow you to make up.

  socializing: will be embarrassed by the bitterness against you that you inspired.

  visiting: someone requires attention.

NEPHEWS
04-08-13-15-31-37

disliking a: good results in own affairs tainted by nephew.

disputes with, having: business rivalry will come to an end.

killed, being: an embarrassment in business, that your nepotism put him in power.

liking your: profit if you offer to support his venture.

of own: great obstacles in adjusting to disagreeable surroundings.

NEPTUNE
01-13-18-25-26-32

of: the bridge between your conscious and unconscious.

NEST
02-08-11-36-38-41

cricket's, a: a fortune in the wonders of silence.

crocodile's, a: friends are gossiping behind your back.

empty, an: termination of business; desire to go home, wherever that is.

finding a bird's: approaching wedding with a mortgage in hand.

with broken eggs: an unconscious craving has been suppressed.

   dead chicks: your honor must be as alert and vigilant as your message.

   only one: poor profit in business as expansion costs financial support.

full, a: fortune of many happy children will be returned to you.

pigeon's, a: have bad humor from your blindness to your instinctive direction.

scorpion's, a: big dissatisfaction needs evasive action and period of woeful revenge.

snake's, a: dishonor from an undercurrent.

NET
09-18-20-25-26-30

catching birds in a: are overly suspicious of innocence.

   fish: must assert yourself and establish your rights.

   something: will receive a surprise; change of temperature and much rain.

   woman, a: family life will be content, with plenty of money.

fish net, drying in the sun: are self-confident that you and your subconscious are one.

   throwing in the sea: are able to handle whatever life gives you.

fly net, breaking a: love affair you would like to forget will go on the rocks.

   catching flies and butterflies with a: have unrighteous desires.

tangled in a: fear of being confined and exposed.

trawler, a: are trying to get the most out of the least effort.

using a: are entangled in an intriguing life situation.

woman dreaming of using a hair: marriage will last, if you take joy in your new honor.

NEW
08-11-13-15-24-32

giving, things to others: will be angry over bad news received from abroad.

having, things: plans have not given you the desired benefit.

   clothes, hats or shoes: big profit will bring contentment.

others with, clothes: don't be misled by superficial changes in their condition.

receiving something: job satisfaction if you refrain from risky ventures.

NEWS   18-23-28-29-37-39

communicating: security in business if you stick to your own.

   bad: must rely upon own vigor to tackle unanticipated problems.

giving good: great curiosity is not misled by appearances.

   bad: will lose a relative by not following another relative's advice.

hearing good: your perseverance has paid off.

   from children: postpone any group trips.

   bad: hostility toward you is festering in places you can't reach.

   from children: must refrain from anger and change direction.

paper: your fraud will be detected and destroy your reputation.

reporter, being interviewed by a: harassment and petty annoyances.

NEWSPAPER
02-14-19-22-35-36

being editor of a: feel a tremendous accomplishment every day.

buying a daily: will receive common gossip of a very great love.

   magazine: will be relieved of worries by reading about another's.

headline, finding name in a: go into hiding, take long trip from the neighborhood.

obituary, a friend's: more comfortable duties will be thrust upon you to accomplish.

   enemy's, an: news of a relocation south.

reading a: feel comfortable in extending yourself to the community.

   an obituary in a: death of an idol reminds you that yours is nearby.

   between the lines of a: are searching for the unwritten truth.

   others, to you: they are telling you untruths.

selling a: the basis of your life's work.

Sunday, a: momentary pleasure from a dignitary.

throwing a, away: dishonor close by; love from a stranger from far away.

weekly, a: advancement in business through careful analysis of the competition.

NEW YEAR'S EVE
05-17-19-32-36-41

being drunk at a, party: your desire to be recognized and acclaimed is dashed.

boy being born on, a: will be driven to become a prominent person.

girl, a: will marry a wealthy person.

committing adultery on: an imminent separation from your integrity.

getting married on: marriage will not last long.

haggis, cutting the: your indiscreet behavior will be exposed to the merriment of all.

of the New Year: an improvement in circumstances is, and should, be anticipated.

proposing on: marriage will last forever.

spending, with friends: be careful of an unscrupulous rival.

even-numbered, an: will have very little money and hopeful career development.

odd-, an: will inherit plenty of money and fail to invest it.

NIECE
01-12-28-29-35-36

beautiful, having a: her affairs will taint your reputation but be out of your control.

being killed, a: how fragile is the tenderness of naïveté.

disliking a: selfish snobbery without participation in the task of family.

disputes with, having: the anger between parent and child is theirs alone.

getting married, a: you have been cheating on your lover.

man flirting with a, a: danger of death from your hand if he doesn't desist.

naked, being: Venus on the half-shell; beauty observed, untouched.

NIGHT
01-07-12-14-17-24

being in the dark: are under heavy influence of harmful personality.

home, at: unexpected hardships in immediate intimate life.

entering a dark place at: will lose at gambling to one who has hurt you in the past.

friends on a dark, with: a fascinating event leads to a discovery about yourself.

children: great satisfaction that your ambitions are fulfilled by your children.

enemies: your lack of clarity allows others to control your thoughts.

of the nighttime: period of crises, secrets are being exposed.

starlit, a: your direction is determined; decisions must be far reaching and accurate.

NIGHTCAP
10-13-15-19-30-42

caught having a, at another's home: wrangling over the hideous sense of being slighted.

lingering over a: are madly in love to commit to the next step.

serving a, to a loved one: will expect a good-night kiss; any more has a price.

wearing a: abundance in business; altercations at home.

with many people, having a: have good fortune to relax for a period.

NIGHTGOWN/NIGHTSHIRT
02-05-11-15-31-33

luxurious, a: your sordid affair will hurt anyone worth your knowing.

pajamas, putting on: your complex passions will be unrequited.

children's: an interminable, agonizing period of waiting.

lounging: a trifling affair of consequence to neither party.

men's: desperate need for affection and a stable home.

women's: are fully displaced from agreement with family.

wearing in wrong setting: need more sleep to clear your perception of reality.

nightwear for daywear: your behavior is too intimate for the occasion.

NIGHTINGALE
01-05-06-7-11-26

cage, in a: if you dare challenge his control, your lover will jilt you.

listening to a, singing at night: seduction without words.

many: restored health to an invalid
through harmony in the home.
night bird, killing a: a joyous event turns to
distress, then to disgrace.
  singing from afar, hearing: will
  receive prosperity; good love
  relationship.

NIGHTSHADE
06-12-13-15-25-29
belladonna ointment, being made into:
approaching harmony of toxin and anti-
toxin.
eating the fruit of this deadly plant: you harbor
forceful antagonism for the wrong source.
mandrake root, eating: fear of castration
from the poisons in your mind.
of this narcotic herb: convolutions from which
health must free itself to heal.
vegetables: will ease your arthritis pain if
you eliminate them from your diet.

NOBILITY
07-11-13-14-20-22
acting nobly: your vanity is unbecoming;
ambition is your master.
ancestors being among: fortune and honor can
be passed down only so far.
appointed duke or earl, being: poverty all
around you cannot affect you.
  nobleman or woman, a: a responsibility
  to defend and support your castle.
approached by a woman of: your spiritual and
financial successes are in her handshake.
aristocrat, being snubbed by an: will rise in
social stature above your peers.
baron, being a: are prone to being proud;
others would strip you of your pride.
  company of a, in the: dignity and distinction is not gained by osmosis.
being with noble people: high honors if you
tone down your arrogance.
belonging to a family of: your social graces will
win only resentment.
knight, being a: your friends are your
weapons; are struggling with your might.
  in full armor: valuable family papers will
  reveal your advantage.
  jousting with a: fight for chivalry no
  longer works; are struggling with your
  might.

looking for a: sterling armored qualities
are yours, as in this sport it should be.
marquis, being a: expect another to accomplish your goals for you.
monarch, being with a: the source of the
rebellion in your home needs to be
challenged.
royal, having delusions of being: will be criticized for your pretentiousness.
  put on, robes: will be reproved for a
  neglected duty, faithfulness to your
  partner.
  throne, on a: a calm confidence of your
  ability to cope with disasters.
scepter, royalty holding a: will be in need of
leadership, a quality still in development.
  at a coronation: extreme misery until you
  make your decision.
throne, sitting on a: a rapid rise to prominence
loses you a valuable friend.
  descending from a: loss of relationship
  with reality.
titles conferred on family members, having:
a move to a higher status in society.
  through inheritance, a: possible loss of
  your fortune before you can gain it.
young girl dreaming of lord in love with her:
will marry a poor man whom you will
fear.

NOISES
11-12-17-21-24-35
hearing: creditors are gossiping about your
ability to pay their high interest.
hearing a loud: refrain from interfering in
quarrels among friends.
  bang: a family member agitates your
  slumber.
  children making: will receive letter with
  long-awaited good news, be patient.
  in the street: defeat in your plans if you
  don't step back for some rest and
  relaxation.
visitors making: success in your affairs
depends on you alone making the
decision.

NOODLES
07-14-31-33-36-40
buying: will carry out a long-intended plan.
cooking: will receive unexpected news.

eating: will cause damages to enemies as
you achieve your ambitions.

  Oriental crisp: an unexpected journey to a
  new abode

making: your uncommon appetite will be
exposed.

of: will be visited by imposing, hungry
people.

NOON
01-20-21-22-27-35

dreaming of, at any other time: may catch
pneumonia in the throes of your mission.

meal, eating a: be sure of taking a trip to
another environment.

meeting with others, having a: the ease of
the cuisine will temper weighty
discussions.

of, time: control yourself in greediness of your
abnormal appetite.

NOOSE
01-19-23-32-33-38

around your neck: a lawsuit threatens to
expose your guilt.

being hanged in a: fear and anxiety at being
persecuted.

  others: your anger and rage at another's
  part in your condition.

having a: use moderation against your obstacles and competition.

woods, in the: commendation for your
actions, the snare has been set.

NORTH
14-18-27-35-36-38

being in northern places: struggles will end
with success and a breath of fresh crisp
air.

birds or planes flying: discovery of a treasure
that everyone is seeking.

Eskimo on a dog sled: your application for a
loan will be denied.

  meeting: will receive a cool reception at an
  affair at which you wished to succeed.

house facing: will receive plenty of money.

northern part of the world, of the: a journey is
ahead of you to see the South.

traveling northward: an inheritance of pure
clear water.

Yankee, being a: will fulfill your duty with
honor.

NOSE
08-23-25-35-36-38

beautiful, having a: are admired for your good
character and sympathetic nature.

  big: be careful with investments, speculation and lending money.

  bleeding: sure sign that you have more
  friends than you think.

  bobbed: your promises are not being kept.

  curved: infidelity of a woman.

  cut off: gossip by friends making relationship with partner difficult.

  frozen: your great powers of imagination
  are underdeveloped.

  long: people hate your influence, but love
  your personality.

  small: your life will be sufficient, no more.

  stuffed-up: unfriendly people expect an
  apology for your noisy interruption.

  ugly: beware of wrong being done to you.

  unusually large: be silent even with the
  truth about others.

beautiful woman's, a: increase in the family.

blowing your: creditors will be relieved at
your payments.

child's, a: friendship is a gift, especially a
child's.

dive, making a: intense, passionate experience
with one of the opposite sex.

enemy's, a: beware of the exposure of your
personal life.

friend's, a: adultery; opposition is encountered.

having no, at all: your blatant curiosity has
been stifled.

hurting your: beware of backlash from sticking your nose where it will annoy others.

mucus, from: unfriendly people expect apology for your noisy interruption.

nosebleed, of having a: will be disillusioned at
being held in contempt by others.

pinching your: the situation is too good to be
true, and it isn't.

  another's: emotions cannot be manufactured.

  someone else's: take care not to display
  your wealth.

running, are unable to stop, from: are blessed
with fertile creativity and imagination.

sneezing, of: will be enlightened suddenly by a salute.

   baby: will have minor stomach trouble.

   children: beware of an infection injuring children.

young girl's: will have many friends to whom you give great gifts.

NOTARY
09-13-14-15-18-39

being a: the absoluteness of your truth is signed and sealed.

going to a, to get papers notarized: have curious friends on a need-to-know basis.

receiving the advice of a: an embarrassment in your business that you can't solve alone.

son becoming a: family satisfaction at in-house capabilities.

taking others with you to a: changes in your life must be witnessed in triplicate.

NOTEBOOK
01-19-21-40-41-42

jotting something down in a: a colleague will surprise you with his detailed records.

losing your: save a second copy of all important data separately.

reading in your: step back, listen, and do not react at the meeting troubling you.

   another's: an important fact has been left out of the proposal.

NOVEL
12-16-28-30-39-40

buying a: refrain from speculation in the stock market.

printing a: a gamble that others are interested in your opinions.

reading a: enjoy the suspension of disbelief for what it is.

writing a: nothing is a substitute for reality for long.

NOVEMBER
02-06-13-15-29-30

being born in: will have financial gains, as playing outside is limited.

   children: will have high position in science world.

of, during other months: money will come easily; keep it.

of the month of, during that month: will be happiest when out in the open air.

NUMB
10-12-19-22-27-30

arms being: are too emotionally numb to allow yourself to feel.

   children's body: plenty of money cannot bring to life what you cannot grow.

   left hand: will receive the visit of an undesirable person.

   legs: can no longer run away from those who would hurt you.

   right hand: will receive the visit of a friend.

feeling: you attain success in your business.

NUMBERS
06-10-22-34-38-40

Arabic numerals, of: dignity in their completeness and sympathy.

checking: your appetite will create enemies if you own the cuisine.

counting: unsettled business conditions require definite, decisive actions.

   of people: will be in command of your affairs.

without finding the correct: will be deceived by your own incompetence.

dreaming of figures and remembering the: will win if you gamble just a little.

   1: self-ambition and passion, communication, versatility, and reason: examine your ideas, then communicate them.

   2: final end to a romance, diligence, care and perfectionism: are unpopular with less meticulous people.

   3: will be fascinated with religion, diplomacy, sensitivity but also indecision: make up your mind and your point tactfully.

   4: will have great power, determination, force, passion and obsessive jealousy: good balance of emotion and feeling.

   5: happiness in married life, study of learning: optimistic member of justice.

   6: perfection in work, sensual emotion directed at stability: long-lasting relationship, wedding ceremony.

   7: will be efficient and active during life; tactless expression of feelings not shared by less adventurous people.

8: complete conservation of property.

9: affliction and happiness.

10: happiness in the near future.

11: will struggle with a litigation.

12: will have the best of everything.

13: will treat things with contempt.

14: will incur loss because of others.

15: will have a merciful disposition.

16: happiness and love.

17: dishonor and shame.

18: will become accustomed to fatigue.

19: unhappiness.

20: will be severe and strict.

21: everything will work out as planned.

22: will discover the secret of a scientific mystery.

23: revenge.

24: will receive rudimentary doctrine.

25: birth of an intelligent child.

26: business will be very beneficial.

27: will be firm and have a good mind.

28: will receive love and affection.

29: will attend a wedding.

30: will become a celebrity.

31: you have active qualities of power.

32: pure in design and expression.

33: if a man, will be honest; if a woman, will have a miscarriage.

34: love for glory.

35: harmony in the family and good health.

36: a genius will be born.

37: affection between loved people.

38: will have an excessive desire for gain.

39: you are envious of others.

40: number of days it takes to totally recharge your body.

41: deprivation of good name.

42: short unfortunate trip.

43: will attend a church service.

44: will become an influential person.

45: loss of virginity.

46: will have big productive powers.

47: long and happy life.

48: will go to court to receive a judgment.

49: will receive affection from a person of the opposite sex.

50: will forgive each other.

60: will become a widow.

70: will be introduced to a prominent person.

71: worship of nature.

75: change in the temperature of the world.

77: will receive a favor from a friend.

80: number of days it takes to go around the world.

81: will soon become a drug addict.

90: will become blind in the near future.

100: will receive a divine favor.

120: will get a government position.

121: will be praised by the community.

200: danger will come through hesitation.

215: calamity is near.

300: will become a philosopher.

313: blessings will soon come.

350: what you hoped for will come soon.

360: change of residence.

365: the stars are in your favor.

400: will undertake a long trip.

490: will hear a sermon by a priest.

500: will win an election.

600: will do everything perfectly.

666: enemies are laying a plot for you.

700: will have strength and power.

800: will be the head of a state.

900: hunger is very near.

1000: will receive clemency.

1095: will be depressed because of loneliness.

1360: will be vexed.

1390: will soon be persecuted.

NUN

05-07-11-19-21-30

abbot, with an: are smart, proud and ambitious, hiding behind a cloak of secrecy.

children, tending: jealous people cause your separation from a lover.

enemies, with your: peril of a contagious illness.

helped by, being: are unable to enact your desires.

leaving your home: keep your many enemies close.

man dreaming of a: his material desires take over his spirituality.

school, a convent: great tranquility as you solve your own problems.

several, with your friends: will attend a funeral.

sick people, helping: a tragedy will reveal your nursing skills.

singing: your high intelligence has picked a compatible partner.

NURSE
05-10-11-12-27-42

child with her: a mother will have another child.

doctor, with a: misery is abating as healing is in progress.

hiring a: need to be cared for on a primal level.

hospital, in a: will occupy position of trust and responsibility.

home, at: financial damages need to be set right and restructured.

impersonating a: potentially disadvantageous news.

needing the help of a: feel unwanted and neglected and are creating pain.

wet, and feeding a child, being a: will receive unpleasant news of family illness.

woman dreaming of being a: will gain high position by sacrifice.

NUTS
09-16-23-32-37-38

almonds, bitter taste of: have unusually strong powers of observation; find your mentor.

buying: temporary sorrow as present ventures fail, but will eventually improve.

eating: a new friend will disappoint you with a stupid indiscretion.

sweet: your friends surround you with sweetness.

Brazil: will contend with obstinate, unreasonable people.

chestnuts, roasted: the warmth of family contentment on the streets of New York.

cracking: success in business through the solving of tough cases.

but not eating: don't spend but reinvest your profits.

and finding it empty: a dependable person will renege on a promise.

eating as a dessert: important wish will be granted.

gathering: are squirreling away creativity for a more propitious time.

hazelnuts: leave the past in the past and recover the present.

hickory: will succeed in a new project.

hiding: discovery of a treasure within yourself that you are afraid to expose.

kernel, a: the essential force guiding your life needs appreciation from you.

nutcracker, holding a: will have unhappy days that will reflect well on your own actions.

pinching your hand with a: happiness in love affairs.

peanuts, eating: will be joined by a room full of strangers.

butter: regret for a lie you can't apologize for without admitting.

pecans: riches.

pistachio: social entertainment honoring a treasured friend.

shells, cracking: happy marriage and success in an undertaking.

stepping on: will receive a large profits from small investments.

throwing away: good luck and a growth of prosperity.

tree, being up in a: your climb is on secure branches with deep roots.

asleep under a: will have good health.

in the shade of a: are shielded from worries caused by an important friend.

picnic with family, having a: frivolity and amusement with your favorite people.

sweetheart, with a: will marry a rather agreeable, affluent person.

walnuts: after a spell of bad luck, you will receive a gift you desire.

NYMPH
03-06-07-15-22-28

beautiful, in a veil: must act properly to avoid criticism.

clouds, in the: peril of death hovers over your happiness.

dancing away from you: passionate desires will find convivial company.

of a naked: will fall in love and be totally faithful.

several people admiring a: termination of business for joys of country life.

O   O   O   O   O

OAK TREE
01-11-23-25-35-36

climbing an: rely on the durability of natural wisdom.

cut down, being: are deceived into an early marriage.

dead, a: remember your background and rely on it.

green leaves, with rich: fortune through another's generosity.

healthy young: build on your growth to live to a ripe old age.

leaves having fallen from an: loss of steadfastness in business.

lovers dreaming of an: contented marriage and numerous healthy children.

lying in your path, an: a rise in your tolerance level in civil pursuits.

many beautiful: immediate prospects flourishing with wise choices.

of an: creative optimism based on strength and stability.

resting under a wide-spreading: your long happy life will be well protected.

white: independence.

withered, a: loss of a sturdy business partner to corruption.

OARS
05-12-16-18-26-28

breaking, a: will be interrupted by obstacles until you get out of the situation.

rowing in a scull: will soon meet a new love interest.

with one oar: need a partner to bounce your theories off of.

others: skimming the issues leaves the difficulties below the surface.

breaking an: an obscure impediment can be unraveled with a clear mind.

handling: your inability to take a relationship seriously means the end of it all.

losing an: your impulsiveness will cause a failure of your own plans.

OASIS
03-14-20-25-38-39

being with others in an: need respite from overwhelming misfortune in love affairs.

finding an: emotional issues need immediate attention.

when wandering in a desert: your new venture will become a phenomenon.

leaving an, on a camel: with long-standing support you will ultimately succeed.

in a jeep: depend on the technical to get the job done.

midnight on an: need a vacation full of dreams and success in your new, unusual plan.

of an: will come out well-nourished from a present danger.

OATH
01-11-13-32-33-39

husband or wife taking a marriage: prosperity is an investment in your future.

after their marriage: foretells divorce.

of taking an: a good position will be yours, if you open up to it.

businesspeople: a setback will trouble you emotionally.

enemies: will suffer humiliation and a wobbling of self-confidence.

others: will receive news of an innocent person suffering.

relatives: complications and vexations in your immediate family.

OATS
09-15-19-20-26-39

cooking oatmeal: varying level of health in concert with your diet.

eating: will enjoy a well-earned fortune.

green unripened: journey will be profitable and of extended length.

growing: a fortunate weather season leading to prosperity.

harvesting: financial gains.

selling: poverty from reckless misuse of funds.

OBEDIENT
14-15-21-24-33-35

being: fear authorities will lower you in their esteem.

children: are worried that they will run out of ambition.

own help: will make big gains in business, if you question orders intelligently.

to others: will have a commonplace career of minimum involvement and action.

woman, a: have profound, genuine and heartfelt emotions for partner.

young woman, a: an admirer is seriously attracted to you.

others being, to you: will command riches and exert wide influence over a former enemy.

OBELISK
02-13-26-32-34-41

being on top of an: be proud of your purchases, maintain them well.

of this four-sided pillar: will move to better surroundings but will be delayed.

several: aspire to wealth above your capabilities.

viewing an: all the wisdom in the world cannot foretell the outcome of feelings.

OBESITY
04-08-16-30-31-36

being potbellied: hold on to your wealth for fear it will be taken away.

others: are these moral examples you wish to follow?

exploding in: fear physical harm if you don't pad your emotions.

mirrors making you look obese: rid your mind of that evil image.

looking at yourself: there are layers of protection against facing your failures.

can't look at: hopelessness against power and authority.

scale, on the: overindulgence, fear and denial weigh heavily.

OBLIGATION
04-07-25-35-36-39

friend being under, to you, a: have powerful friends who will assist you.

others: are being deceived that your will will be honored.

relatives: will take a long vacation at their expense.

of being under, to a: warning of troubles; hard work awaits.

relatives: dignity and distinction to them, not you.

OBSTACLE
13-23-24-30-31-40

clamoring over an: will be challenged by an exciting opportunity.

course: cannot cope with days, if your nights are so confused.

meeting an: face to face does not preclude successful negotiation.

placing an, in another's way: will be confronted with your infringement of privacy.

skirting around an: beliefs have been duly considered; act on them.

OCCUPATION
14-15-16-35-36-38

detesting your: to bring yourself to this level in another occupation will take years.

making good money at: family quarrels over time not spent with them.

little: beware of jealous friends.

OCEAN
17-25-29-31-44-47

calm, a: stormy wedded life, with exciting news at every turn.

deep sea fishing, going: your turbulent life is looking for the ultimate catch.

of the: are harboring emotional anxieties for what you, rationally, cannot see.

rough, a: will have few difficulties as your companion's support is yours.

swimming in the: the condition of the sea is the condition of your emotional life.

vessel on the smooth open, being in a: have a strong moral strength that levels you.

rough: will have big troubles from disrespectful enemies.

that sinks in the: termination of protection to reveal if you can float alone.

voyage, an: are evading an annoying, distressed foe.

waves lashing: until you regain your former calm, negotiations will not go in your favor.

OCTOBER

01-11-21-40-47-48

being born in: prosperity and abundance.

   children: will have a high position at a
     university.

having a dream during: will enjoy the fruits of
   hard work.

of the month of, during this month: profit and
   success.

   during other: will have unhappiness.

ODOR

21-22-30-31-40-42

of a fragrant: contentment with a loved one.

   offensive, an: vexation at being suspected
     by a lover you are pursuing.

   pleasing: will excel in everything.

   unpleasant, an: vexation.

   very strong: unreliable people are in your
     employ.

smelling, body: will be guilty of foolish actions.

   feet: beware of going to prison.

   hand: will suffer because of your own
     careless actions.

smelling a bad, in a house: hard work awaits.

   public room, in a: a change for the better is
     needed.

OFFENSE

07-18-29-32-35-42

committing a public: an enemy has riled you
   sufficiently for you to ruin yourself.

giving cause for an: speak in haste, do penance
   in perpetuity.

offended by relatives, being: are confronted
   with insurmountable obstacles.

   man, by another man: resent another's
     behavior but feel restricted from
     retaliating.

   woman, by a man: will be taken to task for
     speaking what was on your mind.

offending a public person: will suffer humiliation at the loss of an ally.

   someone, a woman: family quarrels will
     create enemies.

receiving an: others are unjustifiably criticiz-
   ing you.

OFFERING

05-8-12-19-31-46

making an, for services: must work hard to
   resist temptation.

   to the church: are embarrassed with
     prominent personalities; you can't
     give more.

   to a man: will have emotional sorrow after
     succumbing to temptation.

   to a public institution: approaching
     money, but you must tithe first.

   to a woman: will be expected to pay more
     than the check.

receiving an: expect a literal improvement in
   your position.

someone making a good, to you: desire to clean
   the slate and return to virtue.

OFFICE

09-14-21-23-37-44

coworkers in an: each one represents a specific
   problem to you.

getting a new, appointment: unhappiness in
   married life.

having an: honesty will bring you prosperity
   and the ability to leave your work at the
   office.

   collecting agency, a: will be a financial
     disaster unless you join the
     collectors.

   job in a newspaper: unfavorable news
     unless you write your own gossip.

holding a government: will suffer humiliation
   at the scope and humbleness of your
   service.

landlord putting you out of your: professional
   esteem doesn't pay the rent.

losing your: your resources include you; your
   assets are in your mind.

opening an: will be insulted if you do not
   have enough work to keep you late.

working in an: guard your healthful environment.

OFFICER

06-13-16-31-37-40

being an: a commanding triumph over all
   affairs.

   among other: will enforce success in
     your affairs, to your detriment.

   appointed: deserve dignity and distinc-
     tion, but are unwilling to earn them.

   dismissed as an: warning of an over-
     inflation of your own command
     of the situation.

of an: rashness does not lead to business transactions in your favor.

ordered by an: your resentment blocks your seeing the necessity of following orders.

OGRE
05-10-14-17-29-42

eating human beings, an: one obstacle between you and your lover is your need for approval.

killing an: your jealous friends are not as critical of you as you are.

of this giant monster: beware of difficulties obtaining credit for your work.

OIL
04-07-20-36-42-46

artists and painters using: large earnings through a more sophisticated, foxy self.

buying: are being deceived by slippery characters.

contractors using: quarrels with partners that may involve violence.

crude, extracting: a depth of resource is within you.

digging for an, well: profit from you presumptuous ambition.

frying food in: big advantages to your health.

having dealings in: fortune through pouring oil on trouble caused by enemies.

kerosene, can of: an unpleasant person will become useful.

   lighting a, lamp: do not repeat a foolish act that will cause irreparable losses.

   spilling a: a fellow exploiter will leave when you change your conscience.

lubricating with: will be boastful of your abundant harvest.

oilcloth, buying: an unjustified apprehension.

   covering furniture with: future delays will block your enjoying what you've earned.

   using an, tablecloth: treachery will cause suffering.

refining: your suspicions are totally without merit.

rich, field: will receive a commendation for a messy, slippery deal.

selling: acknowledgment that your action, against stubborn resistance, is required.

spilling: something is slipping away from you.

suntan: are incompatible with the life of your present friends.

using linseed: exploiting friction will make money.

   vegetable: your exhibitionism will bring you to your boss's notice.

wearing oilskins: delaying expenditures for a full week.

OINTMENT
13-26-27-29-33-40

buying: your direction will lead to good health.

of: will be offended, but the offender will apologize.

using: slight illness to come if you don't soothe another's pain.

   on a sore: have no one to blame but yourself for inability to heal.

      lover: your obsequiousness is flattering one who had the potential to be a foe.

      others: will abandon your friends with thoughtless actions.

OLD
24-27-28-29-32-47

becoming: distance yourself from fame and you will achieve it.

being: he who outlives his opponents wins.

   very: will have bad relationship with a young woman.

geezer, an: will have to justify your innocent act to an inquiring reporter.

having dealings with, people: be prudent; are more satisfied than you allow yourself.

man: distance yourself from the wisdom of questionable actions and their memories.

woman: forgiveness will free the physical stamina to continue emotional involvement.

OLD-FASHIONED
09-17-19-24-25-33

dealing with, people: business will prosper with values you can live with.

drinking an, cocktail: will live in a quaint, old town with solid religious citizens.

having, ideas: short-lived happiness as your opinions are overrun.

of being: keep your rendezvous with the right person.

wearing, clothes: dissension at home, with an attempt to return to an earlier happiness.

OLIVES
05-16-21-24-29-34

bottle, putting, in a: the containment and preservation of your future joy.

> *taking, out of:* social pleasures, delight and favor of influential people.

branch: resolutions of conflicts and reconciliation.

eating: happiness in domestic life if you are realistic.

frying food in, oil: a new job offer is close by.

mixing, oil in a salad: your health will soon improve.

picking, from a tree: work-related skepticism can be solved with pressing work.

> *ground, the:* hard work ahead of you under looming problems.

smelling the scent of an, branch: many favorable solutions in enterprises.

storing, oil: pleasant events will evolve easily through a smooth route.

ONIONS
08-10-19-37-44-45

buying: your feelings will be hurt, but push on to victory over obstacles.

cooking: will be visited by a friend, who will become envious and spiteful.

eating, cooked: a negative lesson to an evil fan will be made palatable.

> *fried, rings:* your over-joyousness will attract an annoying foe.

> *raw:* solutions come through bitter lessons.

peeling: great happiness will soon be yours.

planting: your forceful decisive personality will meet with agreement.

pulling, out of the ground: revelation of a multilayered secret.

seeing, growing: rivals will press you to express your unpleasant thoughts about them.

slicing an: your present ill humor will be short-lived.

OPERA
03-04-18-19-30-43

being at the: the confusion and turmoil in your business is blasted over the airwaves.

theatrical people, with: will be tempted to deceive an innocent.

glasses: someone is watching you from afar.

going to the: family disorder due to your independent ways.

hearing a grand: an old friend will overdramatize his absence.

> *operetta:* are off-key from your surroundings.

house, being backstage in an: your wanderlust is curtailed by the betrayal of friends.

seeing a comical: are jilted in affairs, which turns seriousness to laughter at yourself.

> *complete season of:* your confrontation with domestic chores needs a rest.

> *dramatic:* solid wealth without any froufrou.

> *foolish:* too little work and too much fussing.

> *melodramatic:* are too superstitious to recognize the real thing.

spying with, glasses: don't let appearances stand without close investigation.

OPERATION
01-04-13-16-41-43

another doctor assisting with an: are constantly focused in the public eye.

> *nurse:* successful completion of a time-consuming unmanageable situation.

going to have an: deep issues need to be uncovered, reorganized, cleansed and healed.

incision, making an: your efficiency will be questioned by authorities.

performing an, yourself: rich reward for your patience and skill.

> *brain, a:* your ideas have obstacles within yourself; solve them before presenting your plan.

> *heart transplant:* are a generous and caring person who now needs care.

> *liver:* your decadent lifestyle has caught up with you.

success, being a: an adjustment of organization can mold your truth.

> *not:* corruption must be removed from your business.

undergoing an: will be imposed upon by someone worthy of your confidence.

watching an: your character is too weak to act on the truth.

OPIUM
10-11-17-21-32-38

encouraging friends to take: worries ahead causing setback with partner.

of: are negligent in your affairs as thoughts are confused and lead nowhere.

prescribing: will suffer humiliation through another's underhanded methods.

selling: are ignoring responsibilities that you are not willing to take.

smoking in an, den: are deluding yourself that you have the right to decadence.

smuggler, being an: wealth but inability to openly spend it.

taking: social disgrace through your association with criminals.

> *with others:* changes toward loose morals and jovial inconstancy will occur.

OPPONENT
03-08-12-19-21-32

fighting with an: are doomed if you don't cultivate constructive application of ideas.

having disputes with several: opposition and quarrels disrupt continuity.

of an: will win against rivals with strength of character and determination.

OPTICIAN
08-15-16-18-39-45

being an: money comes easily to you.

buying glasses from an: attempting to hide age because of shame.

> *wearing:* are living an extravagant life; take in every photo opportunity.

going to an: are meeting a serious situation by facing the consequences first.

selling glasses: are fretting loss of your occupation through your poor service.

taking children to an: are executing extra effort to ensure family security.

ORACLE
10-21-33-36-39-40

asking an: an unanticipated and disorienting event has altered your course.

being an: you know your future and fear it.

predicting dire misfortune: the worst is over, pick up the pieces.

happiness, an: are tied to situations that are draining your energy.

ORANGES
08-09-18-21-29-33

being the color of: the state of your liver is murky; consider the stigma of a derelict lifestyle.

> *materials:* the purifying power of a flame.

have clothes: will make small financial gains, but a tremendous impression.

blossoms, picking: balancing intuition with intellect.

> *making a crown of:* a slowly increasing income will allow a steady, rich emotional life.

> *wearing:* your virginity is safe until the love affair you will never forget or regret.

buying: disappointment in love because you bypassed nurturing.

eating an: each segment of your life needs equal attention.

> *nectarines:* a hypocritical woman will cause a calamity to you.

making marmalade: the turning away of impurities.

of an, tree: will shed tears at the beauty of its blossoms.

> *planting:* will make an unsuccessful trip until this fruit of knowledge blooms.

> *with ripe:* abundance of health and spiritual vitality all around.

peeling, an: in the luscious indulgence of the body will come peace.

selling: loss in a venture that was a gamble.

tangerines, peeling a: a death will cause you to take better care of your health.

ORCHARD
03-09-16-24-34-42

being in an: don't favor one good friend over the other.

> *with children:* are overfond of luxuries but will not work for them.

being stripped of fruit: will lose advancement opportunities.

gathering plentiful fruit in an: will never realize desires you don't deserve.

> *scarce:* your fortune will improve if you patiently overcome troubles.

walking in an: every wish will be realized
and well-nourished.

ORCHESTRA

11-16-20-21-46-48

attending an, concert with family: small wealth
ahead; encouragement for the future.

conducting, an: your travel and intense
involvement in work discourages a relationship.

   accompanying a ballet: will pay the cost
of overestimating your value.

hearing an, playing in the distance: mate will
glow in your sunshine.

jazz, a: no muscle will remain unexercised.

performing in an: all aspects of your life can
now play in harmony.

playing an overture: with a new job and with
new people you will score.

   the cymbals: much ado about nothing.

   a stringed instrument in a: previously
insurmountable obstacles can be
triumphed over.

podium, conducting from a: are involved
in a situation you can't extricate yourself
from.

   an empty: are overenthusiastic about an
accomplishment that will turn sour.

   falling from a: your self-congratulations
are premature.

ORCHIDS

02-07-10-17-18-33

buying an: abundant means through faithful
friends.

giving an, to an unmarried woman: short
engagement.

having: will be accused of extravagance over
something that grows itself.

of: flattery must be backed by substance; the
rent still has to be paid.

unmarried girl receiving an, as a gift, an:
prompt engagement.

ORDER

19-22-31-32-43-46

communicating orders: will be grateful for
a service rendered to you.

   obeying: will receive a grave injustice.

   taking: cannot accept that which others
think needs to be listened to.

ordering things through the mail: are too

gullible; return refund must be guaran-
teed.

placing things in correct: many people are
interested in your future.

   wrong: will discover a falseness.

putting things in: must discipline your temper
in order to rise in work or society.

wearing military, or medals: will have setbacks
in hopes.

ORGAN

01-05-10-18-24-26

barrel, of a: sickness in unfamiliar and beautiful surroundings.

   played, hearing a: a rollicking festival into
which you put a great deal of work.

   playing a: after massive long-term effort
comes a happy but solemn occasion.

     others: will be invited to the wedding
of a friend.

buying an: will be in mourning soon for a
discordant friendship.

having, removed: loss of one whom you love
dearly.

having flabby organs: will discover one who
is double-crossing you.

   healthy: renewed hope in spent romance.

   oversized: birth of a boy who is deformed.

   unhealthy: death of father or mother,
which will weary you.

hearing: are courted with personal honors.

   music: loud unpleasant arrival of relatives
bringing family discord into the open.

     funeral march played on an: position in life
is outlined for you.

of a church: friends are endeavoring to assist
you.

organs of sick people: despair a loss of relatives
through your negligence.

pedals of an: your distinct, down-to-earth
personality plays to the soul of the piece.

playing an: will always be an assistant, never
the boss.

   in church: inheritance from plans made
before revisions.

   at home: arrival of unexpected income.

ORGY

04-11-17-35-36-44

debauchery, indulging in: derangement of
family and society.

taking part in an: your actions have become notorious.

   in front of others: cannot accept former friend's intense dislike for you.

watching others at an: envy leads you down the garbage path.

ORIENT
01-06-12-17-20-28

being an Oriental yourself: have the world's blessings.

of the: thoughts alien to you need to be listened to.

Oriental people: romantic happiness that will not last.

   being among: good chance of getting married.

   countries: small measure of deception to further your own interests.

returning from the: are about to take major steps in altering your lifestyle.

   with someone else: are warned, temptation has consequences.

traveling to the: take little stock in people's promises but accept them.

ORNAMENTS
12-14-20-22-45-47

cheap, tacky: your worries are mundane, thus ignored.

church: will have good spirit renewed every week.

flower: will have pleasure and fortune in a vision and perfume.

giving, to others: your extravagance is attracting questions as to your intentions.

jet-polished: will suffer through your own foolishness.

leaf, in a: temptation will come to you; share it.

lose an: the flowering of your life is now decaying.

of fretwork: another person is enjoying what you desired.

   adorned with, being: change in environment does not mean extravagant behavior.

wearing: a contemplated change will bear enactment.

ORPHAN
07-09-21-35-41-44

adopting an: happiness at the implementation of your project.

being an: cry me a river; to be loved you must know how to give love.

   destitute, a: your fear of abandonment is overpoweringly destructive.

child becoming an: will receive a legacy of unhappiness and misfortune.

of an: will receive profits from a stranger and debts from society.

several, in an orphanage: change of surroundings filled with desolation.

OSTRICH
05-12-16-18-44-47

buying, feathers: friends know that you are guilty of miserly habits, ignoring all the facts.

sticking its head in the sand, an: cross-purposes at work will be abruptly appeased.

wearing a hat with, feathers: a slight ailment will cause a flurry of activity for naught.

   others: your effusiveness and tact are tainted with deception.

with head held high: smugness is another's ignoring reality.

OTTER
06-14-19-45-46-48

catching an: good fortune if you let go of controlling others.

eating fish, an: an absent friend will soon return and ask for money.

many: will be harassed by many debts and entertained by many playmates.

of an: untrue friends will hurt your feelings, but cannot touch your spirit.

OVEN
01-05-17-23-34-37

baking in an: affairs will come to a standstill until a great reward.

being lighted: abundance of food symbolizing love.

   very hot on the outside: will be promoted within your community.

brick: big profit in business if you acknowledge old-fashioned techniques.

cooking good food in an: business will improve slightly.

   too long in an: success in love obtained through adulation.

food burning in an: are drifting into bad paths.

overheated, being: friends entice you to their distant shores.

turning off an: will be of service to someone, if you can get past the arguments.

woman dreaming of a hot, a: will be widely loved.

OWL
10-19-26-40-41-48

catching an: don't limit your wisdom; let it fly free.

hooting, an: warning of the approach of a deceitful person.

killing an: shared sacrifices and deprivations.

of an: be watchful of a terrifying action in a terrifying situation.

scaring an, away: life will take a turn against evil.

screaming, an: close associates are the source of the problem.

solemn screech of an: views will be shattered with bereavement.

OXEN
09-13-30-32-46-48

buffalo: use your power to get out of the stampede.

water: your resolution will get the job done.

fighting: have enemies who insist on battle.

herd of, a: prosperity in affairs, felicity at home.

grazing peacefully: should watch speculations for opportunity and take them.

lean: fortune will decrease through partner's hostility.

of buying: will have strength to endure adverse toil.

killing: your obstinacy exceeds your rationality.

selling: be careful in buying and selling shares.

of one ox: profitable business undertakings.

in the pasture: will rise rapidly in present position.

fat: your fortune will increase through influential partner.

plowing: pull together two divergent associates.

pulling a cart: fortunate in love, poor in worldly goods.

sleeping: loss of friends through illness.

without horns: favorable developments in own affairs.

OYSTERS
12-23-31-37-39-41

buying: someone new will fall in love with you.

gathering: will make lots of money garnering unusual sadness.

giving a gift of: courage is needed to succeed in life.

eating: hard work to convince family of legitimacy of your work.

friend's: will have riches, excellent health and trustworthy friends.

marketplace, at a: health had been deteriorating sporadically.

opening an: a rich emotional life is hidden inside your modesty and self-effacement.

spat, catching a young oyster: beware of jealous friends.

eating a: will overcome enemies with perseverance.

widow: be on guard against handsome men attracted to you.

young woman: an influential man will declare his love.

unshelled: your suspicion and resentment besmirch lover.

with pearl: uncover the true core to build a solution.

PACKAGE
13-18-21-36-38-41

carrying a: support from one you thought was a foe.

big: current relationship is materially satisfying but emotionally cold.

small: will have to face trouble from your negative reactions to another's actions.

label on a, putting a: short-lived conflicts ahead; expect a surprise.

mailing a: children's actions will cause enough difference of opinion to become arguable.

opening a: your luck will be affected by its contents.

preparing a: marriage will last forever, if you take infinite care.

receiving a: there is someone in pain who loves you dearly.

    empty, an: deeds must be done first, then the reward.

    from children: profit from an unexpected source and your precise opinions.

refusing to accept a: be firm in your rejecting participation in the actions of others.

PACKING
9-25-31-39-44-45

for a journey: business worries will keep you at home, but significantly change it.

    relatives: reorganization of old relationships you have let lie fallow.

man, clothes for a trip: are guilty of foolish actions.

    woman: may leave your husband without intending to.

something to mail: abuse of confidence will cause failure of proposition.

your home: events cause an entire shift in the environment.

PADLOCK
05-14-30-32-35-36

being unable to open: a solution can be found by approaching a problem from its flanks.

closing a: your unwillingness to participate fully will cause your failure.

having the key to the: avoid speculation of any kind.

    finding: will pull through your troubles.

    losing: be careful in money matters.

open, an: a suitable time to pursue courtship.

opening a: ambitions will be frustrated, leading to a long stretch of dissatisfaction.

    man: are flirting with several women.

    woman: will be unfaithful to the man who loves you.

PAGEANT   13-24-26-28-38-45

children being in a: a distant relative will recognize your connection.

    enemies: unforeseen events will alter their intent and yours.

    friends: are being deceived about a historical incident.

of a: should not judge appearances without uncovering the roots.

watching a, on a float: do not pay attention to other things, deal only with your own.

PAGES
03-14-30-38-47-48

assembling, together: impatience at extent of work required; patience has its purpose.

being paged: your misfortune in business will be publicly announced.

books, of: will be abused by a mésalliance tying together many story lives.

letters, of: will enjoy the confidence of others and the responsibilities it brings.

many, of other things: riches through sound investment in better business practices.

pageboy, a: work is good but not challenging; observing of the workings of others is.

paging others: petty love affairs will cause remorse; are unsuited for a hasty union.

PAGODA
07-10-27-32-40-43

being inside a: solution to a long-standing problem will appear to you.

    with others: duties entrusted to you must be carried out in secret.

    others: beware of jealous friends whose displeasure you have incurred.

lovers dreaming of a pagoda: immediate separation: one will plant a garden, one won't.

of a: unexpected news will cancel a journey, a risky adventure at best.

PAIL
04-11-29-33-38-40

buying a: are cherishing new business ventures of questionable intentions.

clean, a: will have plenty of money to move into a better neighborhood.

dirty, a: will be cheated by friends.

empty, an: poverty to the lowest depths, decayed crops and famine.

full, a: have many close friends, bringing abundance in their wake.

selling a: people will confide in you and value your advice.

PAIN
03-08-09-24-33-39

being in: warning of future idleness caused by the ramification of past sloth.

children: persecution by an enemy will be inflicted on your progeny.

others: learn from your mistakes or they will repeat on you.

farmer in: a good harvest is promised, as is the difficulty of accomplishing it.

having a, in the chest: financial gains are at the expense of others' lives.

   ears: malicious gossip about you causes others to turn against you.

   feet: your troubled foundations cannot sustain growth.

   heart: a camouflaged solution to the reenactment of an illicit passion.

   legs: running away is no longer an option.

   shoulders: others are outflanking your success and being credited for them.

   stomach: pleasant social activities can be overdone.

   teeth: are trying too hard to defend your decision, rather than revisiting it.

   throat: you can't swallow the acceptance of opposing views.

having a painful delivery: death and rebirth.

having pains all over the body: your success is causing a strain on your system.

   lovers dreaming of: their love is secured, yet rejected lover will defame you.

   severe: others would have you feel guilty for doing what they could not.

man in: business prospers if you stop inflicting pain on others.

   woman: suppression of painful memories.

sailor in: the level of tension at sea reflects actual pain.

PAINTER
11-18-31-35-40-43

at work, a: anxiety is constant, as is progress.

   many: worry will be smoothed away with others' support.

being a: your employment is at the vital stage of success or stagnation.

covered with: others will splay their hurts onto you.

going up a ladder: each step brings favor and disfavor and eventual success.

   coming down: unhappiness in love affairs due to failure to communicate fully.

having a, shop: abundant means through much-needed compromise.

others who are a: will meet people who will do you much good.

smudged with lampblack: the forerunner of a barrage of disgrace.

using enamel: long-lasting marriage will be sustained through venomous attack.

PAINTING
02-16-20-25-34-46

buying paint: don't let diversion keep you from obtaining all of the details.

frame, in a: you feel the limitations of your false pride.

job on a house being completed, a: domestic affliction has been healed.

landscape, a: will make good purchases to bring peace to yourself.

oil, in: use the staying power of your artistic talents and creative expression.

   with a palette of many colors: have just begun to show your talents.

pleasing, a: a double-cross by one whose sincerity you trusted.

receiving a gift of a: immediate success of own hopes, the loss of another's.

seascape, a: others see self-absorption as depression.

still life, a: are admired for ability to see through to the truth.

using black paint: health will become a major issue.

   bright colors: have not been honest with a friend.

   white: hiding guilt to cover threats, which you need to hear.

wagon, a: a restoration of your guidance in your career path.

watercolor, in: your situation is uncertain; our pride is extant.

PAINTINGS
11-19-25-34-36-37

buying a: will suffer loss through speculation.

collection of ancient, a: will receive inheritance from a distant relative.

   modern: hostility gained through your false pride.

commissioning a portrait of yourself: your oversell does not gain you prestige.

naked women, of: public disgrace, but will be happy in love affairs.

   men: short-lived victories, long-term retribution.

others having: enemies are endeavoring to destroy you.

owning a collection of: will suffer through the ingratitude of one you adore.

selling: have regrets over a trivial transaction in a paramount project.

taking a, off the wall: your envy is exacerbated by its constant reminder.

wall, on a: honor through a plan devised by an unknown superior.

   relative's, hanging: will be made unhappy by the thoughtless vanity of others.

PAIR
04-09-16-20-40-47

having a, of animals: must find your partner before you can climb the ramp to safety.

   anything: are undecided about marriage plans, don't make them.

   earrings: a friend will share your secrets with others if you lose one earring.

   scissors: gossip concerning private life will turn on its originators.

   shoes: disagreements in family affairs.

   twins: a split of your personality traits into two personas.

husband and wife as a: must do work that you do not like, to gain love you do.

PALACE
02-05-06-08-43-45

being destroyed, a: a heavy burden born out of the failure of romantic liaison.

destroying a: your tyrannical, overbearing behavior will be your undoing.

entering a: beware of enemies who desire to intimidate you.

living in a: people esteem you highly, especially an older, wealthy lover.

many: big real estate dealings will bring competitive jealousies.

of a: pleasures of short duration, uneasiness for long.

owning your own: your superiority is not enhanced by denigrating others.

PALLBEARER
01-05-19-21-22-46

being a: great affection will be a factor in your promotion.

four, carrying a coffin: humiliation from the darts of enemies' eyes.

many: you are a distinguished person who must travel West to benefit from it.

military officers being: will be deceived by a woman.

   poor people: will suffer constant harassment for following your convictions.

pall over a coffin, putting a: will receive a legacy.

   on an altar: great sadness because of a death.

PALM
03-13-17-21-30-44

hand with a telling, a: your history, and how your actions have affected your future.

holding a married woman's: will attain immortality through her children.

   unmarried: will be the object of suspicion unless she marries soon.

kissing a woman's: friendship and a request for a favor she may be unwilling to solicit.

of the, of the hand: inheritance from a distant relative that you have not received.

   child's, a: your power to divine heartfelt love brings domestic peace.

read, having own: will encourage disheartened souls to seek abundance and success.

   showing strong distinct lines: satisfy every one of your ambitions.

   fine delicate: your sensitivity is admirable, but worry doesn't accomplish life.

smelling perfume on a: the attraction is mutual and your suit encouraged.

Sunday, attending church on: will have a heated theological discussion with a friend.

PALM TREE
01-05-12-19-30-48

businessmen dreaming of, a: illusory wall of great success will be breached.

   professional people: will flourish in your profession, if you take vacations regularly.

woman: will have the blessings of children and the abundance to raise them.

young girls: will attract suitors and soon be married.

climbing a: certain failure without sophisticated equipment.

cutting branches from a: revival after much sorrow over the death of an issue.

friends being under a: will enjoy fame and successful speculation.

potted indoor: bring your positive business attitude home.

several: will receive a high and honorable position.

PAN
06-14-19-23-32-39

buying a: a suitable time to pursue courtship.

cooking in a: will enjoy devotion of others and toy with their virtue.

iron, an: a pointless waste of energy and strength.

steel: a decision needs to be made immediately.

frying, cooking in a: your negligence is putting other people at risk.

burning food in a: are about to rebel in the face of impossibilities.

god, the: are being mocked for taking life too seriously.

several: loss of money causes short-lived unhappiness.

others having: receipt of money will be delayed.

PANCAKES
18-21-22-34-42-47

burning: failure in business ventures from overexposure and limited control.

cooking: will have unexpected guests, both ardent suitors.

eating: persevere in present undertakings until you meet dark-eyed lover.

others: business associate will cause difficulties, but venture will stand the test.

making: a flip-flop of interests as each side matures.

others: will find a way out of difficulties by adding more grist to the mill.

PANSIES
12-16-26-38-45-46

garden, in own: misunderstanding with a friend of same sex.

another's: will enjoy dinner with oddly interesting misfits.

growing: will have a big family that will multiply with the time spent on it.

having a bouquet of: will assist at a wedding and plan another in your mind.

receiving a gift of, from a man: your love is secured.

PANTHER
15-24-28-29-33-46

cub: a busybody, gossiping neighbor will cause harm if you let her.

being afraid of a: will be persecuted by a disturbed and misplaced sexuality.

attacked by a: cunning and intrigue will shadow your every move.

triumphant over: slander your rivals without placing yourself as their victim.

cage, being in a: enemies will fail in attempts to injure you.

dying, a: death of a prominent person whose attributes you wish for yourself.

fighting, a: strong emotions bring a challenge to your maturity.

hearing a, roar: will suffer grief from fear, more than actual threats.

killing a: many changes but finally victory, winning a large sum of money.

running, a: the beauty in slick kinetic rhythm is poetry in motion.

scuffling, a: will have cruel suffering from innocent play.

skeleton of a, the: your profits will be reduced to the minimum.

tied with chains, a: a supportive visit from an associate you deemed hostile.

PANTRY
17-22-24-26-39-46

being in a: success in all your affairs.

empty, having an: fear someone has robbed you, but can't figure out who.

fixing drinks in a: news from one you haven't heard from in a long time.

full, having a: will be well loved for your luck and prosperity.

others in a, being with: another is enjoying what you desired while you serve him.

preparing something in a: will succeed in present endeavors.

putting foodstuffs in a: family quarrels over future security and who should receive it.

spilling something in a: a lover is thinking of you; pick it up if you don't want lover.

PANTS

05-12-17-19-36-45

buying: your life is moving in a direction you have chosen.

discarding: clothes don't make the person.

dry cleaning: your self-confidence ensures profitability.

losing: others being indignant toward you is the result of false gossip.

men's: will win competition despite imprudence of your opponents.

taking your, off: have been indiscrete with your actions and nonconformity.

washing: your beliefs are unworthy of you.

wearing: share control of the family and the peace.

women's: taking over another's role does not make you an equal.

PAPERS

13-19-28-36-46-47

being manufactured: will have a good job in your own line of work.

book, of a: your thirst for knowledge will help complete your contracts.

clean: will escape with only slight money losses.

colored: enemies taint your sacrifice of your own pleasures for another's comfort.

dirty: your actions will be questionable, your loss more significant.

empty from another person: are under a negative influence, unspoken and judgmental.

folded: small disappointment should not detract from your trust and sincerity.

losing: even if you read the small print carefully, these are papers you should not sign.

parchment documents, receiving: trouble with legal affairs.

    sending: appointment to new position in which you will be the messenger of losses.

pieces of: your acts will be challenged.

plain: an obscure decision will decide the outcome.

poor quality: will receive disappointing news from a friend.

printed: good faith in the system does not mean system is infallible.

toilet: a well-used solution to a small misfortune.

torn: the fault lies in your actions; admit it and go forward.

used to print newspapers: cull out the one item necessary.

white: innocence.

    empty: possibilities in the making are lost through being underfunded.

written on, that is: you like to argue with yourself before presenting your ideas.

PARACHUTE

05-13-31-32-35-42

backpack, in a: make a choice after carefully rechecking all connections.

coming down in a: optimism in your abilities brings sorrow within the family.

    many people: increase in the family from all branches.

of a, floating downward: be careful not to go to extremes with your self-confidence.

    and not opening: will be criticized by a loved one for faulty equipment.

people killed upon landing in a: dishonor for enemies who would put your health at risk.

PARADE

01-12-13-19-45-47

Boy Scouts, of: will forgive your enemies as you would forgive yourself.

happy people, of: a gift won't pay for your living high above your means.

marching soldiers, of: faithful love makes involvement in a risky venture honorable.

    drilling: a change in life will come through discipline.

national: put all internal disagreement aside when your family is under attack.

protest, of: are being exuberantly indecisive and irrational.

religious: need to forget current emotional problems for a day.

union: are daring others to value your existence.

PARADISE

03-09-13-14-15-27

being in: forgive those who have wronged you and recognize those who support you.

    enemies: they will destroy your illusion of Eden, but retry that failed project.

farmer dreaming of: careful rational actions bring abundant harvest.

    young girls, a: life will not live up to her expectations.

going to: will be a sudden change in family unit.

men being thrown out of: breakup of the family through loss of support.

    women: misery of unfulfilled potential of spiritual and material happiness

not being wanted in: long-lasting finances will not bring you peace.

PARALYZED

04-07-15-18-26-33

becoming: arguments within the family have created a standstill.

children being: listen to their wishes patiently, but react over time.

    enemies: financial losses bring illness of the soul.

    husband or wife: will lose affection for each other and turn away.

    relatives: death of an enemy brings bitter disappointment at his legacy.

having paralysis: self-inflicted dishonor at the inability to control the situation at hand.

left side, on the: your emotional, intuitive side needs equal time.

others that are: are paralyzed between two opposing forces.

PARAPET

03-05-13-15-35-45

falling on a: difficulties will be overcome by your own efforts in facing a partner's jealousy.

    others: your misfortune in love affairs is your responsibility to solve.

kneeling on a: danger from being overcome with gloom and tedium.

leaning over a: a meeting with one you have feared rejection from.

others being on a: shake self-inflicted apathy and reinvolve yourself in project.

PARASOL

14-17-24-37-43-45

beautifully colored, a: your lover will displease you over thoughtless remarks.

borrowing a: misunderstandings with a friend over loyalty to each other.

carrying a, over the head: someone will come to your aid.

having an open: prosperity from a gentleman caller commingling with his deceit.

    to protect you from the sun: wealth will soon be deposited in a savings bank.

lending a: will be hurt by the ingratitude of friends whom you aided.

opening a, in the house: love affairs will be on the rocks over false accusations.

PARDON

01-12-30-31-40-45

asking, for an offense: first is pardonable, second is reprimandable, third is imprisonable.

    children, your: ability to learn from your mistakes is the basis of growth.

    criminal, a: your innocence will ultimately prove to your advantage.

    lover, a: remorse for trust lost takes years to rebuild, if at all.

asking, from God: your punishment will fit your crime.

being pardoned by others: discomfort at their change in attitude toward you.

    priest, a: will have an energetic mind, which needs direction and goals.

pardoning children: will despair after giving pardon, when they repeat the offense.

    another: a secret hurts you deeply, but don't retain the hurt.

    husband and wife, each other: humiliation dissipates to an affirmation of vows.

PARENTS

15-19-33-41-43-44

accompanying: have switched roles with that parent.

another's: a bonus of parental support from left field.

beating their children: unexpectedly good

affairs if you exercise care in their planning.

being accompanied by: new endeavor will succeed.

embracing a: holding onto their ethics despite peer pressure.

grouchy, being a: difficulty instilling their principles into your children.

naked, being: big family disagreement brings fortunate change.

of own after they are dead: closure.

parricide, committing: in your maturity you no longer depend upon them.

questionable parentage, of: major rows within family; your ideas will create enemies.

visiting: business affairs going bad will lead to a quiet life.

PARIS
07-10-29-37-40-41

being in, alone: contentment in being in the far past to heal the near past and present.

with a lover: annoyance of displacement will cause arguments, spoiling your trip.

fashion, looking for: will be excessively extravagant and disappointed with your gain.

going to: are being watched by others wanting your freedom.

living in: will attend the Beaux Arts and live on the right bank.

visiting: you are prone to enjoying amusements too much.

PARK
14-23-25-26-33-47

being lost in a: a controversial judgment call will endanger your career.

children playing in a: are making unbreakable alliances.

keeper of a: have the peace of mind of many under your watch.

national: have burned the bridge of options for career choices.

sitting in a, alone: increase in your fortune will not meet your ambitions.

with sweetheart: enemies must be punished for interfering in your affairs.

strolling through an untidy: reverses in business will cause a major overhaul

of your job.

walking in a beautiful: increase the hours of pleasure with your family.

PARLIAMENT
33-37-38-41-45-48

being a member of: advancement in position after meeting an influential member.

with, officials: much-valued relationship will develop your career prospects.

of a, in session: will be cheated out of your reputation by slanderous remarks.

visiting a: quarrels over long-standing bone of contention will result in a handshake.

PARROT
01-02-11-12-14-32

chattering too much: your gossiping will boomerang and you won't recognize it.

many: avoid encounters with competitive women.

children talking to a: have confidence of friends if you understand what they are saying.

enjoying the chatter of a: flattery from a deceitful person is their opinion of themselves.

laying an egg: increase in the family.

of a: riches through invitation to frivolous actions and idle slander.

talking to a: you expect too many favors from others.

talking to you: mocking parrot's words will come true, but they are not yours.

talks very little, that: difficult, unstable work situation ahead.

young girl dreaming of a: inquire about fiancé's family and defend yours against slander.

PARTRIDGE
10-17-20-28-32-35

flying away, a: a promising future of deserved honors.

killing a: abundant means if you get rid of your jealous partner.

landing, a: assert your way to success, but back it up with worth.

many: will achieve goals by hard work and a sense of humor.

of a: many small troubles from females unable to feel gratitude.

pear tree, in a: celebration will be spoiled by a disappointing act.

PARTY

12-14-23-28-30-41

attending a: good times with harmony and pleasant associations.

   dinner: accord among friends; indiscriminate dealings with your mate.

   others: beware of rivals banding together.

   wild: life's favors will pass you by without recognition.

   without a partner: a peaceful intermission from embroiling family issues.

gala, being at a: will secure profit of pleasure and an accumulation of distress.

   with friends: loss of social friends who weren't your friends in the first place.

     sweetheart: healthful and lively engagement.

     your mate: will believe you to be quarrelsome with other guests.

giving a: uncertain and fluctuating affairs.

   others, for you: unexpected reverses in love.

shy at at, being: will be fortunate in expectations because you have none.

someone getting hurt at a: the use and abuse of pleasure.

taking children to a: hopes are vanishing for you; give your children the baton.

PASSAGE

07-14-15-24-33-38

being with others in a: slow, steady, single-minded progress at work.

deep dark. a: persistence, faith and the belief that the goal is there.

   falling into: let go for a moment and experience the lack of real fear.

   with white light at the end: are particularly worried about the outcome.

finding something in a long: will overcome transition through great difficulties.

   a narrow: are unwilling to involve yourself in another's business.

passing another on the street: your self-centeredness has eliminated any friendship.

reading a, in the Bible: will be captivated by a fine person.

book, a: will have a constant friend from whom there can be no secrets.

dictionary, a: are susceptible to sudden reversals of temper.

PASSENGER

03-06-24-35-45-48

being a: take a backseat in your family, let another be the driver.

   children: family discord over misplaced trust; find it.

   friends: realization of own ambitions is in the hands of another.

on a boat: days without troubles never existed.

   plane: treachery by those upon whom you are dependent.

oncoming: expect others to handle your affairs.

outgoing: will have an opportunity to acquire property through another's loss.

PASSPORT

01-08-15-22-35-52

applying for a new: the decision to move on is yours alone.

foreign, having a: restriction by those you don't know.

invalid, an: are not ready to make the decision required to move.

losing your: your lack of credibility blocks you.

of a: your unconscious is giving you permission to travel.

PASTA

03-05-09-21-31-50

cooking: your stomach craves comfort.

eating: filling up with bland projects spiced with intermittent snags.

elaborate presentation of, an: trying to make a silk purse out of a sow's ear.

PASTOR

19-31-33-38-42-52

being a: must admit a previous failure to solve the problem.

giving advice as a: others have to learn for themselves.

of a: must pay more attention to property holdings.

taking advice from a: increase in possessions.

talking with a: must take better care of personal affairs.

PASTRY

10-14-24-30-39-40

butter in, using plenty of: great satisfaction in small doses.

buying: will find out something startling about your lover.

baking: dissatisfaction with your performance at work.

cake, a: suffering caused by inability to put past behind you.

cookies: will discover the secret to many happy hours with friends.

fancy: will face contradiction with your own actions.

pie, a: beware of spending money on something you can do yourself.

dunking in coffee: your own foolishness will obstruct your congenial work.

eating: melancholy at not being able to share your joy with the world.

children: good results in own enterprises if you don't miss important engagements.

man dreaming of: will fall in love with a teenager.

with almonds: will be justified in your actions.

of a, shop: you love to share good things and are disappointed your mate cannot.

selling: will painfully disconnect from one who cannot return your feelings.

PATCH

05-10-18-35-39-43

being on own clothes: have inherited no false pride in observing your familial obligation.

patching own underclothes: are denying your lover the truth of your character.

relative's garments: are attempting to retrieve some semblance of civility.

patchwork, doing: money will come to you through the acquisition of disputed property.

others: their love for you is sincere; yours for them is not.

for others: another will hold the affection of your lover and keep it from you.

putting a, on children's clothes: are ashamed at not being able to buy clothes.

PATENT

18-23-34-39-47-49

applying for a: act now or people will bother you.

being refused a: in your hesitation you lost a valuable asset.

making money from a: reason has its limits; only intuition creates.

obtaining a: calculate proof positive before proceeding on a venture.

PATH

04-10-27-38-42-51

losing one's way on a: a situation where you appear ridiculous; back up and start over.

meeting obstacles along a: difficulties to be faced if you don't change direction.

struggling along a narrow: with extreme effort you will achieve success.

two people in love walking along a: will meet a prominent person and ignore him.

married woman, with husband: will keep love tryst and divorce her husband.

young girl, with boyfriend: will incur loss of small importance if you marry a rich man.

walking in a broad straight: hidden thoughts bring unhappiness; act on them.

leisurely down a: your affairs will flourish, with clarity of thought.

narrow: adversity if you stray from your goals.

rough: embarrassment if you don't reconsider issues at hand.

wide: take the route of least resistance.

with someone down a: an insignificant event will charm you.

PATRONESS

02-07-08-09-24-49

arguing with a: much commotion with no good results.

being a: a contented life, being able to help those who have helped you.

being insulted by a: people are saying bad things about you.

of a female patron: don't allow a stranger to take over your conversation.

PATTERN

01-05-08-16-23-36

buying a: worries will be overcome by the definite outline of a plan for salvation.

making a: small vexation at a series of radical actions, yours.

of a: quarrels in the family could prove as dangerous as they are impossible to avoid.

ordering a: you will collect money.

PAVEMENT

02-04-07-17-24-30

falling on the: danger ahead for new business venture.

in front of own house: someone in your household has animosity toward you.

street: will fall into a trap; only ingenuity can extricate you from it.

warehouse, in a: resist feelings of envy over friend's success.

PAWN

07-14-24-40-42-50

being a, broker: you barter with another's emotions.

going to a: unleash yourself from others' affairs.

not returning own articles to you: unfaithful sweetheart will request your aid.

renewing pledges at a: indiscretion of mate causes troubles.

shop, going to a: unexpected help will come to you.

receiving money from: your future and troubles are taken care of.

taking articles to be pawned: you do not make plans well.

redeeming: a sudden and unprecedented success.

PAYING

03-14-16-29-32-42

bill that is due, a: misery and poverty due to your exorbitant lifestyle.

bill that you shouldn't, a: will be guilty of making a hurried foolish decision.

debt, a: financial gains if you settle past indebtedness.

for someone else: are taking away their chance to face their own responsibilities.

others, to you: one false move and you

will lose the entire lot.

having to make payments: superiors do not favor you, but their superiors do.

PEACE

07-12-21-29-30-37

having: will have a quarrel over your doubts and suspicious accusations.

making: expect a fight in the near future.

lovers between each other: not until the true animosity is exposed.

mates: increase of affection for children and anger and irritability with each other.

with friends: only the truth will allow acceptance.

remaining peaceful: the supreme sacrifice of unrealizable hopes.

PEACHES

16-20-25-35-41-49

eating, in season: contentment, luscious peace.

out of: the refreshing revival of a past love turns sour again.

with others: your partner is serious; you are not.

many trees loaded with: immortality.

of, on a tree: promised attainment of fondest hopes.

picking, from a tree: unless you correct your injustice, many will suffer.

ripe: your emotions have matured enough to be trusted.

rotten, a: check the subtle references to avoid sickness in the home.

shaking: your impulsiveness brings half-ripened solutions.

PEACOCK

01-13-14-35-46-48

catching a: your ambition will be laughable if you strut it around.

dead, a: your pride will cause your good plans to fail.

fantail spread, with: your arrogance does not serve you well.

farmer dreaming of a: will have a good harvest of your accomplishments.

beautiful woman: are emphasizing another to elevate your position.

man, circling: will have troubles if you unlock the past.

woman: the pride and prejudice of
riches.
hearing a, chirping: don't be enticed to run
with the big boys.
of a: your vanity will be disappointed by
another's beauty.
  beautiful feathers, with: joy without profit
  to your proud spirit.

PEARLS
02-04-28-39-40-50
breaking a string of: grief and a sorrowful
outlook through misunderstanding.
buying: will succeed in your goal at your
new venture.
finding: will earn success through hard work;
don't cast it before those who don't.
gathering, from the sea: are penniless and
unable to take advantage of opportunities.
giving a gift of: desire for an in-depth relationship has been dashed.
  receiving: don't accept if your feelings
  are not reciprocated.
  losing a set of: will fail to make new friends
  at work.
many: unhappiness and tears over insignificant money problems.
of: a serene depth that evolved through
misery to a noble beauty.
restringing a broken strand of: at spiritual
rebirth, don't compromise for anything
less.
threading: loneliness and downheartedness
caused by betrayal.
wearing: each emotional blemish needs to
be restored to health.

PEARS
04-16-19-20-42-52
eating: longevity after a scandal or two.
  children: husband will always be faithful
  to you.
  relatives: husband and wife will always be
  faithful.
  ripe: relationship with partner will be
  rewarding and long-lasting.
picking: amusements become profitable; a
picnic in a profitable scene.
  tree, in bloom: dignity; prospects are
  good, if you are sympathetic and
  understanding.

PEAS
02-12-20-34-51-52
cooking: your robust health will encounter
contagious disease.
dried: large earnings acquired in a shady
manner.
eating: rugged health and increasing riches.
  children: they will succeed in everyday
  activities.
growing in the garden: financial gains through
quick turnarounds.
not completely cooked: exercise patience in
your affairs.
of: will meet that one-in-a-million who can
aid your good health and long life.
on the vines: fortunate undertakings as you
climb the ladder to success.
opening a can of: a talkative neighbor wants
an invitation to dinner.
planting: fulfillment of ambitions with
your physical and mental strength at
a low.
shelling: will take apart your insults and
apologize for them.
sweet: delicate pleasures and a departure.

PEBBLES
01-02-05-27-32-42
handling: competition will cause trouble;
clear up any altercations so they can't.
making a walk with: unhappiness will be
avenged at the first opportunity.
picking up: melancholy if you don't cultivate
leniency toward others' foibles.
sitting on: will be delivered from a difficult
situation.
tossed in the water: jewelry sinks to the
bottom quickly and easily.
  skirting across: should weigh the
  consequences, as some deeds will
  cause you to sink.
various colored: are too proud, causing you
discomfort and uneasiness.

PEDESTRIAN
04-15-23-24-42-52
being: are satisfied with simple fare and
the opinions of acquaintances.
being a: are seeking proportionate enjoyments of a harmonious health.
bumping into a: are confronted with insur-

mountable obstacles in the person of a pedestrian.

coming toward you: while attending a funeral, have an unpleasant task to perform.

falling down: one of married partners is cheating; which one is with you?

hurt, being: fortune in business dealings will bring embarrassment in affairs.

many: will successfully undertake dealing with a series of attacks.

of a: overcome enemies with perseverance and undermine them with a forgiving charm.

PEELING
03-26-29-33-47-48

eggs: will be visited by a loved one who has been preoccupied with another.

facial: are shedding layers of first impressions.

fruits: are voiding the fuzz and dealing with the heart of the matter.

skin: are discarding the pretensions of a suntan to expose your core sincerity.

vegetables: will invite vegetarian friends for dinner.

PEN
02-13-15-26-29-35

ballpoint, a: are intent on sending your message at the best possible cost to you.

blunt, writing with a: are unaware of the negative impression you give.

breaking a, tip: a petty misjudgment could lead to a destructive accident.

buying a: will live a life as long as the expected life of the pen.

children using a pen: are writing what they can't say to your face.

nib, breaking the point of a: all is not what it seems, change direction.

buying a new: advancement for your children with your partiality.

quill, a: a refinement of the writing process with union of mind and pen.

plucking a, for a: a crucial bit of correspondence will explode your luck.

writing with a: nostalgic return to when words spoke volumes.

writing with a: news from absent friends who harbor resentment against you.

fountain: no news from false friends is good news.

letters in bed: annoyance at hidden resentment surrounding you.

love letters, fountain pen: are being deceived, letters are being kept from you.

old-fashioned, an: your reserve and hesitancy cause pessimism in your outlook.

quill: with patience and fortitude your project will be completed.

PENANCE
02-04-08-12-21-35

asking for: will live to an advanced age if you can relieve yourself of heavy cargo.

others: a dangerous influence is near when traveling out of your sphere of influence.

being ordered to give penitence: reparations toward those you have offended are in order.

sorrow for having to pay: will be riled by duties you have been intimidated into doing.

giving, to someone: are led with a serious breach of morality by itinerants.

offering: be reserved with strangers until you establish the best course to follow.

PENCILS
22-26-29-33-35-37

blunt, writing with a: are unaware of the negative impression you give.

buying: your business success is hampered by a lack of commitment by your partner.

children using: they will enjoy good health and comprehend the basics.

erasing: close friend will suffer amnesia and forget you.

giving: will separate from the one to whom you are giving them.

of: are influenced by romantic secrets entrusted to you long ago.

receiving: beware of the person who gave you the pencils.

sharpening: your accounts are in order; your columns are straight.

tip, breaking a: a petty misjudgment could lead to a destructive accident.

PENDULUM
05-15-34-38-40-42

of an inactive: will receive unexpected message from a reliable source.

sitting on a mantel: the balance of your life is continually being challenged.

starting a: will take a long journey with a reliable, steady guide.

stopped, that has: long and healthy life with many hopes bearing fruit.

PENSION
04-06-16-20-24-28

being refused a: have emotional security in one loyal friend.

guesthouse, living in a: your general despondence toward your problems is worrisome.

receiving a: will be called upon to cash in on old debts.

  others: be careful of your decisions involving the family.

  relatives: will make a stock investment that will benefit all.

PEOPLE
04-17-24-41-43-44

affairs of other, attending to: temptation will come; expect profit and demand it.

being clumsy, other: are projecting your anger too quickly; keep it within your control.

bumping into: well-matched matrimony will take place.

calming angry: the truth does not work when passions have been inflamed.

carrying a burden of: expect a large inheritance, but don't plan on it.

chorus of: public opinion is not manipulated or correctly calculated by the polls.

comforting other: will be fortunate in love.

compassion for poor, having: does not include the most devastating insult—pity.

large group of, a: dignity and calm leadership will make a mob constructive.

  dealings with, having: hold firm to principles; don't let your boss mistreat you.

  protection of: are you sure it is not your humility you are protecting?

ordering other, to be calm: will be loved and ridiculed, but sorely needed

seeing many, and counting: to satisfy your ambitions, you need to control the multitudes.

taking advantage of other: prosperity must come from the fruits of your own labor.

visited by big, being: size does not equal threat, nor the winner.

PEPPER
04-22-24-32-37-46

burning the tongue with: idle gossip will cause injury to your digestive tract.

buying: people are whispering bad things about you.

eating: news will spice up your life in a way you would prefer it hadn't.

grinding: will receive bad news about a misappropriation of funds.

of: are satisfied with so little food that you miss the opportunity for a gourmet meal.

smelling, and sneezing: talents within the family lead to financial optimism.

sprinkling, on food: lasting affection in love could turn counterproductive.

white: an innocent situation will turn disastrous.

PEPPERMINT
12-19-24-32-36-38

eating: will attain your goal through a heritage you didn't realize you had.

giving, to others: friends will come to your rescue if needed.

  to children: make sure that your plans are well-intentioned before beginning.

of: are proud of children, and they are proud of you.

receiving, from others: a pleasant end to an evening.

PERFUME
03-04-20-24-25-26

bottle of, empty: your love affair is on the rocks; no aroma of pleasure can save it.

  full: will enjoy much frivolity if you allow yourself to.

  breaking a: disaster to fondest hopes; too much too soon of sensuous desires.

  giving, as a gift: big profit from an elderly man's proposal.

    receiving: will be embraced by an

unknown person of high net
worth.

buying cheap: will have a mediocre harvest.

   expensive: will need sense of humor to
advance in society.

having, not: friends will abuse your confidence and corrupt your image.

   losing: will marry in haste and regret it
at length.

   stealing: a rival will take away your
sweetheart.

man preferring a special: a friend will seduce
his wife.

   woman: are cheating in love affairs; don't
mix up your scents.

man putting, on a woman: adultery in an
exciting taxi ride.

sachet in your clothes: a tender, motherly
woman willing to not judge but to
understand.

smelling: will need a sense of humor to
advance in society.

   children, on: they are doing something
premature to their maturity.

     others: revelation of a secret will lose
you a friendship.

   church, in a: God's blessings on you, but
don't confuse them with secular pleasures.

   expensive, an: will stop only at prostitu-
tion to gain the wealthy man you
want.

   man's, a: beware of people searching for
love and your engaging with them.

spilling: loss of thing that brings pleasure.

using: your pretense of perfection is less
than skin deep.

   another's: have a strong attachment for
this person.

PERJURY
13-17-20-30-33-36

committing: your unethical actions will cause
misfortune.

   husband or wife, against each other: the
storm you now face is your creation.

   others: sacrifice a friendship to offset
impending disaster.

     against you: correct solution may be
illegal.

having committed: postponement of business
affairs.

PERMIT
01-17-19-40-41-43

asking for a: will soon receive relief from
pains and a complicated project.

   permission: will be promoted above your
capabilities.

     giving: have contained your virulence
behind obsequiousness.

being refused a: delay in affairs from your
costly mistakes.

obtaining a: prosperity from your being a
sociable person.

receiving a marriage: many temptations are
ahead of you; seek protection.

   building: will do business with an
ungrateful woman.

   children: will have difficulty persuading
others of your innate talents.

PERSECUTED
09-12-14-19-27-40

being: enjoy a clear conscience by returning
to a practical, rational approach.

   falsely: track down the source and you will
receive a promotion.

   family, by: unhappiness within the family,
as they refuse to support you.

   law, by the: beware of treachery by friends'
malicious remarks.

persecuting others: contentment, as the truth
will out itself.

PERSPIRATION
02-07-35-41-47-48

odors: your sense of deceit in your friends is
correct.

wiping, from forehead: a small fortune, deep
in your psyche, wants out.

   body: you fear a proposal of marriage will
be blocked by those gossiping ill
will.

   children: will succeed in being loved by the
opposite sex.

   enemies: their loss of money is your gain.

   medicine, from taking: health will improve
with less of the exact medicine.

   men: will be badly treated by creditors.

   of perspiring: hard labor will be required
for success.

relatives: will be rewarded for your own good efforts.

PESTS
05-06-11-14-34-48

being in others' houses: must be discrete in social contacts.

facing you, turning around and: are spared from their illness, but not from their wrath.

having, in the bedding: prosperity beyond fondest hopes.

   garden: small prosperity; enjoy it in every detail and it will grow.

   own house: don't give them what they want, but what they need to get what they want.

of a poor: what you give to others comes back threefold.

ugly, an: cosmetics cannot shield your essence.

walking away from you: jealous people are against you.

PETTICOATS
16-19-27-34-45-47

buying, a: exercise moderation in your mode of living.

changing a: your fondest desires will meet with disaster.

colored, a: a multiple marriage will soon take place.

embroidered, an: will contract a contagious disease.

having: will soon have a love affair of petty annoyances.

losing her, a young woman: loss of lover's affection leads to difficulties in married life.

mending a: many amusements will change your love affairs.

torn, a: your reputation has been sullied from your excessive pride in your appearance.

wearing a: warning of conceit and wasteful expenditures.

white, a: will receive a beautiful gift, dignity from a doting, manly husband.

PEWTER
03-07-10-28-34-37

buying utensils made of: a thrifty partner

whose independence will save your wealth.

dishes and pots, using: will overcome the disturbing elements of your digestion.

having: will have money, but not wealth; straitened circumstances, but not be in need.

of things made of various alloys: contentment within the company of your elders.

PHANTOM
01-04-15-32-41-48

dressed in black: avoid temptation to over-impress others.

   white: a new adventure, less than agreeable, will control your fortunes.

lovers dreaming of a: the one you love cannot make up her mind to love you.

   businesspeople: avoid lending money or giving credit.

   married people: do not travel; fate is against you.

   unmarried people: avoid quarrels with friends; disappointment is in store for you.

many: will be in a state of desperation until you befriend your dark side.

PHARMACIST
14-21-28-30-32-37

being a: business affairs are challenged by the incapability of friends.

entering a drugstore: take care; your health is at risk.

   being sick and: recuperation is possible after a long illness.

of a pharmacy: be cautious in business dealings.

PHEASANT
01-07-12-13-17-44

cooking: will slowly become aware of your happiness.

eating: continue to sustain your good digestion.

killing a: abundant temptation taunts and haunts you.

of a: prosperity beyond your own hopes, but save money for a rainy day.

on a finger, holding a: profit and joy from a new source of income.

sitting on shoulders, having a: will have very good health and learn to laugh.

313

PHOTOGRAPH
11-20-27-40-44-46

another taking your: your face blocks your view of the world.

developing a, in the darkroom: wait to see what develops before committing.

of own: bring your sense of direction into focus.

    another's: dignity and distinction when you realize picture is of you.

    unknown person: in right time and place, you will meet your dream image.

old, an: memories of old friends who have reversed their lives.

receiving or giving own: share your self-analysis with appropriate party.

refuses to develop properly: are not seeing clearly and being given undivided loyalties.

smashing down a: are being warned that you are unwittingly the cause of your woes.

    of dead person: listen to your heart, not the deception of your eyes.

someone dear hanging around neck, of: your conduct has been unbecoming.

studio, having a private: reality, not in time, only in your imagination.

taking children's: approaching money from a deceptive source; protect them first.

    dead person's: revisit issues you thought were resolved.

    friend's: you deceive friends when you can't see their goals and insult their every move.

    other's: a rival will take sweetheart's affections.

PHYSICIAN
06-07-20-21-26-45

being a: heal thyself and honor your soul before treating another.

calling a, for children: ask an authority figure for guidance.

    yourself: the remedy is within your soul.

    relatives: rapid recovery from imaginary ailments.

of a: master self-control in your search for answers.

others calling a: a suitable time to pursue courtship.

for you: your body has the resources to heal itself.

visiting patients: big wealth brings ascent on the social ladder.

PIANO
09-11-16-23-28-37

buying a: your expenses exceed your income; chose your priorities.

hearing a: troublesome task requiring more practice.

owning a: your feelings with an indifferent lover must be played out.

pedals of a: an imposing insincere affectation of stage fever.

playing the: disputes over frivolities; stand your ground.

    children: disputes with relatives over qualities of children.

    grand: your overzealous ambitions preclude enjoyment of the music.

    out of tune: slow down; visit your house of worship.

    sweetheart: certain and happy marriage.

selling a: loneliness and disappointment of a cold-hearted family.

tuner, being a: will make your mark and people will listen.

    out of tune: look for another job before you lose this one.

PICKLES
08-10-15-18-19-39

buying: financial loss through misdirected sense of principle.

eating: your life will be marked by lack of ambition.

gherkins, eating: abstain from any alcoholic beverages.

giving, to others: your health and your bank account say thank you.

    receiving, from: false friends will cause a bad experience.

making: temptation in love will come to you; ignore it.

throwing away: your troubles are ended if you concede lover to another.

PICNIC
06-09-22-32-35-40

attending a: deep enjoyment of luck, leisure and prosperity.

happy, a: false friends are gossiping about you.

having a, with children: plans will take years to come to fruition.

   friends: doubtful results in love affairs if attacked by pests.

   relatives: will realize high ambitions and share them.

others having a: are bent on seeking sensual pleasure.

PIE
11-12-13-15-43-44

cooking a: unpleasant complications are developing at home.

crusts, being reduced to eating: business affairs will prosper if you stop being careless.

eating a: indulgence adds dimension, but not to foes.

   others: trouble is hanging over you; follow the luck on the ground.

giving children, to eat: are unusually practical and decisive.

making a, to give to others: will be aided in your perils by hearty friends.

pastry shop, in a: dissension within your close circle must be exposed.

pudding, making a: abundant means in the middle of want is a state of mind.

receiving a: flirting as a side occupation creates a preoccupation with the repercussions.

PIER
04-21-26-31-34-45

being on a, alone: will achieve such heights that present affluence will seem like poverty.

   others: be cautious in all your affairs that you bring happiness to the right person.

   sailors: are seeking relief for your restlessness.

   with others: are in constant search for feedback for what you think you know.

   workmen: are doing all of the taking and none of the giving.

fishing from a: a hopeless engagement in wish fulfillment.

PIGS
04-07-21-37-39-48

being well fed: prosperity to come through your friendliness.

   thin: children will cause petty vexations over dirtiness and overindulgence.

boar, a: someone behind the scenes is fiercely antagonistic to you.

buying: are diligent in your greed.

eating roast pork: take precautions against a rival.

   ribs, barbecued: the core of the problem is disguised as feasting opulence.

many: will receive money after the death of a relative, after others have had their share.

of: with selfishness, your good earnings will disappear and can't be invested to earn more.

selling: will be hated by friends for supporting a failing venture.

sow: a birth, and rebirth, to fortune.

sty, in a: a blissful home, contented progeny and plentiful nutrition.

wild: a friend will attempt to harm you, but take the long shot.

PIGEONS
10-12-19-24-36-45

alighting on ledges: your favorable love affairs are on public view.

brown and white: business enterprises are prosperous and you are seemingly contented.

flying: extend your reaching out for companionship to reciprocal ideas.

gray: your devotion will be subject to reproach.

Jacobin fancy pigeon: will have several lovers; treat them all.

many: are engaged in charitable work; don't support worthless pursuits.

roost, a: imminent marriage of undivided loyalties.

two, fighting: have allowed your low and debasing desires to take you over.

walking on the ground: important news from far away foretelling worthless speculation.

white: consolation of evanescent peace.

PILGRIMS

03-04-13-20-30-43

being a: are too independent to maintain your position at work without a battle.

  on a pilgrimage: with faith you can walk the desert; without it, you fry.

    with a female: the harmony of mutual intentions.

gathering of, a: desires will be satisfied if you trust the one you love.

giving money to: fulfillment of fondest wish, an optimistic future.

migrating to new places: improvement of working conditions.

of a: welcome to all who come to your door.

PILLS

03-10-17-25-34-39

bottle of many: will be indecisive and timid in a journey abroad.

buying: use caution in being psychologically dependent on business ventures.

giving, to children: give confident encouragement to equalize the relationship.

  others: your prejudices will suffer severe criticism.

  relatives: turn past lessons into sweet satisfaction.

taking, yourself: important responsibilities when entrusted to you.

taking a: minor aggravation before emotional healing.

  many, each day: bitterness increases exponentially with each cover-up.

PILOT

02-11-22-26-31-47

ace, of an: stem your impatience or another person will enjoy your winnings.

being a: you are the master in your love affairs, which has you confidently relaxed.

  ace, an: your overconfidence is blind to deception in love matters.

causing damage to a ship: your nervous irritability blocks the benefit of stimulation.

crashing but no one being hurt: your quick thinking will be singled out for high honors.

  and everyone being killed: trouble will come from far away.

directing a ship: monetary benefits if you sail home; death if you don't.

  doesn't know how to fly an: are determined to pass the competency test.

flying an airplane: will accomplish own desires when you care for your responsibilities.

women dreaming of being in love with a: an early marriage by elopement.

PINS

07-21-23-30-35-42

buying: are trying to pin something on another, falsely.

cushion as a gift, giving a: be careful not to give your friends cause to prick you.

  without pins: a life of ease without harassment of envy.

falls out, a: undertakings will be accomplished despite insecurity about a specific person.

having many: serious embarrassment through a friend.

hearing a, drop: attend to even the minutest details now.

others using: will be continually contradicted; readjust plan with each diversion.

pricking yourself with a: will get a great deal more than you expected.

throwing away: stay away from groups of women at a dinner party.

using, while sewing: use people for positive things, not to avenge others for you.

PIPE

03-06-12-19-32-40

breaking a: security and peaceful outcome to adversity.

briar, a: disagreements over extravagant self-indulgent habits.

buying a: wish to soothe your travails with creature comforts.

crawling through a sewer: the relationship is smothering you.

dirty, a: will be publicly rebuked for an indiscretion.

filling a: a disagreeable position should be confronted in your timing.

giving a, as a gift: advancement in your own business.

receiving: advancement in business, if you keep the lines of communication open.

putting out a: you will lose a close friend.

several, having: the contemplation of knowledge brings great peace of mind.

smoking a: a visit will bring sweet satisfaction.

    another: step back from a self-absorbed situation.

utility, a: service to your community through innovative solutions.

PIRATE
01-18-21-22-34-40

being a: journey and financial gains.

    victim of a: a deceitful associate will cause pain, if you allow him.

harmed by pirates, being: a motorcycle accident at your expense.

many: your love affair has reached a very low point; leave it before it is exposed.

of a: beware of friends with adventurous ideas with evil side effects.

PISTOL
07-09-15-18-34-42

carrying a: will be disliked by people who scream their anger in your face.

    being an officer and: struggles with treachery and taunting.

    enemies: loss of temper will require an apology.

    friends: will be annoyed with accusations that are mere hearsay.

firing a: discern who is the enemy before acting.

    hitting a target: discern carefully that the target was the correct one.

    others: will learn of schemes to ruin you; target them.

hearing a, being fired: your self-defense is at stake; verbalize it.

misfiring a: your animosity caused the altercation, refueling the aggression.

owning many: recovery of health after a long, physical ailment.

PIT
04-16-20-23-30-38

being forced to go down into a: will risk fortune and health to find your way out.

falling into a: your indifference and coolness to love will lure uneasiness, not love.

    and being hurt: the character you cultivated will boomerang on you.

going down into a deep: business affairs will decline due to your irreverent risks.

    shallow: decline in love affairs caused your infelicitous scheming designs.

hurting yourself in a: feel helpless with the troubles confronting you.

many people being killed in a: enemies will endeavor to destroy you and any supporter.

others being in a: failure in business will be difficult, but not impossible, to turn around.

walking along and falling into a: an ambitious colleague will connive at your failure.

PITCHER
05-14-24-29-40-42

being full: fidelity in an old-fashioned career.

    empty: infidelity surrounds you; a friend is trying to help you secretly.

breaking a: social activities of a happy nature will be plagued with bitterness.

colored, a: unlucky events manipulated by a force not your own.

drinking from a: your generosity is overwhelming the recipients.

pottery, a: will lose money due to your carelessness.

throwing a, away: will have a new lover with foot trouble.

PITY
08-13-25-32-41-42

asking for: a sizable profit and romantic interlude turn permanent.

being pitied: feel humiliation at the attractive opportunities offered to you.

    by friends: overeagerness leads to accepting risky ventures.

having, on friends: have an unusual level of confidence and decisiveness; use it.

    poor people: affairs are in confusion, deal with your own poverty.

    relatives: expect disappointment when you share your home with in-laws.

    sick people: are giving them the added burden of your negative attitude.

PLAGUE

04-10-23-27-34-37

being bitten by a rat: have a physical checkup immediately.

friends dying of the: delivery from suffering and pain.

  people: poor business, ending in thorough disgust.

having the: a wealthy marriage will be confused with mental instability.

  others: lucky discovery of money if you do not lose self-control.

people recovering from the: show lack of concentration and consistency at work.

rats being killed that caused the: will easily skirt any obstacles put in your way.

someone who can cure the: desires realized through wholehearted commitment to them.

PLAIN

14-22-24-26-36-42

arid, an: unhappiness and distress at a distance.

fruitful, a: will have a life of ease and pleasure.

of a vast open: listen for the sounds of distant messages and their messenger.

  children being on a: will make a pleasure trip with a guilty conscience.

  covered with grass: the remnant of your days will pass in relative comfort.

prairie, life on a: a struggle with your conscience against nature.

PLANE

08-09-22-29-41-42

owning a: are indifferent to the satisfaction of doing good work.

sharpening the blade of a: the recognition of your rights to build your life.

using a carpenter's: life will be shortened, but your ambition will be crowned.

  carpenter, a: your squandering of money will push you to accomplish better work.

  others: your efforts will be rewarded with success in undertakings.

PLANET

12-14-16-24-26-32

black: your ill-advised changes have disrupted progress.

falling: are working in vain to achieve a desire.

golden: your obstinacy has opened the present difficult period with malice.

of a: avoid being so superstitious, enjoy the peace and relaxation.

own horoscope: long life and fortune in old age with knowledge of the universe.

  children's: new expansion of creativity.

PLANKS

18-19-23-26-31-39

buying: will be in a restless state of mind until you establish your goals.

cutting: disappointment at the dimension of your false actions.

falling down a: will be disturbed during a love affair by the indifference of love.

others handling: unfortunate business affairs as others rob you of your profit.

piled up: public disgrace from personal injury perpetrated by one you disgraced.

selling: will have a satisfactory trip on a good sound route.

walking the, to board a ship: are giving up control of your life to another.

  to death: distress at your weakest moment.

  to debark: pending project will culminate auspiciously.

PLANTS

08-17-21-22-40-42

brambles: find your way through your maze with logical analysis, not empirical failure.

elder, ground: strong ambition to root out objectionable parts of yourself.

fern: your future is continually growing in disparate directions.

garden, in a: your friends alternate blooming.

home, in the: unwelcome changes will be, generally, for the better.

hothouse, growing in a: your opinions will attract heated and pointless discussions.

many: must weed out misunderstanding to allow your ideas to bloom.

medicines, used to make: unhappiness will disappear, interests will develop.

nettles, walking through: control of your pessimism is in another's head.

with lover: don't allow an Iago to come between you.

pachysandra: your space is continually invaded by an aggressive authoritarian.

planting: unexpected developments will alter planning.

thistles: antagonism from varied family illnesses causes grave unrest.

watering: children will grow up to be very intelligent.

PLASTER
02-18-20-25-32-35

being on the floor of own home: will suffer humiliation at the debasing of your actions.

coming off the wall of own house: reached the limit of family troubles.

falling on you: false accusations are being made against you.

handling: will soon experience many ups and downs.

mixing: are glossing over past misdeeds with an image of perfection.

PLATEAU
09-11-14-15-23-34

buffalo stampeding over the side of a: achievement without a business plan.

dieting and hitting a: you need a time of rest before you tackle the rest of the plan.

standing on top of a: take in every detail of your future life.

PLATFORM
11-15-17-24-29-38

being on a: be wary of an acquaintance who will not become a lover.

making a political speech on a: avoid hasty judgments for momentary expedience.

of a: will marry one you least expected had put you on a pedestal.

performing on a: accept advice to extract yourself from a difficult event.

watching a parade from a: triumph in a turbulent relationship with a vain, conceited lover.

PLAY
01-05-08-12-24-38

attending a: a short-lived fulfillment of your own dearest desire.

friends: will be escorted by a genial friend who wishes for more.

others: will be dunned by determined creditors.

with family: you can't go home again, but an enactment of it may be palatable.

ground: are making too much noise; nurture more mature relationships.

children at a: in your innocence, you do not notice who is hovering about.

hoop, playing with a: friendships are carefree only in childhood.

taking part in a: will overcome enemies, but not lover's other lover.

fire, a: will receive surprising and bad news about one you learn you care for.

PLEADING
05-09-11-23-25-34

attorney, for you, an: whatever you say will sound facetious; let the professional speak.

for others: the hypocrisy of innocence when you know you are guilty.

in another's defense: beware of being double-crossed, but apologize anyway.

own: aid from friends who are unexpectedly and staunchly loyal.

in defense of children: put mistakes right immediately or consequences will multiply.

of: take confidence in your own powers to spread your talents.

others, for you: the heart of your matter sounds real in another's voice.

PLEASURE
08-14-22-31-32-40

euphoria, having: a short-lived illusion, exposed in harsh light of reality.

having: another person is enjoying what you hoped to win.

children: congenial work and good news from an old playmate.

sweetheart: frivolity is disheartening in its fall into decadence.

PLOT
11-19-21-31-33-38

having a cemetery: if one is prepared, the crisis does not come prematurely.

of a, against you: will gain sufficient retribution to pay off your debts.

   to gain control: be wary of who is scheming against you.

   to injure another: misfortune will harass
you until atonement is met.

of a, of land: correspondence has one main
point—location, location, location.

   buying: the singularity of who you are
needs to be built.

   selling: you do not want to expose your
plan, at least not this one.

PLOWING
04-09-23-24-33-34

being broken, plow: your psychological
blocks can't be overcome; change direction.

farmer, a: field project will be profitable.

field, a: will not achieve success at first, it
will come later.

others: hard work ahead, as are splendid
rewards.

tractor, with a: will turn over real estate profitably.

   horse-drawn cart, a: the fast track is expedient but not always the most successful.

young people: honest, hard work will make up
for your misspent youth.

PLUMBING
09-15-19-36-39-41

being a plumber: your conscience is
following you.

cleaning a blocked drain: will see things in a
different light.

clogged-up drain, cleaning a: anemic emotions
need release to culmination.

leaking: continued obscure irritation from
harassing relatives.

pipe flowing steady: your confidence is missing the emotion.

plumbing for depths: your personality is a well
full of talents.

refitting pipes: are holding on to negative envy
and jealousy.

PLIERS
07-14-15-22-30-39

buying: wish to squeeze every drop out of
the situation.

large, a: don't go where you are being manipulated to go.

mechanics working with: others joke about
your inability to deal with simple parameters.

of: consistent joy and profit require ethics and
a willingness to work.

using: what you seek is within only your
grasp.

PLUMS
04-10-25-29-37-39

eating: will experience a disappointment that
will push you to a position of honor.

green: efforts will fail at a never-ending
friendship.

out of season: are forcing affection upon the
opposite sex.

picking ripe, from a tree: change of position in
employment.

pudding, making: your product is no longer
made with the original essential ingredient.

POCKET
03-04-05-06-10-34

book full of money: immediate success of your
writing.

   empty: shattered hopes of not having
covetous relatives.

catching a pick: would like to defend your
nonpayment of debt.

enemy's: will make up with enemies,
acknowledging each one's peculiarities
and faults.

having your, picked: a friend will turn
against you through the spiteful actions
of others.

hole in your: someone is skimming your
profit and blaming you for it.

knife, closed: your revenge is seething beneath
the surface.

   open: recognize your rage and use it
constructively.

mate's: will win at gambling, line relative's
pockets: misery.

watch: timing is everything; pay attention to
those stingy with it.

POETRY
05-20-23-24-36-41

being a poet: will have a hard life ahead and a
beautiful mind.

reading: study the nuances before you accept the deal.

    out loud: the cadence of your words has additional meaning.

satirical: you hide your intricate thought process behind a barbed attitude.

writing: solutions come in tightly cadenced packages.

    deeply serious: your passion for words needs an outlet.

    humorous: laughing at your own actions is the first step to freedom.

POISON
06-09-18-20-25-38

being poisoned: the gossip you spread remains in your system.

buying arsenic: will meet with contrariness in giving credit and lending money.

    taking: will contract a contagious disease.

dying from taking: a violent rejection of the cause of your suffering is in order.

giving, to someone: your lies will cause separation from a loved one.

of: others disregard you, with venomous actions.

poisoning another's drink: dishonesty of a person you now trust.

poisonous plants, cultivating: protect yourself from the envious, cursing illness.

ptomaine: gluttony has its rewards and its bill collector.

recovering from the effects of: your favorite food or drink may be poison to your system.

sumac: intellectual excellence does not prepare you for a cunning freeloader.

taking, yourself: you participated in spreading a plague.

    friends: do not speculate in stock market, make solid well-researched decisions.

    others: will encounter opposition with painful and distressing news.

throwing, away: success, regardless of all obstacles.

treacle as a cure for: will hear pleasant news that you remember from long ago.

    taking: will be detoxed and recover.

POKER
02-03-24-31-33-38

calling: will not have a decent relationship this year.

man dreaming of playing: attainment of almost every desire seems a bitter memory.

    married woman: are cheating on your husband.

    unmarried woman: should guard your virtue carefully and chose opportunities wisely.

playing: have good tastes and bad luck at attaining them.

    and concealing your hand: you see an enemy in every furrowed brow.

    with friends: total loss in your affairs can be regained in one hand.

        people who cheat: financial gains through embarrassing others for their inadequacies.

        unknown people: doomed to be disappointed by emotional, impressionable people.

winning the jackpot: bet on the dark horse.

POLES
01-19-20-22-25-34

cold isolation: pet project will be frozen out of business plan.

    storage: an obstinate refusal to extend your frozen emotions.

sledding to a: achievement of ambitions beyond your wildest dreams.

POLICE OFFICER
03-13-17-22-28-36

arresting you: will be wrangling with relations over family secret.

    others: believe partners in deal are stealing the profits.

    your friends: their affection will aid you in regaining your confidence.

being arrested by a: your ethics are in question, your actions are not.

    unjustly: a determined ally will win over every rival.

    with cause: guilt feelings for breaching your moral code.

being a witness for a: your evidence can be turned against you.

calling the: your domestic situation has reached a violent end.

feeling stalked by a: have strayed from your moral path, but will profit temporarily.

female, a: you react over-emotionally to your guilt.

handcuffing an arrested person: are a protector of the just to the unjust's detriment.

interrogated, being: the wrong people are inquiring into your credit.

killing a: don't weaken your case by intentionally flouting opposing opinions.

mace-bearer, being a: recover from feeling let down by a friend communicating anger.

of a: reassuring sight that inspires belief in yourself.

of a, station: apprehension over inability to honor commitments.

   being questioning at: will force alliance, that your partner will misinterpret.

     with friends: desire to meddle in other's affairs does not bring happiness.

siccing a, dog on you: will be expected to comply with rules you believe are wrong.

trailing you: your offense will not disappear without an apology.

using a club as a weapon: someone holds enmity against your luck and faithfulness.

POLITICAL
35-40-42-43-46-49

fanatic, being a: resolve the conflict within yourself before you inflict it on another.

man, being a: time to take charge of your life.

   company of a, being seen in the: disgrace to yourself for another's careless words.

party, affiliation with a: argue your conviction, then change party.

   another person's: a change for the better to come.

running a, campaign: your opposition is fruitless without programs for change.

POLLUTION
09-15-18-31-33-49

in the ground: dispose of evils thoroughly or they ultimately return.

   water: examine your thoughts before you expose yourself.

rain, acid: a bad business decision returns to haunt you.

smog, in the air: a change in one's work is needed.

POMEGRANATE
06-07-09-18-21-33

basket full of, having a: will be overbearing in your foolish actions.

breaking a, in two: persecution from tax collector.

eating: happiness, good health and longevity.

   the seeds: will remain in present condition and status.

spoiled, being: will fall heir to riches and pleasant company.

taking the juice from a: will return to be trapped in old patterns every year.

POND
11-15-16-18-29-40

being, in a: check the basic motive before getting involved.

   clear, a: wealth and lasting friendship through your grace and beauty.

full of dead fish: will soon go into bankruptcy.

   live: abundance and riches from being the star speaker of the tour.

muddy, a: quarrels within the home, a hilarity among business associates.

quiet, a: great affection between sweethearts.

PONY
05-19-33-36-39-42

children playing with a: will be seduced by a woman.

   riding: will be freed of bad accusations.

feeding a, in your hand: will be kissed by a woman.

newly born, a: will have a woman who loves you very much.

POOL
14-17-23-32-34-38

full of water: will forgive your enemies.

   with very little: refrain from stock market speculation.

of a garden: fortune is ahead of you, love is at your side.

playing: character is revealed in the choice of each stroke.

   dirty: your business will prosper.

POPE

06-09-20-25-26-36

death of a, the: postponement of success until misfortune is mourned.

receiving his blessing: will be forgiven by one you love.

surrounded with cardinals: your ventures battle the establishment.

talking with the: take a look in the mirror before you criticize another.

visiting the: rely upon own vigor to reach universal truth, though not conforming to it.

POPPIES

28-32-34-36-39-41

field of: money from an illegal source will cause great harm to many.

giving, away: successful pleasure trip, short-lived.

having, in the house: change for the better in your own affairs.

of: will have intelligent children who will be a sentimental delight.

picking: will have a dispute with your sweetheart.

red: your superstitions rule your passions.

seeds, eating: are pushing yourself past your abilities.

various other colors, of: will acquire riches in near future.

PORCH

04-15-18-35-36-37

crawling under a: will hear conversations people have with themselves.

eating on a: will have to be satisfied with present conditions, so that you won't seek more.

  with a lover: proposal is imminent, acceptance should never be.

sleeping on the: an adventure in the wild, under the protection of your home.

PORCUPINE

06-11-12-14-17-21

being stabbed by a, quill: will be maligned in print.

eating, meat: will have a touchy business affair.

killing a: a quick-tempered person can no longer influence you.

of a: are you aware you are a stingy, materialistic, defensive person?

pregnant woman dreaming of a: your husband will disclaim your child.

several: enemies are attempting to bring harm to you.

PORT

04-09-19-22-36-41

arriving at a foreign: happiness in love.

beautiful, a: will be defrauded.

being with others in a: will receive news from far away.

blockading a: will be mistaken for the enemy.

breakwater into a, passing the: must endure guilt.

  with sailors: some person holds secret enmity for you.

drinking: your sparkling intellectual conversations will go down well.

hole, looking through a: an adventure, combining an old friend with a new location.

landing in a: successful completion of a pet venture.

on a lake or river: will take a long voyage.

sailors coming ashore at: troubles in marriage.

sea, a: discovery of a secret.

vessel arriving in: death of a guest in the home.

PORTER

18-20-31-33-35-37

being a: misfortune and fatigue due to overwork and abuse by others.

carrying your luggage: a friend comes to your rescue.

  another's: will lose confidence in yourself.

  loaded with: your demands have been refused, your rationale will not be.

having a, helping you: you are the faithful mate of a hostile person.

PORTRAIT

09-13-33-37-41-42

children, of: will attain a high position in a select social gathering.

friend, of a: the layers will be exposed to salacious scandal.

painting ancestor's: will be gratified, but disillusioned, at his lack of importance.

  another's: will be a victim of artful persuasion.

children's: will abolish any envy and resign yourself to giving.

own: have overblown your own importance in the creation of a new enterprise.

receiving a gift of a: immediate success if you seek a change of location.

relatives, of: deceptive flattery fuels your vanity, but you will reject the giver.

sweetheart, of your: long-lasting love; a season of seductive pleasures.

women of a: your emotions are being thrust aside.

POSTERS

03-09-20-25-30-36

being photographed for a: are an exhibitionist who sees no other way for distinction.

drawing: will argue about a bill for food when there are larger issues at stake.

hanging a: an infirmity, after charges about the poster's content.

making a: reconciliation with your opponent on the issue at stake.

name and face on a: your irascible acts have been noticed.

on another's wall: wish fulfillment, theirs and yours.

POSTMAN

01-05-08-28-39-40

being a: your personal mission is to stamp out misdirected anxieties.

bringing letters: unpleasant news will reach you; avoid those wanting your money.

postcard, a: your deepest emotions and indiscretions will be exposed.

unable to read writing on a: read the small print before signing anything.

special delivery: pleasant distractions consume your attention.

giving a letter to a: will be hurt through jealousy, despite your confrontation of it.

not having letters for you: your decision, even if reversed, would not be accepted.

whistle of a, hearing the: will have an unexpected guest accompany the expected one.

POST OFFICE

03-10-22-29-30-31

being in a: will be victorious through honesty.

buying stamps at a: horizons are limited, expand them.

collecting: are obstinate in your defense of your value.

finding, closed: dissension in love affairs cannot be repaired in writing.

mailing a letter at the: will have obstacles in your path.

parcel post, package by: the return mail will bring a foreign gift.

receiving a: a profitable venture will aid in a relationship with the opposite sex.

receiving, from: inner conflicts will cause a change of residence.

registering: will be offended by someone and change companions.

postmaster, arguing with a: someone is trying to cheat you, but it may be your own stupidity.

POT

04-11-22-24-25-31

aluminum: your health is endangered.

being on a stove: will make good commercial profits.

burning yourself on a: loss of a dearly loved one.

buying new pots: devotion to new direction should dispose of all the old.

a complete set of: must take the wheat with the chaff.

contents are simmering: your emotions need time with themselves.

cooking food in a huge: be careful of plans and keep them to yourself.

copper, burning a: shows a lack of consideration for anxieties of others, but you don't feel.

filling a, with food: will move about, often searching for something you left behind.

overflowing: too much of a good thing leads to stagnation.

pottery, making a: the basic level of the life you wish to live.

stainless steel: an improvement in health comes soon.

throwing away old: people respect you for the wrong reasons.

woman dreaming of a: a baby is on the way.

POTATOES
05-19-20-27-31-37

baking: will have arguments with sweetheart over your lack of understanding.

boiling: will entertain an unwelcome guest to the dissatisfaction of a relative.

digging: big success in own efforts will crown your ambition.

eating mashed: your dreams of a comfortable income will come true.

   salad: investments will bring profits when you make various adverse choices.

feeding, to pigs: will be enticed by a woman, then fed unmerited slights.

frying: will marry a husky girl who will never be hungry yet eat everything off the plate.

peeling: will attempt many tasks and fail in the follow-through.

planting: dearest plans will materialize from the depths.

POULTRY
02-07-16-27-30-40

buying fat: family quarrels over a new proposal you are going to accept.

   fresh: will not be forced to take the consolation prize.

   fryers: brings considerable earnings on a good venture, your dissent on a bad one.

   stewing: no profit without glory, no conscience without arguments.

   uncleaned chicken, an: spiritual and material gains if you are willing to do the work.

   young: will have a change in your own position, due to a vivid imagination.

chick, a: another is displeased with your flitting about.

cleaning: someone will give you money that carries considerable trouble with it.

giving a gift of: much valuable time wasted on frivolous pleasures.

stuffed: friends will stick by you while your money lasts.

POVERTY
03-08-10-26-32-37

being in: will risk your reputation in unearned pleasure.

and very sick: will have many debts to pay before you reach the blissful heights.

indigent, grown children being: have an abnormal appetite to suppress your hunger.

   crippled people: be selective in your choice of companions; sincerity is required.

   others: will give beneficial service to others.

   relatives: shame and sorrow will be weathered until the new dawn.

lowest abject condition, in the: unexpected pleasing prosperity.

POWDER
05-06-10-19-20-38

buying talcum: opposition in your marriage is from displaced ambitions.

   face: will be extravagant in spending money and miserly in using it.

handling gun: the residue of your actions remains on your fingers.

   filling cartridges with: misery.

keg, guarding a: how seriously you take your responsibility depends on its validity.

powdering your face: vanity and hidden scorn; others see only your charms.

spilling: covering up for your actions infects them with guilt.

sprinkling, on sweetheart's body: sweetheart will get sick of your possessiveness.

using body: will have many boyfriends whom you will keep in turmoil.

   face: speak your conscience for lasting love.

POWER
10-13-18-24-31-40

being powerful: the higher the expectations, the bigger the loss.

having, in your position: your dominance must fit your capabilities.

of attorney, canceling a: will have trouble with finances; don't trust the help of strangers.

   giving: will have illness but recover.

   receiving: will place trust in someone under you.

own, going to your head: are overwhelmed with your own power.

taking advantage of your: express your
intentions, explain your motives and
go forward.

using power to hurt others: your disgrace is
proportionate to the time it takes you to
feel it.

PRAISE
19-27-29-30-40-41

giving: people are gossiping about your ability
to feel gratitude they cannot.

hearing others, you: will lead faithful friends
to profit and false ones to debt.

praising God: abundant means to live a
fruitful life.

  your children: will enflame another's ire
with your overblown ego trip.

receiving: are surrounded by scandal; don't
involve yourself in it.

PRAYING
05-14-29-34-36-38

and having prayer heard: will receive
fortunate advice and be asked to give it.

  not being: your lack of humility will
cause misfortune.

church, in: desires will be accomplished.

for someone to do something for you: bad
consequences you don't deserve.

  who has died: are requesting what you
missed and still miss.

God, to: listen carefully to insight within
you.

Jesus Christ, to: the rich comfort of a faithful
lifelong friend.

  cross of, the: infidelity is often what it takes
to get your point across.

others, for you: a simple act of support is with
concrete foundations.

possess a lady, to: your good reputation will be
squandered.

prayer book, reading a: some solace amidst the
chaos of your life.

  losing a: your faith needs bolstering, your
success needs a will.

  receiving a, as a gift: wise advice will come
as needed in every page.

someone else, for: dispute and difficulty
among friends.

with devotion: will have joy and happiness.

  others: change for the better.

PREACHER
07-12-17-21-27-40

being a: will have many ups and downs, but
plans will fail to materialize.

confessing to a: have strayed from moral
ground and need a hand out of the quag-
mire.

listening to a sermon: think deeply until you
have learned its significance.

  to a preacher: good advice is hard to
take; egotistical ramblings are even
harder.

    from out of town: discontent through
another's faultfinding.

preaching at a pulpit: don't follow orders of
one who has ulterior motives.

PRECIPICE
02-07-11-19-34-42

falling into a, and being killed: are at the brink
of being dishonored.

  living: your astral travels have concluded
successfully.

  others: change plans to avoid great outrage
and peril.

  woman dreaming of: will give birth to a
child, not her husband's.

looking up from a: people are making fun of
your external inactivity.

of a: your internal search for meaning in your
distress is exhausting you.

walking away from a: will overcome all losses
and calamities.

PREGNANT
05-13-15-20-28-36

being: your creativity is pushing you to move.

fetus alone in the womb: the birth of an idea,
the seed of which has been long awaiting.

man dreaming that his wife is: she will give
birth to a boy.

married woman dreaming of being: resolve
marital problems before having children.

  unmarried woman: trouble and injury
through scandal.

  widow: will marry very soon and have
more children.

  young girl: don't get married for a while or
it will prove disastrous.

widower dreaming of a, woman: will have to
fight long and hard.

woman dreaming of having a boy: safe delivery
with little suffering.
   girl, a: social pleasures followed by friction
   and misunderstanding.
young man dreaming of getting his girl friend:
remorseful conscience.

PRESCRIPTION
06-07-12-21-23-35

asking doctor for a: an illness protracted
after an ill-conceived adventure.
doctor writing a: good hopes cannot make
up for your careless stupidities.
filling a, for the family: will buy new clothes
whether you need them or not.
handling a: will receive advice on how to
handle problem; take it.
having a: will overcome present unhealthy
condition.
refilling a: will recover completely from an
illness.

PRESIDENT
02-12-17-20-24-32

being a: the greater the honors in the dream,
the lower your assessment of your value.
   elected: will receive blessing from God.
   impeached while: treason by friends; even
     more treason by you.
   reelected: you will be given a chance to
     right past wrongs.
   reelected: you will be given a chance to
     right past wrongs.
losing presidential position: are yielding to the
persuasion of deceit.

PRESS
08-13-14-31-36-39

Fourth Estate, being a member of the:
   guard your tongue and write with
   responsibility.
money-printing, a: will eat bitter bread and
have impoverished ideas.
olive, an: don't rely on friends.
owning a: quarrels over inheritance and the
responsibilities that entails.
printing on a: public disorder through
rumors written with ugly words.
wax, a: will receive an invitation to the
wedding of an unrequited love.
wine, a: are grasping at any known pleasure
not yet experienced.

working at a: your performance merits
distinction.

PRICKED
01-04-05-08-13-40

being, with a needle: are having fitful slumber
for fear that sleep is death.
   thorn, a: misinterpretations of perturbing
     events cause your loss of present posi-
     tion.
of pricking yourself: a gift will be made in a
loving spirit.
others getting: beware of public disgrace.

PRIDE
03-12-21-29-32-35

being harmful to you: people are gossiping
about your selfish ambition.
having, in yourself: you ignore others and
create enemies in the process.
not letting you humble yourself: your relationships are superficial.
others having: suffer from a persecution
complex as you await the success of
others.

PRIEST
04-06-11-23-31-40

aboard a ship, being: bad weather and
shipwreck must be experienced to
move you.
audience with a, having an: will soon be in
trouble for asking for more than your
just deserts.
confessing sins to a: are harboring suspicions
of those dealing in dangerous affairs.
family going to see a: quarrels within the
family need counseling.
in the street, being: humiliation from unjust
publicity.
of a: inheritance is near at hand, bringing
loneliness and troubles.
receiving advice from: many are guarding your
interest; not all are friends.
surplice, wearing a: one with evil intentions is
watching you.
talking to a: will have a position of importance and pride in your achievements.
woman dreaming of confessing to a: will not
marry one you love.
   young girl, a: will break your engagement
     for the wrong reason.

PRINCE

06-17-21-34-35-39

asking permission for audience with a: want church to show your value.

going with a: mate will not be able to live up to your expectations.

killing a: are unable to mount or master professional hurdles.

meeting a princess: splendor with intrigue, honor and the dissolution of decadence.

prince: idealizing romance blinds you to the real thing.

of a: guard against those jealous of a present given to you.

princess, residing with a: peril of death if you act on your desires.

seeing: will be very arrogant with friends who know the real you.

talking with: your self-conceit discourages a helpful woman.

PRINTING

10-14-17-26-29-42

books: rely upon your own vigor and believe in your creativity.

calling cards: patience will not be an advantage to you.

having something printed: an announcement.

letterhead, your: legal troubles over inheritance of your name.

looking at a, proof: beware of gossip, ignore it and write your piece.

newspapers: your well-informed opinions will be listened to.

office, operating a: will experience through others' opportunities.

official documents: will be discredited by the public for reciting another's words.

printer, being a: must exercise extreme economy through a decline in business.

printers, others who are: will experience poverty because of hidden family secrets.

reprinting books: your future is secure, if you continue to remember the past.

watching the printing process: guard against dangerous friends.

PRISON

07-11-12-14-31-32

barbed wire surrounding a: straying has irredeemable consequences.

being in: are dejected at being forced to account for your actions.

others: self-enslavement is an addiction; success in spite of it.

released on parole: you know the seemy side and are unafraid to report on it.

being released from: reject the current offer on the table.

cell, being in a: your behavior patterns need revision.

breaking out of a: feel restraints are unjustified; your addictions rule the roost.

empty: prefer to be left alone in love disputes.

looking from barred windows: whose scruples are blocking your action?

dining hall: food will never be sufficient to feed your hunger.

getting out of a: punishment for a short-lived fortune has been enough.

iron gate: need help of several friends to stimulate your creativity.

others being in a: need to elicit help of several friends.

prisoner, untying a: unexpected events will transpire.

remaining in: a triumph over a restrictive part of yourself.

trapped in a: a big disgrace will come to you from enforced restraint.

tunnel, trying to escape through a: your guilt is a journey, go through it.

visiting another in: your deeds have debilitated the friendship.

windows that are barred: others prevent any new action until you revisit your old actions.

PRIZEFIGHT

03-07-21-23-35-38

being a prizefighter: humiliation and misery if you fight outside the ring.

being in a: good food and a raise in salary within the month.

losing a: will lose at gambling and quarrel with lover.

winning a: you do not have control of yourself.

PROCESSION

01-13-24-30-31-36

happy people, of: are clamoring for attention with your inventive practical jokes.

lovers watching a: happiness, if they wish only to stay in the audience.

married person dreaming of a: long-lasting marriage will contain imperfections.

priests, of: beware of untrustworthy friends who would trick you into temptation.

religious, a: will be threatened with failure; it will take pomp and circumstance to block.

unmarried person being in a: want to be King Midas, if only for a week.

watching a: advancement within own position; hope of mercenary gain.

PROFANITY

05-10-13-20-21-23

others being profane: will have a fight and lose a friendship.

profaning the name of God in vain: financial losses from a disquieting situation.

teaching children not to be profane: will have a happy family but difficult public life.

violating sacred things: will suffer terrible pains due to your culpability.

    friends: will receive a legacy with a codicil attached.

    others: will incur large debts, your assets will drop in value.

    relatives: misery could develop into total degradation.

PROFESSOR

05-07-15-17-27-33

being a: will be conspicuously serious on a solemn occasion.

female: important and very beneficial events ahead.

male, teaching, a: preeminence in the field of endeavor.

teaching only women: material joys will not interfere with your spirituality.

    men: must rebuild the impoverished fortune of spirituality.

PROMISE

04-08-19-30-40-42

accepting a: be wary of expecting something of others you cannot give yourself.

making a: will be disillusioned with the outcome.

not keeping a: unceasing embarrassment at your over-extravagance.

receiving a: keep your own counsel and you will carry others' esteem.

    of matrimony: will accomplish your own desires; successful enterprises.

        refusing: it takes courage to stand by your emotions or lack thereof.

PROMONTORY

17-22-23-36-37-39

being on top of a: keen competition for financial gains changes to nipping at your heels.

    enemies: are in the grip of those who would stop at nothing to gain.

    others: outstanding events are just around the corner.

viewing a, in the distance: will be disillusioned at false accusations of irregular conduct.

PROPERTY

11-19-20-21-30-40

buying: cannot establish the substance of wealth without owning assets.

having a business on own: will not fail because of a raise in the rent.

having community: will sacrifice your own pleasure for the comfort of others.

    disposing of: you don't plan affairs well; sorrow will displace brightest hopes.

    settlement: will have very big projects commanding fortune and high esteem.

large estate of, having a: the enjoyment of worthily earned fortune.

    inheriting a: the forerunner of melancholy tidings will be in mourning.

prospective buyer of: you are a dreamer whose castles will be built if only in your mind.

receiving as a gift: will have agreeable conditions for prosperity.

    giving: will have a big family whom you wish to keep as friends.

selling: swift devaluation of your prominent plan.

    in the country: disgrace from the thoughtless complaints of others, but ultimate gains.

PROPHET

04-14-16-20-26-38

being a: if you don't know what you wish for, you can't get it.

making prophecies: will be involved in dangerous and mysterious things.

> *others, to you:* rely on your own good judgment and inspirational dream message.

of a: don't rely on unfaithful promises of others, make your own.

PROPOSALS

12-13-14-23-28-39

accepting a: will be tormented by doubts; errors in judgment will cause inward rage.

making a: will be invited for dinner and pay the check.

> *others:* family quarrels; you have the solution.

> *relatives:* will have a quiet old age dodging arrows of noisy, nosy neighbors.

receiving a: age can be deceiving until it catches up with you.

refusing a: unsatisfied curiosity is a difficult load to bear.

your, being refused: will put all your resources in the wrong basket.

PROSECUTOR

16-21-24-35-39-48

arguing with a: accusations have scars long after innocence is proven.

being a: have plenty of friends who support your actions.

going against your enemies, a: improper impulse to gain honor at another's expense.

of a: are being deceived that your moral sense has value.

others being prosecuted: business will decline until you clear your conscience.

PROSTATE

09-14-18-23-41-47

having an operation on the gland: damages in the future, in your business.

> *relatives:* will discover a secret and keep it.

others suffering with, troubles: dissension between partners that you could alleviate.

pains in the, having: unwise promises will be made by you.

PROSTITUTE

01-06-10-19-22-34

being a: are coarse and unfeeling to others, thus to yourself.

dancing, a: will go back to your sweetheart, totally committed.

dead, a: a notorious person will fall in love with you.

embracing a: will trample on her feelings unnecessarily.

hearing a, speak without seeing her: that you don't see it, doesn't mean it doesn't exist.

lying with a: security is not portable.

many: honor and blessings from those working for the downtrodden.

pregnant, a: will deceive your betrothed as to your purity.

receiving a, into own house: others will condemn you without proof.

very kind, a: will receive a bad business report on your energetic pursuits.

visiting a: troubles in home life for which you have received righteous scorn.

well-built naked, a: good hopes after a short illness and heavy medication.

who is a man: are a favorite of the opposite sex and your own.

who thinks she is a man: will give birth to a boy.

PROTESTING

03-10-28-31-38-51

actions of enemies: only make you as ugly as them.

making a legal protest: will receive an invitation to dinner.

others, to you: will be deceived in your estimate of the other's honor.

own innocence: are looking for a fortune but unable to find it.

political views: will engage in activities that will detract from your just merits.

PROTOCOL

32-36-37-40-41-43

doing things according to: unmitigated disaster and disclosure of all past misjudgments.

> *against rules of:* people are gossiping about you; take the road less traveled.

handling, documents: make plans for a rainy day, routing each step.

book: will receive a promise of matrimony with rules attached.

PROVIDING
25-35-42-44-46-51

children, for: will receive riches when they add their earnings to your investment.

family, for the: will be compensated with salary for work done.

mate, for a: will live together under favorable circumstances.

means for charity: good earnings and profit require you return your share.

things for business: will be disillusioned over the significance of your contribution.

PROVISIONS
03-06-12-23-31-34

being hungry and can't buy: aims have missed materialization but can be gained.

buying: are discrete in choosing lover from many.

> *others:* new acquaintance will ripen into lasting friendship.

giving, to others: have provided for yourself sufficiently to share.

having plenty of: prosperous surroundings don't mean they are yours.

many, being stored: keep your mind above material frivolity; will live long and well.

PSYCHIATRIST/PSYCHOLOGY
01-18-24-45-51-53

being a: are your own best counsel; perceive yourself.

having hallucinations: not seeing things in actuality for fear of having to change them.

> *nervous condition, a:* all dreams are creatively crazy; will discover a treasure.

> *others:* guard against perjury in testifying on a friend's behalf.

hydrophobia, suffering from: enemies will foil you by dishonoring your friends.

> *multiple personality disorder:* aspects of your personality need to inter-communicate.

> *others:* will be betrayed by one you trust implicitly, after sharing your self-exploration.

inferiority complex, having an: are prone to be apprehensive; protect your flanks.

kleptomaniac, being a: others who see you in the appearance of evil are evil themselves.

maniac, seeing a: will be accused of misappropriating another's belongings.

memory, having a loss of: sometimes it is wise not to remember.

> *amnesia:* will uncover a mixed message about a lucrative job offer.

missed appointment with: want full control to discover yourself and plan your life.

regaining: will acquire skills that you attribute to others.

therapist, seeing a: one who allows you to guide your own path through life's lessons.

transport went in other direction: approach therapy from another's anger.

undergoing: bridge the gap between external and internal.

PSYCHIC
09-14-30-45-50-54

clairvoyant, being: whatever you suspect is most likely true.

power, being possessed with: change of occupation will rile new associates.

reading your fortune, a: gather advice from all sources, then decide your action.

soliciting a: are desperate for sound advice about friction in family.

PUB
01-08-14-25-39-44

being with friends in a: have feelings for one who does not share them.

businessman dreaming of being in a: danger around corner, but not with your peers.

> *farmer:* are wasting precious time on bad crops and ignoring the good.

> *lovers:* deceit by one loved and trusted who became careless with the future.

> *married people:* much false praise, lies and deception fall unstintingly upon you.

drinking in a: carelessness in business affairs brings professional enmity.

owning a: will work hard to recover from losses.

relatives being at a: will be invited to a friend's home.

PUDDING

08-23-34-41-46-51

buying a: terrible gossip is being spread about you.

cooking a: indulgence in insatiable thirst for gain.

eating: will make money, but be disappointed in love.

    at a banquet: a prosperous but uneventful, comfortable life.

    children: financial improvement in the family.

giving a, as a gift: reckless lavishness without substance.

receiving a, as a gift: good returns from a source you expected nothing from.

PULLING

15-27-36-39-46-53

allowing someone to pull you: that rung in your ladder to maturity is lost.

someone, you: change to a direction you choose, even if you have to walk alone.

wagon, a: accomplish by your own steam and carry others.

    others: lead the team, for all to profit from the experience.

    struggling to pull a: want others to work for you without pulling your weight.

PULPIT

07-10-15-28-31-44

being at a: the ability to lead draws the anger of the envious.

giving a sermon from a: hard work ahead to use your influence.

    friends: the truth, as you see it, is not theirs.

    priest, a beautiful: act upon the advice offered.

of a: will achieve a good standing among people.

PUMP

01-04-26-30-40-42

drawing water from a: you will be tormented by your significant other.

of a: will have money, increased freedom and independence in your work.

operating a, by hand: fear of sad news makes you work harder.

priming a: setting parameters for the deal is as important as the deal.

    unable to prime the: your prosperity is temporary.

pumping clear water: temporary gloom with spirits of encouragement.

    muddy: will talk to people who annoy you about your questionable business success.

    others: others, less successful, seek your influence.

using a, to run by a motor: will receive disgusting news that strengthens your resolve.

    fire, a: will receive surprising and bad news about one you learn you care for.

PUMPKIN

02-18-36-40-42-53

buying a: actions will be discovered and criticized publicly.

    pie: misfortune in love affairs is not of a lasting character.

        eating: will contract a serious disease that can be cured with simple remedies.

        making a: a treacherous friend is seeking revenge; throw it back in his face.

growing: your headlong rise will be dishonored by your malicious gossip.

jack-o'-lantern: deceptive signs are tempting, but in the wrong direction.

picking a: the beginning of a relative's demise in the world's eyes and yours.

PUNCH

05-09-11-19-44-53

being punched by someone else: a recent controversial decision will cost you friends.

drinking: unpleasant news shattering your hopes and dreams.

making: a joy of short duration, a hangover of long duration.

offering a drink of, to someone: your bad reputation will be exposed by yourself.

punching an enemy: only new interests and surroundings will relieve your anger.

    friend, a: a serious argument causes misfortune in love affairs.

someone with your fist: annoying emotional reactions that you can't control.

PUNISH

03-05-19-42-44-49

being punished: unexpected pleasure at hand under lowering financial troubles.

court, by a: humiliation but a strong sense of transgressions needing justice.

family, by the: triumph over enemies does not occur with uninvolvement.

others: are being deceived by news from absent people.

others, by: troubles ahead with business partner for not actively participating.

executing punishment to offenders: unjustifiable jealousy.

pilloried, being: will be charged with a debt long since redeemed.

punishing another: will have ill-tempered husband or wife.

children: lasting friendship if you take that well-earned day off.

self-inflicted punishment: is stronger than the crime.

PUPPETS

11-21-26-32-40-46

being a: you succeed with lovers because you put yourself first.

dominated by a, master: desire strong personage to protect and guide you.

pulling your strings: feel helpless in your inferiority; snap the strings.

handling: will have a family argument over your strong organizational capabilities.

important person dreaming of: have faithful help required for future happiness.

of: cannot control your employees' efficiency enough.

PUPPY

05-06-41-43-45-49

buying a: will have much happiness from true friends.

many: are not prone to becoming intimate with people.

of a: will be invited to a joyous party of warm and cuddly friends.

owning a: will give money to charity and love easily.

PURGATORY

07-19-22-37-42-43

ancestors being in: the unhealthy daydreams of a mire-clogged brain.

others: abundant means are temporary, combined with deceitful ambition.

relatives: good luck to one for whom you care through others' generosity.

being sent to: will travel a long distance to assume your dignity.

of: where you wish those you disagree with would end up.

PURPLE

decorating room with: humility becomes you better than ostentation.

riding in a, car: joyful journey through transformation.

wearing: acting royally will bring ill will.

robes: have legal authority to proceed.

regal: develop greater self-confidence by overpreparing.

PURSE

02-04-17-33-37-50

buying a: will be extremely busy attending a wedding, funeral and political event.

finding a, with money in it: loss of power and control of possessions.

without: misunderstanding between relatives about your ill-mannered conduct.

giving a, as a gift: righteous scorn of friend does not alleviate the feud.

receiving: careless routine matters will cause your feelings to be trampled needlessly.

losing your: your past is gone; your indecision is the future.

lovers dreaming of finding a: will receive money you have been looking for.

losing: will misplace something you badly need.

snatching a: are trapped in an inclusive defensive circle of a relationship.

PURSUED

04-12-16-25-26-54

being: the chaser wants to enjoy your clear conscience.

by a man: turn and face who is talking badly about you.

the law: expect significant gains in the future.

vague figure: you must face your dragons and defeat them.

women: contentment if indeed she were your choice.

others: take care of that tax problem.

pursuing others: want what others believe is their right, not yours.

PUTTY

04-05-10-11-16-20

buying: will misplace something you need and replace it with something more useful.

molding: solidify your own thoughts before you try to influence others.

using: results from material work can be corrected.

in own house: will soon have a fight at home about your hazardous choices.

others: don't listen to foolish gossip, unless you make up some of your own.

PUZZLES

08-25-27-28-49-50

a, you can solve: after righting wrongs, labor for the advancement of other.

can't: expect heavy losses with a hasty union that will prove unsuitable.

others working on: many events will attack your integrity.

relatives: expect more trouble with relatives than anticipated.

solving a: pleasant surroundings after taking control of complex problem.

PYRAMIDS

03-17-21-23-28-49

married person dreaming of: with renewed confidence you will attain a high position.

widow: another marriage is ensured after a lengthy journey.

young woman: unhappy in choice of first husband, second is exceptional.

of: the soul acts while you sleep, disturbing your serenity, to create peace.

partially in shadow, a: are self-possessed when facing insurmountable obstacles.

resting on its tip: will face destitution and dependence upon relations.

viewing, with relatives: abundance and prosperity led by a single will.

Q Q Q Q Q

QUACK

08-12-14-39-43-44

being a: will overcome enemies but not suspicions, which will obstruct your healing.

consulting a: only you can tell your true body's health, if you listen.

of a: change of surroundings in your desperation gives false hope.

under the care: will be a nuisance to society when you attribute your remission to him.

others going to a: are stubborn in undertakings; legitimate treatment may be improper.

QUAILS

02-06-25-47-50-54

coming from a pond or sea: someone will steal something from you to torment you.

flushing a covey of: an instant high followed by several lows.

flying: disillusionment over failed expectations.

many: will have remorse over your inability to change bad business ventures.

rotten: arguments over general uncertainty will be hung in public.

QUAKER

05-08-11-22-29-42

being a: conduct your negotiations honorably.

community, a: are surrounded with jealous people; find a group of supportive ones.

dealing with a: you begrudge tenderness shown by your friends.

doctor, a: carelessness in your generosity will cause serious loss.

of a: are confronted with simple truths; act upon them.

QUANTITY

02-05-17-24-32-53

buying in: are blessed with good friends.

of articles: avoid squandering money, when a dollar will do.

selling things in: profit becomes greater when multiplied.

sending or giving, of things: will be persecuted for crossing state lines with contraband.

storing, of things: build yourself a pyramid to protect yourself.

QUARANTINE
02-11-13-16-26-34

being put in: will avoid danger by not fighting the cancellation of your project.

  house: will forgive friends for your being isolated by their argument.

  vessel: will make good earnings slowly and tediously.

isolating yourself in: the connection with your partner has been severed.

QUARREL
07-30-32-37-44-46

having a family: have an opposition of values to face at home.

  business: warning of contact with one contaminated with anger.

  partner, with a: will have mastery over many matters, not the home.

  stranger, with a: this is one person you wish you had never met.

quarreling with a friend: mean deeds by malicious minds.

  sweetheart: making up will make things much better.

  wife or husband: will be guilty of foolish actions against mate's authority.

starting a: pick an opponent to whom you can lose or win, gracefully.

QUARRY
05-12-14-30-32-45

digging in a stone: a high level of energy for an endeavor that protects your energy.

enemies owning a stone: will enjoy success in business after careful savings.

falling into a: will suffer much at the hands of untrustworthy friends.

  and getting out: discovery of the cold truth and having to live with it.

    unable to get out: expect serious troubles, but you're respecting the wrong judgment.

  others: will eke out a modicum of fortune and happiness.

selling stone from a: will be a slave to prejudice, barring your building pyramids.

QUARTER
13-19-28-33-47-48

being given a: loss in business through lack of investment capital.

changing a: misery at its loss in value and in your age.

giving others a: worry will not be smoothed away.

having a: will be unfortunate in business affairs from lack of cash flow.

quarterly payment, receiving a: bringing your debts into manageable form.

  paying a, bill: will begin gambling with the money held for payment.

receiving a, of something: delay in business affairs, when raw materials are delayed.

QUEEN
02-13-22-23-33-43

being a: will be confronted as being over-involved in office politics.

going to see a: you desire your lover's dependence on you.

having an interview with a: rebellion against the influence of a beloved matriarch.

Madonna, of the church: will be pardoned for your sins to keep your stabilizing influence.

of a: your hunger for power and lust for fame offends those with no possibilities.

sending a letter to a: don't expose your intentions until face to face.

surrounded by her court: arrival of news from all parts of the realm.

QUESTIONS
10-11-13-25-35-39

accepting an answer to a: warning of troubles if you force the questioning further.

answering, correctly: all will go well from the beginning of the relationship.

  incorrectly: will go to any length to enforce your right to privacy.

asking, of children: your trusted position carries much weight.

  friends: your integrity is much admired and sought after.

  husband: knowing too much only conflicts the heart of the matter.

  relatives: will overcome petty jealousies only if you question yourself.

wife: congeniality does not hide the threat to your relationship.

inquisitive, being: do not despair in your heart at the close supervision of your work.

others, about you: poverty through desertion.

relatives: don't interfere in another's business; only your boss interferes with yours.

refusing to answer a: your frankness will get you in worse trouble than you are guilty of.

someone asking questions of you: don't answer loaded, prejudiced questions.

QUICKSAND
03-13-15-16-32-34

being sucked into: are bogged down with emotional debt.

handling: do not be indiscreet about your fear of death.

help another out of the: others' affairs are off-limits to your nosy prying.

of: are surrounded with many temptations that will drag you into the mud.

something sinking into: will be cheated by friends forcing their addictions on you.

others: your wish fulfillment for those who have harmed you.

QUIET
18-26-27-33-41-43

asking people to be: a fit of temper playing off another's passive aggression.

being: unhappiness at the nervous shock caused by the interrupting noise.

quieting people fighting: will make peace among enemies.

children: frustrations cannot be dealt with by hitting another.

neighbors: only issues confronted and discussed have a chance at resolution.

QUILT
04-17-25-27-51-52

beautiful, a: will realize own ambitions for the unity and emotional ties of your family.

being straight on a bed: the household is in order: past, present and future.

down: luxury is important in its efficiency and enhancement of practicality.

falling from the bed: a clunk on the head to remind you of reality.

patchwork, a: the rearrangement of life into the protection of bodily warmth.

soiled, a: are burdened with exasperating cares.

QUINCE
10-27-29-30-36-47

cooking: will be persecuted by a woman of ill fame.

eating: will fall heir to money without the experience or ability to manage it.

making jelly from: an expensive investment for meager return.

picking: must reach around the greedy few.

spoiled: your investment in the relationship was for naught.

tree blossoming, a: the temptations of prosperity unearned do not equate to wealth.

shaking: your insistence on perfection strangles your emotions.

with fruit on it: a delicate joy and a simple pleasure.

QUININE
24-26-38-39-42-46

buying: for relief from an untenable feverish condition.

giving, to children: will have riches of self-expression all their life.

engaged couples: temperature of your ardor will drop in time as quarrels increase.

relatives: be cautious, meager and uncertain in all your dealings.

of: be spurred on to live a healthy life of continuous friendship and mutual assistance.

taking: renewed energy will brighten your life and take you away from frustration.

R R R R R

RABBI
07-11-23-35-38-53

arguing with a: will make an advantageous peace with enemies.

being a: will be in financial misery, but live comfortably.

consulting a: will be prosperous in business and invest your profit wisely.

discussing with others, a: your despondency and paranoia are ill-founded.

reading, a: fortune in knowledge at your fingertips.

talking to a: are deceived by the friendly appearance of enemies, when facing the truth.

RABBITS
02-15-20-27-45-47

black, a: failure of enemies to pull your demise out of their hat.

breeding: your money will multiply on its own, as will your family.

eating a: will have a quarrel with a friend and an apology by letter.

foot: prosperity when you will finally appreciate it.

having, in own backyard: time to move to the city and enjoy life with the big kids.

running: a change in occupation, and you will be uncommonly productive.

   several: business ventures move smoothly to bring high returns.

shooting: stop the people trying to take over your life.

white, a: wish fulfillment for purity and fertility.

RACE
13-14-16-41-48-50

dog, a: will have mastery over your enemies if you learn to pace yourself.

marathon: must answer for misdeed you deemed an accident.

running a: must preserve your energy if you desire long-term success.

   and winning: commercial undertakings of import will be consummated.

   losing: will have many competitors in your affairs.

   friends: will stand by you, whether you win or lose.

   jockey, in a: will gain in stature just for finishing the race.

   member of family: are demanding too little of yourself.

others: are being deceived by unsportsman-like behavior.

track, running on a: repeat old patterns for success; others aspire to them.

RACECOURSE
04-07-15-48-49-52

being at a: are making irrational, unstable contracts.

   hurt at a: will visit someone staying at an inn and enjoy comfort for little money.

enemies at a: others aspire to your goals but don't know how to work for them.

   friends: death of a hard-earned success; birth of speculation.

   important personalities: hard work awaits you after a series of misfortunes.

   many people: pleasant company but danger of losses; reality passes at breakneck speed.

   relatives: expected reverses in a peaceful intermission from fighting.

your jockey losing the race: a supporter will rile you with his overconfidence.

   winning: a rival will take sweetheart's affection, caring for her in a worldly way.

your racehorse winning: have many enemies who would still be friends, if you lost.

   losing: will have many competitors, take them on intelligently and singly.

RACEHORSES
01-11-33-40-43-52

betting on a: are demanding your partner face his demons and commit.

owning a: attempt to economize while there is still time.

paddock, exercising, in a: speed up your reaction time, then settle to a reasonable pace.

   being in the inside, pasture: do not speculate with news of an engagement.

   others: an engagement will be called off, due to fluctuating financial affairs.

riding a: loss through indiscriminate speculation by your partner.

training, at a: your character and personality are imitated.

RACKET

12-15-29-37-53-54

creating a very loud: will receive criticism for talking over another's words.

  others: are foiled in participating in amusements.

hearing a: will suffer a nervous spasm at this jar to your system.

operating a: are tempted to interplay with characters and act contrary to your ethics.

racketeer, proposal by a: are likely to suffer an unexplainable malady.

tennis, a: good luck to one for whom you care; an extension of your power.

  own: adjust your gut to be evenly proportioned.

  playing with a: will have mastery over many matters; don't stop gaining more.

    others: beware of the undermining determination of others to win at any cost.

RADIO

13-28-32-41-50-53

listening to a familiar voice on a: secrets have been revealed to you in tone and tenor.

  music on a: are avoiding the issue with busy work.

purchasing a: pleasant encounter with new friends and their varied impassioned opinions.

static from a: your agitation will increase until a decision is made.

  causing: will be reprimanded and have to account for the ramifications of your behavior.

turning off a: are restless at being contained in a relationship.

RADISHES

05-12-28-32-47-48

buying: discovery of domestic secrets; manipulating you through flattery.

eating: passing troubles from bitter remarks.

  others: change your surroundings to avoid critical people.

  horse: put your anger in a letter and do not mail it.

of: an innocent act to you is a sin to your enemies.

raising, to sell: your ambitions will be quickly realized.

  for own use: will suffer from other's ambitions at your expense.

RAFT

01-20-23-25-50-54

buying a: will change residence to a distant country.

sailing on a: others will travel, you will seek peace at home.

  family: uncertain journeys to expand your intimate circle.

  others: will hear false promises.

  saving own life: will have mastery over your own affairs.

selling a: have a solid foundation, be encouraged about the future.

very big and long: will travel until your indolence turns to action.

RAGE

02-04-10-20-40-43

going into a: if not controlled, may terminate in bodily harm.

  man, a: passing love that could only result in unpleasantness.

  relatives: family unhappiness caused by one you loved.

  with friends: concerns health issues that are already on your mind.

  with sweetheart: disappointment over lover's frivolity; it's not with you.

husband being in a: desperation over loss of future wife does not help you today.

  others: business affairs contained in a rut, repeated by rote, wither and fail.

  sweetheart, a: have been snubbed by lover and need to exact revenge.

  wife, a: a better future awaits her, if she divorces her unfaithful mate.

  woman, a: will be justified, but not advantageous to your position.

pacify another in, trying to: your behavior needs reexamination.

RAGS

14-20-23-32-35-52

being a, dealer: must economize for the future and be less lazy today.

children being in: own desires will be granted in short order.

338

enemies: recovery of old problems and issues needing cleansing.

friends: will quarrel with friends over their lack of ambition.

many people: must throw aside difficult routes and find the most direct one.

rich people: a risky venture could prove expensive; a well-considered one, profitable.

gathering: big arguments over your inability to make a decision.

making: your choice will prove accurate and sage.

rag man selling: will be introduced to high-class people who will benefit your project.

red: have left your possessions at risk; but being malfuncting, are not worth stealing.

washing: the arrival of distant relatives reintroduces "opportunity" into your vocabulary.

RAID
04-08-19-22-25-53

air, an: will lose property and the chance to stabilize.

armed forces, an: revenge under the rules of engagement.

being caught up in a: one inadvertent error will cause you to gain irregular income.

observing a, from safe quarters: one false move could prove deadly.

own home being raided: will have emotional sorrow from an uncertain source.

another's: sort out misdeeds or you will lose the love you cherish.

police, a: exposing a minor personal problem before its resolution will avert an arrest.

RAILING
05-09-14-34-38-43

broken: are confronted with insurmountable obstacles; consider alternate, Plan B.

cars stopped at, crossing gates: are awaiting a decision that can turn about your career.

others with hands on a: it's always smart to look before you leap, or are pushed.

racing toward a broken track: be wise to illegal activities in your career.

a damaged bridge: are too weighted down to see the truth or prevent what it warns.

sitting on a: a slight delay while you reevaluate your plans.

that breaks: this is not the time for taking chances.

RAILROAD
04-24-32-41-45-50

being at a, station alone: are preparing for a rapid rise in your business.

with friends: hard times on a new project until you establish momentum.

relatives: abundant means if you leave present situation.

being forced to walk the rails: the long string of tasks you are leaving behind.

being in a, car alone: an odd assortment of Samaritans will aid you.

with children: hard work to raise them in a mobile situation.

friends: a healthy, active social life does not eliminate the possibility of foul play.

relatives: good business transactions from skilled manipulation of affairs.

changing switches: the good, as outlined, is not what you want.

colliding: your plans, as outlined, will be catastrophic.

crossing: are at cross-purposes with your life.

borders: wish to escape from the challenge of success.

enemies being in a, car: a catastrophe is ahead of unfavorable turns.

others: use caution in business activities, others may disappoint you.

jumping track: are ambivalent about a proposed change in direction.

signals, ignoring: move forward with caution on your new job offer.

station, waiting at the: need a boost from a mentor with influence.

for a late train: take time and attention to detail in new relationship.

spending the night in a: an encounter long ago leaves a residue of guilt.

switching engines: reevaluate the leadership and consider the opposition.

underground: an obstacle needs for you to be attentive to it.

walking on the wrong track: have maneuvered yourself into a corner.

RAIN

15-24-35-37-44-46

big downpour of, and bad wind: exclude friends from your confidence.
  and hailstorm ruining crops: abundant means ahead.
  cold: good luck with money, but read the fine print.
businessman dreaming of: misfortune in business.
  farmer, without wind or storm: seek pleasures at the expense of another's prosperity.
dripping into a room: beware of desolation from false friends.
drizzle: less serious emotional situation, fortune will come in minute doses.
forest: a rich source of inspiration and of healing.
getting wet in a downpour of: suffering from suspicious friends for unperformed duties.
hearing patter of, on the roof: great marital happiness, but business is limited.
humidity, suffering from: your arrogance corrupts you, to your ultimate embarrassment.
mist: problems not seen clearly; are guided too easily by emotions.
others being out in the: find a common ground; yield and hear another's view.
  women: disappointment in love will reveal a more fertile direction.
poor people dreaming of, with hail: good opportunities and happy life.
  rich people, a downpour: losses, vexations, and affliction in love.
puddle, step in a: your slightest misstep will be exaggerated.
  over a: leave the old and fertilize the new.
    laying down your coat for another to step over a: your reputation is losing ground.
shelter from the: have found your niche; designs will mature with springtime growth.
soaked by a cloudburst: success through luck, not brains.

sun shining through the: cry your heart out, and let it go.
very bad, and windstorm: lover will leave you out in the cold.

RAINBOW

03-15-19-24-25-31

at noon: betterment of fortune followed by troubles like you have never known.
  sunrise: big riches as your horizons open up.
  sunset: happy and contented times of rest and relaxation are ahead.
being near a: the end reveals path to be taken and the means to do so.
children seeing a: will be healthy and intelligent and frolic in their youth.
  lovers, together: happy marriage and riches after a period of the worst trouble.
married woman dreaming of a: change in love affairs to permanence before long.
  unmarried woman: a beautiful present is received for passing on tempting indiscretions.
  young girl: will have an agreeable sweetheart.
over your head, being: will show false pride without acclaim to match.

RAISINS

28-33-35-39-41-45

buying: be cautious in business ventures as wealth will come slowly.
cooking: several small presents will soften the blow.
drying: will receive an unexpected visit from the past.
eating: will spend money faster than you earn it.
selling: ignoring displeasure does not equate to happiness.

RAKE

03-34-39-42-52-54

buying a: are industrious in a tricky situation.
of a: beware of talkative thieves who alienate you from your love.
raking leaves: a wedding to occur soon to solve financial problems.
  hay: your considerable physical stamina is guided by a strong will.

stepping on a, and being bonked by it: a series of incidents laughable in their tragedy.

using a driveway: are too cautious in forming new relationships.

   farmers: good friends will take care of your necessities; you, the luxuries.

RAMS

01-11-30-39-40-45

buying: expect nothing but respect and you will get it.

having many: energy, aggressiveness and impulsiveness without contemplation.

killing a: will lose a lawsuit for requests not serviced.

of a: are falling into a trap that will require tact and judiciousness to free yourself from.

raising a: will receive an unexpected visitor, running headlong toward you.

selling: big gains.

RANCH

18-21-40-41-42-47

buying a: must endure unhappiness for a short time.

owning a: joy and prosperity in your social circle from the theater.

rodeo, riding in a: a reunion with cause for much celebration.

selling a: will gain flack for parroting unproven gossip.

working on a: a wedding will soon take place.

RANCOR

10-12-26-28-34-37

existing between mates: a violent assault will cause a separation that will soon take place.

   relatives: will have a devastating blow to your peace and contentment.

having secret, for someone: will have good friendships if you open up to them.

of: will harbor hate for others, causing your loneliness and pessimism.

others having, against you: will make good earnings in business.

RANGE

10-17-18-22-32-46

cooking on a wood: will be professional in your economy.

having a coal: are prone to incurring too many debts.

of an open expanse of: will be visited by sweet-talking people.

shooting, a: will keep busy and enjoy happiness.

   being with others at: persecutions will be rejected; there's meager, if any, evidence.

working on the open: will have unhappiness.

RAPED

08-20-40-44-47-51

being: dispense feelings of self-degradation, to match your outward dishonor.

   by a woman: acute feelings of dishonor and embarrassment.

   friends: envy their social graces and want to degrade them.

   over twenty-one: unconscious criticism should be kept to yourself.

   raping someone underage: someone is libeling you unjustly.

RARE

05-09-34-38-40-50

buying, items: will have big disputes with friends over nostalgia.

eating, meat: your joy at work accomplishments is attracting praise from superiors.

gems: will have affliction and uneasiness in seeking adulation.

of, items: have a highly egotistic nature, you desire what no one else can have.

book: your sensitivity needs a less hyper outlet.

stamps: are astute to understand history before it repeats itself.

RASCAL

12-20-39-43-45-48

being a, yourself: your public esteem is exasperating to an outsider.

businessman dreaming of a: increase of trade and comfortable income.

   woman: will lose a friend's high regard; keep your own counsel.

   young girl: will receive a proposal of marriage.

many: are recognized as a perfect gentleman at the height of his career.

RASH
13-32-42-45-47-53

children having a: have an honest conscience and dishonest enterprise.

  friend, on the face: must use strenuous means to establish your rights.

having a, on the body: beware of speaking too hastily.

  face: one you haven't seen for a long time will visit.

  legs: embarrassment without being too serious.

RASPBERRIES
22-35-36-43-48-54

buying: will suffer disillusionment, as they are never as good as straight from the bush.

eating black: a tiny disloyalty is a relationship breaker.

  red: seek out friends who are salt of the earth.

making jam from: lover will be industrious and a good provider.

picking: friends are concealing something from you, trust your visions.

RATS
18-24-38-42-44-53

bait for, putting out: your intelligence determines your future.

being bitten by a: envy will create an arch-enemy out of a best friend.

catching, in a trap: are disliked by others for your cowardice.

  cat, in the house: unfinished business will become successful.

gnawing: an acquaintance is envious of your life.

killing a: deviousness will attend all undertakings.

many: serious trouble from another's dishonesty, leading to poverty.

of: injury caused through deceit and decay of trust.

placing hands on a: will succeed by dealing with the worst, first.

rat catcher, of a: you will soon attract a new lover.

  catching rats in a field: are committing treason by betraying another's confidence.

many: will receive vindication from people who did you wrong.

  white: wish ruin of very bad enemies; get over it.

sweethearts dreaming of: fear a rival does not believe you deserve to be so fortunate.

swimming from a sinking ship: row your boat in the other direction.

trap, setting a: that which you have feared will be tempted to expose itself.

white: don't follow the leader; take the tunnel with the light at the end.

RAVENS
06-12-17-24-35-47

flapping wings: death through lack of cleanliness and abundance of decay.

flock of, flying together: avoid disaster by going tried and true route.

flying: your present life is in danger; transform it before it transforms for you.

hearing the noise of: unhappiness due to the resistance of your feelings.

husband dreaming of a: make plans to be free of your wife.

  wife: warn husband against checking on you, if he wants to keep you.

killing: quarrels over your defiance of authority will reverse your fortune.

of a: will receive diabolically evil news from an unknown source.

RAVINE
07-09-22-40-47-51

falling into a: troubles will be multiplied with a simple error; correct it and climb out.

much water running through a: people have faith in your ability to not be seduced.

nearly dry: a friend will render you a service despite your disagreeableness.

of a: will have plenty of self-confidence to lead you; strengthen your independence.

small, a: peace and prosperity in an early and comfortable union.

RAZOR
02-29-32-33-35-44

broken, a: hidden pain denotes the flaw in upcoming deal; correct it or get out.

buying a: will be persecuted for questionable conduct before it gets out of the box.

cutting yourself with a: must control your conflicting emotions.

killing someone with a: disagreeable events must be rebelled against.

>*yourself:* your inner calm and contentment do not balance with outer world.

>*of a:* danger will be encountered in confusion with a loved one.

straight, a: your precise execution of your work may be old-fashioned.

>*sharpening a:* meet adversity at the point of its inception.

using a: warning of a coming quarrel if you don't confront the signs.

>*dull:* confusion and ill-temper of loved one can be rectified by you.

>*electric:* easy actions can falter for lack of attention.

READING
15-27-33-34-45-49

book, a: spoken words have fleeting nuances, pirated ones stand alone.

but not understanding: will excel at a venture appearing difficult to others but not to you.

children: will enjoy the friendship of many people in words alone.

comic: are engaged in difficult work; a synopsis of treasures for deeper reading.

hieroglyphics: your newest discovery will bring you notability.

newspaper, a: success will attend any undertakings.

out loud: will come to the notice of an influential mentor.

>*making children read:* as long as it's a book that piques their interest to read more.

poetry: will overcome obstacles with the use of insightful phrases.

scientific books: will meet a highly intelligent person and his connection with reality.

REAPERS
03-06-28-33-41-51

being a, yourself: all the abundance you need is at home.

friends being: don't listen to their advice; consult the quantity and quality of their work.

many at work: will have a picnic after a hard morning's work.

>*idling:* misery, when your efforts provide no results in the midst of other's prosperity.

reaping wheat: will receive a blessing.

>*wild hay:* don't worry over trifles when there is vast work to do.

REAR ADMIRAL
05-11-37-43-48-52

battleship, on a: will not tolerate insubordination in others, yet choose to be insubordinate.

being a: people have a high opinion of you outside of your home.

>*at the Pentagon:* an abuse of confidence will threaten your integrity and honor.

>*young:* are a great lover of women when not on duty.

being the wife of a: are surrounded by lovers but want only one.

dock, on a: will receive a visit from a superior with new orders.

friend who is a: a secret of his frequent absences will soon be explained.

REBELLION
03-04-24-30-46-52

being in a: people will cease to annoy you if you cease to be annoying.

>*friends:* your prospects at work will be secretly aided by a friend.

>>*with:* infidelity exists on both sides.

>>*wounded:* you are the source of the problem.

being a rebel: emotional setback caused by an unanticipated breakup.

foreign, a: are too ambitious in expecting to solve problems quickly.

of a: someone inferior to you is causing much trouble for you.

people being killed in a: have found a clever solution to a sticky problem.

put a stop to a, having: advancement within own position.

taking leadership part in a: self-satisfaction will turn into turmoil.

watching a: disruptive events interfere with your business.

RECEIVING
01-09-25-35-47-50

being received by others: support and custodial aid from influential sources.

compliment, a: your depression is from disbelief in your light.

document, a: don't put too much trust in your future.

family letter, a: peril is ahead of you, but your family is behind you.

gift at own house, a: harmony in domestic life.

important personalities: riches through a distant admirer.

love letter, a: your suffering, unhappiness and persecution will lead to reconciliation.

money: business matter will be rectified in your favor.

ring as a gift secretly, a: will have a promise of matrimony with a hint of betrayal.

RECEPTION
03-05-07-21-28-29

attending a: will receive compensation by being invited into a social circle.

public dinner, alone: postponement of success until emotional eggs are in a row.

giving a: will be highly thought of in society for your financial well-being.

wedding, for children: will realize high ambitions for them.

in your honor: are not accustomed to the praise of others.

noisy informal, a: bad advice is forthcoming.

of a: family quarrels over your exciting new romantic venture.

sitting in: don't overthink, act honestly.

solemn, a: your originality lives to imagine risks and take them.

RECOGNIZING
07-10-11-36-38-50

being recognized by others after many years: your patience will be tried.

dead person, a: will be afflicted with heart trouble.

of, people: will lead a quiet life until current project is revealed to public.

old friend, an: will become very upset at the ramifications of your mistake.

recognition, gaining: your seemingly never-ending task will be successful.

giving: are able to achieve what others failed to complete.

soiled legal document, a: are confident in your abilities, use them.

RECONCILING
06-15-22-23-48-50

reconciling an argument: sensible initiatives first, risky ones after foundation is laid.

business transaction: heavy involvement needs to be unraveled.

with a creditor: will fall into a trap, causing wide financial loss.

with father: a business trip will be constructive and profitable.

friend, a: quarrels over your open-hearted sociability not being loyal.

mother: fearlessness and decisiveness in the execution of your abilities.

RECORDS
05-12-20-36-44-50

being a court recorder: will fall in love instantly, but cannot act upon it.

buying musical: your confidence needs bolstering by a mentor.

making: will enjoy social activities and a strong will.

playing: your impulsive, jumpy overreactions have found a forum.

selling: financial gains by recognizing a favorable opportunity.

of: are unfitted to fill the family position.

recording legal matters: will enjoy much security with unexpected good news.

record time, ready in: satisfaction from a job well done.

requesting a: old ideas and habits are replaced by innovative interactions with others.

world: strong need for freedom and independence drives you.

RECOVERING
16-25-26-30-45-47

children: will be protected by God during unforeseen changes.

family member, from illness: desperately need to solve your detachment from others.

furniture: are prone to being imprudent with your originality.

not: beware of treacherous people who disrupt your daily routine.

of: will live a long life if you pay intricately close attention to your health.

stolen goods: are full of imaginative ideas.

RECRUITS
17-25-32-41-43-44

barracks, in the: freedom without direction leads to humiliation.

being recruited: traumas at work have brought out your strength of character.

lined up for inspection: disciplining yourself has not succeeded.

sports, for: major disagreements with opinionated relatives.

RECUPERATING
02-09-22-23-26-33

business loss, from a: will have happiness in near future.

of, from an illness: you enjoy amusements too much.

  children: unhappiness will be over in 48 hours.

  mate: misinterpretations are over, but the hurt needs time to heal.

RED
01-11-13-14-15-29

crimson: pleasant news from a racy profligate friend.

  using things of: long trip in the heat of passion.

Cross, the: will be recruited to nurse a relative through distress.

face being: anger overcomes any positive action.

fire engine: a warning to avoid a quarrel with friends.

scarlet: family quarrels will take years to resolve.

seeing: vital aggression is required for positive actions.

sports car: are asking for a speeding ticket.

traffic light turning: another's behavior is blocking your energy.

wearing: are burning your energy foolishly.

REEDS
10-15-19-20-21-33

bamboo, swaying in the breeze: faith flows with your river; do not delay the lawsuit.

bent by your boat: be guided by your wise instinct.

handling: are deceived by businesspeople.

  others: prove people before trusting them.

oboe: crisp determination and accurate eyes and ears are vital to your success.

playing a, instrument: be wary of the motive behind your friend's determination.

  another: with quiet confident optimism you will attain a good life.

  broken: an intense, short-lived attachment will help reconciliation with enemies.

  recorder, the: will fall in love and sacrifice everything to attain it.

section of the orchestra: staccato tactics will work.

REFEREE
06-20-21-23-24-29

being a: have power to change position in life.

  of sports: are too egocentric to have a happy healthy home.

court, a: battle between own ideas and values, and those imposed by the community.

ignoring the: will receive an injustice; whom must you bypass to counter it?

protesting the, call: who wants to strike you out?

REFINING
09-13-19-26-27-35

making thinner by: will make undreamed-of progress if you can.

of: have many enemies, cherish your friends.

people working at a refinery: time for spring cleaning of your soul.

purifying while: you waste too much time with pleasures.

REFLECTION
08-11-13-17-33-36

of own, in water: lonely life as you fail to recognize any love but your own for yourself.

  children: will achieve success because you cannot run away from the problem.

  family: visit from a strange person, who may be ideally suited to you.

  loved one: your unladylike contact will not impress your lover.

strange face reflected, a: your lack of staying power causes separation from loved ones.

REFORMING
09-20-23-25-29-34

obstinate children needing: their companions are unsympathetic to your discipline.

of a, institution: prove friends before trusting them in high important position.

reformatory, being sent to a: are running with the wrong crowd.

stubborn animals needing: will receive a present from a stranger.

REFRESHMENTS
02-03-16-24-27-28

being offered: check the career ladder, make sure each rung is nourished.

buying: joy for the woman in the family.

giving family: are serious and sincere about their emotional well-being.

   children: they will achieve prominence in community.

   friends: will receive a present from a rich man.

serving: will receive a small vexation over otherwise perfect health.

REFRIGERATOR
04-25-33-40-49-50

emptying a: the dinner guest won't leave, starve him out.

loading up the: will fill your home with a gay social life.

of a: will injure a friendship with your selfishness.

opening a: emotional frigidity will cause you to be discourteous.

   full: will have the mental nourishment to sustain your goals.

taking ice from a: project will be delayed through your selfish injury.

REFUGE
15-18-19-23-24-35

being in a: are reevaluating and making lifestyle changes.

going into, with family: have constricted your thoughts to concern only you.

harboring a refugee: what you do will be misinterpreted and condemned.

of a: being displaced in time and space and seeking a harbor.

taking, against enemies: present insecurity belies that you will soon gain money.

from a bad storm: concern for the whole community, not just your family.

   hurricane: beware of another's bad judgments of you behind your back.

others: will be unhappy with present condition but are afraid to confront it.

REFUSAL
06-10-11-23-24-31

being refused by your children: conditions must be met for happiness in the near future.

   relatives: old ideas need to be discarded before prospects of better times.

   friends: jealousy and dissension must be erased from your consciousness.

others refusing: misery and desperation until old ideas are disposed of.

refusing a gift: are too certain of receiving another gift.

   others, your: will be embraced by sweetheart; finally, acceptance.

refusing to accept a letter: secret pains over opinions that need revisiting.

   others, your: business will not turn around unless you face facts.

REGATTA
01-09-16-20-23-30

being the master of a: will be courted by many women.

losing a: will have to find a new lover; yours was thrown overboard.

taking part in a: will soon be decorated with medals.

watching a: immediate change of plans is required as you follow the course.

   rowing in a: will take long trip abroad with sweetheart.

   sailing on a: joy and festivity over news of future career opportunities.

winning a: will inherit money from an old woman.

REGIMENT
11-21-22-25-32-34

annihilated, being: will be surrounded by beautiful women.

being in a: have confidence that you will be actively involved in civic affairs.

losing a battle: are surrounded by creditors; apply for a different credit card.

winning: will rise above your present society of friends and equals.

marching in a parade: change in own position within a large family.

REGISTRAR
04-17-21-28-29-33

being a: will receive a proposal of marriage and be married for a long time.

court: will receive news of many deaths, none related to you.

election, an: happiness and contentment.

of a, office: are at the crossroads of life; you are directing the traffic.

going to: make decisions and don't look back.

with loved one: announcement of marriage.

others: will win a large lottery.

registering at a hotel: your original project will be taken over and finished by others.

under an assumed name: will engage in guilty enterprises that will create uneasiness.

REGRETS
04-05-12-14-29-32

being remorseful: well-meant advice will guide you through seeming impenetrability.

expressing, to mate: some things are better left unsaid.

others: your unhappiness will soon come to an end with peaceful settlements.

having: your changeable mood will be harmful to the stability of your relationships.

regretting actions: will have a bad aspect of the moon in its final phase.

children: don't be so particular in your demands; more creative uses are available.

first love: will meet a wealthy, honorable person who will not erase your memories.

present condition: will be induced to leave your home under false pretenses.

wrongdoings: you are cultivating perfection.

in business: will have domestic difficulties as mate turns deceitful and unworthy.

RELATIVES
09-16-21-25-30-33

age of: death in the family brings disappointments in affairs

arrival of many: loss in business through exposure of your evil intents.

contradicted by, being: bad luck to come from family arguments.

crazy, being: will receive many costly gifts.

discussing matters with: the relationship of different aspects of your heritage.

rejection from, feeling: dispose of cluttered, worn-out ideas and opinions.

worried about a, conscience, being: struggles with others' overabundant self-esteem.

RELEASED
01-16-20-25-26-32

being, from business venture: are not carrying out your commitments.

contract, a: the wrong love will end, leaving room for the right one.

matrimony, from: unexpected joy at your generous and congenial disposition.

prison: will be well accepted in society for your congeniality.

releasing someone else from a contract: will leave home under false pretenses.

RELIGIOUS
10-11-12-15-16-29

affiliation with God: will go far and deflate an imagined worry.

attending a church every day: your ingeniousness will block the squandering of money.

being a very, person: will break or dishonor something you hold dear.

believing in own religion: big family argument disrupts quiet and contentment.

belonging to a, institution: will be exposed to evil designs of false friends.

campaign against sin: will substantially support charitable deeds.

relic, a: your lack of pretensions allows you practicality to accomplish much.

REMEDY
04-09-16-20-28-29

advising others of a: have confidence and are decisive in what you believe.

aloe to skin, applying: domestic problems are resolved.

   drinking juice: will heal the cuts in your stomach and the bruises on your heart.

antidote, taking an: for any thesis there is an antithesis; healing is synthesis.

camphor, using in the house: failure of the plans of a moth; will risk vengeance.

castor oil, being ordered to take: recovery from a short bout of argumentativeness.

chamomile: peaceful settlements of adverse energies.

cupping, the process of: usury will be only to your advantage.

finding a, for business affairs: will economize and foil a scheme to ruin your interests.

giving children a: will be highly considered by others who are not worthy of you.

iodine, swallowing: snap out of your depression.

liniment, rubbing a pain with: a valuable legacy of simple treasures.

manna as a mild laxative: everything in nature has medicinal properties.

   divinely supplied: your health issues are nutritional.

poultice, applying a: climb out of that pit and develop that crazy obscure idea.

taking a: will recover from an illness very soon.

   aspiration: neither listen to nor respect gossip.

   belladonna: failure to meet debts, which cramps your hands.

     giving: vain efforts to win affections away from the throes of poison.

   cod liver oil: a love episode full of ecstatic charm.

   ipecac: your disgusting needs amuse you; will stand firm against deceitful adventurers.

   lozenge, throat: your disagreeable chatter does not make the job go away.

REMOVING
02-08-12-20-21-23

clothes to another place: reassuring prognosis for a relative's health.

   yourself: your aspirations exceed your abilities; push to your limit no more.

obstacle, an: your personality is too strong-minded to be willing to change.

others, things: need financial help; use your possessions as collateral, not as power.

your house: will enjoy working hard through major changes you initiated.

   false teeth: expect a visitor to your home; be sure you know where you left them.

RENOUNCING
05-12-14-26-30-31

good position, a: are foolishly distancing yourself from a constructive environment.

mates, each other: control issues create unreasonable demands.

of: must avoid contradictions by discarding your emotions.

others, their position: will have many enemies, by refusing to listen to the whole story.

political career, a: will maneuver out of embarrassment; affairs will turn for the better.

REPEATING
17-13-47-43-3-51

mistake: your lack of industriousness is blocking any recognition.

scientific experiment, a: your rational analytical mind sees God in the details.

yourself: have droned yourself into mediocrity so as not to offend others.

REPLY
01-02-13-14-26-39

receiving a good: will receive a settlement of money you thought was gone.

   unfavorable: affairs will improve after an uncomfortable journey and depressing work.

     from a man: your smooth progress has hit a snag.

       woman: your liberality will highly commend your efforts.

replying in a business affair: worries will be ended with a fortunately situated reply.

   to a man's letter: conditions will become worse as anger is renewed.

     woman's: a mystery will be solved, bringing discomfort and loneliness.

waiting for a: bitterness of friends will be sweetened by sincerity.

REPRIMANDING
04-07-14-18-23-28

being reprimanded: your jumpiness is causing serious errors in your judgment.

  by an officer: will discover secret enemies within yourself.

    superior: keep an eye out for where money is sent.

children: your job is at jeopardy: speak your mind at work.

employees: will be sincerely loved, but don't realize it.

friends: delightful surprise is ahead as friends agree to go forward with your plans.

others: will receive unpleasant news that you have been reproached about by others.

partners, each other: your tranquility and fortune are at risk.

relatives: will receive an important offer from a superior; take it.

servants: domestic arguments over your irrational behavior.

REPTILES
02-08-16-32-34-36

being bitten by a: business is going fine, but rivals are out to destroy your family.

  relatives: people are slandering your name, slander theirs.

catching a live: people are gossiping against you, prove them wrong.

crocodile, a: a powerful adversary is submerged, ready to emerge from hiding.

dying from the bite of a: are surrounded by enemies, punt.

having a, in a cage: will win at gambling, but not the high stakes.

  others: be cautious in business affairs as finances are in jeopardy.

killing: deal with treacherous people before they damage you.

many, in the woods: are too egotistic to believe enemies would lie in wait for you.

of: have hidden enemies who would cause your partner to deceive you.

REQUEST   05-06-24-26-29-36

receiving a: will be put under interrogation for your success.

  for money: have sufficient competency to live above penury; review your priorities.

  from several women: will suffer humiliation for exceeding your expectations.

requesting things from others: you expect too many favors from others.

  mates, of each other: relationship is on shaky ground; sharing was not part of the deal.

RESCUING
04-11-12-21-24-34

being rescued without injury: slight business loss from rotten apples shaken loose.

by an animal: situation needs to be faced before it becomes threatening.

  by a hero: friends in high places come to your rescue.

  from drowning: avoid travel on the sea and disclosure of intimates.

children: big inheritance from an unknown person will not prove as solid as imagined.

enemies from killing themselves: be unusually careful; dangers have not disappeared.

one who wants to die: will feel keenly the indifference shown by insincere friends.

others: your good reputation for civic duties will culminate in honor.

  from drowning: will make big financial gains in pleasure and presents.

relatives: your defense of honor is in danger of collapse in family quarrels.

seaman, a: to his humiliation and shame, he will be ever indebted to you.

RESERVOIR
04-07-08-18-27-30

being filled up with water: many are depending upon you for their basic welfare.

  clean: plenty of money to enhance your wardrobe.

  half-filled: declining business needs emotional input.

empty: destruction of all available nurturance.

RESIGNATION
13-16-19-26-31-35

abdicating, king or president: disorder in business caused by major change.

  prominent position, from a: a peaceful influence will eventually reach you *being informed of enemy's:* discussions about your own resignation as well.

handing in own: are relinquishing your hard-earned public esteem.

> *friends:* will have disagreeable arguments, with the first impression being wrong.
>
> *husband:* money gained through legal matters.
>
> *others:* advancement in near future due to your grace in defeat.

of resigning: you are seceding defeat at the hands of weaker foes.

> *enemies:* you are an accomplice to incorrectly acting spontaneous.
>
> *friends:* will win a lawsuit, but success is delayed.
>
> *husband or wife:* your impression of your mate has turned sour.
>
> *others:* an enemy is trying to make up with you.
>
> *relatives:* the joy of your intuitive and reflective personality.

RESISTING
05-08-10-12-28-36

love of someone, the: will be persecuted for your innate desire for independence.

not, advances: discovery of lost valuables; your ability to love.

others, love: will gain confidence in yourself; gaining every aspect of love.

progress at work: your elders have learned something in your many years.

wrongdoing: luck and prosperity are plagued with adversity.

RESPECTED
03-04-10-28-32-34

being by others: will receive money and achieve riches with your joy and friendship.

> *highly, by children:* increase in wealth from this constructive support.

of respect: will attempt a venture fraught with danger and earn its reward.

> *showing, to others:* tremendous catastrophe ahead; are influenced by base thought.

respectable person, being a: will lead a touchy irritable life with love dove.

> *considered:* big rain and change of temperature of your companion's affection.

having business dealings with: your work will be compensated, your heart will not.

> *of, people:* will enjoy all the pleasures and desires of life, even if others cannot.

RESPONSIBLE
04-06-07-16-29-30

being, for wrongdoings: beware escaping creditors do not block your enterprise.

> *good actions:* beware of a double-cross from a heckler.

being given a, job: worries will not be smoothed away, clear things up.

dealing with, people: are doomed with your excessive preoccupation with the past.

having, children: relatives will come asking for help.

RESTAURANT
08-11-27-31-33-34

buffet, all you can eat: your ideas need to be digested.

Dutch, paying: each will expect the other to insist on picking up the tab.

eating at a: will receive a proposition too lucrative to refuse.

> *enemies:* your bitterest foes will wear the garb of friendship.
>
> *husband and wife, alone:* sensual appetites are sated in a long happy marriage.
>
> *others:* are envious of other's sociability as they are of yours; join forces.
>
> *with children:* their health is not very good because of bad nutrition.
>
> > *relatives:* will overcome enemies with patience.
> >
> > *sweetheart:* are timid in solving a bad financial condition.

entering a: overindulgence does not feed your soul.

menu, reading the: if you order by price, you shouldn't be eating there.

of a: need to be served, for once.

RESTING
04-05-14-22-30-35

of: the physical and mental stress in sporting matters needs to be relaxed.

> *children:* overzealous in creating happiness in family affairs.

friends: will be informed of sad news for which you are definitely responsible.

others: will acquire a new home and lose your job.

relatives: affairs are going backwards from your being worn out.

RESTRICT
03-07-09-17-32-35

actions being restricted: hindrances to your development are self-imposed.

> *by government and complying:* should diet during the alarming fluctuations in the affair.

> *by others:* wisdom to accept another's counsel.

restricting actions of businesspeople: will successfully outstrip your rival.

> *children from wrongdoing:* are exceptionally decisive with constructive criticism.

> *impositions of family members:* family will ask for money whether allowed or not.

RESURRECTION
01-06-11-14-17-29

attending Easter sunrise services with family: rebirth of an ambition.

being at the, site: religious interest will bring hope for happiness.

being resurrected: recovery from an illness and altercations with friends.

> *another:* an oppression you didn't realize has lifted; deal with what it hid.

of the: long journey to religious shrines to receive faith previously lost.

RETURNING
01-02-10-12-28-31

friends, to their home: have received a blessing that you have not acknowledged.

from a trip: great prosperity when your considerable talents and qualities are put to use.

of: unexpected joy when jealousy and bitterness, however justified, are lifted.

others, after a long time: losses soon to be made good.

prison: your patience and perseverance are on the verge of extremism.

relatives, from a trip: jealousy within the family over your emotional relationship.

sweetheart, home: he has been untrue to you.

war: are overconfident that your battles are over.

REVENGE
01-03-10-17-24-25

against family: solve the small arguments immediately.

> *enemies:* a rival will take your sweetheart's affection.

> *friends:* use talents to enrich your mind, not pleasure to destroy your morality.

> *man, a:* humiliating and heartless act on your part.

> *relatives:* quarrels will cause you to lose many a good ally.

> *woman, a:* are considered to be very vulgar.

seeking: anxious times leading to bitter disappointments.

REVIEWING STAND
01-02-05-07-22-26

being a reviewer: the reviewed are likely to be hostile in their response.

being on a: a joy of short duration, your ambitions drive you on.

> *high officials:* you have a bad temper when your creative ideas aren't recognized.

> *military officers:* ambiguous situation could lead to accusations of treason.

> *people:* a sick friend will recover after you visit.

> *politicians:* are rash and hasty in your conceit; your ambitions will haunt you.

REVOLVER
05-10-14-20-22-35

children holding a: parents are unworthy of your self-control.

firing a: your strongarm tactics debilitate your team.

handling a: learn the proper use of your jealousy.

killing with a: be aware of your ability to hurt and be hurt.

officers with a: responsibility requires total knowledge.

using a: be careful and considerate in your activities.

enemies: the return of your lively use of initiative after complications are solved.

policemen: your sensibility and intelligence need to be revived.

REWARD
02-16-19-20-23-27

accepting a: will have a big argument over money.

declining an unjustified: put forth the corrected version of events.

giving a: will enjoy things that money cannot buy.

receiving a: your overconfidence and under-utilization of kindness will cause failure.

enemies: interference with your closest affections.

others: beware of the danger of fire in your home.

RHEUMATISM
01-05-16-17-28-30

having: your bitterness and anger are avenging themselves in you.

enemies: disappointment in wishing another's downfall.

friends: will yield yourself captive to another's chaos.

relative: keep track of your promises and fulfill them.

of: hiding hurt from the indiscretion of friends.

suffering with: will overcome rejection of one's value and contribution.

RHINOCEROS
04-05-07-14-27-32

cage at a zoo, in a: disillusionment for those in love, in your revealed secrets.

fighting: someone is seeking revenge upon you; block them with your chaos.

killing a: appearances do not reveal the whole man.

of a: use steady powerful common sense when faced with the work jungle.

RHUBARB
02-03-09-10-21-30

buying: warning of taking the bitter with the sweet doesn't always work.

cooking: will free yourself from destructive associations.

eating: are dissatisfied with occupation, move forward in another direction.

growing: change in affairs will culminate propitiously.

making, pie: will have an unexpected visitor and move with him.

of a: new and strong friendship of common philosophy.

RIBBONS
05-09-15-29-31-36

buying many: another is dividing your social bonus and pleasures.

handling: big satisfaction in the final touches of your success.

fluttering: open yourself up to new friends of the opposite sex.

measuring: entanglement in lawsuits over your being too lighthearted.

of: sincerity in love matters is not necessarily reciprocal.

tying: will make a good trade of something with your rival for lover's affections.

untying: sweetheart is sowing wild oats, keep a distance.

wearing: unexpected pleasant news concerning love.

relative: ignoring contradictions to unexpected prosperity.

RIBS
01-11-15-30-32-33

breaking: beware of treachery among those trusted and vastly apply your talents.

wife, her: will divorce her husband; events will bring no show of emotions.

children having broken: unfitted to hold their own in the sports of life.

having a misplaced: people are gossiping about you; unhappiness caused by relatives.

having strong: moderate speculations and full use of your talents.

own, being injured: will bow in servitude to the will of a master of your own choosing.

RICE
04-10-19-27-32-34

buying: will realize high ambitions and survive conflicts victoriously.

cooking: prosperity in a variety of trades, though remaining in same location.

others: abolishment of ill-feelings of
possessiveness.

eating: a season of seductive pleasures and
domestic bliss.

friends: will entertain an unwelcome guest
whose intentions are doubtful.

pudding: will be a victim of flattery and
sinful persuasion.

so much, that you are full: the fair was for
another's charity, not yours.

growing: abundance will come from a visit
to foreign lands.

selling: be careful in making plans too soon
for financial gains.

throwing: enemies thrust your interest aside
through your inability to stop them.

RICH
12-13-16-22-29-32

being: high honors and success.

relatives: they will have trouble in their
life.

becoming: your aggressive, firm approach will
bring just deserts.

not: will obtain small employment under
wealthy person.

others who are: turmoil in business affairs
as competition enlivens.

talking with, people: will have beneficial
compensation.

RIDING
23-25-31-34-35-36

horse, a: business will go out of control, ride it
out.

and being thrown off: change direction for
satisfactory business.

children: will give up the one you love for
mercenary gain.

falling off a: prosperity under
hazardous conditions.

red: step back and reuse your anger
constructively.

white: a message from heaven.

in full gallop: in your speed you veered from
your goal.

in a car: peril of death if you go the wrong
direction.

fast: prosperity may not develop, as
you waste valuable time in frivolous
pleasures.

carriage: are surrounded by unscrupulous
people; be watchful to detect them.

taking a ride: will reap the benefits of
another's labor.

with others: plans will turn out unsatisfactorily.

RIDDLES
05-10-11-16-21-32

talking in, yourself: keen disappointment
from pointed responses.

children: will receive an unexplained
visit from a old friend.

hearing others: unexpected offer from an
unscrupulous relative.

relatives: luxury and unobstructed
progress.

sweetheart: must control passions to let
them evolve and grow.

RIFLE
04-10-16-21-23-32

firing a: expressing your repressed ego will
be explosive.

at an enemy: success is postponed as
another steals your winnings.

man dreaming of a: trying to impress her is
futile; enjoy it yourself.

woman: fear of an aggressive suitor.

RING
8-22-27-30-31-35

breaking a wedding: disquieting moments
of domestic unrest lead to divorce.

fiancée's: separation of lovers, reunion
of old ones.

buying a: loss of old investments; new
ventures will prosper.

having a diamond: old love affair revived
and consummated.

gold: it will take strenuous efforts to avert
losing your dignity.

put on your finger: commitment to
a relationship or marriage.

iron: infidelity of your spouse; hard work
ahead to repair the damage.

of precious stones: release yourself from
a unrequited love; a night of passion is
shared.

on a chain: marriage problems are
short-lived.

losing your: large quarrel results in a budding
love.

man dreaming of losing his: fiancée will marry
another man.

single girl, her: will be left by boyfriend.

taking a, off your finger: unsavory aftermath
to an affair.

wearing many rings: multiple ventures will
prove enterprising.

RIOT

03-07-14-16-23-35

ending, a: your secret is causing others'
actions to be misconstrued.

leading a: your misuse of the opposite sex
will put you in an emotional prison.

of a: your affection shortage won't be alleviated by debauchery.

taking part in a: misfortune in business if you
do not moderate your opinions.

enemies: watch them make mistakes and
take advantage.

friends: persecution by an enemy on a
very tiring business trip.

relatives: are too independent from the
support of friends.

RITUAL

03-15-16-28-33-37

of a: your commitment is to minister an
ongoing change in your life course.

watching a: you need to bring your follow-
ers into setp.

sacrifice, making a: your martyrdom is under-
appreciated and self-serving.

friends, for you: reproaches will fall heavily
on you.

sacrificing an animal: character is set by how
you lead those dependent upon you.

child: being required to chose will ruin the
relationship.

sacrilege, committing a: will suffer much misery
from overbearing egotistical people.

RIVAL

05-08-18-21-27-29

being defeated by a: will turn around situation
and lead it to success.

competing with a: will soon experience the
ups and downs of your temper.

defeating a: will prove successful in business
with unhasty actions.

lover dreaming of having a: need to assert
your rights in love affairs.

married people: are weak and wavering in
your decision for full commitment.

young woman: will accept her present
lover for fear of not having another.

of a: will undertake an unpleasant enterprise
and succeed.

RIVER

06-08-11-17-21-36

cataract with rapid clear water: an adventurer
threatens your domestic happiness.

murky: the flow of life is neverending and
never smooth.

creek, wading in a dry: new experiences;
taking a trip of short duration.

others: another is enjoying what you had
rejected as insufficient.

drifting on the, in a boat: imminent danger;
take a decisive hand in your life.

enemies committing suicide in a: a long-
desired move is imminent.

falling into a: danger is awaiting your misstep;
seek professional advice.

children: are passing from one growth
period to the next one.

sweetheart: a restful break to allow feelings
to soar above the conflicts.

fishing in a: change of environment brings
contact with person of influence.

flooding, a: will receive good news concerning
pending lawsuits.

escape from a: long-lasting lawsuits
through indiscrete actions of others.

being unable to: disillusionment when
you correct your faults.

fording a river: security is on the other side,
find the right ford.

palisades, of a: cautious optimist will guide
you through obstructers.

embankment, being on a: will hear news of
the engagement of your love to another.

others: engagement will be called off
from your obsession with personal
ease.

riding the rapids: gaining strength against
a repressive relationship.

swimming in a: meet the imminent danger
directly and head to the source.

upstream: your actions go against your
instincts; reverse them to coincide.

throwing someone into a: will be befriended by another more faithful friend.

walking the shores: inspirations is at hand; grasp it.

water, of clear: good business practices coming to fruition.

  dirty: disgrace for disputing another's tainted emotional state.

ROAD
03-11-14-17-25-33

avenue stretches in the distance: project will extend for decades.

  strolling down the: focus on the path you have chosen.

being lost on a: an error in a decision to not confront something directly will cause losses.

busy, a: are faced with complex choices, which may all lead to the same fortune.

dark unlit, an: your mistaken questioning has made your goals unreachable.

detour, taking a: simplify, simplify, simplify until the course is straight.

  making a: your inflexibility blocks your reaching your goal.

going downhill with others: stop the elevator and get off before it hits bottom.

  sweetheart: new relationship brings new problems and a disabuse of confidence.

  uphill: your noble aspirations are reachable.

gravel, driving on coarse: beware of skidding from heights of success.

  others doing, work: new undertakings will bring grief and loss of time, little else.

  walking on a rough, path: will fail to please others in your selection of friends.

highway: road is clear for racing.

lane, country: a lengthy burdensome task will be a reward in itself.

  blockaded off: personal dilemmas come from major financial difficulties.

  meeting in a shady: will be fortunate in love if you keep your actions discreet.

  narrow: must accommodate others with concessions and compromises.

of a: good health through following your differing opinion for treatment.

bad: new undertakings will bring sorrow and losses.

crooked: your project is vague and all-inclusive; nothing can be accomplished.

full of obstacles: change of plans is wise.

narrow, winding: obstacles can be overcome with compromise.

paved with macadam: honest intentions will receive their own reward.

rocky: meet your strange encounter head on.

straight: lasting but limited happiness, don't stray from the course.

turns back on you: reroute.

wide: relationships are smoothly progressing.

rough neighborhood, in a: chosen life is straying from intended route.

sign, reading a: changing directions will bring annoyances.

traveling on a: security is a long road to haul.

  at edge of a cliff: a review of one's finances is needed.

  down a steep hill: turn around, the original grass was greener.

  up: your goals are reachable with extensive travel.

turns back on you: reroute your entire itinerary.

unstable bridge, on an: double back and take another route.

wet slick, a: lack of inner balance leaves you exposed to the elements.

ROAR
10-12-16-19-23-26

hearing the, of animals: an enemy is watching your every move and listening intently.

  in a barn: advancement within the confines and comfort of your own position.

  in the distance: an unpleasant encounter in the near future will disconcert you now.

  of water: a traveler will return after an unjustified attack.

  wind: will waste your heritage and throw a pall on the proceedings.

ROAST

03-05-11-22-23-36

buying beef: pleasure and profitable undertakings.

    eating: will receive affectionate greetings that will detract from your real merit.

    serving: are sharing a wealth of opportunity with friends.

    slicing: will win at gambling, a bet with each cut of the cards.

carving a: a celebration amongst those closest to you.

roasting beef: minimal danger to your comfortable living.

    lamb: blessings and nutritious support.

    on a spit: will be invited to a meeting that will last for days.

    pork: losses from gambling.

    veal: desires will be accomplished in proportion to your effort.

ROBBED

03-05-18-30-31-33

being: will receive money from a guilty source.

    of jewels: will receive an inheritance and a jealous relative.

    of money: will sustain an injury that is easily curable.

    of securities: will emerge well from present troubles.

    of your clothes: will have good friends supporting your insecurities.

organizing a robbery: inner anxiety with no outward effect causes permanent damage.

people robbing others: lack of self-control in approaching money.

robbing someone else: a warning: you persist in taking credit for other's work.

while traveling: slow your pace and be more observant.

ROBBER

06-16-19-23-25-36

arrested, being: your identity is in crisis, only you can pay its bail.

back door, breaking down the: new money will be taken from you through deviousness.

being a: prepare to give back all that you have taken.

    molested by a: loss of relative's children and property.

escaping injury by a: possessions can be replaced; you cannot.

friends rifling through your belongings: will be kidnapped by the dissolution of your hopes.

killing a: will lose yourself over your robbing the cradle.

running away: disappointment in love affairs dissipating; live only in your mind.

ROBINS

07-12-13-14-24-25

feeding: a new opportunity presents itself every day, take advantage of it.

killing a: unhappiness to all concerned.

lawn, on a: malicious gossip is being spread about you.

nest, making a: domestic unhappiness until you become more constructive.

pulling worms from the ground: will build your dream home.

resting: will become learned and polished in social skills.

several, flying: will receive something for which you wished, long ago.

singing: great happiness in the thrill of the trill.

ROCKET

17-21-26-28-30-32

building a: must have firmer foundations for business.

enemies being killed by a: will hear false news of an unhappy union.

exploding a: expansion of the family, figuratively and monetarily.

many: triumph over enemies in a short-lived success.

observing a, launch: an advantage from an unlikely source.

taking off: your ideas need a more robust market analysis.

ROCKING CHAIR

18-27-28-29-31-35

buying a: your extravagance in your personal life needs a rest.

children playing in a: approaching money.

empty, rocking an: death of someone in the family.

selling a: will move on to active participation.

sitting in a: are confronted with insurmountable obstacles.

ROCKS
04-10-13-16-33-34

children climbing up: desire for abundance of money will be fulfilled.

down: will confront reverses and obstacles to gain a good education.

climbing, with sweetheart: will be married soon, based on a solid foundation.

climbing down: shoulder your share of the responsibilities.

easily: a new venture launched with a shaky future.

the hard way: realization of desires will be slow, commitment must be solved.

having trouble: you pushed yourself too far.

kissing sweetheart on top of a: marriage will last forever.

large, in the sea, a: will overcome enemies with perseverance.

ROLLERBLADING
02-11-12-14-19-36

buying rollerblades: success depends on timing and the treatment of your opponents.

competing: get in the game or others will overtake you.

down the sidewalk: your skill is still undeveloped.

watching another: are too far out of the action to be effective.

ROOF
01-02-04-22-23-25

climbing a ladder to a: solve your problems one at a time to unbounded success.

falling off a: a major relapse in judgment; have no firm hold on the positive.

fixing a leak in a: will soon take a journey faraway to increase your fortune.

flames, in: you live in fear of impending illness.

walking toward house with: retreat from present path to the fork in the road.

gutter, standing beneath a rain: will be corrected, cleansed and sent on a new mission.

leaking: new information is breaking the barriers of your obstinacy.

of own house: predictive of the state of your health.

putting a, on a building: an enemy is watching.

others: will have a vigorous mind occupied with petty vexations.

shingle: security in life but disappointment in love.

tile falling from a: separation of states of consciousness is deteriorating.

walking around on a: you are at the height of your profession.

ROOM
04-05-06-12-14-23

apartment, in an: be on the lookout for treachery.

bath, a: your overpossessiveness is annoying the family.

being in own: your good humor will not ease slow suffocation.

of someone you love: will be cheated by friends who lure you into ill health.

boardinghouse, in a: bad business ventures absorb all of your living costs.

children's: privacy and comfort are your greatest aims.

dark, a: a wealth of images reenergizes emotional progress.

decorating own: losses in business affairs bring unexpected guests.

empty, an: have to earn to appreciate whatever you own.

entering a: certainty of good earnings and pleasant company.

home, at: emotional poverty looms over you.

hotel, a: suggestions put forth are not what they seem.

mortuary, at a: a danger of immediate death.

newly painted, a: will be deceived, if you trifle with lover's affections.

office, an: will have bad dealings with creditors; consolidate your debts.

prison, a: feel repressed, confined and trapped in your present situation.

waiting, a: are pacing the floor with uncertainty when you just need to open the door.

ROOSTER
14-17-25-30-32-35

girl hearing a cock crow, a: will soon have a new lover.

lover: you have a formidable rival.

married man: someone else is in love with your wife.

 woman: are in love with a handsome man.

laying an egg: big profit from communicating a message.

of a: are alert, vigilant and an early riser.

two, fighting: are vain and unbearable in your actions.

ROOTS

03-06-10-20-24-33

digging up roots: the source of your problems will surprise you.

 and finding truffles: are ingenious at making a profit.

eating: return your extended health to its point of origin.

plants, of: sickness will soon come unless you nourish yourself.

pulling, of plant from ground: others are credited with your ideas.

teeth, of children's: do not weaken to friends' desires or a child's plea.

 own: do not give any money on credit.

 pulled, having: a deep-seated pain is exposed.

trees, of: will have a difficult task to accomplish.

uncovering: your abilities need to develop with rapid effectiveness.

ROPES

07-14-15-17-19-29

being bound with: others wish to threaten your expansion.

 by others: will fall into a trap as troubles overtake you.

binding heavy things together: will have trouble with Justice Department.

 others with: embarrassment and loss of money from your irrational behavior.

climbing up a: are self-willed and obstinate; perseverance furthers loneliness.

coil of new hemp, a: successful termination of a long and arduous project.

coming down a: will overcome all who may seek your downfall.

hanging people: interference from friends foisted upon you by circumstances.

lasso, throwing a: your insistence on control denies you the joy of creating.

noose of: an unfortunate solution to a mystery brings you harm.

sailors using, on a ship: will have work using all of your vigorous mind.

ship, of a: will have news from people to whom you owe money.

strung too tight: your limit has been reached.

tightrope, walking a: take on dangerous adventures for the sake of friends.

tying: have an unusually high-flying physical resistance.

untangling: eliminate the one who set the trap.

ROSARY

01-11-12-19-21-36

others: good times are coming for them.

 relatives: will have sorrow from your apathy and indifference.

someone wearing a: will suffer through bereavement to better living conditions.

telling the: will suffer because of sins and gain with acts of kindness.

telling the beads of own: reconciliation with an influential adviser.

ROSES

02-12-22-28-30-35

artificial: speak low if you speak love, even lower if you speak deceit.

blossoms being withered and falling away: are deceived, the passion is gone.

buds: courage to develop capricious beauty against all odds.

deep-red: joyous times and fun lie ahead.

giving, as a gift: joyous times and fun, emotional relationships.

 receiving: pleasant memories of old friends; relieve your anxiety.

holding, in hands during season: happiness is the highest form of love.

 out of season: the misfortune of infatuation.

picking: are a good lover or sweetheart unconscious of your beauty.

 yellow: envy for missing love is still a beautiful emotion.

pricked by a, being: are feeling sexually subjugated by an early attachment.

pruning: love life pricked your heart only once.

red: will be a bachelor or old maid if you don't control your passion.

sick people smelling: there is danger in the death of transient impressions.

slightly faded: success will come after loss of a dear friend.

smelling, during season: empathy for Mother Nature and all that is lovely.

white: innocence and purity; an ambassador of love.

ROWING
14-15-18-27-35-36

canoe, in a: will receive a promotion.

club, a: will need to curb impulsiveness against a strong rival.

Erg, on the: be persistent toward your goal.

kayak, in a: the promotion you expected goes to another.

others: don't confide secrets to friends, but impress them with your competitiveness.

people: headed toward misfortune with your high-strung irritability.

> *in a race:* advancement within own position.

racing shell with another: others assist you, if you work in unison; against you, if not.

> *with eight:* success, where others have failed, is in synchronicity.

> *with four:* will be reassigned to another territory with a new team.

upstream: contradiction with your superior at work.

yourself: others have become aware of your considerable abilities.

RUBBER
03-05-10-12-13-18

articles made from: rebellion among relatives; stick to your honor among those thieves.

erasing writing with a: uncertainty in your own actions threatens the effect of other's actions.

> *love letters:* are giving a lover the brush-off to allow wooing by another.

using, for various things: friends will fail to understand your conduct.

wearing: protect your health and freedom with practical insurance.

RUBBISH
03-09-16-20-24-27

handling: are about to make a valuable discovery amidst the trash.

> *others:* have a secret enemy who hides behind other's facades.

of: will clean your home in anticipation of meeting a stingy person.

rubble, hauling: you have left nothing to bar your success.

> *pile of:* the solution can be found in the rejected file.

throwing, away: recovery from an illness, during which your affairs were badly managed.

RUBIES
02-04-07-16-29-34

buying jewelry with: the deeper the consolation, the more valuable the experience.

> *selling:* loss of money through shaky investments.

> *wearing:* will triumph over enemies and be indifferent to your present love.

of: true humanity generated by the depth of color in the stone.

ring, a: will have a very faithful love, many of them.

RUDDER
01-12-26-34-38-44

broken, a: business is in distress through faulty speculation.

new, a: expect the visit of a dear friend with advice long needed.

of a: have an undecided, inner confidence and no specific route to take.

ship swaying without a: avoid taking a voyage with enemies appearing to be friends.

> *losing a, at sea:* big profit to pirates and fortune hunters.

RUINED
05-07-09-21-34-47

causing another's ruin: will have prosperity at a huge expense of conscience.

city, a: will receive fortune to aid in the rebuilding.

financially, a family being: will receive money unexpectedly.

home, own: the moment to begin reconstructing your life.

ruining yourself because of wrongdoing: will be gravely embarrassed.

marriage: are well-known for being stingy.

RULER
04-15-28-37-44-45

being the, of a nation: will receive unhappy news concerning love.

carpenter using a: use perspective when viewing your aspirations.

measuring with a: will become financially destitute.

professional person using a: will overcome unhappiness.

ruling a nation with a strong hand: will be asked for money by relatives.

RUNNING
02-12-13-14-26-48

afraid, because of being: will go into exile to avoid facing your guilt.

after an enemy: victory and profit at another's disastrous expense.

　deer or a rabbit: you are a miserly person who extracts blood as profit.

catch someone, to: forever trying to keep up with others, forgetting yourself.

children, with clubs: a slow pace is indicated.

　people: dissension between labor and management.

circles, in: friends do not think very much of your roundabout methods.

jogging at a steady pace: are bored with present exercise.

madman, like a: your progress is being sabotaged.

many people, in confusion: will receive dreadful news of chaotic events.

naked: will be overtaken by your overdestructive impulses.

others: great profit if you apprehend your opponent.

too fast: unexpected fortune at the expense of your health.

wanting to run but can't: are torn by inner conflict.

while hunting: are more afraid of your prey than they are of you.

RUPTURE
07-09-16-19-42-46

having a, in the body: family worries will afflict you, physically.

of a: will be very envious of others as you fail in your overexertion.

operation on a, having an: arguments, not reconciled, within the organs operated upon.

　others: the physical condition will become a major contention.

RUSTY
12-26-27-32-35-45

articles: beware of loss through your inattention.

　handling: you neglect the sensitivity of lovemaking.

　　others: warning, your reputation is in trouble; false friends control your sphere.

of rust: enemies will celebrate your misfortune.

RYE
03-09-11-15-41-46

flour, grinding: a disagreeable function for which you dress to perfection.

liquor, drinking: your attendance at social functions is required.

of bread: have all the nourishment you need; share the rest.

　baking: good days to come, in the popularity of your home.

　buying a loaf of: adventure will stir your ambitions; temper it with sound judgment.

　eating: popularity with opposite sex; displeasure caused by children.

serving, at a meal: fortune is secured in the company of friends.

SABLE
03-04-06-27-30-41

buying a, fur coat: a seductive woman mysteriously manifests in your presence.

having, altered: will have honor and social distinction among fools.

owning: cultivate influential mentors, through appearing to be wealthier than you are.

relatives: will be cheated by your foes, who
think you share your relative's wealth.

selling: loss of money in a double-cross by
your partner.

wearing: will meet an adventurous person of
the opposite sex.

SACKS
13-27-33-34-40-44

carrying a heavy: unexpected money is
received.

coal, of: a productive heart-warming project
that no one wanted to do.

  potatoes: severe restraint is required
  toward sexual temptation.

empty: your astuteness and acumen are
needed to build your business.

emptying a: a season of sorrow, unemploy-
ment and embezzlement.

  filling a: acquisitiveness on a dull and
  ordinary level.

full: are obstructing justice in your drive for
financial gains.

SADDLE
10-31-37-43-44-47

being a, maker: big profits from unsavory
deeds.

falling from a: an abrupt turnover of responsibility.

  headfirst: your control deadens another's
  creativity.

of a: good friends continue to support you.

riding a horse with a: your progress is on solid
footing.

  new: are confronted with insurmountable
  obstacles.

  old, an uncomfortable: are being lax in
  your work performance.

    children: revise your plans to impose
    your will on them.

    others: a catastrophe is caused by those
    you misused.

  sidesaddle: your lack of commitment
  thwarts your project.

  without a: your maverick tactics will fail
  you.

SAFE
10-22-25-32-44-46

empty: so worried about being safe you've
become claustrophobic.

emptying a: serious disaster when you
discover something you had lost in your
home.

filled with money: are hiding your worth
and value behind an underutilized
position.

locking a: plans for personal security will go
well.

of a: repercussions for recent action you
wish to conceal.

unlocking a: anxiety caused by your
failure, keeps your secrets from your
family.

SAILBOAT
16-18-21-44-45-46

handling a: business plans as at present may
prove futile.

of sailing a boat in open sea: your knack for
adventure should be put to constructive
use.

  with small children: will have mastery
  over many matters, but not money.

  sailor, a: present business plans will
  prove futile.

  sweetheart, alone: will have emotional
  sorrow in love matters.

others in a: your desires will not exceed your
ability to retain, once you possess.

owning a: will come out well from a present
danger.

sailing in a: many difficulties will be faced
then released.

  calm sea, in a: will be fortunate in trade.

    stormy: hindrances will thwart your
    passage, but you are immune.

SAILOR
04-07-09-10-23-26

Bacchus, dreaming of the Greek god: will
recover latent vitality and win a promotion.

being a: restlessness and changes in affairs will
lose you your lover.

falling overboard: speculation will cause loss
of rank.

man dreaming of being with a: convert your
emotions into friends and cope with
them.

  woman: overanxious desire for admiration from afar.

of a: will take a perilous trip that proves to be an exciting adventure.

several: misery: you go down with your captain.

SAILS

11-14-15-24-31-48

handling the, in your boat: are being deceived into making an embarrassing choice.

handling several: your responsibilities include leadership where others have failed.

hoisting a, on a boat: with proper organization your innovative ideas will catch the wind.

of a, for a vessel or boat: an enemy is seeking your ruin.

square, a: problems must be confronted squarely from all points of view.

SAINT

15-21-25-42-44-47

being very close: a long-anticipated reconciliation will bring peace and well-being.

ill person dreaming of a: a suggestion that the wrong illness is being treated.

sinful person: must repent, but confess first.

of a: listen to the message, act on its wisdom.

praying to a: will overcome hurdles to ambitious venture with perseverance.

SALADS

02-06-28-31-37-41

anchovies on a: will receive a legacy with stringent conditions.

eating: your body is asking for more nourishment.

in company of others: will be guilty of foolish actions at a party of strangers.

large bowl of, a: are being swayed by bad press, who belittle your harmonious family.

of: your own qualities will ensure advancement within present position.

preparing a mixed: health may worsen while you are cleansing your colon.

others: are being deceived into feigning an uptight positive.

watercress, buying: will be insulted by neighbors whose snobbery demeans you.

eating: expect an increase in your cash flow.

SALAMI

01-06-11-12-19-40

eating: family arguments over boring, disagreeable relatives.

making a, sandwich: will receive good news from close friends.

of many kinds of: your love is very changeable and unsteady.

slicing: beware of a trap being laid for you.

SALARY

01-05-13-24-40-46

paying: hard work awaits your determination of each person's real value.

others: beware of jealous friends blocking your way.

raise, asking for a: be wise and do not waste time spent doing your job.

and being refused: will create new source of income before you leave this job.

and spending recklessly: everything goes awry; a demotion and cut in pay.

your well deserved: self-confidence comes from wise spending.

receiving a: achievements will be belittled and your job restructured.

others: triumph over enemies, but another will get the spoils.

SALE

10-15-24-35-39-43

of a public: are in the grip of deceitful, frenzied people; hide the family heirlooms.

others selling things: secret enmity of some person is directed at you.

private, a: will do good business without conniving competition.

buying things at: without a challenge to the price, worth cannot be determined.

selling merchandise: don't include a part of yourself in the deal.

own property: a better income brings a change of surroundings.

yourself: are your material gains worth what you paid for them?

SALESMAN

01-14-16-24-25-33

being a: will come out well if you sell with love and affection.

friend: beware of being cheated by friends.

others buying from a: postponement of success until you get what you need.

selling to you, a: there are no stupid questions; if he belittles your questions, don't buy it.

arms, an: your temptation should stop at harming another.

SALIVA
01-04-08-15-20-48

animal, of an: you will overcome your enemies.

coming out of the mouth of a dog: have loyal friends who wish to shower you with gifts.

horse: you can lead yourself to opportunity, but you alone must take it.

others spitting: a foe is endeavoring to destroy your hunger to get on with your project.

sick person, of a: self-destruction is contagious; build up your immune system.

your children, of: their excitement should be moderated for their talents to be developed.

your own: your future happiness is ensured.

SALMON
08-19-29-40-41-44

catching a: accord among friends you meet in an unconventional manner.

eating fresh: a loyal friend will support you through lover's quarrel and reconciliation.

canned: altercations with neighbors over waste disposal.

cooked: even purity needs modification to be palatable.

salad, a: will have sorrow and strife with those controlling your nourishment.

sandwich: opponents will accuse you of the wrongdoing they have secretly done.

smoked: continual dissatisfaction drives your ambition.

SALT
02-06-11-21-23-31

adding, to food: entertain, but do not interfere with another's affairs.

being a, merchant: will make a fixed amount of money as need is steady.

buying: dependable earnings will last a long time for steadfast work.

cooking food with: will receive a mild attack of food poisoning.

of: share your abundant vitality on solid foundations.

pillar of: bury past hurts caused by jealousy on your part and move on.

spilling: are on the right path to money if you throw salt over your shoulder.

others: give no one an opportunity to quarrel over their dissatisfaction.

sprinkling, on a bird's tail: will feel a deep dampening of your social exposure.

using a, shaker: will throw yourself wholeheartedly into the study of science.

on food: religious arguments over errors you wish not to be downcast about.

too much: will miss the perfect opportunity amidst the many offers.

SALVO
02-03-13-14-21-25

hearing a gun salute: recovery of illness comes in small spurts in regular succession.

army giving: contentment at being acknowledged for distinguished source.

navy: progress in enterprises goes quicker with boundaries.

of a: are amidst a war of nerves.

ordering a: with a quibbling evasion, your enemy is saving his pride.

receiving a: a dishonest mental reservation will taint the jury.

SAMPLES
07-09-13-26-31-47

taking, of: are testing the ones you love for things they cannot control.

food: will unwillingly pay a bill you incurred without knowing it.

materials: sickness cannot be cured with experiments on your body.

metals: will be invited to a concert to absorb a previously unknown experience.

minerals: prosperity if you own the source of the raw materials.

various seeds: security in business.

SANATORIUM
03-14-18-40-43-46

being put in a: treachery by relatives who misrepresent your actions.

enemies: financial improvements for the present; prepare for future vengeance.

friends: triumph over persecution with the cleansing of a life.

relatives: avoid being alarmed by the revelation of family secrets, and showing it.

being released from a: big fortune gained in gambling at the tables, not with your sanity.

friends: another who had you committed is promoted above you.

relatives: postponement of success while you rebuild the family name.

of a: you'll make yourself ill if you don't step back from the situation.

working in a: others may not be able to appreciate your contribution.

SAND
05-12-20-29-38-45

bags, using: someone is flooding you with requests from fans.

castles, building: your period of easy fortune is over.

colored: will receive a favor that will reverse into owing one.

dune, a: will be justified by friends as you defend their honor.

handling: will have many small vexations from those wishing to use your influence.

lying on the: reverse the tide before you get soaked.

mixing, with cement: your manipulations are unchangeable.

of: embarrassment and uneasiness, as another puts the grain of his idea in your venture.

others using: will receive unexpected money, which will slip through your fingers.

storm, heading into a: open your eyes to the deception, but don't imagine it everywhere.

property being damaged by a: will build a new house on more solid foundations.

through an hourglass: begin another project while you are waiting.

walking on shifting sand: forced psychological growth with the defense of each step.

working with: defend years of hard work, keeping others from slipping off with your ideas.

SANDALS
08-25-32-33-35-41

Birkenstocks, walking in: the imprint of your dreams; a walking tour of your life.

changing: will have a headache from one badgering for payment of a small loan.

of: good health if you know when to step out of the heat.

taking off: will receive a small unexpected inheritance from stranger.

throwing away: your talents are unknown and undervalued until you express them.

wearing: will have healthy feet and romance at midnight.

SANDWICHES
18-21-22-27-30-46

buying at a fast food restaurant: be wary of falling into a conversation with a stranger.

eating a, with white bread: a delicate approach will yield enormous profit.

dark bread: density does not make your problems less digestible.

made with fish: an opportunity to better your condition in life.

toasted, a: an unfortunate adventure in which you were burned.

various meats: a thin sliver is sufficient.

making, for others: a love affair will explode in your face, your job, your life.

SANITARY
03-18-26-29-33-48

condemning a thing for being unsanitary: your guilt cannot be cleansed that way.

doing, chores: a constant humbling reminder that you are alone.

family helping with: important events, very beneficial to the entire lot.

working in a, department: improvement of career through responsible leadership.

SAPPHIRE
02-13-15-16-17-30

friends wearing a, ring: will receive very pleasant news.

others: disputes with best friends; the solution will be seduced by force.

woman dreaming of: a quieting of the anxiety of material possessiveness.

dark blue: husband will protect you from being molested.

wearing jewelry with: love without sexual expression, but religious fervor.

    bracelets: omen of future gain through foiling many secret enemies.

    not: will attract people of stature and rank.

    rings: a hasty retreat from an emotional situation that projected a hint of evil.

SARDINES
01-07-20-21-30-35

buying, in a tin: troubles are ahead for you, make the decision now.

catching, in a net: those envious of your accomplishments will malign you.

    eating: discontent within the home kitchen; fertility in the bedroom.

frying: will quarrel with a person who is distasteful to you.

making, pie: disagreement among relatives can be combined with your argument with yourself.

marinating: distress rolls over into distraught, a deeper mental illness.

of: have a black mark of dishonor on you.

shoal of: extended family reunion brings pleasant news.

SATISFACTION
07-10-19-28-29-30

being satisfied: are sated with momentary wealth you have not yet paid for.

giving, to friends: will be persecuted for giving to others and lauded for taking away.

    others: loss of present position allows others to fill your shoes; move on.

receiving, from others: a bad lawsuit, where payment will be extracted for gift recovery.

SATURATING
05-12-17-31-32-46

being given something saturated: will receive sad news that you will hang out to dry.

    of something being: your abundance will become in proportion to the saturation.

others, articles: you are seeking a new business.

relatives, something: are unable to find employment in the family field.

SATYR
02-27-31-33-43-44

being a lewd person: will be criticized by the community; give them their just desserts.

doing indecent actions: your immoral pleasures will crush every kindly feeling.

having, friends: will be forced to scheme to keep honor.

others who are: will contract an incurable disease in their company.

Pan, of: your secret liaisons will become known through musical lyrics.

SAUCE
06-14-16-27-32-40

brown: will invite friends in from the cold for a meat and potatoes dinner.

chili: don't trust your first reaction, steel yourself for the fifth.

curry: the harsh blight of reality will be sweetened through time.

gravy, passing a bowl of: will overlook an opportunity that would bring you fame.

    making: loss of rugged health.

        others: financial success through gambling on a new venture.

green: you will suffer from indigestion.

of a ready-made: you have a love of good food.

pan, using a: future from debt is secured if you spend within your means.

preparing a mushroom: will receive favors from an important person.

putting, on food: your pride will not be satisfied with the basics.

tartar, eating: are prone to be malicious in your quick-witted, tart reply.

white: depend on your imagination to gloss over your difficulties.

SAUSAGES
01-08-21-24-27-38

buying: a fortune in business and contentment in life if you avoid promiscuity.

cooking: contentment in home affairs if you use your influence for harmony.

eating: pull together what is left of the situation to create something new.

    liver: poverty, the last resort, the one intuitive value you need.

pork: will win in gambling; your life will not be made toxic.

veal: find new ways to embellish your present career.

with sauerkraut: will steal another's lover and marry.

making: are a very passionate person with a strong sense of your place in the food chain.

SAVANT

03-11-19-39-40-48

being a: intelligence is an incredible burden to bear.

enemies going to a: don't trust that another understands you better than you do yourself.

of a man of learning: wisdom is not learning, but insight.

taking the advice of a: the step you are hop-scotching over will need to be revisited.

SAVING

02-14-22-32-34-42

account, putting money in a financial: will surprise your enemies with friendships.

life of children: your savings enable you to buy a home.

money: have a changeable mind and a flexible bank account.

children: family financial secret will be revealed, leaving little legacy.

other team from scoring, the: a deserved windfall of unimaginable proportions.

someone from drowning: will have dealings with honest people.

committing suicide: public disgrace for putting yourself before another's basic needs.

wrongdoings: reconciliation with enemies.

SAW

04-8-16-31-33-39

buying a: gossip will endanger your reputation and your credit; cut your own work.

dull, a: upgrade your systems to fit the challenge.

hack, to cut metal, using a: the intricacies of your job will take more time with extra pay.

hand: will alter your politics to fit your reality.

of a: progression in business if you reuse the shavings.

rusty with broken teeth, a: your disgrace leads to failure.

sawing wood: your honesty irritates others; reevaluate your methods of sharing.

enemies: move on the issue while they are asleep.

others: accept responsibility for others' failure, not yours.

SCAFFOLD

10-13-14-26-40-43

being executed on a: pass this one deception back to the originator.

being on top of a: sick people will get well with your insightful thoughts.

climbing a: walking the straight and narrow does not raise your stature.

erecting a: your wishing ill will cause another's sickness.

falling from a: are supporting the wrong side of the issue.

many people: will cause injury by disillusioning others.

several, lined up: a rival competitor will press you hard and ruin your dignity.

standing under a: disgrace will fall upon your family with your taking risks.

taking down a: bleeding the company dry leaves nothing to build future means.

under the gallows, a: examine your risks, then move forward on your new venture.

SCALE

03-06-13-37-38-45

balancing a: the only solution is where all parties are satisfied.

being on a: will have dealings with the Justice Department.

others: denotes an arrest causing disappointment and worry.

relatives: will be summoned before a court for relying on what others say as truth.

of a: have not given full weight to one side of the argument.

old-fashioned, an: flattering results in a lawsuit do not equate with justice.

scraping scales from a fish: investigate until you uncover the plot to discredit you.

several: arrest and appearance before a court for an ancestral misdeed.

weighing children on a: will be badly deceived if you expect each time to be the same.

   food: should reexamine the quantities, not what food you eat.

   various things: arguments with friends over the importance of serious issues.

   yourself: your measure is not in your possessions.

SCANDAL

06-09-13-25-40-43

being involved in a: expect to be offended in a social gathering.

   enemies: will be accused of false accusations and gossip.

   farmers: would destroy your neighbors to have a good harvest.

   friends: will underestimate their value by being indifferent to their pain.

creating a: an unwise action will compromise your future.

hearing of a: others are attempting to raise their stature into your confidence.

of a: solving a difficulty will bring honor and triumph.

SCAR

06-15-24-30-39-44

face disfigured by: secret in your past torments you.

having a: dishonor will come to the inflicter of the wound.

   because of a fight: your avoidance of confrontations leaves a scar of guilt.

   from an operation: will attempt to conceal a shameful act.

other's face disfigured with: must learn to forgive them and yourself.

vaccination, a: will have short-lived bitterness with a permanent sin.

SCHOOL

10-25-39-43-47-48

being in, yourself: increase of life's lessons will make the grade.

building, a: learning does not stop when you leave school.

can't open locker: gain access to needed equipment.

children becoming teachers: have promising business affairs and the time to pursue them.

   getting good grades at: need new intellectual challenges.

   going to, alone: broaden your intellectual life before including others.

classroom, being in a: the soul attends classes on the inner planes.

dormitory: are mulling over several plans for the future.

forget class project: fear of failure blocks your new attempts.

going to: business will be in good standing; still, check other options.

   back to: will reencounter a close school friend who had traveled far away.

   dancing, a: your morals make you unfit to fill position.

   elementary, an: are attending basic classes on the spiritual plane.

   grammar, a: will benefit from listening to the suggestions of youth.

   high, a: modesty, feelings of inadequacy; pulling together basic knowledge.

   swimming. a: take precautions against potential risk of being robbed.

grades: a level of distinction that must be earned.

graduation: have completed this stage, go on to a new job and a bigger mortgage.

   attending: rise in social stature.

grammar, correcting another's: will make a wise venture that will prove profitable.

   teaching: will need your strong powers of persuasion.

having a good foundation for: will make good resolutions to build upon.

high school, at your: look for those qualities in a mate.

   night: gift will arrive on schedule, despite roundabout route.

homework, preparing: depends on whether you view this as drudgery or an opportunity.

   correcting another's: will be faced with the truth about another's abilities.

house burns down: don't overspend from a streak of luck that will prove temporary.

integration, being in the process of: will lose staunch friends and gain others.

kindergarten, attending: early marriage and healthy offspring.

of a: will suffer humiliation in the shadow of your past misery.

primer, reading a: learning should be a happy adventure.

reunion, attending a: a resource for the furthering of your career.

spelling bee, being in a: will compete at your own level.

   misspelling: beware of untrue friends who make a minor league, major.

spending money for: boisterous people help you avoid making an adult decision.

students, parents becoming: your life experience is invaluable learning.

   teacher having many good: will have the respect of others for a short time.

   bad: will fall in love with one of them.

superintendent, being a: will have arguments and suffer abuse.

   of a: accept your destiny with resignation and move on.

taking children to: will set a good example if you study your unpredictability.

tassels: will accomplish your goals in cheerful company.

unfamiliar: a surprise from the blue will restructure your opinions.

SCIENCE
01-17-19-20-22-32

Einstein, of: some perplexing problem needs a flash of genius to solve.

   being in a laboratory: security will be tighter than empirical milieus.

   people working in a: singlemindedness runs hand-in-hand with absentmindedness.

scientist, of being a: will obtain a position at the bottom of the laboratory ladder.

   and forgetting something: eccentricity in itself is a creative venture.

   using intricate instruments: your extensive zealous work will finally be recognized.

SCISSORS
03-12-27-30-31-33

buying: you are a precise and proper person, except with jealousy and suspicion.

cutting materials with: will be a victim of prank you inflicted on another.

   cleanly: decisive actions needed to control situation.

   paper: want to put your past behind you, but it keeps rearing its ugly head.

enemies using: feel cut off from your circumstances, keep it that way.

   married couple: your rebelliousness will cause a big love quarrel.

   others: future is not secure if you remain in the battle.

lovers handling: accusations without proof will sever the affair.

of: will be appointed editor of a well-known newspaper.

using manicure: cannot separate yourself from your criticism, which will turn on you.

   left-handed: change to a more visual profession, where your talents are needed.

SCORPION
01-11-23-30-35-42

being bitten by a: discard one fault and the business will succeed.

eating lizards: your idealism will be stung with conscience.

in a cage, a: you are surrounded by boisterous people.

killing a: will suffer loss through the gossip of pretend friends.

killing its mate after sex: get out of that relationship.

nest of, a: overcome enemies by returning their sarcasm in kind.

of a: damages caused by the cynicism of your enemies begun by your overconfidence.

several: enemies spread bitterness behind your back, which may be well-grounded.

SCRATCHING
02-06-8-17-30-34

being scratched by a cat: have disrupted another's inner dissatisfaction.

   children: will experience unexpected personal failure.

dog, a: another's sudden aggressiveness needs explaining.

rosebushes: an annoying setback to your freedom.

woman's nails, a: your love is secured, but will not bring satisfaction.

drawing blood from a scratch: faults of a close friend will irritate you.

others: worries will be smoothed away as you are the one relied upon.

own back: don't break your arm bragging about your approaching money.

head: an ingenious solution to serious doubts.

sweethearts, each other: will injure the connecting tissue between you.

your head: flattery does not equal sincere favors.

yourself: your overambitiousness causes a rashness that precludes success.

not: opponents' plans will be foiled by your reserve.

SCREAMING
07-08-23-25-28-47

calming, of someone suffering: have a violent temper against other's self-destruction.

children: will see your misdeeds avenged on them.

for help: will discover a plot to destroy your disreputable love affairs.

of: will join social forces to demand their betterment.

others: an enemy is seeking your ruin through another.

relatives: quarrels and arguments over the revelation of a family skeleton.

SCREENS
16-25-35-45-47-48

beautiful: double-cross by friends cannot be sugarcoated.

buying a: overexposure is not required.

dividing a room: will attend a comedy, listening to two speakers at once.

folding into the wall: attempt to hide mistakes that will be exposed with a flourish.

undressing behind a: will enjoy beautiful things and the distinction of wearing them.

SCREW
10-12-19-38-42-47

losing a: an element of your life will be voided.

loose, a: find the deal breaker and make them at fault for your reneging.

of: others will try to take your possessions.

turning a: your creative work matches your talents.

vise, working on a: an opportunity to be equitable toward another.

others: turn their screw, make the deal and leave.

SCULPTOR
13-19-30-35-42-43

being friendly with a sculptor: will bring about love but less money.

of a: will be tempted to chisel others' affairs to your specifications.

posing for: expect too many favors from others.

married woman: will be left by her husband.

model, naked: will realize high ambitions if you mind your own business.

virgin: will marry a rich man who fell in love with your image.

widow: a suitable time to pursue your desires, but don't expect permanence.

visiting a: will receive honors for your exciting new centerpiece.

SCYTHE:
12-13-19-21-27-42

cutting grain with a: will use your abilities to gain all nature.

very tall: will receive much attention for your bushwhacking techniques.

dried: sickness from malnutrition.

sharpening a: shame for wrongdoings will prevent you from performing your duties.

small, a: weakness of character leads you to splay out; the blame is yours.

SEA
06-08-13-26-29-38

being adrift in a: loss of control in determining your life's direction.

dead calm, a: a lonely life due to your reserved, self-centered tendencies.

with a loved one: have a sense of security though business is slow.

blue, a: business affairs are running smoothly.

dirty-colored, a: small profit from a weary, unfruitful and toxic life.

falling into the: go back to the beginning and regroup.

   and clutching a piece of wood: will attain goal with hard work.

   waking upon: a woman's love will cause ruin and dishonor.

girl dreaming of a stormy: deep anguish because of a double-cross.

gull in flight: freedom to overcome danger by the safest method.

   hovering over the: pick your belief system and commit to it.

   many, in formation: your courageous defiance within corporate situation.

horse, harnessing a: will join an RV caravan.

lagoon, mooring in a: desire privacy to face your fears.

lonely person dreaming of the: a life without love is a life unlived.

looming above the surface of the: time for you to participate instead of control.

   of the open, with small waves: the tranquility before the complete disruption of your career.

overwhelmed by waves: possessions rapidly increase in value, more than you can handle.

sucked into the depths: an experience with cosmic consciousness.

swimming in the warm: wisdom that does not require words will soon be yours.

taking a bath in the: honor is supporting your indiscriminate pleasures, for now.

   men and women: connubial bliss without honor or profit.

thrown by force into the, being: an agreement cannot be reached.

traveling across a very rough: business affairs threaten to dissolve.

   man and wife: great and lasting love in material pleasures of true refinement.

   smooth: devoted love within the family will support you in any venture.

   typhoon, during a: adversity cannot be calmed or fought, only withstood.

walking out of the: a refreshing start to a venture with a clear vision of your mission.

waves on the, large: will receive unexpected help when you think you need it least.

SEAL

11-14-24-30-35-41

breaking the, on a letter: loss of present position through your obsessive ambition.

of the, of the government: are striving for a place above your power to maintain.

opening a sealed letter: the beginning of a new regime; establish your place.

putting own, on legal papers: have exhausted any objections to your scheme.

   letter, a: will escape danger if you keep the secret.

sealing a letter: are seeking security.

wax: your reservation precludes your putting your mark on the decision.

SEALS

01-02-19-26-34-45

catching a: secret enemies are working against you.

coming onto the beach: will soon become pregnant.

diving: abundant means does not mean indiscriminate extravagance.

killing a: the last resort, after an impossible task in business.

of: are pushed on by abnormal ambitions, but will never attain your goal.

   Navy, a: will accomplish what you set out to do.

sealskin coat, a: approaching money from a sensitive and excited aggression.

small, in an aquarium: security.

taking oil from a: if you have to destroy another to win, it is not a victory.

SEARCHING

03-06-23-29-36-45

for a lost object: family dishonor can be rectified.

   something: infidelity cannot be recovered from.

others: will prate about what you wish were in your life.

own house being searched by the law: tranquility of conscience is required.

through the house: warning of an impish foe who sabotages your efforts.

husband's pockets: your action will be defended with your findings.

for lost personal effects: beware of thieves within your mind.

SEARCH WARRANT
02-08-13-30-34-43

being found innocent: suspicion is destructive, no matter how mature.

given to others: financial gains.

handed a: will be unable to gratify your ambitions.

the cause of a: your guilt is no longer yours alone.

SECRETARY
05-06-07-30-31-39

being a male: will enjoy, by osmosis, riches that you cannot live with.

female: keep your boss from falling in love with you.

cabinet, of a: this decision cannot be delegated, and will be accompanied by a large raise.

female at work: will have a good fortune ahead.

male: don't underestimate talents—no matter how they are packaged.

firing a male: he will fall in love with a member of the family.

female: family discord over their criticism of your choices.

hiring a male: business disputes must be free of emotional involvement.

female: will be well situated for the rest of your life, but will not rise above it.

taking dictation: are responsible for others' words and subsequently your ideas.

SECRETS
16-27-34-40-44-45

being told a: a tremendous burden you may not want.

whispered in ear: public dignity to be bestowed on you.

betraying a: divine punishment on your malicious gossip, results will be the same.

children keeping, from parents: a prompt engagement of friendly inquiry is required.

couples, each other: diligence without truth cannot equal love.

communicating a: don't expect your own secrets to be kept.

friends telling you a: intrigue among people you trust is still intrigue.

having a: everyone knows the secret you think you are hiding.

among themselves: introducing friends allows them to unite against you.

telling a: if of another, your secrets are not safe either.

SECURITY
07-09-12-16-24-43

having financial: will do your duty as a good citizen; invest money in government bonds.

for old age: future ambitions are overzealous; try anyway.

mates feeling secure about each other: family happiness is based on sincerity.

putting money in, for children: the least you can do; don't expect any back.

receiving, from others: good financial speculation done by others for your benefit.

SEDUCING
12-20-25-27-32-41

being seduced: a complicated situation needs rectifying before it becomes violent.

but escaping: are too sentimental and impressionable to recognize a seducer.

Lothario, flirting with a: be on the lookout for the seducer among seeming innocents.

man being arrested for, a woman: many perplexities in proving your innocence.

marrying the man who seduced you: are dealing with frivolousness, not love.

teenager, girl of same age: death of the family in divisive accusations.

very young girl, a: business will run as you desire and stall on legal formalities.

woman by force, a: your actions will turn on you.

SEEDS
04-06-09-15-27-47

bird: dishonor among the greedy.

making your own: your life experiences are germinating.

planting flower: prosperity by following up on your latest idea.

   grain: matrimony is being planned among children.

   vegetable: discomfort in your work will prove fruitful if allowed.

shop, a: an unknown person is talking about you; listen carefully.

sowing: if you follow your nurturing route, your deeds will sprout to success.

sprouting: all the materials for success are within yourself.

SEESAW
06-15-23-25-39-43

breaking a: will have an unexpected visitor of equal weight and prominence.

children playing on a: many delightful ups and downs in your future.

   being hurt when: your relationship with them is one-sided.

handling a: unexpected love affairs that will not last long.

SELLING
02-04-07-16-29-34

business, a: will have family arguments over your failure to observe your heritage.

credit, on: are uncertain the price given is equal to the emotional drain at its loss.

jewelry: your morbid imagination creates scenarios you wish it hadn't.

mechanical things: unhappiness if you don't supply technical support.

milk and cheese: have taken on the responsibility of another's health.

own belongings: how much do you need to feel comfortable with yourself?

   poor man, to a rich man too cheaply: only money makes money.

property: illness through toxicity not revealed at closing.

small quantities of merchandise: lack the confidence to gain abundance and riches.

things of steel: are allowing others to build your life.

tobacco: a high of peaceful origins turns destructive when overexposed.

SEMINARY
01-06-11-19-28-36

being the dean of a: will suffer misery to the depth of your responsibility.

student: a false friend is attempting to cause harm.

not being accepted into a: new life will bring good profits and little else.

visiting a: will have a son who will become a priest.

SENATE
03-05-20-26-29-41

being a member of the: will be pursued by those asking favors.

   making love to a: will feel social prominence by being the one most gossiped about.

listening to arguments of senators: will have ability to fool some people, but not all of them.

of the: will have disputes over ridiculous things.

visiting the: avoid telling lies or you will be misled by friends.

SENDING
06-10-19-38-43-51

business merchandise: are supporting the proliferation of wealth.

clothes in a package: what you wish to throw away is always of use to another.

foodstuffs to poor people: will receive a sad announcement; turn it pleasant.

gift to a loved one, a: a good harvest must be shared to be repeated.

letter or package, a: are making your wishes known in a palatable form.

SENTENCE
10-29-32-41-43-51

being sentenced to death: what have you done for which you feel such insane guilt?

   to prison: are wrong and have to comply with another's decision.

   unjustly in a lawsuit: people are telling lies about you, as you are to yourself.

reading a, from a book: waste time with many pleasures instead of concentrating on you.

receiving a: do not confide in others your guilt or innocence.

writing an incorrect, in a letter: have not got a clear conscience; settle the confusion.

SENTINEL
02-04-31-32-46-50

being a: your surroundings are well-guarded, with little flexibility.

being killed by a: desires and hopes will be accomplished.

warned by a: death is near for whoever crosses the line.

lonely, a: new business will take you on a journey south.

many a: beware of those in whom you have placed trust.

shooting to sound an alarm: be cautious in your affairs.

SEPARATION
15-18-27-31-34-41

children's marriage, of: an inheritance of flaws unsealed and thoughts unsaid.

friends, of: sickness of children who depended upon their attention.

having a final: the dissolution of an unsupported union.

husband and wife, of: gossip by friends becomes more lascivious than the truth.

others desiring your: beware of shady people; look for their motives.

planning a, from someone: feel you must introduce old lover to the new lover.

separating from a business partner: success in your portion of the business.

those you love: failure of some cherished plan because no one asked what they wanted.

sweethearts, of: idle talk by people around you does not constitute truth.

sweetheart wanting a: be cautious in business transactions involving mate.

SEPTEMBER
05-11-27-28-39-42

being born in: abundant means to accomplish growth of your talents.

children: your future is secured in their commitment to it.

of, during the month of: gather the fruits of your labor and store them for the winter.

of, during other months: changes that you can take advantage of.

SEPULCHER
04-05-18-23-36-53

being in a, with sweetheart: a letter will bring happiness.

building a: you live by a cavalier moral code, which makes you vulnerable to misery.

for family: birth of a boy who will establish the family name.

going into a: will go into ruin, unless you break out of the family heritage.

visiting a, alone: sad news can be born only in spirit.

with others: unpleasant family news requires discussion.

partner: good news concerning a birth or rebirth of generosity.

white, a: noble, respectable and virtuous.

SERENADE
08-10-14-17-46-48

enjoying a: will receive a proposal within the month and have a lasting love.

hearing a: be cautious not to cast a flower unless the one who serenades is your choice.

lovers listening to a: will quarrel and break up over frivolous attention of others.

singing a: will suffer financial embarrassments.

SERMON
26-38-40-41-42-51

being a preacher and giving a long: are conflicted between Utopia and practical reality.

delivering a short: your amiable friends enjoy an irresponsibility you cannot.

following the advice of a: are very superstitious with those who mean well.

hearing a: approaching temporary illness over a problem not solved.

SERPENT
01-04-15-30-34-53

arguing with a: unfulfilled sexual desires cannot be consummated.

being bitten by a: enemies are accusing you of hatred and illness.

biting its own tail: your situation has come full circle.

crawling through your legs: awakened sexual energy.

killing a: are too boisterous to acknowledge a seduction even you want.

moving away, a: ungrateful people you aided demand your imprisonment.

physician's caduceus: healing is taking place within yourself.

psychic energy from a blue: religiosity.
   golden: glory to God.
   green: budding emotional desires.
   orange: idealism, emotions and sexuality.
   red: seduction.
   violet: intellectual power.
   white: spiritual insight.
shedding skin: new opportunities are close
   by and need uncovering
unwinding, a: sickness.
water, a: recovery from an illness; the
   treatment is acceptance of nightmares
   as reality.
white, a: wisdom will be received by open
   minds and ears.
with several heads: will seduce a beautiful girl
   on all fronts.
   catching a: will go fishing in polluted
      waters.
   killing a: victory over enemies with your
      bare hands; your demons will be
      released.

SERVANT
01-02-04-16-34-40
being a: act like a servant and you will be
   treated like one.
female, a: another's gossip will be harmful.
   male, a: wish to exercise your authority to
      someone, anyone.
firing a: will sustain heavy losses that you will
   regret through subsequent actions.
   hiring: someone will steal from you.
manservant, being a: someone of evil intent is
   watching for a breach of etiquette.
   firing a: good manners taken to the
      extreme bring unexpected repercus-
      sions.
of own, waiting on you: mold your inferiority
   complex into humility.
   others': friends are endeavoring to destroy
      you.
   several: persevere and stick close to your
      affairs; listen for any sign of dissent.
quarreling with: are too involved with ideal
   business arrangement to see what exists.
served by a, being: infidelity; work smarter,
   not harder.
   having a: a childhood friend will resurface
      and call you on your arrogance.

work, a, at: may wish to turn your anger to
   aiding a worthy cause.

SERVICE
09-15-16-36-46-47
asking for, from others: may need time to
   absorb disgrace in the family.
attending a church: wish to share the contentment in your own heart.
being of, to friends: time to restore your faith
   in yourself.
china, a: gossip by neighbors can be stopped
   by having a dinner party.
giving, to others: will incur debts, but your
   talents must be shared.
silverware, a: a servant is stealing from you
   and is self-righteous about it.

SEWER
08-10-16-21-27-46
being chased in the: are drained of emotion;
   time for regeneration.
flowing out to fresh water: don't forgot the
   step about confirming evidence before
   slandering.
of a: all waste is reusable by someone.
overcome by the stench in a, being: forgot to
   take out the garbage.
splashing through the: dispose of mild irritation to allow elimination of noxious
   fumes.

SEWING
16-24-26-30-44-50
basting: extravagance opens you to much
   vexation.
clothes for yourself: bring aspects of your life
   together.
daughter: engagement will soon be
   announced; a trousseau prepared.
fashioning new garments: will manipulate
   your work into a more lucrative position.
for the home: make specific adjustments to
   your personal reality.
seam, a: a melding of contradictions only you
   can comprehend.
stitching: repairs are needed in some area.
tailor, a: will receive news from abroad.

SEX
12-15-16-24-46-52
female, a: will live a life of constant giving and
   later exacting a price for it.

daughter: an urge to bond with a refreshing view of yourself.

homosexual, being a: acceptance of who you are with no apology or hostility.

Lolita, being a: your amorous intentions are being rejected.

desiring a: age is only a state of mind.

male, a: are responsible for the survival of the species.

boy: luck and prosperity and a continuation of the family name.

man changing his: time to pay attention to your anima.

woman, her: a son will be born to bring honor to family.

man having sexual desires: public disgrace and private horror.

woman: immediate success of hopes if you follow through with them.

SEXUAL ADVANCES
01-03-04-11-19-41

groping, of: affairs are improving, do not despair.

your way along: an introduction will cheer you shortly.

of a lewd person: will be jilted by your lover for a momentary fling.

being arrested: be cautious in your dealings that the truth is self-evident.

reprimanding: freedom includes making a supreme fool of yourself.

SEXUAL INTERCOURSE
05-16-25-34-44-53

being impotent yourself: will have unforeseen wealth you are powerless to activate.

of uniting in: happiness is ensured if intent is pure.

others who are having: unless it's your mate, it's none of your business.

with several people: have lost all sense of boundaries, exposing yourself to harm.

SEXUAL ORGANS
03-11-20-33-42-45

being in good condition: there is no end to your capabilities.

exposing the: danger of losing potency in full disclosure.

man having a disease of the: poverty is insufficient punishment for a crime.

woman: warning of troubles with conception until virtuous son is born.

sterile, being: are too generous with loved ones; must adopt a child of your own.

uterus, having pains in the: are seizing property to which you have no legal right.

removed, having the: will make good money, but will be unable to establish credit.

woman having ovaries removed: death of a member of the family.

SHADOW
02-11-14-33-35-55

being afraid of a: will be threatened by a great enemy; you need to excise yourself.

your own: acknowledge your negatives and integrate them.

enemies, of: negative parts of yourself projected onto others.

evil spirits, of: what moral defect of yours is this expressing?

friends, of: beware of being tricked into believing their view of you.

many: an unrecognized negative will overwhelm you.

misty, a white: blissful remembrance of your mother checking you in your sleep.

own: financial gains through legal affairs.

The: represents everything about yourself that you hate.

tree, of a: a friend you thought was faithful will cheat you.

being in the: will receive a proposal of love.

SHAMROCK
04-06-23-31-44-45

giving a, to others: suitable time to pursue courtship.

having a: prosperity in love affairs and joy in life.

others: arrival of three unexpected invitations for the same date.

picking: your lightheartedness will bring you big fortune.

receiving a: news of old matters will change your affairs.

wearing a: a false friend is nearby.

SHARK

02-07-21-30-35-52

being killed by a: will overcome obstacles, but lose friends.

   bitten, but not killed: bad results in business if you allow it.

   others: will help others escape from serious trouble.

catching a: affairs are running too smoothly.

escaping from a: serious illness from another's deceit.

of a: troubles if you deceive another.

SHARPENING

09-10-25-26-37-40

blade, a: congenial partnership can only improve.

knives: speak with a sharp tongue to the traitor, a soft one to a friend.

of a person who sharpens knives: good fortune for adventurers.

pencil, a: dissension within the family.

scissors: someone is attempting to break up a marriage.

tools: loss of occupation is not a forgone conclusion.

SHAVING

13-14-32-34-47-53

beard, having a thin: are unwilling to share your potency with others.

   red: will be annoyed by creditors for debts you didn't incur.

   thick: will make sufficient money on the edge and will not be overdrawn.

being shaved by a barber: don't buy the shares and stocks he suggests.

having completed: are guilty of molesting women with your gossip.

head of a man, the: losses in gambling.

   nun: unprofitable ambitions, well meant and well received.

lathering before: will solve a pressing problem by looking in the mirror.

neckline: don't refuse the proposition, combine it with your ideas.

someone else is, you: do not rise to the bait, no matter how provoked.

woman dreaming of, under her arms: are liked by men because of a passion for travel.

legs: will refuse a proposal without understanding its significance.

woman shaving a man: women give you the brush-off.

yourself: use succinct analysis in the difficulties ahead.

SHAWL

06-09-17-27-35-54

black: grief at being careless with your discretion.

buying a: will receive a visit from a doctor.

giving a, as a gift: will have deep affection from one you love.

large white, a: purity and virtue.

red: are too loose with your affections.

various other colored shawls: affairs will run smoothly and adventurously.

wearing a: someone will be cruel to you, with no long-term intent or effect.

   embroidered, given as a gift, an: unjustified gossip about you.

   friends: must pay more attention to business.

   poor people: enemies are plotting against you.

   relatives: will go to a funeral parlor.

   young girls: are surrounded by fast-talking people.

SHEARS

06-12-18-24-25-45

buying: long life full of necessities and few luxuries.

using: prosperity if you sell the cuttings.

   on animals: are sharing your survival instincts.

   to cut own hair: have little respect or use for professional talents.

      prisoner's: are embarrassed by attempted cleanliness, destroying any respect for yourself.

SHEEP

02-18-32-44-45-53

black, being the family: temptation will send your life away.

bleating of one lamb, hearing: your business will prosper with good advertising.

   several lambs: have patience with pain and it will disappear.

buying: good earnings in stock speculation.

counting: quibbling invitations and transient hindrances drive you to distraction.

drinking milk of: will be molested for no apparent reason.

ewe, of an: a large family and prosperity to come.

> *many together:* riches and abundance, if you economize and plan for old age.
>
> > *fighting among themselves:* hard work without a goal breeds discord.
>
> *milking:* abundant means are offered to you at present.

fighting: your compliancy will fail you; challenge your detractors.

flock of, a: your manipulating to stand out in the herd will cost you.

having a herd of fine quality: are overly obedient.

losing: will be abandoned if you agree too quickly.

ram, of a: your assertiveness is overpowering.

sacrificial, on an altar: resolve challenges without making yourself a martyr.

seeing lambs: diligent work will be seen as silly, bringing moderate abundance.

selling: your tactics will ruin an enemy and salvage your reputation.

shearing: success through well-conceived plans of others.

squirting milk of, into own mouth: are letting others provide your nourishment.

SHEETS
03-13-17-27-39-40

clean-colored sheets on: arrival of unexpected guests; be prepared.

escaping out the window with: a venture consummated quickly will be paid for over time.

sleeping in decorated: a promotion satisfying your need for just recompense.

> *dirty:* come clean with an apology for your present intolerant bitterness.
>
> *pure white:* will have little cause to worry, as never before.

tangled in, being: too many hearts are involved in your affairs.

washing: letting another do the work doesn't work.

SHELF
07-25-27-40-45-54

putting books on a: will soon have an accident you could have prevented.

> *groceries on shelves:* family disputes over cooking.
>
> *hats:* business affairs are all confused; will attain goal with hard work.
>
> *linen:* your conscience is not clear; you are not a virgin but an experienced lover.
>
> *pans:* unavoidable loss of money.
>
> *pillows and blankets:* will be deceived by one you love and warned by one you don't.
>
> *shoes:* death of a member of the family in the bed of another.

several: your desires will be opposed; defending them, futile.

SHELLFISH
02-07-33-35-40-44

abalone, eating: unusual experience with envious acquaintances.

clean, a: will go into bankruptcy if you cook the books.

crawfish, a: in meeting deceit, retreat, regroup and engage in battle.

gathering: fleeting pleasures at a séance.

many live: are in a protected environment; are sheltered and nourished.

> *cockle:* bad news from afar clears the way for romantic developments at home.
>
> *dead:* are suddenly thrust into reality.
>
> *gathering:* will receive a sad letter, to your family's profound embarrassment.
>
> *mollusk, a:* mysterious happenings claim your attention; do not believe what you hear.
>
> > *of shells:* extravagance earned from victory in the field.
>
> *rough, a:* change of residence will improve your own circumstances.
>
> *smooth, a:* the passion in your love affairs has been worn down.

scallops, eating: a movement toward a peaceful, well-furnished home.

SHEPHERD
07-23-25-33-35-55

being far away from his flock: misfortune

will be brief, leading to a long and healthy life.

farmer dreaming of a: need outside support from your unusually bountiful harvest.

leading herd of sheep to pasture: are full enough to give spiritual nurturance to others.

through a forest: will find valuable things if you dig in the underbrush.

living in a forest: profit from a secret well-kept and well-cultivated.

losing some of his flock: your preoccupation with your own affairs neglects your work.

several, gathering flocks: honor of short duration on your route to success.

watching: good earnings ahead if you take yourself seriously.

very young: prosperity and good reputation will take years of minor upsets to develop.

whose flock is scattered: big earnings will be taken from you bit by bit.

SHINGLES

05-20-14-32-40-43

being debilitated by: your grief must be addressed

buying: will fall into much money, which you must invest to keep.

nailing: loss of a friend.

painting: will get out of debt for a momentary concealment of funds.

putting, on a house: will achieve security and warmth through hard work.

selling: will make inevitable errors of salesmanship.

suffering from: will experience a personal loss.

SHIP

04-08-11-13-25-44

ballast, a broken: friends are not trustworthy when the going gets rough.

full, a: partner can be trusted if you are trustworthy.

battle, a: the sense of security allows you to be more productive.

being afloat, a big ship: the boat will stop rocking only if you accept responsibility.

being on the bridge of a: a sail across the sea is a lonely introverted journey.

boarding a: make amends, then leave and see who distrusts you.

the wrong: your direction is being influenced by the wrong person.

build a model of a: will marry your beloved within a year.

deck of a, being on the: will contribute a valuable discovery to mankind.

during calm weather: unhappiness and inferiority await you.

stormy: a productive adventure will deserve both praise and riches.

with opposite sex: temporary temptations must be overcome to gain a long-term love.

dreadnought in a battle, a: disastrous quarrels with in-laws.

frigate, a: a dangerous adventure is eased by knowing true north.

going aboard a, with all of immediate family: are tending to the security of your flock.

gong of a, the: avoid trifling with problems in present job, return to old one.

keel: news from a lover at sea whose loneliness matches yours.

damaged, being: have lost your sense of proportion.

longshoreman loading a: a job offer you should accept within the month.

man-of-war, a: dissension in political affairs calls you to arms.

merchant seamen, embarking on a: the ultimate productive escape.

marine troops: failure of enemies at your capable hands.

navy sailors: enemies must be defeated at whatever the cost.

mermaid at the bow of a: brute seduction leads to misfortune for the seducer.

mooring a vessel, yourself: now is the time for courage, not fear.

narrows on a, passing through: will obtain what you dared not hope for.

poop deck of a: will hold up the rear of a team you wish to be part of.

prisoner dreaming of a: your stratagem will be unveiled and taint your reputation.

lovers, docking: marriage will not be realized; must rely upon your own vigor.

scraped, being: warning of trouble in the offing.

setting sail, a: separation anxiety from a needed change.

> *with all sails up:* will receive unexpected good news to support your adventures.

sinking: will have to do more than tread water to save your good name.

> *after a collision:* good ventures in the future if you change partners.

stateroom, being in a: each aspect of your life has its own pigeonhole.

stern of a, the: will be double-crossed by a loved one when disaster strikes.

submarine, being in a: have hidden from reality too long.

> *and firing a torpedo:* a secret business plan comes to fruition.

> *yellow:* joy is 90 percent under water.

traveling on a, with business people: very good fortune among fellows.

two, going in opposite directions: a problem you can't solve, another you perhaps can.

yard, building vessels in a: honor above your present life style.

> *repairing a, in a:* will be in financial distress from which you can be salvaged.

> *working in a:* will have money during old age if you keep your intrigues private.

SHIPWRECK
12-17-24-34-38-43

abandoning ship: affairs will soon take a turn for the worse.

> *but reaching land:* good financial earnings, but loss of your good name.

being shipwrecked with family: mutual support will aid the whole.

> *saved after a:* your health needs a consultation with an expert.

> *sinking into the sea:* anxieties over others' moral lapses are affecting your reputation.

> *with one you love:* a big catastrophe will be shared, strengthening the relationship.

broken pieces of a ship after a: a life must include all bits and pieces to work.

landing on rocks, and: sickness will interrupt your progress.

losing your life in a: arrival of an unexpected friend to relieve the pressure on you.

others in a: beware of rivals you created.

raft after an, in a: must endure troubles before realizing desires.

SHIRT
02-08-25-42-46-48

button missing, with a: your error of omission will be exposed.

buying: will be told many falsehoods.

changing shirts: don't throw away old relationships.

dirty, a: will contract a contagious disease.

evening, an: a dramatic upturn of operatic proportions.

ironing a: you love someone who doesn't love you.

losing a: hedge your bets with multiple projects.

putting on a: will be neglected but must protect yourself.

taking off a: will be disillusioned over estrangement from loved one.

torn, a: good fortune if you are not careless with the details.

washing a: your central nervous system requires restoration to its initial working order.

wearing a fancy sport: sweethearts will break up through frivolous insensitivity.

SHIVERING
02-03-10-27-46-56

children: loss of a member of the family through kidnapping.

dressing warmly to keep from: loss of an inheritance.

others: will lose money in stock market transactions.

relatives: they will soon receive new clothes.

wife and husband: will buy something they both like.

SHOCK
06-27-38-39-41-47

being shocked by bad news: will have mastery over your affairs if you are resilient.

> *by a loved person:* will overcome enemies with perseverance.

shocking a loved one: your love is changeable, as is theirs.

members of own family: will overcome difficulties only by confessing their source.

others: beware of a trap being laid for you.

SHOE POLISH
01-04-19-28-46-54

being a shoeblack: pride has gone beyond reason; its value is yours alone.

polishing shoes: perfection is a doable activity.

having shoes polished by professional: will have legal dealings with an attorney.

shoeshine boy shining others' shoes: joy and contentment.

of dreamer's husband: will receive invitation to a dance.

SHOES
13-17-20-41-46-52

being without: expect a difficult route to business success.

buying a pair of: the beginning of a lengthy project of many parts.

children's: are overly concerned about the health of those dependent upon you.

buying new, for: unexpected good results in long-term business.

clogs, buying: are prying overly into other's affairs; your findings will shock you.

putting on: prepare for a wedding in the near future.

wearing: stride over your previous boundaries; continue on the route you chose.

cobbler, being a: the essence of probation.

having, repaired by: salvaging the positive from amidst the downtrodden.

finding one: a stranger will bring a promising offer.

pair of, a: break off the oppressive relationship.

gaiters of: will be very fortunate in love affairs if you follow your hunches.

wearing: have delusions of grandeur about your bank account.

others: will be snubbed by a person you esteem.

regular shoes with: a tiresome journey is ahead, pleasantries tainted by rivalries.

having black: desertion of friend will create bad times.

blue: a friend will be lost to you through sickness.

suede: will have happy days that can easily be ruined.

high boots: will need to pay bribery to keep a secret.

new: will have a large profit from a short journey.

old comfortable: have become too married to your couch.

other qualities of leather shoes: your timidity will cause you to fall into ruin.

white: your future is completely secure and will be uplifting.

with holes in the soles: your lack of confidence causes you to miss an appointment.

heel, injured: others will exploit your weakness; take up the opportunity offered.

holes in soles, with: a major overhaul of a project is needed.

laces or buckles coming undone: quarrels with relatives over ill-founded opinions.

lacking, when not appropriate: your approach is outmoded; share the new ideas.

leather: don't listen to the flattery of others.

losing: only poverty can come from continuing on this path.

maker, a: a project you thought was dead will revive.

repairing your: a failing project can be saved with fresh investors.

men's: postponement of success in business affairs until your superior notices you.

of: will have no obstacles in path to achieving your goal.

pain, which cause: your physical problems should be diagnosed.

pair of, in store window: if you relax, the goal is yours.

patched: your tactless, outspoken bluntness is causing you financial difficulties.

repairing: your tactfulness will lead to a tranquil productive life.

resoling a woman's: flirting, however innocent, breeds deceitful desires.

spats, of men's: recovery from an illness, with an advancement in position.

wearing: will have mastery over love matters, but lose your job.

others: someone with evil intentions is watching you.

tack into, driving a: will be asked to perform a small service—will profit only if done willingly.

tight, wearing: a foe is constricting your progress and taking liberties during your delay.

tree, putting shoes in a: unfavorable news.

boots: will be worn out from overwork.

wearing high heels: your efforts are finally rewarded.

for weather conditions: greater flexibility is needed now.

spike: no one buys a cow when the milk is free.

wrong, for the occasion: are not listening to your heart.

women's: expressing who you are, walking on to get what you want.

worn out, going into the mud with: period of despondency from poverty of the soul.

SHOOTING
02-20-23-25-35-49

artillery: condemnation of your ideas and overusing them.

being shot: abuse from a source you had depended upon.

birds: false gossip by friends flutters about and must be squelched.

contest, in a: will have an opportunity to better yourself.

enemies: domestic troubles from outside sources.

hearing: misunderstandings between married people.

killing someone, and: hostile disputes from an unforeseen source.

only one shot: big profit if you find a partner; disaster if you solo.

others, at you: will be disgraced for acting without your evidence.

people, at other: family roughhousing can get out of hand.

something but missing: will overcome difficulties of a temporary nature.

target, and hitting the: your candor will produce success.

SHOPPING
02-12-15-21-29-47

cosmetics in a drugstore, for: the invitation is in the mail.

different articles, buying in a: trouble ahead in financial matters.

food staples, for: the beginning of security, the basis of your wealth.

going into a, with others: opinions must be accumulated because they do matter.

that does small business: love affairs are insecure if not continually expanded.

having purchases delivered: the contract has not been signed.

mall, of a: good fortune follows efforts.

being at a: ruin of another's business.

mannequin, fixing a, in a window: beware of being left standing while others party.

with no clothes on: financial gains.

operating a: success.

paying too much: are trying to impress lover, unsuccessfully.

sales, in: the sale price may indeed be the fair price.

store, buying things in a department: rapid advancement climbing the ladder to success.

SHORE
02-07-16-33-40-47

being at the: an internal conclave of your conscious and unconscious selves.

friends: the disposition of your morale; God will provide for you.

relatives: will be able to avoid perils, being without their inertia and laziness.

boardwalk, walking on the: an expected, long delayed legacy.

boat coming into: will receive a rich gift unexpectedly.

going to a seaside: a distant person will change your mood to sudden anger.

people shoring up something: have overblown impractical ambitions.

surf, being hit by the: you will be guilty of foolish actions.

    receding: succeeding at something no matter how small encourages success.

tide, at high: will eventually get the praise you deserve.

    low: will make your fortune in waste management.

used to prop something up, a: will receive help you sorely need from someone.

using a, inside the house: don't fail to help needy people.

SHOULDERS
01-07-08-16-19-37

beautiful naked: an explanation can forestall a setback in matters of the heart.

bony: sickness through being overburdened with other's ills.

children's: will receive a letter containing good news.

heavy: are carrying weight others should take back.

large muscular: will enjoy excellent health to master your life.

others': must rely upon your own vigor and not let others rely on you.

placing your head on another's: need a reprieve from your plight.

    and crying: choose wisely which friend you depend upon.

    someone, your: an appeal for support, which should be given.

prisoner dreaming of having large: will remain in prison.

SHOVEL
05-07-29-40-46-51

buying a: will be robbed of time and energy, but still complete the task.

of a: friends will come to the rescue financially.

owning a: you foolishly desire credit for work done.

using a: must rely upon your own good judgment as responsibilities increase.

    children: problems leave as quickly as they arrive.

    laborer's: good health and shaky finances.

    others: friends will come to your rescue financially.

SHOWER
02-16-18-35-40-41

being showered upon: the kudos are going to their rightful owner.

showering upon another: need to transfer the onus to its creator.

taking a: cleanse yourself of negative press.

    children: their mother is smothering their individuality.

    guests: an all-embracing problem to organize creature comforts.

    others: purge the false, support the truth.

SHOWING
06-15-24-32-27-42

childish qualities: must revert to earlier times to enjoy a long life.

figure, your: people can't see beyond your beauty, to your intelligence.

personal belongings: pride attracts the envious.

teeth: will have a dispute about personal integrity versus power.

yourself: have too much vanity to hide yourself, too much fear to expose it.

zealous actions: all desires will be realized through the chances you take.

SHRIMP
01-10-17-20-28-45

cooking: death of a friend from overexposure.

crayfish, cooked: disappointment due to poor judgment in love affairs.

eating: disgrace of highly respectable people you depended on.

fishing for: will have a big honor bestowed on you.

raw: will have a bad business transaction rectified.

SHRUBS
04-17-28-30-40-53

boughs, several evergreen: work hard for your true and steady friend.

boxwood hedge, a: the solution may be a leap, but you will solve a vexing problem.

cutting down: danger through a secret exposed and inflicted upon your privacy.

green leaves, full of: news brings great joy in your home.

hedge clipping: will overcome any obstacle your unruly partner presents to you.

crawling through a: will be ostracized by a socially prominent couple.

hiding behind: imminent danger from exposure of depressing love affairs.

others: speedy recovery from opposition in love to a bright future.

seeing someone purposefully: beware of gossips.

holly, giving: nostalgic memories of Christmas and hearth.

picking: beware of vexations that taunt you into depression.

wreaths of: luck materially and socially will continually renew itself.

juniper, of: someone will speak evil about you and it will be exposed in your favor.

berries, cooking with: be warned against associating with loose immoral characters.

laburnum, of a: someone will attempt to poison your vigorous mind.

lavender, of: take the unsavory actions of others with a grain of salt.

leafless, brittle or bare: your plan's failure cannot be reversed.

pushing through: will have a change for the better.

tangled undergrowth: are nervous about a threat of a secret affair.

whacking way through the bushes: disadvantages eventually will prove for the best.

SHUTTING
06-14-20-36-37-49

box, a: the contents of your life need not be exposed just yet.

door, a: will be highly considered for a new position but not for an old one.

in someone's face: as one door closes, another opens.

down, of: big neighborhood scandal will tarnish your estate.

office or business: should have made plans for your old age long ago.

drawers: finalize the organization of your life.

jewelry box, a: protect your dearest heritage from another's envy.

safe, a: jealousy in the family cannot be contained with restrictions.

SHY
13-27-28-31-38-41

being: others' confidence in your abilities matches yours.

children: are surrounded by jealous people, but you are not their object of envy.

mate: trust relatives for advice in your obstacle course at work.

others: plans will turn out unsatisfactorily, if you make them that way.

work, at: modesty never gained a promotion.

SICK
10-12-27-30-37-42

being: are inclined to being melancholy, which will encourage rivals.

children: the challenge of life is to avoid sadness.

mentally: you're coddling grief where lamentation exceeds the cause of the sorrow.

to the stomach: squandering of possessions; overeating to gain them back.

caring for, people: count on giving with no return expected.

loved ones who are: will succumb to a temptation that will impair others' progress.

visiting, people: will find a way to reach your goal without endangering your health.

at a hospital: listen to the anger of helplessness and let it go.

SIDEWALK
06-37-38-41-46-48

being with a loved one on a: will have an argument over love and harmony making up.

children walking on a: prosperity if you avoid the cracks.

falling on a: are prone to having a bad temper, which disrupts your coordination.

on the left: bad times are ahead; sinister, inauspicious anarchy.

right: good times are ahead; adroit adept mastery.

walking with mate on a: will be invited to a wedding.

SIEGE
17-26-31-35-48-55

being inside an area under: you have false friends.

castle surrendering under: are confident your financial venture will yield benefits.

continuous state of: limit your expenses to withstand unwarranted pressure.

relatives being in a: will become an actor or actress to cope with family distress.

SIEVE
20-23-26-35-36-43

others: sickness for those using it, if not thoroughly cleaned before.

sifting flour through a: your neglect of the project was correct, it was hopeless.

straining with a: will be judged on account of your actions.

> *a cooked sauce:* will make acquaintance of a stage personality.

using a: your extravagance will turn to hardship.

SIGHING
08-11-13-17-22-37

hearing children, from fatigue: continue the nourishment.

> *others:* secret enmity of someone you thought highly of.

making a very deep sigh: clear the air with your peers.

of: big joy if you acknowledge your desires.

waking yourself from: need fresh air and a new outlook.

SIGNAL
04-20-27-35-43-47

danger, a: conditions are unfavorable to an improvement in your affairs.

> *overlooking a:* will struggle to humor your pride.

hearing a fire: will be informed of unpleasant happenings.

> *police:* will be cheated by a woman but will gain in some other pursuit.

of a, station: be cautious to protect the integrity of your system.

red light, a: are placing your life in dangerous hands.

seeing a, but not heeding it: misfortune of friends will depress you.

semaphore, a: warning of emotional trouble; the competition is not yours.

> *alphabet flags:* state your case; if they don't accept it, move on.

street, a: contagious diseases will confront you.

> *officer directing traffic at a:* the competency is yours and can't be shared.

woman dreaming of a police siren: be cautious whom you let approach you familiarly.

SIGNATURE
07-39-40-42-43-45

high official's, on documents: children's lives are in peril.

judge's, on a law decision: will uncover deceitful friends.

of own: father and mother make you very happy.

putting, on a birth certificate: riches.

> *death:* be careful of eyesight as your office work increases.

> *diploma:* joy.

> *wedding license:* good health.

SIGNING
10-15-27-31-43-45

agreement, an: as an idealist your work has just begun.

check, a: will penny-pinch your way to poverty.

communicating with the deaf by: it is easier to touch a soul that is reaching out.

contract, a: someone will confide a secret; put it in your safety deposit box.

legal document, a: will abandon the family home for richer fare.

letter, a: will make new friends if you correctly present yourself.

> *love:* if you can't tell the truth, don't tell anything.

making signs with fingers: it's vanity that you think you will be understood.

> *hands:* beware of being seduced by agreeing to something unsaid.

note to borrow money, a: a recent outburst will taint your credit.

SIGNPOST
07-08-14-17-32-55

being hit by a: cruel gossip is being spread about you.

destroying a: will embarrass others far more than you will yourself.

hitting a: have envious domestic enemies who wish you to fail.

painting a: have a faithful friend who looks past your flaws to you.

pasting something on a: your dishonor was not defended.

putting up a new: will overcome those trying to harm you.

reading a: will do much work without profit.

seeing a, but not heeding it: a corporation will be dissolved, your license revoked.

    blank: either move in or get on with your life.

SILK
06-14-24-27-33-34

buying: are contemplating a new venture and making the first investment.

dress, a: sensual love but not with your partner.

    cleaning: are replacing contention with auspicious actions moving toward prosperity.

    getting dressed up in: someone is undermining your happiness.

    making: riches will provide you with life's necessities.

    receiving, as a gift: would love the admiration of the giver.

    tearing: a simulation of joy will turn to shredded dreams.

    throwing away: will contract a contagious illness you are not immune to.

    wearing: don't believe anything you hear without proof.

    wedding: purity beyond the realm of the earthly.

garments: have a maid that is cheating you.

    black, of: will receive news of damages to your own affairs.

        blue: live wisely with compassion and in the tranquility of your own conscience.

        red: will be wounded by a bullet of passion intended for another.

        white: the beginning and end of emotional immaturity.

        yellow, buying: will be deceived by a loved one and joyous to be rid of him.

    for children: prosperous affairs that are impossible to care for.

nightgowns: will be singled out for promotion for the wrong reason.

other colors of: tranquility of conscience.

selling: are incurring too many debts.

spinning, thread: wish to treat life more delicately.

wearing a negligee without a nightgown: will receive a proposition and take it.

    young girl, a: success will crown your efforts but not hers.

SILVER
02-24-31-34-40-47

buying, things: need to reflect on how you appear to others.

changing, money: will be visited by a quiet friend whose politeness will disturb you.

    finding: prosperity with great civic responsibility.

counting: invest in a venture that makes money honorably.

gathering: your miserliness gives pause to those you wish to impress.

giving, gifts: are overly materialistic and void of concern for the spiritual.

handling: will receive damages in business matters.

having a large amount of valuable: will escape danger if careful and not greedy.

having one-dollar and fifty-cent pieces: advancement within own position.

    twenty-five- and ten-cent pieces: loss of present position.

inheriting: ungratified ambition to equal your ancestors.

moon: your affections are pure and restrained.

of, money: are vexed at being provoked into completing compulsory actions.

plate with a calling card: a formal invitation to an elegant affair.

plating: must have more courage.

receiving, gifts: anniversaries are a celebration of endurance.

selling, things: promotion will be delayed indefinitely.

ware, polishing: annoying critical in-laws will make their yearly visit.

wearing a, dress: will be fortunate in all dealings if you remain cool.

SIN

14-18-30-32-36-47

Avarice: will lose someone of great value to you.

Envy: take care or you may lose that which you have.

Gluttony: only by changing your habits can you survive.

Lust: that which you own, owns you.

Pride: be careful that they see you through the fog.

Sloth: be one who makes things happen rather than someone things happen to.

Wrath: forgive those who wounded you.

committing a: be careful of menacing dangers nearby.

   children: days of melancholy ahead as remembrances don't subside.

   family members: will make a long trip through purgatory and back.

   friends: your many desires will be harmful to you; is that what you want?

repenting a: ruing repeats again and again.

SINGING

07-09-15-18-21-40

being a singer: all moments will be as deeply emotional as a death in the family.

   folk: pleasures of your extended family and their simple joys.

   jazz: the array of emotions is never-ending, the music unstoppable.

   karaoke: indulge yourself in an admiring audience.

duet, applauding a: your being molested by ruffians will encourage your business.

hearing: optimistic tidings and melodious moments with a crowd of jolly performers.

   bass voice, a: a discrepancy leads to uncovering an employee's deceit.

   birds: the thrill of awakening from a long hibernation.

   church, in: merry companionship, wholesome and positive.

   heavenly choir, a: will leave the accident unharmed but have scars on your mind.

   love song, a: irrational moves may be lovely but could be harmful to your career.

   others: are too fast-tracked to spend the time to deal with others.

singer with a raspy voice, a: disputes over your outlandish pretensions.

   soft sweet: are harboring quarrelsome aggressive tendencies.

   soprano, a: are temporarily irritable and shrill-tempered.

   tenor, a: the height of masculine sensitivity.

listening to bad: beware that jealousy does not ruin your happiness.

   falsetto: will charm the woman of your dreams.

   rock and roll: exercise free emotions without restraint.

   solo: will escape to a place where your anonymity will not be questioned.

   vibrato, of: instantaneous satisfaction of desires.

   watching, perform: small sickness in the family can be compensated for.

operatic songs: will be afflicted with tears at the time you wasted gossiping.

others: your life will be gladdened by many friends.

song, a: are in harmony with your surroundings.

   melancholic: allow your sadness to run its course.

SINGLE

12-17-21-30-35-36

being: a sin of omission will follow you if you accept this opportunity.

person dreaming of an attic: prompt engagement in future family affairs.

   baron, a: your greed is commanding you to get it all.

   Cain: a risky chance offer will affect the rest of your life.

   getting married: indecision in choice of husband.

   loving someone: are prone to having a short temper.

man or woman dreaming of being, again: gossip will cause you worry.

man taking advantage of a, girl: are fighting against the natural instinct to protect.

old maid, being an: will be offended by a proposition from a temperamental musician.

woman accepting the advances of a, man: will marry a tall, dark-eyed, handsome stranger.

   giving birth to a child: will be abandoned by her lover.

woman dreaming of having a small beard: gambling losses.

   baby: obstacles on the home front will cause acute anxiety.

   baking: friends are lost because of your temper.

SINKING
10-24-28-32-34-35

and drowning in the sea: big profit will be lost unnecessarily.

because of another's negligence: your judgment in selecting whom you trust is weak.

being saved from: good business ventures.

escaping from: consider the proper placement of selfish pleasure.

haystack, into a: will depart on the capriciousness of others for pleasure.

mud, into the: ruin is coming, will fall into disgrace.

poaching in soft ground: hasty conclusions signal reverses and trying times.

SIPHON
12-19-27-28-43-45

breaking a: your property is in danger of leaving family hands.

man dreaming of a: will be invited to a bachelor party.

   woman: will be complimented on your choice of fiancé.

using a: gossip within own home will be waylaid before it gets to another.

   others: something new will happen that is good.

SISTER
05-14-15-22-30-31

arguing with a: family disgrace.

   with a sister-in-law: dissension within the family must be nipped in the bud.

in-law, a: your husband is cheating on you.

   two sisters-in-law arguing with a sister: family shame of irreparable damage.

insulting each other: beware of an illness from heartbreak.

marrying your: gossip by people of society; your familiarity breeds the content.

parting from your: develop your own life, not an ideal of hers.

several: fortune in a communion of spirit can turn to vicious gossip sessions.

SITTING
08-15-19-21-33-38

being asked to sit in a chair: a long-awaited solution to your financial affairs.

inviting people to sit down: honors will be conferred upon you.

   in a waiting room: sit still, drop your usual frantic pace.

on a bench in a park: will be treated well by loved one and poorly by strangers.

on a divan: will live a comfortable life.

SITUATION
06-19-31-32-42-45

being in a complex: humiliation at the hands of those who are not in control.

   serious: watch that the envious guard their tongues.

friends being placed in a bad: think twice before you make a move you will regret.

   objects: use caution in business affairs.

own, in life improving: the goal is being true to your inner spirit.

own job, not being good: opponents are involved in preparing your demise.

SKATING
02-10-19-33-38-43

children: luck and prosperity to those who speed past the envious.

falling while: will be solicited for contributions for the underprivileged.

in-line: speed up the pace; will encounter opposition to your exhilaration.

others: may be connected with a scandal peripherally.

relatives: an opportunity to make your mark.

roller: your anxiety and nerves are resting firmly.

skateboarding: disapproval, change your route.

speed: speed up your ambitious plans.

SKELETON

01-02-06-19-45-47

ancestors, of: cease to define yourself by their terms.

animal, of an: will have fear because your wrongdoing may be exposed.

being a: flesh out your character for others to see its value.

chased by a: aches in joints are caused by disease.

man, of a: will inherit property to which a secret is attached.

of a: will have spells of nausea from a pervading fear.

someone you know, of: get down to the bare bones of the problem.

woman, of a: your depression can be shaken off.

SKIING

02-12-38-44-49-53

jumping: your impatience has become desperation, rely on your psychological strength.

skiing, on the bunny slope: they won't wait for you to make up your mind.

  downhill: will reach bottom and have to be carried up again.

  racing: have left too many ideas unsolidified.

  through the trees: be alert to every turn of events and avoid fits of anger.

  with sweetheart: meeting life's challenges in unison.

SKIN

05-07-15-30-38-45

acne, having: your nastiness is bubbling to the surface.

animal, buying: kindness from those you least expected.

  dyed, having: will be unpleasantly surprised with the turn of affairs.

  having things made from, of tiger: will find out who your enemies are before proceeding.

  into a coat: will soon be rich and continually required to defend your self.

  skinning an: will drag your ancestral-chest-thumping pride in disgrace.

hives, contracting: unexplainable occurrences for which you must find an explanation.

  riding yourself of: problem allowed to fester without solution becomes serious.

molting: are aware of the need to bare the real you, again and again.

scaled with eczema: have acted without due consideration of others.

scarred: emotional hurt not healed will become a health problem.

sunburned: will cheat your friends with the gall of endurance.

  peeling own, off: changing one's old way of life.

using, for drums or tambourines: will receive good news through a unique message.

washing own: death of someone you knew and wish you hadn't.

wrinkled: after fifty you cannot hide who you are from your face.

yellowish: have trouble processing other's depression with your own.

SKINNY

15-35-40-43-46-53

being: your dreams are undernourished; allow them more breadth.

  others: success improves at the hands of other's ruin.

  very: your health is in jeopardy through your self-denial.

emaciated, seeing yourself: your actions alienate others while drying up their supply.

feeling: your inner reserve has shrunk.

gaining weight, of: increased material gain shouldn't equal increased girth.

SKIRT

04-20-25-30-37-49

black, a: adversity with the opposite sex, the limitations of being all-inclusive.

buying a: are overanxious over a relatively unimportant action.

long, a: are hiding your deception beneath the flow of fabric.

man dreaming of a: one does not win with improper advances.

of a: are too lazy to take what you desire, thus others will take theirs.

of other colors: your ambition exceeds your romantic conquest.

short, tight, a: attraction bypasses clothes; make sure it is your desires that are realized.

tattered, a: must heal past hurts to be ready for new love.

white, a: your tastes are high class, your fortunes less worldly.

SKULL
01-02-10-39-48-53

ancestor, of an: will do good business if you ignore family trade.

animal, of: domestic troubles will prove psychotically embarrassing.

being in a museum: will receive money for further expeditions.

crossbones, and: a warning that danger is pursuing you.

dead person's, a: after the shock, allow yourself to discover a hidden secret.

> *holding, in hands:* revelation of an enemy's well-kept secrets.

handling a: are too absorbed in the written word to communicate with others.

of a: repentance for your imperfections.

relative's: your fickle loyalties have injured your reputation.

SKUNKS
08-13-16-19-29-37

killing a: will have an unexpected after-death experience.

man dreaming of many: will love a young girl who will cheat you.

> *woman:* will be defrauded by one who will turn his back on you.

unmarried person dreaming of: are a cunning person who will cheat others at will.

SKY
01-02-10-39-48-51

ascending into the: can expect honors to be bestowed in good time.

azure blue, a clear: contentment in love affairs if you conduct yourself very properly.

bright, a: a joyous love affair that will melt with the first days of rain.

cloudy, a: a tempestuous affair will end in misfortune.

descending from the: beware of falling into traps set by foes.

falling on your head, the: expect to be killed in an accident.

full of clouds: arguments between business partners.

golden, a: will be threatened by a well-known personality.

great expanse of flaming red: desolation in your inability to be the center of it all.

laden with heavy gray clouds: a less-obvious friend will staunchly support you.

skyscraper, living in a: you scream to be treated as an individual.

> *without windows:* lover is moving away from you.

> *working:* aim high, recognize your limit.

stars looking like diamonds in the: certain good earnings in everything.

> *falling from the:* will be given messages of universal truth.

things falling out of the: expect war from a previously unobtrusive source.

without clouds: conclusion of own hopes must be brought to the fore.

SLAPPING
15-16-22-30-35-45

being slapped: will find yourself in bad company.

> *by a good friend:* happiness in the family.

children: will be treated unjustly by friends.

children, each other: are continually insensitive.

> *friends:* will enjoy good results in enterprises.

man, a woman: marriage will last forever.

woman, a man: unfaithfulness of a loved one.

SLAUGHTERING
08-13-16-19-29-37

animal, an: a catastrophe is ahead.

being done: will be feared more than loved by lover.

being slaughtered: unkind insinuations.

farmer, a: will have a family reunion with a cornucopia of basic fare.

horse, a: early warning of a life-threatening disease; get a checkup.

lamb, a: will enjoy peace in the illumination of the problem's solution.

pig, a: the sustenance of physical needs in every rib.

veal, a: youth regenerating itself upward in the food chain.

working at a slaughterhouse: caution, criticism cannot be taken lightly.

SLEDGE
27-34-40-42-44-54

being pulled by several dogs, a: be careful of the quality of the friends you choose.

  turned over: time to bring your comic talent to the stage.

of a, hammer: cruelty within yourself perpetrated on others.

  driving in a: do not venture too far in your business; keep to the warmth.

  someone using a: oppression by force of physical mobility.

SLEEPING
01-13-16-33-43-52

alarm while, hearing: be alert to indications of an accident you can prevent.

  awakening others: are optimistic of the trust you have garnered.

  frightened by: be on guard against future troubles not yet seen in dreams.

alone: with energy and vitality gained and retained, temptations seem irrelevant.

being asleep: be cautious in your actions.

boat, in a: have lost a relationship with the solidness of reality.

  covered wagon: your trek through the prairie needs your undivided attention.

dreaming one is napping: your body needs emotional sustenance.

daughter, with her mother, a: adoption of a boy disrupts family balance.

family, awakening the: are trusting that the day will bring success.

going to sleep: will inadvertently make an influential business contact.

man, with one he doesn't love: your supervisor respects your talents.

  woman, she: advancement through pillow talk is tenuous at best.

outdoors: relate to the order of the universe.

sleepwalker, being a: have your actions monitored for safety and curiosity.

sweethearts, together: need the interchange of psychic energy.

waterbed, on a: place too much confidence in a persuasive friend of unreliable morals.

with a beautiful young girl: are gullible to think she is in it for anything but your money.

  little child, a: return of simple love and domestic joy.

  own wife: will conform to the desires of a woman of substance.

  person of opposite sex: affairs will go well if you accept ramifications of deeds.

  person of own sex: imminent perplexing differences over trivial matters.

  prostitute, a: will be in pain the next day and spread it to undeserving loved ones.

  very ugly man, a: great unhappiness, sickness and displeasure.

woman, with a man during husband's absence: adversity due to your character weakness.

SLIDING
03-15-16-22-36-40

children: they will grow up normally and healthily.

friends: will receive news of a wedding.

of: will have ridiculous disputes incompatible with your nature.

of a slide: pleasure is fleeting and addictive.

others: aid your friends when they fall.

  downhill: your obligation is to yourself, not your greed.

SLINGSHOT
06-11-25-28-34-35

snapping a: prepare to defend yourself against attack.

  at a teacher: face it, you do not know everything.

  others: another deceit will destroy you.

SLIPPERS
01-09-12-18-33-41

buying: will receive a small kindness, a trip that will turn in your favor.

having many: will receive a large reward from proposal you made.

men, for: will live a long life in a strong relationship.

moccasins: will be hired to supervise others.

wearing: security and contentment in your own heart.

> *man, a:* will lead a relaxed life if satisfied with your choice of mate.

> *tattered:* are throwing away your relationship.

> *torn:* a major rift threatens your relationship; the next one will be a step up.

> *unmarried person dreaming of:* be careful in choice of mate.

> *woman, a:* you are in a good financial position.

women, for: will have to pardon enemies to accept disarmed relationships.

SMALLPOX
02-18-25-31-32-52

being vaccinated for: will have plenty of money and live a long life.

having: all will go well for the dreamer.

mark from a, vaccination, the: sign of beauty compared to the ugliness of the disease; vaccinate.

nursing a, victim: an unexpected promotion or legacy.

SMELL
06-11-25-28-34-35

pleasant: will attract lover with the wrong bait.

scent, a bad: loss of friendship with neighbors.

> *breath:* someone will trick you with advice you had best ignore.

> *in the air:* will be deceived by your best friend.

sweat, of: your avoidance will push you into the arms of a new lover.

unpleasant: an intimate secret will reveal your exertion was unnecessary.

SMILING
02-06-17-19-27-33

children: compromises made at each step will hamper your career or your child's.

family: will suffer opposition for from forty-eight to seventy days.

friends: beware; they may not be true friends.

girls: have found the man you want to marry.

grinning: success at or in the theater.

husband: will be relieved of pains, as he has made good money.

secretly to yourself: others talking will cause concern, but not to you.

walking with a smile on your face: an unwelcome encounter will prove surmountable.

wife, at her husband: will tell him of pregnancy.

woman, at you on the street: her lack of morals will be alarming news.

SMOKING
07-08-16-42-43-45

children: as fortune smiles upon the dreamer, a child suffers from a delicate constitution.

cigars: are stating your right in vain to trample over others.

friends: will enjoy fortunate new acquaintance.

in smoke-free areas: defy the requests of those around you for your financial gains.

narghile oriental water pipe, a: realization of desired love affairs, in mind only.

> *tobacco through the water in:* many women will pursue you, none will catch you.

of smoke: tears and disorientation from a clear direction.

> *being overcome by:* are choked up with confusion; clear it up.

> *coming from a building:* glory that is short-lived is displeasing you.

> *from a chimney:* a blackened reputation through machinations of an overzealous friend.

> *very thick:* hostile attacks are obscuring your view.

others who are: one you highly respect is behaving badly.

rising smoke: will find asylum in another's place.

> *dense biting:* no escaping from a delusion or the depths of your disappointment.

> *white:* your peacefulness is temporal.

yourself: are disgruntled with your present success.

SMUGGLING
26-37-38-42-46-48

being a smuggler: unexpected relief from a secret finally shared.

enemies: will soon be imprisoned for wacky exploits you hardly know you did.

friends: rash, hasty plans bring no end of crises.

others who are: not all of your plans will succeed, everything will turn out for the best.

SNAILS
01-18-21-33-36-47

being in a garden: work without financial expectations brings rewards.

cooking: regular inconsistency within the family.

eating: will have a good financial standing.

   at a special party: are fond of risqué talk with obscene gestures.

   children: they will have a brilliant career.

horns showing out of the shell: infidelity and continuous change of lovers.

picking up, from the ground: a family reunion that you will wish you had not attended.

retreating into its shell, a: someone is hiding a puzzle piece.

tramping on a: your intolerance will gain only enemies.

very huge: will receive a high and honorable position.

SNAKE
13-18-28-31-35-49

adder, of an: disputes with your lover.

   killing an: victory over internal enemies.

   many: the evil of temptation does not give up after one try.

   seeing in a cage: a friend can no longer be trusted.

beaten, being: your plans will be wrecked by the dire actions of enemies.

being chased by a: your conscience needs to shed its armor.

   unable to kill a: unfortunate events that were not anticipated.

being in a cage at a zoo: your ungrateful friends weave your anxieties into a false portent.

boa constrictor, a: challenge the devil but don't deal with him.

cobra, of a: awakening of the cosmic power of the spine.

coiled, a: stormy times and much danger.

fangs of a: the mysterious poisons spread by the spoken word.

garter, a: hurtful gossip is being spread about you.

   handling a: repeating ugly rumors makes you just as ugly.

grass, in the: what you hide is more powerful than what you express.

hissing, a: will make a weighty mistake losing your temper.

killing a: will have victory over enemies.

of: beware the primordial spiritual personage.

python, a: a stranger is instigating an intimidation of you.

rattle, encountering a: stand still and watch those who can't look you in the eye.

   ready to strike: treachery from one you least expect.

several: jealous people would like to cause your ruin, your plan would reverse this.

shedding skin, a: will be offered a new business opportunity.

surrendering, a: an enemy will deeply provoke you into a regrettable response.

water, being attacked by a: to recover from this illness, you must prevent the next one.

with two heads: seduction and disenchantment with humanity.

SNOW
01-16-26-37-48-49

boots trudging through the: a chilling physical upheaval with possible ties to growth.

businessman dreaming of, falling out of season: business difficulties.

   farmer: abundant harvest.

   merchant: poor business.

   military person: battle plans will fail, as they are out of proportion to the risks at hand.

caught in a storm, being: mate is having an affair.

children playing in the: will not need a doctor for a long time.

drifts of, in a city: solve problem or lose all previous gains.

driving through: will cause grief through your emotional distance.

   at night or dawn: a satisfactory reply to your request does not merit your enthusiasm.

eating: have left your place of birth.

falling in a warm climate: will recognize those you disregarded as beneath you.

  during the winter: ensure that all of your abundance is harvested.

    other seasons: you are an industrious farm laborer.

flakes, thick: your doubts and difficulties are being glossed over.

flurries: prosperity for the moment, capriciousness forever.

footprint in the: are entering a period of inner conflict and indecision.

man, going skiing with a: extend your reach and pull in your partner.

melting: hurry before the thought disappears.

mountains, in the: unexpressed thoughts of singular beauty.

shoveling: it is better to argue in silence with those who control you.

sparkling crisp air after a: clarity prevails after blinding yourself to truth.

storm: the warmth of your lover's arms will sustain you.

very deep, on the street: people are talking falsely, use discretion in what you repeat.

washing yourself with: relief from pain and unexpected pleasure.

SNUFF
06-09-17-23-24-44

being up to: will soon receive a bonus or promotion.

  not: work habits need to be examined.

box, of a: hanging on to old problems is of questionable value.

nose, up the: will lose your temper over lost horizons.

offering a pinch of, to a friend: are squandering your goodwill on others' destructive habits.

putting, in the mouth: are squandering money on instant gratification.

SOAP
01-03-04-07-11-23

bubbles: ground your illusions or they will burst.

buying: business affairs are all confused, due to unwillingness to understand one another.

foaming: the fury feeds on itself, renew the old attachment.

liquid: grab what you want before it floats away.

making: will never experience want, just perpetual ill ease.

powdered, dissolving: will settle puzzling matters for a productive meeting.

selling: are deluding yourself with bad business.

using, to take out a stain: dishonor from an inability to satisfy excessive demands.

washing own body with: asking for help from friends will be a good transaction.

  clothes: do not overreact to unjust accusations.

  face: cannot match the face in the mirror with your opinion of yourself.

  hands: leave the situation you cannot solve, solve the one you can.

SODA
02-03-06-13-26-51

buying caustic: your outlook appears full of contradictions.

buying sparkling: have some impossible desires.

  drinking: are surrounded by undesirable friends.

    with alcohol: will receive many gifts.

fizz: will have to justify your inappropriate behavior.

fountain, at a: will meet a celebrity doing normal things.

making, water: will rejoice in your power over the simplest of matters.

SOFTWARE
05-30-33-36-37-49

business: look for hidden profit leaks.

graphics: your business logo and ad campaign are weak.

modem: an associate is selling your secrets to others

search tool: a new product or service is needed.

virtual reality: people you have placed in charge are failing you.

virus protection: the skills of your attorney are questionable.

word processing: have failed to communicate

your goals to your employees or associates.

SOLDIERS

10-11-25-40-45-55

artillery: have difficulty persuading others to your long-standing viewpoint.

being chased by a: are stimulated to face torment with record speed.

   shot at: are being repaid for a debt that is long overdue.

counting: are prone to being stingy with your protection.

drilling: realization of hopes and desires, which have been long troubling you.

fighting: will be victorious in a fierce mental confrontation at work.

hearing, singing: a superior has a greater interest in you than you realize.

infantry: will follow the decision of your superior against your better judgment.

many, marching: the wrongs you experienced need expiating.

of: aim high and follow the prescribed route.

own son being a: will atone for parent's misconduct.

participating in sports: your children will be very intelligent spatially.

shifting loyalty to other side: will be double-crossed by friends if you do not change first.

that you know: represent the angels of God's retribution.

turning against you: to lead you must be willing to listen to the truth.

wounded: will lose sleep until you solve the difficulty, dreams will show you the way.

young girl dreaming of: will have many changes before settling down.

SON

05-26-31-37-43-45

adopting a: own children will dislike the adopted son.

being killed: misery caused by parents and returned to them.

dreaming of his father: advice should be acknowledged, but the honor is yours alone.

father dreaming of his: imitation is the best form of flattery.

giving birth to a, when not pregnant: an internal return to your youth.

having several: a multiple re-creation of each aspect of your self.

own, being crippled: trouble awaits, but can be ambushed itself.

   sick: obstacles are ahead for you; live your life despite them.

rescuing your, from danger: he will rise to eminence.

talking to own: will achieve happiness by allowing him his own efforts.

SORES

13-35-40-46-47-54

children with, on their body: will heal, only with your close cooperation in their growth.

   others: anger at how others have been treating you.

dressing: will sacrifice much for others on receipt of disquieting news.

having, on own body: your career is at a critical stage.

   face: will sort out problems with a deal you risked money on.

of: anger at how you have been treating others.

SOUP

02-05-17-22-30-44

boiling: a spattering of light difficulties tower collectively as a large burden.

eating: make your ingredients work.

   barley: will have good health.

   bean: poverty stretched to its limit changes course to prosperity.

   bread and wine: your relationship must be restructured to succeed.

   chicken: a heavy date with your sorrow in the comfort zone.

   clam chowder: big fortune will evolve from small investments.

   onion: a brief argument over your disregard for family peace.

   rice: a few obstacles on your road to prosperity.

of, in cans: will be aided by a source you will strain to trust.

SOUTH AMERICA

01-06-36-43-47-48

being a citizen of a, country: an enrichment of purpose with much work.

being deported from: loss of present position due to dissension in the family.

going to several countries in: an exposure to culture through the centuries.

returning from: your devoted marriage partner renews vows.

having business with: will dissolve your partnership and form a new one.

touring: have seen all the glories of God's handiwork.

SPACE

05-15-18-24-48-52

seeing a: messengers of the gods are appealing to them for confirmation.

ship, being on a: a spiritual journey into all that is not known.

staring into: your inner compass is reorienting you.

SPADE

15-18-20-26-31-36

buying a: abundant alternatives below the surface are promising.

having a, hanging at your side: stay on beaten track when out alone.

killing an enemy with a: will live a long life with secure honest friendships.

of a: a new vista of contentment is ahead for you.

rusty, a: your tactfulness and care will benefit your delicate constitution.

using a: what you dig up you may wish to cover up.

laborers: hard times come before the good.

wounding an enemy with a: will be guilty of foolish actions.

SPARROW

18-19-26-30-35-44

chasing a, away: neighbors covet your possessions and blame you for their not having them.

flock of: period of overwork and being frugal results in affluence.

killing a: signifies the secret enmity of some person for you.

many: ugly gossip will cause you to have a lean purse and obnoxious, unpopular children.

nest, in a: need protective support.

twittering, a: hard work is ahead but among friends.

SPEAKING

07-16-32-33-40-47

enemy, to an: will submit to injustice to salvage another's honor.

foreign accent, with: caution needed in health matters.

hearing another: be cautious how you interpret the meaning behind the words.

at length: will be driven to make restitution for an old error.

you cannot understand: life is only a mystery if you continue to live it as such.

husband and wife, to each other: beware of neighbors spying on your conversation.

lisp, with a: friends are attempting to cheat you.

microphone, into a: are you ready to reveal your problem?

mother, with own children: enjoy many kinds of entertainment in-house.

placing an accent between words: submit yourself to your man's will.

slang to dignified people, in: will be invited to an impressive charity gala.

stuttering: only the truth is worth speaking; all else should remain unsaid.

with someone: have to listen to more difficult opinions.

SPEAR

01-07-08-16-19-37

of a: you avenge being hurt by hurting other people.

grasping a: are the symbolic aggressor rather than the harmful one.

lance: others will incite a battle, your strength of will will commit to it.

stabbing a, fish: will receive an inheritance, to your great dissatisfaction

spearman: a rapid succession of major obstacles.

using a, to catch fish: concentrate your powerful mind against the distractions.

SPEECH

01-05-09-21-31-42

being an orator: are infatuated with your own
eloquence.

  enthused with message of: a tremulous
  appeal will touch your heart
  completely.

  in love with an: are an indolent, pliant,
  emotional parasite.

being a speaker: beware of minor troubles, as
not everyone agrees with everything.

delivering a: loss of a friend through your
ambitious oratory.

  another: are more persuasive when incorrect.

giving a, on a platform: your affability hides
your lack of courage in disputes.

hoarse in, being: an affair will put you in an
embarrassing situation.

listening to a: will submit to injustice to allow
another his rights.

political, a: owe the public an explanation for
your misdeeds.

sermon, a: are being justifiably overcritical of
a friend.

silent, being: speech is silver, but silence is
golden.

speaking aloud: are admonishing yourself for
a grievance you have been silent about.

speechless, being: the inspiration of your life is
yours to share.

SPENDING

06-14-20-36-37-49

amusements, for: will quarrel with friends
over what makes you happier.

charity, for: affairs will improve after a long
while until the next need surfaces.

children, on: will give service to an ungrateful
person.

family, on the: domestic happiness if shared
equally.

foolishly: be careful and economize for a short
time.

man, on other women: will desert his home
for a short-lived love affair.

traveling, for: overindulgence in frivolity
decreases the internal quality of life.

spree: a desire to possess what you have not
earned.

SPHINX

01-05-10-17-28-45

being a: great wisdom that you dare not
impart, as it will be misused.

meeting with a: no words can ask a question
that has no answer.

questioning a: are trying to answer unanswer-
able questions.

standing guard, a: what is keeping you from
befriending others?

SPICES

02-16-18-35-40-41

chives on a windowsill: a boring person begins
to distract you.

  in an omelet: reject overbearing people
  advancing your ideas.

curry or ginger, eating: your life needs some
stimulation.

nutmeg, buying: changes in business will lead
to overland travel.

  cane of, using a: big quarrels between business associates.

paprika, buying: your profit will be
resented.

  spilling, on the floor: a heated argument
  with an overheated person.

  using, on food: will become very irritated
  with the many pleasures in others'
  lives.

rosemary, cooking with: a child born in its
own home will leave.

  growing: desire for food will be satisfied.

  smelling: will have melancholy and annoyance.

saffron powder, buying: will receive money
and fall into disgrace from its source.

  cooking with: momentary sex energies will
  turn to destruction.

sage, buying: have homesickness for domestic
virtue.

  of the plant: recovery from an illness with
  the mere hint of odor.

thyme, seasoning with: abundant means
happiness in love affairs.

SPIDER

02-04-06-17-25-31

being bitten by a: marital unfaithfulness
and being confined with it.

businessman dreaming of a: your fortune

will be devoured by a seductive partner.

unmarried woman: do not accept being married to a clinging mate.

crawling on your skin: an envious hatred needs to be unraveled.

another's: your immature spite and hatred will do you in.

eating a: are a very voluptuous person entrapped in your own web.

killing a: a time for great pleasure.

of a: a provocation will lead to entanglement in a sticky situation.

seeing a, at night: plenty of money from illicit means.

morning, in the: will be entrapped in a lawsuit with trumped-up charges.

several: domestic quarrels in a web you have intricately spun.

spinning a web: thrift and conscientious actions will sustain the power to amass a fortune.

being caught in a: realization of own desires can be squelched with one wrong move.

children finding a: they will be prominent in life.

tarantula, being bitten by: your safety is in great danger.

SPILLING
07-08-14-17-32-55

blood: loss in business affairs as partner is losing his footing.

drink: be wary of who is hitting you from behind.

food: will receive a refusal from a friend.

hot liquids: health concerns over a high fever and flushed face.

oil: are not bargaining based on your abilities, but your needs.

other: small dissension within the family.

of, something: are prone to being too egotistical.

salt: have opened the door for family problems to surface.

water: are acting like a hurt child in an adult world.

wine: family arguments over a deception that won't dissipate.

SPINNING
08-09-13-14-21-37

of, cotton: wealth from completion of an industrious task.

old woman dreaming of, an: annoyance and anxiety from your fable of events.

operating a, wheel: will not be recompensed for your own diligence.

owning: new acquaintances may prove untrustworthy.

spinner at work, a: good earnings from using all of your resources.

wool: don't neglect children if they are to become prominent.

SPIRAL   10-12-27-30-37-42

spiraling upward: your inflated ego is accepting all credit.

downward: feel out of control and are blaming others.

staircase, walking up a: your going round in circles is leading somewhere.

down: escape the situation now!

SPIRITS
04-17-28-30-40-53

attending a séance: will regret turning down an offer you were suspicious of.

being in good: something is preying on your conscience.

family: beware of people who are teasing you; their comments are serious.

spiritualist, being a: will be criticized and damned for being too sensitive.

talking to a spirit of dead relative: keep certain abilities to yourself.

The Holy Spirit: must endure fatalities, unless you listen before you speak.

SPONGES
10-15-27-31-43-45

diver, a: will soon receive greater earnings for a job well done.

dreaming of gathering: misery if you don't ask for a raise.

squeezing a dry: the odds are against your winning at gambling.

a wet: lover will have a prominent admirer in the military.

using a, to wash: waiting anxiously for something to come through.

young single girl: is in a hurry to marry a man with money.

woman dreaming of: are prone to being stingy.

SPOONS

20-23-26-35-36-43

being fed by a: have been acting like a hungry baby.

> *silver:* your envy is interfering in your life.

buying: are building the foundation of domestic bliss.

eating with a: poor relationships are made with your ingredients.

looking into a: your view of the situation is distorted.

losing a: will receive sad news of infidelity.

> *and retrieving it, from a large kettle:* the invitation is in the mail.

silver, a: a supposed life of ease is as fraught with issues as anyone's.

spooning out liquid: take emotional traumas one at a time.

> *medicine:* accept the situation and deal with it.

> *peanut butter:* want to hold onto someone.

> *solids:* want to protect someone.

table, a: flexibility of service and adapts well to sharing.

tea, a: are ridiculing a simple act and overlooking its value.

using a baby, a: joy and happiness within the home.

> *to stir:* will have company for dinner.

wooden: the control is out of your hands in a tryst that can only bring trouble.

SPORTS

15-17-26-31-35-48

arena, being in a: consider carefully before taking your new position.

> *winning in a:* insight into how to win and not just play the game.

bungee jumping from a bridge: check all of your equipment before making a move.

> *being pushed:* are terrified of making the wrong move.

cheering at a, event: avoid spending too much money on the inessentials.

children's: begin with basics, then advance to adult exercise.

cricket, of: feel bound by others' rules, from which you will escape.

> *ball:* your impatience needs to be checked at the gate.

> *bat:* petty jealousies create rivalries out of irrelevant objects.

cycling: will encounter bumps on your visit to a distant place.

> *children:* expect a new employment opportunity.

> *others:* misfortune in love affairs.

football tackle: trouble caused by your prying into another's affairs.

handicap, succeed despite a: a better position will be offered to you.

hockey: success through close attention to the disparate paths to your goal.

javelin, throwing the: a broken friendship can be repaired by good business ethics.

jujitsu, practicing: intricately conceived plot is on the brink of collapsing.

losing at: a delayed decision must finally be made.

medal, receiving a: are on the right track; proceed fully aware of your goal.

Olympic Games, participating in the: you exaggerate the importance of your work.

> *visiting Mount Olympus:* trust a higher power that will not give you the will.

penalties, imposing: charge the instigator of the action first.

> *being imposed on you:* you created the altercation; placate your opponent.

score, keeping: your judgment will be disputed by a person passed over for your job.

soccer, playing: your flexibility appears as nonchalance.

> *scoring a goal:* coordination is essential; persistence and skill are in demand.

sportsmanship, displaying: will be in fashionable, influential, discriminating company.

team, playing on a: all inner aspects of self must team up for life's game.

tennis against a concrete wall, playing: your toughest opponent is yourself.

> *balls:* certain high birth of a child.

trophy, drinking from a gold: have passed your life's most difficult task.

raising the, over your head: enjoy the fact that you have earned it.

silver, a: honors received will never be enough.

your side winning a: loneliness amidst the crowd.

SPRAYING
01-07-10-27-34-35

incense in the house: will improve present condition by attracting wise friends.

insecticides inside of house: will enjoy fine surroundings cleansed of sloth.

perfume, woman dreaming of: will be strong and healthy during your frivolous life.

   body: awaiting a visitor who will come for your folly alone.

SPRING
01-02-10-39-48-53

cleaning: each aspect of the past as it comes to completion clears the way for the new.

drinking from a pure: large wealth coming later, affection is available now.

dry, a: poverty and sickness.

fine, day, a: your new and stimulating ideas will be insulted by a foolish person.

gushing water, a: wealth, honor and dignity.

season: will make news with your creative endeavor.

   during winter: a wedding will soon take place.

used in furniture: are not materialistic and can manage with little.

   bed, a: will have the resilience to rest every part of your body.

SPY
06-22-25-34-36-46

being a: adventures will come your way whether you want them or not.

   on a mission: check your conspiracy theories at the door.

dealing with a: your distrust is developing into a persecution complex.

of a: your offer to render a service will be refused.

recognizing a: protect yourself from bad influences and inquiring eyes.

SQUANDERING
08-09-19-22-25-51

of: will suffer misery unless you settle down and use common sense.

others: will suffer with the pain when it is all gone, but need not replace it.

others, your money: unhappy future from allowing others to control your life.

your fortune: will have a better future if you stop trying so hard to live in the present.

SQUARES
17-21-30-35-36-52

checkerboard, of a: will be happy in all ventures; which ones, you will have to decide.

empty, an: have lost the will to communicate with others.

fear of walking on the cracks of: walk boldly on the solid pavement to your opportunity.

   in the floor, a: confidence and security.

populated: increasing energy needs a corresponding activity.

public, a: touch base with the stability of the community.

various colored, wearing a skirt with: will encounter debts from squandering money.

SQUINTING
07-09-15-21-40-48

man dreaming of: the time has come to examine your life myopically.

   woman: will have many lovers, but concern for only one.

   young girl: will be married within the year.

of, the eyes: have the affection of one whom you love.

SQUIRRELS
21-23-35-41-49-55

being bitten by a: the family black sheep will marry for money.

chasing each other in trees: are playing at being financially responsible.

eating: take a breath before every bite of food.

feeding nuts to a: will soon return to the faith of your father.

hiding nuts: with the rising condition in business begin your retirement account.

killing a: will acquire a few friends with an equal lack of tact.

man dreaming of, a: will make love to his maid.

  children, a: will surprise a thief.

  woman, a: will be surprised while doing wrong.

  young girl, a: will be untrue to her boyfriend.

petting a: without preparation, winter brings fear.

STABLE
07-39-40-42-43-45

illuminated by the moonlight: happiness in love outside of the marriage.

of a, for horses: the possibility of producing wealth.

  pigs: have a weak character that wallows in other's misery as your own.

  sheep: patience will be advantageous to your sensitivity.

stall in a: if you have to ask the cost, you can't afford it.

  Christ child in a: the God you seek has been born in your heart.

STAG
13-19-22-41-47-53

attending a, party: the all-inclusive ego is opening up its vulnerability.

avoiding a: plans will be ruined when you receive an inheritance.

hunting a male deer: are chasing the one you should join to gain distinction.

of a: your chance to be lord of the hill, but behind the scenes.

  party: don't be disillusioned, take the opportunity offered.

several: a great friendship is yours.

taking a prominent part in a, party: separation from friends.

STAGE
24-31-34-40-47-50

applying greasepaint: deceit with the best of intentions, to entertain.

audition, being at an: the rehearsal for an interview.

being on a: disappointment in projects begun for early exposure.

  prompted: are not sure of your words, actions or exits.

thrown out of a, door: will have pains in the heart over missed opportunity.

building a: will mourn over the loss of relatives.

coach, driving a: your adventures have become wild and wooly.

  being a passenger on a: will be stirred from innocence to pursue a love affair.

  family name on the: will be nominated for a leadership position.

floor of a, the: have been searching the pleasures of love for free.

of a: remarkable events in which you are on show.

performing on: are concerned with how you appear to others.

sitting in a box near the: endure terrible pangs of jealousy to be the center of attention.

STAIRS
05-14-15-22-30-44

becoming dizzy on the: a premature, severe turn downward for a seedling venture.

climbing of your house: progress in overcoming all obstacles to your ambitions.

  with others: will share your heights with loyal friends.

descending: disappointments in business and social status.

  with others: check your partner's lack of contribution to the venture.

falling down the: own envy will cause you to be drawn into a conspiracy.

of a broad staircase: wealth and honor as you absorb another's conscience into your own.

scrubbing the: your children will gain in stature and status.

short, a: are not exerting your influence when appropriate.

steep, a: overexertion over an extended period can cause a physical harm.

stone, a: will take all of your heroism to free your work from another's credit.

very high: will attain well-deserved credit at work and be jilted by your lover.

wooden, a: your errors and careless gestures are jeopardizing your career.

STAKE

02-12-19-38-44-49

being burned at the: creativity by its very nature is unorthodox.

another: will take control of a bully.

driving a, into the ground: will dig as deep as you wish to rise.

for a tent: the beginning of a massive venture.

through the heart: generations will thank your selfless act.

STAMMER

01-02-06-19-27-45

of stammering: have a very determined mind yet can't express yourself.

children: they will have a good position in the future.

friends: beware of them; they will suggest wrongdoing.

others who: fresh interests will lead to happiness.

STAMPS

06-19-31-32-42-45

approval, of, a: will advance your position by knowing socially influential people.

buying: reconciliation with an enemy by accepting some of their control.

collecting: will find a rare chance to gain income.

putting, in an album: will associate with a high official.

on letters: will be criticized by the press.

STARCHING

08-15-19-21-33-38

collars: must make plans for your old age.

of a lady's dress: some worry but much gain.

ladies' blouses: are prone to being stingy in carrying out a project.

men's shirts: will receive unexpected fortune if you stop being too cocky.

woman dreaming of, linen: will marry an industrious person.

STARS

05-07-15-30-38-45

behind clouds: in an instant you could lose direction.

Bethlehem, of: purity, guidance toward love.

dim: everything will go wrong, so don't place confidence in others.

falling from the sky: disaster to those who close their eyes to the quest for knowledge.

on your house: will move quickly up in power.

with a tail: will abandon house because of fire.

North, being guided by the: advice is being given surreptitiously; take it.

observatory, of an: the expanse of your business is broadening.

being in an: a solitary life will be your fate.

with friends: are unable to reject unreliable friends and begin a new life.

one, lighting your path: listen to a friend to map the route to your ambition.

seeing brilliant: prosperity and gratification of your every wish on your pleasant journey.

several, close together: danger of war and the emergence of a savior.

shining into a room, a: danger of death for the head of the family.

shooting: aiming for your goals needs only your singular attention.

unusually bright, an: losses in business are due to others' blindness, not yours.

STARVING

02-10-33-38-43-49

eating while dreaming of: curtail your expenses, invest sparingly and intelligently.

of: will acquire riches through courage against deprivation.

several days, for: it's hard to make headway in worldly affairs without intelligent support.

suffering from starvation: much wealth is coming to you.

STATUE

14-18-30-32-36-47

adoring a: your relationship has become inflexible.

being a: have armored yourself behind a rigid facade.

bronze: are prone to lose willpower at the slightest diversion.

clay: the slightest hedge could leave you open to a countercharge.

marble: an unrequited love tortures your self-control.

   being a: perfection must bury the real person.

naked man, of a: have removed yourself from reality.

   woman: your message has reached cold hard lust.

saint, of a: wealth for one you thought had little respect for you.

several in a museum: your love is not wanted, except in your work.

STEALING
08-13-16-19-29-37

being robbed: have attained your possessions legitimately.

clothes: have taken something that does not belong to you.

furs: return what you have attained illegally and you will be paid your due.

of: a gift of jewelry will be offered to you that is not the giver's to give.

others: feeling deprived doesn't justify your taking from others.

valuable things: the great misery you have caused others will be returned to you.

STEAM
04-20-25-30-37-49

boiling pot, from a: let them work their off-color life out themselves, drink your own tea.

   engine: your anger is at risk, turn it into positive energy.

   locomotive: your one-track goals will be derailed.

burned by, being: exposure of a covert plot against you.

full, ahead, going: have resolved your issues and are ready to accomplish.

radiator, pounding with: do not incite anyone to blackmail you.

   releasing: if problems aren't dealt with when they happen, they explode exponentially.

roller, operating a: be wary against stepping across bounds of humanity.

steaming: your angry part of yourself has taken over.

taking a, bath: will clear away tasks previously impossible.

using: doubts and differences between you and the one you love.

   for cleaning: time to allow your steam to work for you.

STEEPLE
10-16-37-38-45-54

being hurt on a: will have health difficulties that must be dealt with and overcome.

chase race, riding in a: much social activity at your expense.

climbing a: achievement of own greatest wish after handling a mass of problems.

falling from a: ambitions thwarted by an acquaintance.

of steeples: warning of serious troubles.

STEPCHILD
19-22-24-29-34-43

arguing with a: make your own decisions without others' advice.

being a: time for you to grow up and become an adult yourself.

disliking a: are unhappy with the choices you have made.

STEPFATHER
06-11-25-28-34-35

arguing with a: your decisive personality is persecuting other's emerging individuality.

being a: it is tempting to take total control and be life consuming.

   good: family arguments will cause you to be distracted and make mistakes.

disliking a: are abusing the confidence of an extrovert.

STEPMOTHER
01-09-12-18-33-54

arguing with a: persecution for making jokes at her expense.

being a: are apt to contract a disconcerting un-diagnosable disease.

   good: you don't need another mother, but like what she does for you.

disliking a: family quarrels over the maliciousness of a fertile imagination.

STEPS
02-18-25-31-32-51

coming down: will be condemned for carelessness.

going up the: support from your superior in your advancement.

marble: will be forced to do something against your will.

one step at a time: moderation and perseverance succeed.

steppingstone, walking on a in bare feet: sudden love affairs push into everything.

stepping towards something: defining your goal is only the first step.

STICK   03-15-16-36-40-52

hitting relatives with a: good hopes will be dominated by a woman.

leaning on a, with branches broken off: will discover a thief.

pressing gunpowder into a gun with a: will enjoy better days.

using a truncheon: warning of thieves coming to collect money.

STILETTO
07-12-17-29-31-48

being struck by a: many distractions discourage your attention to your regular work.

of a sharp-pointed dagger: don't antagonize anyone of whom you are not sure.

plunging a, into someone: will press your exacting habits on others.

walking on, heels: your tongue can slice through another's heart.

wearing a, on a uniform: will persuade your unfaithful friends so as to be understood.

STILTS
08-13-16-19-29-37

being mounted on: are puffed up with vain pride and missing the point.

buying: don't offend associates by your conceit.

others on: will have a good future after you fail once.

seeing: pleasant news concerning own your children.

STING
02-05-17-22-30-44

being stung: your self-destructive tendencies cause you to withdraw into yourself.

by an insect: a deep depression will assail you, then another ailment is caused by the cure.

others: uncovering a colleague's misdeeds will bring you to the attention of your boss.

being wounded with a poisonous: will feel remorse from mistrust of yourself.

of a: your cleverness at knowing just how much to say and when to say it.

STOCK
06-11-25-28-34-35

clerk, being a: a simple transaction has the potential of risk.

giving out items from a: small arguments will bring a new dimension to your romance.

receiving: will be double-crossed by friends bringing self-doubt to your judgment.

man, being a: will reach your goal slowly but surely.

dealings with a: will be unfavorably accepted by society; refuse their conditions.

moving a: will be involved in a public altercation and are headed toward a lawsuit.

pile, buying a: your obsession with an easy deal misses a golden opportunity.

selling, merchandise: will receive a legacy.

room, an empty: will hear of the violent death of an enemy.

yard, being at a busy: ingratitude for good deeds done, will cause no more to be done.

working at a: will have good fortune in the future.

STOCKINGS
07-08-15-16-42-43

cotton: your ideas bring you big pleasure, but can never be realized.

dark-colored: satisfaction will be your only reward.

darning: salvaging your home will be temporary.

hanging up Christmas: many friends whose company alone is your present.

knitting: will meet with the opposition in your present romance.

light-colored: sorrow.

losing a: your lover is looking elsewhere and indifferent to your concern.

putting on: honor and profit from services rendered by friends.

tearing while: gains from harming another are not yours to enjoy.

silk: will be tempted to encourage a man's attention.

wearing: will barter your body and soul for financial reward.

with a hole in them: will be required to defend your actions.

woolen: affluence.

STOCK MARKET
09-27-29-30-33-42

being a member of the: will deal with debtors skirting between riches and poverty.

dealing in stocks: patience will be advantageous in uncovering an unknown enmity.

losing at the: a loss of riches will leave you temporarily disoriented.

making gains at the: only tell of your profits to those who have proved their loyalty.

portfolio in the, having a: investing in the wealth of your country as well as your own.

selling stocks, methodically: your finances are secure.

frantically: fix the disappointing results of your risk-taking.

stockman, being a: will reach your goal slowly but surely.

having dealings with a: will be accepted into society but refuse their tainted conditions.

STOMACH
01-16-26-29-37-48

aching: a change in diet is in order if problems are to be solved.

being full and satisfied: riches according to the amount eaten.

too: had to absorb an unpleasant event.

digestion: your life has too much to chew on.

having a beer: your finances are tipsy, your friends are embarrassing.

distended: must cover a wide range before you discover the culprit.

flat: your risks have debilitated your financial standing.

full, children: they will make progress in their studies.

empty: will not be invited to a dinner party.

relatives: disappointment in your own hopes not being possible for others.

large: digest your misery before turning toward your fortune.

pregnant, a swelling: the progress of your accomplishments are showing.

small: no one will know your secrets because you can't stomach them.

strong: perhaps these are situations you should avoid handling.

illness: finish the first project before starting another.

indigestion: your temptation is to avoid the solution you're blocking.

STONES
01-03-04-07-11-23

lodestone: are attracting favorable opportunities.

of: angry discussions and time-consuming provisions for a solid project.

precious: your generosity has been ill received.

quartz, clear: are overconfident about uncertain prospects for the future.

pink: excessive qualms cause confrontation in a long-term relationship.

rough: barbs in your thought process have to be polished.

skipping: the repetitive boredom of the search for perfection.

tablet, inscribed: your inflexibility limits your positive action.

throwing: reassure yourself that your actions are not perpetuated in a glass.

tomb, a: respect and recognition for a deed long past due.

walking on: will have to suffer for a while.

STORKS
13-19-24-33-34-41

being very quiet: arrival of enemies and holdup people.

flying in the air: will be responsible for many children.

group of, a: foretells that you will be robbed, but by which one is still in question.

nest of chicks: toddlers are in your future.

seeing a, in the winter: big disaster ahead will leave you worse off than before.

sleeping: change to a more harmonious residence.

two, together: will marry and have good children.

STORM

16-19-22-34-37-44

being in a: unfortunate business deals will cause distress.

tempest, a: slander leaves ruin in its wake.

thunder, a: have barged into a delicate situation with a simplistic solution.

demolishing your house: people with evil intentions await your misstep.

damaging: keep to your morals while others project their anger.

hitting: abrupt changes at work reveal your bosses' confidence in you.

homes of others: big dangers ahead.

seeking shelter from a: ventures will break apart and drift into despair.

sleet, being in a: be more patient with people around you.

others: will receive interesting information.

watching a: unhappiness in love will quickly blow over.

STORY

03-08-22-37-42-49

hearing a: will have much hard work ahead.

from a friend: will be amazed at the similarity to your thoughts.

performer: are doomed for disappointment as an appointment is suddenly cancelled.

reading a: wishes will not be realized through unjust criticism being taken for fact.

selling a, to a magazine: beware of being seduced by disorder; be precise.

telling a: your efforts must build upon each other to a climax.

writing a: arguments within the family over who first acknowledged your brilliance.

STOVE

07-10-19-38-48-49

being heated by a, that heats well: your home life nourishes you.

burned by a, being: accept the truth based on a number of trusted sources and move on.

coal, a: expect a business proposition from an old friend.

electric, an: the uncertainty in a certain situation is sharpening its focus.

filled with burning coal: prosperity from an oddly favorable consequence.

fireless: if your partner doesn't leave, you should.

gas, a: bounteous energy uplifts your health.

grate, with a burned-out: the home as you knew it, is over.

kerosene, a: changes for the better if you keep it burning.

wood burning, a: the solution will emerge with input from several sources.

STRANGERS

02-03-06-13-26-31

approached by, being: put adversity aside and invest in a future relationship.

beating children of: have a cruel bent represented by your abusive childhood.

being a: have the raw material to shape yourself into a person you can respect.

chased by sinister, being: a part of yourself you never cared for and ignored.

with a weapon: anger that you never addressed, catches up with you.

of a: will be reminded of a past misdeed for which you never paid the consequences.

receiving a: arrival of a friend who will dredge up an old foe, who defeated you.

STRANGLE

26-31-32-37-43-45

being strangled: need to extricate yourself from a shady business deal.

others: rapid success of own hopes can be thwarted with one wrong twist.

of strangling: are denying expression that can bring satisfaction in life.

someone yourself: your wish will come true.

STRAW

04-22-33-35-36-45

broken: the rupturing of a contract.

burning: will attend a big festivity, and leave a victim of an out-of-control situation.

buying: must work hard to overcome troubles.

cutting: will have much residual pain from an embarrassing situation.

hat, a: your sociability interferes with your progress in investigating your worth.

selling: prosperity and security in your business.

stable, in a: the heavy burden of a multiple mission.

STRAWBERRIES
03-06-26-28-39-48

blossoms: will have foresight to esteem, but not love.

eating: big joy in love life and security in business.

making jam with: unexpected affection for an old friend.

> *pie:* a love affair will turn into a serious relationship.

> *rhubarb:* a bitter pill will be sweetened.

picking wild, from the vines: a forbidden love affair will make you many new friends.

with cream: your lack of objectivity in dealing with an issue.

STREAM
12-14-22-29-41-45

dried up, a: your work has taken every ounce of energy and still will not be done.

streamlined, becoming: will soon have a proposal of marriage.

> *having difficulty:* will receive an unwelcome visitor.

swimming in a: will be insinuated into a project unwillingly.

taking dirty water from a: due to the ingratitude of others, you will fall into disgrace.

wading in a, alone: passing time with an effortless joy.

STREET
11-16-21-27-35-51

bad condition, in: success of own hopes after strenuous effort.

baggage being on the: your belongings will be stolen.

being lost in several muddy and dirty: will be molested.

being on a, you've never been on before: will do a lot of traveling.

deserted, a: your sole courage will bring great joy.

long, with nice homes, a: will receive a happy surprise.

many curves, with: unhappiness if you continue down this path.

many people on it, with: despite your afflictions, you will be welcomed by everyone.

straight, full of people: prosperity.

walking along an endless: success, if a distant vision.

STREETCAR
06-12-19-24-34-38

driving a: take a course of first aid to counteract maliciousness.

jumping off a: your own path is the only one for you.

platform of a, on a: a perilous affair could put your future in jeopardy or in bliss.

running on rails: are unable to deviate from controlled route.

rushing to catch a: an unfinished symphony needs to be played.

STRETCHING
24-30-36-37-38-42

being unable to stretch something: postponement of success.

of: will play a solo on an instrument.

others, ropes: another person received what you desired.

something after washing it: someone is attempting to destroy you.

STRIKE
10-16-20-43-45-50

being a, breaker: an unknown person is in love with you.

> *leader:* will be robbed of a position you never wanted.

being damaged financially by a: will have a very delicate sense of dignity.

ending a: will be falsely accused of something you didn't do.

organizing a: will help people in need of money.

STRING
14-15-22-28-39-47

ball of, winding a: your project will be successful.

cutting: will have quarrels and danger; your lifelines will be severed.

putting, around a package: have a strong power of attraction.

tying: the confusion should be resolved one knot at a time.

untangling: take safety measures before dealing with your problem.

using: must be careful in all your affairs.

STRIPTEASE

14-28-29-31-42-53

being a, girl: will have money troubles all your life.

    sweetheart: will not be accepted in society.

many, dancers on a stage: prosperity and success in business.

stripping yourself: have a great desire to do good for others, but they won't have it.

    woman of ill fame, herself: an unhappy surprise is ahead.

STROKE

15-29-30-46-47-54

being paralyzed by a: will have a weak mind, but a large heart.

having a: will make progress in personal affairs.

    mate, a: must rely upon your own good judgment.

    others: someone is trying to steal your sweetheart.

    relatives: will receive plenty of money in the future.

not being affected by a: there is part of your life where you are prevented from taking action.

STUBBORN

02-16-18-36-43-45

being: hopes will not be realized; offer was made under false pretences.

    children: correct your mistakes before your children imitate them.

    others: will have many loving people around who will be menaced by danger.

dealing with, animals: are asserting your rights; your responsibility is love.

friends, having: unhappiness in love; have ulterior motives.

    mate: will lead a pleasant life in old age, if you put off some hobbies until then.

    relatives: a new love is growing for your professional prestige.

obstinate, being: will be degraded, but stand by your well-thought-out beliefs.

STUDYING

09-10-27-28-41-44

children: all desires will be realized if you open yourself up to the fun of learning.

    not: will abuse the confidence of others with deceitful flattery.

mate: have renewed hope that your marriage will be saved by two agreeing.

math: will disagree with an indefensible solution.

professor: your engrossment in your project leaves you absentminded about others.

SUGAR

05-10-18-24-45-50

buying: an unfaithful friend is seeking your ruin.

cane: arguments between friends over who can interfere the most.

cooking with: are overindulging your sweet tooth.

eating: have made a correct assessment, you are surrounded by sycophants.

on fruit to sweeten it: sweet words from friends do not equal sincerity.

putting, in coffee or tea: will experience the bitterness of a false friend.

SUICIDE

04-16-19-29-33-41

committing, husband or wife: permanent change in surroundings and marriage.

    others: frustrations with others' inabilities and their blindness to it.

    thinking of: must conform yourself to real life, or accept that you live without it.

    woman: another's opposition in love and despair will directly affect you.

hara-kiri, committing: guilt over your having distressed others' circumstances.

having committed: unhappiness at inability to cope.

    by hanging: other's are misusing your generosity.

of a: have overstrained your mind in misjudging others.

overboard, by jumping: will sacrifice a treasured possession to help a relative.

planning to commit: troubles were brought on by yourself.

SUITCASE

23-32-38-41-42-47

buying a: an uncovered secret cannot be escaped.

leather: will be called upon to attend a distant meeting.

packing a: a tiresome newsmonger will be accompanying you on a trip, pack earplugs.

receiving a, as a gift: an enticing offer.

taking, from closet: are ready to leave the relationship.

SUMMER

03-09-13-24-30-32

landscape, a: your optimism and trust fulfilled themselves.

of, during: will seek pleasure at the expense of another's sense of propriety and justice.

autumn: will regret some duty unperformed.

spring: must try to think things out very well, excluding friends from your confidence.

winter: be in earnest in your undertakings.

SUMMIT

23-24-30-36-37-40

celebrating with others reaching the: will have powerful friends with your best interest.

climbing a very high: a challenge to be sought after and solved.

descending unharmed from: your assessment of the challenge was exaggerated at best.

planting a flag on a: your unrequited emotions are beginning to be reciprocated.

SUMMONS

04-14-30-38-40-49

accepting a: your strength of character will dispel any slander.

being served with a: adverse criticism and scandal will vex your agitated mind.

issuing a: unhappiness in love life can be redirected by enthusiasm.

refusing a: will suffer humiliation from your partner's unpredictable behavior.

SUN

24-32-33-36-45-48

arising with the: happiness through willpower and a fulfilling future in money matters.

sunset: time to retire from the intensity of the past.

being in the: your self-confidence will bring joy, eventually.

blind person dreaming of the: will have his sight again.

prisoner: will be let out of prison to a more frightening life.

eclipse of the: a temporary, leaky period of decreasing fortune.

entering a house and seeing the sunshine: will purchase a particular piece of real estate.

excessive, light: will dry up your ideas and parch your creations.

going toward the moon: will have in-fighting among friends.

golden: the source of your vitality.

lamp, using a: will be scarred by an experience in your former active life.

married woman dreaming of sunshine in a room: will have a virtuous child.

of the: masculine energy will bring success in love.

peeping through the clouds: troubles will soon vanish with news from far away.

people who have enemies dreaming of the: false news of losses will cause you losses.

ray of sunlight: have a guardian angel at work for you.

falling from the sky: obstacles will come from left field.

shining on your bed: apprehension over threat of illness.

red, a: sick children will turn for the better when you least expect them to.

shining brightly in a room: big gains and prosperity.

on the top of a house: will have ups and downs; in danger of fire.

on your head: sins are pardoned, all glory and honor.

spot on the: be sure to accept a forthcoming promotion.

sunstroke, having a: others will have reason to envy you very much.

relatives: family quarrels as you increase your responsibility by default.

SUNDAY

15-20-24-27-28-47

going to church on: will realize delightful promises and the maturity of high ambitions.

having a restful: care for your interests with renewed vigilance.

of: coming change of affairs in renewed forms.

sundae, eating a: a celebration of another epiphany.

working on: will lose mastery over many matters without touching them.

SUNDIAL

03-04-12-17-39-53

checking a: marriage within own immediate circle.

handling a: enjoy every hour of your happiness in love.

of a: coming events will never be as good as now.

watching a: an unrealistic aspect of life, long out of fashion.

SUNFLOWER

03-09-18-26-33-49

eating, seeds: will conquer someone who will rise again and conquer you.

of a: your love is not reciprocated, go to another garden.

picking a: don't rush your affairs and make a spectacle of yourself.

tall: your naughtiness could use some informality.

turning toward the sun: worries ahead as you meet again those who bested you.

SUPPER

07-10-28-29-30-51

giving, to animals: pleasure will wipe out misfortune, only to see it rear its ugly head again.

having: will let the little things interfere with your big picture.

alone: will recapture your zest for youth.

business, a: a public disgrace cannot be hidden behind a fancy facade.

of the Last: will receive blessings of a new and valuable friend.

SUPREME COURT

06-11-31-32-39-48

being a member of the: the ultimate responsibility.

having a case before the: arguing the truth as you deeply believe it.

losing: infidelity can be placated by winning at gambling.

of the: will attain goals slowly after discovering the lies of others.

SURPASSING

18-28-33-39-42-52

being surpassed in sports: will have many discouragements and a few hard-won victories.

children, others: will be refused a requested favor by a false friend.

others: will work hard on a new enterprise that will end talk.

you in the same business: vexation in affair; you are envious of lover's belongings.

SURPLUS

3-6-26-28-39-48

buying a: invest against future famine.

farmer, a: will enjoy a happy life in the future.

selling: a skillful manipulation of affairs.

having a, of merchandise: will be cheating others, entangling you in future losses.

in the home: should cultivate independence in planning and executing affairs.

store selling: will enrich your possessiveness with economy.

SURPRISE

06-12-18-19-24-34

astonishing others: have ignored convention and make original art.

being astonished: are in line to receive a cabinet post.

actions of others, by: if you don't expect anything, you will be receptive to learning.

family member, by action of: will receive good news.

children in wrongdoings: will be victimized and robbed of your clean record.

mate, a: your arrogant selfishness will offend those who make an honest living.

receiving a: are surrounded by unfaithful people who get religion.

others: unexpected jolt to your love life; are now free to pursue your true love.

SURRENDERING
15-18-20-26-31-36

army, an: are unable to defend yourself from the encroachments of adversity.

lover, to a: will become even stingier in the future, to raise your standard of living.

police, to the: are determined to overcome any charges, legally.

stolen items: must endure several sleepless nights guarding your property.

will of your mate, to the: you are feeling great confidence in your ability to win.

SUSPECTING
05-10-18-20-24-45

being suspected: are accustomed to doing wrong to others; now it's your turn.
  with cause: needs will be granted; your wishes are your responsibility.

mate, the other, a: beware of a tender friendship with someone else.

relative, a: a woman will play a dirty trick on you.

SUSPENDERS
03-26-33-41-42-46

buying: your careless words will cause anxiety, your practical foresight success.

having old: look out for gossiping behind your back and take the assistance offered.
  new: temptations to stretch to the limit must be restrained.

lover wearing: will lose your rose-colored glasses with his ill-mannered behavior.

of: must have faith in your will and determination to succeed.
  broken: will have to make an apology after your true ambitions are gained.

suspended animation, in: decide which traits you want to keep and discard the others.
  being, in the air: will enjoy honor and consideration by others.

SWALLOW
04-16-19-29-33-41

lawn, on a: peace and domestic harmony.

lovers seeing a: throw a pebble in the air and leave ill will where it lands.
  married couples, when together: domestic happiness after many perplexities.

nest, a swallow's: are ready to begin your family.

destroying a: in destroying your enemies, you destroy yourself.

with eggs: a child waits to be born.

of swallowing: the seeds of a potentially highly profitable company.
  having pains when: will live to be over ninety years old.
  pills: make sure everything you put in your body needs to be there.
  story that you don't believe, a: frivolity will hang heavily over you.

SWAMP
11-16-21-27-31-35

being swamped with letters: unwise stratagem with a distant relative.

Everglades, walking in the: entanglement with foreign animals.

full of dead fish: will soon be overworked and go hungry.

sinking into a: the harder you work, the less you will be rewarded.

walking through a: heavy burdens from which there is no escape.

SWAN
04-13-35-40-46-47

black, a: a feared evil will be diminished by your staunch principles.

feeding a: a friendship will fail you, but love will not.

hearing the noise of a: harsh criticism for an innocent gesture.

killing a: business affairs need care, beauty, grace and dignity.

many, together: good health and revelation of a mystery.

of a: there is grace above, and power beneath the surface.

song, singing your: your old position won't miss you.

water, on: material contentment, grace, beauty.

white, a: riches and a faithful discharge of duties.

SWEARING
02-04-06-22-26-34

blasphemy: are turning your will against potential guidance from within.

having sworn: will know about the insincerity of a blood oath participant.

of: your actions deny your latent capabilities.

> *others:* will be blamed for actions you thought, but did not act upon.
>
> *relatives:* your worry is well-founded, your family is at stake.

SWEETHEART
16-19-20-22-34-37

calming a: atonement for accidental harm will prove exceedingly enjoyable.

caressing each other: will receive dreadful news that only others can assuage.

going bathing with, at sea: current love affair ends; be clear and open for next one.

having a changeable: happiness will vanish and estrangement will appear.

old, embracing an: will receive a gift followed by a phone call.

SWEETS
02-03-06-10-13-26

making: will be cheated by friends' false maneuvers and rash indecision.

receiving: be on the lookout for a message causing a permanent break.

sending: be cautious in love ventures; bitterness abounds.

tasting: prosperity will come at a great cost to your happiness.

SWIMMING
03-08-22-37-42-49

afloat, having trouble staying: expect troubles instantaneously.

back, on your: will have a big quarrel over your revisiting portions of the venture.

lifeguard, meeting a: will meet a likable mate who understands honor.

muddy water, in: your path is beset with many obstacles and mortification.

of: staying afloat depends upon the strength of your character.

open sea, in the: prosperity among your recent acquaintances.

pool, floating in a: heed importance of relaxation; allow yourself to feel secure.

> *underwater:* allusion to the process of birth.

reaching your objective, and: will be successful in everything.

river, in a: will encounter danger in the near future.

shore, to a: hard work is ahead for you, alongside someone you just met.

tangled in seaweed: a resolute mercenary will be persuasive, but you know it is wrong.

water in a pool, no: new prospect will cause considerable work for very little profit.

SWINDLER
26-31-32-37-43-45

being a: are rendering services too easily and others take advantage.

> *swindled:* will enjoy fortune in a risky venture with temperance and fortitude.

having a, for a partner: are too much of an idealist to believe another's bad intentions.

of a: are a very courteous person prone to foolhardiness.

swindling others: be cautious with friends who disapprove of your actions.

SWINGING
02-09-13-27-36-39

around in circles: a change of plans will prove very successful.

of a swing: postponement caused by your fickleness.

others: your old ideas are rejected for being outside the ropes.

yourself: be cautious in believing satisfaction and freedom exist in your love affairs.

SWORD
04-22-33-35-36-45

being a swordsman: your distinction will be menaced by indifference.

being wounded by a: there is great danger at the hands of the impassioned law.

> *by an acquaintance:* will receive a service from an honorable person.
>
> *in the hand:* your defense will be belittled and discarded.

blood coming from a, wound: are cut off from your senses.

broken, a: deep discouragement that obstacles can't be severed.

hitting an unknown person with a: success in your enterprises.

life being endangered by a: big benefits if you stand your ground.

sharpening a: security through fixing the most subtle threats to your finances.

wearing a: will have a position of public trust.

woman dreaming of wounding someone: will receive many presents.

pregnant: will give birth to a boy.

wounding others with a: expect a commitment to your authority.

SYRUP   06-09-14-17-23-24

buying: beware of thieves.

making: beware of enemies.

maple: fortunate gathering of the joys of remembrance.

of: will suffer humiliation and shame.

putting on food: business affairs will become very confused.

children's: will make good collection of money.

T T T T T

TABLE

01-09-12-34-38-39

banquet, a: find a start date for the project; a new team is arriving.

being seated at a, with children: luck, prosperity and comfortable circumstances.

card: an opportunity to make money will arise.

conventioneers: misunderstandings and rowdy disagreements.

marriage guests: happiness is ensured.

relatives: too much to say, no chance to speak.

round: all guests have an equal say, listen to the new stimulating conversation.

boardroom, the: your seat reflects your position in the power structure.

broken, a: pleasure that will bring misery and poverty.

empty, an: family deserts you, along with their support.

library, a: promotion through self-initiative and home study.

marble top, with a: are entering a period of new sensations and partnerships.

of a, set for dinner: you work hard for others' indulgence in oral enjoyment.

sitting at a, with own family: happy married life, convivial times ahead.

TABLECLOTH

09-18-42-45-47-55

buying a: your irritability stifles your growth.

clean, on a table: will reap unexpected rewards.

soiled: expect troubles of your own making; you are untrustworthy and unfaithful.

colored, a: advancement within own position as your just reward.

embroidered lace, an: important and very beneficial event to come.

of a: will receive a favor from an important person.

putting a, on a table: your time is well-apportioned and busy.

torn, a: trust has been lost with a loved one.

white, a: dignity and distinction.

TABLOIDS

03-12-21-34-45-46

being exposed in the: enemies seek to destroy you.

featured: will receive a promotion.

declaring end of your marriage: great happiness is around the corner.

scandalizing your children: a family outing is planned.

you: expect a price with your bonus.

your career: will make an unpredictable career change.

TAIL

02-08-09-19-40-47

burned, a: will suffer adversities in remedying your past misjudgments.

curly: the joke is on you.

cutting your: will be guilty of foolish actions; guard your tongue.

having a: will have to apologize for the actions of one of your relations.

lady's dress, of a: will soon have plenty of money.

long, of a horse: will receive assistance from friends.

separated from the: will be abandoned by friends.

pulling an animal's tail: are asking to be kicked.

red, a: will have good business dealings.

restraining an animal by the: you're in danger of being kicked.

tame animal, of a: will marry an unstable person.

very long, a: the cart gets heavier as projects drag on.

wagging, a: will have long-lasting comforts in life.

wild animals, of: will meet intelligent people.

TAILOR

02-40-41-42-52-53

alterations being made by a: reassess your eating habits, you're going overseas.

becoming a: will receive an offer to change your position.

being a: change of surroundings will require tailoring your patience.

girl dreaming of a: will marry a man beneath your standing.

male, a: exercise caution in business ventures.

ordering clothes from a: joy without profit.

TALISMAN

03-13-14-18-33-39

of a: a mystery will be solved with the honest counsel of a friend.

woman wearing a: danger from the lover of your choice, not your soulmate.

young girl: walk carefully when crossing streets.

TALKING

19-29-30-35-52-53

against another: your ill temper comes straight from your unconscious.

business partner, to a: premature doubts will disrupt the enactment of your plan.

dog: significant financial losses and future expenses.

enemy: the embarrassment of family arguments, theirs.

parrot: you will be an embarrassment to your enemies.

who fails to respond: a supposedly auspicious venture will come to naught.

hearing much, around you: send the malicious gossip back to the instigator.

man: will be accused of aiding the breakup of lovers, for your own romantic benefit.

mother and father, to: will be granted what you asked for.

of: are confronted with insurmountable obstacles.

relatives, to you: warning of troubles from your impulsiveness.

too loud: your major obstacle is your own malicious gossip.

much: will be exposed to malicious plans causing the downfall of another.

your superior, to: will become a victim and suffer humiliation.

TALONS

02-14-19-27-28-43

being scratched by: an enemy will triumph over you.

animal's, and it's running away: victory over enemies who will suffer loss.

bird's, and it's flying away: are being watched by one with evil intentions.

others: a friend is helping you secretly.

defending yourself using: faithful friends look out for you.

TAMBOURINE

04-06-08-12-37-52

dancing to a: ecstatic delight.

of a: rewarding prospects mingled among the slow route to success.

playing a: should control your spending of money on things that are most important.

husband, a: your inconsistent explanations of your absences raise suspicions.

musicians: will be cheated by friends.

sweetheart, a: a rival will take your place.

young girl, a: an old man will propose marriage.

TANGLED

05-07-13-21-36-50

becoming, up: patience will be well-rewarded when you backtrack to the problem's source.

being, in a business deal: hard work awaits your extrication from embarrassment.

of a, skein of wool: will have to contend with difficult persons.

others being, up: the confusion of mixed-up ideas includes the elements of a solution.

undergrowth in the woods: are thwarted by

your inability to establish good foundations.

web, in a: secret love affair will complicate your life.

TANK
07-18-23-25-40-42

driving a: face the threats without aggression.

filled with gas: will overcome rivals and competitors.

filled with oil: your sins will disappear in suppressed emotions.

filled with overflowing: your ideas are wasted in sloth.

filled with wine: the fermentation of ideas, the bliss of their imagined execution.

TANTRUM
14-21-30-37-41-50

being caught up in own: selfish lack of consideration for others.

having a: recent behavior has been childish, exhibiting an ugly image of your shortcomings.

   children: a mirror of your actions.

   others: will cause your own predicament through careless speech.

TAP
09-12-40-42-48-52

drawing beer through a: exercise caution in your business.

   wine: danger through a secret.

of a, dance: a change in life will come soon, but you must control your passions.

tapping hole to start a screw into wood: things will run smoothly.

   telephone wires: an enemy watches over you; tell him what he doesn't want to know.

taps, playing: your chance to step up to the gate and outwit your opponents.

TAPESTRY
06-19-20-23-26-51

admiring a: an abuse of confidence; the story cannot be judged fairly.

burning a: death of the head of the family.

buying a: extravagant taste denotes culture and refinement.

decorating a: utilize the knots of your struggles to create a beautifully patterned life.

decorating with a: huge satisfactions for little expense.

designing, pictures: your experience joy at work, but little profit.

painting on a: will be deceived by friends in the plot against your reputation.

TAR
06-18-32-36-46-48

buying: beware of a double-cross of one taking advantage of your self-condemnation.

of: gossip will cause much vexation, as the truth cannot be known.

pitch used to repair cracks on the bottom of ships: have dishonored your dignity.

tarred and feathered: your success will be belittled, your very existence derided.

   and run out of town: others begrudge your prestige as unearned.

using: exercise great care in the choice of companions.

workers applying: will be cheated of credit due.

TARGET
07-32-33-35-37-46

hitting a: attunement to your ideals.

making a bull's-eye on a: are open-minded and original and must make your own mark.

missing a, completely: repressed desires cloud your vision.

of a: will fully succeed in getting what you desire.

shooting at a: architectural plans need your disciplined attention.

TARTS
05-18-20-28-35-38

baking a: approaching money is limited.

buying a: fortune ahead of you; time to reexamine your life.

eating a: a pleasant piece of news is a sign of mastery over many matters.

   apple, an: you expect to be highly rewarded for doing what is your job.

   cherry: life as you know it is not all there is.

   chocolate: fatigue as the pressure rises to your head; let your ideas out the top.

   jelly: will have an unforgettable experience with your mate.

of a woman of loose morals, being a: will
have a memorable encounter with your
mate.

TATTOO
05-06-29-46-48-53

having a, on your body: beginning the initiation into a new stage of your life.
>*another:* will receive a story in confidence
you dare not repeat

having your arms tattooed: will suffer because
of an insatiable jealousy.

hearing a call on drums or fife before taps: your
ego has announced itself.

ordering the military to return to quarters, a:
estrangements from the family hierarchy.

watching someone tattooing: others' success
will deplete your confidence.

TAX
02-21-23-31-41-47

being a, collector: will have to press yourself
unduly to feel pride in yourself.

cheating on calculations: be wary of even
bigger losses; ask friends for aid.

filling out a, return: discontent and foreboding over loss of good earnings.

lien, having a: your financial embarrassment
will be published.

of taxes: will have to endure a great sacrifice
to meet the obligation of another.
>*being unable to pay:* are placing an unnec-
essary burden on yourself.
>
>*paying:* will be stretched beyond your
limit to render service to a friend.

receiving a, refund: change for the better on
your own, not with your stingy relations.

TAXI
09-18-23-27-45-46

driving a: beware of jealous friends, when
you feel they have so little to be jealous
about.

escaping from the path of an oncoming:
your love life will be besieged with war
games.

hailing a: manual labor with little financial
future.

riding in a: hasty news of an inheritance from
someone you met once.
>*with another person:* be on guard against
false news.

TEA
07-16-28-46-47-49

bags: dignity and distinction through your
sharp wit.

buying: will experience many ups in your
resources and downs with heavy burdens.

drinking: return to the basics, free from bad
influences.
>*iced:* relationship will have an abrupt
hiatus because you feel drained by it.
>
>*large party, at a:* are interacting with
other's spiritual center.
>
>*lemon, with:* your decisive clarity and
reserved caution will gain your
promotion.
>>*milk:* subtle intelligent actions will
gain you what you want.
>>
>>*others, with:* use a velvet glove to deal with
the situation.
>>
>>*shop, at a:* abandon the hare, join forces
with the tortoise.

grounds: will be solicited for many social
duties helping the unfortunate.

making: be cautious in your dealings because
of an indiscreet act.

teetotaler, being a: will contend with unacceptable opinions from friends.

TEACHER
02-03-13-22-35-43

becoming a: your first student is yourself, as is
your best teacher.

being a: a chance to build character at its base,
with your own in tandem.\
>*foreign language:* listen to both sides of
the story, judge as you would be
judged.
>
>*high school:* growing up is a process, not
an instantaneous event.

being taught: anger over a small, trifling
matter will block your ability to learn.

hiring a: mix amusement with your mission.

small children: will be asked to contribute to
charity.

talking to a: refrain from lecturing another
and take instruction from a judicial figure.

teaching classes: passions are awakened when
your receptivity is open.
>*night school:* will be invited to a solemn
occasion of punitive power.

school: prohibited love, when authority is present, brings physical and mental heartache.

TEARING
01-16-21-23-39-45

dress, a: friends gossip about you.

love letters: will fall in love with someone new, who will tear your heart apart.

money: will attain your goals slowly but surely.

of: desire to hurt yourself as you are guilty of wanting to hurt another.

papers: misfortune in love.

valuable documents: will have a change of mind.

TEARS
02-12-16-20-27-37

crying: empathy is constructive when accompanied by the truth.

of: opposition will awaken your truth and push you to defend it.

shedding, children: awakening of awareness within a very short time.

husband: suppressed anger will never allow happiness in marriage.

relatives: will soon experience many ups and downs in affairs that are not yours.

sweetheart: will have consolation after emotional cleansing.

teenagers: release of frustration you were unable to defend twelve years before.

TEASING
10-12-31-40-43-49

being teased by children: secret desires will be discovered, which will redirect their lives.

friends: your cleverness offends your enemies and solidifies the loyalty of your friends.

relatives: will come out ahead of them in the end.

dog, a: will have difficulty explaining yourself and your actions.

others: will see a naked woman.

others, you: will be deserted by your wife.

TEDDY BEAR
01-10-28-30-34-40

cuddling your: must give yourself unconditional love before you are able to share it.

of a: unconditional devotion and support.

talking with your: an immature fear of talking it out.

TEETH
13-20-28-31-33-52

ache, having a: displeasure at losing quarrels that disgrace a close associate.

braces, wearing: your speech has been distorted; correct it.

brushing: trials, which will seemingly rob you of your pride, will end in self-esteem.

not: even with your faithful friends, you would get lost.

of children: will borrow money from relatives, and lose them as friends in the process.

covered with tartar: time to reexamine your speech.

falling out: personal affairs are brutally discussed by your close neighbors.

and crumbling: do exercises to relax your jaw while on alert for enemies.

drop out: you spoke out of turn; some team members will defect.

loose and, being: your inner anger has pushed someone away.

false, wearing: taking credit for something not yours will backfire.

flossing your: unscrupulous, malicious gossip will be revealed.

foam created from brushing: your singular distress will arouse empathy in others.

forceps used to extract: difficult period to which you will return every decade.

friend, of a: will receive good news from relatives far away.

fungus growing on your: are allowing others to speak for you.

gnashing your: humiliation at the hands of lowly creatures, put your teeth in them.

gold, a: corruption and sorrow surrounds you.

of any other metal: humiliating quarrels, which, if you fight on, will bring lawsuits.

grinding your: swallowing silent anger at authority to allow digestion.

growing in, a: will receive news of a death.

having big: will be very short of money.

black: have neglected your teeth, see a dentist.

cleaned by a dentist: will lend money to neighbors.

dirty: affliction caused by heredity.

filled: a mistake has to be rectified before you can go on.

healthy: success is unquestionable.

knocked out: are aggressively struggling for control of your sudden misfortune.

pulled: your profit from another's tragedy is tainted.

> *wisdom tooth, a:* fear losing something you treasure: your ability to speak your mind.

infected: must give an explanation for your fears to overcome them.

injected with Novocain, being: will be honored with a vacation, at your expense.

losing, in a fight: your physical suffering is not diagnosable.

> *baby, a:* your inner anger has pushed even the tooth fairy away.

> *your front:* loss of your grasp of the circumstances of power.

loved one, of a: court action over an inheritance.

moving: a major obstacle of emotional stability caused by the inconstancy of friends.

one, being longer than the rest: are full of fears of affliction from relatives.

perfectly straight white: the wish of happiness for the rest of your life will be realized.

prominent: need dental checkup.

staring at another's: are assessing their worth at an amicable divorce.

TELEGRAM
08-13-37-49-50-56

friend sending you a: loss of a friend, because of a failure to communicate.

receiving a: unpleasant news will be received and processed, if you stay centered.

> *business:* to receive guidance, you must be willing to receive it.

sending a: are controlling your emotions until a confident friendship ends, but it does.

> *business:* decline in business due to your unwillingness to communicate.

TELEMARKETER
03-07-11-33-41-44

buying from a: an intimate friend will challenge you, and upon losing talk ill of you.

hanging up on a: an aggressive intrusion of your privacy can be aggressively repelled.

of a: a new profitable influence is about to enter your life.

talking to a: be reserved with present associates and terrifying to new ones.

TELEPHONE
04-09-10-26-36-42

being without a: balance and confidence so you control what you do.

can't reach child by: what message do you not understand?

> *deceased person:* will inherit a small sum of money from an old friend.

> *friend:* boredom is difficult to rise out of when you continue to be boring.

> *lover/mate:* are trying too hard to gain their attention.

> *parent:* are slipping into an apathetic state even a parent could not love.

desperately trying to get through: frustrated at not being able to state your opinion.

dialing 911: your difference of opinion is seriously jeopardizing your relationships.

> *incorrect number:* others would not know about it, until you accused them of it.

> *odd:* are ignoring communications from your unconscious.

> *wrong:* change direction; differences of opinion are seriously jeopardizing your love.

hanging up the: who on the other end of the other line do you wish to avoid?

interference with the: rivals will talk much to persuade others against you.

making a, call: whomever you are thinking about needs you.

> *and no answer:* are not getting your point across.

> *receiving:* postponement of a date for you to sort out your problems.

not answering a ringing: are marrying or are married to the wrong person.

party won't answer: someone is crying for your support, but the relationship is over.

> *hangs up on you:* mate knows he will become your ex.

pick up, but no one speaks: confront your feelings or a telemarketer.

receiving a, message: are less observant than
you should be.

talking long distance on the: your curiosity will
be satisfied.

wrong, connection: caller wants you out of his
life.

wrong party, get: you feel for someone other
than your mate.

TELEVISION

03-08-21-37-41-52

completely involved in the: an unconscious
choice between your reality and another's.

surfing channels: unable to focus on the major
thrust of your life.

   and finding nothing: have a low level
of confidence that you are entertaining.

   flipping though them again: involvement in a potentially adverse state
of affairs.

talking back to the: live a balanced life;
making sensible decisions and brute
judgments.

watching: time to make some positive
changes in your personal life.

   laying on a couch: too lazy to pay attention
to real life and your lack of a financial
future.

   while doing housework: missing out
because you are preoccupied with
irrelevancies.

TEMPER

10-21-22-30-33-52

cold, a: you gain warmth by being empathetic
to those less fortunate.

having a: are surrounded by liars who won't
admit to their lies.

hot, a: passions drive your actions.

losing, at children: have something on your
conscience.

medium: will become the arbitrator of a
dispute.

TEMPEST

13-14-16-24-32-44

approaching, a: affliction swirls around you
because of the malicious words of the
envious.

being blown about by a: people trick you
because of your good faith.

children: outspoken controversies
become resolved and improve your
position.

damaging property of relatives, a: will be
exiled because of a love affair.

of a: will suffer humiliation when slander
leaves ruin in its wake.

something falling on own house during a: will
be wounded by accident.

TEMPLE

11-20-23-33-37-47

country, in your own: death of a very close
friend: your adolescence.

   foreign, a: unusual experience is coming to
you soon.

entering a: discretion will bring rewards.

worshipping in a: stop neglecting your spiritual side

   idols in a: will do something socially
unjustifiable yet essential to your
spirit.

TEMPTED

08-10-18-26-32-45

being: will encounter obstacles in your path.

   to commit sin: difficulties will be
surmounted.

   to leave sweetheart: will meet a charming
person and will yield to your
emotions.

resisting a: a tempest of fresh air will build
support for your work.

wrongdoing, with: guard your tongue and use
common sense.

TENNIS

01-08-19-23-35-39

against a concrete wall: your toughest opponent is yourself.

balls: certain high birth of a child.

doubles: have a sensible and a rational reason
for your actions.

lawn court, playing on a: will secure employment; will take interest in your own
friends.

   winning, and: warning of falling in love;
will have a minor illness.

playing: have a strong need for self-expression
within a flexible framework.

racquets: your courageous aggressive assertion in a fair and balanced court.

TENT

25-26-31-43-45-47

camping in a, with children: remembering the freedom and independence of your youth.

family: your family will undergo many changes, strengthening itself with each hit.

friends: will take pleasure in helping others in love affairs.

sweetheart: arguments over the impermanence of love.

military camp of tents, a: will take a very tiresome trip to find your permanent identity.

TERNS

15-19-32-35-37-42

coming into a house or a ship, a: will receive news from friends.

flying over land: newly marrieds will be intelligent and faithful.

ocean: visit from someone from far away.

nest of: fortune and blessings on the house where the nest is made.

of this gull-like bird: will receive unexpected good news.

TERRACE

03-04-06-25-44-53

being on a, alone: will rise to a worldly position and not take anyone with you.

with children: will have many ups and downs.

friends: will suffer humiliation.

prominent officials: will be master of your affairs.

relatives: will receive an inheritance.

TERRIER

02-08-16-17-19-30

barking: beware of quarrels in social activities of a happy nature.

biting a friend of yours: double-cross from someone you trust.

playing with children: will have good earnings in the future.

sleeping: leave the issue alone.

TERROR

18-28-31-32-46-49

being a terrorist: get more honey from the bees by singing than by kicking over the hive.

using violence against you, a: an enemy causes friends a sorrowful predicament.

being in: the rage must be resolved within yourself.

children causing: emerging sexual energy directed toward creative expression.

political party: you want your own freedom, but cannot allow others theirs.

confronting a: guard against any who would rend your means of support away from you.

TESTIFYING

02-11-18-19-24-32

against others: liars tend to accuse others of what they do.

in favor of: speak only the truth, as you know it, and only if specifically asked.

on own behalf: others have revealed the truth; their accusations describe themselves.

testimony, giving a: people will honor your distinction.

under oath: a desperate felon will resort to any manipulation of the facts.

TESTING

01-03-08-15-22-26

doctor, you, a: analyze your entire system and build health into it.

faithfulness of mate: awareness of all of the forces that stabilize your lover.

others, you: will have sorrow at the lack of trust where you were confident of it.

machinery: your false hopes of another's love will be solidified in reality.

taking a: intuitive guesswork is knowledge well-stored in your brain.

oral test, an: are reserved and diplomatic and think well on your feet.

your ability: discovery of lost valuables: your talents.

THANKSGIVING

27-30-37-43-49-52

being alone on: will have blessings from God to rebuild your family.

entire family expressing thankfulness: will lead a quiet and happy life.

of, Day: will have good health in a happier and more prosperous life.

spending, with others not of family: contentment of heart.

THAWING

03-08-14-16-17-42

being with others during a thaw: a former adversary will become a friend.

frozen food: danger through a secret energy aimed in the wrong direction.

ice: will be cheated by friends, but can turn it around to your profit.

of your emotions: will suffer unforeseen trouble with your relaxed attitude.

THEATER

08-19-20-35-39-48

aisle in a, the: others will taunt and belittle you into reacting; don't.

   walking down an: are guilty of bad actions; change tickets and sit in a different seat.

applause, giving: are unselfish and not envious of others, but they are envious of you.

   hearing: forget present plans, begin an entirely new venture.

   others: wish to receive the adulation of a star, to make up for none at all.

   prominent person, to a: trust your instincts, not their credentials, in choosing allies.

   receiving: are prone to snobbishness over the life you wish you were living.

     catcall, a: approval isn't a prerequisite in life unless it's your own.

     jeering: someone will cancel an agreement.

attending a, alone: a disagreeable encounter with reality over the pretense of being what you are not.

audience, an: putting through a deal, first you need a viable deal.

   being on stage before an: face them boldly with your response.

   political person, with a: an intense but temporary adventure.

     social: pleasure with high distinction.

bored, being: will be expected to accompany a dull, plodding guest.

cabaret, being in a: a charming insincerity on the part of newfound acquaintance.

can't find: rethink your plan for self-growth.

drama, acting in a: the gracious appearance of a traffic cop can be deceiving.

   having the jitters: will take an important part in amateur theatricals.

   writing: will expose secret foolish act and lose best friend.

enjoying a theatrical spectacle: beware the double-dealings of your unrealistic ambitions.

floodlights, at the: public confrontations expose your inferiority complex.

   looking into: the future is yours to see.

   on your path: your focus is unfaltering.

   shining on you: your sins are over-exposed.

forgetting own line of a play: uncomfortable visit from people you dislike.

green room of a, being in the: will soon relax into your accomplishments, or lack of them.

harlequin, dancing with a: delightful time with beloved.

hissing an actor: will be held in contempt by those you respect.

   being hissed: will be anxious at the disregard and rudeness you receive.

late for a performance, being: make extra preparations for your day.

made it just in time: take a deep breath and start slowly.

matinee, attending a: a lapse from your stolid path.

not listening: have not formulated your presentation with updated input.

pantomime, a: an indiscrete blabbermouth will cause a stumble in your route to success.

   in a troop: minor disagreements can be removed from those unwilling to solve them.

   watching a: observe movements without words to understand motives.

performing: your escapades will journey deeply into your shame.

prima donna, meeting a: your social circle is of glittery images and unreal characters.

rehearsing: need not stammer and stutter in one aspect of your life.

a musical scene: if you do not know how to behave, learn.

revue, taking part in a: take stock of your talents and develop those unique to you.

scenery, making the: will opt out of a frolicking good time because of a minor infection.

seeing a dramatic spectacle: will suffer through emotional crises and emerge.

good play with a loved one, a: matrimony.

large group, a: will be forced to associate with unpleasant companions.

sweetheart: prosperity in the company of those in the pursuit of pleasure.

with family: are entertaining the idea that you too could be entertaining.

taking children to a: be cautious in discussing plans, but prepare for any eventuality.

usher won't seat you: try another approach for a missed chance.

ventriloquist, being a: people disregard what you say: your face says the opposite of what you feel.

THEFT
04-31-37-38-40-53

being robbed: are being correctly accused of false behavior.

committing a: loss of money on business ventures.

friends, by: be circumspect in dealings.

money, someone steals your: someone is stealing time, energy or ideas.

stealing clothing: others are stealing your identity, but they can't create your ideas.

food: have suffered a financial loss and want only to feed your family.

money: are overstepping the bounds of civilized society.

THERMOMETER
06-09-13-25-27-47

buying a: will make many trips to ensure the correct functioning of your ventures.

of a: gossip over your clothes being unkempt is damaging your reputation.

taking a temperature with a: decisions should be made only after careful analysis.

children's: your strong sense of responsibility gets things done; others do their own thing.

fever rising in the: your emotions are high and eagerness is uncontrollable.

falling: the calm will bring a moment of clarity before the storm.

THIEF
01-19-27-36-43-47

arresting a: your self-centered wittiness will cause your misstep.

being a: will overrate your value to the business and steal to make the finances equitable.

being discovered while: your anger is without warrant.

catching a: will be reimbursed for damages sustained and secure your financial affairs.

entering your house: unusually good business ahead.

killing a: will have misfortune and must exercise great economy in everyday life.

of thieves: will incur big damages in your enemy's eyes, but shrewdly not in yours.

being robbed by a: is that mistrust within yourself?

robbing others, a: are skeptical of the idea that possession is nine-tenths of the law.

pickpocket, a: don't waste your reserves on careless people.

THIMBLE
23-25-36-39-41-44

borrowing a: many friends will make your life happy.

buying a: will be unable to secure employment with your misbehavior.

having a, on when sewing: your excessive arrogance will secure you reprisals.

losing a: will have difficulty justifying your bad judgment.

woman dreaming of a: are being criticized for not being able to earn your own living.

THIN
07-10-27-45-47-52

being: are more sensual, your nerve ends are closer to the surface.

girl dreaming of becoming: will cry over a lost lover; don't die over him.

man: lack the strength and endurance to play in the big leagues.

woman: happy love affairs.

reducing to become: unexpected riches.

suffering in order: will receive a marriage proposal.

THIRST
09-10-23-40-42-43

being thirsty: desire to be fulfilled by love.

children: children's high ambitions will be realized.

with an empty bottle: unhappiness

drinking cloudy water to satisfy your: will be afflicted with worse trouble.

and not being satisfied: an unrequited love.

hot water: will be corrupted with your overeagerness for knowledge.

until, is satisfied: riches and contentment.

giving a drink to a person: are by nature kind and generous.

having a great: big catastrophe ahead, if you don't aspire to leadership.

satisfying your: with your fine leadership your affair will exceed your expectations.

satisfy your, being unable to: will not realize desires you really don't want.

THISTLES
01-28-31-33-36-46

being pricked by a: you stand alone with your ideas.

of: each prick is a trial you have avoided facing.

pulling: antagonism in the tangled confusion of your mind.

family: determination takes a team.

relatives, out: quarrels can be avoided with tact.

sprinkling a field of: watering down the effect of your disappointment.

THORNS
05-09-24-26-40-41

being irritated by a: an intelligent change after a hiatus from torment on the job.

pricked: warning of trouble in your sex life.

children: are making a martyr of yourself over caring for your child.

of: contentment when you accept your emotional pain.

having, on your body: divorce yourself from the bickering of envious neighbors.

THRASH
19-25-42-43-46-53

beating copper or lead: will have good days ahead.

out a fire: will have hard times ahead.

being thrashed: good times are ahead.

by friends: things will go wrong in love affairs.

of thrashing corn: you confide in others too much.

THREADS
08-14-24-34-37-46

brass: will be introduced to artists and enjoy the benevolent sharing of their creativity.

broken: faithless friends cause your losses, strengthen bonds of those committed to you.

cotton: your arguments with a lover over rational things are irrational.

gold: will search for the truth in the tapestry that is your life.

knotted: a mystery is resolved and will bring certain profit.

silk: a pointless hoax perpetrated by one with an age-old anger.

silver: the binding together of delicate feelings.

spinning: wealth gained by thrifty ways and a steady pace.

steel: will have to fight with opposition over the credit for a prosperous yield.

unraveling: an indiscreet friend will cause your secret to become public property.

wasting: discovery of a secret can aid your recovery from a psychotic episode.

wool: will come out well from a time-consuming hindrance.

THREATENED
01-31-33-42-43-50

but not injured: friends seek to discredit you.

by animals: repressed instincts eventually erupt.

dog: loosen up, let your natural instincts guide you.

in last minute of sleep: a fear of inadequacy to deal with your day.

insanity: reflect on your connection, not the quandary itself.

intruder, an: identity will clarify the reason for the invasion.

pet, a: leave civilization and come down to earth.

unharmed assailant, an: hidden shame needs expression.

THROAT
21-22-30-32-40-43

cutting your: troubles caused by others are insignificant compared to what you caused.

children's: your imagination is painfully inflamed.

someone else's: an unconscious indiscretion will cause the victim to cut off a necessity.

having trouble with your: your metabolism has been brought to a standstill.

difficulty swallowing: too much richness without the finances to back it up.

pressure in your: the truth hurts but must be expressed before pessimism digs in.

sore, a: what you say must speak to the truth.

THUNDER
06-10-11-29-34-49

hearing crashes of: imminent perils require action when first exposed.

lightning following: a quick decision is appropriate, you have analyzed long enough.

being hit by: see what was damaged by your lack of attention?

of a, storm: the disapproval of the gods.

stranded in a, storm, being: an unconsidered thought will gain in importance.

THYROID
07-10-35-37-42-45

goiter, having a: depressing, petty anxieties overcome your ability to handle real problems.

Graves' disease, having: accept the fact that someone loves you.

hyperactive: slow down and smell the roses.

hypoactive: blaming others for your failures accomplishes nothing.

TICKETS
02-05-15-19-41-43

can't find window: your plans will be thwarted.

forgot: your love life needs examination.

for wrong date: are in the wrong job or wrong company.

destination: have moved too fast to remember where you should have been.

having a lottery: will quarrel with the person you love best.

that did not win: will receive long-awaited good news.

lost: an opportunity is at hand that comes only once in a lifetime.

waiting hours to purchase: a person in line will become important.

TICKLING
03-13-14-29-37-45

being tickled by someone: an error caused by your indiscreet behavior will be cleared up.

others: are telling only parts of the truth to incite others to riot.

own nose: will be asked to lend money, which will cause a fight.

throat: your lies will be repeated to those who know the truth.

TIDE
02-05-27-40-46-49

flowing in: favorable events to increase your fortune will soon happen.

going out: make that decision now, to eliminate added worry.

low: life is stagnating, prepare to build by facing and handling the muddy situation.

tidal wave: are under the emotional weight of your entire heritage.

high: take immediate advantage of the first opportunity offered.

TIGERS
07-10-15-22-23-36

being attacked by a: a quiet person will become lethal.

caged at the zoo: social advancement through the death of a prominent person.

surprised by a: will suffer great embarrassment from a far-reaching family quarrel.

tied with a chain: will be surprised by the deviousness of an enemy.

dying when delivering babies: limit aggression and you eliminate degeneration.

having a small, as a pet: a marriage proposal that would be dangerous to accept.

killing a: beware of fiercely jealous friends; attack their flanks before they attack yours.

performing at a circus: will have helpful friends, but your life's performance is yours alone.

roaring: will suffer grief if you listen to those who speak the loudest, as the only truth.

running: will successfully ward off serious illness.

watching a: enemies beset your path to a family fortune; keep them within your view.

TIGHTROPE
05-11-26-36-39-44

riding a bicycle on a: business associates are supporting you.

teetering on a: are too thoughtless of the ramifications of your actions.

using a pole to balance on a: are an overloading your schedule.

walking a: enemies at work seek your destruction.

TILES
06-07-11-21-27-48

breaking: are destructive to your own positive influences.

falling from a roof: be careful to avoid an accident.

handling: are happily optimistic and take your challenges as they come.

many: a protective covering to allow good business profits.

of: attempt to increase your earnings.

TIME
02-11-13-25-37-49

arriving on: be wary of false alarms, which threaten your eccentric lifestyle.

checking the: your self-centered concept of time doesn't work.

> *asking someone for:* an agitation in your love life will bring pessimistic results.

clock, punching a: will be tempted by a smooth-talking stranger.

timetable: will react with unusual impulsiveness to an action that will prove valuable.

> *ignoring the:* your production level has decreased, your mind being distracted.

traveling in: a vision of astounding importance will deflate to inconsequentiality.

TIN
04-06-15-24-37-39

buying: will raise your own financial position.

ear: don't hear what you don't wish to.

of: people are talking behind your back.

of a tinker: do not meddle in the affairs of friends, or you will have to explain your actions.

> *mending kettles and pans:* will repair aspersions to your character.
> > *being unable to mend:* will have a vigorous mind.

selling: test friends before trusting them.

shining, objects: will accept untrue friends as good friends.

working with: don't lend money too freely.

TIPS
24-31-33-37-39-44

dividing, among people: will achieve a fortune dishonestly.

giving: someone is attempting to bribe your overbearing arrogance.

> *secretly:* rebellion is pointless; only you can change your attitude.

making a living on: cannot make your children obey only the traits you choose.

receiving a: must be less welcome to one who is attempting to bring harm to you.

TIPTOEING
18-20-22-35-36-40

children: unexpected happenings for separated lovers.

many people: will meet people who do not have high morals.

others: be sure to mend your quarrels before nightfall.

tulips, in the: contentment and happiness as you stop a plot to harm you.

424

TIRED

02-08-28-36-39-42

being: will receive a big favor from someone.

children: are expecting them to grow up too fast.

employees: you care more for amusements than work.

fatigued: your rundown vitality is open to disease.

friends: are endeavoring to diminish your power.

mate: ill health causing depression will pull energy out of relationships.

TIRES

08-12-13-18-36-44

blowing out: will suffer a slight, annoying accident and be ridiculed by your associates.

changing a: having to pay a debt you thought was canceled.

flat: massage those thighs and walk every day.

making a rut: your route has been hampered by conflicting opinions.

punctured, a: will secure safety measures that will prevent an accident.

repairing a: relations with your mate need repairing.

TITLES

05-07-29-40-46-55

carrying on a family: don't let people disturb your thoughts within or without the family.

earning an academic: your decisions are interminably discussed, but never acted upon.

receiving a: financial investments turned reckless through gossip by neighbors.

renouncing a: loss of prestige will bring a chance for the real you to grow up.

TOADS

08-10-15-18-19-39

catching a: a self-inflicted injury precludes your rival from challenging you full force.

hearing croaking of: pleasure awaits, but you are too rash and foolhardy to accept it.

hopping away: hard work solves your situation; trading up for a new one brings success.

killing: an unreliable friend demands constant praise and your undivided attention.

stepping on a: friends will desert you when they are needed most.

stones, picking up: will have to combat impending danger alone.

TOAST

01-07-12-13-17-44

answering a, made at a banquet: will lose a loved one by taking a new community position.

eating: will make a big profit and incur a vicious prejudice.

making a, during a meal: good humor at the arrival of unexpected news.

  hearing others: your overenthusiasm will be free of embarrassment.

master, being a: an opportunity to improve others' opinions of you.

serving, to others: will be invited to a dinner party with a group of influential friends.

toasting dark bread: great annoyances on your route to riches.

  white: increased expenses.

TOBACCO

16-18-23-24-29-43

bundle of leaves: will receive false news.

buying: plan and save for your old age.

leaves: failure in love, but success in business.

pouch, a: are squandering the money left you by one you distrusted.

putting, in the nose: will be very irritable when meeting a selfish woman.

selling: will meet someone very interesting.

shop, a: extensive gossiping behind your back will open up a friend to your face.

smoking: what you have to say could get you into trouble.

TOBOGGAN

13-14-31-32-37-44

coasting downhill on a: will come out well from a present peril, but without a job.

having a: an opening for lost souls to join in convivial companionship.

of a: be careful of your every step and slide accurately to your course.

others riding on a: the success of the team is dependent upon he who sets the pace.

TOILET
16-18-23-28-44-49

fixing hair or face in a, room: will receive a request for funds you cannot ignore.

flushing the: purge yourself of extraneous attitudes that are poisoning you.

going to the: have gleaned from life its cherries and are ready for a happy retirement.

of a: being timid with forgiving and relinquishing negative attitudes that cause hurt to others.

sitting on a: wish to forgive your enemies.

stopped up, being: are constipated, denying experiences you deep down cannot forget.

TOMATOES
06-08-11-17-30-32

eating: will have comfortable circumstances through your own efforts.

   children: return of splendid health and considerable travel.

   cooked: recent innovations brighten your future prospects.

fried green: a celebration is at hand for the simple things in life.

growing: your hands will be cramped by overeating nightshade vegetables.

half-mature, on the vines: persecution for demanding full pay for half work.

juice, drinking: the rebalancing of your system the morning after.

making a, sauce: your love will last forever.

picking: peace and happiness in the home.

rotten: beware of approaching danger in the midst of plenty.

splitting open a: persecution by a woman of ill fame.

TOMBS
02-13-15-21-23-26

being put into a: are adaptable to self-sacrifice, when misery befalls your family.

building a: will be required to perform duties that are distasteful.

catacombs, in the: exploration of deep conflicts with reincarnation.

   lost: your long-lost power will energize your pleasant family events.

church or convent, at a: will receive an ill-tempered accusative communication.

epitaphs on: will perform unpleasant duties of a grave nature.

falling into ruins: will overcome obstacles through research work into your heritage.

   over a: a narrow escape as your enemies fail to harm you.

of a: searching for your ability to live according to your values.

prominent people, of: advancement to honor and wealth will lose you many a friend.

stones in a rural cemetery: will reconnect with an alienated friend.

   new, amidst the old: new chance to make a good impression.

   setting a: call a friend to extricate you from trouble.

viewing, with another person: will find a suitable business partner.

walking among: marriage into a prominent family.

your name on a: exciting distant news favors you immensely.

TONGUE
03-05-11-15-16-37

biting the: are a romantic person with an inability to let go of your anger.

burning the: slander will severely criticize your character.

children showing their: their intelligence will defend them from detrimental gossip.

dirty, a: your behavior is misunderstood, causing false accusations.

extra-long, an: cure your nervous condition or you will be wrongly accused for your actions.

man dreaming of a large: will be able to discipline oneself with reason.

   woman: slander will strike your character and reputation.

of a: will become a victim of indiscreet actions, your own.

sharp, a: the truth is never heard from another's voice.

sticking, out at another: your gossip will return to haunt you.

wagging: cannot tell when people are speaking truthfully.

TOOLS
08-09-11-12-17-44

buying: many raises to your income due to good business prospects.

carrying: will serve under others, but battle your fears individually.

having carpenter's: will receive a proposition from a woman.

machinist's: will repair, renew and restart your life process.

many: manifesting the wealth of your empirical knowledge.

losing: time to start a new project.

art: what don't you want to see?

receiving, as a gift: pleasant things will be done for you.

selling, at a good price: an opportunity to be promoted if you control your temper.

TOOTHACHE
12-20-21-23-27-30

going to a dentist to cure a: an unbudgeted expense will cause you to borrow money.

having a: family squabbles upset business ventures.

children: happiness over letter from an old friend far away.

persisting: will soon hear news of fortune in the future.

receiving relief from a: excellent opportunities for investment.

TOOTHPICKS
01-12-13-15-28-35

buying: an enemy is watching your actions.

of: careless actions will cause damages.

others using: indiscreetly communicate your fury to indecent people.

picking teeth with a: will receive financial damages.

throwing, away: will lead a sanitary life.

toothbrush, using a: need to cleanse spiteful thought.

TORCH
07-14-19-24-32-37

enemies holding torches: honor and distinction will be clarified to all eyes.

others, in hands: discovery of wrongdoings better left unexposed.

women: a love affair under strange ritualistic circumstances.

holding a, at a public place: will be blessed with reasoning.

flaming, a: a secret revealed; respecting others brings respect to you.

that has gone out: a wave of apathy and resignation after being rejected for lack of fire.

holding a love, for a beautiful woman: will fall back into sin again to gain your desires.

married woman, a: what you take from another will be taken from you.

lighted, a: troubles will vanish quickly.

lighting a: will find a way to vanquish your troubles quickly.

torcherre, a: will be blessed with reasoning; but don't go directly into the light.

light parade, a: the illumination of the unconscious can prove deadly.

TORNADO
02-18-19-35-37-46

damages caused by a: honesty over repressed rage will bring victory for you.

furious, a: are wrapped up in a conflict over the loss of your friends.

mild, a: will be overwhelmed and out of control in your own affairs.

of a: warning of disaster in home and business.

others' property being damaged by a: there will be a tremendous agitation.

TORPEDO
19-21-27-30-41-42

exploding, an: are surrounded by envious people who will ruin you.

firing a: changes in your life once those who will destroy you are destroyed themselves.

handling a: love at first sight will bring personal miseries and profound regret.

hitting a target: will have joy with children.

TORRENT
20-24-29-33-37-44

crossing a: will accomplish your aims through personal miseries and profound regret.

falling into a: achieving power is not the most important thing.

of a: adversity, which will require your even-tempered practicality.

others saving themselves from a: a friend's double-cross leads you to an influential ally.

swimming to save yourself from a: dangers ahead for you, be cautious with each stroke.

walking beside a: desires realized after a short delay, but you must become involved.

watching a, with others: do not rush things; step back carefully into tranquility

TORTURING
06-09-22-30-31-34

animals: big money losses due to the defensive actions of deceiving minds.

being tortured: solutions for domestic hardships will prove fruitless.

chamber, a: repressed feelings of anger need to be expressed.

lovers, each other: a propitious relationship will prove that you are unreasonable.

others: injustice is anathema on either side; your suspicions are unjust.

watching news of torture: do not take responsibility for what you cannot change.

yourself: you kill your love with your own misconstrued thoughts.

TOTEM
01-14-24-26-34-54

defending others from: actions of deceptive friends will incur much hardship for you.

  your: the social structure based on your ancestral kinship is held in high regard.

pole, a: will meet distant relative for the first time and realize you two have led parallel lives.

  your: your life will be built one story at a time.

TOWEL
15-19-24-27-40-49

clean: after a period of cleansing, you must be careful to admit only cleansed values.

dirty: your secrets and hidden agendas are making you ill.

having guest, in the bathroom: beware of a double-cross by friends and losing your position.

using a, to dry face: will undergo a brief illness to find happiness in love.

  children: will accomplish your aims with a small amount of money.

  others: recovery from an illness very soon.

wipe hands: approaching money through devious means.

TOWER
06-10-22-26-27-28

at a distance, church: have chosen your path, which uses all of your inner resources.

  climbing up a: map out your area of operations.

being destroyed: another's envy has reached psychotic proportions.

bells peeling, the: make your move, now or never.

coming down from a: your wishes will not all be realized.

fortress, of a: will resist your enemy's obstinacy and drive him until he is compromised.

  going up into a: freedom from embarrassment but loss of money.

  gun salute being fired from a: will be cheated in a wasted effort to impress a lover.

locked up in a, being: are so wrapped up in own pain you cannot relate to another's.

standing on top of the: think with your heart and intellect before leaping in.

  in the belfry: timing is everything; leave before the bells begin to toll.

  others: much affliction when an unscrupulous person swindles you.

  overlooking a city: outline the entire project before you begin.

very high, a: will have a long life and a pleasant old age.

TOWN
19-21-29-35-36-47

coming from a big city to a small: a loss of money for a personal gain.

farmer dreaming of being in a big: warning against bad ambitions.

hall, entering: have become a responsible citizen with a very honest heart.

  heading a meeting in: must integrate differing views.

  paying a fine in: a chance to learn from your mistakes.

townsman going to a big city: increase in business and gains.

woman, from a: employer is dissatisfied with you.

TOYS
03-19-34-40-43-46

buying: your plan would be considered clever in kindergarten, but not after graduation.

giving, to children: are acting possessively toward others.

> *receiving, for your:* have loyal friends and are greatly beloved.

losing a: change the name of your game.

playing with: lighten up your thoughts for all the creative tools to work.

popgun, a: a malicious attack will broadside your reputation.

TRAFFIC
02-10-18-21-29-30

an accident in being in: are injured more than you realize; the blame could fall on you.

> *others, hurt:* will undergo persecution for what you inadvertently did to another.

being in: public dignity and many friends are in store for you.

> *big city:* don't buck the flow; go where your business will prosper.

> *held up by stopped:* infidelity and inconstancy of lover.

> *jam, a:* quarrel with one whom you need as an ally.

being stopped by a, officer: enjoy an active life; be adventurous but stay within the law.

light, a: your life is currently out of control.

sign, a: the direction has been given; there is no other way out.

TRAILING
03-07-18-20-27-31

behind someone: are prone to being arrogant, but your health is far from perfect.

being trailed: have a guilty conscience and are carrying it on your back.

> *by a mate:* arrival of a friend will cause you sacrifice, if you want to keep your mate.

> > *investigator, an:* your good faith is in doubt, put your own affairs in order first.

> > *sweetheart:* will have an adventure with one of the opposite sex.

TRAIN
14-20-27-46-48-49

brakeman turning the, switch: all changes for the better will happen eventually.

buying tickets for a: are restless and yearn for the open road.

cargo, a: present complex concerns will ultimately prove beneficial to you.

cogwheel, a broken: approaching money will change your outlook.

> *many:* plans will succeed from now on.

conductor, being a: your ambitions are overburdened with too many steps to your goal.

> *engineer:* your ambition will be crowned as difficulties are overcome easily.

freight, a: improved business circumstances if you stay on track.

locomotive, of a: ask to be allowed precious time to observe travel.

> *coming toward you:* your desire to relive an experience can't be done.

> *going away from you:* will be jilted by a lover after your deceptive actions are revealed.

> *going full speed:* quick rise to wealth for a contented life.

> *two hooked together:* wish to move forward and solidify the relationship.

> *wrecked:* loss of prosperity has left you with nothing but a movie of your life.

mail, a: are frustrated at a letter unanswered, or never sent.

missing a: opportunity will pass you by, if you are not prepared.

> *connection:* something to blame your inferiorities on; stop running others' lives.

of a: will take care of a contemplated project with speed.

sleeping cars, being in: your lewd actions taint your selfish struggle to amass wealth.

> *spending all night on a:* will arrive at the decision on another's timetable.

station, arriving at a: take a deep breath and proceed with your journey of life.

> *leaving:* check all systems and slowly gain momentum.

> *unable to get to the:* that is one trip you should not take.

subway, riding in a: must keep stiff upper lip through irritating incidents.

   being in a wreck: will have a car full of friends to support your next venture.

switching tracks in a: an outside source will cause your change of direction.

traveling on a: are optimistic that a lawsuit will be ruled in your favor.

   through a tunnel: can avoid a mass of work by following your instincts.

   with the family: take advantages in your life; do not let yourself be taken advantage of.

      friends: a major professional move is imminent; keep your approach to it rational.

watching one leave on a: your breadth of vision deters your accepting the first offer.

wreck with another train, in a: distress and many disappointments.

TRAMP
12-24-45-46-50-52

begging, a: a letter from a friend whom you regard as a material and moral failure.

being a: an absent friend is thinking about you.

   hobo: your nefarious actions will be shamed in public.

owning a, vessel: are carrying the responsibility for dirty things no one else wants to acknowledge.

preparing a: take precautions against being caught in your own trap.

setting a trap for another: will be a victim of your own devices.

tramping your feet on the floor: your arguments will clarify the true passions.

TRAP
02-13-19-21-28-39

door, closed, a: have limited yourself to reconciliation without love.

   falling through a: have been duped into limiting your true self, exit gracefully.

going trapping: are sabotaging your actions with delusions of grandeur.

   others, with: are trapped in a circle of relationships.

of a: will receive a surprising and unpleasant letter; don't respond without a lawyer.

snaring another in: disregard another's influence and take back your governance.

   animals: family will not approve of your choice of profession.

   birds: will collect a small amount of money.

trapped, being: have hardened your emotions against a dead issue.

   passage, in an underground: will abuse the confidence of others.

TRAVELING
04-12-17-37-38-39

abroad, being: if your mind is unsettled, consider potential results long and hard before acting.

   going: your childish unreliability will lose you needed respect.

      others: triumph over enemies will bring a sudden and large increase of income.

   others: someone will belittle your accomplishments when their fortunes rise.

alone: will avoid unpleasant events if you avoid the interference of noisy neighbors.

another: a visit from a distant friend; consider results before acting.

arranging for a trip: beware of friend's gossip as to why you are taking your trip.

commuting, a married man: a fellow worker has no excuse for his poor performance.

   by subway: are attacking your ambitions by utilizing your subconscious drives.

   single man, a: another's interests may not be in line with the business focus.

      woman: will receive important help from your superiors.

   woman: someone with evil intentions is watching you.

galaxy, in the: spiritual journey of self-expansion and heightened awareness.

home from another town, to: present conditions are moving toward positive growth.

in a car: separation from immediate family to journey in an area you alone can go.

   carriage: will enjoy large fortune, if you accept new ideas in your job.

on a horse: will have dealings with obstinate people, one of them is yourself.

foot: hard work is ahead for you; take care, your health is dubious.

small boat: need to nurture every bit of your self-awareness.

train: think before you act and only after a well-deserved rest.

tourist, being a: your nervousness is restraining your developing a relationship.

in a group: do not avoid another's opinion, their advice may be useful.

with business associates: dashed hopes in all present ventures until you find new ones.

firearms: will soon find a wife, but not before you solve your nervous irritability.

loved one: delays in personal matters due to hiding your insincerity.

others: feel you are stagnating as others leave you in their wake.

your family: will avoid unhappiness by making necessary sacrifices.

TREASURE
04-27-28-33-39-49

burying: your egocentricity is isolating your spirit from friends.

buying: do not expect any resale value; your disgrace is caused by your greed.

digging for a: your unsettled state interferes with your seeing opportunity.

finding a: your interpretation of the symbols unearthed will provide your direction.

chest, a: an inheritance from an obscure source releases your creative powers.

hidden: in danger of being robbed of your abilities.

going to the treasury: big headaches ahead for you in justifying your finances.

of a treasurer: will receive money from relatives to complete your project.

stealing a: beware of double-cross from those you now trust.

treasuring your children: have good friends in them.

sweetheart, a: will leave home of father and mother.

TREES
12-15-24-25-42-47

almond in blossom, of an: a duplicitous relationship with indiscretion and stupidity.

ripe fruit, with: a propitious time for happiness in the home.

apple, an: will be tempted by deceitful charms in your pursuit of perfection.

ash, an: it is prudent to separate your ego from the surrounding grandeur.

mountain: be prudent with your magical moments that they don't deny you rest.

aspen, an: lament your actions, as they are the cause of your loneliness.

banyan, a: a never-ending acrimonious argument.

bark of a: keep your inner life to yourself, but be supported by its strength.

damaged: redraw the boundaries to your intimate space.

deformed: the elements of your life have taken their toll.

barren, a: someone is cheating you through their lack of support.

bay, a: guard against self-pity being your merit badge.

beech, a: your cruel narrow-mindedness will limit the prosperity of your new ventures.

big, without fruit: have total lack of sensibility in your extravagant spending.

birch, a: your love is virtuous and honorable and too meek to appreciate your worth.

birds in a: reflect on the words of others and the songs of a few.

blossoms, with: joy and sweet satisfaction.

without: business will be increased.

box, a: will benefit from stoicism and loneliness through the loss of a young person.

branches: family will divide and spread for each to have room to grow.

burning: nuisance and unhappiness.

cedar, a: have an incorruptible strength of character.

cherry, a: sickness will block distractions for you so you can concentrate on your education.

chestnut, a: you deserve luxury, if only for a day.

climbing, children: a pleasing variety of knowledge, leisure and diversion.

falling while: restructure your goals to be just beyond realistic.

fruit: are an extroverted, imaginative personality enjoying the forbidden and unusual.

limb, breaking while: usual routes to success are not open to you; be original.

with a ladder: will attain an important high position and be difficult to live with.

Christmas, a: joy and happiness, peace on earth.

crooked, a: will limit prosperity of your new ventures.

cutting down timber: will incur losses and become another's servant.

dead: short engagement ending in new growth in a happy marriage.

in someone else's land: are protected by influential people from the mate of your choice.

cutting up a, in a building: an interesting discovery about your project.

cypress tree, of a: a friend's help will bring despair when health problems are discovered.

blowing in the wind: a sad setback will bring meaning into your home.

diseased, a: your present path is up for ridicule.

elm, a: dignity in a carefree life.

escaping from a forest fire: will have an unusual accident.

evergreen, an: your strong faith in yourself bodes well for a long life.

fig, a: will be prolific in your arguments and adamant in your idleness.

finding a fallen, in the road: misfortune will cross your path.

fir, a: ever hopeful in the midst of darkening despair.

forest of pine: a family reunion will provide security and staunch support.

fruit, without fruit, a: your talents cannot be recognized if you don't expose them.

unripened: your vitality is being sapped by another's growth.

green, a: unbounded joy will make you forget all sadness.

grove of, a: will chair a meeting of several opposing viewpoints.

heavily fruit-laden: riches and fortune in business.

hickory, a: hard, heavy-laden travails in business.

horse chestnut, eating a: failure due to the timing of a short illness.

Judas, a: your disbelief at being betrayed.

leaves falling in the fall: must overcome situation or ramifications will follow you.

rustling: the voice of Mother Nature manifesting your talents.

turning yellow: illness to come soon, then everything will return to normal.

linden, cutting down a: dangerous love affair; security is in conjugal love.

locust: an elegant affection.

logs floating down a river: honor among fellows who can outrun the flow.

sawing: a comfortable home is satisfaction for hard work.

sitting on a: leisure to carry out the life you want.

magnolia, a: the dignity of perseverance in strong friendships unaffected by distance.

mast of a ship made from a, a: will get assistance in time of need.

mulberry, a: will survive by your wisdom, but not your mate's.

oak, an: sound financial and organized, hospitable family life.

live, hung with moss: a home you find it impossible to leave.

of a: will receive favors from friends with good intentions.

olive, cutting branches from an: peace, serenity and happiness in all desires.

orange, an: passing discontent at unreciprocated generosity.

palm, a: victory, if you don't attempt to climb above your abilities.

peach, a: will have fights because of opposition to your ideas, but never consider separation.

pear, a: opposition in love affairs will lead to a search for a comforting one.

picking fruit from a: inheritance received from elderly people.

pine, a: tremendous happiness with an honest person.

cone on the ground: a concurrence of events will redirect your income concerns.

cutting branches from a: will enjoy congenial work and well-being.

pineapple, a: fertility—the greatest nutrition per calorie.

plum, a: fidelity to, and from those, who count on you.

   wild: independence from vicious gossip.

pomegranate: will enjoy a quiet future amidst your foolishness.

poplar, a: will enjoy a large reputation for small adventures.

   twisted: reanalyze your views and prejudices.

prune, to: brings your health to light.

redwood, a: your expansion possibilities are majestic.

resting under a: have the influence of friends, but are alone responsible for your growth.

   flowering: are asserting your creative principle.

   sleeping: health and vigor are being drained by your responsibilities.

rings of a: wisdom gained from past experiences can be invested in your future growth.

roots of a: depths of the past will inform the present.

sap from a: will be happily surprised by a visitor, once the blood of your life.

spruce, a: hope in adversity against those who bear down until they get the advantage.

stump, digging out a: your vigorous inquisitiveness will prove to be justified.

sycamore, a: curiosity.

tiny sapling: fertility, procreation and poverty until fruition.

trunk, a: continue your family tradition and contribute to your heritage.

unhealthy: your potential has receded into itself.

willow, a: bravery in defense of humanity.

yew, cutting branches from a: death of an aged relative.

TRELLIS
01-02-16-23-28-32

at your summer house: will come out well from a present peril.

being on a: will have many children.

bower alone, being under a: will receive a marriage proposal.

   others, with: will be visited by lover.

picking grapes from a: will have a happy married life.

having a: a firm friendship will be the foundation of success.

TRENCH
20-21-23-30-42-44

being in a: hopes for new employment.

digging a: are weak with initiative and enterprise; follow the leader.

fighting in a: one is never cut off from an evil influence or the power to destroy it.

of a, coat: are gradually building up a brilliant career, don't squander money.

   wearing a: will fight with a temperamental person.

   others: will be jilted by friends.

of a, filled with soldiers: will be astonished that so tiring a labor could be so lucrative.

soldiers being killed in a: beware of being trapped.

TRESPASSING
07-08-19-36-40-45

animals, on your property: allow serious illness to intrude upon your creative powers.

being caught: are imposing your self-expression on another's rights.

being forbidden to trespass a premise: attraction for a married person.

enemies, on your property: inevitably damages should be handled by legal means.

of a no, sign: prosperity is coming soon for you to hide behind.

TRIAL
01-11-17-35-41-44

being at a: an admirer merits your attention, but not your harsh judgment.

being on: will enjoy lifelong security if you detach yourself to see the real truth.

   condemned for wrongdoings: your conscience is not clear.

   woman: will receive bad news.

enemies: are a determined stubborn individual who stands up for his rights.

friends: death of an acquaintance.

justly accused: take responsibility for your actions and apologize, now!

    unjustly: are enjoying much passion and little compassion.

relatives: will play well in the lottery.

tried on a business matter: will witness an injustice done to another.

losing in a: your adversary has more to lose than you do.

    winning in a: you know the truth, act on it.

suing someone in a: the absolute certainty of your truth will win in the end.

TRIANGLE
29-30-35-50-54-55

being in the middle of a: either/or doesn't work, keep both friends and make a trio.

children figuring geometry: will receive a fortune in the near future.

drawing a: will discover you can integrate talents and balance the rational with the emotional.

    others: will have to choose between two lovers.

laborer cutting out a, a: happiness will follow suffering.

TRIP
02-08-22-28-29-38

anticipating a: what you have planned for is happening.

being driven on a: relax; others are supporting you.

buying a ticket for a: the battle with addictions and attitudes is over, go your own way.

    on the Internet: rise above your problems to get an unobstructed view.

    through a travel agent: need someone you trust.

driving yourself on a: don't hesitate; take the decided direction.

leaving on a: scout the possibilities for your next move.

    suddenly: your guilt has been exposed.

preparing for a: it takes layers of learning to prepare for all eventualities.

TROUBLE
10-18-28-30-35-37

avoiding: are very gullible; your introversion confines you to solitude.

being in: your overbearing arrogance will break any friendship.

    lover: failure in love.

facing: will have success, now is the time to make plans.

TROUSERS
12-16-17-27-39-42

hole in your, having a: flirtation with a married woman, which will never come to light.

laborer's dirty, a: better days will not come in the future; these *are* the better days.

of: are prone to talking too much without meaning it.

pantaloons, women wearing: have established an irresistible attachment.

putting on: increase within the family as your confidence in your future increases.

taking off: a woman will be faithful to you.

wearing tight: do not lend any money that you cannot afford to lose.

TROUT
21-25-29-34-37-38

buying: advancement through a presentation, with your amiable and courteous demeanor.

catching: will receive improvements in finances.

    others: looming doubts bring misfortune in love affairs.

cooking: will quarrel with relatives over alarming news.

eating: your troubles will be over.

fish market, at a: advancement within own position.

swimming upstream: with freedom comes responsibility.

TRUCK
02-20-23-25-35-49

being on a: have difficulty maneuvering your love life.

carrying away a load: clutter is useless garbage.

driving a: your entire life is on the move.

    pick up: be on guard against spiteful gossip.

    van: are hiding your talents behind tinted windows.

hauling a trailer: test each burden and discard unwanted luggage with care.

running on rails, a: suitable time to pursue courtship.

TRUMPET
03-08-29-30-31-49

blowing on a: your ego is fragile and will be severely humiliated.

hearing a: will receive a surprise revelation about an incident at home.

   several: make plans for a family reunion.

large, a: pleasant activities in the near future.

playing a: people are curious about your affairs, don't tell them.

   children: will be very fortunate in the future.

TRUNK
21-27-29-34-41-48

car, a: a secret you are intent on keeping.

elephants, an: are satisfied with small pleasures.

filling a: be selective as to whom you include.

full, a: plans for a trip have been canceled, until you rise above the situation.

many: take the trip, to more appreciate what you left and will return to.

of an empty: resist the temptation to change jobs, your promotion is imminent.

opening the lid: are on a voyage of self-discovery.

   closing: dispose of undesirable elements.

relative's, a: a traveler will return from abroad.

taking a, on a trip: a wish will be realized.

unfolding layers in a: a potential is to be developed.

TRYST
18-22-30-51-55-59

of a: a reconciliation will end romantically.

rendezvous, planning a: your reputation will not survive it.

waiting at an appointed place: misfortune in love affairs.

   in an ambush: you are wasting your time destroying another's life instead of building you own.

   others: will have sorrow that you are not the one your love meets.

TUB
05-13-21-23-38-57

being in a: are doing extravagant things for little, lasting reward.

bringing a, into the house: will receive mysterious news; take the prospective offer.

empty, an: hard times are ahead due to your indecision and the ensuing uncertainty.

full of water, a: happiness in married life if moderation is used in disputes with in-laws.

TUBES
01-08-09-12-29-35

buying: your birth was successful, so you will prosper.

filled with water, a: will meet someone and have an argument.

fixing and putting, in place: will have a good reputation.

pile of many big: prosperity according to the amount of tubes.

selling: grab your fortune before it passes.

TUMOR
12-19-27-28-35-39

having a, on the neck: take advantage of good luck when it comes.

   children: family will be bothered by undermining annoyances.

   in the throat: your reluctance to change your opinions to the truth you now know.

   on the waist: unhappiness caused by an inheritance.

   others: will meet the beautiful wife of a friend.

TUNNEL
18-22-30-31-32-33

being built: victories in many business transactions if you can clearly see the dealers.

chamber in a, in a locked: your unconscious is speaking deep thoughts loud and clear.

dark, a: troubles are looming on the horizon; trust is not possible with present company.

escaping injury in a: business satisfaction; you can't get off track.

exiting from a: put your sunglasses on; reality is cruel.

going through on a train: wish to return to

the womb rather than face the tasks at hand.

driving a car: unsatisfactory business undertakings trap you in a womblike state.

meeting another train: will confront them with fortitude in impossible conditions.

light at the end of a: relief and rebirth from past deleterious conditions.

lit, a brightly: misunderstandings are solvable no matter how confined and dim.

mud in a, walking in the: are disturbing yourself by plodding.

narrow, a: ambition has been constricted until you expand your world.

trapped in a, being: are unable to understand belief systems not your own.

　　pitch black: your eye prescription needs to be changed; a happy period is in prospect.

wandering in circles in a: dependence upon mother and inability to sever apron strings.

wide, a: your considerable ambition may cause a wrong; keep it justified and trudge on.

TURKEY
01-11-13-17-35-37

being a Turk: beautiful women will seek after you.

buying a: can expect something good to come to you.

carving a: quarrels over an unwise but common method of procedure.

eating a: dissent within communal fellowship.

killing a: your vivid imagination leads to infidelity.

making, sandwiches: will be visited by hungry people.

of a: abundant harvest for the farmer.

people of, the: will be subjected to the will of others.

plucking a: will have a nervous breakdown.

roasting a: with your inconsistency and unfaithfulness you will lose those who matter most.

TURNIPS
09-10-20-34-55-56

buying: have no foundation for your hopes, until those whom you befriend join you.

cooking: improvement of own health.

eating: poor health will recede as you begin to look better.

growing: your questionable prospects turn you into a self-made man.

harvesting: combine your investments.

white, a: complications in love life.

TURTLES
08-18-21-22-26-49

catching a sea: opportunity for advancement will come to you.

dead, a: support diminished without your knowing.

drinking bouillon made from sea: are slow moving to make changes.

killing a: have destroyed the hand that fed you.

of a tortoise: will retreat into your shell with little provocation.

　　buying: some new person will fall in love with you.

TWINE
03-20-26-29-33-48

buying: suitable time to pursue your courtship.

dark ball of: use energy frugally; avoid flirtations.

having very thick: will suffer tears because of a love affair.

saving old: will have an argument with a friend over small matters.

unraveling: problem must be faced.

wrapping something with: will be guilty of foolish actions.

TWINS
03-22-31-32-37-41

having: split the conflict between the ideas, and the decisions that implement them.

　　horses: will come out well from a present peril.

　　of the same sex: keep a state of mental poise about your overwhelming responsibility.

　　　different: dignity and distinction, one of each.

man dreaming of wife having: change of surroundings brings balance.

sickly, being: daily meditation is needed.

woman dreaming of having: will verbalize thoughts and fears.

UGLY
08-18-34-44-50-54

being: misunderstandings make all things unattractive.

can't help: are being watched by one with evil intentions because of your attractiveness.

children: love quarrels with your mate over responsibilities you share.

young lady dreaming of: break your engagement, love makes everyone beautiful.

others who are: your chilly indifference will cause others to react with anger.

ULCERS
05-08-21-24-50-56

having: your affection needs to be shared to be returned.

in the mouth: your impulsiveness needs to delay your tongue; take a few deep breaths.

stomach: must fulfill your destiny no matter how time consuming and difficult it is.

throat: will be ignored by everyone.

on the arms: another is blocking your initiatives.

legs: will suffer affliction from another taking credit for your accomplishment.

UMBRELLA
07-09-13-33-35-59

borrowing an: shelter your emotions from the downpour.

carrying an: will be annoyed by trouble and many vexations.

open, over the head: someone will come to your aid.

closing an: have protected your emotions long enough, let them run free.

having a broken rib: financial troubles will destroy confidence, yours and others in you.

fixing many: petty tribulations will test your patience until they come to a head.

several: one will come to your rescue with a trial to build your self-confidence.

having an: will be shielded against the storms of life.

open inside the house: are broadminded, practical, open and adapt with ease.

leaking, a: distrust a close associate and suspect him of divulging company secrets.

leaving a wet umbrella to dry: your distrust of others will belittle your reputation.

lending an: will be hurt by false friends, causes a total estrangement.

opening an: shielding yourself from experience stunts your growth.

others with an: will fail to meet the requirements of a venture you initiated.

wind turning, inside out: will have a joyous reunion with a childhood confidante.

UNCLE
06-09-29-33-52-57

being an: a successful matrimony if you distance your family from in-laws.

of a husband's: his displeasure in being the skeleton-in-the-closet in a controversy.

another's: shame and sorrow caused by a difficult predicament brings on family arguments.

wife's: beware of jealous in-laws causing a rift in your home.

UNDERTAKER
18-26-28-34-40-49

being an: are taking on necessary, painful job for one who cannot do it himself.

going to the parlor of an: are harboring the death wish but will live a long life.

parlor of an, the: will receive announcement of a wedding.

preparing the body for a funeral: will sustain a loss, but guilt feelings need to be placed.

removing a body from the house: an authority figure no longer has authority.

UNDERWEAR
15-17-19-28-34-36

dressing without: a fearless performance will succeed, but end in uncertainty.

garter, adjusting a: will hear scandalous reports of you in a situation that never happened.

shopping for: expose your hidden talents, not your lack of virtue.

at a sale: don't sell yourself short; you desire what others have and are willing to work to get it.

wearing, underwear: hopes are temporarily dashed.

suit, a: will have unpleasant events ahead.

wrapping something in: are guilty of wrongdoing.

wearing in public: intimacy is missing from your satisfaction.

black: are hiding from your true self.

dirty: are not fooling others by your performance.

panties: an intimate liaison is needed.

underpants: just ask others for what they need.

undershirt: someone close to you is unfaithful.

UNDRESSING
14-23-28-31-37-40

before others: people are talking about your unfaithfulness behind your back.

being undressed: gossip and malice will cause sorrow.

children: pleasant events will occur in your life.

husband and wife, in same room: business affairs will go bad.

in another's house: are exposing your unadulterated feelings.

in a hotel room: a dangerous situation is looming; spies are in your bedroom.

in privacy: your secret about a previously hidden incident will reveal your lack of scruples.

in public: distress will come to you; stand up for your rights.

others: will be visited by a loved one.

yourself: will have an unusual experience with a new acquaintance.

UNFAITHFUL
03-09-19-23-35-39

being: someone is taking advantage of your trust in them.

boy, to his girlfriend: doubt and distrust without reason causes doubt.

girl, her boy: will receive an invitation from a prominent person.

man dreaming of being, to his wife: two wrongs don't equal a right.

others, to each other: will receive money from a dishonest man.

woman, husband: are uncertain of the father of your child.

UNGRATEFUL
01-05-13-18-25-31

children being: will earn money in winnings.

family: must rely on your own good judgment.

people: something is preying on your conscience.

relatives: will be visited by someone asking a favor.

others, being, to: will be visited by a judge who will grant you what you deserve.

UNICORN
04-11-23-35-43-49

cage, in a: will be avoided by acquaintances because you won't share.

killing a: losses in real estate.

many, together: are facing new acquain-tances whose pleasant coats hide their deceit.

of an animal with one horn: will have anxiety caused by falsehoods.

UNIFORMS
02-03-09-25-45-47

enlisted personnel in: will be unable to extricate yourself from big afflictions.

khaki, wearing a: wish to take care of unpleasant visitors with frivolity.

army people in: a rival will take your sweetheart.

member of own family in: glory and dignity.

men wearing, for their business: abundance in money.

women: strict self-expression will bring about happiness.

military: are unfitted to fill position in life; must change, using wise, deliberate actions.

officers in: will receive a promotion in the eyes of those you respect.

selling: friends will exert influence to help you in more than one onerous task.

wearing a: valor and prominence have to be earned; the opportunity is warranted.

enemies: will have much dignity in your chosen calling and distinction.

helmet, a: an internal disturbance of serious consequences.

lover: will be guilty of foolish actions toward a stage actress.

others: will become a military or naval officer.

with epaulets: have honor and consideration for your defeated foes.

UNIVERSITY
13-16-17-29-37-43

attending a: are fortunate in your talents; develop them.

children: your mood alternates between creative elation and inept depression.

being a professor at a: are inventive, with a strong will to follow through.

of a: essentially, be perfect in your studies so as to be prepared for fresh challenges at work.

others going to a: triumph over enemies.

UNLOCKING
02-15-23-24-37-38

being unable to unlock a door: beware of trouble ahead.

drawer: don't keep secrets from those who love you.

not finding the key to unlock something: be careful in money matters.

of, something: a discovery will be made in your home.

URINATING
23-25-28-29-30-36

children: will have to sweep the floor.

drinking urine: feel others are depleting your energy.

having to urinate: are avoiding facing annoying obstacles; reality does not disappear.

others: completion of a business transaction after a heated argument with an investor.

urinal pot, a: are retaining malice aforethought and wish to purge yourself.

wall, on a: apologizing for past transgressions becomes increasingly difficult the longer you wait.

wet your bed, having: an unconscious act showing your disdain for another.

URN
20-37-40-41-46-48

broken, a: unhappiness as plans unfold badly.

empty, an: death among neighbors reveals your shyness.

full of ashes: are not very enthusiastic about the conditions of your inheritance.

of a relative: will receive news from a new acquaintance.

handling an: death of a friend.

others: will achieve distinction and destroy your credibility with nervous chatter.

putting hands in an: will turn a struggling venture into a good business.

UTERUS
04-09-14-24-26-29

having pains in the: are seizing property to which you have no legal rights.

having the, removed: will make good money but be unable to establish credit.

V V V V V

VACATION
04-05-31-34-44-46

being on an: be on guard against married associates.

family, with: important and beneficial event to come.

friends: beware, this friend may not be true.

husband and wife: postponement of realizing your desires.

others, without you: will have financial gains unexpectedly.

going on a: the project will not let you loose from cherished opinions.

others: will enjoy an increased earning capacity.

with a loved one: will be persecuted for feeling entitled to what you deserve.

making plans for a: your employer is overworked himself.

resort, visiting a: an amusing seduction and a wake-up call rebuke you.

returning from a: overwork does not equate with prosperity.

VACCINATED
12-14-25-32-41-52

being: are showering affections on an unworthy person.

  by a nurse: will have opposition to your showering of flattery, but disregard it.

  children: beware of squandering money.

  family: prosperity proportioned to number vaccinated.

  others: let your head rule your heart or your enemies will occupy your time.

needing to be: suspicion will lead to your being forced to prove your innocence.

VAGABOND
01-04-05-15-22-23

being a: dishonor through lack of morals of those you helped feed.

  friends: will be acquainted with dignified people who will consider you an interloper.

of a: as you free yourself from the boundaries set by society.

wandering around, a: a good time on a picnic, and a bad time with food poisoning.

wayfarer, being in the company of a: attempt to avoid bad company.

  meeting a lonely, on a path: a new friend with whom you will combat annoying obstacles.

  others: restructure your finances to reevaluate your self-worth.

VALENTINES
01-02-04-16-26-27

married people exchanging: will receive an unexpected invitation, don't accept it.

of St., Day: will kiss one of the opposite sex who will promptly forget you.

receiving a: will take advantage of available opportunities, thereby missing the best one.

  sweetheart: victory over enemies, but no sharing of the spoils.

sending a: will lose an opportunity to make money.

  children, to parents: inheritance within a year.

  sweetheart: contradiction in the terms of your love will alienate those you love.

VALIDATING
02-03-08-09-10-26

check, a: will fall into the grip of creditors.

document, a: don't rely too much on your fortune.

having a valid fortune: will hear stupid gossip.

ticket, a: will have an abundance of property.

VALLEY
01-06-11-19-28-36

barren, a: your rollicking devil-may-care attitude will leave you dissatisfied and wanting.

being in a: an energetic, independent, determined person needs to focus these qualities.

  relatives: warning of very bad health; do not overexert yourself.

  with children: will unexpectedly receive money due you.

bottom of a, at the: are at a low point, but have aimed yourself out of the ballpark.

crossing a green: contentment and ease are insufficient to keep the fields cultivated.

dark, wandering in a: being a wastrel is not a legitimate occupation, tranquil though it is.

VAMPIRE
02-07-23-25-30-39

being bitten by a: all of your fears point to an unpleasant encounter that must be faced.

  chased by a: choose your companions stringently, no negative thinkers.

dead person coming back to life: your destructive habits have a seductive hold over you.

fighting with a: are responsible for maintaining your own envy level.

kissing your neck, a: a lover is draining your energy and you emotionally.

married person dreaming of a: have made a bad bargain with a selfish bloodsucker.

of a: will triumph over resistance to your lowly class and marry for money.

VANISHING
16-20-30-31-32-38

friends: other's difficulties with you can be traced to your unwillingness to share.

mate: will cause unhappiness with your extreme impulsiveness.

members of family: will have good business, though minor problems are stifling your profits.

of: rumors will irritate you and their suppression will be your lasting goal.

own possessions: have a hard life ahead: hardwood floors, doors, windows and frames.

VARNISHING
04-09-13-15-22-40

doors of a house, the: bigotry and biting interferences will bring harm to your business.

floor: hypocrisy, as your thriftiness and work attire are used and abused by superiors.

furniture: glossing over mistakes and transgressions.

of: your outward appearances will not fool others.

VASE
07-18-27-29-42-51

breaking a, and spilling the water: your concern with appearances shatters your hopes.

broken, a: overwhelming sorrow, causing you doubts and indecision you had hidden.

cracked, a: are still able to hold your own, but outlook is weakening.

full of flowers: exposure of your overspending on luxuries.

made of fine pottery: value highly loved one's attributes.

receiving a gift of a: there will be a radical restoration of your finances.

silver, a: past debts will be repaid and your coffers will remain full.

full of flowers: friends will aid you when distress appears.

unmarried person dreaming of a: immediate marriage and birth of a son.

VAULT
09-10-16-19-21-30

being at a sarcophagi: your search for meaning, and not finding it, has caused depression.

empty, an: put a different slant on your rejection of the past.

full, a: are docking your abilities for fear of premature exposure.

of a: make a clean break with past dangers before undertaking new ventures.

opening a: difficulty in persuading others your conduct was an attempt to make them think.

VEGETABLES
07-08-09-21-31-33

artichokes, eating: family dissension over your ridiculous acts.

growing: will be able to surmount present troubles.

asparagus, cooking: success in own enterprises if you admit when you are wrong.

eating: be careful what you wish for, because you will get it.

buying: family quarrels.

eating: are reaping the benefits of what you have sown.

broccoli: your ambitions will be misinterpreted, leaving your real motives undigested.

endives: a foreigner will communicate love, which will be sufficient conversation.

leek: improvement of health.

string beans: long-awaited plans come to fruition.

summer squash: opportunities will be wide open for increasing your wealth.

turnips: will quarrel in the company of friends.

eggplant, preparing: success in gradual increments by entertaining business associates.

fennel, a: spiritual clear-sightedness of life's cycles.

green: continue to persevere and retain high hopes on the romantic front.

growing: your labor will bear fruit if you nurture it, and financial gain if you water it.

horseradish: doubts as to your friend's fidelity and stability.

lentils, of: in training for the fight of your life.

lettuce, eating: make excuses for the behavior of relative; jealousy has come to full flower.

picking from own garden: faithful finances

will be destroyed by your super-sensitivity.

of: hard work with small rewards and a continual threat of a reversal of fortune.

parsley, buying: security in the pleasantries of society.

   growing: success will be achieved through hard work.

parsnips, buying: sickness will not last long.

   cooking: are indebted to someone; pay him back before he turns on you.

   eating: success will not come in business if you are too easily satisfied.

   picking: money worries will be greatly lessened by economical measures.

   others: your quarrels are attracting strong criticism.

planting: reexamine your health and feed the spiritual side.

smelling odors of, cooking: will discover unpleasant secrets, then pleasant ones.

spinach, cooking: will receive gratitude from family with a serving of grit.

   eating: will be bothered by thoroughly detestable neighbor.

still in the ground, that are: will suffer afflictions to your supposedly solid foundations.

vegetarian, being a: self-discipline through diet should follow your true nature.

zucchini, eating: have the good habit of attending church regularly.

   growing: will receive unexpected news that makes you happy.

VEIL
04-10-12-22-33-37

arranging a, on your head: a pretentious cover-up, making sacred what never was.

bridal, a: propitious prospects for great happiness.

having a: are disguising a forbidden thought in a spiritual overtone.

losing a: will lose your lover after your dispute with his superior.

opening a, or folding it: an important truth has been unveiled.

over a dead person: favorable circumstances will assist at a wedding.

tear in a veil: will lose protective support

when your insincerity is exposed.

wearing a: your secretive actions are for self-preservation, not self-enhancement.

   others: mystery and modesty.

VEINS
05-07-15-27-32-38

blood being taken from: take a new perspective toward your health.

   a relative's: don't believe all you hear, but defend your name against what you suspect.

children's, being cut: be cautious in all your actions, your anxiety will lead to illness.

cutting: riches if you let your talents flow.

extracting blood from: will enjoy a very great love.

VELVET
16-22-38-40-42-48

being a, merchant: wealth will be amassed by questionable methods.

buying: will be industrious, soft, sensuous and elegant.

dress, a: another's honor and riches will rub off on you.

of: the opposition will resent your rise in stature.

sewing with: will receive assistance from a friend and return it tenfold.

splitting: will offer little resistance to advances.

VENUS
01-03-04-16-22-37

marrying: will be respected and loved by everyone.

naked picture of: intercourse as a form of celebration.

of: will write poetry, songs, anything to seduce her man.

   goddess, the: attend to your sensual but wayward emotions.

   planet, the: a vision of aesthetic harmony.

   statue of, having a: riches in proportion to the size of the statue.

VERDICT
04-11-15-18-31-45

being a juror and deciding a: will get money from a friend if you guard your tongue.

hearing a, against you: will prepare for a journey in a hurry.

hearing a juror give a: will win a case.

jury who decides the: your cunning and shrewdness causes others to reject your society.

VERMIN
09-13-21-32-41-47

having, on your body: don't be overly severe with wrongdoers due to your insecurity.

many: good luck if you avoid certain peoples' poisonous attitudes.

of: will receive an abundance of gold and silver, but still lack love for yourself.

on others: your hatred of yourself is visited upon others.

VERMOUTH
15-17-29-31-35-38

buying: will suffer humiliation.

drinking: must economize with earnings.

giving a gift of: a foolish person will cause annoyance.

of: will soon have much pain in the body.

selling: will suffer embarrassment and humiliation.

VERSES
08-22-23-27-40-45

being read aloud by others: happiness in the family.

of: a stupid person is causing annoyances; your irritability is not helping.

reading: will succeed in your plans because you are clear about the true issues you face.

> *Bible:* happiness with your mate, but must fend off the hostility of both in-laws.

writing: will not succeed if you work alone, deal with the setbacks and annoyances.

VEST
06-07-11-12-32-47

being vested with authority: high honors are earned; the route is seldom explained.

buying a colored: conceal your suspicions but not behind alcohol.

man, for a: hostility surrounds you, protect your heart.

taking off a: are too easygoing in your gluttony.

vesting authority in another: are giving up your control for the betterment of the whole.

VEXATION
14-28-38-39-42-44

being vexed: feel anxious to solve a problem but helpless to enact a solution.

causing: will be deceived by one in whom you confided.

> *children:* improve conditions with correct activities.

vexing others: everything will turn out for the best.

VICAR
03-13-16-26-27-31

being a: will have ups and downs.

of a: honor and dignity.

receiving blessings from a: will live a long life.

talking to the, of a church: people will cause annoyance.

VICE
33-7-34-35-19-50

immoral conduct, having: friends will cheat you.

> *others:* will suffer humiliation.

mechanical, having a: you will have hard work.

of a vice-president or governor: will have mastery over many matters.

physical defect, a: will live a long life.

> *moral:* your secret agenda becomes known.

working with a: will have fortune in your affairs.

VICTORY
02-09-12-21-36-41

being a member of a victorious team: don't take sides in others' quarrels.

gaining, over someone: riches and honor.

military, a: people are laughing at your attempts to block their injurious moves.

political, a: will expose and exaggerate your opponent's flaws with impeccable timing.

VIEW
05-06-14-19-21-30

houses and tree, of: good results from your building and the growth of your enterprises.

in the distance: your health needs careful tending.

lake: recent friendships are formed at basic levels of agreement.

losing something from: death of a relative.

misty, a: will not be successful in affairs and suffer misery.

of a beautiful: all your desires will be realized.

    panorama of a mountain: your inconsistency is exaggerated by your solidness.

seascape: your hypersensitivity exaggerates the slightest problem.

VILLA
04-07-11-13-17-23

beautiful, a: proportions can be diagrammed, but beauty comes from the ability to see within.

being wrecked by an earthquake: starvation from the death of beauty and proportion.

burning, a: will serve in a war, and set your sights lower due to the devastation.

rebuilding a: preserve the structure of your soul by periodic renovation.

rustic, a: you will succeed in your hopes and desires.

VILLAGE
04-10-26-27-35-36

burning, a: will make a pilgrimage to the source of your ability to love.

far away, a moonlit: a golden opportunity may have corrupting repercussions.

several, in the distance: changes in your own position as you hop from job to job.

where you live, the: improved conditions and perfect contentment in the future.

VILLAIN
10-14-16-37-38-45

bad, a: stop being a victim to discover your role in society.

being a: are unwilling to take responsibility for creating your own life.

many, doing wrong: inability to determine what can or cannot change.

meeting a female: a love letter, revealing deep affection for you, has been posted to you.

    male, a: are living up to expectations not your own.

VINEGAR
06-12-18-19-24-34

cooking with: have agreed to an action that could bring disaster to your industry.

drinking: family discord over your extravagance; balance is in more basic pleasures.

fresh: will retain good health with care.

making: the project carries too many problems to succeed.

    dressing for a salad: will participate in an orgy of healthy delights.

    from good wine: will have a legal fight over an obstructing bitterness.

making pickles with: business will be at a standstill until fermentation begins.

of: labors will bring results at a later date, after you deal with twelve obstacles.

red: will be insulted by others, deepening an already distressing affair.

spilling: loss of a friend will drive you away from accustomed haunts.

white: ruin is near at hand, with inharmonious and unfavorable aspects.

VINES
01-02-10-39-48-53

grape: abundance and fruits of your labor.

green leaves, of: success will be attained soon.

harvesting fruit from: good earnings if your relationship with partner is trustworthy.

having a large: the older you are, the more capable will be your production.

healthy: successful operation of business with good friendship; peril can be averted.

picking from a: misunderstandings will not end in your favor.

pruning down: must have faith in your own enterprise to achieve fortune.

strolling among: favorable speculation, auspicious lovemaking and many children.

vineyard, checking a: impatiently expect results without working for them.

withered: depleted vitality has left your rundown system open to fraud.

VIOLENCE
04-08-26-35-46-47

being attacked with: an upheaval of which you are a part, but not the instigator.

being done to others: have lost all sense of control over your power.

mate showing: infidelity in a delicate situation is undoable.

    yourself: are a sensitive, timid person who needs tranquility.

VIOLETS
0-14-28-50-51-52

African, growing: nostalgic for a breath of beauty in the harsh cold.

buying: will have a lawsuit, sanctity cannot be bought for you.

making a bouquet of: chastity and religious devotion.

picking: humility will lead to a happy marriage.

receiving, from a loved one: will be very fortunate in love.

wearing violet: modesty and temperance, power and passion.

VIOLIN
15-18-27-32-40-43

arch of: others will interfere in love affairs.

base, a: will be visited by an old friend.

bass viol: your talents are an essential part of the team project.

breaking a string of a: will soon have sorrow that causes tears.

broken, a: bliss between husband and wife.

hearing the sweet music of a: will be crowned to the height of your domestic desires.

playing a: will have considerable trouble untangling complicated situations.

at a concert: consolation of a beautiful mind.

cello, a: your confidence is steady, deep and heartfelt.

in solitude: will attend a funeral.

others: joy if you give up the jealousy.

string quartet, in a: your decision should not be based on malicious gossip.

VIRGIN
01-18-21-33-36-47

being introduced to a: fortune smiles on pleasures without secrecy.

embracing a: will outrage her innocence in a depraved manner.

holding a: with full commitment to each other, there are no bars to the expression of love.

kidnapping a: your obsession with gaiety will create slander of unreal proportions.

knowing a, with many boyfriends: be on guard that your naïveté is respected.

making advances toward a: your own guilt will not allow another's purity.

picture of a: temptations threaten your every direction.

realizing a person is not a: grief for believing you need what is unessential to a relationship.

sick person dreaming of the, Saint: your recovery speed will be equal to your sincerity.

talking to the, Saint: the consolation prize will be quick in coming and unwarranted.

VIRTUOUS
10-12-23-35-39-41

being a, person: many enemies are nearby, protect yourself by standing firm.

children: don't listen to the lies of others without confronting your own lies.

mates: will be in a precarious situation.

friends, having: will fall into a trap expecting others to live up to your expectations.

of virtue: are keeping bad company.

hidden, a: proceed with your involvement with a new friend with an easy heart.

VISION
01-05-16-17-18-27

hampered: are unable to decipher your own errors in judgment.

imaginative, an: your insightful point of view should be expressed in totality.

lovely and charming, a: the spiritual message of your significant role in the world.

of God: horror and fright denoting impending illness.

goddesses: public humiliation is likely.

saints: an unexpected promotion is offered.

weird confusion: are overextended and must slow down.

seeing a visual image: danger in the vain, selfish person who appears to you.

VISITING
11-18-23-25-28-31

doctor, you: will have advantages over him, you live in your body and know it best.

friend, you: will have business losses if an urgent problem is not dealt with.

several: will receive good news soon.

paying a visit: obstacles in your plans to iron out a difference of opinion.

returning: have a problem, as you deserve to, with patience.

receiving business visits: will have sorrow that will cause tears.

> *from someone in distress:* solve their problem for them and earn indebtedness for life.

relative, with: slackers will be suspicious of your strong organizational skills.

your friends: your situation is not good; put off making a decision.

VISITORS
04-12-17-22-27-28

being a: embrace their admirable characteristics.

deals with a, having: you want skills of the person dreamt about.

many: are slowly regaining your energies, after a trauma, with the help of friends.

of: discard your reluctance to proceed with revisions; you need a fresh approach.

receiving: arrival of an unexpected and unwelcome friend.

VOICES
06-08-13-15-16-34

having no voice: no one is listening to you, nor are you listening to your inner psyche.

> *laryngitis:* expressions of your deep concern will stir others' defenses.

hearing friend's: one near you will become ill and need you as a guardian.

> *happy:* strangers will aid your solution to many worries.

> *lover's, your:* atone for all your negligence to the relationship—now!

> *several, at the same time:* reverses in business for your failure to meet obligations.

> *strange, speaking to you, a:* business opposition will leave your position precarious.

> *well-known, a:* use discretion but accept the good advice of your friends.

weeping: guard your tongue and listen well while at the height of your emotion.

VOLCANO
11-15-25-26-29-31

erupting, a: emotions are pouring out of a crack in your outer self.

extinct: toss old, painful memories in the crater to conclude matters.

hot, active: your passion is about to erupt over a pressing need for money.

lava covering town: are consumed with anger.

lover dreaming of a: deceit and intrigue by another.

> *man:* have dishonest servants leading you astray.

> *woman:* have frightened up old emotions and pain.

of a: are involved in high-risk activities, let off some steam first.

VOLLEYBALL
05-13-16-18-31-36

getting lost: don't expect letters from those you love.

playing: make an effort to control yourself; attend to your needs at home.

> *children:* will receive good news, but payment will be delayed.

VOMITING
03-09-15-18-28-32

food: are purging yourself of a nauseating situation.

inducing: need to take back your power or you will incur damages.

liquor, after drinking: will easily spend money won in gambling.

of: eruption of suppressed emotions for fear of participating in a big event.

others: will ask the service of someone else to get things up and out.

sick to your stomach, being: will be framed, based on your extravagant living.

wine: what you are holding will make you ill.

VOTING
05-08-19-25-28-33

ballot, being on a: an accomplishment beyond wish fulfillment.

casting a ballot: a change for the better, in companionship, comes soon.

> *others, their:* defeat in present affairs through a lack of self-expression.

> *opening a, box:* have a choice to make.

for people to hold position in church: virtue and blessings of God.

> *political offices:* an accomplishment beyond wish fulfillment.

someone you know: must be at peace with yourself to attain desires.

VOYAGE

11-14-16-20-27-34

taking a: will receive a message soon from far away and return one.

alone: good times will come again if you remember them from your past.

and being in a foreign country: reflect upon actions towards those who don't know you.

foreign, with family, a: expand your horizons to give everyone a goal.

with sweetheart: will receive remuneration above what you earn.

VULGAR

06-09-26-27-28-36

being: will be ridiculed by others, rightly so.

friends: will enjoy happiness in the future.

hearing, talk: will make the friendship of a well-known person.

talking, to others: will be able to rely on the success of good wishes.

others who are: will make unpleasant acquaintances.

VULTURE

09-17-21-24-27-31

being attacked by a: be careful what you eat, it will return on you.

circling, a: deceptive people will push until they get their way; trip them up.

dead, a: vanquish aged beliefs and opinions, victory to the new alive ones.

devouring its prey, a: people are trying to live off of you.

flying, a: someone is enjoying your troubled times.

killing a: will gain victory over dangerous enemies, finally.

many: will have a long illness that may bring misery and death.

of a: will be unable to reconcile misunderstandings with a friend.

WADING

07-09-10-16-17-36

lovers, in clear water: their love is not secure.

muddy: disillusionment will lead to illness of the heart.

rough: their love will fade completely; their vows will remain intact.

of: will commit a sin to gain a desire dear to your heart.

others: will find the real truth concerning a secret.

WAFERS

01-08-13-17-32-34

communion, receiving a: are accepting responsibility unduly.

eating a: trying to deal with too many civil matters.

making, for family to eat: have overextended yourself and are unable to finish the job.

receiving a, from a priest: feel inappropriate in your new circumstances.

seal, of a: will receive something you desire.

using a, to close an envelope: legal matters will be to your benefit.

WAGES

12-18-20-22-31-36

being refused payment of: a deception caused by those who dislike you.

paying: will lose money received from a legacy.

laborers, to: will have to work hard all during life.

weekly: a better future awaits you.

white-collar workers, to: a beautiful woman will be married.

preparing the payroll: bad temper and disappointment of those you highly esteem.

receiving: danger of small thefts will threaten your profitable undertakings.

not, for work performed: bankruptcy of the soul.

own: secure your possessions and leave others to theirs.

WAGON

11-13-16-22-25-27

coming to your door: you are without a source of power, restore your balance.

cover for a: are hiding information from malicious gossipers.

driving a: hope to counter discouraging evidence.

falling off a moving: restructure your priorities and struggle for your rights.

leasing a: another person is enjoying what you hoped to win.

loaded, a: unexpected fortune from illicit entanglements you would prefer to forget.

losing a wheel from a: replace the dissident and move on.

pulled by a donkey: change jobs to work with intelligent leadership.

riding in a: are working with the right group on the right job.

   with family: inheritance from a distant relative.

      loved one: will have tremendous good fortune at an auction.

WAIST
02-08-15-17-24-36

fastening clothes around the: a happy romance is viewed differently by each lover.

   things, another's: will assist this person soon.

having pains in the: will have plenty of money from an agreeable dispersal of funds.

naked, a: will be censured for illicit enjoyments.

of a blouse: fortune will soon slip away as you are distracted by social demons.

putting a belt around the: will win admiration through your ingenuity.

small, a: displeasing dishonor that you did not own up to wrongdoing.

waistcoat, a large: resist your shyness and throw yourself into the affair.

WAITER
04-07-13-14-16-20

at a saloon: are too confident.

being served by a: will become an invalid requiring a nurse.

many, serving others: have dishonest help and gain money from another's sacrifice.

   banquet, a: will be pleasantly entertained by a friend.

serving as a: your opinions are being dismissed, be more vigilant in presenting them.

waitress, a: will receive false news that's creating family problems.

   at a saloon: gossip will be nurtured, you can reject its sustenance

WAITING
03-09-12-22-29-31

for a loved one to arrive: fear of delay may be blocking acceptance of an important plan.

   who is delayed: timing of a relationship takes two.

in readiness for action: a friend is secretly pushing you to proceed.

   someone: a friend with questionable motives is nearby.

people, on: advancement within own position.

WALKING
11-23-25-26-33-35

backward: loss of money because an old debt remains unpaid.

behind rivals: rearrange your schedule to take a different form of transportation.

crutches, on: loss through gambling.

down a dry canal: your insecurity is caused by people working against you.

   riverbank: your stress level is lowering.

forward: will have a change in fortune that will bring profit.

gravel, on: will suffer unless you take everything in stride.

heavily: will be acquainted with a scientist and follow his research carefully.

lightly: advice from someone will bring profit.

limp, with a: struggles and complications make headway dangerous.

muddy streets, in: only hard work will overcome your difficulties.

night, at: annoyance at being molested, whether real or imagined.

over burning things: your feet are being tested to their limit.

slowly: disgrace dissolves into calm contentment.

speed: need to be more energetic with your winnings.

stick, buying a: attend to pressing matters more carefully.

   putting weight on a: your prosperity will be given assistance.

      others: will be slapped by someone over a dispute.

water, in: are in control of your triumph and success.

zigzag: opposition can be left unchallenged in your wake.

WALL

05-06-07-20-28-36

being built higher: whatever you deny gains strength in your denial.

    constructed: will enjoy an industrial gain if you persuade others to your point of view.

    torn down: conclude your affairs before laying new foundations.

building a: are prone to being very stingy and locked in rigid roles and fears.

climbing a: will overcome financial obstacles.

    with a ladder: rise above pointless arguments to joy.

falling down: a serious comment on the fabric of your life.

    from a: assert your independence from your mate.

having a, in front of own house: troublesome, pointless arguments need compromises.

jumping over a: will realize own ambitions if you don't change jobs in mid-project.

moat surrounding a: if you can believe it, you can be it.

stone, a: don't say "yes" when you mean "no."

    being blocked by: step back, is this the direction you want?

    climbing over: despite obstacles, you know what to do.

    standing on top of a: have raised your station in life.

wainscot, of sheets of oak: exercise caution in business.

    attaching a: your financial accounts must be audited

walking on top of a: negotiate a settlement by helping both sides.

    woman dreaming of: your happy marriage is potentially adverse to your health.

WALLET

08-09-16-17-26-28

empty, an: will gain fortune, but lose yourself.

filthy, a: the source of your lucrative state may not be altogether legal.

finding a: cease the paralyzing indecision; an achievement will do to start.

and returning it: a profitable relationship will ensue.

woman's: will receive a small amount of money and take a prosperous meeting.

full, a: discovery of an inner power influences your choice of a sensible approach.

leather, a: have serious ambitions to overcome.

of a lost: your identity is unexpressed, no one can find the true you.

stolen, being: you lacked the confidence to go on, now it is too late.

WALNUTS

04-07-17-26-29-30

buying: satisfaction in business after past is regretted, rued and healed.

cracking: will have an unsettled mind until the first opportunity appears.

eating: expectations will turn bitter when they collapse.

gathering: significant gains in business are ensured.

growing: embarrassment in business when your sourness is noticed.

making a pie with: your intellectual stratagem brings riches.

    cookies: will discover a treasure in each morsel.

tree, a: a wealth of health surrounds you.

    climbing a: find the congestion and rebuild your health.

    sitting in the shade of: security and abundant peace.

WALTZ

01-12-21-25-31-33

dancing a, in a ballroom: good humor toward an elegant romance.

hearing music: being lost in the melody and ignoring the faithful mate next to you.

waltzing with children: will win the friendship of an influential person.

    lover or sweetheart: an admirer is concealing his affections.

    person of ill fame: a minor error in judgment may cause permanent damage.

WANDERING

17-20-28-29-32-34

aimlessly: are limited by your imagination and the restrictions of your inner self.

children: advancement in business.

enemies: your searching will end at the beginning; go back to your roots.

in the streets: wealth will be put in your path.

of: are advancing toward achieving your desires.

others: be decisive and strong-willed to block being cheated by people.

WANTING

14-16-17-19-32-34

being in want: you are a visionary person.

relatives: will receive censure from those you most respect.

most wanted list, being on the: will narrowly avoid a very public scandal.

of, something: will make friends with a new acquaintance.

children various things: happiness is giving them what they need to get what they want.

mate: arguments over your dissatisfaction with the services he renders.

sweetheart: will receive an important letter with money.

WAR

01-05-23-36-47-49

armistice, making an: no one wins at the peace talks.

being in a: danger of illness.

prisoner, a: your opponent has won, change battlefields.

chemical weapons used in a: an end to the hostilities is nearby.

conquest of, a: expect too many favors from others.

documents of: expand your workspace to contain the truth.

ending hostilities in your favor: peace must be fair to last.

losing a: loss of important papers justifying your actions.

making, with someone: persecution of yourself will stop.

mobilizing for: peace will soon be announced.

rescuing others from a: have great fortitude, which is appreciated

are rescued from a: friends support your efforts.

town ruined in a, your: make your suspicions public.

trapped by a: break out of the mold set by others.

trying to save self and others: will be vindicated.

failing: seek legal assistance now.

watching a: misfortune.

winning a: happiness if you rehabilitate your enemy.

WARBLE

10-15-17-33-35-36

hearing the, of a bird: happiness in love.

children: don't allow people to threaten you.

famous singers: be wise to their lyrics before being caught in their tune.

many: discord between married people.

WARDEN

02-17-21-29-30-31

being a: your controlling, restrictive, rejecting tendencies.

having trouble with prisoners: death of a relative will spark a furor.

of a: will have much happiness for a long time.

receiving a favor from a: are squandering your good intentions.

removing a, from his position: watch whom you attract as allies.

talking to a: happy holiday soon to come, when what you say is listened to.

WARDROBE

03-06-16-18-23-26

adding clothes to a: disillusionment at being called to defend an unworthy foe.

giving away clothes from a: a surprise awaits when you recycle.

going through own: are pretending to be rich.

having a large: are very sure of what you want and make rapid strides toward it.

sloppy, a: others are suspicious of you.

small: will meet a very influential person, and influence with words, not clothes.

seeing old clothes from a: will have fortune at the expense of your community.

WAREHOUSE

03-14-16-24-29-36

being in a: you catalog your life experiences.

goods being dispatched from a: are emptying your emotional resources.

of a: your tremendous potential will come easily all your life.

storing things in a: your miserliness controls your talent as well.

    taking, out of: expect others to make your decisions.

van, a: another's infidelity will lead you to your future partner.

WARM
04-06-11-27-29-32

disliking a, climate: desires will cause damages to your ability to enjoy life.

enjoying weather: will be reprimanded for inability to appreciate all aspects of your life.

keeping warm: unhappiness at the imbalance of emotional temperature.

    children: arrival of a friend eases the pressure on you to be entertaining.

warming food: your timid inaction will cause hurt when it could help another.

    water: will have bad thoughts towards those weaker than you.

WARTS
06-12-15-24-25-32

having: are expulsing the gossip from your past.

    many, on the hands: much money will come to you.

    on the body: reputation will suffer because of generous actions.

of: are surrounded by hidden, hard-calloused hostility.

WASHING
13-17-18-20-23-28

body: will suffer through a misjudgment of immoral conduct.

clear water, in: will enjoy many pleasures in life, with minor setbacks.

dishes: friends will visit at your home in the midst of an argument.

face, your: a welcome relationship is on the horizon.

feet: anxiety over where you have been.

food: may have to pocket your pride to rid yourself of another's polluting your character.

hair or beard: sorrow interrupted by a short-lived euphoria.

hands in cold water: contentment, a purifying stillness.

    hot: others blame you for your success.

linen: feel you are sleeping with the enemy.

machine: are on the road to bettering yourself.

window: a service will be rendered by an unknown person.

WASPS
02-10-12-20-29-30

being stung by a: losses through opposition that spiteful opponents have wrought.

    children: an injustice will be done to you; bitter recriminations on your part.

    relatives: enemies among those you trust are endeavoring to malign you.

hive of, a: many blame you for their sorrows; look after your own interests.

hornet, killing a: a rival will seek to injure you twice as much as you did him.

    others: another is conducting your battles.

    being a: the spark needed for the success of the venture.

queen, the: will try to destroy you to rebuild herself.

WATCH
03-12-19-21-23-25

being a, maker: will have to do some hard work before being noticed by an influential person.

breaking a: check stability of the bank that holds your money.

buying a pocket: will take an overland journey.

    having a: will make successful speculations and receive added responsibilities.

    wrist: like learning vicariously.

fixing watches: rivals will come to your aid.

guarding a secret: integrate what's important in your life and guard it well from enemies.

    something: good health and pleasant recreation.

maker, a: have a highly developed analytic ability.

melting, a: are not making the best use of your time.

of a wrist: time to take positive steps to settle down.

   selling a: time is running short.

   wearing a: precious time has been lost.

young girl receiving a gift of a: will receive a marriage proposal.

WATCHING
06-09-19-29-33-36

from a high window: people are spying on you; return the favor.

keeping watch: fear that by participating, you will acquire all of the culpability.

others: you are a voyeur, dependent upon others for your pleasures.

   acting out a dream: you view life from the sidelines.

people's hair floating: will be hired by an enemy; keep your surprise hidden.

someone's hand: infidelity is a priority that should be lost in your reorganization.

   you don't care for: the moon will bring rain and needless worry about your career.

WATCHMAN
18-33-34-35-36-45

animal, an: are an exhibitionist who lives through others' performances.

bank, a: have a very kind heart to care for that which cannot return your love.

being a: will be persecuted for an immoral desire or impulse.

   night: will be saved from danger by detaching yourself from the situation.

   taken away by a: your conscience finally has some control over others.

catching a prowler: will be misled by a mental snoop.

   you: fear your closely guarded guilt will be exposed.

hitting a: jump hurdles to finish your project.

of a: are protected by silent love.

park, a: are content to watch while others do.

patrol, a: expect too many favors from others while you do favors for cash.

several: recognize dangerous coworkers.

WATER
14-18-23-29-32-36

aqueduct, much water flowing through an: will receive a fortune from parents.

being built: postponement of success.

   repaired: will realize high ambitions.

being bloated with: desire to return to the womb is being thwarted.

being thrown into the: strenuous internal diologue in your mind; reconciliation will take both sides.

boiling: passions must be moderated.

carrying, into the bedroom: will be visited by a man with loose morals.

   in a jug without spilling it: avoid trusting others with valuables.

     and spilling it: difficulties in retaining wealth through an unfavorable deal.

   in a leaky container: abuse of confidence and theft by insidious means.

cascade, being alone near a: success will pour down on you because it's within you.

   with a loved one: a love affair beyond remembering will be hidden in the cave beneath.

coming from a hole in the ground: affliction.

dike, held back by a: your dike must last, or it will ruin you.

dirty: don't settle for the first offer, let the air settle.

drawing, from a fountain: a beautiful young wife will bring fortune.

   well, a: will be tormented by your mate.

dredger, using a: a nagging problem will not go away until it is solved.

drinking, blessed by a priest: wish to wash away your sins to have purity of soul.

   hot: will be molested and persecuted by enemies.

   ice: prosperity and triumph over enemies.

   spring: refresh yourself every day for your health.

face mirrored in: perfect yourself, then move on to enjoying others.

falling into, and waking immediately: entire life will be ruined by your marriage partner.

fire with, dousing a: cool down your thought process.

hose, a: explosive regeneration of creative ideas.

hot, being in: plans in progress need to be reconsidered.

jumping into the very cold: persecution.

mineral, of: will recover from illness to complete health.

    carbonated: exciting events are bubbling.

muddy: the repercussions of your being unable to collect money will settle in a few days.

objects floating in: connotations of explicit sex.

putting roses in: have too great an imagination.

refreshing: renewal when you receive what you have been anxiously awaiting.

running: your health will improve greatly

salt: will loose respect of employers when they ignore a confrontation you need to succeed.

smelly: great struggle to resist the odors of sickness.

spilling: your anger obstructs your advancement.

spout, of a: you worry too much for no reason.

stagnant: will suffer from a stubborn lack of ambition.

throwing dirty, away: troubles created by others must be fixed by you.

whirlpool of, the movement of a: will be pulled unwillingly into a confrontation.

WATERFALL
03-11-27-35-38-42

clear, a: swiftly running stream of activities.

clear water running easily: expect the domestic happiness of a life of affluence.

    murky, not: swept along by events not of your choosing.

muddy water: are releasing repressed emotions with a continuous thud.

of a: your patience and tolerance will be required when invited to a place of amusement.

taking water from a: exciting social windfall.

viewing a, with others: your reasonable nature is being watched for one hypocrisy.

WAVES
10-14-21-40-46-48

breaking against rocks: friendship will be short-lived; contend with the next problem.

    on the bow of a ship: abundance of money from the accumulation of wisdom.

capsizing a boat: will be cheated by friends through your lack of proper judgment.

coming onto a beach: are absorbing energy into yourself for renewal.

high crashing on the shore: expect resistance and face the danger within your community.

riding a: are motivated by potent emotions.

WAX   11-18-27-34-35-46

buying: are easily molded into squandering money.

using: avoid lending money and refuse to help friends with financial problems.

waxing the floors of own house: will borrow money to keep an important appointment.

    others: will not be successful in enterprises when you fail to keep appointments.

WEAK
07-17-22-27-30-48

being: taking back your powers from others allows rapid success of your own hopes.

    children: refuse to accept their lack of potential and self-esteem.

    friends: cannot have good earnings if you give away power to others.

    mate: ambitions thwarted by your inability to recognize your own potential.

WEALTHY
01-29-30-39-40-45

being: your high ideals and the wherewithal to accomplish them.

    affluent: success in immediate plans; tread softly in the future.

having, friends: they will endeavor to destroy you; a period of self-doubt and depression.

    mate, a: your stamina will aid you in reverses.

    relatives: a heritage of talents to achieve aims found within.

receiving a, inheritance: your heritage of knowledge and wisdom will serve you well.

WEAPONS
04-09-17-26-28-43

armory full of, an: credibility is gained by works, not by force.

bludgeon, hitting a person with a: correct the source of the gossip, not the messenger.

boomerang, throwing a: be wary of revealing information unintentionally.

damaged, a: have misused valuable information for your defense.

grenade, throwing a: a stark adjustment of confidence after missing your target.

lance, a: impossible odds against formidable enemies can be overcome.

    wounded by a: an error in judgment in a crucial experiment will aggravate you.

possessing a: learn the correct defense method before proceeding.

sharp, pointed, a: your words do the damage; insight and love can heal the wound.

WEASEL
06-08-10-31-37-47

having a fur coat made of: a smile, a giggle, an abundant hug does not equal love.

    buying: try to save your money, to not be dependent on others.

    selling: will foil schemes deeply involved in your defeat.

of a: beware of one who appears to be a friend, but whose illegalities will disgrace you.

WEATHER
03-07-08-10-24-42

beautiful, of: your security lies in your decisive confidence.

forecast, a: exercise great concern with each item of advice.

rainy: a letter will end the sadness, but an undertone of depression will remain.

stormy: enemies are seeking your ruin, but you create the flood.

    with lightning: a past indiscretion resurfaces aggressively.

sunny: self-confidence with outbursts of passion; you jitter back and forth.

terrible: a psychotic episode brings unpleasant news that overheats you.

vane, changing direction from north to south: loss of money.

    south to north: gain of money.

    viewing a: are overly complimented; don't allow your ego to be inflated.

windy: an old friendship will revitalize your physical welfare.

WEAVING
03-05-13-25-40-44

cloth: are bogged down in a repetitive routine.

dress, a: blend endeavor, intuition and motivation to create your life as you want it.

of: are too embarrassed to speak for fear of exposing your plotting.

ordering something from a weaver: good news will come in a letter.

suit, a: trouble can be straightened out with patience and fortitude.

tapestry, a: an embarrassment of riches as your mate is overly frugal.

wedding dress, a: pleasant days doing constructive work for another's happiness.

WEDDING
19-20-23-27-38-45

attending a: recovery from illness will be replaced with an obsession with petty jealousies.

    brother's: many tears from young woman assembled.

    daughter's: whirlwind courtship and marriage within a year.

    relative's: expect trouble in the family circle that will cause divorce.

    sister's: discontent and bitterness over her getting what you did not.

    son's: long life with a loving partner.

best man, being a: plans fail because of a false friend whose plans succeed.

    woman, dreaming of: are marrying the wrong man.

betrothed, becoming: expect the family to circle around to mar your happiness.

    being, but not engaged: are not prepared for sexual relations you regard as degrading.

    friends: high ambitions will be realized if you integrate their positive qualities.

    relatives: are uniting all parts of your heritage into aspects of your self.

eloping: gossip attacking your character requires a quick reversal.

guests, many: exposure of a doomed affair foreshadows friction for the marriage.

ring of a diamonds, receiving: domestic happiness, if you don't accept the first offer.

losing: vexation at partner's disregard.

returning: the relationship is over.

widow's: are integrating the qualities of a deceased husband into you.

WEEDS
18-24-33-35-36-38

burning dry: all your negative thoughts have been eliminated.

destroying: destroying bad habits causes embarrassment in business.

nettles, being stung by: will be discontented with the painful.

　　walking among, without: have wasted your usefulness and gone to seed.

of: will face hindrances in an undertaking that promises great honor.

pulling: destroy the nonessential completely before proceeding.

smoking: repressed wild urges are piling up.

WEEPING
14-28-33-35-46-49

along with grief: will enjoy pleasures, financial position and a healthy marriage.

friends: limit your expenditures; will receive an unexpected gift.

others: will panic unnecessarily over bad news that is irrelevant to your life.

wailing, animals: feel pain of a victim's helplessness at the loss of someone dear to you.

　　children: at least someone loves you unequivocally.

with the family: fortify your strength against others' scandalous escapades.

with happiness: are worried and anxious about others' gossip, not grief.

WEIGHING
01-06-09-11-16-37

food: an opportunity will prove to be advantageous to your financial business.

grain: are being subsidized and supported from a powerful source—God.

large things: will overcome objections to present position and remain.

meat: an advantageous move.

packages: are prone to have too many prejudices; send the care packages anyway.

precious metals: your extravagances are provoked by your vivid imagination.

yourself: will make an advantageous move that will prove expensive.

WEIGHT
12-15-16-29-44-48

gaining: money will come easily during a prosperous period.

losing: breakdown in relationship with partner.

making for a sport: will overcome troubles and have a large business.

of own: your worry will cause anxiety, which causes physical weakness.

　　children: immediate success of your hopes of subordinating them to your own interests.

　　gold: your imagination is excessively vivid.

　　grain: lasting prosperity.

　　relatives: realization of your ambitions despite family deceitfulness.

　　silver: are supported by someone in power

　　your mate: financial worries; make a go of your present job despite misgivings.

weights yourself, lifting: will impose a burden on another's life to make him dependent.

　　children: family reunion where they begin to care about you.

　　mate: financial gains will be favorable to you.

　　others: resent taking on more burdens than you caused.

WELL
06-15-23-27-38-41

artesian, an: a moderate but uninterrupted income.

digging a: what is the means of exposing your fiery trapped emotions?

dirty water in a: situation will turn sour and bring loss of your estate.

drawing water from a: success and profit from fulfillment of schemes.

dry, a: will have some damages in old affairs, not your risky new ventures.

falling into a: troubles ahead for you; a vital decision is needed.

full of clear water: expectations will bring luck and prosperity.

giving, water to animals to drink: enemies' schemes will challenge your own.

　　others: big fortune will be wasted on misapplied energies.

having a, in your yard: will be robbed of your abundance if you share with strangers.

overflowing, an: have opportunity to advance your prospects.

throwing someone in a, of water: strong elements direct your course.

WEST
03-11-19-39-40-47

going, alone: exploring your possibilities, which are still in a subconscious state.
   with your family: union of light and darkness created by motherhood.

of the western part of the world: aggressive adventure to civilize their world.

traveling westward: exploration to build your dream.

WHALE
16-26-28-32-40-46

bones of: are prone to be conceited and reject appropriate opportunities as beneath you.

catching a: an enemy is seeking your struggles and loss of property.

dolphin on the deck of a ship, a: beware of seducers with emotional power agendas.

engaging in, fishing: an opportunity for recovery of lost money.

killing a: have found the source of good luck, now swallow up your opponent.

of a: large profits in one check, a wholesome relationship with yourself.

watching a: another is handling well a project you rejected as too enormous.

WHARF
05-11-12-31-42-45

being in poor condition: will become drunk.

bidding good-bye to someone at a: will buy jewelry for loved one.

of a: will enjoy modesty and chastity.

quay, being along on a: will suffer grief from being overloaded.
   with sailors: secret enmity of a person with emotions of stone.

sailors and workmen on a: loss of friends.

walking on a: will have a happily married life, with not one day of sadness.

WHEAT
06-08-19-21-25-30

buying: propensity for trouble and starvation will diminish gradually.

harvesting: beware of jealous friends when accomplishing an arduous task.

of ripe: will have a big fortune if you can separate the wheat from the chaff.

selling: increasing money from encouraging prospects.

WHEEL
05-28-29-41-43-44

axle, of a broken: will suffer much embarrassment in amazing arguments with partner.
   on a car: others will guide your recovery from illness.
      truck: will be thrifty and energetic in gaining abundant means.

barrow, carrying load in a: moving back and forth with no progress.

fortune, of: fortune will not come without your effort.

gambling, a: unimaginable disruption of affairs is imminent.

grinding, a: a disagreement and a fight begun by your premature worry and doubt.

many, in operation: recovery of money in a roundabout way.

mill: are faced with great danger from a heavy burden.

moving, a: unseen progress is being made.

steering: your will can empower you.

still, a: another will have to start the project.

water: will come into a great deal of money.

WHIP
14-15-17-28-32-42

being whipped: will travel abroad to find a gullible victim.
   enemies: will recover from an illness caused by self-punishment.
   several people: are doomed for disappointment if you expect problems to end.

having a: will receive an affectionate message of forthcoming mischief.

lashing a: others recognize the aggression behind your sweet facade.
   horse with a: your abusiveness is an occasion for guilt and shame.
   someone else: one you admire doesn't need force to convince you, but is using it.

using a: domination, superiority, authority whether you deserve them or not.

WHIRLWIND
03-12-16-22-24-44

devastation caused by a: discovery of a disposition not in accordance with your wishes.

losing property in a: your emotions are running away with you.

of a: dangerous reports are impossible to analyze well with your schedule.

watching a: will be lifted up and resettled in a new Oz.

WHISKEY
07-18-24-30-47-48

being offered a drink of: will sacrifice friends to your selfishness.

buying: will have debts and difficulties, but pay them with illicit schemes.

drinking: warning of your own bad behavior, of which you are totally unobservant.

offering, to friends: your self-centeredness will cause animosity with friends.

  lover: temptation will come to you.

  mate: realization of high ambitions through scheming seductions.

  relatives: be on the lookout for a double-cross in your struggle for your goal.

WHISPERING
08-27-34-38-48-49

children, to: make your intentions and rules clear.

friends: are being deceived by advice coming from one with ulterior motives.

others: they are endeavoring to destroy you; catch them.

relatives: a rumor will be confirmed; are holding yourself back.

your mate: financial gains are at hand.

WHISTLING
04-05-20-38-40-49

calling attention by: will lose in prospective ventures to others, who treat it as a game.

children: will participate in a joyous event of comedic intent.

dog, for a: will be disturbed by changes to your innocent pleasures.

hearing others: bad talk will injure your reputation, but not your success.

  in the quiet of the night: are protected from your enemies

theater, at a: have an adaptable, flexible personality.

  catcall: a personal liaison is soon to take place.

whistle, of a broken: scandal is being spread about you unjustly.

  being blown during a game: change your strategy before you get a penalty.

  fixing: will receive good advice; heed its message.

  shrill: be wary of minor aggressions.

WHITE
03-05-09-30-43-44

painting a room: limit your responsibility, accept your ascent from darkness.

room, in a: aspire to an all-inclusive perfection of mystical illumination.

seeing, light: erase all previous problems and begin again.

washing vice and crime: use caution in business ventures.

  investigation, an: will be called upon to extricate a friend from trouble.

  walls: be on the lookout for a double-cross.

wearing: new start in a wholesome life.

WIDOW
02-05-17-24-32-35

baking: expect favors from others to deal with responsibilities you deem weighty.

dreaming of expecting a baby: are driving yourself toward shattered ambitions.

giving birth to a child: will be guilty of foolish actions.

marrying: have reached the last resort of thwarted hopes.

  distant relative, a: change of surroundings will rid you of malicious people.

  rich old man, a: money will arrive by mail; happiness is ensured.

    poor: insurmountable obstacles are ahead for someone close to you.

    young: misfortune in love affairs as weighty responsibilities become yours.

of a: achieve balance by allowing your masculine traits to evolve.

WIDOWER
01-10-20-24-38-45

marrying a rich woman: your cherished

desires will crumble to emotional sorrow.

aged, young girl: unconscious desire to be emotionally alone while among friends.

sister-in-law: have moved away to avoid temptation.

woman his own age: realization of high ambitions; will have mastery over many things.

young widow: are seriously concerned, but it will not last long.

of a: bring out your feminine aspects of self.

remain a, determined to: are concerned that someone close to you will desert you.

WIFE
04-19-25-29-35-37

afflicted, being: rapid success in business, to your detriment.

arguing with your: will have a quarrel lasting several days.

beating her husband: a long-lasting marriage.

being beautifully dressed: whom are you trying to impress with her?

being called by your: will be tormented by internal grieving for your love.

calming one's: will have a violent family quarrel.

caressing her husband: her suspicion is magnified, as is your resistance to defeat.

checking on your: are doing wrong to an innocent person.

house, being a: will marry a professional who is always traveling.

lying in the sun at the beach: avoid present peril by developing the quality of selfishness.

man being with his beautiful: pleasing time in love if you can extricate her from mother.

in a bathtub: misfortune in love affairs until you create your home.

married to another: sudden separation or death of husband.

man dreaming of beating his: great happiness in marriage.

his, betraying him: she has cause to suspect foul play, he does not.

nagging: your frivolous wife, who is too fond of amusements, is echoing your actions.

neglecting your: events are going against you.

of your own: must control your passions and jealousy; be patient and caring.

being naked: she is cheating on you.

undressing: must mend your ways and commit yourself to one woman.

swimming at a pool: a rival will steal her affections.

taking a: the accomplishment of your desires and of your confinement.

WIG
02-18-20-32-41-46

man wearing a light-colored: several women refuse you, and your partner unfairly judges you.

dark-: will be loved best by women who induce you to make a change you will regret.

wearing a: feel insignificant without a crutch: your eccentric behavior.

others: look to your past appearances for a motive, ill is being projected onto you.

woman wearing a blond, a: will have many admirers of your idealism, but not yourself.

brunette: will exaggerate your sexuality to marry a poor man.

dark: should mend your naïveté and lack of common sense.

white: will marry a rich man much older than yourself.

WILD BEAST
18-27-28-34-41-42

being attacked by a: get past the adversity to live a long life.

being pursued by a: disgraced by a friend's offense.

cage, in a: enemies will fail in their attempts to injure you.

dead, a: death of a prominent person.

ears of a: a boost from an enemy.

head of a: victory over enemies is foiled by your careless act.

hearing the roar of a: unexpected promotion.

horns of a: magnificence.

killing a: many changes will occur, but finally victory.

of a: will have the protection and favor of people of distinction.

running, a: misfortune through serious
mental illness and unaccountable distur-
bances.

WILDERNESS
02-18-19-20-28-48
inhabited only by wild beasts: everyone, no
matter how threatening, has a purpose in
your life.
of the: will have a festive occasion in your
home.
uncultivated, an: expect too many favors from
others when only you can build your life.
uninhabited, an: retain your old friends for
your new adventures.

WILL
22-25-33-47-51-52
bequest being made in own favor, a: to inherit
money requires tact and diplomacy.
from an unknown person: financial gains.
canceling a bequest: will reach a ripe old age
with concrete decisions and family fights.
disinheriting a, in a: you will sustain a serious
loss.
other: changing your environment will
not right wrongs done to you.
executor, being the: you will receive an unexpected legacy.
induced against you, others: your solitude
needs breaking; your conscience, defining.
leaving nothing to relatives: imminent death
of your relationship.
all to strangers: the melancholic trials
of a discontented mind.
relative, a: will live a long time and have a
continuous string of vulturine relatives.
wife, your: wife will pass away first to
avoid the disorderly proceedings.
losing a: have forgotten a rival in your quest
for the inheritance.
willing a legacy to someone: fights within the
family will make you unhappy for a day.
charity, a: will have a very long illness;
request wise counsel.
children: will spend a long time in
momentous trials and speculations.
friend, a: a friend will pass away very soon
and you will be upset with his difficulties.

writing a, for another person: will become
entangled in a delicate situation.

WILLOW
03-06-08-14-41-42
creeping: forsaken love; will be consoled by
faithful friends.
making baskets out of, branches: approaching
money.
of, trees: a rival will take the affections of your
sweetheart, if you are not faithful.
others working with, wood: warning of troubles if you are not flexible.
pussy: humility brings the comfort of peace.
using a machine to cut down a, tree: are being
deceived.
weeping, a: your shoulder will be cried on
interminably.

WINCH
02-03-08-22-27-34
farmer using a: are in the grip of a deceitful
person.
yourself: control of your life sometimes
has to be artificially manipulated.
lifting a heavy load: will be protected by businesspeople.
machinery from a window: envious people
surround you, but only you can live
your life.
loading a ship: will make plenty of money
through speculation.
ships, being broken: your fortune is secured,
but will be postponed.

WIND
05-06-07-08-18-29
battling with the: rapid success of your
own hopes, if you face difficulties head
on.
blowing: are forewarned, litigation will
take untiring energy and attending
success.
away a boat's sail: approaching emotional
turmoil; future conditions will
improve.
breeze, being out in a gentle: will be
insulted by a man with poor manners.
enjoying a, at night: a gift is received from
a stranger.
own hat away: a suitable time for business
transactions with strangers.

soft cooling, a: take this inspiration and run with it.

strong: pull yourself together; show some spunk in your speculations.

candle in the: will receive an inheritance or promotion at work.

gale, being in a: financial gains if you plod carefully and ingeniously with every step.

  on a ship during a strong: will realize high ambitions, battered but undaunted.

    in a small boat: financial troubles and losses.

mystic: start of a new adventure only you can travel on.

not blowing at all: a need for recovery from the dashed hopes of a cherished wish.

ship battling against the: you will discover a secret.

sinking a vessel: money will come easily from successful speculation.

strong, of a: have the energy resources within you to move mountains.

swirling around you: consider previously refused ideas.

walking with the: abundant means through the support of friends.

  against: agony at the hands of tormenting competitors.

    tingling: will be insulted by a man with poor manners.

west, being in the woods and feeling a: modesty.

WINDMILL
04-10-24-27-35-42

changing directions: untrustworthy people surround you, but you make the decisions.

married people dreaming of a: untruthfulness between mates.

  sweethearts: will enjoy much happiness.

  unmarried people: will soon marry.

moving a grinding machine: will have to take care of many things.

operating a: will make some gains of small monetary value.

stopped, a: will receive inheritance from a rich relative.

very tall, a: will be content and receive a large fortune.

WINDOW
10-19-26-34-48-49

back of your home, at the: disputes between sisters turns malicious.

blocked, a: a determined denial of sight.

breaking a glass: trouble is ahead; form your response.

broken, a: be suspicious of theft by friends and hounded by the disloyalty of loved ones.

changing glass of a: are changing your outlook in life for a more romantic flare.

cleaning a glass: your happiness is in danger from your tendency to exaggerate it.

climbing from a, on a fire escape: will become bankrupt from overt intrigues.

  in a: have used dishonorable means to gain a distinguished position.

closed, a: will suffer desertion by your friends.

  standing behind a: absorb the atmosphere around you and be still.

decorating a show: take advantage of opportunities to fulfill your obligations.

dormer, looking out of a: brighter horizons presage a rapid recovery.

fire coming from a: a long life is promised.

glass breaking: sad news you don't want to see or be taken to court for.

jumping from a: wish to find some outlet for your impulses without risking your health.

looking out a: change your orientation to bring in more light.

open, an: success will attend your excellent health.

opposite your home: dispute between brothers comes to blows.

seeing people kissing in front of a: a pet bird will be the victim of your folly.

throwing things from a: advancement within position through insight into your world.

very big, a: very good success in business.

viewing something from a: victory over enemies by letting them destroy each other.

WINE
02-11-12-14-28-46

barrel of, having a full: you fret and stew with no cause or consequence.

bottle of, a: feasting, prosperous times and consequent friendships.

 broken: others will deceive you into thinking you have committed immoral acts.

 empty, an: a life devoid of pleasure.

buying: will have new employment with congenial colleagues.

corks, having several: perseverance will give you much-needed confidence.

 pushing a, into a bottle: an unexpected high-spirited visitor will ease your troubles.

 removing from: a friend will aid your rise above your circumstances.

corkscrew, opening a bottle with a: danger through an inability to control sordid desires.

 others: a mystery will be solved: it's all in your head.

drinking: will receive many good things, then be shocked by realizing you're in trouble.

 claret: will be offered a noble assignment.

 from a flagon of: your love and passion will border on excessive shame and sorrow.

 Marsala: business conditions will improve if you avoid excess.

 misty: allowing for an emotion you don't allow yourself to feel in public.

 Muscatel: high honors will be varied and from distant shores.

 nearly black in color: fortune and satisfaction.

 red: will become inebriated with cheerfulness and optimism.

 very fine: intelligent conversations with friends.

 white: happiness in sincere friendships.

fermenting: temporary mental illness will disturb your family.

getting drunk on: an illegitimate son will be born.

making: superior amusement, pleasure and good results in all affairs.

of a shop: will give financial help to others.

receiving, as a gift: the transforming power of truth, shared.

selling: beware of double-cross, when you sell your services.

sipping at the liturgy: the transformative significance of Christ.

sour: your inaction has turned your talent to vinegar.

spilling a glass of: someone will be injured and lose much blood.

 red, on a white tablecloth: you shoulder others' disasters.

WINTER
15-21-29-31-41-49

being sick during the: relatives are envious of your lack of emotional involvement.

farmer dreaming of a severe: good harvest will be renewed each year.

 navigators: financial gains will not pass to the payout stage.

living through a hot: ill health and dreary prospects won't leave you.

 mild: are prying into affairs of others when your own life is unfruitful.

 severe: invalidism threatens you.

 very: work on handicrafts to beautify your home.

weather causing damages: death of an enemy with your complete support and guilt.

WIRE
11-14-22-32-35-36

barbed, being caught in a: reword your stern defense to waylay your opponent's fears.

 climbing over a: leave enemies to their own devices.

 electrified, an: be careful of those who love to hate.

connecting multiple work stations, a: your new proposal at work will be accepted

tripping over a: an unexpected glitch caused by a friend's uncontrollable temper.

WIRELESS
09-12-13-16-22-29

being at an office of, machines: money will come easily from outside sources.

machine being broken: have many enemies who would sabotage your efforts.

operating a, machine: prompt engagement in a connection.

 aboard a ship: will receive unexpected good news concerning money.

phone, a: your side of a family dispute will be believed.

receiving messages by: are very cruel when you expose the truth.

sending: family afflictions cannot be shared with strangers.

WISDOM

12-19-24-32-36-38

being sapient: confusion in business affairs when what is wise isn't practical.

person giving advice: are being deceived into believing because it is said to be correct.

following advice of: avoid rivals, who advise your adviser.

of an eminent person of wisdom: there is no end to wisdom available, if you need it.

sage, consulting a: have a vigorous mind and are prone to talk too much.

WISHING WELL

04-28-37-41-47-48

dropping money into a: choose friends carefully; listen to criticism gingerly.

making a wish over a: a fortune for those who feed you.

of a: two admirers seeking your company are at odds.

stealing money from a: death in the near future to any possibility of luck.

WITCH/WIZARD

04-14-22-24-29-43

becoming nervous because of a: men snubbed by sweethearts.

being a: face your irrational fear and seek to explain it.

being chased by a, on a broom: beware of double-crossing, a disillusioning experience.

scared by a: an abuse of confidence, this sleight of hand.

with wand: accept strange hints as valid until you have proven them otherwise.

hazel: a cleansing spell will discard the lull in business.

ignoring a: are being watched by one with evil intentions.

seeing a hag: gossip and scandal from female friends over losing your looks.

talking with a: your instigations will backfire, mend your ways.

wife, of a: wish your wife would take better care of herself and stop nagging.

woman dreaming of a: fear your actions have been far from considerate.

WITNESS

09-15-22-35-45-46

being in contempt as a: insecurity in your affairs.

false: will go to prison, and if not behind bars, then beyond your sight.

being a, in court: false accusations are made against you.

at any civil action: good earnings in business.

divorce case, a: do not reveal your prosperity.

for someone else: a big catastrophe is ahead.

murder, a: small profits.

having a, for an alibi: be on guard against false friends.

someone witnessing a document: your actions are always proper.

unfaithfulness of mate: family legal problems.

witnesses testifying on your behalf: good results in business affairs.

WOLF

04-08-35-44-45-48

being attacked by a: secret enemies seek your destruction.

chased by a: friends save you from scandal.

frightened by a: are so anxious that you will be robbed by thieves, that you will be.

catching a: abundance of money.

dead, a: are confronted with insurmountable obstacles.

head of a: honor and an obscure success are imminent.

killing a: will have dealings with smart and treacherous enemies.

pack of, following you: your game is well played with your sharp scheming.

running, a: the majestic guide to the source of sacred wisdom.

several: employees are abusing your trust.

trained, a: will be kissed often; your love is badly placed.

two, playing together: have false friends who wait for you to let down your guard.

with small cubs: disappointment and an end to love.

WOMAN

14-25-33-34-36-40

accosted by a, being: envy destroys honor.

amorous, being: you demand too much with your confidence and decisiveness.

approached by a, being: will be humiliated.

bachelor to marry her, getting a: a rich woman is found for you to marry.

bald, going: difficult love affairs.

beating her suitor: great triumph in love.

beautiful naked, a: symbolizes your feelings and your opinion about her.

birth to a child, divorced giving: will inherit a large legacy.

buttocks of a: happiness and love

carrying a: difficulties will soon be overcome.

conquest of a beautiful: must rely upon your own good judgment.

dancing, a: illness.

desiring to have children: unfriendliness of others.

dreaming of being a man, a: birth of son who brings honor to family.

   Cain: will be highly considered by others.

   dead, a: will be abandoned.

   divorcing husband: will marry a very wealthy man.

   Greek god Bacchus, the: are preoccupied with appearances.

   handsome, a: love will not last long.

   having a baby: pregnancy.

flirting with a man: that woman is competing with you.

   your: your lover is having an affair with your best friend.

gambling: will be deprived.

hair, with black: your envy destroys any chance of a relationship.

   beautiful blond: will enjoy a happy life.

      long: are preoccupied with appearances.

   brunette: seduction without success.

   red: acknowledge your temper and work with it.

white: dignity and distinction.

hearing the voice of a: permanent change of residence.

ill repute, of: will suffer humiliation.

laughing, a: be wary of a confidante with a loose tongue.

lying on a bed: security.

making advances to your man: jealousy.

man dreaming of a beautiful: are insincere and bitter that he did not approach you

   committing adultery with a: the hurt never goes away, nor does the need for revenge.

   dead: will soon be loved by a wealthy lady.

   delivering a baby: prosperity.

   ill repute, of: serious disaster as an unscrupulous person is stealing your reputation.

   talking to him: big gossip.

   with hair as long as she is tall: have an adulterous wife.

man being with a: pastimes will be agreeable after earlier misunderstandings are righted.

married, dreaming of being pregnant: your envy destroys any chance of a relationship.

   baking: unlucky events to come.

   delivering a fish: very smart children.

   slapping a man on the face: complete faithfulness to her husband.

   wearing an apron: will have ups and downs.

   when pregnant dreaming of having a baby: big success in love.

      when not: happiness.

naked, a: recognize the object of your passions and act on it.

nursing a baby: will be deceived by a trusted friend and nurtured by a perfidious foe.

of a: the more emotional, intuitive and irrational part of yourself.

receiving services from a: will have a bad reputation.

several at a maternity ward: much happiness.

strong, a: speculating on an undervalued gamble.

turning her back on you, a: opposition in love

from one for whom your desires are intense.

unknown, an: will entertain an unwelcome guest.

unmarried, wearing an apron: will soon be engaged.

   dreaming of being pregnant: trouble and injury through scandal.

     the Greek god Bacchus: will receive a marriage proposal.

      having a small beard,: gambling losses.

visiting your house, a: good hopes.

WOOD

02-07-15-19-29-30

being cut by a, burr: withdraw from unpleasant people.

buying: are in need because your efforts are not rewarded.

carving a, piece: wish to share your talents.

cutting trunks of trees: misery and affliction.

   fallen: happiness is ensured.

   hatchet, with a: work smarter, not harder, in your reaction to scandal.

dry: success will be yours through hard work.

green: life and springtime.

logs, of: abundant means.

   carrying: will be offended by a friend.

   fagot of, a: nostalgia for home and hearth.

   splitting: persuade your partner to act sensibly.

selling: abundant means.

shavings, of: defend yourself against scandal.

sorrel: maternal tenderness.

splinters: reinforce your defenses against a bitter dispute with relatives.

   removing a: will misplace sensitive, confidential document.

straight piece of: approaching money.

   crooked: disgrace.

stubbing your toe on a log: vulgar people dare to insult you.

woodcutter, being a: efforts will not result in much profit.

   in a wood shop: your projects will be successful.

WOODS

24-27-30-40-48-49

broken trees in the: pleasant social activities.

burning: affliction.

clearing in the, a: a reprieve from uncertainties.

getting lost in the: expect a new opportunity to present itself.

many people being in the: caution in business ventures.

many trees in the: will enjoy very satisfactory business.

walking in the: will have hard work ahead.

WOOL

07-12-17-27-41-47

buying: prosperity and success.

   clothes: loss of a friend.

lamb's: are a very kind and easygoing person.

making material from raw: will suffer from being allergic to other's ideas.

   worsted: will receive a comfortable income.

owning bales of: success at home, in business and in influence with the community.

selling: will enjoy a comfortable life.

   clothes made of: great unhappiness.

sheep's: are prone to using flattery to cover up your gift for being stubborn.

WORK

05-08-09-14-17-39

being at: a mountain of past experience has molded your views and actions.

   your family: financial gains.

   your help: realization of high ambitions.

children at: happiness.

delegating: your business will profit from other's labors.

others working: will be pleasantly situated in life.

   friends, busily: be cautious in business ventures.

suffocated from, being: intellectual deprivation from lack of work.

workhouse, being in a: a big legacy will come to you soon.

workman, being a: satisfy your curiosity over how a major change affects your career.

   hiring: you are stagnating because of a lack of willpower and enthusiasm.

   lumber, a: you handle your affairs in good order; avoid any askew temptations.

plumbing: enterprises must be free-flowing and contiguous to bring profit.

steel, a: will receive a visitor who will accomplish affairs as you desired.

workshop, being in a: on an out-of-state trip your character will be revealed in full.

buying a: have ambitious projects for the future.

others: are decisive in taking the initiative to compete on a level plane and win.

WORLD
05-17-21-38-41-47

discussing the, situation: will be molested by enemies.

going bad: will be double-crossed by someone nearby.

end of the, the: a part of your past is being stripped away.

map of the, a: contentment and tranquility are the goal.

turning the, upside down: everything will turn in your favor.

WORMS
04-11-12-31-19-40

being on plants: will receive unexpected money through holding on to old friends.

destroying: are blindsided by an acquaintance's betrayal.

on own body: are easily discouraged with your lack of self-reliance and goals.

on, of children: danger of an infectious disease.

of: will be the victim of intrigue but foil their cabal with your assertiveness.

others killing: the source of the destruction will go to prison.

WOUND
01-21-24-38-39-44

being wounded: a new opportunity to advance yourself at work.

accident, in a: tell the loved one that they hurt you.

another: take extra care when driving.

attack, in a: be careful where you eat.

children: good times are coming.

fall, in a: ask a relative for help.

gun, by a: will make plenty of money.

knife: good friendship.

sword: bad news.

lovers: will have serious quarrels.

mate: warning of troubles.

old people, on the breast: will have misfortune.

young: will have splendid future.

others: will be untrue to marriage vows.

lint to wrap, buying: your life is protected.

large amount of: must exercise prudence.

wrapping a, with: be forgiving or you will regret it.

pus emitting from a: an accident will cause permanent scars.

WREATH
09-24-30-32-40-42

beautiful flowers, of a: high hopes and well-deserved honors.

being crowned with a: unconscious guilt for a lack of sympathy.

crepe paper, a: will have an illness and can't pay for the care.

gold, of: will be protected by influential people.

of a: looking down on life and not living it creates hostility.

placing a, on someone's head: will have the respect of people.

tomb, a: dignity.

weaving a: the hope of your future is in your head.

WRESTLING
09-12-14-19-27-40

losing at arm: a colleague is out to deprive you.

of a, match: disputes over a difficult problem.

losing: bow out of the controversy and restrain yourself.

winning: leave your opponent with some dignity.

others, with crazy people: change sports.

with children: unexpected fortune.

crazy people: death.

debtors: will receive assistance.

friends: will be elevated to a better position.

prisoners: liberated yourself from the workforce, to being taken care of.

professionals: enemies will be punished, but you can't be known as the punisher.

sheep: continual, plodding, hard work ahead.

snakes: severe entitlement of enemies to create their own punishment.

very strong people: infirmity and sickness will not last long.

wild beasts: will escape some danger by befriending when confronted.

WRINKLES
06-14-28-37-39-48

clothes, in: will have small disagreements, but the total still stands.

elderly man with: loss of friendship through incorrigible comments.

middle age: are very gullible; time is of the essence, use it wisely.

without: compliments and social pleasures; will achieve all desires in life.

face, in own: long life after a sickness.

friends having, at an early age: will have ulcers and very bad skin disease.

no, having: will have good looks the rest of life.

WRITING
04-22-24-32-37-46

addresses: remember friends and spy on your enemies.

agenda, an: infirmity from a blunder in scheduling.

another: renege on the contract; are not pleasing those who will then make false accusations.

article for a magazine: successful works of literary import.

capital letters, in: be leery of those persuasive in their scheming.

inscriptions, dated: tragedy in your immediate circle.

undecipherable: continue to seek guidance, but not from envious people.

journal, in a: a dividend from a stock you thought worthless.

reading your: will receive a telegram.

letter, a: someone has stolen from you and you are exacting revenge.

business, a: need to send a long overdue letter that reflects your satisfaction.

children, to: must put out money or be depressed.

love, to mate: happiness and unity.

relatives: will make a mistake that will prove your undoing.

manuscript, completing a: ambitions need to be expanded for your next effort.

having, returned: criticisms should be taken as the critic's own qualms.

not: go to plan B; writer's block has an expanded dimension—a new project.

memoirs: your dishonor foretells a serious error, which will threaten your peace.

opinions: consult friends before they interfere where you don't want them to.

paper, on: will be falsely accused of something.

reminder of payment due: no success in collecting money.

report, a: will be accused of slander by your own conscience.

you: a handshake will not stand up in court.

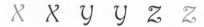

XENOPHOBIA
02-08-27-28-36-46

deporting a foreigner: loss of a faithful friend.

disliking: family quarrels.

having hatred for: happiness.

insulting: a mystery will be solved.

man being married to a foreign woman: luck and prosperity.

woman, man: congenial work and good news.

melting pot, of the: a marriage outside the family causes upset.

of xenogamy: will have unexpected friends come to dinner.

X RAY
08-22-25-32-42-47

having a favorable, report: an important and very beneficial event to come.

unfavorable: others are not fooled by your confident facade.

having own, taken: have doomed yourself for disappointment.

of an, machine: worry will be smoothed away as your involvement intensifies.

operating an: time for reflection and reappraisal of your mission in life.

reports of another's: new relationship with one of the opposite sex.

YACHT

06-13-23-28-30-33

being on a: realization of your own ambitions.

of a: connections will bring you good luck.

owning a: do not depend on anyone else for your funds.

sailing on rough sea: have confidence your talents will gain you wealth.

  smooth: optimism that your efforts will be enhanced by influential contracts.

stranded, a: business ventures will cause you distress and disappointments to friends.

under full engine speed: big joy for those pleasure bent.

  full sail: pleasant visit in a nice place.

YARD

24-25-31-44-46-48

being in a: an unwelcome friend will visit you.

  friend's, a: persecution.

  neighbor's, a: must rely on your own efforts.

having an untidy: will have sorrow that causes tears.

  well-kept: family arguments over details.

picking flowers from a: news of the engagement of friends will reach you.

  planting things in a: are so involved in the details you miss the future.

scrap, a: are you sure of not being cheated on purchases?

stick, using a: are measuring the length of your commitment to life.

  mate: are judging mate by another standard, not your own.

  salespeople: are disliked by others and are often snubbed.

working in a: an admirer will soon be married.

YARN

10-21-29-30-37-43

balling: can easily extract yourself from a trap.

buying: a present from a recently developed friendship that must remain secret.

  man dreaming of: will attain success with the revelation of your unique techniques.

woman: will encourage husband by thrift and peace, not obstinate demands.

unmarried person: show indifference when you should be kind.

tangled: your obstinacy is self-destructive; allow another's way of doing things.

untangling: your enemy's case is easily destroyed, if you don't reveal it now.

YAWNING

12-17-22-30-31-40

at social events: are unfitted to fill your position; find one more appropriate.

at the office: pick a realistic career goal and request better ventilation.

in church: will be humiliated by being over-tired.

in the morning: will be jilted by your lover so brutally that you become ill.

of: small troubles that are not serious are holding you back.

YEAST

14-16-28-30-35-37

baking with: will receive money under strange circumstances.

  bread with: abundance will rise out of your creative spirit.

buying: unusual wealth from the smallest investment.

of: money accumulated by thrift will be left to you.

YELLING

11-14-15-16-24-34

hearing children: many family quarrels over minor issues.

  hideous yells: worry will be smoothed away.

    noisy: will have peace and money.

    others: will have strife followed by peace.

howling, people: will have difficulties quelling the resentment within the family.

mates, at each other: an introduction will alter your plans.

yourself: be cautious that you don't act out of turn in business ventures.

YOGA

21-26-28-29-36-46

meditation: a family member is in need.

yogi, a: must turn your attention to spiritual things.

YOKE

01-08-17-30-41-43

hanging garments, a: try to develop your own
personality.

having a, on shoulders carrying two pails:
punishment and slavery.

of a gallows: are influenced by an older person.

two animals yoked together: teamwork when
timing fits perfectly.

YOUTH

09-14-17-29-32-42

aged person dreaming of: remembering a
younger aspect of your life.

   woman: will have a devoted husband.

being: a positive change lasts as long as you
keep optimistic.

of becoming, again: important and very beneficial events to come.

ZEALOUS

02-07-17-31-33-50

being a, zealot: will fight for your cause to the
detriment of the world.

   not: peril and misfortune when you let
sentiment rule your decision.

      others who are: short courtship will
end with mutual agreement.

being unable to work with zeal: discovery
of a treasure is wished for and
unattained.

ZEBRA

05-08-15-18-23-43

being attacked by a wild: your honor is in
danger from a venture with little credibility.

mother, with her young: disagreements with
friends will dissipate to satisfaction.

of a: will do extensive travel abroad, to a
source of surprising profitability.

zoo, at a: friendship is badly placed and will
cause you much harm.

   fed: ingratitude from those you worked to
set up in a venture.

ZENITH

04-12-20-32-42-47

divorced people dreaming of the: will marry a
rich man or rich woman.

   married person: unusual wealth.

      unmarried: good choice of husband or
wife.

widow: will marry a younger man.

widower: will never get married again.

of that point of the heavens directly above you:
happiness.

ZEPPELIN

03-04-07-36-39-40

being in a: will be molested for achievements
causing a great hazard.

   on fire: your passion, not your intellect,
will achieve your goal.

coming down in a: will receive good news
when your feet are on solid ground.

crashing in a: your indecision is the maker of
your failure.

flying through the clouds: your evaluation of
yourself is not true.

going up in a: will be insulted by a poorly
mannered man.

helium, inflating a, with: safe and profitable
investments.

of a, airship: have ambitions far beyond your
reach.

watching a, moving slowly: people are
meddling in your affairs.

ZIGZAG

16-24-30-31-36-49

walking: business will suffer due to your
inability to commit.

   children: will go out of your mind; forget
control, use gentle nudging.

   friends: avoid hesitation in making decisions, but make them your own.

zigzagging with a car: your changeable moods
could prove harmful.

   horse: changes in business will put you in
a different bracket.

ZINC

02-15-19-32-35-37

buying: your future will be built on a firm
foundation.

   articles made of: avoid speculations in
gold.

handling: you participate in too many amusements.

of: will achieve solid success through untiring
efforts.

others using things made of: are going in too
many directions for a long-lasting
romance.

ZIPPER

08-14-28-50-51-52

buying a: desire to develop an easier relationship with someone.

stuck, a: social embarrassment in opening and closing remarks.

unzipping own clothes: a release of tension from trying to be who you aren't.

man, a woman's dress: will receive news of the coming birth of a child.

zipping up own clothes: minor irritation will clear the way for a proposal of love.

child's, a: will preserve family dignity in the face of all odds.

others, their: will be lucky at gambling and chagrined at your friend's ill luck.

ZODIAC

08-17-25-49-50-53

of any sign of the: will have a big fortune in the future.

children's: will be greatly loved by the children.

family's: riches.

own sign: will win a lottery.

relative's: will have arguments with relatives.

ZOO

07-13-21-36-50-57

going to the, alone: are humiliated and your instincts confined.

with family: good hopes if the future will allow.

friend: do not confide your secrets; select friends after close observation.

husband or wife: hopes will not be realized; will have a varied fortune.

sweetheart: confined and molested by others.

keeper of game, the: financial gains with close attention.

visiting a, with children: need to tidy up a situation and wish joy and admiration.

wild animals, being in a, with: success will require a new way to make money.

working in a: your jealousy will make your married life miserable.

others: they have a reputation for gossip.